PHYSICAL ANTHROPOLOGY 96/97

Fifth Edition

Editor

Elvio Angeloni
Pasadena City College

Elvio Angeloni received his B.A. from UCLA in 1963, his M.A. in anthropology from UCLA in 1965, and his M.A. in communication arts from Loyola Marymount University in 1976. He has produced several films, including *Little Warrior,* winner of the Cinemedia VI Best Bicentennial Theme, and *Broken Bottles,* shown on PBS. He most recently served as an academic adviser on the instructional television series, *Faces of Culture.*

A Library of Information from the Public Press

Cover illustration by Mike Eagle

Dushkin Publishing Group/
Brown & Benchmark Publishers
Sluice Dock, Guilford, Connecticut 06437

The Annual Editions Series

Annual Editions is a series of over 65 volumes designed to provide the reader with convenient, low-cost access to a wide range of current, carefully selected articles from some of the most important magazines, newspapers, and journals published today. Annual Editions are updated on an annual basis through a continuous monitoring of over 300 periodical sources. All Annual Editions have a number of features designed to make them particularly useful, including topic guides, annotated tables of contents, unit overviews, and indexes. For the teacher using Annual Editions in the classroom, an Instructor's Resource Guide with test questions is available for each volume.

VOLUMES AVAILABLE

Abnormal Psychology
Africa
Aging
American Foreign Policy
American Government
American History, Pre-Civil War
American History, Post-Civil War
American Public Policy
Anthropology
Archaeology
Biopsychology
Business Ethics
Child Growth and Development
China
Comparative Politics
Computers in Education
Computers in Society
Criminal Justice
Developing World
Deviant Behavior
Drugs, Society, and Behavior
Dying, Death, and Bereavement
Early Childhood Education
Economics
Educating Exceptional Children
Education
Educational Psychology
Environment
Geography
Global Issues
Health
Human Development
Human Resources
Human Sexuality

India and South Asia
International Business
Japan and the Pacific Rim
Latin America
Life Management
Macroeconomics
Management
Marketing
Marriage and Family
Mass Media
Microeconomics
Middle East and the Islamic World
Multicultural Education
Nutrition
Personal Growth and Behavior
Physical Anthropology
Psychology
Public Administration
Race and Ethnic Relations
Russia, the Eurasian Republics, and Central/Eastern Europe
Social Problems
Sociology
State and Local Government
Urban Society
Western Civilization, Pre-Reformation
Western Civilization, Post-Reformation
Western Europe
World History, Pre-Modern
World History, Modern
World Politics

Cataloging in Publication Data
Main entry under title: Annual editions: Physical anthropology. 1996/97.
        1. Physical anthropology—Periodicals. I. Angeloni, Elvio, comp.
II. Title: Physical anthropology.
ISBN 0–697–31527–4   573'.05

Fifth Edition

Printed in the United States of America

To the Reader

In publishing ANNUAL EDITIONS we recognize the enormous role played by the magazines, newspapers, and journals of the *public press* in providing current, first-rate educational information in a broad spectrum of interest areas. Within the articles, the best scientists, practitioners, researchers, and commentators draw issues into new perspective as accepted theories and viewpoints are called into account by new events, recent discoveries change old facts, and fresh debate breaks out over important controversies.

Many of the articles resulting from this enormous editorial effort are appropriate for students, researchers, and professionals seeking accurate, current material to help bridge the gap between principles and theories and the real world. These articles, however, become more useful for study when those of lasting value are carefully *collected, organized, indexed,* and *reproduced* in a *low-cost format,* which provides easy and permanent access when the material is needed.

That is the role played by *Annual Editions.* Under the direction of each volume's *Editor,* who is an expert in the subject area, and with the guidance of an *Advisory Board,* we seek each year to provide in each ANNUAL EDITION a current, well-balanced, carefully selected collection of the best of the public press for your study and enjoyment.

We think you'll find this volume useful, and we hope you'll take a moment to let us know what you think.

This fifth edition of *Annual Editions: Physical Anthropology 96/97* contains a variety of articles relating to human evolution. The articles were selected for their timeliness, relevance to issues not easily treated in the standard physical anthropology textbook, and clarity of presentation.

Whereas textbooks tend to reflect the consensus within the field, *Annual Editions: Physical Anthropology 96/97* provides a forum for the controversial. We do this in order to convey to the student the sense that the study of human development is an evolving entity in which each discovery encourages further research, and each added piece of the puzzle raises new questions about the total picture.

Our final criterion for selecting articles is readability. All too often, the excitement of a new discovery or a fresh idea is deadened by the weight of a ponderous presentation. We seek to avoid that by incorporating essays written with enthusiasm and with the desire to communicate some very special ideas to the general public.

Included in this volume are a number of features designed to be useful for students, researchers, and professionals in the field of anthropology. While the articles are arranged along the lines of broadly unified subject areas, the *topic guide* can be used to establish specific reading assignments tailored to the needs of a particular course of study. Other useful features include the *table of contents abstracts,* which summarize each article and present key concepts in bold italics, and a comprehensive *index.* In addition, each unit is preceded by an overview that provides a background for informed reading of the articles, emphasizes critical issues, and presents *challenge questions.*

In contrast to the usual textbook, which by its nature cannot be easily revised, this book will be continually updated in order to reflect the dynamic, changing character of its subject. Those involved in producing *Annual Editions: Physical Anthropology 96/97* wish to make the next one as useful and effective as possible. Your criticism and advice are welcomed. Please fill out the postage-paid article rating form on the last page of the book and let us know your opinions. Any anthology can be improved, and this one will continue to be.

Elvio Angeloni

Elvio Angeloni

Editor
(Internet address: Evangeloni@pcc.cc.ca.us)

Contents

Unit
1

Natural Selection

Seven articles examine the link between genetics and the process of natural selection.

The concepts in bold italics are developed in the article. For further expansion please refer to the Topic Guide and the Index.

Unit 2

Primates

Six selections examine some of the social relationships in the primate world and how they mirror human society.

The concepts in bold italics are developed in the article. For further expansion please refer to the Topic Guide and the Index.

Unit 3

Sex and Society

Five articles discuss the relationship between the sexes and the evolution of a social structure.

Unit 4

The Hominid Transition

Six articles examine the enigma of human evolution from the ape. A definitive common fossil link between apes and humans has yet to be made.

The concepts in bold italics are developed in the article. For further expansion please refer to the Topic Guide and the Index.

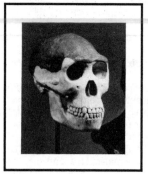

Unit 5

The Fossil Evidence

Five selections discuss some of the fossil evidence for hominid evolution.

The concepts in bold italics are developed in the article. For further expansion please refer to the Topic Guide and the Index.

Unit 6

Late Hominid Evolution

Seven articles examine archaeological evidence of human evolution.

The concepts in bold italics are developed in the article. For further expansion please refer to the Topic Guide and the Index.

Unit
7

Living with the Past

Seven articles discuss evolutional theory and how genetic
heritage impacts on our present and our future.

The concepts in bold italics are developed in the article. For further expansion please refer to the Topic Guide and the Index.

Topic Guide

This topic guide suggests how the selections in this book relate to topics of traditional concern to students and professionals involved with the study of physical anthropology. It is useful for locating articles that relate to each other for reading and research. The guide is arranged alphabetically according to topic. Articles may, of course, treat topics that do not appear in the topic guide. In turn, entries in the topic guide do not necessarily constitute a comprehensive listing of all the contents of each selection.

TOPIC AREA	TREATED IN	TOPIC AREA	TREATED IN
Aggression	8. Machiavellian Monkeys 9. What Are Friends For? 11. Young and the Reckless 14. These Are Real Swinging Primates 18. Apes of Wrath 19. Dim Forest, Bright Chimps 20. To Catch a Colobus 24. Ape Culture and Missing Links 31. Hard Times among the Neanderthals 38. Eugenics Revisited 40. Farmers and Baboons in the Taita Hills	**Creationism**	1. Growth of Evolutionary Science 2. Struggle for the Schools
		Cro-Magnons	25. Dawson's Dawn Man 34. Old Masters 35. Dating Game 36. Neanderthal Peace
Anatomy	10. Gut Thinking 16. Sex and the Female Agenda 17. What's Love Got to Do with It? 21. Flesh and Bone 22. Ape at the Brink 23. Human Ancestors Walked Tall, Stayed Cool 24. Ape Cultures and Missing Links 26. New Fossils Take Science Close to Dawn of Humans 30. *Erectus* Rising 31. Hard Times among the Neanderthals 36. Neanderthal Peace 37. No Bone Unturned	**Disease**	3. Curse and Blessing of the Ghetto 4. Arrow of Disease 5. Future of AIDS 7. Racial Odyssey 38. Eugenics Revisited 42. Reasonable Sleep 43. Saltshaker's Curse
		DNA (Deoxyribonucleic Acid)	3. Curse and Blessing of the Ghetto 5. Future of AIDS 6. Black, White, Other 38. Eugenics Revisited 39. DNA Wars
		Dominance Hierarchy	9. What Are Friends For? 11. Young and the Reckless 14. These Are Real Swinging Primates 17. What's Love Got to Do with It? 18. Apes of Wrath
Archeology	30. *Erectus* Rising 32. Ancient Odysseys 34. Old Masters 35. Dating Game 36. Neanderthal Peace 37. No Bone Unturned	**Fluorine Testing**	25. Dawson's Dawn Man
		Forensic Anthropology	37. No Bone Unturned 39. DNA Wars
Australopithecines	10. Gut Thinking 21. Flesh and Bone 25. Dawson's Dawn Man 27. Sizing Up Human Intelligence 28. East Side Story	**Genes**	3. Curse and Blessing of the Ghetto 5. Future of AIDS 6. Black, White, Other 38. Eugenics Revisited 39. DNA Wars 43. Saltshaker's Curse
Biostratigraphy	28. East Side Story		
Bipedalism	17. What's Love Got to Do with It? 21. Flesh and Bone 23. Human Ancestors Walked Tall, Stayed Cool 29. Scavenger Hunt	**Genetic Drift**	1. Growth of Evolutionary Science 3. Curse and Blessing of the Ghetto
		Genetic Testing	3. Curse and Blessing of the Ghetto 38. Eugenics Revisited 39. DNA Wars
Blood Groups	6. Black, White, Other 7. Racial Odyssey 39. DNA Wars	**Homo erectus**	25. Dawson's Dawn Man 27. Sizing Up Human Intelligence 30. *Erectus* Rising
Brain Size	10. Gut Thinking 27. Sizing Up Human Intelligence	**Homo habilis**	27. Sizing Up Human Intelligence
Catastrophism	1. Growth of Evolutionary Science	**Homo sapiens**	27. Sizing Up Human Intelligence 32. Ancient Odysseys 33. Rhinos and Lions and Bears (Oh, My!) 35. Dating Game 36. Neanderthal Peace
Chain of Being	1. Growth of Evolutionary Science		

TOPIC AREA	TREATED IN	TOPIC AREA	TREATED IN
Hunting and Gathering	19. Dim Forest, Bright Chimps 20. To Catch a Colobus 29. Scavenger Hunt 31. Hard Times among the Neanderthals 34. Old Masters	Race	6. Black, White, Other 7. Racial Odyssey
Hunting Hypothesis	9. What Are Friends For? 15. Myth of the Coy Female 21. Flesh and Bone 29. Scavenger Hunt	Reproductive Strategy	5. Future of AIDS 9. What Are Friends For? 10. Gut Thinking 11. Young and the Reckless 14. These Are Real Swinging Primates 15. Myth of the Coy Female 16. Sex and the Female Agenda 17. What's Love Got to Do with It? 18. Apes of Wrath 20. To Catch a Colobus
Locomotion	14. These Are Real Swinging Primates 17. What's Love Got to Do with it? 21. Flesh and Bone 23. Human Ancestors Walked Tall, Stayed Cool	Sexuality	14. These Are Real Swinging Primates 16. Sex and the Female Agenda 17. What's Love Got to Do with It? 18. Apes of Wrath 20. To Catch a Colobus 24. Ape Cultures and Missing Links
Mutation	1. Growth of Evolutionary Science 5. Future of AIDS		
Natural Selection	1. Growth of Evolutionary Science 3. Curse and Blessing of the Ghetto 4. Arrow of Disease 5. Future of AIDS 6. Black, White, Other 7. Racial Odyssey 10. Gut Thinking 43. Saltshaker's Curse	Social Relationships	9. What Are Friends For? 11. Young and the Reckless 13. Dian Fossey and Digit 14. These Are Real Swinging Primates 15. Myth of the Coy Female 16. Sex and the Female Agenda 17. What's Love Got to Do with It? 18. Apes of Wrath 19. Dim Forest, Bright Chimps 20. To Catch a Colobus 24. Ape Cultures and Missing Links 34. Old Masters 40. Farmers and Baboons in the Taita Hills
Neanderthals	25. Dawson's Dawn Man 31. Hard Times among the Neanderthals 35. Dating Game 36. Neanderthal Peace		
Paleoanthropology	24. Ape Cultures and Missing Links 26. New Fossils Take Science Close to Dawn of Humans 28. East Side Story 30. Erectus Rising 35. Dating Game 36. Neanderthal Peace	Species	1. Growth of Evolutionary Science 36. Neanderthal Peace
		Taxonomy	1. Growth of Evolutionary Science 6. Black, White, Other 7. Racial Odyssey 26. New Fossils Take Science Close to Dawn of Humans 30. Erectus Rising
Piltdown Hoax	25. Dawson's Dawn Man		
Primates	8. Machiavellian Monkeys 9. What Are Friends For? 10. Gut Thinking 11. Young and the Reckless 12. Mind of the Chimpanzee 13. Dian Fossey and Digit 14. These Are Real Swinging Primates 15. Myth of the Coy Female 16. Sex and the Female Agenda 17. What's Love Got to Do with It? 18. Apes of Wrath 19. Dim Forest, Bright Chimps 20. To Catch a Colobus 21. Flesh and Bone 22. Ape at the Brink 24. Ape Cultures and Missing Links 27. Sizing Up Human Intelligence 40. Farmers and Baboons in the Taita Hills 41. Macaque See, Macaque Do	Technology	4. Arrow of Disease 5. Future of AIDS 22. Ape at the Brink 30. Erectus Rising 34. Old Masters 35. Dating Game 36. Neanderthal Peace
		Territoriality	40. Farmers and Baboons in the Taita Hills
		Theology	1. Growth of Evolutionary Science 2. Struggle for the Schools
		Uniformitarianism	1. Growth of Evolutionary Science
		Viruses	4. Arrow of Disease 5. Future of AIDS

Natural Selection

As the twentieth century draws to a close and we reflect upon where science has taken us over the past 100 years, it should come as no surprise that the field of genetics has swept us along a path of both insight into the human condition and heightened controversy as to how to handle this potentially dangerous knowledge of ourselves.

Certainly, Gregor Mendel in the late nineteenth century could not have anticipated that his study of pea plants would ultimately lead to a greater understanding of over 3,000 genetically caused diseases, such as sickle-cell anemia, Huntington's chorea, and Tay-Sachs. Nor could he have foreseen the present-day controversies over such matters as surrogate motherhood, cloning, and genetic engineering.

The significance of Mendel's work, of course, was his discovery that hereditary traits are conferred by particular units that we now call "genes," a then-revolutionary notion that has been followed by a better understanding of how and why such units change. It is knowledge of the process of "mutation," or alteration of the chemical structure of the gene, that is now providing us with the potential to control the genetic fate of individuals.

The other side of the evolutionary coin, as discussed in "The Growth of Evolutionary Science," is natural selection, a concept provided by Charles Darwin and Alfred Wallace. This refers to the "weeding out" of unfavorable mutations and the perpetuation of favorable ones. The pace and manner in which such forces become evident in the fossil record have been the subject of a great deal of discussion among scientists and, indeed, of some controversy among nonscientists (see "The Struggle for the Schools" by Eugenie Scott).

It seems that as we gain more understanding of both of these processes, mutation and natural selection, and grasp their relevance to human beings (as described by Jonathan Marks in "Black, White, Other" and by Boyce Rensberger in "Racial Odyssey"), we draw nearer to that time when we may even control the evolutionary direction of our species. Knowledge itself, of course, is neutral—its potential for good or ill being determined by those who happen to be in a position to use it. Consider the possibility of eliminating some of the harmful hereditary traits discussed in "Curse and Blessing of the Ghetto," by Jared Diamond. While it is true that many deleterious genes do get weeded out of the population by means of natural selection, there are other harmful ones, Diamond points out, that may actually have a good side to them and will therefore be perpetuated. It may be, for example, that some men are dying from a genetically caused overabundance of iron in their blood systems in a trade-off that allows some women to absorb sufficient amounts of the element to guarantee their own survival. The question of whether or not we should eliminate such a gene would seem to depend on which sex we decide should reap the benefit.

The issue of just what is a beneficial application of scientific knowledge is a matter for debate. Who will have the final word as to how these technological breakthroughs will be employed in the future? Even with the best of intentions, how can we be certain of the long-range consequences of our actions in such a complicated field? Note, for example, the sweeping effects of ecological change upon the viruses of the world, which in turn seem to be paving the way for new waves of human epidemics. Generally speaking, there is an element of purpose and design in our machinations. Yet, even with this clearly in mind, the whole process seems to be escalating out of human control. As Jared Diamond (in "The Arrow of Disease") and Geoffrey Cowley (in "The

Future of AIDS") point out, it seems that the whole world has become an experimental laboratory in which we know not what we do until we have already done it.

As we read the articles in this section and contemplate the significance of genetic diseases for human evolution, we can hope that a better understanding of these diseases will lead to a reduction of human suffering. At the same time, we must remain aware that, rather than reduce the misery that exists in the world, someone, at some time, may actually use the same knowledge to increase it.

Looking Ahead: Challenge Questions

In nature, how can design occur without a designer, orderliness without purpose?

Should "equal time" be devoted to "scientific creationism" in the public classroom?

Why is it difficult to study natural selection in humans?

Why are epidemic diseases more common today than in our hunting and gathering past?

How and why might the ABO blood group be related to epidemic diseases?

Discuss whether or not people should be told that they are going to die of a disease from which they are suffering and for which there is no cure.

How is it possible to test for deleterious genes?

Why is Tay-Sachs disease so common among Eastern European Jews?

How do ecological changes cause new viruses to emerge?

Why was post-Columbian disease transmission between Europe and the Americas so unidirectional?

What do you predict for the future of the AIDS epidemic?

Discuss whether or not the human species can be subdivided into racial categories.

How and why did the concept of race develop?

Charles R. Darwin.

The Growth of Evolutionary Science

Douglas J. Futuyma

Today, the theory of evolution is an accepted fact for everyone but a fundamentalist minority, whose objections are based not on reasoning but on doctrinaire adherence to religious principles.

—James D. Watson, 1965*

In 1615, Galileo was summoned before the Inquisition in Rome. The guardians of the faith had found that his "proposition that the sun is the center [of the solar system] and does not revolve about the earth is foolish, absurd, false in theology, and heretical, because expressly contrary to Holy Scripture." In the next century, John Wesley declared that "before the sin of Adam there were no agitations within the bowels of the earth, no violent convulsions, no concussions of the earth, no earthquakes, but all was unmoved as the pillars of heaven." Until the seventeenth century, fossils were interpreted as "stones of a peculiar sort, hidden by the Author of Nature for his own pleasure." Later they were seen as remnants of the Biblical deluge. In the middle of the eighteenth century, the great French naturalist Buffon speculated on the possibility of cosmic and organic evolution and was forced by the clergy to recant: "I abandon everything in my book respecting the formation of the earth, and generally all of which may be contrary to the narrative of Moses." For had not St. Augustine written, "Nothing is to be accepted save on the authority of Scripture, since greater is that authority than all the powers of the human mind"?

When Darwin published *The Origin of Species,* it was predictably met by a chorus of theological protest. Darwin's theory, said Bishop Wilberforce, "contradicts the revealed relations of creation to its Creator." "If the Darwinian theory is true," wrote another clergyman, "Genesis is a lie, the whole framework of the book of life falls to pieces, and the revelation of God to man, as we Christians know it, is a delusion and a snare." When *The Descent of Man* appeared, Pope Pius IX was moved to write that Darwinism is "a system which is so repugnant at once to history, to the tradition of all peoples, to exact science, to observed facts, and even to Reason herself, [that it] would seem to need no refutation, did not alienation from God and the leaning toward materialism, due to depravity, eagerly seek a support in all this tissue of fables."[1] Twentieth-century creationism continues this battle of medieval theology against science.

One of the most pervasive concepts in medieval and post-medieval thought was the "great chain of being," or *scala naturae.*[2] Minerals, plants, and animals, according to his concept, formed a gradation, from the lowliest and most material to the most complex and spiritual, ending in man, who links the animal series to the world of intelligence and spirit. This "scale of nature" was the manifestation of God's infinite benevolence. In his goodness, he had conferred existence on all beings of which he could conceive, and so created a complete chain of being, in which there were no gaps. All his creatures must have been created at once, and none could ever cease to exist, for then the perfection of his divine plan would have been violated. Alexander Pope expressed the concept best:

Vast chain of being! which from God
  began,
Natures aethereal, human, angel, man,
Beast, bird, fish, insect, what no eye
  can see,
No glass can reach; from Infinite to
  thee,
From thee to nothing.—On superior
  pow'rs
Were we to press, inferior might on
  ours;
Or in the full creation leave a void,
Where, one step broken, the great
  scale's destroy'd;
From Nature's chain whatever link you
  strike,
Tenth, or ten thousandth, breaks the
  chain alike.

Coexisting with this notion that all of which God could conceive existed so as to complete his creation was the idea that all things existed for man. As the philosopher Francis Bacon put it, "Man, if we look to final causes, may be regarded as the centre of the world . . . for the whole world works together in the service of man . . . all things seem to be going about man's business and not their own."

"Final causes" was another funda-

*James D. Watson, a molecular biologist, shared the Nobel Prize for his work in discovering the structure of DNA.

mental concept of medieval and post-medieval thought. Aristotle had distinguished final causes from efficient causes, and the Western world saw no reason to doubt the reality of both. The "efficient cause" of an event is the mechanism responsible for its occurrence: the cause of a ball's movement on a pool table, for example, is the impact of the cue or another ball. The "final cause," however, is the goal, or purpose for its occurrence: the pool ball moves because I wish it to go into the corner pocket. In post-medieval thought there was a final cause—a purpose—for everything; but purpose implies intention, or foreknowledge, by an intellect. Thus the existence of the world, and of all the creatures in it, had a purpose; and that purpose was God's design. This was self-evident, since it was possible to look about the world and see the palpable evidence of God's design everywhere. The heavenly bodies moved in harmonious orbits, evincing the intelligence and harmony of the divine mind; the adaptations of animals and plants to their habitats likewise reflected the divine intelligence, which had fitted all creatures perfectly for their roles in the harmonious economy of nature.

Before the rise of science, then, the causes of events were sought not in natural mechanisms but in the purposes they were meant to serve, and order in nature was evidence of divine intelligence. Since St. Ambrose had declared that "Moses opened his mouth and poured forth what God had said to him," the Bible was seen as the literal word of God, and according to St. Thomas Aquinas, "Nothing was made by God, after the six days of creation, absolutely new." Taking Genesis literally, Archbishop Ussher was able to calculate that the earth was created in 4004 B.C. The earth and the heavens were immutable, changeless. As John Ray put it in 1701 in *The Wisdom of God Manifested in the Works of the Creation,* all living and nonliving things were "created by God at first, and by Him conserved to this Day in the same State and Condition in which they were first made."[3]

The evolutionary challenge to this view began in astronomy. Tycho Brahe found that the heavens were not immutable when a new star appeared in the constellation Cassiopeia in 1572. Copernicus displaced the earth from the center of the universe, and Galileo found that the perfect heavenly bodies weren't so perfect: the sun had spots that changed from time to time, and the moon had craters that strongly implied alterations of its surface. Galileo, and after him Buffon, Kant, and many others, concluded that change was natural to all things.

A flood of mechanistic thinking ensued. Descartes, Kant, and Buffon concluded that the causes of natural phenomena should be sought in natural laws. By 1755, Kant was arguing that the laws of matter in motion discovered by Newton and other physicists were sufficient to explain natural order. Gravitation, for example, could aggregate chaotically dispersed matter into stars and planets. These would join with one another until the only ones left were those that cycled in orbits far enough from each other to resist gravitational collapse. Thus order might arise from natural processes rather than from the direct intervention of a supernatural mind. The "argument from design"—the claim that natural order is evidence of a designer—had been directly challenged. So had the universal belief in final causes. If the arrangement of the planets could arise merely by the laws of Newtonian physics, if the planets could be born, as Buffon suggested, by a collision between a comet and the sun, then they did not exist for any purpose. They merely came into being through impersonal physical forces.

From the mutability of the heavens, it was a short step to the mutability of the earth, for which the evidence was far more direct. Earthquakes and volcanoes showed how unstable terra firma really is. Sedimentary rocks showed that materials eroded from mountains could be compacted over the ages. Fossils of marine shells on mountaintops proved that the land must once have been under the sea. As early as 1718, the Abbé Moro and the French academician Bernard de Fontenelle

had concluded that the Biblical deluge could not explain the fossilized oyster beds and tropical plants that were found in France. And what of the great, unbroken chain of being if the rocks were full of extinct species?

To explain the facts of geology, some authors—the "catastrophists"—supposed that the earth had gone through a series of great floods and other catastrophes that successively extinguished different groups of animals. Only this, they felt, could account for the discovery that higher and lower geological strata had different fossils. Buffon, however, held that to explain nature we should look to the natural causes we see operating around us: the gradual action of erosion and the slow buildup of land during volcanic eruptions. Buffon thus proposed what came to be the foundation of geology, and indeed of all science, the principle of uniformitarianism, which holds that the same causes that operate now have always operated. By 1795, the Scottish geologist James Hutton had suggested that "in examining things present we have data from which to reason with regard to what has been." His conclusion was that since "rest exists not anywhere," and the forces that change the face of the earth move with ponderous slowness, the mountains and canyons of the world must have come into existence over countless aeons.

If the entire nonliving world was in constant turmoil, could it not be that living things themselves changed? Buffon came close to saying so. He realized that the earth had seen the extinction of countless species, and supposed that those that perished had been the weaker ones. He recognized that domestication and the forces of the environment could modify the variability of many species. And he even mused, in 1766, that species might have developed from common ancestors:

If it were admitted that the ass is of the family of the horse, and different from the horse only because it has varied from the original form, one could equally well say that the ape is of the family of man, that he is a degenerate man, that man and ape have a common origin; that, in fact, all the families among plants as well as animals have come from a single stock, and that all animals are descended from a single animal, from which have sprung in the course of time, as a result of process or of degeneration, all the other races of animals. For if it were once shown that we are justified in establishing these families; if it were granted among animals and plants there has been (I do not say several species) but even a single one, which has been produced in the course of direct descent from another species . . . then there would no longer be any limit to the power of nature, and we should not be wrong in supposing that, with sufficient time, she has been able from a single being to derive all the other organized beings.[4]

This, however, was too heretical a thought; and in any case, Buffon thought the weight of evidence was against common descent. No new species had been observed to arise within recorded history, Buffon wrote; the sterility of hybrids between species appeared an impossible barrier to such a conclusion; and if species had emerged gradually, there should have been innumerable intermediate variations between the horse and ass, or any other species. So Buffon concluded: "But this [idea of a common ancestor] is by no means a proper representation of nature. We are assured by the authority of revelation that all animals have participated equally in the grace of direct Creation and that the first pair of every species issued fully formed from the hands of the Creator."

Buffon's friend and protégé, Jean Baptiste de Monet, the Chevalier de Lamarck, was the first scientist to take the big step. It is not clear what led Lamarck to his uncompromising belief in evolution; perhaps it was his studies of fossil molluscs, which he came to believe were the ancestors of similar species living today. Whatever the explanation, from 1800 on he developed the notion that fossils were not evidence of extinct species but of ones that had gradually been transformed into living species. To be sure, he wrote, "an enormous time and wide variation in successive conditions must doubtless have been required to enable nature to bring the organization of animals to that degree of complexity and development in which we see it at its perfection"; but "time has no limits and can be drawn upon to any extent."

Lamarck believed that various lineages of animals and plants arose by a continual process of spontaneous generation from inanimate matter, and were transformed from very simple to more complex forms by an innate natural tendency toward complexity caused by "powers conferred by the supreme author of all things." Various specialized adaptations of species are consequences of the fact that animals must always change in response to the needs imposed on them by a continually changing environment. When the needs of a species change, so does its behavior. The animal then uses certain organs more frequently than before, and these organs, in turn, become more highly developed by such use, or else "by virtue of the operations of their own inner senses." The classic example of Lamarckism is the giraffe: by straining upward for foliage, it was thought, the animal had acquired a longer neck, which was then inherited by its offspring.

In the nineteenth century it was widely believed that "acquired" characteristics—alterations brought about by use or disuse, or by the direct influence of the environment—could be inherited. Thus it was perfectly reasonable for Lamarck to base his theory of evolutionary change partly on this idea. Indeed, Darwin also allowed for this possibility, and the inheritance of acquired characteristics was not finally prove impossible until the 1890s.

Lamarck's ideas had a wide influence; but in the end did not convince many scientists of the reality of evolution. In France, Georges Cuvier, the foremost paleontologist and anatomist of his time, was an influential opponent of evolution. He rejected Lamarck's notion of the spontaneous generation of life, found it inconceivable that changes in behavior could produce the exquisite adaptations that almost every species shows, and emphasized that in both the fossil record and among living animals there were numerous "gaps" rather than intermediate forms between species. In England, the philosophy of "natural theology" held sway in science, and the best-known naturalists

continued to believe firmly that the features of animals and plants were evidence of God's design. These devout Christians included the foremost geologist of the day, Charles Lyell, whose *Principles of Geology* established uniformitarianism once and for all as a guiding principle. But Lyell was such a thorough uniformitarian that he believed in a steady-state world, a world that was always in balance between forces such as erosion and mountain building, and so was forever the same. There was no room for evolution, with its concept of steady change, in Lyell's world view, though he nonetheless had an enormous impact on evolutionary thought, through his influence on Charles Darwin.

Darwin (1809–1882) himself, unquestionably one of the greatest scientists of all time, came only slowly to an evolutionary position. The son of a successful physician, he showed little interest in the life of the mind in his early years. After unsuccessfully studying medicine at Edinburgh, he was sent to Cambridge to prepare for the ministry, but he had only a half-hearted interest in his studies and spent most of his time hunting, collecting beetles, and becoming an accomplished amateur naturalist. Though he received his B.A. in 1831, his future was quite uncertain until, in December of that year, he was enlisted as a naturalist aboard *H.M.S. Beagle,* with his father's very reluctant agreement. For five years (from December 27, 1831, to October 2, 1836) the *Beagle* carried him about the world, chiefly along the coast of South America, which it was the *Beagle's* mission to survey. For five years Darwin collected geological and biological specimens, made geological observations, absorbed Lyell's *Principles of Geology,* took voluminous notes, and speculated about everything from geology to anthropology. He sent such massive collections of specimens back to England that by the time he returned he had already gained a substantial reputation as a naturalist.

Shortly after his return, Darwin married and settled into an estate at Down where he remained, hardly traveling even to London, for the rest of his life. Despite continual ill health, he pursued an extraordinary range of biological studies: classifying barnacles, breeding pigeons, experimenting with plant growth, and much more. He wrote no fewer than sixteen books and many papers, read voraciously, corresponded extensively with everyone, from pigeon breeders to the most eminent scientists, whose ideas or information might bear on his theories, and kept detailed notes on an amazing variety of subjects. Few people have written authoritatively on so many different topics: his books include not only *The Voyage of the Beagle, The Origin of Species,* and *The Descent of Man,* but also *The Structure and Distribution of Coral Reefs* (containing a novel theory of the formation of coral atolls which is still regarded as correct), *A Monograph on the Sub-class Cirripedia* (the definitive study of barnacle classification), *The Various Contrivances by Which Orchids are Fertilised by Insects, The Variation of Animals and Plants Under Domestication* (an exhaustive summary of information on variation, so crucial to his evolutionary theory), *The Effects of Cross and Self Fertilisation in the Vegetable Kingdom* (an analysis of sexual reproduction and the sterility of hybrids between species), *The Expression of the Emotions in Man and Animals* (on the evolution of human behavior from animal behavior), and *The Formation of Vegetable Mould Through the Action of Worms.* There is every reason to believe that almost all these books bear, in one way or another, on the principles and ideas that were inherent in Darwin's theory of evolution. The worm book, for example, is devoted to showing how great the impact of a seemingly trivial process like worm burrowing may be on ecology and geology if it persists for a long time. The idea of such cumulative slight effects is, of course, inherent in Darwin's view of evolution: successive slight modifications of a species, if continued long enough, can transform it radically.

When Darwin embarked on his voyage, he was a devout Christian who did not doubt the literal truth of the Bible, and did not believe in evolution any more than did Lyell and the other English scientists he had met or whose books he had read. By the time he returned to England in 1836 he had made numerous observations that would later convince him of evolution. It seems likely, however, that the idea itself did not occur to him until the spring of 1837, when the ornithologist John Gould, who was working on some of Darwin's collections, pointed out to him that each of the Galápagos Islands, off the coast of Ecuador, had a different kind of mockingbird. It was quite unclear whether they were different varieties of the same species, or different species. From this, Darwin quickly realized that species are not the discrete, clear-cut entities everyone seemed to imagine. The possibility of transformation entered his mind, and it applied to more than the mockingbirds: "When comparing . . . the birds from the separate islands of the Galápagos archipelago, both with one another and with those from the American mainland, I was much struck how entirely vague and arbitrary is the distinction between species and varieties."

In July 1837 he began his first notebook on the "Transmutation of Species." He later said that the Galápagos species and the similarity between South American fossils and living species were at the origin of all his views.

During the voyage of the *Beagle* I had been deeply impressed by discovering in the Pampean formation great fossil animals covered with armour like that on the existing armadillos; secondly, by the manner in which closely allied animals replace one another in proceeding southward over the continent; and thirdly, by the South American character of most of the productions of the Galápagos archipelago, and more especially by the manner in which they differ slightly on each island of the group; none of these islands appearing to be very ancient in a geological sense. It was evident that such facts as these, as well as many others, could be explained on the supposition that species gradually become modified; and the subject has haunted me.

The first great step in Darwin's thought was the realization that evolution had occurred. The second was his brilliant insight into the possible cause of evolutionary change. Lamarck's theory of "felt needs" had not been convincing. A better one was required. It came on September 18, 1838, when after grappling with the problem for fifteen months, "I happened to read for amusement Malthus on Population, and being well prepared to appreciate the struggle for existence which everywhere goes on from long-continued observation of the habits of animals and plants, it at once struck me that under these circumstances favorable variations would tend to be preserved, and unfavorable ones to be destroyed. The result of this would be the formation of new species. Here, then, I had at last got a theory by which to work."

Malthus, an economist, had developed the pessimistic thesis that the exponential growth of human populations must inevitably lead to famine, unless it were checked by war, disease, or "moral restraint." This emphasis on exponential population growth was apparently the catalyst for Darwin, who then realized that since most natural populations of animals and plants remain fairly stable in numbers, many more individuals are born than survive. Because individuals vary in their characteristics, the struggle to survive must favor some variant individuals over others. These survivors would then pass on their characteristics to future generations. Repetition of this process generation after generation would gradually transform the species.

Darwin clearly knew that he could not afford to publish a rash speculation on so important a subject without developing the best possible case. The world of science was not hospitable to speculation, and besides, Darwin was dealing with a highly volatile issue. Not only was he affirming that evolution had occurred, he was proposing a purely material explanation for it, one that demolished the argument from design in a single thrust. Instead of publishing his theory, he patiently amassed a mountain of evidence, and finally, in 1844, collected his thoughts in an essay on natural selection. But he still didn't publish. Not until 1856, almost twenty years after he became an evolutionist,

1. NATURAL SELECTION

ORIGINAL ANCESTOR

Figure 1. *Some species of Galápagos finches. Several of the most different species are represented here; intermediate species also exist. Clockwise from lower left are a male ground-finch (the plumage of the female resembles that of the tree-finches); the vegetarian tree-finch; the insectivorous tree-finch; the warbler-finch; and the woodpecker-finch, which uses a cactus spine to extricate insects from crevices. The slight differences among these species, and among species in other groups of Galápagos animals such as giant tortoises, were one of the observations that led Darwin to formulate his hypothesis of evolution. (From D. Lack, Darwin's Finches [Oxford: Oxford University Press, 1944].)*

page "abstract" that was published on November 24, 1859, under the title *The Origin of Species by Means of Natural Selection; or, the Preservation of Favored Races in the Struggle for Life.* Because it was an abstract, he had to leave out many of the detailed observations and references to the literature that he had amassed, but these were later provided in his other books, many of which are voluminous expansions on the contents of *The Origin of Species.*

The first five chapters of the *Origin* lay out the theory that Darwin had conceived. He shows that both domesticated and wild species are variable, that much of that variation is hereditary, and that breeders, by conscious selection of desirable varieties, can develop breeds of pigeons, dogs, and other forms that are more different from each other than species or even families of wild animals and plants are from each other. The differences between related species then are no more than an exaggerated form of the kinds of variations one can find in a single species; indeed, it is often extremely difficult to tell if natural populations are distinct species or merely well-marked varieties.

Darwin then shows that in nature there is competition, predation, and a struggle for life.

Owing to this struggle, variations, however slight and from whatever cause proceeding, if they be in any degree profitable to the individuals of a species, in their infinitely complex relations to other organic beings and to their physical conditions of life, will tend to the preservation of such individuals, and will generally be inherited by the offspring. The offspring, also, will thus have a better chance of surviving, for, of the many individuals of any species which are periodically born, but a small number can survive. I have called this principle, by which each slight variation, if useful, is preserved, by the term natural selection, in order to mark its relation to man's power of selection.

Darwin goes on to give examples of how even slight variations promote survival, and argues that when populations are exposed to different conditions, different variations will be favored, so that the descendants of a species become diversified in structure, and each ancestral species can give rise to sev-

did he begin what he planned to be a massive work on the subject, tentatively titled *Natural Selection.*

Then, in June 1858, the unthinkable happened. Alfred Russel Wallace (1823–1913), a young naturalist who had traveled in the Amazon Basin and in the Malay Archipelago, had also become interested in evolution. Like Darwin, he was struck by the fact that "the most closely allied species are found in the same locality or in closely adjoining localities and . . . therefore the natural sequence of the species by affinity is also geographical." In the throes of a

malarial fever in Malaya, Wallace conceived of the same idea of natural selection as Darwin had, and sent Darwin a manuscript "On the Tendency of Varieties to Depart Indefinitely from the Original Type." Darwin's friends Charles Lyell and Joseph Hooker, a botanist, rushed in to help Darwin establish the priority of his ideas, and on July 1, 1858, they presented to the Linnean Society of London both Wallace's paper and extracts from Darwin's 1844 essay. Darwin abandoned his big book on natural selection and condensed the argument into a 490-

eral new ones. Although "it is probable that each form remains for long periods unaltered," successive evolutionary modifications will ultimately alter the different species so greatly that they will be classified as different genera, families, or orders.

Competition between species will impel them to become more different, for "the more diversified the descendants from any one species become in structure, constitution and habits, by so much will they be better enabled to seize on many and widely diversified places in the polity of nature, and so be enabled to increase in numbers." Thus different adaptations arise, and "the ultimate result is that each creature tends to become more and more improved in relation to its conditions. This improvement inevitably leads to the greater advancement of the organization of the greater number of living beings throughout the world." But lowly organisms continue to persist, for "natural selection, or the survival of the fittest, does not necessarily include progressive development—it only takes advantage of such variations as arise and are beneficial to each creature under its complex relations of life." Probably no organism has reached a peak of perfection, and many lowly forms of life continue to exist, for "in some cases variations or individual differences of a favorable nature may never have arisen for natural selection to act on or accumulate. In no case, probably, has time sufficed for the utmost possible amount of development. In some few cases there has been what we must call retrogression of organization. But the main cause lies in the fact that under very simple conditions of life a high organization would be of no service. . . ."

In the rest of *The Origin of Species,* Darwin considers all the objections that might be raised against his theory; discusses the evolution of a great array of phenomena—hybrid sterility, the slave-making instinct of ants, the similarity of vertebrate embryos; and presents an enormous body of evidence for evolution. He draws his evidence from comparative anatomy, embryology, behavior, geographic variation,

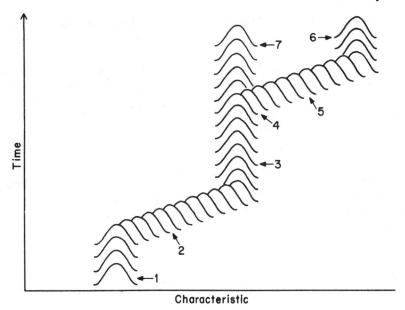

Figure 2. *Processes of evolutionary change. A characteristic that is variable (1) often shows a bell-shaped distribution—individuals vary on either side of the average. Evolutionary change (2) consists of a shift in successive generations, after which the characteristic may reach a new equilibrium (3). When the species splits into two different species (4), one of the species may undergo further evolutionary change (5) and reach a new equilibrium (6). The other may remain unchanged (7) or not. Each population usually remains variable throughout this process, but the average is shifted, ordinarily by natural selection.*

the geographic distribution of species, the study of rudimentary organs, atavistic variations ("throwbacks"), and the geological record to show how all of biology provides testimony that species have descended with modification from common ancestors.

Darwin's triumph was in synthesizing ideas and information in ways that no one had quite imagined before. From Lyell and the geologists he learned uniformitarianism: the cause of past events must be found in natural forces that operate today; and these, in the vastness of time, can accomplish great change. From Malthus and the nineteenth-century economists he learned of competition and the struggle for existence. From his work on barnacles, his travels, and his knowledge of domesticated varieties he learned that species do not have immutable essences but are variable in all their properties and blend into one another gradually. From his familiarity with the works of Whewell, Herschel, and other philosophers of science he developed a powerful method of pursuing science, the "hypothetico-deductive" method, which consists of formulating

a hypothesis or speculation, deducing the logical predictions that must follow from the hypothesis, and then testing the hypothesis by seeing whether or not the predictions are verified. This was by no means the prevalent philosophy of science in Darwin's time.[5]

Darwin brought biology out of the Middle Ages. For divine design and unknowable supernatural forces he substituted natural material causes that could be studied by the methods of science. Instead of catastrophes unknown to physical science he invoked forces that could be studied in anyone's laboratory or garden. He replaced a young, static world by one in which there had been constant change for countless aeons. He established that life had a history, and this proved the essential view that differentiated evolutionary thought from all that had gone before.

For the British naturalist John Ray, writing in 1701, organisms had no history—they were the same at that moment, and lived in the same places, doing the same things, as when they were first created. For Darwin, organisms spoke of historical change. If there has indeed been such a history, then fossils in the oldest rocks must differ from those in younger rocks: trilobites, dinosaurs, and mammoths will not be mixed together but will appear in some temporal sequence. If species come from common ancestors, they will have the same characteristics, modified for different functions: the same bones used by bats for flying will be used by horses for running. If species come from ancestors that lived in different environments, they will carry the evidence of their history with them in the form of similar patterns of embryonic development and in vestigial, rudimentary organs that no longer serve any function. If species have a history, their geographical distribution will reflect it: oceanic islands won't have elephants because they wouldn't have been able to get there.

Once the earth and its living inhabitants are seen as the products of historical change, the theological philosophy embodied in the great chain of being ceases to make sense; the plenitude, or fullness, of the world becomes not an eternal manifestation of God's bountiful creativity but an illusion. For most of earth's history, most of the present species have not existed; and many of those that did exist do so no longer. But the scientific challenge to medieval philosophy goes even deeper. If evolution has occurred, and if it has proceeded from the natural causes that Darwin envisioned, then the adaptations of organisms to their environment, the intricate construction of the bird's wing and the orchid's flower, are evidence not of divine design but of the struggle for existence. Moreover, and this may be the deepest implication of all, Darwin brought to biology, as his predecessors had brought to astronomy and geology, the sufficiency of efficient causes. No longer was there any reason to look for final causes or goals. To the questions "What purpose does this species serve? Why did God make tapeworms?" the answer is "To no purpose." Tapeworms were not put here to serve a purpose, nor were planets, nor plants, nor people. They came into existence not by design but by the action of impersonal natural laws.

By providing materialistic, mechanistic explanations, instead of miraculous ones, for the characteristics of plants and animals, Darwin brought biology out of the realm of theology and into the realm of science. For miraculous spiritual forces fall outside the province of science; all of science is the study of material causation.

Of course, *The Origin of Species* didn't convince everyone immediately. Evolution and its material cause, natural selection, evoked strong protests from ecclesiastical circles, and even from scientists.[6] The eminent geologist Adam Sedgwick, for example, wrote in 1860 that species must come into existence by creation,

a power I cannot imitate or comprehend; but in which I can believe, by a legitimate conclusion of sound reason drawn from the laws and harmonies of Nature. For I can see in all around me a design and purpose, and a mutual adaptation of parts which I *can* comprehend, and which prove that there is exterior to, and above, the mere phenomena of Nature a great prescient and designing cause. . . . The pretended physical philosophy of modern days strips man of all his moral attributes, or holds them of no account in the estimate of his origin and place in the created world. A cold atheistical materialism is the tendency of the so-called material philosophy of the present day.

Among the more scientific objections were those posed by the French paleontologist François Pictet, and they were echoed by many others. Since Darwin supposes that species change gradually over the course of thousands of generations, then, asked Pictet, "Why don't we find these gradations in the fossil record . . . and why, instead of collecting thousands of identical individuals, do we not find more intermediary forms? . . . How is it that the most ancient fossil beds are rich in a variety of diverse forms of life, instead of the few early types Darwin's theory leads us to expect? How is it that no species has been seen to evolve during human history, and that the 4000 years which separates us from the mummies of Egypt have been insufficient to modify the crocodile and the ibis?" Pictet protested that, although slight variations might in time alter a species slightly, "all known facts demonstrate . . . that the pro-

longed influence of modifying causes has an action which is constantly restrained within sufficiently confined limits."

The anatomist Richard Owen likewise denied "that . . . variability is progressive and unlimited, so as, in the course of generations, to change the species, the genus, the order, or the class." The paleontologist Louis Agassiz insisted that organisms fall into discrete groups, based on uniquely different created plans, between which no intermediates could exist. He chose the birds as a group that showed the sharpest of boundaries. Only a few years later, in 1868, the fossil *Archaeopteryx,* an exquisite intermediate between birds and reptiles, demolished Agassiz's argument, and he had no more to say on the unique character of the birds.

Within twelve years of *The Origin of Species,* the evidence for evolution had been so thoroughly accepted that the philosopher and mathematician Chauncey Wright could point out that among the students of science, "orthodoxy has been won over to the doctrine of evolution." However, Wright continued, "While the general doctrine of evolution has thus been successfully redeemed from theological condemnation, this is not yet true of the subordinate hypothesis of Natural Selection."

Natural selection turned out to be an extraordinarily difficult concept for people to grasp. St. George Mivart, a Catholic scholar and scientist, was not unusual in equating natural selection with chance. "The theory of Natural Selection may (though it need not) be taken in such a way as to lead man to regard the present organic world as formed, so to speak, *accidentally,* beautiful and wonderful as is the confessedly haphazard result." Many like him simply refused to understand that natural selection is the antithesis of chance and consequently could not see how selection might cause adaptation or any kind of progressive evolutionary change. Even in the 1940s there were those, especially among paleontologists, who felt that the progressive evolution of groups like the horses, as revealed by the fossil record, must have had some unknown cause other than natural selection. Paradoxically, then, Darwin had convinced the scientific world of evolution where his predecessors had failed; but he had not convinced all biologists of his truly original theory, the theory of natural selection.

Natural selection fell into particular disrepute in the early part of the twentieth century because of the rise of genetics—which, as it happened, eventually became the foundation of the modern theory of evolution. Darwin's supposition that variation was unlimited, and so in time could give rise to strikingly different organisms, was not entirely convincing because he had no good idea of where variation came from. In 1865, the Austrian monk Gregor Mendel discovered, from his crosses of pea plants, that discretely different characteristics such as wrinkled versus smooth seeds were inherited from generation to generation without being altered, as if they were caused by particles that passed from parent to offspring. Mendel's work was ignored for thirty-five years, until, in 1900, three biologists discovered his paper and realized that it held the key to the mystery of heredity. One of the three, Hugo de Vries, set about to explore the problem as Mendel had, and in the course of his studies of evening primroses observed strikingly different variations arise, *de novo*. The new forms were so different that de Vries believed they represented new species, which had arisen in a single step by alteration or, as he called it, mutation, of the hereditary material.

In the next few decades, geneticists working with a great variety of organisms observed many other drastic changes arise by mutation: fruit flies (*Drosophila*), for example, with white instead of red eyes or curled instead of straight wings. These laboratory geneticists, especially Thomas Hunt Morgan, an outstanding geneticist at Columbia University, asserted that evolution must proceed by major mutational steps, and that mutation, not natural selection, was the cause of evolution. In their eyes, Darwin's theory was dead on two counts: evolution was not

gradual, and it was not caused by natural selection. Meanwhile, naturalists, taxonomists, and breeders of domesticated plants and animals continued to believe in Darwinism, because they saw that populations and species differed quantitatively and gradually rather than in big jumps, that most variation was continuous (like height in humans) rather than discrete, and that domesticated species could be altered by artificial selection from continuous variation.

The bitter conflict between the Mendelian geneticists and the Darwinians was resolved in the 1930s in a "New Synthesis" that brought the opposing views into a "neo-Darwinian" theory of evolution.[7] Slight variations in height, wing length, and other characteristics proved, under careful genetic analysis, to be inherited as particles, in the same way as the discrete variations studied by the Mendelians. Thus a large animal simply has inherited more particles, or genes, for large size than a smaller member of the species has. The Mendelians were simply studying particularly well marked variations, while the naturalists were studying more subtle ones. Variations could be very slight, or fairly pronounced, or very substantial, but all were inherited in the same manner. All these variations, it was shown, arose by a process of mutation of the genes.

Three mathematical theoreticians, Ronald Fisher and J. B. S. Haldane in England and Sewall Wright in the United States, proved that a newly mutated gene would not automatically form a new species. Nor would it automatically replace the preexisting form of the gene, and so transform the species. Replacement of one gene by a mutant form of the gene, they said, could happen in two ways. The mutation could enable its possessors to survive or reproduce more effectively than the old form; if so, it would increase by natural selection, just as Darwin had said. The new characteristic that evolved in this way would ordinarily be considered an improved adaptation.

Sewall Wright pointed out, however, that not all genetic changes in

species need be adaptive. A new mutation might be no better or worse than the preexisting gene—it might simply be "neutral." In small populations such a mutation could replace the previous gene purely by chance—a process he called random genetic drift. The idea, put crudely, is this. Suppose there is a small population of land snails in a cow pasture, and that 5 percent of them are brown and the rest are yellow. Purely by chance, a greater percentage of yellow snails than of brown ones get crushed by cows' hooves in one generation. The snails breed, and there will now be a slightly greater percentage of yellow snails in the next generation than there had been. But in the next generation, the yellow ones may suffer more trampling, purely by chance. The proportion of yellow offspring will then be lower again. These random events cause fluctuations in the percentage of the two types. Wright proved mathematically that eventually, if no other factors intervene, these fluctuations will bring the population either to 100 percent yellow or 100 percent brown, purely by chance. The population will have evolved, then, but not by natural selection; and there is no improvement of adaptation.

During the period of the New Synthesis, though, genetic drift was emphasized less than natural selection, for which abundant evidence was discovered. Sergei Chetverikov in Russia, and later Theodosius Dobzhansky working in the United States, showed that wild populations of fruit flies contained an immense amount of genetic variation, including the same kinds of mutations that the geneticists had found arising in their laboratories. Dobzhansky and other workers went on to show that these variations affected survival and reproduction: that natural selection was a reality. They showed, moreover, that the genetic differences among related species were indeed compounded of the same kinds of slight genetic variations that they found within species. Thus the taxonomists and the geneticists converged onto a neo-Darwinian theory of evolution: evolution is due not to mutation *or* natural selection, but to both. Random mutations provide abundant genetic variation; natural selection, the antithesis of randomness, sorts out the useful from the deleterious, and transforms the species.

In the following two decades, the paleontologist George Gaylord Simpson showed that this theory was completely adequate to explain the fossil record, and the ornithologists Bernhard Rensch and Ernst Mayr, the botanist G. Ledyard Stebbins, and many other taxonomists showed that the similarities and differences among living species could be fully explained by neo-Darwinism. They also clarified the meaning of "species." Organisms belong to different species if they do not interbreed when the opportunity presents itself, thus remaining genetically distinct. An ancestral species splits into two descendant species when different populations of the ancestor, living in different geographic regions, become so genetically different from each other that they will not or cannot interbreed when they have the chance to do so. As a result, evolution can happen without the formation of new species: a single species can be genetically transformed without splitting into several descendants. Conversely, new species can be formed without much genetic change. If one population becomes different from the rest of its species in, for example, its mating behavior, it will not interbreed with the other populations. Thus it has become a new species, even though it may be identical to its "sister species" in every respect except its behavior. Such a new species is free to follow a new path of genetic change, since it does not become homogenized with its sister species by interbreeding. With time, therefore, it can diverge and develop different adaptations.

The conflict between the geneticists and the Darwinians that was resolved in the New Synthesis was the last ma-

jor conflict in evolutionary science. Since that time, an enormous amount of research has confirmed most of the major conclusions of neo-Darwinism. We now know that populations contain very extensive genetic variation that continually arises by mutation of pre-existing genes. We also know what genes are and how they become mutated. Many instances of the reality of natural selection in wild populations have been documented, and there is extensive evidence that many species form by the divergence of different populations of an ancestral species.

The major questions in evolutionary biology now tend to be of the form, "All right, factors x and y both operate in evolution, but how important is x compared to y?" For example, studies of biochemical genetic variation have raised the possibility that nonadaptive, random change (genetic drift) may be the major reason for many biochemical differences among species. How important, then, is genetic drift compared to natural selection? Another major question has to do with rates of evolution: Do species usually diverge very slowly, as Darwin thought, or does evolution consist mostly of rapid spurts, interspersed with long periods of constancy? Still another question is raised by mutations, which range all the way from gross changes of the kind Morgan studied to very slight alterations. Does evolution consist entirely of the substitution of mutations that have very slight effects, or are major mutations sometimes important too? Partisans on each side of all these questions argue vigorously for their interpretation of the evidence, but they don't doubt that the major factors of evolution are known. They simply emphasize one factor or another. Minor battles of precisely this kind go on continually in every field of science; without them there would be very little advancement in our knowledge.

Within a decade or two of *The Ori-*

gin of Species, the belief that living organisms had evolved over the ages was firmly entrenched in biology. As of 1982, the historical existence of evolution is viewed as fact by almost all biologists. To explain how the fact of evolution has been brought about, a theory of evolutionary mechanisms—mutation, natural selection, genetic drift, and isolation—has been developed.[8] But exactly what is the evidence for the fact of evolution?

NOTES

1. Andrew Dickson White, *A History of the Warfare of Science with Theology in Christendom* vol. I (London: Macmillan, 1896; reprint ed., New York: Dover, 1960).

2. A. O. Lovejoy, *The Great Chain of Being* (Cambridge, Mass.: Harvard University Press, 1936).

3. Much of this history is provided by J. C. Greene, *The Death of Adam: Evolution and its Impact on Western Thought* (Ames: Iowa State University Press, 1959).

4. A detailed history of this and other developments in evolutionary biology is given by Ernst Mayr, *The Growth of Biological Thought: Diversity, Evolution, Inheritance* (Cambridge, Mass.: Harvard University Press, 1982).

5. See D. L. Hull, *Darwin and His Critics* (Cambridge, Mass.: Harvard University Press, 1973).

6. *Ibid.*

7. E. Mayr and W. B. Provine, *The Evolutionary Synthesis* (Cambridge, Mass.: Harvard University Press, 1980).

8. Our modern understanding of the mechanisms of evolution is described in many books. Elementary textbooks include G. L. Stebbins, *Processes of Organic Evolution,* (Englewood Cliffs, N.J.: Prentice-Hall, 1971), and J. Maynard Smith, *The Theory of Evolution* (New York: Penguin Books, 1975). More advanced textbooks include Th. Dobzhansky, F. J. Ayala, G. L. Stebbins, and J. W. Valentine, *Evolution* (San Francisco: Freeman, 1977), and D. J. Futuyma, *Evolutionary Biology* (Sunderland, Mass.: Sinauer, 1979). Unreferenced facts and theories described in the text are familiar enough to most evolutionary biologists that they will be found in most or all of the references cited above.

The Struggle for the Schools

Despite a 1987 rebuff from the Supreme Court, creationists are still pushing for equal time in science classes

Eugenie C. Scott

Eugenie C. Scott, executive director of the National Center for Science Education, located in Berkeley, California, studies the activities of the religious right and scientific creationists and helps teachers around the nation keep evolution at the core of the science curriculum. She finds her work satisfying but is often dismayed by the extent of scientific illiteracy in America.

Late last year, a letter received at the National Center for Science Education from one of our Alaskan members reminded me that even though some things change in the creation-evolution conflict, old battles continue. My job is to help teachers teach evolution when they are pressured not to, and to help people cope with attempts to insert the biblical story of the Creation into science classes. The letter alerted me that the Alaska State Board of Education was debating a requirement that teachers give creationism equal status alongside evolution in science classes, even though the Supreme Court outlawed such "equal time" provisions in 1987. In Alaska, as usually happens when such attempts are made to legally enforce creationism, cooler heads prevailed and the requirement was not added to the guidelines. But more frequently, I am confronted by evolved forms of creationism designed to sidestep the legal prohibitions.

By the turn of the twentieth century, evolutionary theory had captivated the world of science and had even begun to take hold in American textbooks. Some citizens, distressed at these developments, lobbied for legislation against the teaching of evolution in the public schools. John Scopes was convicted under Tennessee's antievolution law in 1925, in the so-called Monkey Trial. Although the Supreme Court struck down such laws in 1968, antievolutionists have never given up the struggle.

Antievolutionism in America is largely the creature of a Christian fundamentalist theology that was built upon five core beliefs, called "the Fundamentals," which had crystallized by about 1915. The first of these argued that the Bible should be read literally, not interpreted. The Bible said not only that God created the universe, but also how—all at one time, over six 24-hour days, and only a few thousand years ago. Evolution contradicted the biblical account of the Creation by proposing that the universe came into being over a vast period of time, and that living forms descended with modification from earlier ones. Most Catholic and Protestant clergy, while stressing the ultimate creative role of the Deity, were willing to leave the details to science, but fundamentalists rejected any such compromise.

Fundamentalists did not oppose evolution just because they believed it contradicted God's Word. After all, so did spherical-earth geology and heliocentrism; but by the early twentieth century, few Christians interpreted the Bible literally on those issues. The evidence of science on the shape and location of the earth is also accepted by most creationists today, although some still argue that the earth is the center of the solar system.

But turn-of-the-century fundamentalists were convinced, as are their modern descendants, that acceptance of evolution breeds not only theological problems but also moral ones. The most influential creationist of this century, Henry M. Morris. has blamed evolutionary theory for "communism, fascism, Freudianism, social Darwinism, behaviorism, Kinseyism, materialism, atheism, and, in the religious world, modernism and neo-orthodoxy." The worry is that if children learn evolution they will reject God. Lacking faith, children may accept "nature red in tooth and claw" as the only morality and fall into evil ways. Believers in evolution, according to Morris, will be lost to salvation and face eternal damnation.

After 1968, when the attempt to exclude evolutionary teaching from the public schools was outlawed by a decision of the Supreme Court (*Epperson v. Arkansas*), creationists sought equal time for their own views. Since the teaching of religious beliefs would violate the constitutional separation of church and state, creationists repackaged the Bible as science to give it a legitimate position in the curriculum. The result was the birth of "scientific creationism," the idea that scientific data exist to document the sudden creation of the universe in the not-too-distant past.

Overwhelmingly, scientists who have analyzed these arguments have concluded that creation science misstates evolutionary theory, presents erroneous data, and reveals a gross misunderstanding of the nature of science (see "The Flood of Antievolutionism," by Laurie R. Godfrey, *Natural History,* June 1981). But during the 1970s, several organizations, the largest being Morris's Institute for Creation Research, in California, and the Bible-Science Association, in Minnesota, successfully promoted the idea that creationism and evolution should be taught side by side in science classes as "two models" or "two theories." Their appeal for fairness won creation scientists more support than their science.

By the late 1970s, at least twenty-six state legislatures were considering "equal time" laws. Two states, Arkansas and Louisiana, passed such legislation, and both laws were immediately challenged in the courts and struck down. In 1987, the Louisiana case reached the Supreme Court, which proclaimed in *Edwards v. Aguillard* that creationism is inherently a religious idea. Its teaching thus represents a state advocacy of religion, violating the establishment clause of the first amendment to the Constitution.

Since 1987, the attempts to give equal time to creation science have dwindled, although they still occur. For example, a school district in Vermont passed a resolution in late 1992 that "creation be presented as a viable theory on an equal status with the various theories of evolution." Once shown to school district lawyers, such resolutions are usually rescinded.

But the Supreme Court decision left a loophole that encouraged creationists to persevere. In *Edwards,* the court recognized that teachers are free to teach "all scientific theories about the origins of humankind." Justice Brennan wrote that "teaching a variety of scientific theories about the origins of humankind to school-children might validly be done with the clear secular intent of enhancing the effectiveness of science instruction." This suggested that alternative theories could be taught, but it ignored that there are no reputable alternatives to evolution as a

scientific explanation. Antievolutionists were further encouraged by Justice Antonin Scalia's dissenting opinion, when he stated that residents of Louisiana had a right "as a secular matter, to have whatever scientific evidence there may be against evolution presented in their schools."

Antievolutionists thus adopted a new strategy: avoiding Creation, Creator, or any term that implied creationism, they called for equal time to teach that evolution did not occur. This new language appeared quite soon after the *Edwards* decision, in the Texas textbook guidelines for 1990. The Texas Educational Agency told publishers that books submitted for adoption should discuss "scientific evidence of evolution and reliable scientific theories to the contrary." This language also cropped up in August 1991 in Louisville, Ohio, where a school board's science curriculum stated that teachers should "develop an appreciation of theories on evolution and its alternatives." Teachers were supposed to "contrast, compare and discuss alternatives to evolutionary theory."

In May of 1993, the school board in Vista, California, presented a resolution stating that "weaknesses that substantially challenge theories in evolution should be presented." And in December, the Tangipahoa Parish (Louisiana) school board, quoting from the *Edwards* decision itself, drafted a policy that would allow the teaching of "other theories of the origin of man" besides evolution "if done with the clear secular intent of enhancing the effectiveness of science instruction."

The "weaknesses in evolution" and "evidence against evolution" that have been put forward include such arguments as: there are no transitional forms; life is so improbable that it could not have originated "randomly"; the second law of thermodynamics (which refers to a tendency toward increased disorder) disproves evolution; radiometric dating is invalid and the earth is young. On examination these views turn out to be identical to what in pre-*Edwards* days was called scientific creationism. But the lack of obvious religious content and purpose

may help insulate these antievolution arguments from legal challenge. A judge might decide that regardless of scholarly merit, these teachings did not obviously promote religion. Just because the first amendment protects against the government establishment of religion doesn't mean it will be a protection against bad science.

So far this strategy seems to have failed, at least in the cases that have been brought to the attention of the National Center for Science Education. This is partly because we are often able to offer information or other assistance to the local opposition, including finding scientists to testify on behalf of evolution and against creationism. For example, in the Vista, California, case, members of a citizens' group testified vociferously at several school board meetings that they wanted evolution, not creationism, taught and threatened to sue if the board pushed the issue. Similarly, in Tangipahoa Parish, Louisiana, scientists from the local state university and others protested at school board meetings, as well as in such public forums as "letters to the editor" columns and radio talk shows, against the teaching of "other theories" besides evolution. In March 1994 the board gave up its plan.

Students in Texas and elsewhere are not now reading science textbooks that present "scientific" theories that contradict evolution because members of our organization and others, such as People for the American Way, helped promote a change in the final wording of Texas's very influential guidelines. The curriculum now calls for adopting textbooks that provide "scientific evidence of evolution and reliable scientific theories to the contrary, if any." The "if any" allows the textbook publishers some wiggle room—they can argue that they cannot find any such theories. And the Louisville, Ohio, situation is currently on hold while the district awaits the release of a state curriculum. Protest from community members and a threatened lawsuit by the Ohio chapter of the American Civil Liberties Union probably encouraged this delay.

The evolution of creationism has taken another turn, however. In 1989, the Foundation for Thought and Ethics, a Texas-based creationist organization, published *Of Pandas and People* as a supplement to high-school biology texts. *Pandas* claims to be a balanced treatment of evolution and "intelligent design theory." In familiar creationist fashion, it presents evolution as a largely chance process that cannot account for the impressive complexity of such intricate structures as the vertebrate eye. The alternative to this allegedly random process is "intelligent design," a term that obviously suggests divine creation, although the authors deny that the intelligence is necessarily supernatural. All in all, the text parades the usual creationist arguments, only without identifying them as such.

The publisher promotes *Pandas* through a grass-roots campaign, encouraging parents to approach school curriculum committees to adopt the book. According to the publisher, *Pandas* is being used in more than forty states, although in which states and in which districts is not made clear. The book was submitted for state adoption in Idaho and Alabama and rejected in both places. A creationist school board member in Vista, California, asked teachers there to consider it as a supplementary textbook. Armed with reviews prepared by our scientists and educators, they, too, soundly rejected it. Despite these successes, however, individual teachers may be using the book. In a case in northern California,

the colleagues of one teacher directed him to return the classroom copies he had ordered for his students, on the grounds that the book had not passed normal district review.

Compared with those of other industrialized nations, the American public school system is very decentralized. Local school districts make the majority of curriculum decisions, sometimes guided by state curricula but not always bound by law to obey them. State agencies may influence school districts by requiring them to spend state funds only on approved books, but what is taught in the classroom will vary locally. Not only the local school board but also the individual teacher has considerable leeway. Unless students report on what happens when the door is closed, no one else may know.

In Stanwood, Washington, for example, local residents didn't know, until a student mentioned it to a parent, that a creation scientist had been invited to lecture on the "latest scientific findings" about how humans and dinosaurs lived at the same time. In another Washington community, a teacher who was teamed up with another for a high-school science class was astounded to hear his colleague advocating the creationist view that the earth was very young. Until the two shared the same classroom, no one had known that this teacher presented creation science.

From kindergarten through high school, public school teachers face pressure to teach creation science or "evidence against evolution," or at

least to downplay evolution. Our caseload at the National Center for Science Education has been steadily increasing over the last six years. Part of this increase has been brought about by a shift in American politics. The religious right, disappointed by its lack of success on the national level, has focused on winning local elective offices, including representation on school boards and curriculum committees.

When the religious right wins a majority of seats on a school board, as in Vista, California, the teaching of evolution becomes a contentious issue. Even if not forced to do so, some teachers just quietly stop teaching it. Others feel a chilling effect. One teacher wrote me that he makes sure to collect all the handouts when he teaches evolution so that parents won't know what he is teaching. That teachers have to sneak good science into the classroom is regrettable. Unfortunately, in the face of parental pressure, principals and superintendents frequently fail to support teachers, even when the curriculum mandates the teaching of evolution.

If public school teachers shrink from teaching evolution, many students will not learn about it unless they go to college—if then. Others will be deprived of one of the great enriching ideas of science. If, as the geneticist Theodosius Dobzhansky said, "Nothing in biology makes sense except in the light of evolution," these students will learn nonsensical biology, a "pile of sundry facts" unconnected by an organizing theory.

Curse and Blessing of the Ghetto

Tay-Sachs disease is a choosy killer, one that for centuries targeted Eastern European Jews above all others. By decoding its lethal logic, we can learn a lot about how genetic diseases evolve—and how they can be conquered.

Jared Diamond

Contributing editor Jared Diamond is a professor of physiology at the UCLA School of Medicine.

Marie and I hated her at first sight, even though she was trying hard to be helpful. As our obstetrician's genetics counselor, she was just doing her job, explaining to us the unpleasant results that might come out of the genetic tests we were about to have performed. As a scientist, though, I already knew all I wanted to know about Tay-Sachs disease, and I didn't need to be reminded that the baby sentenced to death by it could be my own.

Fortunately, the tests would reveal that my wife and I were not carriers of the Tay-Sachs gene, and our preparenthood fears on that matter at least could be put to rest. But at the time I didn't yet know that. As I glared angrily at that poor genetics counselor, so strong was my anxiety that now, four years later, I can still clearly remember what was going through my mind: If I were an evil deity, I thought, trying to devise exquisite tortures for babies and their parents, I would be proud to have designed Tay-Sachs disease.

Tay-Sachs is completely incurable, unpreventable, and preprogrammed in the genes. A Tay-Sachs infant usually appears normal for the first few months after birth, just long enough for the parents to grow to love him. An exaggerated "startle reaction" to sounds is the first ominous sign. At about six months the baby starts to lose control of his head and can't roll over or sit without support. Later he begins to drool, breaks out into unmotivated bouts of laughter, and suffers convulsions. Then his head grows abnormally large, and he becomes blind. Perhaps what's most frightening for the parents is that their baby loses all contact with his environment and becomes virtually a vegetable. By the child's third birthday, if he's still alive, his skin will turn yellow and his hands pudgy. Most likely he will die before he's four years old.

My wife and I were tested for the Tay-Sachs gene because at the time we rated as high-risk candidates, for two reasons. First, Marie was carrying twins, so we had double the usual chance to bear a Tay-Sachs baby. Second, both she and I are of Eastern European Jewish ancestry, the population with by far the world's highest Tay-Sachs frequency.

In peoples around the world Tay-Sachs appears once in every 400,000 births. But it appears a hundred times more frequently—about once in 3,600 births—among descendants of Eastern European Jews, people known as Ashkenazim. For descendants of most other groups of Jews—Oriental Jews, chiefly from the Middle East, or Sephardic Jews, from Spain and other Mediterranean countries—the frequency of Tay-Sachs disease is no higher than in non-Jews. Faced with such a clear correlation, one cannot help but wonder: What is it about this one group of people that produces such an extraordinarily high risk of this disease?

Finding the answer to this question concerns all of us, regardless of our ancestry. Every human population is especially susceptible to certain diseases, not only because of its life-style but also because of its genetic inheritance. For example, genes put European whites at high risk for cystic fibrosis, African blacks for sickle-cell disease, Pacific Islanders for diabetes—and Eastern European Jews for ten different diseases, including Tay-Sachs. It's not that Jews are notably susceptible to genetic diseases in general; but a combination of historical factors has led to Jews' being intensively studied, and so their susceptibilities are far better known than those of, say, Pacific Islanders.

Tay-Sachs exemplifies how we can deal with such diseases; it has been the object of the most successful screening program to date. Moreover, Tay-Sachs is helping us understand how ethnic diseases evolve. Within the past couple of years discoveries by molecular biologists have provided tantalizing clues to precisely how a deadly gene can persist and spread over the centuries. Tay-Sachs may be primarily a disease of Eastern European Jews, but through this affliction of one group of people, we gain a window on how our genes simultaneously curse and bless us all.

The disease's hyphenated name comes from the two physicians—British ophthalmologist W. Tay and New York neurologist B. Sachs—who independently first recognized the disease, in 1881 and 1887, respectively. By 1896 Sachs had seen enough cases to realize that the disease was most common among Jewish children.

Not until 1962, however, were researchers able to trace the cause of the affliction to a single biochemical abnormality: the excessive accumulation in nerve cells of a fatty substance called G_{M2} ganglioside. Normally G_{M2} ganglioside is present at only modest levels in cell membranes, because it is constantly being broken down as well as synthesized. The breakdown depends on the enzyme hexosaminidase A, which is found in the tiny structures within our cells known as lysosomes. In the unfortunate Tay-Sachs victims this enzyme is lacking, and without it the ganglioside piles up and produces all the symptoms of the disease.

We have two copies of the gene that programs our supply of hexosaminidase A, one inherited from our father, the other from our mother; each of our parents, in turn, has two copies derived from their own parents. As long as we have one good copy of the gene, we can produce enough hexosaminidase A to prevent a buildup of G_{M2} ganglioside and we won't get Tay-Sachs. This genetic disease is of the sort termed recessive rather than dominant—meaning that to get it, a child must inherit a defective gene not just from one parent but from both of them. Clearly, each parent must have had one good copy of the gene along with the defective copy—if either had had two defective genes, he or she would have died of the disease long before reaching the age of reproduction. In genetic terms the diseased child is homozygous for the defective gene and both parents are heterozygous for it.

None of this yet gives any hint as to why the Tay-Sachs gene should be most common among Eastern European Jews. To come to grips with that question, we must take a short detour into history.

From their biblical home of ancient Israel, Jews spread peacefully to other Mediterranean lands, Yemen, and India. They were also dispersed violently through conquest by Assyrians, Babylonians, and Romans. Under the Carolingian kings of the eighth and ninth centuries Jews were invited to settle in France and Germany as traders and financiers. In subsequent centuries, however, persecutions triggered by the Crusades gradually drove Jews out of Western Europe; the process culminated in their total expulsion from Spain in 1492. Those Spanish Jews—called Sephardim—fled to other lands around the Mediterranean. Jews of France and Germany—the Ashkenazim—fled east to Poland and from there to Lithuania and western Russia, where they settled mostly in towns, as businessmen engaged in whatever pursuit they were allowed.

It seems unlikely that genetic accidents would have pumped up the frequency of the same gene not once but twice in the same population.

There the Jews stayed for centuries, through periods of both tolerance and oppression. But toward the end of the nineteenth century and the beginning of the twentieth, waves of murderous anti-Semitic attacks drove millions of Jews out of Eastern Europe, with most of them heading for the United States. My mother's parents, for example, fled to New York from the Lithuanian pogroms of the 1880s, while my father's parents fled from the Ukrainian pogroms of 1903–6. The more modern history of Jewish migration is probably well known to you all: most Jews who remained in Eastern Europe were exterminated during World War II, while most the survivors immigrated to the United States and Israel. Of the 13 million Jews alive today, more than three-quarters are Ashkenazim, the descendants of the Eastern European

Jews and the people most at risk for Tay-Sachs.

Have these Jews maintained their genetic distinctness through the thousands of years of wandering? Some scholars claim that there has been so much intermarriage and conversion that Ashkenazic Jews are now just Eastern Europeans who adopted Jewish culture. However, modern genetic studies refute that speculation.

First of all, there are those ten genetic diseases that the Ashkenazim have somehow acquired, by which they differ both from other Jews and from Eastern European non-Jews. In addition, many Ashkenazic genes turn out to be ones typical of Palestinian Arabs and other peoples of the Eastern Mediterranean areas where Jews originated. (In fact, by genetic standards the current Arab-Israeli conflict is an internecine civil war.) Other Ashkenazic genes have indeed diverged from Mediterranean ones (including genes of Sephardic and Oriental Jews) and have evolved to converge on genes of Eastern European non-Jews subject to the same local forces of natural selection. But the degree to which Ashkenazim prove to differ genetically from Eastern European non-Jews implies an intermarriage rate of only about 15 percent.

Can history help explain why the Tay-Sachs gene in particular is so much more common in Ashkenazim than in their non-Jewish neighbors or in other Jews? At the risk of spoiling a mystery, I'll tell you now that the answer is yes, but to appreciate it, you'll have to understand the four possible explanations for the persistence of the Tay-Sachs gene.

First, new copies of the gene might be arising by mutation as fast as existing copies disappear with the death of Tay-Sachs children. That's the most likely explanation for the gene's persistence in most of the world, where the disease frequency is only one in 400,000 births—that frequency reflects a typical human mutation rate. But for this explanation to apply to the Ashkenazim would require a mutation rate of at least one per 3,600 births—far above the frequency observed for any human gene. Furthermore, there would be no precedent for one particular gene mutating so much more often in one human population than in others.

As a second possibility, the Ashkenazim might have acquired the Tay-Sachs gene from some other people who already had the gene at high frequency. Arthur Koestler's controversial book *The Thirteenth Tribe,* for example, popularized the view that the Ashkenazim are really not a Semitic people but are instead descended from the Khazar, a Turkic tribe whose rulers converted to Judaism in the eighth century. Could the Khazar have brought the Tay-Sachs gene to Eastern Europe? This speculation makes good romantic reading, but there is no good evidence to support it. Moreover, it fails to explain why deaths of Tay-Sachs children didn't eliminate the gene by natural selection in the past 1,200 years, nor how the Khazar acquired high frequencies of the gene in the first place.

The third hypothesis was the one preferred by a good many geneticists until recently. It invokes two genetic processes, termed the founder effect and genetic drift, that may operate in small populations. To understand these concepts, imagine that 100 couples settle in a new land and found a population that then increases. Imagine further that one parent among those original 100 couples happens to have some rare gene, one, say, that normally occurs at a frequency of one in a million. The gene's frequency in the new population will now be one in 200 as a result of the accidental presence of that rare founder.

Or suppose again that 100 couples found a population, but that one of the 100 men happens to have lots of kids by his wife or that he is exceptionally popular with other women, while the other 99 men are childless or have few kids or are simply less popular. That one man may thereby father 10 percent rather than a more representative one percent of the next generation's babies, and their genes will disproportionately reflect that man's genes. In other words, gene frequencies will have drifted between the first and second generation.

Through these two types of genetic accidents a rare gene may occur with an unusually high frequency in a small expanding population. Eventually, if the gene is harmful, natural selection will bring its frequency back to normal by killing off gene bearers. But if the resultant disease is recessive—if heterozygous individuals don't get the disease and only the rare, homozygous individuals die of it—the gene's high frequency may persist for many generations.

These accidents do in fact account for the astonishingly high Tay-Sachs gene frequency found in one group of Pennsylvania Dutch: out of the 333 people in this group, 98 proved to carry the Tay-Sachs gene. Those 333 are all descended from one couple who settled in the United States in the eighteenth century and had 13 children. Clearly, one of that founding couple must have carried the gene. A similar accident may explain why Tay-Sachs is also relatively common among French Canadians, who number 5 million today but are descended from fewer than 6,000 French immigrants who arrived in the New World between 1638 and 1759. In the two or three centuries since both these founding events, the high Tay-Sachs gene frequency among Pennsylvania Dutch and French Canadians has not yet had enough time to decline to normal levels.

The same mechanisms were once proposed to explain the high rate of Tay-Sachs disease among the Ashkenazim. Perhaps, the reasoning went, the gene just happened to be overrepresented in the founding Jewish population that settled in Germany or Eastern Europe. Perhaps the gene just happened to drift up in frequency in the Jewish populations scattered among the isolated towns of Eastern Europe.

But geneticists have long questioned whether the Ashkenazim population's history was really suitable for these genetic accidents to have been significant. Remember, the founder effect and genetic drift become significant only in small populations, and the founding populations of Ashkenazim may have been quite large. Moreover, Ashkenazic communities were consid-

erably widespread; drift would have sent gene frequencies up in some towns but down in others. And, finally, natural selection has by now had a thousand years to restore gene frequencies to normal.

Granted, those doubts are based on historical data, which are not always as precise or reliable as one might want. But within the past several years the case against those accidental explanations for Tay-Sachs disease in the Ashkenazim has been bolstered by discoveries by molecular biologists.

Like all proteins, the enzyme absent in Tay-Sachs children is coded for by a piece of our DNA. Along that particular stretch of DNA there are thousands of different sites where a mutation could occur that would result in no enzyme and hence in the same set of symptoms. If molecular biologists had discovered that all cases of Tay-Sachs in Ashkenazim involved damage to DNA at the same site, that would have been strong evidence that in Ashkenazim the disease stems from a single mutation that has been multiplied by the founder effect or genetic drift—in other words, the high incidence of Tay-Sachs among Eastern European Jews is accidental.

In reality, though, several different mutations along this stretch of DNA have been identified in Ashkenazim, and two of them occur much more frequently than in non-Ashkenazim populations. It seems unlikely that genetic accidents would have pumped up the frequency of the same gene not once but twice in the same population.

And that's not the sole unlikely coincidence arguing against accidental explanations. Recall that Tay-Sachs is caused by the excessive accumulation of one fatty substance, G_{M2} ganglioside, from a defect in one enzyme, hexosaminidase A. But Tay-Sachs is one of ten genetic diseases characteristic of Ashkenazim. Among those other nine, two—Gaucher's disease and Niemann-Pick disease—result from the accumulation of two other fatty substances similar to G_{M2} ganglioside, as a result of defects in two other enzymes similar to hexosaminidase A. Yet our bodies contain thousands of different enzymes. It would have been an incredible roll of the genetic dice if, by nothing more than chance, Ashkenazim had independently acquired mutations in three closely related enzymes—and had acquired mutations in one of those enzymes twice.

All these facts bring us to the fourth possible explanation of why the Tay-Sachs gene is so prevalent among Ashkenazim: namely, that something about them favored accumulation of G_{M2} ganglioside and related fats.

For comparison, suppose that a friend doubles her money on one stock while you are getting wiped out with your investments. Taken alone, that could just mean she was lucky on that one occasion. But suppose that she doubles her money on each of two different stocks and at the same time rings up big profits in real estate while also making a killing in bonds. That implies more than lady luck; it suggests that something about your friend—like shrewd judgment—favors financial success.

What could be the blessings of fat accumulation in Eastern European Jews? At first this question sounds weird. After all, that fat accumulation

was noticed only because of the curses it bestows: Tay-Sachs, Gaucher's, or Niemann-Pick disease. But many of our common genetic diseases may persist because they bring both blessings and curses (see "The Cruel Logic of Our Genes," *Discover*, November 1989). They kill or impair individuals who inherit two copies of the faulty gene, but they help those who receive only one defective gene by protecting them against other diseases. The best understood example is the sickle-cell gene of African blacks, which often kills homozygotes but protects heterozygotes against malaria. Natural selection sustains such genes because more heterozygotes than normal individuals survive to pass on their genes, and those extra gene copies offset the copies lost through the deaths of homozygotes.

So let us refine our question and ask, What blessing could the Tay-Sachs gene bring to those individuals who are heterozygous for it? A clue first emerged back in 1972, with the publication of the results of a questionnaire that had asked U.S. Ashkenzaic parents of Tay-Sachs children what their own Eastern European-born parents had

We're not a melting pot, and we won't be for a long time. Each ethnic group has some characteristic genes of its own, a legacy of its distinct history.

died of. Keep in mind that since these unfortunate children had to be homozygotes, with two copies of the Tay-Sachs gene, all their parents had to be heterozygotes, with one copy, and half of the parents' parents also had to be heterozygotes.

As it turned out, most of those Tay-Sachs grandparents had died of the usual causes: heart disease, stroke, cancer, and diabetes. But strikingly, only one of the 306 grandparents had died of tuberculosis, even though TB was generally one of the big killers in these grandparents' time. Indeed, among the general population of large Eastern European cities in the early twentieth century, TB caused up to 20 percent of all deaths.

This big discrepancy suggested that

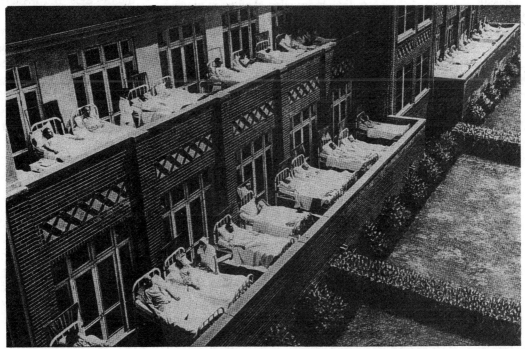

Records at a Jewish TB sanatorium in Denver indicated that among patients born in Europe between 1860 and 1910, Jews from Austria and Hungary were overrepresented. (Photo credit: AMC Cancer Research Center, Denver)

Tay-Sachs heterozygotes might somehow have been protected against TB. Interestingly, it was already well known that Ashkenazim in general had some such protection: even when Jews and non-Jews were compared within the same European city, class, and occupational group (for example, Warsaw garment workers), Jews had only half the TB death rate on non-Jews, despite their being equally susceptible to infection. Perhaps, one could reason, the Tay-Sachs gene furnished part of that well-established Jewish resistance.

A second clue to a heterozygote advantage conveyed by the Tay-Sachs gene emerged in 1983, with a fresh look at the data concerning the distributions of TB and the Tay-Sachs gene within Europe. The statistics showed that the Tay-Sachs gene was nearly three times more frequent among Jews originating from Austria, Hungary, and Czechoslovakia—areas where an amazing 9 to 10 percent of the population were heterozygotes—than among Jews from Poland, Russia, and Germany. At the same time records from an old Jewish TB sanatorium in Denver in 1904 showed that among patients born in Europe between 1860 and 1910, Jews from Austria and Hungary were overrepresented.

Initially, in putting together these two pieces of information, you might be tempted to conclude that because the highest frequency of the Tay-Sachs gene appeared in the same geographic region that produced the most cases of TB, the gene in fact offers no protection whatsoever. Indeed, this was precisely the mistaken conclusion of many researchers who had looked at these data before. But you have to pay careful attention to the numbers here: even at its highest frequency the Tay-Sachs gene was carried by far fewer people than would be infected by TB. What the statistics really indicate is that where TB is the biggest threat, natural selection produces the biggest response.

Think of it this way: You arrive at an island where you find that all the inhabitants of the north end wear suits of armor, while all the inhabitants of the south end wear only cloth shirts. You'd

be pretty safe in assuming that warfare is more prevalent in the north—and that war-related injuries account for far more deaths there than in the south. Thus, if the Tay-Sachs gene does indeed lend heterozygotes some protection against TB, you would expect to find the gene most often precisely where you find TB most often. Similarly, the sickle-cell gene reaches its highest frequencies in those parts of Africa where malaria is the biggest risk.

But you may believe there's still a hole in the argument: If Tay-Sachs heterozygotes are protected against TB, you may be asking, why is the gene common just in the Ashkenazim? Why did it not become common in the non-Jewish populations also exposed to TB in Austria, Hungary, and Czechoslovakia?

At this point we must recall the peculiar circumstances in which the Jews of Eastern Europe were forced to live. They were unique among the world's ethnic groups in having been virtually confined to towns for most of the past 2,000 years. Being forbidden to own land, Eastern European Jews were not peasant farmers living in the countryside, but businesspeople forced to live in crowded ghettos, in an environment where tuberculosis thrived.

Of course, until recent improvements in sanitation, these towns were not very healthy places for non-Jews either. Indeed, their populations couldn't sustain themselves: deaths exceeded births, and the number of dead had to be balanced by continued emigration from the countryside. For non-Jews, therefore, there was no genetically distinct urban population. For ghetto-bound Jews, however, there could be no emigration from the countryside; thus the Jewish population was under the strongest selection to evolve genetic resistance to TB.

Those are the conditions that probably led to Jewish TB resistance, whatever particular genetic factors prove to underlie it. I'd speculate that G_{M2} and related fats accumulate at slightly higher-than-normal levels in heterozygotes, although not at the lethal

levels seen in homozygotes. (The fat accumulation in heterozygotes probably takes place in the cell membrane, the cell's "armor.") I'd also speculate that the accumulation provides heterozygotes with some protection against TB, and that that's why the genes for Tay-Sachs, Gaucher's, and Niemann-Pick disease reached high frequencies in the Ashkenazim.

Having thus stated the case, let me make clear that I don't want to overstate it. The evidence is still speculative. Depending on how you do the calculation, the low frequency of TB deaths in Tay-Sachs grandparents either barely reaches or doesn't quite reach the level of proof that statisticians require to accept an effect as real rather than as one that's arisen by chance. Moreover, we have no idea of the biochemical mechanism by which fat accumulation might confer resistance against TB. For the moment, I'd say that the evidence points to some selective advantage of Tay-Sachs heterozygotes among the Ashkenazim, and that TB resistance is the only plausible hypothesis yet proposed.

For now Tay-Sachs remains a speculative model for the evolution of ethnic diseases. But it's already a proven model of what to do about them. Twenty years ago a test was developed to identify Tay-Sachs heterozygotes, based on their lower-than-normal levels of hexosaminidase A. The test is simple, cheap, and accurate: all I did was to donate a small sample of my blood, pay $35, and wait a few days to receive the results.

If that test shows that at least one member of a couple is not a Tay-Sachs heterozygotre, then any child of theirs can't be a Tay-Sachs homozygote. If both parents prove to be heterozygotes, there's a one-in-four chance of their child being a homozygote; that can then be determined by other tests performed on the mother early in pregnancy. If the results are positive, it's early enough for her to abort, should she choose to. That critical bit of knowledge has enabled parents who had gone through the agony of bearing a Tay-Sachs baby and watching him die to find the courage to try again.

The Tay-Sachs screening program launched in the United States in 1971 was targeted at the high-risk population: Ashkenazic Jewish couples of childbearing age. So successful has this approach been that the number of Tay-Sachs babies born each year in this country has declined tenfold. Today, in fact, more Tay-Sachs cases appear here in non-Jews than in Jews, because only the latter couples are routinely tested. Thus, what used to be the classic genetic disease of Jews is so no longer.

There's also a broader message to the Tay-Sachs story. We commonly refer to the United States as a melting pot, and in many ways that metaphor is apt. But in other ways we're not a melting pot, and we won't be for a long time. Each ethnic group has some characteristic genes of its own, a legacy of its distinct history. Tuberculosis and malaria are not major causes of death in the United States, but the genes that some of us evolved to protect ourselves against them are still frequent. Those genes are frequent only in certain ethnic groups, though, and they'll be slow to melt through the population.

With modern advances in molecular genetics, we can expect to see more, not less, ethnically targeted practice of medicine. Genetic screening for cystic fibrosis in European whites, for example, is one program that has been much discussed recently; when it comes, it will surely be based on the Tay-Sachs experience. Of course, what that may mean someday is more anxiety-ridden parents-to-be glowering at more dedicated genetics counselors. It will also mean fewer babies doomed to the agonies of diseases we may understand but that we'll never be able to accept.

The Arrow of Disease

When Columbus and his successors invaded the Americas, the most potent weapon they carried was their germs. But why didn't deadly disease flow in the other direction, from the New World to the Old?

Jared Diamond

Jared Diamond is a contributing editor of Discover, *a professor of physiology at the UCLA School of Medicine, a recipient of a MacArthur genius award, and a research associate in ornithology at the American Museum of Natural History. Expanded versions of many of his* Discover *articles appear in his book* The Third Chimpanzee: The Evolution and Future of the Human Animal, *which won Britain's 1992* copus *prize for best science book. Not least among his many accomplishments was his rediscovery in 1981 of the long-lost bowerbird of New Guinea. Diamond wrote about pseudohermaphrodites for* Discover's *special June issue on the science of sex.*

The three people talking in the hospital room were already stressed out from having to cope with a mysterious illness, and it didn't help at all that they were having trouble communicating. One of them was the patient, a small, timid man, sick with pneumonia caused by an unidentified microbe and with only a limited command of the English language. The second, acting as translator, was his wife, worried about her husband's condition and frightened by the hospital environment. The third person in the trio was an inexperienced young doctor, trying to figure out what might have brought on the strange illness. Under the stress, the doctor was forgetting everything he had been taught about patient confidentiality. He committed the awful blunder of requesting the woman to ask her husband whether he'd had any sexual experiences that might have caused the infection.

As the young doctor watched, the husband turned red, pulled himself together so that he seemed even smaller, tried to disappear under his bed sheets, and stammered in a barely audible voice. His wife suddenly screamed in rage and drew herself up to tower over him. Before the doctor could stop her, she grabbed a heavy metal bottle, slammed it onto her husband's head, and stormed out of the room. It took a while for the doctor to elicit, through the man's broken English, what he had said to so enrage his wife. The answer slowly emerged: he had admitted to repeated intercourse with sheep on a recent visit to the family farm; perhaps that was how he had contracted the mysterious microbe.

This episode, related to me by a physician friend involved in the case, sounds so bizarrely one of a kind as to be of no possible broader significance. But in fact it illustrates a subject of great importance: human diseases of animal origins. Very few of us may love sheep in the carnal sense. But most of us platonically love our pet animals, like our dogs and cats; and as a society; we certainly appear to have an inordinate fondness for sheep and other livestock, to judge from the vast numbers of them that we keep.

Some of us—most often our children—pick up infectious diseases from our pets. Usually these illnesses remain no more than a nuisance, but a few have evolved into far more. The major killers of humanity throughout our recent history—smallpox, flu, tuberculosis, malaria, plague, measles, and cholera—are all infectious diseases that arose from diseases of animals. Until World War II more victims of war died of microbes than of gunshot or sword wounds. All those military histories glorifying Alexander the Great and Napoleon ignore the ego-deflating truth: the winners of past wars were not necessarily those armies with the best generals and weapons, but those bearing the worst germs with which to smite their enemies.

The grimmest example of the role of germs in history is much on our minds this month, as we recall the European conquest of the Americas that began with Columbus's voyage of 1492. Numerous as the Indian victims of the murderous Spanish conquistadores were, they were dwarfed in number by the victims of murderous Spanish microbes. These formidable conquerors killed an estimated 95 percent of the New World's pre-Columbian Indian population.

Why was the exchange of nasty germs between the Americas and Europe so unequal? why didn't the reverse happen instead, with Indian diseases decimating the Spanish invaders, spreading back across the Atlantic, and causing a 95 percent decline in *Europe's* human population?

Similar questions arise regarding the decimation of many other native peoples by European germs, and regarding the decimation of would-be European conquistadores in the tropics of Africa and Asia.

Naturally, we're disposed to think about diseases from our own point of view: What can we do to save ourselves and to kill the microbes? Let's stamp out the scoundrels, and never mind what *their* motives are!

In life, though, one has to understand the enemy to beat him. So for a moment, let's consider disease from the microbes' point of view. Let's look beyond our anger at their making us sick in bizarre ways, like giving us genital sores or diarrhea, and ask why it is that they do such things. After all, microbes are as much a product of natural selection as we are, and so their actions must have come about because they confer some evolutionary benefit.

Basically, of course, evolution selects those individuals that are most

effective at producing babies and at helping those babies find suitable places to live. Microbes are marvels at this latter requirement. They have evolved diverse ways of spreading from one person to another, and from animals to people. Many of our symptoms of disease actually represent ways in which some clever bug modifies our bodies or our behavior such that we become enlisted to spread bugs.

The most effortless way a bug can spread is by just waiting to be transmitted passively to the next victim. That's the strategy practiced by microbes that wait for one host to be eaten by the next—salmonella bacteria, for example, which we contract by eating already-infected eggs or meat; or the worm responsible for trichinosis, which waits for us to kill a pig and eat it without properly cooking it.

As a slight modification of this strategy, some microbes don't wait for the old host to die but instead hitchhike in the saliva of an insect that bites the old host and then flies to a new one. The free ride may be provided by mosquitoes, fleas, lice, or tsetse flies, which spread malaria, plague, typhus, and sleeping sickness, respectively. The dirtiest of all passive-carriage tricks is perpetrated by microbes that pass from a woman to her fetus—microbes such as the ones responsible for syphilis, rubella (German measles), and AIDS. By their cunning these microbes can already be infecting an infant before the moment of its birth.

Other bugs take matters into their own hands, figuratively speaking. They actively modify the anatomy or habits of their host to accelerate their transmission. From our perspective, the open genital sores caused by venereal diseases such as syphilis are a vile indignity. From the microbes' point of view, however, they're just a useful device to enlist a host's help in inoculating the body cavity of another host with microbes. The skin lesions caused by smallpox similarly spread microbes by direct or indirect body contact (occasionally very indirect, as when U.S. and Australian whites bent on wiping out "belligerent" native peoples sent

them gifts of blankets previously used by smallpox patients).

From our viewpoint, diarrhea and coughing are "symptoms" of disease. From a bug's viewpoint, they're clever evolutionary strategies to broadcast the bug. That's why it's in the bug's interests to make us "sick."

More vigorous yet is the strategy practiced by the influenza, common cold, and pertussis (whooping cough) microbes, which induce the victim to cough or sneeze, thereby broadcasting the bugs toward prospective new hosts. Similarly the cholera bacterium induces a massive diarrhea that spreads bacteria into the water supplies of potential new victims. For modification of a host's behavior, though, nothing matches the rabies virus, which not only gets into the saliva of an infected dog but drives the dog into a frenzy of biting and thereby infects many new victims.

Thus, from our viewpoint, genital sores, diarrhea, and coughing are "symptoms" of disease. From a bug's viewpoint, they're clever evolutionary strategies to broadcast the bug. That's why it's in the bug's interests to make us "sick." But what does it gain by killing us? That seems self-defeating, since a microbe that kills its host kills itself.

Though you may well think it's of little consolation, our death is really just an unintended by-product of host symptoms that promote the efficient transmission of microbes. Yes, an untreated cholera patient may eventually die from producing diarrheal fluid at a rate of several gallons a day. While the patient lasts, though, the cholera bacterium profits from being massively disseminated into the water supplies of its next victims. As long as each victim thereby infects, on average, more than one new victim, the bacteria will spread, even though the first host happens to die.

So much for the dispassionate examination of the bug's interests. Now let's get back to considering our own selfish interests: to stay alive and healthy, best done by killing the damned bugs. One common response to infection is to develop a fever. Again, we consider fever a "symptom" of disease, as if it developed inevitably without serving any function. But regulation of body temperature is under our genetic control, and a fever doesn't just happen by accident. Because some microbes are more sensitive to heat than our own bodies are, by raising our body temperature we in effect try to bake the bugs to death before we get baked ourselves.

Another common response is to mobilize our immune system. White blood cells and other cells actively seek out and kill foreign microbes. The specific antibodies we gradually build up against a particular microbe make us less likely to get reinfected once we are cured. As we all know there are some illnesses, such as flu and the common cold, to which our resistance is only temporary; we can eventually contract the illness again. Against other illnesses, though—including measles, mumps, rubella, pertussis, and the now-defeated menace of smallpox—antibodies stimulated by one infection confer lifelong immunity. That's the principle behind vaccination—to stimulate our antibody production without our having to go through the actual experience of the disease.

Alas, some clever bugs don't just cave in to our immune defenses. Some have learned to trick us by changing their antigens, those molecular pieces of the microbe that our antibodies recognize. The constant evolution or recycling of new strains of flu, with differing antigens, explains why the flu you got two years ago didn't protect you against the different strain that arrived this year. Sleeping sickness is an even more slippery customer in its ability to change its antigens rapidly.

We and our pathogens are now locked in an escalating evolutionary contest, with the death of one contestant the price of defeat, and with natural selection playing the role of umpire.

Among the slipperiest of all is the virus that causes AIDS, which evolves new antigens even as it sits within an individual patient, until it eventually overwhelms the immune system.

Our slowest defensive response is through natural selection, which changes the relative frequency with which a gene appears from generation to generation. For almost any disease some people prove to be genetically more resistant than others. In an epidemic, those people with genes for resistance to that particular microbe are more likely to survive than are people lacking such genes. As a result, over the course of history human populations repeatedly exposed to a particular pathogen tend to be made up of individuals with genes that resist the appropriate microbe just because unfortunate individuals without those genes were less likely to survive to pass their genes on to their children.

Fat consolation, you may be thinking. This evolutionary response is not one that does the genetically susceptible dying individual any good. It does mean, though, that a human population as a whole becomes better protected.

In short, many bugs have had to evolve tricks to let them spread among potential victims. We've evolved countertricks, to which the bugs have responded by evolving counter-countertricks. We and our pathogens are now locked in an escalating evolutionary contest, with the death of one contestant the price of defeat, and with natural selection playing the role of umpire.

The form that this deadly contest takes varies with the pathogens: for some it is like a guerrilla war, while for others it is a blitzkrieg. With certain diseases, like malaria or hook-worm, there's a more or less steady trickle of new cases in an affected area, and they will appear in any month of any year. Epidemic diseases, though, are different: they produce no cases for a long time, then a whole wave of cases, then no more cases again for a while.

Among such epidemic diseases, influenza is the most familiar to Americans, this year having been a particularly bad one for us (but a great year for the influenza virus). Cholera epidemics come at longer intervals, the 1991 Peruvian epidemic being the first one to reach the New World during the twentieth century. Frightening as today's influenza and cholera epidemics are, though, they pale beside the far more terrifying epidemics of the past, before the rise of modern medicine. The greatest single epidemic in human history was the influenza wave that killed 21 million people at the end of the First World War. The black death, or bubonic plague, killed one-quarter of Europe's population between 1346 and 1352, with death tolls up to 70 percent in some cities.

The infectious diseases that visit us as epidemics share several characteristics. First, they spread quickly and efficiently from an infected person to nearby healthy people, with the result that the whole population gets exposed within a short time. Second, they're "acute" illnesses: within a short time, you either die or recover completely. Third, the fortunate ones of us who do recover develop antibodies that leave us immune against a recurrence of the disease for a long time, possibly our entire lives. Finally, these diseases tend to be restricted to humans; the bugs causing them tend not to live in the soil or in other animals. All four of these characteristics apply to what Americans think of as the once more-familiar acute epidemic diseases of childhood, including measles, rubella, mumps, pertussis, and smallpox.

It is easy to understand why the

combination of those four characteristics tends to make a disease run in epidemics. The rapid spread of microbes and the rapid course of symptoms mean that everybody in a local human population is soon infected, and thereafter either dead or else recovered and immune. No one is left alive who could still be infected. But since the microbe can't survive except in the bodies of living people, the disease dies out until a new crop of babies reaches the susceptible age—and until an infectious person arrives from the outside to start a new epidemic.

A classic illustration of the process is given by the history of measles on the isolated Faeroe Islands in the North Atlantic. A severe epidemic of the disease reached the Faeroes in 1781, then died out, leaving the islands measles-free until an infected carpenter arrived on a ship from Denmark in 1846. Within three months almost the whole Faeroes population—7,782 people—had gotten measles and then either died or recovered, leaving the measles virus to disappear once again until the next epidemic. Studies show that measles is likely to die out in any human population numbering less than half a million people. Only in larger populations can measles shift from one local area to another, thereby persisting until enough babies have been born in the originally infected area to permit the disease's return.

Rubella in Australia provides a similar example, on a much larger scale. As of 1917 Australia's population was still only 5 million, with most people living in scattered rural areas. The sea voyage to Britain took two months, and land transport within Australia itself was slow. In effect, Australia didn't even consist of a population of 5 million, but of hundreds of much smaller populations. As a result, rubella hit Australia only as occasional epidemics, when an infected person happened to arrive from overseas and stayed in a densely populated area. By 1938, though, the city of Sydney alone had a population of over one million, and people moved frequently and quickly by air between London, Sydney, and other Australian cities. Around then, rubella

for the first time was able to establish itself permanently in Australia.

What's true for rubella in Australia is true for most familiar acute infectious diseases throughout the world. To sustain themselves, they need a human population that is sufficiently numerous and densely packed that a new crop of susceptible children is available for infection by the time the disease would otherwise be waning. Hence measles and other such diseases are also known as "crowd diseases."

Crowd diseases could not sustain themselves in small bands of hunter-gatherers and slash-and-burn farmers. As tragic recent experience with Amazonian Indians and Pacific Islanders confirms, almost an entire tribelet may be wiped out by an epidemic brought by an outside visitor, because no one in the tribelet has any antibodies against the microbe. In addition, measles and some other "childhood" diseases are more likely to kill infected adults than children, and all adults in the tribelet are susceptible. Having killed most of the tribelet, the epidemic then disappears. The small population size explains why tribelets can't sustain epidemics introduced from the outside; at the same time it explains why they could never evolve epidemic diseases of their own to give back to the visitors.

That's not to say that small human populations are free from all infectious diseases. Some of their infections are caused by microbes capable of maintaining themselves in animals or in soil, so the disease remains constantly available to infect people. For example, the yellow fever virus is carried by African wild monkeys and is constantly available to infect rural human populations of Africa. It was also available to be carried to New World monkeys and people by the transatlantic slave trade.

Other infections of small human populations are chronic diseases, such as leprosy and yaws, that may take a very long time to kill a victim. The victim thus remains alive as a reservoir of microbes to infect other members of

the tribelet. Finally, small human populations are susceptible to nonfatal infections against which we don't develop immunity, with the result that the same person can become reinfected after recovering. That's the case with hookworm and many other parasites.

All these types of diseases, characteristic of small, isolated populations, must be the oldest diseases of humanity. They were the ones that we could evolve and sustain through the early millions of years of our evolutionary history, when the total human population was tiny and fragmented. They are also shared with, or are similar to the diseases of, our closest wild relatives, the African great apes. In contrast, the evolution of our crowd diseases could only have occurred with the buildup of large, dense human populations, first made possible by the rise of agriculture about 10,000 years ago, then by the rise of cities several thousand years ago. Indeed, the first attested dates for many familiar infectious diseases are surprisingly recent: around 1600 B.C. for smallpox (as deduced from pockmarks on an Egyptian mummy), 400 B.C. for mumps, 1840 for polio, and 1959 for AIDS.

Agriculture sustains much higher human population densities than does hunting and gathering—on average, 10 to 100 times higher. In addition, hunter-gatherers frequently shift camp, leaving behind their piles of feces with their accumulated microbes and worm larvae. But farmers are sedentary and live amid their own sewage, providing microbes with a quick path from one person's body into another person's drinking water. Farmers also become surrounded by disease-transmitting rodents attracted by stored food.

Some human populations make it even easier for their own bacteria and worms to infect new victims, by intentionally gathering their feces and urine and spreading it as fertilizer on the fields where people work. Irrigation agriculture and fish farming provide ideal living conditions for the snails carrying schistosomes, and for other flukes that burrow through our skin as we wade through the feces-laden water.

If the rise of farming was a boon for our microbes, the rise of cities was a veritable bonanza, as still more densely packed human populations festered under even worse sanitation conditions. (Not until the beginning of the twentieth century did urban populations finally become self-sustaining; until then, constant immigration of healthy peasants from the countryside was necessary to make good the constant deaths of city dwellers from crowd diseases.) Another bonanza was the development of world trade routes, which by late Roman times effectively joined the populations of Europe, Asia, and North Africa into one giant breeding ground for microbes. That's when smallpox finally reached Rome as the "plague of Antonius," which killed millions of Roman citizens between A.D. 165 and 180.

Similarly, bubonic plague first appeared in Europe as the plague of Justinian (A.D. 542–543). But plague didn't begin to hit Europe with full force, as the black death epidemics, until 1346, when new overland trading with China provided rapid transit for flea-infested furs from plague-ridden areas of Central Asia. Today our jet planes have made even the longest intercontinental flights briefer than the duration of any human infectious disease. That's how an Aerolíneas Argentinas airplane, stopping in Lima, Peru, earlier this year, managed to deliver dozens of cholera-infected people the same day to my city of Los Angeles, over 3,000 miles away. The explosive increase in world travel by Americans, and in immigration to the United States, is turning us into another melting pot—this time of microbes that we previously dismissed as just causing exotic diseases in far-off countries.

When the human population became sufficiently large and concentrated, we reached the stage in our history when we could at last sustain crowd diseases confined to our species. But that presents a paradox: such diseases could never have existed before. Instead they had to evolve as new diseases. Where did those new diseases come from?

The explosive increase in world travel by Americans, and in immigration to the United States, is turning us into another melting pot— this time of microbes that we'd dismissed as causing disease in far-off countries.

Evidence emerges from studies of the disease-causing microbes themselves. In many cases molecular biologists have identified the microbe's closest relative. Those relatives also prove to be agents of infectious crowd diseases—but ones confined to various species of domestic animals and pets! Among animals too, epidemic diseases require dense populations, and they're mainly confined to social animals that provide the necessary large populations. Hence when we domesticated social animals such as cows and pigs, they were already afflicted by epidemic diseases just waiting to be transferred to us.

For example, the measles virus is most closely related to the virus causing rinderpest, a nasty epidemic disease of cattle and many wild cud-chewing mammals. Rinderpest doesn't affect humans. Measles, in turn, doesn't affect cattle. The close similarity of the measles and rinderpest viruses suggests that the rinderpest virus transferred from cattle to humans, then became the measles virus by changing its properties to adapt to us. That transfer isn't surprising, considering how closely many peasant farmers live and sleep next to cows and their accompanying feces, urine, breath, sores, and blood. Our intimacy with cattle has been going on for the 8,000 years since we domesticated them—ample time for the rinderpest virus to discover us nearby. Other familiar infectious diseases can similarly be traced back to diseases of our animal friends.

Given our proximity to the animals we love, we must constantly be getting bombarded by animal microbes. Those invaders get winnowed by natural selection, and only a few succeed in establishing themselves as human diseases. A quick survey of current diseases lets us trace four stages in the evolution of a specialized human disease from an animal precursor.

In the first stage, we pick up animal-borne microbes that are still at an early stage in their evolution into specialized human pathogens. They don't get transmitted directly from one person to another, and even their transfer from animals to us remains uncommon. There are dozens of diseases like this that we get directly from pets and domestic animals. They include cat scratch fever from cats, leptospirosis from dogs, psittacosis from chickens and parrots, and brucellosis from cattle. We're similarly susceptible to picking up diseases from wild animals, such as the tularemia that hunters occasionally get from skinning wild rabbits.

In the second stage, a former animal pathogen evolves to the point where it does get transmitted directly between people and causes epidemics. However, the epidemic dies out for several reasons—being cured by modern medicine, stopping when everybody has been infected and died, or stopping when everybody has been infected and become immune. For example, a previously unknown disease termed *o'nyong-nyong* fever appeared in East Africa in 1959 and infected several million Africans. It probably arose from a virus of monkeys and was transmitted to humans by mosquitoes. The fact that patients recovered quickly and became immune to further attack helped cause the new disease to die out quickly.

The annals of medicine are full of diseases that sound like no known disease today but that once caused terrifying epidemics before disappearing as mysteriously as they had come. Who alive today remembers the "English sweating sickness" that swept and terrified Europe between 1485 and 1578, or the "Picardy sweats" of eighteenth- and nineteenth-century France?

A third stage in the evolution of our

major diseases is represented by former animal pathogens that establish themselves in humans and that do not die out; until they do, the question of whether they will become major killers of humanity remains up for grabs. The future is still very uncertain for Lassa fever, first observed in 1969 in Nigeria and caused by a virus probably derived from rodents. Better established is Lyme disease, caused by a spirochete that we get from the bite of a tick. Although the first known human cases in the United States appeared only as recently as 1962, Lyme disease is already reaching epidemic proportions in the Northeast, on the West Coast, and in the upper Midwest. The future of AIDS, derived from monkey viruses, is even more secure, from the virus's perspective.

The final stage of this evolution is represented by the major, long-established epidemic diseases confined to humans. These diseases must have been the evolutionary survivors of far more pathogens that tried to make the jump to us from animals—and mostly failed.

Diseases represent evolution in progress, as microbes adapt by natural selection to new hosts. Compared with cows' bodies, though, our bodies offer different immune defenses and different chemistry. In that new environment, a microbe must evolve new ways to live and propagate itself.

The best-studied example of microbes evolving these new ways involves myxomatosis, which hit Australian rabbits in 1950. The myxoma virus, native to a wild species of Brazilian rabbit, was known to cause a lethal epidemic in European domestic rabbits, which are a different species. The virus was intentionally introduced to Australia in the hopes of ridding the continent of its plague of European rabbits, foolishly introduced in the nineteenth century. In the first year, myxoma produced a gratifying (to Australian farmers) 99.8 percent mortality in infected rabbits. Fortunately for the rabbits and unfortunately for the farmers, the death rate then dropped in the second year to 90 percent and eventually to 25 percent, frustrating hopes of eradicating rabbits completely from Australia. The prob-

lem was that the myxoma virus evolved to serve its own interests, which differed from the farmers' interests and those of the rabbits. The virus changed to kill fewer rabbits and to permit lethally infected ones to live longer before dying. The result was bad for Australian farmers but good for the virus: a less lethal myxoma virus spreads baby viruses to more rabbits than did the original, highly virulent myxoma.

For a similar example in humans, consider the surprising evolution of syphilis. Today we associate syphilis with genital sores and a very slowly developing disease, leading to the death of untreated victims only after many years. However, when syphilis was first definitely recorded in Europe in 1495, its pustules often covered the body from the head to the knees, caused flesh to fall off people's faces, and led to death within a few months. By 1546 syphilis had evolved into the disease with the symptoms known to us today. Apparently, just as with myxomatosis, those syphilis spirochetes evolved to keep their victims alive longer in order to transmit their spirochete offspring into more victims.

How, then, does all this explain the outcome of 1492—that Europeans conquered and depopulated the New World, instead of Native Americans conquering and depopulating Europe?

Part of the answer, of course, goes back to the invaders' technological advantages. European guns and steel swords were more effective weapons than Native American stone axes and wooden clubs. Only Europeans had ships capable of crossing the ocean and horses that could provide a decisive advantage in battle. But that's not the whole answer. Far more Native Americans died in bed than on the battlefield—the victims of germs, not of guns and swords. Those germs undermined Indian resistance by killing most Indians and their leaders and by demoralizing the survivors.

The role of disease in the Spanish conquests of the Aztec and Inca empires is especially well documented. In

1519 Cortés landed on the coast of Mexico with 600 Spaniards to conquer the fiercely militaristic Aztec Empire, which at the time had a population of many millions. That Cortés reached the Aztec capital of Tenochtitlán, escaped with the loss of "only" two-thirds of his force, and managed to fight his way back to the coast demonstrates both Spanish military advantages and the initial naïveté of the Aztecs. But when Cortés's next onslaught came, in 1521, the Aztecs were no longer naive; they fought street by street with the utmost tenacity.

What gave the Spaniards a decisive advantage this time was smallpox, which reached Mexico in 1520 with the arrival of one infected slave from Spanish Cuba. The resulting epidemic proceeded to kill nearly half the Aztecs. The survivors were demoralized by the mysterious illness that killed Indians and spared Spaniards, as if advertising the Spaniards' invincibility. By 1618 Mexico's initial population of 20 million had plummeted to about 1.6 million.

Pizarro had similarly grim luck when he landed on the coast of Peru in 1531 with about 200 men to conquer the Inca Empire. Fortunately for Pizarro, and unfortunately for the Incas, smallpox had arrived overland around 1524, killing much of the Inca population, including both Emperor Huayna Capac and his son and designated successor, Ninan Cuyoche. Because of the vacant throne, two other sons of Huayna Capac, Atahuallpa and Huáscar, became embroiled in a civil war that Pizarro exploited to conquer the divided Incas.

In the century or two following Columbus's arrival in the New World, the Indian population declined by about 95 percent. The main killers were European germs, to which the Indians had never been exposed.

---

1. NATURAL SELECTION

When we in the United States think of the most populous New World societies existing in 1492, only the Aztecs and Incas come to mind. We forget that North America also supported populous Indian societies in the Mississippi Valley. Sadly, these societies too would disappear. But in this case conquistadores contributed nothing directly to the societies' destruction; the conquistadores' germs, spreading in advance, did everything. When De Soto marched through the Southeast in 1540, he came across Indian towns abandoned two years previously because nearly all the inhabitants had died in epidemics. However, he was still able to see some of the densely populated towns lining the lower Mississippi. By a century and a half later, though, when French settlers returned to the lower Mississippi, almost all those towns had vanished. Their relics are the great mound sites of the Mississippi Valley. Only recently have we come to realize that the mound-building societies were still largely intact when Columbus arrived, and that they collapsed between 1492 and the systematic European exploration of the Mississippi.

When I was a child in school, we were taught that North America had originally been occupied by about one million Indians. That low number helped justify the white conquest of what could then be viewed as an almost empty continent. However, archeological excavations and descriptions left by the first European explorers on our coasts now suggest an initial number of around 20 million. In the century or two following Columbus's arrival in the New World, the Indian population is estimated to have declined by about 95 percent.

The main killers were European germs, to which the Indians had never been exposed and against which they therefore had neither immunologic nor genetic resistance. Smallpox, measles, influenza, and typhus competed for top rank among the killers. As if those were not enough, pertussis, plague, tuberculosis, diphtheria, mumps, malaria, and yellow fever came close behind. In countless cases Europeans were

actually there to witness the decimation that occurred when the germs arrived. For example, in 1837 the Mandan Indian tribe, with one of the most elaborate cultures in the Great Plains, contracted smallpox thanks to a steamboat traveling up the Missouri River from St. Louis. The population of one Mandan village crashed from 2,000 to less than 40 within a few weeks.

The one-sided exchange of lethal germs between the Old and New worlds is among the most striking and consequence-laden facts of recent history. Whereas over a dozen major infectious diseases of Old World origins became established in the New World, not a single major killer reached Europe from the Americas. The sole possible exception is syphilis, whose area of origin still remains controversial.

That one-sidedness is more striking with the knowledge that large, dense human populations are a prerequisite for the evolution of crowd diseases. If recent reappraisals of the pre-Columbian New World population are correct, that population was not far below the contemporaneous population of Eurasia. Some New World cities, like Tenochtitlán, were among the world's most populous cities at the time. Yet Tenochtitlán didn't have awful germs waiting in store for the Spaniards. Why not?

One possible factor is that the rise of dense human populations began somewhat later in the New World than in the Old. Another is that the three most populous American centers—the Andes, Mexico, and the Mississippi Valley—were never connected by regular fast trade into one gigantic breeding ground for microbes, in the way that Europe, North Africa, India, and China became connected in late Roman times.

The main reason becomes clear, however, if we ask a simple question: From what microbes could any crowd diseases of the Americas have evolved? We've seen that Eurasian crowd diseases evolved from diseases of domesticated herd animals. Significantly, there were many such animals in Eurasia. But there were only five animals that became domesticated in the Americas: the turkey in Mexico and parts of

North America, the guinea pig and llama/alpaca (probably derived from the same original wild species) in the Andes, the Muscovy duck in tropical South America, and the dog throughout the Americas.

That extreme paucity of New World domestic animals reflects the paucity of wild starting material. About 80 percent of the big wild mammals of the Americas became extinct at the end of the last ice age, around 11,000 years ago, at approximately the same time that the first well-attested wave of Indian hunters spread over the Americas. Among the species that disappeared were ones that would have yielded useful domesticates, such as American horses and camels. Debate still rages as to whether those extinctions were due to climate changes or to the impact of Indian hunters on prey that had never seen humans. Whatever the reason, the extinctions removed most of the basis for Native American animal domestication—and for crowd diseases.

The few domesticates that remained were not likely sources of such diseases. Muscovy ducks and turkeys don't live in enormous flocks, and they're not naturally endearing species (like young lambs) with which we have much physical contact. Guinea pigs may have contributed a trypanosome infection like Chagas' disease or leishmaniasis to our catalog of woes, but that's uncertain. Initially the most surprising absence is of any human disease derived from llamas (or alpacas), which are tempting to consider as the Andean equivalent of Eurasian livestock. However, llamas had three strikes against them as a source of human pathogens: their wild relatives don't occur in big herds as do wild sheep, goats, and pigs; their total numbers were never remotely as large as the Eurasian populations of domestic livestock, since llamas never spread beyond the Andes; and llamas aren't as cuddly as piglets and lambs and aren't kept in such close association with people. (You may not think of piglets as cuddly, but human mothers in the New Guinea highlands often nurse them, and they frequently live right in the huts of peasant farmers.)

The importance of animal-derived diseases for human history extends far beyond the Americas. Eurasian germs played a key role in decimating native peoples in many other parts of the world as well, including the Pacific islands, Australia, and southern Africa. Racist Europeans used to attribute those conquests to their supposedly better brains. But no evidence for such better brains has been forthcoming. Instead, the conquests were made possible by Europeans nastier germs, and by the technological advances and denser populations that Europeans ultimately acquired by means of their domesticated plants and animals.

So on this 500th anniversary of Columbus's discovery, let's try to regain our sense of perspective about his hotly debated achievements. There's no doubt that Columbus was a great visionary, seaman, and leader. There's also no doubt that he and his successors often behaved as bestial murderers. But those facts alone don't fully explain why it took so few European immigrants to initially conquer and ultimately supplant so much of the native population of the Americas. Without the germs Europeans brought with them—germs that were derived from their animals—such conquests might have been impossible.

The Future of AIDS

*New research suggests HIV is not a new virus but an old one that grew deadly.
Can we turn the process around?*

Geoffrey Cowley

Ten years ago, Benjamin B. got what might have been a death sentence. Hospitalized for colon surgery, the Australian retiree received a blood transfusion tainted with the AIDS virus. That he's alive at all is remarkable, but that's only half of the story. Unlike most long-term HIV survivors, he has suffered no symptoms and no loss of immune function. He's as healthy today as he was in 1983—and celebrating his 81st birthday. Benjamin B. is just one of five patients who came to the attention of Dr. Brett Tindall, an AIDS researcher at the University of New South Wales, as he was preparing a routine update on transfusion-related HIV infections last year. All five were infected by the same donor. And seven to 10 years later, none has suffered any effects.

The donor turned out to be a gay man who had contracted the virus during the late 1970s or early '80s, then given blood at least 26 times before learning he was infected. After tracking him down, Tindall learned, to his amazement, that the man was just as healthy as the people who got his blood. "We know that HIV causes AIDS," Tindall says. "We also know that a few patients remain well for long periods, but we've never known why. Is it the vitamins they take? Is it some gene they have in common? This work suggests it has more to do with the virus. I think we've found a harmless strain."

He may also have found the viral equivalent of a fossil, a clue to the origin, evolution and future of the AIDS epidemic. HIV may not be a new and inherently deadly virus, as is commonly assumed, but an old one that has recently acquired deadly tendencies. In a forthcoming book, Paul Ewald, an evolutionary biologist at Amherst College, argues that HIV may have infected people benignly for decades, even centuries, before it started causing AIDS. He traces its virulence to the social upheavals of the 1960s and '70s, which not only sped its movement through populations but rewarded it for reproducing more aggressively within the body.

The idea may sound radical, but it's not just flashy speculation. It reflects a growing awareness that parasites, like everything else in nature, evolve by natural selection, changing their character to adapt to their environments. Besides transforming our understanding of AIDS, the new view could yield bold strategies for fighting it. Viruses can evolve tens of thousands of times faster than plants or animals, and few evolve as fast as HIV. Confronted by a drug or an immune reaction, the virus readily mutates out of its range. A few researchers are now trying to exploit that very talent, using drugs to force HIV to mutate until it can no longer function. A Boston team, led by medical student Yung-Kang Chow, made headlines last month by showing that the technique works perfectly in a test tube. Human trials are now in the works, but better drug treatment isn't the only hope rising from an evolutionary outlook. If rapid spread is what turned HIV into a killer, then condoms and clean needles may ultimately do more than prevent new infections. Used widely enough, they might drive the AIDS virus toward the benign form sighted in Australia.

I. WHERE DID HIV COME FROM?

Viruses are the ultimate parasites. Unlike bacteria, which absorb nutrients, excrete waste and reproduce by dividing, they have no life of their own. They're mere shreds of genetic information, encoded in DNA or RNA, that can integrate themselves into a living cell and use its machinery to run off copies of themselves. Where the first one came from is anyone's guess, but today's viruses are, like any plant or animal, simply descendants of earlier forms.

Most scientists agree that the human immunodeficiency viruses—HIV-1 and HIV-2—are basically ape or monkey viruses. Both HIVs are genetically similar to viruses found in African primates, the so called SIVs. In fact, as the accompanying tree illustrates, the HIVs have more in common with simian viruses than they do with each other. HIV-2, found mainly in West Africa, is so similar to the SIV that infects the sooty mangabey—an ash-colored monkey from the same region—that it doesn't really qualify as a separate viral species. "When you see HIV-2," says Gerald Myers, head of the HIV database project at the Los

From *Newsweek*, March 22, 1993, pp. 47-52. © 1993 by Newsweek, Inc. All rights reserved. Reprinted by permission.

Alamos National Laboratory, "you may not be looking at a human virus but at a mangabey virus in a human." HIV-1, the virus responsible for the vast majority of the world's AIDS cases, bears no great resemblance to HIV-2 or the monkey SIVs, but it's very similar to SIV cpz, a virus recovered in 1990 from a wild chimpanzee in the West African nation of Gabon.

The prevailing theory holds that humans were first infected through direct contact with primates, and that the SIVs they contracted have since diverged by varying degrees from their ancestors. It's possible, of course, that the HIVs and SIVs evolved separately, or even that humans were the original carriers. But the primates-to-people scenario has a couple of points in its favor. First, the SIVs are more varied than the HIVs, which suggests they've been evolving longer. Second, it's easier to imagine people being infected by chimps or monkeys than vice versa. Humans have hunted and handled other primates for thousands of years. Anyone who was bitten or scratched, or who cut himself butchering an animal, could have gotten infected.

Until recently, it was unclear whether people could contract SIV directly from primates, but a couple of recent accidents have settled that issue. In one case, reported last summer by the Centers for Disease Control, a lab technician at a primate-research center jabbed herself with a needle containing blood from an infected macaque. The infection didn't take—she produced antibodies to SIV only for a few months—but she was just lucky. Another lab worker, who handled monkey tissues while suffering from skin lesions, has remained SIV-positive for two years. In a recent survey of 472 blood samples drawn from primate handlers, health officials found that three of those tested positive as well. No one knows whether the people with SIV eventually develop AIDS, but the potential for cross-species transmission is now clear.

Far less clear is when the first such transmission took place. The most common view holds that since AIDS is a new epidemic, the responsible vi-

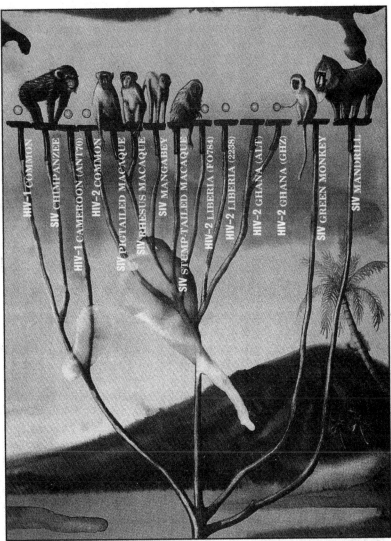

ILLUSTRATION BY ALEXIS ROCKMAN

HIV'S EXTENDED FAMILY: Today's viruses are descendants of earlier forms. This family tree shows that the human AIDS viruses, HIV-1 and HIV-2, are more closely related to viruses found in primates (the SIVs) than to each other.

ruses must have entered humans within the past few decades. That's a reasonable suspicion, but it raises a sticky question. Why, if people have been handling primates in Africa for thousands of years, did SIV take until now to jump species?

One possibility is that humans recently opened some avenue that hasn't existed in the past. Some theorists argue, for example, that AIDS was spawned by a polio-vaccination program carried out in Africa during the late 1950s. During that four-year effort, 325,000 Africans received an oral polio vaccine produced in kidney cells from African green monkeys. Even if the vaccine was contaminated with SIV—which hasn't been estab-

lished—blaming it for AIDS would be hasty. For the SIVs found in African green monkeys bear too little resemblance to HIV-1, the primary human AIDS virus, to be its likely progenitor. In order to link HIV-1 to those early lots of polio vaccine, someone would have to show that they contained a monkey virus never yet found in actual monkeys.

The alternative view—that the HIVs are old viruses—is just as hard to prove, but it requires fewer tortured assumptions. Dr. Jay Levy, an AIDS researcher at the University of California, San Francisco, puts it this way: "We know that all these other primates harbor lentiviruses [the class that includes the SIVs and HIVs]. Why should humans be any exception?" If the HIVs were on hand before the AIDS epidemic began, the key question is not where they came from but whether they always caused the disease.

II. WAS HIV ONCE LESS DEADLY?

If HIV had always caused AIDS, one would expect virus and illness to emerge together in the historical record. Antibodies to HIV have been detected in rare blood samples dating back to 1959, yet the first African AIDS cases were described in the early 1980s, when the disease started decimating the cities of Rwanda, Zaire, Zambia and Uganda. When Dr. Robert Biggar, an epidemiologist at the National Cancer Institute, pored over African hospital records looking for earlier descriptions of AIDS-like illness he didn't find any. It's possible, of course, that the disease was there all along, just too rare to be recognized as a distinct condition. But the alternative view is worth considering. There are intriguing hints that HIV hasn't always been so deadly.

Any population of living things, from fungi to rhinoceri, includes genetically varied individuals, which pass essential traits along to their progeny. As Charles Darwin discerned more than a century ago, the individuals best designed to exploit a particular environment tend to produce the greatest number of viable offspring. As generations pass, beneficial traits become more and more pervasive in the population. There's no universal recipe for reproductive success; different environments favor different traits. But by preserving some and discarding others, every environment molds the species it supports.

Viruses aren't exempt from the process. Their purpose, from a Darwinian perspective, is simply to make as many copies of themselves as they can. Other things being equal, those that replicate fastest will become the most plentiful within the host, and so stand the best chance of infecting other hosts on contact. But there's a catch. If a microbe

reproduces too aggressively inside its host, or invades too many different tissues, it may kill the host—and itself—without getting passed along at all. The most successful virus, then, is not necessarily the most or the least virulent. It's one that exploits its host most effectively.

As Ewald and others have shown, that mandate can drive different microbes to very different levels of nastiness. Because they travel via social contact between people, cold and flu viruses can't normally afford to immobilize us. To stay in business, they need hosts who are out coughing, sneezing, shaking hands and sharing pencils. But the incentives change when a parasite has other ways of getting around. Consider tuberculosis or diphtheria. Both deadly diseases are caused by bacteria that can survive for weeks or months outside the body. They can reproduce aggressively in the host, ride a cough into the external environment, then wait patiently for another host to come along. By the same token, a parasite that can travel from person to person via mosquito or some other vector has little reason to be gentle. As long as malaria sufferers can still feed hungry mosquitoes, their misery is of little consequence to the microbe. Indeed, a

host who can't wield a fly swatter may be preferable to one who can.

These patterns aren't set in stone. A shift in circumstances may push a normally mild-mannered parasite toward virulence, or vice versa. One of the most devastating plagues in human history was caused by a mere influenza virus, which swept the globe in 1918, leaving 20 million corpses in its wake. Many experts still regard the disaster as an accident, triggered by the random reshuffling of viral genes. But from an evolutionary perspective, it's no coincidence that the flu grew so deadly when it did. World War I was

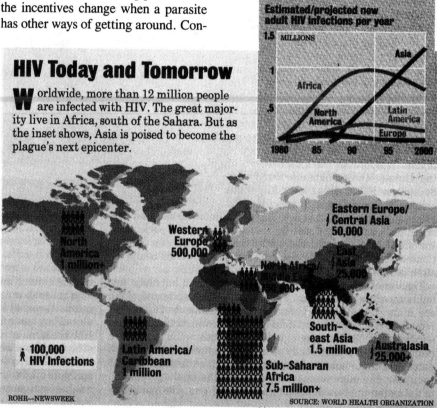

HIV Today and Tomorrow

Worldwide, more than 12 million people are infected with HIV. The great majority live in Africa, south of the Sahara. But as the inset shows, Asia is poised to become the plague's next epicenter.

Estimated/projected new adult HIV infections per year

100,000 HIV Infections

North America 1 million+
Western Europe 500,000
Eastern Europe/ Central Asia 50,000
North Africa/ Middle East 100,000+
East Asia 25,000
Southeast Asia 1.5 million
Australasia 25,000+
Latin America/ Caribbean 1 million
Sub-Saharan Africa 7.5 million+

ROHR—NEWSWEEK

SOURCE: WORLD HEALTH ORGANIZATION

raging in 1918. Great numbers of soldiers were huddled in the European trenches, where even the most ravaged host stood an excellent chance of infecting many others. For a flu virus, the incentives favoring restraint would have vanished in those circumstances. Rather than rendering the host useless, extreme virulence would simply make him more infectious.

Ewald suspects that HIV has recently undergone a similar transformation. Unlike influenza viruses, which infect cells in the respiratory tract and spread through coughs and sneezes, the HIVs insinuate themselves into white blood cells. Infected cells (or the new viruses they produce) can pass between people, but only during sex or other exchanges of body fluid. Confined to an isolated population where no carrier had numerous sex partners, a virus like HIV would gain nothing from replicating aggressively within the body; it would do best to lie low, leaving the host alive and mildly infectious for many years. But if people's sexual networks suddenly expanded, fresh hosts would become more plentiful, and infected hosts more dispensable. An HIV strain that replicated wildly might kill people in three years instead of 30, but by making them more infectious while they lasted, it would still come out ahead.

Is that what actually happened? There's no question that social changes have hastened the spread of HIV. Starting in the 1960s, war, tourism and commercial trucking forced the outside world on Africa's once isolated villages. At the same time, drought and industrialization prompted mass migrations from the countryside into newly teeming cities. Western monogamy had never been common in Africa, but as the French medical historian Mirko Grmek notes in his book "History of AIDS," urbanization shattered social structures that had long constrained sexual behavior. Prostitution exploded, and venereal disease flourished. Hypodermic needles came into wide use during the same period, creating yet another

mode of infection. Did these trends actually turn a chronic but relatively benign infection into a killer? The evidence is circumstantial, but it's hard to discount.

If Ewald is right, and HIV's deadliness is a consequence of its rapid spread, then the nastiest strains should show up in the populations where it's moving the fastest. To a surprising degree, they do. It's well known, for example, that HIV-2 is far less virulent than HIV-1. "Going on what we've seen so far, we'd have to say that HIV-1 causes AIDS in 90 percent of those infected, while HIV-2 causes AIDS in 10 percent or less," says Harvard AIDS specialist Max Essex. "Maybe everyone infected with HIV-2 will progress to AIDS after 40 or 50 years, but that's still in the realm of reduced virulence." From Ewald's perspective, it's no surprise that HIV-2, the strain found in West Africa, is the gentle one. West Africa has escaped much of the war, drought and urbanization that fueled the spread of HIV-1 in the central and eastern parts of the continent. "HIV-2 appears to be adapted for slow transmission in areas with lower sexual contact," he concludes, "and HIV-1 for more rapid transmission in areas with higher sexual contact."

The same pattern shows up in the way each virus affects different populations. HIV-2 appears particularly mild in the stable and isolated West African nation of Senegal. After following a group of Senegalese prostitutes for six years, Harvard researchers found that those testing positive for HIV-2 showed

virtually no sign of illness. In laboratory tests, researchers at the University of Alabama found that Senegalese HIV-2 didn't even kill white blood cells when allowed to infect them in a test tube. Yet HIV-2 is a killer in the more urban and less tradition-bound Ivory Coast. In a survey of hospital patients in the city of Abidjan, researchers from the U.S. Centers for Disease Control found that HIV-2 was associated with AIDS nearly as often as HIV-1.

The variations within HIV-1 are less clear-cut, but they, too, lend support to Ewald's idea. Though the evidence is mixed, there are hints that IV drug users (whose transmission rates have remained high for the past decade) may be contracting deadlier strains of HIV-1 than gay men (whose transmission rates have plummeted). In a 1990 study of infected gay men, fewer than 8 percent of those not receiving early treatment developed AIDS each year. In a more recent study of IV drug users, the proportion of untreated carriers developing AIDS each year was more than 17 percent.

Together, these disparities suggest that HIV assumes different personalities in different settings, becoming more aggressive when it's traveling rapidly through a population. But because so many factors affect the health of infected people, the strength of the connection is unclear. "This is exactly the right way to think about virulence," says virologist Stephen Morse of New York's Rockefeller University. "Virulence should be dynamic, not static. The question is, how dynamic?

A Hypothetical History of AIDS

Why did HIV suddenly emerge as a global killer? According to one theory, the virus has infected people for centuries, but recent social changes have altered its character.

BEFORE 1960
Rural Africans contracted benign ancestral forms of HIV from primates. Because the viruses spread so slowly

among people, they couldn't afford to become virulent.
1960 TO 1975
War, drought, commerce and urbanization shattered African social institutions. HIV spread rapidly, becoming more virulent as transmission accelerated.
1975 TO PRESENT
Global travel placed HIV in broader circulation. Shifting sexual mores and

modern medical practices, such as blood transfusion, made many populations susceptible.

THE FUTURE
If social changes can turn a benign virus deadly, the process should be reversible. Simply slowing transmission may help drive fast-killing strains out of circulation.

1. NATURAL SELECTION

We know that a pathogen like HIV has a wide range of potentials, but we can't yet say just what pressures are needed to generate a particular outcome."

The best answers to Morse's question may come from laboratory studies. A handful of biologists are now devising test-tube experiments to see more precisely how transmission rates shape a parasite's character. Zoologist James Bull of the University of Texas at Austin has shown, for example, that a bacteriophage (a virus that infects bacteria) kills bacterial cells with great abandon when placed in a test tube and given plenty of new cells to infect. Like HIV in a large, active sexual network, it can afford to kill individual hosts without wiping itself out in the process. Yet the same virus becomes benign when confined to individual cells and their offspring (a situation perhaps akin to pre-epidemic HIV's). With a good animal model, researchers might someday manage to test Ewald's hypotheses about HIV with the same kind of precision.

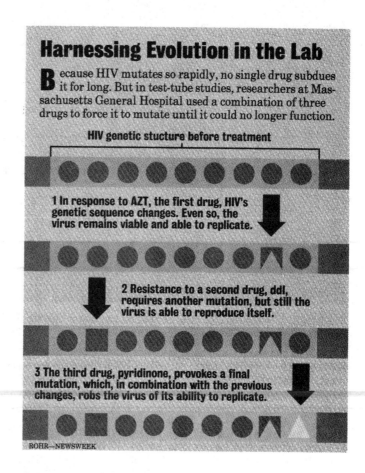

Harnessing Evolution in the Lab

Because HIV mutates so rapidly, no single drug subdues it for long. But in test-tube studies, researchers at Massachusetts General Hospital used a combination of three drugs to force it to mutate until it could no longer function.

HIV genetic structure before treatment

1 In response to AZT, the first drug, HIV's genetic sequence changes. Even so, the virus remains viable and able to replicate.

2 Resistance to a second drug, ddI, requires another mutation, but still the virus is able to reproduce itself.

3 The third drug, pyridinone, provokes a final mutation, which, in combination with the previous changes, robs the virus of its ability to replicate.

ROHR—NEWSWEEK

III. CAN HIV BE TAMED?

Until recently, medical science seemed well on its way to controlling the microbial world. Yet after 10 years and billions of dollars in research, HIV still has scientists over a barrel. The secret of its success can be summed up in one word: mutability. Because HIV's method of replication is so error prone (its genes mutate at a million times the rate of our own), it produces extremely varied offspring, even within an individual host. Whenever a drug or immune response successfully attacks one variant, another arises to flourish in its place. Even when an AIDS drug works broadly enough to check HIV's growth, it rarely works for long. AZT, for example, can help prevent symptoms for a couple of years. But people on AZT still get AIDS, as the viral populations in their bodies evolve toward resistant forms.

There may not be a drug or vaccine on earth that could subdue such a protean parasite. But from a Darwinian perspective, killing HIV is not the only way to combat AIDS. We know the virus changes rapidly in response to outside pressures. Logic suggests that if we simply applied the right pressures—within a community, or even within a patient's body—we might begin to tame it.

It's well known that condoms and clean needles can save lives by preventing HIV infection. From an evolutionary perspective, there is every reason to think they could do more. Used widely enough, those same humble implements might push the virus toward more benevolent forms, simply by depriving virulent strains of the high transmission rates they need to survive. Gay men are already engaged in that exercise. Studies suggest that, thanks to safer sex, the rate of new infections among gays declined five to tenfold during the 1980s. There are tantalizing hints that HIV has grown less noxious in the same population over the same period. In a 1991 study, researchers at the National Institutes of Health (NIH) calculated the rates at which infected people from different risk groups were developing AIDS each year. They found that as of 1987, the rate declined sharply among gay men, suggesting the virus was taking longer to cause illness. Part of the change was due to AZT, which can delay the onset of symptoms. But when the NIH researchers corrected for AZT use, there was still a mysterious shortage of AIDS cases. From Ewald's viewpoint, the shortfall was not only unsurprising but predictable.

How far could such a trend be pushed? Would broader, better prevention efforts eventually turn today's deadliest HIV-1 into something as benign as Senegal's HIV-2? No one knows. But the prospect of domesticating the AIDS virus, even partially, should excite public-health officials. Condoms and clean needles are exceedingly cheap medicine. They can save lives even if they fail to change the course of evolution—and judging from the available evidence, they might well succeed.

In the meantime, more than 12 million people are carrying today's HIV,

5. Future of AIDS

and those who get AIDS are still dying. Fortunately, as Yung-Kang Chow and his colleagues at Massachusetts General Hospital showed last month, there's more than one way to manipulate viral evolution. The researchers managed, in a test-tube experiment, to outsmart HIV at its own game. Their trick was to combine three drugs—AZT, ddI and pyridinone—that disarm the same part of the virus (an enzyme called reverse transcriptase).

Any of those drugs can foil HIV's efforts to colonize host cells. When HIV encounters them individually, or even in pairs, it gradually mutates into resistant forms and goes on about its business. But each mutation makes the virus slightly less efficient—and as Chow's group demonstrated, there comes a point where mutation itself hobbles the virus (see chart on previous page). By engineering an HIV mutant that contained three different mutations (one in response to each of the three drugs), the researchers ended up with a virus that was too deformed to function at all. If virgin HIV can't function in the presence of the three drugs—and if triply mutated HIV can't function at all—then the three-drug regimen should, theoretically, do wonders for patients.

It's a long way from the test tube to the clinic; many treatments have shown great promise in lab experiments, only to prove ineffective or highly toxic in people. Upcoming clinical trials will determine whether patients actually benefit from Chow's combination of drugs. The beauty of the new approach, however, is that it's not limited to any particular combination. While the Boston team experiments with drugs directed against reverse transcriptase, researchers at New York's Aaron Diamond AIDS Research Center are trying the same tack against another viral target (an enzyme called protease). "This virus has impressed us again and again with its ability to change," says Dr. David Ho, director of the Aaron Diamond Center. "It always has a new strategy to counter our efforts. Now we're asking it to make a tradeoff. We're saying, 'Go ahead and mutate, because we think that if you mutate in the right place, you'll do less damage to the patient'."

IV. CAN THE NEXT AIDS BE AVOIDED?

The forces that brought us this plague can surely bring us others. By encroaching on rain forests and wilderness areas, humanity is placing itself in ever-closer contact with other animal species and their obscure, deadly parasites. Other activities, from irrigation to the construction of dams and cities, can create new diseases by expanding the range of the rodents or insects that carry them. Stephen Morse, the Rockefeller virologist, studies the movement of microbes among populations and species, and he worries that human activities are speeding the flow of viral traffic. More than a dozen new diseases have shown up in humans since the 1960s, nearly all of them the result of once exotic parasites exploiting new opportunities. "The primary problem," Morse concludes, "is no longer virological but social."

The Ebola virus is often cited as an example of the spooky pathogens in our future. The virus first struck in August 1976, when a trader arrived at a mission hospital in northern Zaire, fever raging and blood oozing from every orifice. Within days the man died, and nearly half of the nurses at the hospital were stricken. Thirty-nine died, and as hospital patients contracted the virus, it spread to 58 neighboring villages. Ebola fever ended up striking 1,000 people in Zaire and nearby Sudan, killing 500. Epidemiologists feared it would spread more widely, but the outbreaks subsided as quickly as they had begun. From a

As Human Habits Change, New Viruses Emerge

VIRUS, DISEASE	SYMPTOMS	ORIGIN	STATUS
JUNIN Argentine Hemorrhagic Fever	Fever, muscle pain, rash, internal bleeding and, sometimes, tremors or convulsions. Mortality rate: 10 to 20 percent.	First recognized in 1953, Junin has emerged as a result of an increase in corn cultivation in northern Argentina. Carried by mice.	A rodent-control program brought the virus's Bolivian cousin, Machupo, under control, but Junin has expanded its reach in recent decades. It strikes 400 to 600 people annually.
EBOLA African Hemorrhagic Fever	Fever, vomiting, rash, muscle pain, gastrointestinal bleeding, shock. A deadly virus, Ebola kills at least half its victims.	Virtually identical to Marburg, a virus found in Germany in 1967, Ebola was first reported in 1976. Its origin is unknown.	An outbreak in Africa killed 500 in 1976. Philippine monkeys sent to a Reston, Va., research lab brought a related—but not lethal—virus here in 1989, leading to curbs on monkey imports.
DENGUE Dengue Fever	Headache, fever, muscle pain, chills. More severe dengue hemorrhagic fever can cause internal bleeding and death.	Dengue has long plagued tropical Asia, South America and the Caribbean, favoring densely populated, mosquito-infested areas.	Infects more than 30 million people annually. Rare in U.S. but could spread more widely since a shipment of used tires brought virus-transmitting Asian tiger mosquitoes ashore in 1985.
HTLVs Leukemia, TSP	Leukemia is a cancer of white blood cells which can spread to other organs. TSP is a degenerative neurological disorder.	HTLV-1 was first reported in 1980, but studies suggest that it and the related virus HTLV-2 have attacked humans for millenniums.	HTLVs are transmitted in the same manner as HIV but, so far, appear less deadly. One recent study found that up to 20 percent of IV drug users in Los Angeles are infected.

SOURCE: STEPHEN S. MORSE—THE ROCKEFELLER UNIVERSITY, PAUL EWALD—AMHERST COLLEGE

Darwinian perspective, that's no great surprise. A parasite that kills that rapidly has little chance of sustaining a chain of infection unless it can survive independently of its host.

More worrisome is a virus like HTLV, a relative of HIV that infects the same class of blood cells and is riding the same waves through new populations. Though recognized only since the 1970s, the HTLVs (HTLV-1 and HTLV-2) appear to be ancient. About one in 20 HTLV-1 infections leads eventually to leukemia, lymphoma or a paralyzing neurologic disorder called TSP. The virus is less aggressive than HIV-1—it typically takes several decades to cause any illness—but its virulence seems to vary markedly from one setting to the next. In Japan, the HTLV-related cancers typically show up in 60-year-olds who were infected by their mothers in the womb. In the Caribbean, where the virus is more often transmitted through sex, the average latency is much shorter. It's not unusual for people to develop symptoms in their 40s.

HTLV may not mutate as readily as HIV, but it is subject to the same natural forces. If human activities can turn one virus into a global killer, it's only prudent to suspect they could do the same to another. "HTLV is a threat," says Ewald, "not because it has escaped from some secluded source, but because it may evolve increased virulence." HTLV-1 is only one tenth as prevalent as HIV in the United States, but it has gained a strong foothold among IV drug users, whose shared needles are a perfect breeding ground for virulent strains.

No one knows whether HTLV could cause an epidemic like AIDS. Fortunately, we don't have to wait passively to find out. We're beginning to see how our actions mold the character of our parasites. No one saw the last epidemic coming. This time, that's not an excuse.

Black, White, Other

Racial categories are cultural constructs masquerading as biology

Jonathan Marks

New York-born Jonathan Marks earned an undergraduate degree in natural science at Johns Hopkins. After getting his Ph.D. in anthropology, Marks did a post-doc in genetics at the University of California at Davis and is now an associate professor of anthropology at Yale University. He is the coauthor, with Edward Staski, of the introductory textbook Evolutionary Anthropology *(San Diego: Harcourt, Brace Jovanovich, 1992). His new book,* Human Biodiversity: Genes, Race, and History *is published (1995) by Aldine de Gruyter.*

While reading the Sunday edition of the *New York Times* one morning last February, my attention was drawn by an editorial inconsistency. The article I was reading was written by attorney Lani Guinier. (Guinier, you may remember, had been President Clinton's nominee to head the civil rights division at the Department of Justice in 1993. Her name was hastily withdrawn amid a blast of criticism over her views on political representation of minorities.) What had distracted me from the main point of the story was a photo caption that described Guinier as being "half-black." In the text of the article, Guinier had described herself simply as "black."

How can a person be black and half black at the same time? In algebraic terms, this would seem to describe a situation where $x = \frac{1}{2}x$, to which the only solution is $x = 0$.

The inconsistency in the *Times* was trivial, but revealing. It encapsulated a longstanding problem in our use of racial categories—namely, a confusion between biological and cultural heredity. When Guinier is described as "half-black," that is a statement of biological ancestry, for one of her two parents is black. And when Guinier describes herself as black, she is using a cultural category, according to which one can either be black or white, but not both.

Race—as the term is commonly used—is inherited, although not in a strictly biological fashion. It is passed down according to a system of folk heredity, an all-or-nothing system that is different from the quantifiable heredity of biology. But the incompatibility of the two notions of race is sometimes starkly evident—as when the state decides that racial differences are so important that interracial marriages must be regulated or outlawed entirely. Miscegenation laws in this country (which stayed on the books in many states through the 1960s) obliged the legal system to define who belonged in what category. The resulting formula stated that anyone with one-eighth or more black ancestry was a "negro." (A similar formula, defining Jews, was promulgated by the Germans in the Nuremberg Laws of the 1930s.)

Applying such formulas led to the biological absurdity that having one black great-grandparent was sufficient to define a person as black, but having seven white great grandparents was insufficient to define a person as white. Here, race and biology are demonstrably at odds. And the problem is not semantic but conceptual, for race is presented as a category of nature.

Human beings come in a wide variety of sizes, shapes, colors, and forms—or, because we are visually oriented primates, it certainly seems that way. We also come in larger packages called populations; and we are said to belong to even larger and more confusing units, which have long been known as races. The history of the study of human variation is to a large extent the pursuit of those human races—the attempt to identify the small number of fundamentally distinct kinds of people on earth.

This scientific goal stretches back two centuries, to Linnaeus, the father of biological systematics, who radically established *Homo sapiens* as one species within a group of animals he called Primates. Linnaeus's system of naming groups within groups logically implied further breakdown. He consequently sought to establish a number of subspecies within *Homo sapiens*. He identified five: four geographical species (from Europe, Asia, Africa, and America) and one grab-bag subspecies called *monstrosus*. This category was dropped by subsequent researchers (as was Linnaeus's use of criteria such as personality and dress to define his subspecies).

While Linnaeus was not the first to divide humans on the basis of the continents on which they lived, he had given the division a scientific stamp.

1. NATURAL SELECTION

But in attempting to determine the proper number of subspecies, the heirs of Linnaeus always seemed to find different answers, depending upon the criteria they applied. By the mid-twentieth century, scores of anthropologists—led by Harvard's Earnest Hooton—had expended enormous energy on the problem. But these scholars could not convince one another about the precise nature of the fundamental divisions of our species.

Part of the problem—as with the *Times's* identification of Lani Guinier—was that we humans have two constantly intersecting ways of thinking about the divisions among us. On the one hand, we like to think of "race"—as Linnaeus did—as an objective, biological category. In this sense, being a member of a race is supposed to be the equivalent of being a member of a species or of a phylum—except that race, on the analogy of subspecies, is an even narrower (and presumably more exclusive and precise) biological category.

The other kind of category into which we humans allocate ourselves—when we say "Serb" or "Hutu" or "Jew" or "Chicano" or "Republican" or "Red Sox fan"—is cultural. The label refers to little or nothing in the natural attributes of its members. These members may not live in the same region and may not even know many others like themselves. What they share is neither strictly nature nor strictly community. The groupings are constructs of human social history.

Membership in these *un*biological groupings may mean the difference between life and death, for they are the categories that allow us to be identified(and accepted or vilified) socially. While membership in (or allegiance to) these categories may be assigned or adopted from birth, the differentia that mark members from nonmembers are symbolic and abstract; they serve to distinguish people who cannot be readily distinguished by nature. So important are these symbolic distinctions that some of the strongest animosities are often expressed between very similar-looking peoples. Obvious examples are Bosnian Serbs and Muslims, Irish and English, Huron and Iroquois.

Obvious natural variation is rarely so important as cultural difference. One simply does not hear of a slaughter of the short people at the hands of the tall, the glabrous at the hands of the hairy, the red-haired at the hands of the brown-haired. When we do encounter genocidal violence between different looking peoples, the two groups are invariably socially or culturally distinct as well. Indeed, the tragic frequency of hatred and genocidal violence between biologically indistinguishable peoples implies that biological differences such as skin color are not motivations but, rather, excuses. They allow nature to be invoked to reinforce group identities and antagonisms that would exist without these physical distinctions. But are there any truly "racial" biological distinctions to be found in our species?

Obviously, if you compare two people from different parts of the world (or whose ancestors came from different parts of the world), they will differ physically, but one cannot therefore define three or four or five basically different kinds of people, as a biological notion of race would imply. The anatomical properties that distinguish people—such as pigmentation, eye form, body build—are not clumped in discrete groups, but distributed along geographical gradients, as are nearly all the genetically determined variants detectable in the human gene pool.

These gradients are produced by three forces. Natural selection adapts populations to local circumstances (like climate) and thereby differentiates them from other populations. Genetic drift (random fluctuations in a gene pool) also differentiates populations from one another, but in non-adaptive ways. And gene flow (via intermarriage and other child-producing unions) acts to homogenize neighboring populations.

In practice, the operations of these forces are difficult to discern. A few features, such as body build and the graduated distribution of the sickle cell anemia gene in populations from western Africa, southern Asia, and the Mediterranean can be plausibly related to the effects of selection. Others, such as the graduated distribution of a small

deletion in the mitochondrial DNA of some East Asian, Oceanic, and Native American peoples, or the degree of flatness of the face, seem unlikely to be the result of selection and are probably the results of random biohistorical factors. The cause of the distribution of most features, from nose breadth to blood group, is simply unclear.

The overall result of these forces is evident, however. As Johann Friedrich Blumenbach noted in 1775, "you see that all do so run into one another, and that one variety of mankind does so sensibly pass into the other, that you cannot mark out the limits between them." (Posturing as an heir to Linnaeus, he nonetheless attempted to do so.) But from humanity's gradations in appearance, no defined groupings resembling races readily emerge. The racial categories with which we have become so familiar are the result of our imposing arbitrary cultural boundaries in order to partition gradual biological variation.

Unlike graduated biological distinctions, culturally constructed categories are ultrasharp. One can be French or German, but not both; Tutsi or Hutu, but not both; Jew or Catholic, but not both; Bosnian Muslim or Serb, but not both; black or white, but not both. Traditionally, people of "mixed race" have been obliged to choose one and thereby identify themselves unambiguously to census takers and administrative bookkeepers—a practice that is now being widely called into question.

A scientific definition of race would require considerable homogeneity within each group, and reasonably discrete differences between groups, but three kinds of data militate against this view: First, the groups traditionally described as races are not at all homogeneous. Africans and Europeans, for instance, are each a collection of biologically diverse populations. Anthropologists of the 1920s widely recognized *three* European races: Nordic, Alpine, and Mediterranean. This implied that races could exist within races. American anthropologist Carleton Coon identified *ten* European races in 1939. With such protean use, the term race came to have little value in describing actual biological entities within *Homo sapiens*. The scholars were not only grappling with a broad north-south gradient in human appearance across Europe, they were trying to bring the data into line with their belief in profound and fundamental constitutional differences between groups of people.

But there simply isn't one European race to contrast with an African race, nor three, nor ten: the question (as scientists long posed it) fails to recognize the actual patterning of diversity in the human species. Fieldwork revealed, and genetics later quantified, the existence of far more biological diversity within any group than between groups. Fatter and thinner people exist everywhere, as do people with type O and type A blood. What generally varies from one population to the next is the *proportion* of people in these groups expressing the trait or gene. Hair color varies strikingly among Europeans and native Australians, but little among other peoples. To focus on discovering differences between presumptive races, when the vast majority of detectable variants do not help differentiate them, was thus to define a very narrow—if not largely illusory—problem in human biology. (The fact that Africans are biologically more diverse than Europeans, but have rarely been split into so many races, attests to the cultural basis of these categorizations.)

Second, differences between human groups are only evident when contrasting geographical extremes. Noting these extremes, biologists of an earlier era sought to identify representatives of "pure," primordial races presumably located in Norway, Senegal, and Thailand. At no time, however, was our species composed of a few populations within which everyone looked pretty much the same. Ever since some of our ancestors left Africa to spread out through

the Old World, we humans have always lived in the "in-between" places. And human populations have also always been in genetic contact with one another. Indeed, for tens of thousands of years, humans have had trade networks; and where goods flow, so do genes. Consequently, we have no basis for considering *extreme* human forms the most pure, or most representative, of some ancient primordial populations. Instead, they represent populations adapted to the most disparate environments.

And third, between each presumptive "major" race are unclassifiable populations and people. Some populations of India, for example, are darkly pigmented (or "black"), have Europeanlike ("Caucasoid") facial features, but inhabit the continent of Asia (which should make them "Asian"). Americans might tend to ignore these "exceptions" to the racial categories, since immigrants to the United States from West Africa, Southeast Asia, and northwest Europe far outnumber those from India. The very existence of unclassifiable peoples undermines the idea that there are just three human biological groups in the Old World. Yet acknowledging the biological distinctiveness of such groups leads to a rapid proliferation of categories. What about Australians? Polynesians? The Ainu of Japan?

Categorizing people is important to any society. It is, at some basic psychological level, probably necessary to have group identity about who and what you are, in contrast to who and what you are not. The concept of race, however, specifically involves the recruitment of biology to validate those categories of self-identity.

Mice don't have to worry about that the way humans do. Consequently, classifying them into subspecies entails less of a responsibility for a scientist than classifying humans into sub-

species does. And by the 1960s, most anthropologists realized they could not defend any classification of *Homo sapiens* into biological subspecies or races that could be considered reasonably objective. They therefore stopped doing it, and stopped identifying the endeavor as a central goal of the field. It was a biologically intractable problem—the old square-peg-in-a-round-hole enterprise; and people's lives, or welfares, could well depend on the ostensibly scientific pronouncement. Reflecting on the social history of the twentieth century, that was a burden anthropologists would no longer bear.

This conceptual divorce in anthropology—of cultural from biological phenomena was one of the most fundamental scientific revolutions of our time. And since it affected assumptions so rooted in our everyday experience, and resulted in conclusions so counterintuitive—like the idea that the earth goes around the sun, and not vice-versa—it has been widely underappreciated.

Kurt Vonnegut, in *Slaughterhouse Five,* describes what he remembered being taught about human variation: "At that time, they were teaching that there was absolutely no difference between anybody. They may be teaching that still." Of course there are biological differences between people, and between populations. The question is: How are those differences patterned? And the answer seems to be: Not racially. Populations are the only readily identifiable units of humans, and even they are fairly fluid, biologically similar to populations nearby, and biologically different from populations far away.

In other words, the message of contemporary anthropology is: You may group humans into a small number of races if you want to, but you are denied biology as a support for it.

Racial Odyssey

Boyce Rensberger

The human species comes in an artist's palette of colors: sandy yellows, reddish tans, deep browns, light tans, creamy whites, pale pinks. It is a rare person who is not curious about the skin colors, hair textures, bodily structures and facial features associated with racial background. Why do some Africans have dark brown skin, while that of most Europeans is pale pink? Why do the eyes of most "white" people and "black" people look pretty much alike but differ so from the eyes of Orientals? Did one race evolve before the others? If so, is it more primitive or more advanced as a result? Can it be possible, as modern research suggests, that there is no such thing as a pure race? These are all honest, scientifically worthy questions. And they are central to current research on the evolution of our species on the planet Earth.

Broadly speaking, research on racial differences has led most scientists to three major conclusions. The first is that there are many more differences among people than skin color, hair texture and facial features. Dozens of other variations have been found, ranging from the shapes of bones to the consistency of ear wax to subtle variations in body chemistry.

The second conclusions is that the overwhelming evolutionary success of the human species is largely due to its great genetic variability. When migrating bands of our early ancestors reached a new environment, at least a few already had physical traits that gave them an edge in surviving there. If the coming centuries bring significant environmental changes, as many believe they will, our chances of surviving them will be immeasurably enhanced by our diversity as a species.

There is a third conclusion about race that is often misunderstood. Despite our wealth of variation and despite our constant, everyday references to race, no one has ever discovered a reliable way of distinguishing one race from another. While it is possible to classify a great many people on the basis of certain physical features, there are no known feature or groups of features that will do the job in all cases.

Skin color won't work. Yes, most Africans from south of the Sahara and their descendants around the world have skin that is darker than that of most Europeans. But there are millions of people in India, classified by some anthropologists as members of the Caucasoid, or "white," race who have darker skins than most Americans who call themselves black. And there are many Africans living in sub-Sahara Africa today whose skins are no darker than the skins of many Spaniards, Italians, Greeks or Lebanese.

What about stature as a racial trait? Because they are quite short, on the average, African Pygmies have been considered racially distinct from other dark-skinned Africans. If stature, then, is a racial criterion, would one include in the same race the tall African Watusi and the Scandinavians of similar stature?

The little web of skin that distinguishes Oriental eyes is said to be a particular feature of the Mongoloid race. How, then, can it be argued that the American Indian, who lacks this epicanthic fold, is Mongoloid?

Even more hopeless as racial markers are hair color, eye color, hair form, the shapes of noses and lips or any of the other traits put forth as typical of one race or another.

NO NORMS

Among the tall people of the world there are many black, many white and many in between. Among black people of the world there are many with kinky hair, many with straight or wavy hair, and many in between. Among the broad-nosed, full-lipped people of the world there are many with dark skins, many with light skins and many in between.

How did our modern perceptions of race arise? One of the first to attempt a scientific classification of peoples was Carl von Linné, better known as Linnaeus. In 1735, he published a classification that remains the standard today. As Linnaeus saw it there were four races, classifiable geographically and by skin color. The names Linnaeus gave them were *Homo sapiens Africanus nigrus* (black African human being), *H. sapiens Americanus rube-*

scens (red American human being), *H. sapiens Asiaticus fuscusens* (brownish Asian human being), and *H. sapiens Europaeus albescens* (white European human being). All, Linnaeus recognized, were members of a single human species.

A species includes all individuals that are biologically capable of interbreeding and producing fertile offspring. Most matings between species are fruitless, and even when they succeed, as when a horse and a donkey interbreed and produce a mule, the progeny are sterile. When a poodle mates with a collie, however, the offspring are fertile, showing that both dogs are members of the same species.

Even though Linnaeus's system of nomenclature survives, his classifications were discarded, especially after voyages of discovery revealed that there were many more kinds of people than could be pigeonholed into four categories. All over the world there are small populations that don't fit. Among the better known are:

- The so-called Bushmen of southern Africa, who look as much Mongoloid as Negroid.
- The Negritos of the South Pacific, who do look Negroid but are very far from Africa and have no known links to that continent.
- The Ainu of Japan, a hairy aboriginal people who look more Caucasoid than anything else.
- The Lapps of Scandinavia, who look as much like Eskimos as like Europeans.
- The aborigines of Australia, who often look Negroid but many of whom have straight or wavy hair and are often blond as children.
- The Polynesians, who seem to be a blend of many races, the proportions differing from island to island.

To accommodate such diversity, many different systems of classification have been proposed. Some set up two or three dozen races. None has ever satisfied all experts.

CLASSIFICATION SYSTEM

Perhaps the most sweeping effort to impose a classification upon all the peoples of the world was made by the American anthropologist Carleton Coon. He concluded there are five basic races, two of which have major subdivisions: Caucasoids; Mongloids; full-size Australoids (Australian aborigines); dwarf Australoids (Negritos—Andaman Islanders and similar peoples); full-size Congoids (African Negroids); dwarf Congoids (African Pygmies); and Capoids (the so-called Bushmen and Hottentots).

In his 1965 classic, *The Living Races of Man,* Coon hypothesized that before A.D. 1500 there were five pure races— five centers of human population that were so isolated that there was almost no mixing.

Each of these races evolved independently, Coon believed, diverging from a pre-*Homo sapiens* stock that was essentially the same everywhere. He speculated that the common ancestor evolved into *Homo sapiens* in five separate regions at five different times, beginning about 35,000 years ago. The populations that have been *Homo sapiens* for the shortest periods of time, Coon said, are the world's "less civilized" races.

The five pure races remained distinct until A.D. 1500; then Europeans started sailing the world, leaving their genes—as sailors always have—in every port and planting distant colonies. At about the same time, thousands of Africans were captured and forcibly settled in many parts of the New World.

That meant the end of the five pure races. But Coon and other experts held that this did not necessarily rule out the idea of distinct races. In this view, there *are* such things as races; people just don't fit into them very well anymore.

The truth is that there is really no hard evidence to suggest that five or any particular number of races evolved independently. The preponderance of evidence today suggests that as traits typical of fully modern people arose in any one place, they spread quickly to all human populations. Advances in intelligence were almost certainly the fastest to spread. Most anthropologists and geneticists now believe that human

beings have always been subject to migrating and mixing. In other words, there probably never were any such things as pure races.

Race mixing has not only been a fact of human history but is, in this day of unprecedented global mobility, taking place at a more rapid rate than ever. It is not farfetched to envision the day when, generations hence, the entire "complexion" of major population centers will be different. Meanwhile, we can see such changes taking place before our eyes, for they are a part of everyday reality.

HYBRID VIGOR

Oddly, those who assert scientific validity for their notions of pure and distinct races seem oblivious of a basic genetic principle that plant and animal breeders know well: too much inbreeding can lead to proliferation of inferior traits. Crossbreeding with different strains often produces superior combinations and "hybrid vigor."

The striking differences among people may very well be a result of constant genetic mixing. And as geneticists and ecologists know, in diversity lies strength and resilience.

To understand the origin and proliferation of human differences, one must first know how Darwinian evolution works.

Evolution is a two-step process. Step one is mutation: somehow a gene in the ovary or testes of an individual is altered, changing the molecular configuration that stores instructions for forming a new individual. The children who inherit that gene will be different in some way from their ancestors.

Step two is selection: for a racial difference, or any other evolutionary change to arise, it must survive and be passed through several generations. If the mutation confers some disadvantage, the individual dies, often during embryonic development. But if the change is beneficial in some way, the individual should have a better chance of thriving than relatives lacking the advantage.

DISEASE ORIGINS

The gene for sickle cell anemia, a disease found primarily among black people, appears to have evolved because its presence can render its bearer resistant to malaria. Such a trait would have obvious value in tropical Africa.

A person who has sickle cell anemia must have inherited genes for the disease from both parents. If a child inherits only one sickle cell gene, he or she will be resistant to malaria but will not have the anemia. Paradoxically, inheriting genes from both parents does not seem to affect resistance to malaria.

In the United States, where malaria is practically nonexistent, the sickle cell gene confers no survival advantage and is disappearing. Today only about 1 out of every 10 American blacks carries the gene.

Many other inherited diseases are found only in people from a particular area. Tay-Sachs disease, which often kills before the age of two, is almost entirely confined to Jews from parts of Eastern Europe and their descendants elsewhere. Paget's disease, a bone disorder, is found most often among those of English descent. Impacted wisdom teeth are a common problem among Asians and Europeans but not among Africans. Children of all races are able to digest milk because their bodies make lactase, the enzyme that breaks down lactose, or milk sugar. But the ability to digest lactose in adulthood is a racially distributed trait.

About 90 percent of Orientals and blacks lose this ability by the time they reach adulthood and become quite sick when they drink milk.

Even African and Asian herders who keep cattle or goats rarely drink fresh milk. Instead, they first treat the milk with fermentation bacteria that break down lactose, in a sense predigesting it. They can then ingest the milk in the form of yogurt or cheese without any problem.

About 90 percent of Europeans and their American descendants, on the other hand, continue to produce the enzyme throughout their lives and can drink milk with no ill effects.

NATURAL SELECTION

If a new trait is beneficial, it will bring reproductive success to its bearer. After several generations of multiplication, bearers of the new trait may begin to outnumber nonbearers. Darwin called this natural selection to distinguish it from the artificial selection exercised by animal breeders.

Skin color is the human racial trait most generally thought to confer an evolutionary advantage of this sort. It has long been obvious in the Old World that the farther south one goes, the darker the skin color. Southern Europeans are usually somewhat darker than northern Europeans. In North Africa, skin colors are darker still, and, as one travels south, coloration reaches its maximum at the Equator. The same progressions holds in Asia, with the lightest skins to the north. Again, as one moves south, skin color darkens, reaching in southern India a "blackness" equal to that of equatorial Africans.

This north-south spectrum of skin color derives from varying intensities of the same dark brown pigment called melanin. Skin cells simply have more or less melanin granules to be seen against a background that is pinkish because of the underlying blood vessels. All races can increase their melanin concentration by exposure to the sun.

What is it about northerly latitudes in the Northern Hemisphere that favors less pigmentation and about southerly latitudes that favors more? Exposure to intense sunlight is not the only reason why people living in southerly latitudes are dark. A person's susceptibility to rickets and skin cancer, his ability to withstand cold and to see in the dark may also be related to skin color.

The best-known explanation says the body can tolerate only a narrow range of intensities of sunlight. Too much causes sunburn and cancer, while too little deprives the body of vitamin D, which is synthesized in the skin under the influence of sunlight. A dark complexion protects the skin from the harmful effects of intense sunlight. Thus, albinos born in equatorial regions have a high rate of skin cancer. On the other hand, dark skin in northerly latitudes screens out sunlight needed for the synthesis of vitamin D. Thus, dark-skinned children living in northern latitudes had high rates of rickets—a bone-deforming disease caused by a lack of vitamin D—before their milk was routinely fortified. In the sunny tropics, dark skin admits enough light to produce the vitamin.

Recently, there has been some evidence that skin colors are linked to differences in the ability to avoid injury from the cold. Army researchers found that during the Korean War blacks were more susceptible to frostbite than were whites. Even among Norwegian soldiers in World War II, brunettes had a slightly higher incidence of frostbite than did blonds.

EYE PIGMENTATION

A third link between color and latitude involves the sensitivity of the eye to various wavelengths of light. It is known that dark-skinned people have more pigmentation in the iris of the eye and at the back of the eye where the image falls. It has been found that the less pigmented the eye, the more sensitive it is to colors at the red end of the spectrum. In situations illuminated with reddish light, the northern European can see more than a dark African sees.

It has been suggested that Europeans developed lighter eyes to adapt to the longer twilights of the North and their greater reliance on firelight to illuminate caves.

Although the skin cancer-vitamin D hypothesis enjoys wide acceptance, it may well be that resistance to cold, possession of good night vision and other yet unknown factors all played roles in the evolution of skin colors.

Most anthropologists agree that the original human skin color was dark brown, since it is fairly well established that human beings evolved in the tropics of Africa. This does not, however, mean that the first people were Negroids, whose descendants, as they moved north, evolved into light-skinned Caucasoids. It is more likely that the skin color of various populations changed several times from dark to light and back as people moved from one region to another.

Consider, for example, that long before modern people evolved, *Homo erectus* had spread throughout Africa, Europe and Asia. The immediate ancestor of *Homo sapiens, Homo erectus,* was living in Africa 1.5 million years ago and in Eurasia 750,000 years ago. The earliest known forms of *Homo sapiens* do not make their appearance until somewhere between 250,000 and 500,000 years ago. Although there is no evidence of the skin color of any hominid fossil, it is probable that the *Homo erectus* population in Africa had dark skin. As subgroups spread into northern latitudes, mutations that reduced pigmentation conferred survival advantages on them and lighter skins came to predominate. In other words, there were probably black *Homo erectus* peoples in Africa and white ones in Europe and Asia.

Did the black *Homo erectus* populations evolve into today's Negroids and the white ones in Europe into today's Caucasoids? By all the best evidence, nothing like this happened. More likely, wherever *Homo sapiens* arose it proved so superior to the *Homo erectus* populations that it eventually replaced them everywhere.

If the first *Homo sapiens* evolved in Africa, they were probably dark-skinned; those who migrated northward into Eurasia lost their pigmentation. But it is just as possible that the first *Homo sapiens* appeared in northern climes, descendants of white-skinned *Homo erectus.* These could have migrated southward toward Africa, evolving darker skins. All modern races, incidentally, arose long after the brain had reached its present size in all parts of the world.

North-south variations in pigmentation are quite common among mammals and birds. The tropical races tend to be darker in fur and feather, the desert races tend to be brown, and those near the Arctic Circle are lighter colored.

There are exceptions among humans. The Indians of the Americas, from the Arctic to the southern regions of South America, do not conform to the north-south scheme of coloration. Though most think of Indians as being reddish-brown, most Indians tend to be relatively light skinned, much like their presumed Mongoloid ancestors in Asia. The ruddy complexion that lives in so many stereotypes of Indians is merely what years of heavy tanning can produce in almost any light-skinned person. Anthropologists explain the color consistency as a consequence of the relatively recent entry of people into the Americas—probably between 12,000 and 35,000 years ago. Perhaps they have not yet had time to change.

Only a few external physical differences other than color appear to have adaptive significance. The strongest cases can be made for nose shape and stature.

WHAT'S IN A NOSE

People native to colder or drier climates tend to have longer, more beak-shaped noses than those living in hot and humid regions. The nose's job is to warm and humidify air before it reaches sensitive lung tissues. The colder or drier the air is, the more surface area is needed inside the nose to get it to the right temperature or humidity. Whites tend to have longer and beakier noses than blacks or Orientals. Nevertheless, there is great variation within races. Africans in the highlands of East Africa have longer noses than Africans from the hot, humid lowlands, for example.

Stature differences are reflected in the tendency for most northern peoples to have shorter arms, legs and torsos and to be stockier than people from the tropics. Again, this is an adaptation to heat or cold. One way of reducing heat loss is to have less body surface, in relation to weight or volume, from which heat can escape. To avoid overheating, the most desirable body is long limbed and lean. As a result, most Africans tend to be lankier than northern Europeans. Arctic peoples are the shortest limbed of all.

Hair forms may also have a practical role to play, but the evidence is weak. It has been suggested that the more tightly curled hair of Africans insulates the top of the head better than does straight or wavy hair. Contrary to expectation, black hair serves better in this role than white hair. Sunlight is absorbed and converted to heat at the outer surface of the hair blanket; it radiates directly into the air. White fur, common on Arctic animals that need to absorb solar heat, is actually transparent and transmits light into the hair blanket, allowing the heat to form within the insulating layer, where it is retained for warmth.

Aside from these examples, there is little evidence that any of the other visible differences among the world's people provide any advantage. Nobody knows, for example, why Orientals have epicanthic eye folds or flatter facial profiles. The thin lips of Caucasoids and most Mongoloids have no known advantages over the Negroid's full lips. Why should middle-aged and older Caucasoid men go bald so much more frequently than the men of other races? Why does the skin of Bushmen wrinkle so heavily in the middle and later years? Or why does the skin of Negroids resist wrinkling so well? Why do the Indian men in one part of South America have blue penises? Why do Hottentot women have such unusually large buttocks?

There are possible evolutionary explanations for why such apparently useless differences arise.

One is a phenomenon known as sexual selection. Environmentally adaptive traits arise, Darwin thought, through natural selection—the environment itself chooses who will thrive or decline. In sexual selection, which Darwin also suggested, the choice belongs to the prospective mate.

In simple terms, ugly individuals will be less likely to find mates and reproduce their genes than beautiful specimens will. Take the blue penis as an example. Women might find it unusually attractive or perhaps believe it to be endowed with special powers. If so, a man born with a blue penis will find many more opportunities to reproduce his genes than his ordinary brothers.

Sexual selection can also operate when males compete for females. The moose with the larger antlers or the lion with the more imposing mane will stand a better chance of discouraging less well-endowed males and gaining access to females. It is possible that such a process operated among Caucasoid males, causing them to become markedly hairy, especially around the face.

ATTRACTIVE TRAITS

Anthropologists consider it probable that traits such as the epicanthic fold or the many regional differences in facial features were selected this way.

Yet another method by which a trait can establish itself involves accidental selection. It results from what biologists call genetic drift.

Suppose that in a small nomadic band a person is born with perfectly parallel fingerprints instead of the usual loops, whorls or arches. That person's children would inherit parallel fingerprints, but they would confer no survival advantages. But if our family decides to strike out on its own, it will become the founder of a new band consisting of its own descendants, all with parallel fingerprints.

Events such as this, geneticists and anthropologists believe, must have oc-

curred many times in the past to produce the great variety within the human species. Among the apparently neutral traits that differ among populations are:

Ear Wax

There are two types of ear wax. One is dry and crumbly and the other is wet and sticky. Both types can be found in every major population, but the frequencies differ. Among northern Chinese, for example, 98 percent have dry ear wax. Among American whites, only 16 percent have dry ear wax. Among American blacks the figure is 7 percent.

Scent Glands

As any bloodhound knows, every person has his or her own distinctive scent. People vary in the mixture of odoriferous compounds exuded through the skin—most of it coming from specialized glands called apocrine glands. Among whites, these are concentrated in the armpits and near the genitals and anus. Among blacks, they may also be found on the chest and abdomen. Orientals have hardly any apocrine glands at all. In the words of the Oxford biologist John R. Baker, "The Europids and Negrids are smelly, the Mongoloids scarcely or not at all." Smelliest of all are northern European, or so-called Nordic, whites. Body odor is rare in Japan. It was once thought to indicate a European in the ancestry and to be a disease requiring hospitalization.

Blood Groups

Some populations have a high percentage of members with a particular blood group. American Indians are overwhelmingly group O—100 percent in some regions. Group A is most common among Australian aborigines and the Indians in western Canada. Group B is frequent in northern India, other parts of Asia and western Africa.

Advocates of the pure-race theory once seized upon blood groups as possibly unique to the original pure races. The proportions of groups found today,

they thought, would indicate the degree of mixing. It was subsequently found that chimpanzees, our closest living relatives, have the same blood groups as humans.

Taste

PTC (phenylthiocarbamide) is a synthetic compound that some people can taste and other cannot. The ability to taste it has no known survival value, but it is clearly an inherited trait. The proportion of persons who can taste PTC varies in different populations: 50 to 70 percent of Australian aborigines can taste it, as can 60 to 80 percent of all Europeans. Among East Asians, the percentage is 83 to 100 percent, and among Africans, 90 to 97 percent.

Urine

Another indicator of differences in body chemistry is the excretion of a compound known as BAIB (beta-amino-isobutyric acid) in urine. Europeans seldom excrete large quantities, but high levels of excretion are common among Asians and American Indians. It had been shown that the differences are not due to diet.

No major population has remained isolated long enough to prevent any unique genes from eventually mixing with those of neighboring groups. Indeed, a map showing the distribution of so-called traits would have no sharp boundaries, except for coastlines. The intensity of a trait such as skin color, which is controlled by six pairs of genes and can therefore exist in many shades, varies gradually from one population to another. With only a few exceptions, every known genetic possibility possessed by the species can be found to some degree in every sizable population.

EVER-CHANGING SPECIES

One can establish a system of racial classification simply by listing the features of populations at any given moment. Such a concept of race is, however, inappropriate to a highly mobile and ever-changing species such as *Homo sapiens*. In the short view, races may seem distinguishable, but in biology's long haul, races come and go. New ones arise and blend into neighboring groups to create new and racially stable populations. In time, genes from these groups flow into other neighbors, continuing the production of new permutations.

Some anthropologists contend that at the moment American blacks should be considered a race distinct from African blacks. They argue that American blacks are a hybrid of African blacks and European whites. Indeed, the degree of mixture can be calculated on the basis of a blood component known as the Duffy factor.

In West Africa, where most of the New World's slaves came from, the Duffy factor is virtually absent. It is present in 43 percent of American whites. From the number of American blacks who are now "Duffy positive" it can be calculated that whites contributed 21 percent of the genes in the American black population. The figure is higher for blacks in northern and western states and lower in the South. By the same token, there are whites who have black ancestors. The number is smaller because of the tendency to identify a person as black even if only a minor fraction of his ancestors were originally from Africa.

The unwieldiness of race designations is also evident in places such as Mexico where most of the people are, in effect, hybrids of Indians (Mongoloid by some classifications) and Spaniards (Caucasoid). Many South American populations are tri-hybrids—mixtures of Mongoloid, Caucasoid and Negroid. Brazil is a country where the mixture has been around long enough to constitute a racially stable population. Thus, in one sense, new races have been created in the United States, Mexico and Brazil. But in the long run, those races will again change.

Sherwood Washburn, a noted anthropologist, questions the usefulness of racial classification: "Since races are open systems which are intergrading, the number of races will depend on the purpose of the classification. I think we should require people who propose a classification of races to state in the first place why they wish to divide the human species."

The very notion of a pure race, then, makes no sense. But, as evolutionists know full well, a rich genetic diversity within the human species most assuredly *does*.

Primates

Primates are fun. They are active, intelligent, colorful, emotionally expressive, and unpredictable. In other words, observing them is like holding up an opaque mirror to ourselves. The image may not be crystal clear or, indeed, what some would consider flattering, but it is certainly familiar enough to be illuminating.

Primates are, of course, but one of many orders of mammals that adaptively radiated into the variety of eco-logical niches vacated at the end of the Age of Reptiles about 65 million years ago. Whereas some mammals took to the sea (cetaceans), and some took to the air (chiroptera, or bats), primates are characterized by an arboreal or forested adaptation. Whereas some mammals can be identified by their food-getting habits, such as the meat-eating carnivores, primates have a penchant for eating almost anything and are best described as omnivorous. In taking to the trees, primates did not simply develop a full-blown set of distinguishing characteristics that set them off easily from other orders of mammals, the way the rodent order can be readily identified by its gnawing set of front teeth. Rather, each primate seems to represent degrees of anatomical, biological, and behavioral characteristics on a continuum of progress with respect to the particular traits we humans happen to be interested in.

None of this is meant to imply, of course, that the living primates are our ancestors. Since the prosimians, monkeys and apes, are our contemporaries, they are no more our ancestors than we are theirs; as living end products of evolution, we have all descended from a common stock in the distant past.

So, if we are interested primarily in our own evolutionary past, why study primates at all? Because, by the criteria we have set up as significant milestones in the evolution of humanity, an inherent reflection of our own bias, they have not evolved as far as we have. They and their environments, therefore, may represent glimmerings of the evolutionary stages and ecological circumstances through which our own ancestors may have gone. What we stand to gain, for instance, is an educated guess as to how our own ancestors might have appeared and behaved as semierect creatures before becoming bipedal. It is in the spirit of this type of inquiry that Peter Radetsky (in "Gut Thinking") investigates the relationship between diet, social organization, and intelligence, and that Robert Sapolsky (in "The Young and the Reckless") asks why, in the case of "adolescent transfer," young primate males will risk life and limb to move from one troop to another. Aside from being a pleasure to observe, then, living primates can teach us something about our past.

Another reason for studying primates is that they allow us to test certain notions too often taken for granted. For instance, Barbara Smuts, in "What Are Friends For?" reveals that friendship bonds, as illustrated by the olive baboons of East Africa, have little if anything to do with a sexual division of labor or even sexual exclusivity between a pair-bonded male and female. This article challenges the traditional male-oriented idea that primate societies are dominated solely by males and for males.

This unit demonstrates that relationships between the sexes are subject to wide variation, that the kinds of answers obtained depend upon the kinds of questions asked, and that we have to be very careful in making inferences about human beings from any one particular primate study. We may, if we are not careful, draw conclusions that say more about our own skewed perspectives than about that which we claim to understand. Still another benefit of primate field research is that it provides us with perspectives that the bones and stones of the fossil hunters will never reveal: a sense of the richness and variety of social patterns that must have existed in the primate order for many tens of millions of years. (See James Shreeve's essay "Machiavellian Monkeys," Jane Goodall's "The Mind of the Chimpanzee," and Sy Montgomery's "Dian Fossey and Digit.")

Finally, there is a sense of urgency in the study of primates as we contemplate the dreaded possibility of their imminent extinction. We have already lost 14 species of lemurs in the past thousand years (most of which were larger than the contemporary forms), and the fate of most other free-ranging primates is in the balance. It is with considerable irony that future generations may come to envy us as having been among the first and last people to be able to observe our closest living relatives in their natural habitats. If for no other reason, we need to collect as much information as we can about primates while they are still with us.

Looking Ahead: Challenge Questions

What is the role of deception among primates, and how might it have led to greater intelligence?

Why is friendship important to olive baboons, and what implications does this have for the origins of pair-bonding in hominid evolution?

What are the advantages to a primate species of "adolescent transfer"?

How is it possible to objectively study and assess emotional and mental states of nonhuman primates?

Why is the mountain gorilla in danger of extinction?

What makes fruit-eating spider monkeys so much smarter than leaf-eating howlers? What are the implications of this for human evolution?

Machiavellian Monkeys

The sneaky skills of our primate cousins suggest that we may owe our great intelligence to an inherited need to deceive.

James Shreeve

This is a story about frauds, cheats, liars, faithless lovers, incorrigible con artists, and downright thieves. You're gonna love 'em.

Let's start with a young rascal named Paul. You'll remember his type from your days back in the playground. You're minding your own business, playing on the new swing set, when along comes Paul, such a little runt that you hardly notice him sidle up to you. All of a sudden he lets out a scream like you've run him through with a white-hot barbed harpoon or something. Of course the teacher comes running, and the next thing you know you're being whisked inside with an angry finger shaking in our face. That's the end of recess for you. But look out the window: there's Paul, having a great time on *your* swing. Cute kid.

Okay, you're a little older now and a little smarter. You've got a bag of chips stashed away in your closet, where for once your older brother won't be able to find them. You're about to open the closet door when he pokes his head in the room. Quickly you pretend to be fetching your high tops; he gives you a look but he leaves. You wait a couple of minutes, lacing up the sneakers in case he walks back in, then you dive for the chips. Before you can get the bag open, he's over your shoulder, snatching it out of your hands. "Nice try, punk," he says through a mouthful,

"but I was hiding outside your room the whole time."

This sort of trickery is such a common part of human interaction that we hardly notice how much time we spend defending ourselves against it or perpetrating it ourselves. What's so special about the fakes and cheaters here, however, is that they're not human. Paul is a young baboon, and your big brother is, well, a chimpanzee. With some admittedly deceptive alterations of scenery and props, the situations have been lifted from a recent issue of *Primate Report*. The journal is the work of Richard Byrne and Andrew Whiten, two psychologists at the University of St. Andrews in Scotland, and it is devoted to cataloging the petty betrayals of monkeys and apes as witnessed by primatologists around the world. It is a testament to the evolutionary importance of what Byrne and Whiten call Machiavellian intelligence— a facility named for the famed sixteenth-century author of *The Prince,* the ultimate how-to guide to prevailing in a complex society through the judicious application of cleverness, deceit, and political acumen.

Deception is rife in the natural world. Stick bugs mimic sticks. Harmless snakes resemble deadly poisonous ones. When threatened, blowfish puff themselves up and cats arch their backs and bristle their hair to seem bigger than they really are. All these animals could be said to practice deception because they fool other animals—usu-

ally members of other species—into thinking they are something that they patently are not. Even so, it would be overreading the situation to attribute Machiavellian cunning to a blowfish, or to accuse a stick bug of being a lying scoundrel. Their deceptions, whether in their looks or in their actions, are programmed genetic responses. Biology leaves them no choice but to dissemble: they are just being true to themselves.

The kind of deception that interests Byrne and Whiten—what they call tactical deception—is a different kettle of blowfish altogether. Here an animal has the mental flexibility to take an "honest" behavior and use it in such a way that another animal—usually a member of the deceiver's own social group—is misled, thinking that a normal, familiar state of affairs is under way, while, in fact, something quite different is happening.

Take Paul, for example. The real Paul is a young chacma baboon that caught Whiten's attention in 1983, while he and Byrne were studying foraging among the chacma in the Drakensberg Mountains of southern Africa. Whiten saw a member of Paul's group, an adult female named Mel, digging in the ground, trying to extract a nutritious plant bulb. Paul approached and looked around. There were no other baboons within sight. Suddenly he let out a yell, and within seconds his mother came running, chasing the startled Mel over a small cliff. Paul then took the bulb for himself.

In this case the deceived party was Paul's mother, who was misled by his scream into believing that Paul was being attacked, when actually no such attack was taking place. As a result of her apparent misinterpretation Paul was left alone to eat the bulb that Mel had carefully extracted—a morsel, by the way, that he would not have had the strength to dig out on his own.

If Paul's ruse had been an isolated case, Whiten might have gone on with his foraging studies and never given it a second thought. But when he compared his field notes with Byrne's, he noticed that both their notebooks were sprinkled with similar incidents and had been so all summer long. After they returned home to Scotland, they boasted about their "dead smart" baboons to their colleagues in pubs after conferences, expecting them to be suitably impressed. Instead the other researchers countered with tales about their own shrewd vervets or Machiavellian macaques.

"That's when we realized that a whole phenomenon might be slipping through a sieve," says Whiten. Researchers had assumed that this sort of complex trickery was a product of the sophisticated human brain. After all, deceitful behavior seemed unique to humans, and the human brain is unusually large, even for primates—"three times as big as you would expect for a primate of our size," notes Whiten, if you're plotting brain size against body weight.

But if primates other than humans deceived one another on a regular basis, the two psychologists reasoned, then it raised the extremely provocative possibility that the primate brain, and ultimately the human brain, is an instrument crafted for social manipulation. Humans evolved from the same evolutionary stock as apes, and if tactical deception was an important part of the lives of our evolutionary ancestors, then the sneakiness and subterfuge that human beings are so manifestly capable of might not be simply a result of our great intelligence and oversize

brain, but a driving force behind their development.

To Byrne and Whiten these were ideas worth pursuing. They fit in with a theory put forth some years earlier

---

Suddenly Paul let out a yell, and his mother came running, chasing Mel over a small cliff.

---

by English psychologist Nicholas Humphrey. In 1976 Humphrey had eloquently suggested that the evolution of primate intelligence might have been spurred not by the challenges of environment, as was generally thought, but rather by the complex cognitive demands of living with one's own companions. Since then a number of primatologists had begun to flesh out his theory with field observations of politically astute monkeys and apes.

Deception, however, had rarely been reported. And no wonder: If chimps, baboons, and higher primates generally are skilled deceivers, how could one ever know it? The best deceptions would by their very nature go undetected by the other members of the primate group, not to mention by a human stranger. Even those ruses that an observer could see through would have to be rare, for if used too often, they would lose their effectiveness. If Paul always cried wolf, for example, his mother would soon learn to ignore his ersatz distress. So while the monkey stories swapped over beers certainly suggested that deception was widespread among higher primates, it seemed unlikely that one or even a few researchers could observe enough instances of it to scientifically quantify how much, by whom, when, and to what effect.

Byrne and Whiten's solution was to extend their pub-derived data base with a more formal survey. In 1985 they sent a questionnaire to more than 100 primatologists working both in the field and in labs, asking them to report back any incidents in which they felt their subjects had perpetrated decep-

tion on one another. The questionnaire netted a promising assortment of deceptive tactics used by a variety of monkeys and all the great apes. Only the relatively small-brained and socially simple lemur family, which includes bush babies and lorises, failed to elicit a single instance. This supported the notion that society, sneakiness, brain size, and intelligence are intimately bound up with one another. The sneakier the primate, it seemed, the bigger the brain.

Byrne and Whiten drew up a second, much more comprehensive questionnaire in 1989 and sent it to hundreds more primatologists and animal behaviorists, greatly increasing the data base. Once again, when the results were tallied, only the lemur family failed to register a single case of deception.

All the other species, however, represented a simian rogues' gallery of liars and frauds. Often deception was used to distract another animal's attention. In one cartoonish example, a young baboon, chased by some angry elders, suddenly stopped, stood on his hind legs, and stared at a spot on the horizon, as if he noticed the presence of a predator or a foreign troop of baboons. His pursuers braked to a halt and looked in the same direction, giving up the chase. Powerful field binoculars revealed that no predator or baboon troop was anywhere in sight.

Sometimes the deception was simply a matter of one animal hiding a choice bit of food from the awareness of those strong enough to take it away. One of Jane Goodall's chimps, for example, named Figan, was once given some bananas after the more dominant members of the troop had wandered off. In the excitement, he uttered some loud "food barks"; the others quickly returned and took the bananas away. The next day Figan again waited behind the others and got some bananas. This time, however, he kept silent, even though the human observers, Goodall reported, "could hear faint choking sounds in his throat."

Concealment was a common ruse in sexual situations as well. Male monkeys and chimpanzees in groups have fairly strict hierarchies that control their access to females. Animals at the top of the order intimidate those lower down, forcing them away from females. Yet one researcher reported seeing a male stump-tailed macaque of a middle rank leading a female out of sight of the more dominant males and then mating with her silently, his climax unaccompanied by the harsh, low-pitched grunts that the male stump-tailed normally makes. At one point during the tryst the female turned and stared into his face, then covered his mouth with her hand. In another case a subordinate chimpanzee, aroused by the presence of a female in estrus, covered his erect penis with his hand when a dominant male approached, thus avoiding a likely attack.

In one particularly provocative instance a female hamadryas baboon slowly shuffled toward a large rock, appearing to forage, all the time keeping an eye on the most dominant male in the group. After 20 minutes she ended up with her head and shoulders visible to the big, watchful male, but with her hands happily engaged in the elicit activity of grooming a favorite subordinate male, who was hidden from view behind the rock.

Baboons proved singularly adept at a form of deception that Byrne and Whiten call "using a social tool." Paul's scam is a perfect example: he fools his mother into acting as a lever to pry the plant bulb away from the adult female, Mel. But can it be said unequivocally that he intended to deceive her? Perhaps Paul had simply learned through trial and error that letting out a yell brought his mother running and left him with food, in which case there is no reason to endow his young baboon intellect with Machiavellian intent. How do we know that Mel didn't actually threaten Paul in some way that Byrne and Whiten, watching, could not comprehend? While we're at it, how do we know that any of the primate deceptions reported here were really deliberate, conscious acts?

"It has to be said that there is a whole school of psychology that would deny such behavior even to humans," says Byrne. The school in question—strict behaviorism—would seek an explanation for the baboons' behavior not by trying to crawl inside their head but by carefully analyzing observable behaviors and the stimuli that might be triggering them. Byrne and Whiten's strategy against such skepticism was to be hyperskeptical themselves. They accepted that trial-and-error learning or simple conditioning, in which an animal's actions are reinforced by a reward, might account for a majority of the incidents reported to them—even when they believed that tactical deception was really taking place. But when explaining things "simply" led to a maze of extraordinary coincidences and tortuous logic, the evidence for deliberate deception seemed hard to dismiss.

Society, sneakiness, brain size, and intelligence are intimately bound up with one another.

Paul, for instance, *might* have simply learned that screaming elicits the reward of food, via his mother's intervention. But Byrne witnessed him using the same tactic several times, and in each case his mother was out of sight, able to hear his yell but not able to see what was really going on. If Paul was simply conditioned to scream, why would he do so only when his mother could not see who was—or was not—attacking her son?

Still, it is possible that she was not intentionally deceived. But in at least one other, similar case there is virtually no doubt that the mother was responding to a bogus attack, because the alleged attacker was quite able to verbalize his innocence. A five-year-old male chimp named Katabi, in the process of weaning, had discovered that the best way to get his reluctant mother to suckle him was to convince her he needed reassurance. One day Katabi approached a human observer—Japanese primatologist Toshisada Nish-

ida—and began to screech, circling around the researcher and waving an accusing hand at him. The chimp's mother and her escort immediately glared at Nishida, their hair erect. Only by slowly backing away from the screaming youngster did Nishida avoid a possible attack from the two adult chimps.

"In fact I did nothing to him," Nishida protested. It follows that the adults were indeed misled by Katabi's hysterics—unless there was some threat in Nishida unknown even to himself.

"If you try hard enough," says Byrne, "you can explain every single case without endowing the animal with the ability to deceive. But if you look at the whole body of work, there comes a point where you have to strive officiously to deny it."

The cases most resistant to such officious denials are the rarest—and the most compelling. In these interactions the primate involved not only employed tactical deception but clearly understood the concept. Such comprehension would depend upon one animal's ability to "read the mind" of another: to attribute desires, intentions, or even beliefs to the other creature that do not necessarily correspond to its own view of the world. Such mind reading was clearly evident in only 16 out of 253 cases in the 1989 survey, all of them involving great apes.

For example, consider Figan again, the young chimp who suppressed his food barks in order to keep the bananas for himself. In his case, mind reading is not evident: he might simply have learned from experience that food barks in certain contexts result in a loss of food, and thus he might not understand the nature of his own ruse, even if the other chimps are in fact deceived.

But contrast Figan with some chimps observed by Dutch primatologist Frans Plooij. One of these chimps was alone in a feeding area when a metal box containing food was opened electronically. At the same moment another chimp happened to approach. (Sound familiar? It's your older brother again.) The first chimp quickly closed the metal box (that's you hiding your chips), walked away, and sat down, looking around as if nothing had happened. The second chimp departed, but after going some distance away he hid behind a tree and peeked back at the first chimp. When the first chimp thought the coast was clear, he opened the box. The second chimp ran out, pushed the other aside, and ate the bananas.

Chimp One might be a clever rogue, but Chimp Two, who counters his deception with a ruse of his own, is the true mind reader. The success of his ploy is based on his insight that Chimp One was trying to deceive *him* and on his ability to adjust his behavior accordingly. He has in fact performed a prodigious cognitive leap—proving himself capable of projecting himself into another's mental space, and becoming what Humphrey would call a natural psychologist.

Niccolò Machiavelli might have called him good raw material. It is certainly suggestive that only the great apes—our closest relatives—seem capable of deceits based on such mind reading, and chimpanzees most of all. This does not necessarily mean that chimps are inherently more intelligent: the difference may be a matter of social organization. Orangutans live most of their lives alone, and thus they would not have much reason to develop such a complex social skill. And gorillas live in close family groups, whose members would be more familiar, harder to fool, and more likely to punish an attempted swindle. Chimpanzees, on the other hand, spend their lives in a shifting swirl of friends and relations, where small groups constantly form and break apart and reform with new members.

"What an opportunity for lying and cheating!" muses Byrne. Many anthropologists now believe that the social life of early hominids—our first non-ape ancestors—was much like that of chimps today, with similar opportunities to hone their cognitive skills on one another. Byrne and Whiten stop just short of saying that mind reading is the key to understanding the growth of human intelligence. But it would be disingenuous to ignore the possibility. If you were an early hominid who could comprehend the subjective impressions of others and manipulate them to your own ends, you might well have a competitive advantage over those less psychosocially nimble, perhaps enjoying slightly easier access to food and to the mating opportunities that would ensure your genetic survival.

Consider too how much more important your social wits would be in a world where the targets of your deceptions were constantly trying to outsmart *you*. After millennia of intrigue and counterintrigue, a hominid species might well evolve a brain three times bigger than it "should" be—and capable of far more than deceiving other hominids. "The ability to attribute other intentions to other people could have been an enormous building block for many human achievements, including language," says Whiten. "That this leap seems to have been taken by chimps and possibly the other great apes puts that development in human mentality quite early."

So did our intellect rise to its present height on a tide of manipulation and deceit? Some psychologists, even those who support the notion that the evolution of intelligence was socially driven, think that Byrne and Whiten's choice of the loaded adjective *Machiavellian* might be unnecessarily harsh.

"In my opinion," says Humphrey, "the word gives too much weight to the hostile use of intelligence. One of the functions of intellect in higher primates and humans is to keep the social unit together and make it able to successfully exploit the environment. A lot of intelligence could better be seen as driven by the need for cooperation and compassion." To that, Byrne and Whiten only point out that cooperation is itself an excellent Machiavellian strategy—sometimes.

The Scottish researchers are not, of course, the first to have noticed this. "It is good to appear clement, trustworthy, humane, religious, and honest, and also to be so," Machiavelli advised his aspiring Borgia prince in 1513. "But always with the mind so disposed that, when the occasion arises not to be so, you can become the opposite."

What Are Friends For?

*Among East African baboons, friendship means companions, health, safety . . .
and, sometimes, sex*

Barbara Smuts

Virgil, a burly adult male olive baboon, closely followed Zizi, a middle-aged female easily distinguished by her grizzled coat and square muzzle. On her rump Zizi sported a bright pink swelling, indicating that she was sexually receptive and probably fertile. Virgil's extreme attentiveness to Zizi suggested to me—and all rival males in the troop—that he was her current and exclusive mate.

Zizi, however, apparently had something else in mind. She broke away from Virgil, moved rapidly through the troop, and presented her alluring sexual swelling to one male after another. Before Virgil caught up with her, she had managed to announce her receptive condition to several of his rivals. When Virgil tried to grab her, Zizi screamed and dashed into the bushes with Virgil in hot pursuit. I heard sounds of chasing and fighting coming from the thicket. Moments later Zizi emerged from the bushes with an older male named Cyclops. They remained together for several days, copulating

often. In Cyclops's presence, Zizi no longer approached or even glanced at other males.

Primatologists describe Zizi and other olive baboons (*Papio cynocephalus anubis*) as promiscuous, meaning that both males and females usually mate with several members of the opposite sex within a short period of time. Promiscuous mating behavior characterizes many of the larger, more familiar primates, including chimpanzees, rhesus macaques, and gray langurs, as well as olive, yellow, and chacma baboons, the three subspecies of savanna baboon. In colloquial usage, promiscuity often connotes wanton and random sex, and several early studies of primates supported this stereotype. However, after years of laboriously recording thousands of copulations under natural conditions, the Peeping Toms of primate fieldwork have shown that, even in promiscuous species, sexual pairings are far from random.

Some adult males, for example, typically copulate much more often than

others. Primatologists have explained these differences in terms of competition: the most dominant males monopolize females and prevent lower-ranking rivals from mating. But exceptions are frequent. Among baboons, the exceptions often involve scruffy, older males who mate in full view of younger, more dominant rivals.

A clue to the reason for these puzzling exceptions emerged when primatologists began to question an implicit assumption of the dominance hypothesis—that females were merely passive objects of male competition. But what if females were active arbiters in this system? If females preferred some males over others and were able to express these preferences, then models of mating activity based on male dominance alone would be far too simple.

Once researchers recognized the possibility of female choice, evidence for it turned up in species after species. The story of Zizi, Virgil, and Cyclops is one of hundreds of examples of female primates rejecting the sexual advances of particular males and enthusiastically cooperating with others. But what is the basis for female choice? Why might they prefer some males over others?

This question guided my research on the Eburru Cliffs troop of olive baboons, named after one of their favorite sleeping sites, a sheer rocky outcrop rising several hundred feet above the floor of the Great Rift Valley, about 100 miles northwest of Nairobi, Kenya. The 120 members of Eburru Cliffs spent their days wandering through open grassland studded with occasional acacia thorn trees. Each night they retired to one of a dozen sets of cliffs that provided protection from nocturnal predators such as leopards.

Most previous studies of baboon sexuality had focused on females who, like Zizi, were at the peak of sexual receptivity. A female baboon does not mate when she is pregnant or lactating, a period of abstinence lasting about eighteen months. The female then goes into estrus, and for about two weeks out of every thirty-five-day cycle, she mates. Toward the end of this two week period she may ovulate, but usually the female undergoes four or five estrous cycles before she conceives. During pregnancy, she once again resumes a chaste existence. As a result, the typical female baboon is sexually active for less than 10 percent of her adult life. I thought that by focusing on the other 90 percent, I might learn something new. In particular, I suspected that routine, day-to-day relationships between males and pregnant or lactating (nonestrous) females might provide clues to female mating preferences.

Nearly every day for sixteen months, I joined the Eburru Cliffs baboons at their sleeping cliffs at dawn and traveled several miles with them while they foraged for roots, seeds, grass, and occasionally, small prey items, such as baby gazelles or hares (see "Predatory Baboons of Kekopey," *Natural History,* March 1976). Like all savanna baboon troops, Eburru Cliffs functioned as a cohesive unit organized around a core of related females, all of whom were born in the troop. Unlike the females, male savanna baboons leave their natal troop to join another where they may remain for many years, so most of the Eburru Cliffs adult males were immigrants. Since membership in the troop remained relatively constant during the period of my study, I learned to identify each individual. I relied on differences in size, posture, gait, and especially, facial features. To the practiced observer, baboons look as different from one another as human beings do.

As soon as I could recognize individuals, I noticed that particular females tended to turn up near particular males again and again. I came to think of these pairs as friends. Friendship among animals is not a well-documented phenomenon, so to convince skeptical colleagues that baboon friendship was real, I needed to develop objective criteria for distinguishing friendly pairs.

I began by investigating grooming, the amiable simian habit of picking through a companion's fur to remove dead skin and ectoparasites (see "Little Things That Tick Off Baboons," *Natural History,* February 1984). Baboons spend much more time grooming than is necessary for hygiene, and previous research had indicated that it is a good measure of social bonds.

Although eighteen adult males lived in the troop, each nonestrous female performed most of her grooming with just one, two, or occasionally, three males. For example, of Zizi's twenty-four grooming bouts with males, Cyclops accounted for thirteen, and a second male, Sherlock, accounted for all the rest. Different females tended to favor different males as grooming partners.

Another measure of social bonds was simply who was observed near whom. When foraging, traveling, or resting, each pregnant or lactating female spent a lot of time near a few males and associated with the others no more often than expected by chance. When I compared the identities of favorite grooming partners and frequent companions, they overlapped almost completely. This enabled me to develop a formal definition of friendship: any male that scored high on both grooming and proximity measures was considered a friend.

Virtually all baboons made friends; only one female and the three males who had most recently joined the troop lacked such companions. Out of more than 600 possible adult female-adult male pairs in the troop, however, only about one in ten qualified as friends; these really were special relationships.

Several factors seemed to influence which baboons paired up. In most cases, friends were unrelated to each other, since the male had immigrated from another troop. (Four friendships, however, involved a female and an adolescent son who had not yet emigrated. Unlike other friends, these related pairs never mated.) Older females tended to be friends with older males; younger females with younger males. I witnessed occasional May-December romances, usually involving older females and young adult males. Adolescent males and females were strongly rule-bound, and with the exception of mother-son pairs, they formed friendships only with one another.

Regardless of age or dominance rank, most females had just one or two male friends. But among males, the number of female friends varied greatly from none to eight. Although high-ranking males enjoyed priority of access to food and sometimes mates, dominant males did not have more female friends than low-ranking males. Instead it was the older males who had lived in the troop for many years who had the most friends. When a male had several female friends, the females were often closely related to one another. Since female baboons spend a lot of time near their kin, it is probably easier for a male to maintain bonds with several related females at once.

When collecting data, I focused on one nonestrous female at a time and kept track of her every movement toward or away from any male; similarly, I noted every male who moved toward or away from her. Whenever the female and a male moved close enough to exchange intimacies, I wrote down exactly what happened. When foraging together, friends tended to remain a few yards apart. Males more often wandered away from females than the reverse, and females, more often than males, closed the gap. The female behaved as if she wanted to keep the male within calling distance, in case she needed his protection. The male, however, was more likely to make approaches that brought them within actual touching distance. Often, he would plunk himself down right next to his friend and ask her to groom him by holding a pose with exaggerated stillness. The female sometimes responded by grooming, but more often, she exhibited the most reliable sign of true intimacy: she ignored her friend and simply continued whatever she was doing.

In sharp contrast, when a male who was not a friend moved close to a female, she dared not ignore him. She stopped whatever she was doing and held still, often glancing surreptitiously at the intruder. If he did not move away, she sometimes lifted her tail and presented her rump. When a female is not in estrus, this is a gesture of appeasement, not sexual enticement. Immediately after this respectful acknowledgement of his presence, the female would slip away. But such tense interactions with nonfriend males were rare, because females usually moved away before the males came too close.

These observations suggest that females were afraid of most of the males in their troop, which is not surprising: male baboons are twice the size of females, and their canines are longer and sharper than those of a lion. All Eburru Cliffs males directed both mild and severe aggression toward females. Mild aggression, which usually involved threats and chases but no body contact, occurred most often during feeding competition or when the male redirected aggression toward a female after losing a fight with another male. Females and juveniles showed aggression toward other females and juveniles in similar circumstances and occasionally inflicted superficial wounds. Severe aggression by males, which involved body contact and sometimes biting, was less common and also more puzzling, since there was no apparent cause.

An explanation for at least some of these attacks emerged one day when I was watching Pegasus, a young adult male, and his friend Cicily, sitting together in the middle of a small clearing. Cicily moved to the edge of the clearing to feed, and a higher-ranking female, Zora, suddenly attacked her. Pegasus stood up and looked as if he were about to intervene when both females disappeared into the bushes. He sat back down, and I remained with him. A full ten minutes later, Zora appeared at the edge of the clearing; this was the first time she had come into view since her attack on Cicily. Pegasus instantly pounced on Zora, repeatedly grabbed her neck in his mouth and lifted her off the ground, shook her whole body, and then dropped her. Zora screamed continuously and tried to escape. Each time, Pegasus caught her and continued his brutal attack. When he finally released her five minutes later she had a deep canine gash on the palm of her hand that made her limp for several days.

This attack was similar in form and intensity to those I had seen before and labeled "unprovoked." Certainly, had I come upon the scene after Zora's aggression toward Cicily, I would not have understood why Pegasus attacked Zora. This suggested that some, perhaps many, severe attacks by males actually represented punishment for actions that had occurred some time before.

Whatever the reasons for male attacks on females, they represent a serious threat. Records of fresh injuries indicated that Eburru Cliffs adult females received canine slash wounds from males at the rate of one for every female each year, and during my study, one female died of her injuries. Males probably pose an even greater threat to infants. Although only one infant was killed during my study, observers in Botswana and Tanzania have seen recent male immigrants kill several young infants.

Protection from male aggression, and from the less injurious but more frequent aggression of other females and juveniles, seems to be one of the main advantages of friendship for a female baboon. Seventy times I observed an adult male defend a female or her offspring against aggression by another troop member, not infrequently a high-ranking male. In all but six of these cases, the defender was a friend. Very few of these confrontations involved actual fighting; no male baboon, subordinate or dominant, is anxious to risk injury by the sharp canines of another.

Males are particularly solicitous guardians of their friends' youngest infants. If another male gets too close to an infant or if a juvenile female plays with it too roughly, the friend may intervene. Other troop members soon learn to be cautious when the mother's friend is nearby, and his presence provides the mother with a welcome respite from the annoying pokes and prods of curious females and juveniles obsessed with the new baby. Male baboons at Gombe Park in Tanzania and Amboseli Park in Kenya have also been seen rescuing infants from chimpanzees and lions. These several forms of male protection help to explain why females in Eburru Cliffs stuck closer to their friends in the first few months after giving birth than at any other time.

The male-infant relationship develops out of the male's friendship with the mother, but as the infant matures, this new bond takes on a life of its own. My co-worker Nancy Nicolson found that by about nine months of age, infants actively sought out their male friends when the mother was a few yards away, suggesting that the male may function as an alternative caregiver. This seemed to be especially true for infants undergoing unusually early or severe weaning. (Weaning is generally a gradual, prolonged process, but there is tremendous variation among mothers in the timing and intensity of weaning. See "Mother Baboons," *Natural History,* September 1980). After being rejected by the mother, the crying infant often approached the male friend and sat huddled against him until its whimpers subsided. Two of the infants in Eburru Cliffs lost their mothers when they were still quite young. In each case, their bond with the mother's friend subsequently intensified, and—perhaps as a result—both infants survived.

A close bond with a male may also improve the infant's nutrition. Larger than all other troop members, adult males monopolize the best feeding sites. In general, the personal space surrounding a feeding male is inviolate, but he usually tolerates intrusions by the infants of his female friends, giving them access to choice feeding spots.

Although infants follow their male friends around rather than the reverse, the males seem genuinely attached to their tiny companions. During feeding, the male and infant express their pleasure in each other's company by sharing spirited, antiphonal grunting duets. If the infant whimpers in distress, the male friend is likely to cease feeding, look at the infant, and grunt softly, as if in sympathy, until the whimpers cease. When the male rests, the infants of his female friends may huddle behind him, one after the other, forming a "train," or, if feeling energetic, they may use his body as a trampoline.

When I returned to Eburru Cliffs four years after my initial study ended, several of the bonds formed between males and the infants of their female friends were still intact (in other cases, either the male or the infant or both had disappeared). When these bonds involved recently matured females, their long-time male associates showed no sexual interest in them, even though the females mated with other adult males. Mothers and sons, and usually maternal siblings, show similar sexual inhibitions in baboons and many other primate species.

The development of an intimate relationship between a male and the infant of his female friend raises an obvious question: Is the male the infant's father? To answer this question definitely we would need to conduct genetic analysis, which was not possible for these baboons. Instead, I estimated paternity probabilities from observations of the temporary (a few hours or days) exclusive mating relationships, or consortships, that estrous females form with a series of different males. These estimates were apt to be fairly accurate, since changes in the female's sexual swelling allow one to pinpoint the timing of conception to within a few days. Most females consorted with only two or three males during this period, and these males were termed likely fathers.

In about half the friendships, the male was indeed likely to be the father of his friend's most recent infant, but in the other half he was not—in fact, he had never been seen mating with the female. Interestingly, males who were friends with the mother but not likely fathers nearly always developed a relationship with her infant, while males who had mated with the female but were not her friend usually did not. Thus friendship with the mother, rather than paternity, seems to mediate the development of male-infant bonds. Recently, a similar pattern was documented for South American capuchin monkeys in a laboratory study in which paternity was determined genetically.

These results fly in the face of a prominent theory that claims males will invest in infants only when they are closely related. If males are not fostering the survival of their own genes by caring for the infant, then why do they do so? I suspected that the key was female choice. If females preferred to mate with males who had already demonstrated friendly behavior, then friendships with mothers and their infants might pay off in the future when the mothers were ready to mate again.

To find out if this was the case, I examined each male's sexual behavior with females he had befriended before they resumed estrus. In most cases, males consorted considerably more often with their friends than with other females. Baboon females typically mate with several different males, including both friends and nonfriends, but prior friendship increased a male's probability of mating with a female above what it would have been otherwise.

This increased probability seemed to reflect female preferences. Females occasionally overtly advertised their disdain for certain males and their desire for others. Zizi's behavior, described above, is a good example. Virgil was not one of her friends, but Cyclops was. Usually, however, females expressed preferences and aversions more subtly. For example, Delphi, a petite adolescent female, found herself pursued by Hector, a middle-aged adult male. She did not run away or refuse to mate with him, but whenever he wasn't watching, she looked around for her friend Homer, an adolescent male. When she succeeded in catching Homer's eye, she narrowed her eyes and flattened her ears against her skull, the friendliest face one baboon can send another. This told Homer she would rather be with him. Females expressed satisfaction with a current consort partner by staying close to him, initiating copulations, and not making advances toward other males. Baboons are very sensitive to such cues, as indicated by an experimental study in which rival hamadryas baboons rarely challenged a male-female pair if the female strongly preferred her current partner. Similarly, in Eburru Cliffs, males were less apt to challenge consorts involving a pair that shared a long-term friendship.

Even though females usually consorted with their friends, they also mated with other males, so it is not surprising that friendships were most vulnerable during periods of sexual activity. In a few cases, the female consorted with another male more often than with her friend, but the friendship survived nevertheless. One female, however, formed a strong sexual bond with a new male. This bond persisted after conception, replacing her previous friendship. My observations suggest that adolescent and young adult females tend to have shorter, less stable friendships than do older females. Some friendships, however, last a very long time. When I returned to Eburru Cliffs six years after my study began, five couples were still together. It is possible that friendships occasionally last for life (baboons probably live twenty to thirty years in the wild), but it will require longer studies, and some very patient scientists, to find out.

By increasing both the male's chances of mating in the future and the likelihood that a female's infant will survive, friendship contributes to the reproductive success of both partners. This clarifies the evolutionary basis of friendship-forming tendencies in baboons, but what does friendship mean to a baboon? To answer this question we need to view baboons as sentient beings with feelings and goals not unlike our own in similar circumstances. Consider, for example, the friendship between Thalia and Alexander.

The affair began one evening as Alex and Thalia sat about fifteen feet apart on the sleeping cliffs. It was like watching two novices in a singles bar. Alex stared at Thalia until she turned and almost caught him looking at her. He glanced away immediately, and then she stared at him until his head began to turn toward her. She suddenly became engrossed in grooming her toes. But as soon as Alex looked away, her gaze returned to him. They went on like this for more than fifteen minutes, always with split-second timing. Finally, Alex managed to catch Thalia looking at him. He made the friendly eyes-narrowed, ears-back face and smacked his lips together rhythmically. Thalia froze, and for a second she looked into his eyes. Alex approached, and Thalia, still nervous, groomed him. Soon she calmed down, and I found them still together on the cliffs the next morning. Looking back on this event months later, I realized that it marked the beginning of their friendship. Six years later, when I returned to Eburru Cliffs, they were still friends.

If flirtation forms an integral part of baboon friendship, so does jealously. Overt displays of jealousy, such as chasing a friend away from a potential rival, occur occasionally, but like humans, baboons often express their emotions in more subtle ways. One evening a colleague and I climbed the cliffs and settled down near Sherlock, who was friends with Cybelle, a middle-aged female still foraging on the ground below the cliffs. I observed Cybelle while my colleague watched Sherlock, and we kept up a running commentary. As long as Cybelle was

feeding or interacting with females, Sherlock was relaxed, but each time she approached another male, his body would stiffen, and he would stare intently at the scene below. When Cybelle presented politely to a male who had recently tried to befriend her, Sherlock even made threatening sounds under his breath. Cybelle was not in estrus at the time, indicating that male baboon jealousy extends beyond the sexual arena to include affiliative interactions between a female friend and other males.

Because baboon friendships are embedded in a network of friendly and antagonistic relationships, they inevitably lead to repercussions extending beyond the pair. For example, Virgil once provoked his weaker rival Cyclops into a fight by first attacking Cyclops's friend Phoebe. On another occasion, Sherlock chased Circe, Hector's best friend, just after Hector had chased Antigone, Sherlock's friend.

In another incident, the prime adult male Triton challenged Cyclops's possession of meat. Cyclops grew increasingly tense and seemed about to abandon the prey to the younger male. Then Cyclops's friend Phoebe appeared with her infant Phyllis. Phyllis wandered over to Cyclops. He immediately grabbed her, held her close, and threatened Triton away from the prey. Because any challenge to Cyclops now involved a threat to Phyllis as well, Triton risked being mobbed by Phoebe and her relatives and friends. For this reason, he backed down. Males frequently use the infants of their female friends as buffers in this way. Thus, friendship involves costs as well as benefits because it makes the participants vulnerable to social manipulation or redirected aggression by others.

Finally, as with humans, friendship seems to mean something different to each baboon. Several females in Eburru Cliffs had only one friend. They were devoted companions. Louise and Pandora, for example, groomed their friend Virgil and no other male. Then there was Leda, who, with five friends, spread herself more thinly than any other female. These contrasting patterns of friendship were associated

with striking personality differences. Louise and Pandora were unobtrusive females who hung around quietly with Virgil and their close relatives. Leda seemed to be everywhere at once, playing with infants, fighting with juveniles, and making friends with males. Similar differences were apparent among the males. Some devoted a great deal of time and energy to cultivating friendships with females, while others focused more on challenging other males. Although we probably will never fully understand the basis of these individual differences, they contribute immeasurably to the richness and complexity of baboon society.

Male-female friendships may be widespread among primates. They have been reported for many other groups of savanna baboons, and they also occur in rhesus and Japanese Macaques, capuchin monkeys, and perhaps in bonobos (pygmy chimpanzees). These relationships should give us pause when considering popular scenarios for the evolution of male-female relationships in humans. Most of these scenarios assume that, except for mating, males and females had little to do with one another until the development of a sexual division of labor, when, the story goes, females began to rely on males to provide meat in exchange for gathered food. This, it has been argued, set up new selection pressures favoring the development of long-term bonds between individual males and females, female sexual fidelity, and as paternity certainty increased, greater male investment in the offspring of these unions. In other words, once women began to gather and men to hunt, presto—we had the nuclear family.

This scenario may have more to do with cultural biases about women's economic dependence on men and idealized views of the nuclear family than with the actual behavior of our hominid ancestors. The nonhuman primate evidence challenges this story in at least three ways.

First, long-term bonds between the sexes can evolve in the absence of a sexual division of labor of food sharing. In our primate relatives, such relationships rest on exchanges of social, not economic, benefits.

Second, primate research shows that highly differentiated, emotionally intense male-female relationships can occur without sexual exclusivity. Ancestral men and women may have experienced intimate friendships long before they invented marriage and norms of sexual fidelity.

Third, among our closest primate relatives, males clearly provide mothers and infants with social benefits even when they are unlikely to be the fathers of those infants. In return, females provide a variety of benefits to the friendly males, including acceptance into the group and, at least in baboons, increased mating opportunities in the future. This suggests that efforts to reconstruct the evolution of hominid societies may have overemphasized what the female must supposedly do (restrict her mating to just one male) in order to obtain male parental investment.

Maybe it is time to pay more attention to what the male must do (provide benefits to females and young) in order to obtain female cooperation. Perhaps among our ancestors, as in baboons today, sex and friendship went hand in hand. As for marriage—well, that's another story.

Gut Thinking

What makes fruit-eating spider monkeys so much smarter than leaf-eating howlers? Their gourmet diet, apparently—it's gone to their heads.

Peter Radetsky

Peter Radetsky is a contributing editor of Discover *and teaches science writing at the University of California at Santa Cruz. His most recent book,* Invisible Invaders: Viruses and the Scientists Who Pursue Them, *is now available in paperback. In the March* Discover, *Radetsky wrote about the elusive stem cell and the controversy over patenting it.*

Life should be a breeze in the tropical forest. The weather is warm, and there's plenty of food for the asking. In theory, you need only reach out and luscious fruits and other tidbits will fall into your hands. Sadly, it's not so, says Katharine Milton—particularly if you're a monkey. Milton, a physical anthropologist at the University of California at Berkeley, has spent the last 20 years studying howler and spider monkeys in the forests of Panama. Life, she's concluded, is tough in the forest—animals need to devise all sorts of ingenious tactics just to get enough food to survive. Finding food is *so* tough, Milton thinks, that successful strategies have driven the evolution of the species. "It is the solutions to the problems of diet that have made primates primates," she says. And what pertains to forest primates pertains as well to their city-slicker cousins—us. In other words, the food we eat has made us human.

Milton began her observations in 1974 on the island of Barro Colorado in Panama. For the fledgling anthropologist—Milton was then a New York University graduate student—it was an ideal spot. The island offered a protected forest inhabited by numerous species of wild animals, including howler monkeys—13- to 18-pound primates notorious for their terrifying, unearthly howls. It was also the site of a Smithsonian Institution research station, complete with an extensive herbarium for identifying indigenous plants.

Milton threw herself into her work. "I'd get up every morning at 4:30, go to the dining hall, stuff as much food in my face as I could, make a bunch of peanut butter sandwiches, fill my water bottle, then walk into the forest to where I'd left the monkeys the night before," she recalls, in the twang of her native Montgomery, Alabama. "I'd sit on a log in the dark, and as soon as they started to wake up at dawn, about 6, I'd start taking notes." She would then follow the monkeys as they meandered along the forest canopy some 80 feet above, note where they stopped to eat, and collect the scraps of food that dropped to the ground.

"I'd follow them until 6 P.M., when it got dark, and watch them settle down for the night. Then I'd run back with a flashlight, jumping down the trail like a little goat. I'd get to the dining hall, nobody there, but the cook would have made a plate for me and covered it with tinfoil. I'd gobble down my dinner, run to the herbarium and identify my plant scraps, take a shower, and go to bed. And the next day the same thing."

Thus passed the bulk of three years. Milton found that most of the time the howlers ate leaves and fruit in almost equal measure, but when seasonal fruits were in short supply, the animals filled up on leaves. Howler monkeys were finicky, though. They ate only tender, young leaves, and only the tips at that.

Typically, soon after awakening, a howler troop of 19 individuals would set off through the trees in single file. The group traveled with no apparent leader, but after about 45 minutes, they'd arrive at a source of food.

"They know where they're going," says Milton. "I don't know how, but they know. They appear to use a collective information pool to locate their foods. They'll just set off in a straight line right to it."

For example, one of the howlers' favorite delicacies was the leaf of the *Ceiba pentandra* tree, a 100-foot-tall monster with room-size buttresses and limbs large enough for a grown man to walk on. "It has a five-fingered leaf that's pinkish brown when it first comes out on the tree but within hours turns green," Milton says. "After that, the monkeys don't want it anymore. Somehow they know how to get there just when the emerging leaves are beginning to expand. They eat the tips, which are far more nutritious than the middles or bases."

The howlers conducted these expeditions over 75 acres, searching out as many as 25 species of plants daily. Some, like the *Ceiba pentandra* tree, were edible for only a few hours a year; others were available more often. Unerringly, the howlers tracked them down. The ranges of various howler troops overlapped, so Milton would occasionally come upon a tree filled with monkeys, with other groups in adjoining trees politely waiting their turn at the table. All of which suggested that the animals had an extraordinary collective memory, an unfailing sense of direction, refined social manners, and a built-in barometer of what foods were good for them.

_____

Spider monkeys lead a varied and independent life, which requires a lot of training. As a result, infant spider monkeys mature slowly and are nursed and carried by their mothers for two years.

_____

This aggregate intelligence allows infant howlers to mature quickly. "After 12 to 14 months, howler mothers don't want to see their babies again," Milton says. The babies soon declare independence and rely on the group for support.

Still, despite the obvious group intelligence, the monkeys individually didn't seem particularly smart to Milton. They were relatively dull and placid—and unobservant. "I ate lunch for months in full view of dozens of howlers, and not one ever seemed to realize that I was eating, much less that what I was eating might be something they would enjoy, too," she says. "You could make noises and slurp and carry on—whatever cognitive processes are required to identify the act of eating, they don't seem to use them."

But spider monkeys did. "I saw them all the time when I was studying howlers," says Milton. "They'd go roaring by like greased lightning." Spider monkeys are the same size as howlers, and the two animals share parts of each other's ranges on Barro Colorado. But there the similarities end. Whereas howlers travel through the canopy on all fours, spiders swing along like Tarzan. Unlike the placid howlers, spiders are playful and mischievous. "They're terrible teases," says Milton. "And they're mean little devils. They remind me of people," she confides with a laugh. "Although not specifically any of my close friends."

Spider monkeys had no trouble recognizing Milton's lunch. *"Food!"* they'd shout. *'Let's see if we can get it!'* They'd swing down toward you; they'd threaten you. They know what a banana is. They have a keen idea of what a peanut butter sandwich is. You simply cannot eat in front of them."

Intrigued, Milton decided she'd add spider monkeys to her observations. She thought it might be interesting to compare how the two species evolved from a common ancestor. But while the comparatively sedate howlers were a researcher's dream, dealing with the spider monkeys was something else again. "They were too fast for me," says Milton. "So I hired a young man to work with me. He would run through the forest as fast as he could, following the monkeys, and I would come behind. We communicated by calls. *'Whooooo!'* Like that. The sound really carries through the forest."

When the barnstorming spider monkeys found food, they'd finally screech

to a stop, allowing Milton to catch up. "They'd just stuff themselves. Then they'd lie around and take naps."

Unlike the howlers, Milton discovered, the spider monkeys almost exclusively ate fruit, which often made up 90 percent of their diet. Even when fruit was out of season or in short supply, it constituted over half their food. But ripe fruit is even harder to find than tender leaves. To get enough, the 18 spider monkeys on the island would resort to splitting up and trying their luck on their own. "During most of the year the distribution patterns of their foods are such that if they went around in a big group, there wouldn't be enough at any one site to feed everyone," says Milton. "So they'd spend almost the whole day foraging in small subunits or by themselves. Then around twilight they'd begin to call and coalesce, and then they'd spend the night together."

As a result of this extended exploring, the spiders' territory was huge, some 750 acres, ten times that of the howler monkeys. "And that's a conservative estimate," says Milton. "Two thousand acres might be right." If the howlers displayed impressive feats of memory and direction by finding young leaves, the spider monkeys' long-distance forays after fruit were astounding. Within an enormous area they had to remember at least 100 species of fruit and where to find thousands of fruit-bearing trees. They had to remember when each fruit was ripe, how best to approach the site, and how best to return home. If a howler forgot a food source or a travel route, the others were there to take up the slack. The spiders, though, had to fend for themselves.

And they had to know how to stay in touch. Howler monkeys tended to be quiet, communicating through subtle clucks and rattles in the throat, except at daybreak, when their eerie howls declared "This is where we are this morning." ("All the howler troops on the island participate," says Milton. "It's called the dawn chorus. The sound comes rolling by as light moves across the forest.")

Spider monkeys, on the other hand, were conspicuously noisy. They'd yelp and cry, whinnying like horses, barking like dogs—sometimes for hours at a time. "When they're cross about something," says Milton, "they'll bark incessantly, until you think they're going to fall out of the tree." And in contrast to the howlers' community messages, spider monkeys believed in individual expression. "Spider monkey vocalizations are generally individualistic. It's George giving a food call, or Mary hailing Susie, whereas a howler monkey is not saying 'Hi, Susie' but rather 'Okay, everyone, we're getting ready to move to a new food tree.' "

All that variety and independence requires lots of training. As a result, infant spider monkeys mature slowly. They are nursed and carried by their mothers for two years, and they continue to associate almost exclusively with her until they're about three or three and a half years old. Milton remembers watching female spider monkeys patiently waiting for their offspring to take off into the trees. "The mother would then slowly tag along behind," she says. "It was her way of instructing the youngster, forcing it to become independent by learning to move through the trees on its own."

Always, of course, leaving time for mischief. For example, spider monkeys loved to torment howlers. "They would steal howler babies," says Milton. "A howler mother doesn't know what to do—she's too dopey to get her baby back. Howlers would move out of the tree when they saw spiders coming. They'd sit quietly and hope the spiders didn't pick on them."

Why were the two monkeys so dissimilar? Milton wondered about the differences in their diets. Howler monkeys ate mainly leaves, sometimes exclusively leaves, a low-quality source of nutrition. Leaves are plentiful and relatively high in protein, but they're low in energy-rich carbohydrates. They also consist of some 60 percent indigestible fiber and sometimes contain toxic chemicals. How in the world did howlers get enough energy from this unpromising diet? And why did they stick to it even during seasons when there was plenty of ripe fruit in the forest?

Fruits are loaded with easily digested carbohydrates and are relatively low in fiber—they're high-quality, nutritious food. They mean instant energy. On the other hand, fruits provide little protein. So, Milton wondered, how did spider monkeys get enough protein? And why, when fruits were scarce, didn't they fill up on leaves, as howlers did? Why did they go to such extremes to find fruits?

The howler and spider monkeys live in the same forest, they are roughly the same size, but they have evolved in totally different ways.

Milton began finding some answers to these questions in 1977, when she returned to Barro Colorado after completing her doctoral thesis. She soon conducted an experiment measuring how long it took the monkeys to process their food. "I needed to look at internal features of the monkeys," she says. "I thought that perhaps the structure of their guts or efficiency of their digestion might be influencing their behavior."

She trapped howler and spider monkeys, confined them in pens, and fed them food in which she had concealed tiny plastic markers. "I used a type of thin plastic material that I cut with very fine manicure scissors into little colored plastic worms," she explains. When the monkeys excreted the remains of their food, out came the markers. Milton could therefore measure the time it took any one meal to pass through a monkey's digestive tract. The results were dramatic: howlers took 20 hours to digest their food, five times as long as spiders. "That was a *humongous* surprise," says Milton. "The difference in transit times blew me away. There had to be an explanation—they don't have a *door* in there. So I went in and looked at their guts."

When Milton came upon monkeys that had died in the forest, she took them back to the research station, dissected them, and measured their gastrointestinal tracts. She then confirmed her figures against published material on differential gut measurements in various primates. She found that the colons of howlers were considerably wider and longer than those of spider monkeys. Food had to travel much farther and remained much longer in howler guts, and the monkeys had room for much more bulk. As a result, bacteria had a chance to ferment masses of fibrous leaves in the monkeys' colons, producing energy-rich fatty acids. Milton eventually found that howlers receive more than 30 percent of their daily energy from such fatty acids.

In contrast, spider monkey food resembled the speedy monkeys themselves, hurtling through the animals' more compact guts. Spiders were far less efficient at extracting energy from the fiber in their diet—but they didn't have to be efficient. They ate easily digestible fruits. By moving a steady stream of fruit through their gastrointestinal tracts every day, they obtained all the carbohydrates they needed and some of the protein. The rest came from supplements of young, tender leaves.

It was a striking example of evolutionary adaptation. Each monkey's physiology fit its particular diet. Spider monkeys couldn't get away with eating a howler diet of mostly leaves. With their smallish guts, they'd never keep enough bulk around long enough for fermentation to provide energy. And howlers wouldn't manage for long if they used the spider monkey tactic of eating fruit—their slow digestive tracts couldn't process nearly enough of it.

Besides, it took smarts to track down sufficient fruit, and Milton thought it unlikely that the howlers were up to the job. Nor was the howler diet of leaves up to the job of fueling the amount of brainpower necessary. The brain, a big, hungry organ, requires a disproportionate amount of energy, and leaves just don't provide enough. All of which led to the second part of the puzzle: the difference in the monkeys' mental capacities.

"I kept thinking, spider monkeys are so smart, and howler monkeys don't seem so smart. The more I thought about it, the more it seemed to make sense that if you have a high-energy diet and widely distributed foods, you're going to need a certain amount of ability to locate those foods. I became curious—I wondered how big their brains were."

Luckily for Milton, that information was available without her having to cut apart more monkeys. A scientist named Daniel Quirling had published extensive statistics about the sizes of primate brains. Spider monkey brains, he had determined, weigh twice those of howlers, 107 grams compared with 50.4. No wonder spiders are smarter.

With that, everything came together. "It was a *eureka* moment," says Milton. Here were two monkeys, the same size, living in the same forest, but so different. Compared with the howlers, spider monkeys were brighter and more lively. They matured more slowly and had more to learn; they made more ruckus, with a greater variety of vocalizations; they ate widely dispersed, high-energy foods that were harder to find—and their brains were twice as large. Why?

As far as Milton was concerned, diet was the key to these discrepancies. Eating fruits fueled the evolution of the spider monkeys' large brains. Says Milton, "It would have been a feedback process in which some slight change in the monkeys' foraging behavior conferred a benefit, which in turn permitted a modest improvement in the quality of their diet, which led to an excess of energy. Over generations, the monkeys that spent the energy on making their brain slightly bigger and more complex had an evolutionary advantage. Their improved brain allowed for more helpful changes in their behavior, and so on."

Milton realized that if such a scenario was correct, similar differences in brain size should show up in other primates with similar differences in diet—monkeys and apes that eat fruits should have larger brains than their leaf-eating counterparts. Sure enough, when Milton checked the literature, she found the pattern held true. For example, of the three great apes, lively, quick chimpanzees, our closest animal relatives, have a bigger brain for their body size than do the slower, more placid gorillas and orangutans. Chimps take some 94 percent of their diet from plants, largely in the form of ripe fruits. Gorillas and orangutans eat 99 percent plant foods, but mainly lower-quality leaves, pith, even bark. Diet had to be the key to their disparate evolution.

And what about the primate with the largest brain of all? Might large human brains also have initially been the result of a high-quality diet? Milton thinks so. "I view dietary conditions as the key pressure leading to the emergence of humans."

Her scenario goes like this: When our australopithecine ancestors emerged in Africa more than four and a half million years ago, their brains were not appreciably larger than those of today's apes, and they had massive, grinding jaws and molar teeth, suggesting that they ate mostly tough, low-quality plant material. Eventually the australopithecines were supplanted by another series of early humans with increasingly larger brains and smaller jaws and teeth, indications that their diet had become higher in quality, less fibrous and abrasive. In time these brainy ancestors refined their diet. With the introduction of meat, early humans started to eat in ways that no primates had before.

"The fossil evidence offers strong support for the view that early humans made a dietary breakthrough," Milton says. No longer were we, like spider monkeys and chimps, primarily fruit eaters. Now, drawing on the power of our large brains, we introduced tools to help us prepare food and learned to divide the responsibility for meals—a uniquely human characteristic—so that different people became experts in different diets. Eventually we became what Milton calls cultural omnivores. "We will eat anything, from other human beings to sea squids," she says. "But if our culture tells us not to eat something, it doesn't matter if it is the most nutritious, digestible food in the world—we won't eat it. Food for humans is more in the mind than in the item."

A case in point may involve meat itself. It is usually thought that early humans began eating meat to satisfy their need for protein, but ongoing research by Milton's former student Craig Stanford, now an anthropologist at the University of Southern California, suggests that eating meat is as much a social gesture as a dietary necessity. With Jane Goodall, Stanford studies chimpanzees at Gombe National Park in Tanzania. He has found that Gombe chimps eat about 3 percent of their diet as meat; primarily they hunt colobus monkeys.

Chimps don't routinely hunt monkeys, though. They separate into small groups to forage for fruits, and they go after a monkey only when they come upon it by chance. Even then they might not hunt—they tend to do so when a female in heat happens to be part of the foraging group. Then, once a male makes the kill, a fascinating ritual often ensues. "Immediately, within seconds, the female comes racing over with her hand out," says Stanford. "The male pulls away the carcass until the female allows him to copulate with her. Then the male shares the meat. Sometimes he will induce her to copulate, then wave the carcass in her face and pull it away until they copulate again. Then she gets some meat."

The chimps thus use meat as a commodity exchange—in this case, to elicit sexual favors. Stanford has found that foods more nutritious than meat, such as oil palm nuts, are available year-round. Such immobile foods are much easier to procure than monkeys, which fight like the dickens and provide no more than a few ounces of meat per chimp. "It's not just a nutritional decision when they decide to hunt," Stanford says. "They have more in mind."

"Chimps appear to eat meat for social reasons more than nutritional reasons," agrees Milton. "It's kind of like a date. It's a party, a community event."

2. PRIMATES

Did we humans start eating meat for similar reasons? Stanford wouldn't be surprised: "Other researchers have shown that dominant chimps withhold meat from enemies and dole it out to allies, using it in a cleverly calculated political way."

The similarity to people is reinforced by other chimp behaviors. "The whole life cycle of chimps is not that different from people's," says Stanford. Chimp babies, for example, are totally dependent on their mothers for their first four years, and they continue to hang around Mom until the age of 10 or 11. Females become sexually mature at about the age of 12; males go out into the world with the other guys at about 15. "Chimps defend their territory with lethal aggression," says Stanford. "Humans are the only other primates to do so."

Milton sees strong parallels between humans and chimps, and spider monkeys as well. Similar diet; similar aggressive, individualistic bent; similar long-term rearing of young; similar social system—and similarly large brains. All of us—spider monkeys, chimps, and humans alike—are what we eat. The behaviors and physiology that define us are the consequences of dietary-driven evolution.

"Everything comes back to diet," says Milton. "It's the pivotal feature, the kickoff. When you get right down to it, the way we behave had better translate ultimately into groceries—we're not going to be around to behave that way much longer."

The Young and the Reckless

*Every day young primates leave the comfort of home to live through weeks
and months of abuse at the hands of beastly strangers.
Why in the world do they—and we—do it?*

Robert Sapolsky

I remember going off to college. I was so nervous and excited that I had the runs for a week beforehand. What if they had made a mistake by admitting me? Suppose I never made any friends? Would these really turn out to be the best years of my life? Queasy and vertiginous, I packed my bags onto a Greyhound bus, squirreling a bottle of Kaopectate into my knapsack.

Actually, getting my bowels into such an uproar proved to be quite justified, given the momentous freshman-year events that awaited me: the epiphany when I knew I was never going to understand photosynthesis and should give up on being a biology major (I switched to bioanthropology); the realization, as I contemplated four years of purple yogurt and Polynesian meatless meatballs in the cafeteria, that my mother was a fabulous cook; my first lesson in political correctness—I learned that I was now surrounded by women and not by girls; the infinitely pleasant discovery that some of those women were willing to talk to me now and then; the wonder of watching older guys suavely work references to Claude Lévi-Strauss and Buckminster Fuller into casual conversation; the giddy pleasure at finding that a joke that worked in high school worked equally well here too; the calming ritual of fighting with my roommate every evening over whether to open or close the window.

Growing up, and growing away. Off to college, off to war, off to work in the city, off to settle in a new world—home is never the same again, and sometimes home is never even seen again. What is striking about this maturational event is that it is central not only to us humans but to many of our primate relatives as well. The process of growing up and growing away has a remarkably familiar look of excitement and discovery and challenge.

Some primates, such as orangutans, lead solitary lives, meeting only for the occasional mating. But the average group of primates is supremely social, whether it is a family of a dozen gorillas living in a mountain rain forest, a band of 20 langur monkeys on the outskirts of an Indian village, or a troop of 100 baboons in the African grasslands. In such groups an infant is born into a world filled with relatives, friends, and adversaries, surrounded by intrigue, double-dealing, trysts, and heroics—the staples of great small-town gossip. Pretty heady stuff for the kid that's learning who it can trust and what the rules are, along with its species' equivalent of table manners.

Most young primates get socialized in this way quite effectively, and home must seem homier all the time. Then, inevitably, a lot of the young must leave the group and set out on their own. It is a simple fact driven by genetics and evolution: if everyone stayed on, matured, and reproduced there, and if their kids stayed on, and their kids' kids too, then ultimately everyone would be pretty closely related. You would have the classic problems of inbreeding—lots of funny-looking kids with six fingers and two tails (as well as more serious genetic problems).

Thus essentially all social primates have evolved mechanisms for adolescent emigration from one group to another. Not all adolescents have to leave. The problem of inbreeding is typically solved so long as all the adolescents of one sex go and make their fortune elsewhere; the members of the other sex can remain at home and mate with the newcomers immigrating to the group. In chimpanzees and gorillas, it is typically the females who leave for new groups, while the males stay home with their mothers. But among most Old World monkeys—baboons, macaques, langurs—it is the males who make the transfer. Why one sex transfers in one species but not in another is a complete mystery, the sort that keeps primatologists arguing with each other ad nauseam.

This pattern of adolescent transfer solves the specter of inbreeding. But to look at it just as a solution to an evolutionary problem is absurdly mechanistic. You can't lose sight of the fact that those are real animals going through the harrowing process. It is a remarkable thing to observe: every day, in the world of primates, someone young and frightened picks up, leaves Mommy and everyone it knows, and heads off into the unknown.

The transfer pattern I know best is the one among the baboons I study in the grasslands of East Africa. Two troops encounter each other at midday at some sort of natural boundary—a river, for example. As is the baboon propensity in such settings, the males of the two troops carry on with a variety of aggressive displays, hooting and hollering with what they no doubt hope is a great air of menace. Eventually everyone gets bored and goes back to eating and lounging, ignoring the interlopers on the other side of the river. Suddenly you spot the kid—some adolescent in your troop. He stands there at the river's edge, absolutely riveted. New baboons, a whole bunch of 'em! He runs five steps toward them, runs four back, searches among the other members of his troop to see why no one else seems mesmerized by the strangers. After endless contemplation, he gingerly crosses the river and sits on the very edge of the other bank, scampering back down in a panic should any new baboon so much as glance at him.

A week later, when the troops run into each other again, the kid repeats the pattern. Except this time he spends the afternoon sitting at the edge of the new troop. At the next encounter he follows them for a short distance before the anxiety becomes too much and he turns back. Finally, one brave night, he stays with them. He may vacillate awhile longer, perhaps even ultimately settling on a third troop, but he has begun his transfer into adulthood.

And what an awful experience it is—a painfully lonely, peripheralized stage of life. There are no freshman orientation weeks, no cohorts of newcomers banding together and covering their nervousness with bravado. There is just a baboon kid, all alone on the edge of a new group, and no one there could care less about him. Actually, that is not true—there are often members of the new troop who pay quite a lot of attention, displaying some of the least charming behavior seen among social primates, and most reminiscent of that of their human cousins. Suppose you

are a low-ranking member of that troop: perhaps a puny kid a year or so after your own transfer, or an aging male in decline. You spend most of your time losing fights, being pushed around, having food taken from you by someone of higher rank. You have a list of grievances a mile long and there's little you can do about it. Sure there are youngsters in the troop that you could harass pretty successfully, but if they are pretransfer age, their mothers—and maybe their fathers and their whole extended family—will descend on you like a ton of bricks. Then suddenly, like a gift from heaven, a new even punier kid shows up: someone to take it out on. (Among chimps, where females do the transferring, the same thing occurs; resident females are brutally aggressive toward the new female living on the group's edge.)

Yet that's only the beginning of a transfer animal's problems. When, as part of my studies of disease patterns among baboons, I anesthetize and examine transfer males, I find that these young animals are just teeming with parasites. There is no longer anyone to groom them, to sit with them and methodically clean their fur, half for hygiene, half for friendship. And if no one is interested in grooming a recent transfer animal, certainly no one is interested in anything more intimate than that—in short, it is a time of life filled with masturbation. The young males suffer all the indignities of being certified primate geeks.

They are also highly vulnerable. If a predator attacks, the transfer animal—who is typically peripheral and exposed to begin with—is not likely to recognize the group's signals and has no one to count on for his defense. I witnessed an incident like this during one of my first research stints in Africa. The unfortunate animal was so new to my group that he rated only a number, 273, instead of a name. The troop was meandering in the midday heat and descended down the bank of a dry streambed into some bad luck: a half-asleep lioness. Panic ensued, with animals running every which way as the lioness stirred—while Male 273 stood bewildered and terribly visible.

He was badly mauled and, in a poignant act, crawled for miles to return to his former home troop and die near his mother.

In short, the transfer period is one of the most dangerous and miserable times in a primate's life. Yet, almost inconceivably, life gets better. One day an adolescent female will sit beside our transfer male and briefly groom him. Some afternoon everyone hungrily descends on a tree in fruit and the older adolescent males forget to chase the newcomer away. One morning the adolescent and an adult male exchange greetings (which, among male baboons, consists of yanking on each other's penises, a social gesture predicated on trust if ever I saw one). And someday, inevitably, a terrified new transfer male appears on the scene, and our hero, to his perpetual shame perhaps, indulges in the aggressive pleasures of finding someone lower on the ladder to bully.

In a gradual process of assimilation, the transfer animal makes a friend, finds an ally, mates, and rises in the hierarchy of the troop. It can take years. Which is why Hobbes was such an extraordinary beast.

Three years ago my wife and I were spending the summer working with a baboon troop at Amboseli National Park in Kenya, a research site run by the behavioral biologists Jeanne and Stuart Altmann from the University of Chicago. I study the relationships between a baboon's rank and personality, how its body responds to stress, and what sorts of stress-related diseases it gets. In order to get the physiological data—blood samples to gauge an animal's stress hormone levels, immune system function, and so on—you have to anesthetize the baboon for a few hours with the aid of a small aluminum blow-gun and drug-filled darts. Fill the dart with the right amount of anesthetic, walk up to a baboon, aim, and blow, and he is snoozing five minutes later. Naturally it's not quite that simple—you can dart only in the mornings (to control for the effect of circadian rhythms on the animal's hormones). You must ensure there are no predators around to shred the guy, and you must make certain he doesn't climb a tree before passing out. And most of all, you have to dart and remove him from the troop when none of the other baboons are looking so that you don't alarm them and disrupt their habituation to the scientists. So essentially, what I do with my college education is creep around in the bushes after a bunch of baboons, waiting for the instant when they are all looking the other way so that I can zip a dart into someone's tush.

It was about halfway through the season. We were just beginning to get to know the baboons in our troop (named Hook's troop, for a long-deceased matriarch) and were becoming familiar with their daily routine. Each night they slept in their favorite grove of trees; each morning they rolled out of bed to forage for food in an open savanna strewn with volcanic rocks tossed up eons ago by nearby Mount Kilimanjaro. It was the dry season, which meant the baboons had to do a bit more walking than usual to find food and water, but there was still plenty of both, and the troop had time to lounge around in the shade during the afternoon heat. Dominating the social hierarchy among the males was an imposing character named Ruto, who had joined the troop a few years before and had risen relatively quickly in the ranks. Number two was a male named Fatso, who had had the misfortune of being a rotund adolescent when he'd transferred into the troop years before and was named by a callous researcher. Fat he was no longer. Now a muscular prime-age male, he was Ruto's most obvious competitor, though still clearly subordinate. It was a fairly peaceful period for the troop; mail was delivered regularly and the trains ran on time.

Then one morning we arrived to find the baboons in complete turmoil. It is not an anthropomorphism to say that everyone was mightily frazzled. There was a new transfer male, and not someone meekly scurrying about the periphery. He was in the middle of the troop, raising hell—threatening, chas-

ing, and whacking everyone in sight. This nasty, brutish animal was soon named Hobbes (in deference to the seventeenth-century English philosopher who described the life of man as solitary, poor, nasty, brutish, and short).

This is an extremely rare, though not unheard of, event among baboons. The transfer male in such cases is usually a big, muscular, intimidating kid. Maybe he is older than the average seven-year-old transfer male, or perhaps this is his second transfer and he picked up confidence from his first emigration. Maybe he is the son of a high-ranking female in his old troop, raised to feel cocky. In any case, the rare animal with these traits comes on like a truck. And he often gets away with it for a time. As long as he keeps pushing, it will be a while before any of the resident males works up the nerve to confront him. Nobody knows him yet; thus no one knows if he is asking for a fatal injury by being the first fool to challenge this aggressive maniac.

And this was Hobbes's style. The intimidated males stood around helplessly. Fatso discovered all sorts of errands he had to run elsewhere. Ruto hid behind females. No one else was going to take a stand. Hobbes rose to the number one rank in the troop within a week.

Despite his sudden ascendancy Hobbes's success wasn't going to last forever. He was still a relatively inexperienced kid, and eventually one of the bigger males was bound to cut him down to size. Hobbes had about a month's free ride. At this point he did something brutally violent but which made a certain grim evolutionary sense. He began to selectively attack pregnant females. He beat and mauled them, causing three out of four to abort within a few days.

One of the great clichés of animal behavior in the context of evolution is that animals act for the good of the species. This idea was discredited in the 1960s but continues to permeate *Wild Kingdom*–like versions of animal behavior. The more accurate view is that animals usually behave in ways

that maximize their own reproduction and the reproduction of their close relatives. This helps explain extraordinary acts of altruism and self-sacrifice in some circumstances, and sickening aggression in others. It's in this context that Hobbes's attacks make sense. Were those females to carry through their pregnancies and raise their offspring, they would not be likely to mate again for two years—and who knows where Hobbes would be at that point. Instead he harassed the females into aborting, and they were ovulating again a few weeks later. Although female baboons have a say in whom they mate with, in the case of someone as forceful as Hobbes they have little choice: within weeks Hobbes, still the dominant male in the troop, was mating with two of those three females. (This is not to imply that Hobbes had read his textbooks on evolution, animal behavior, and primate obstetrics and had thought through this strategy. The wording here is a convenient shorthand for the more correct way of stating that his pattern of behavior was almost certainly an unconscious, evolved one.)

As it happened, Hobbes's arrival on the scene—just as we had darted and tested about half the animals for our studies—afforded us a rare opportunity. We could compare the physiology of the troop before and after his tumultuous transfer. And in a study recently published with Jeanne Altmann and Susan Alberts, I documented the not very surprising fact that Hobbes was stressing the bejesus out of these animals. Their blood levels of cortisol (also known as hydrocortisone), one of the hormones most reliably secreted during stress, rose significantly. At the same time, their numbers of white blood cells, or lymphocytes, the sentinel cells of the immune system that defend the body against infections, declined markedly—another highly reliable index of stress. These stress-response markers were most pronounced in the animals getting the most grief from Hobbes. Unmolested females had three times as many circulating lymphocytes as one poor female who was attacked five times during those first two weeks.

An obvious question: Why doesn't every new transfer male try something as audaciously successful as Hobbes? For one thing, most transfer males are too small at the typical transfer age of seven years to intimidate a gazelle, let alone an 80-pound adult male baboon. (Hobbes, unusually, weighed a good 70 pounds.) Most don't have the personality needed for this sort of unpleasantry. Moreover, it's a risky strategy, as someone like Hobbes stands a good chance of sustaining a crippling injury early in life.

But there was another reason as well, which didn't become apparent until later. One morning, when Hobbes was concentrating on who to hassle next and paying no attention to us, I managed to put a dart into his haunches. Months later, when examining his blood sample in the laboratory, we found that Hobbes had among the highest levels of cortisol in the troop and extremely low lymphocyte counts, less than one-quarter the troop average. (Ruto and Fatso, sitting on the sidelines now, had three and six times as many lymphocytes as Hobbes had.) The young baboon was experiencing a massive stress response himself, larger even than those of the females he was harassing, and certainly larger than is typical of the other, meek transfer males I've studied. In other words, it doesn't come cheap to be a bastard 12 hours a day—a couple of months of this sort of thing is likely to exert a physiological toll.

As a postscript, Hobbes did not hold on to his position. Within five months he was toppled, dropping down to number three in the hierarchy. After three years in the troop, he disappeared into the sunset, transferring out to parts unknown to try his luck in some other troop.

All this only reaffirms that transferring is awful for adolescents—whether they're average geeks opting for the route of slow acceptance or rare animals like Hobbes who try to take a troop by storm. Either way it's an ordeal, and the young animals pay a heavy price. The marvel is that they keep on doing it. Transferring may solve the inbreeding problem for a population; but what's in it for the individual?

Adolescent transfer is a feature of many social mammals, not just primates, and the mechanisms can differ. Sometimes transfer can arise from intrasexual competition—a fancy way of saying that the adolescents are driven from the group by a more powerful same-sex competitor. You see this in species like gazelles and impalas, for example. The core social group consists of a single breeding male, a large collection of females, and their offspring. At any given point some of those male off-spring are likely to be entering puberty. But since the breeding male typically doesn't hold on to his precarious position for long, he is probably not the father of these adolescent males. He doesn't view them as sons coming of age but as unrelated males becoming reproductive competitors. At their first signs of puberty he violently drives them out of the group.

In primates, however, forced dispersion almost never happens. Critically, these adolescents choose to go—even though the move seems crazy. After all, they live in a troop surrounded by family and friends. They know their home turf—which trees are fruiting at what time of year, where the local predators tend to lurk. Yet they leave these home comforts to endure parasites, predators, and loneliness. And why? To dwell among strangers who treat them terribly. It makes no sense, from the standpoint of the individual animal. Behaviorist theories state this more formally: animals, including humans, tend to do things for which they are rewarded and tend not to do things for which they get punished. Yet here they are, leaving their comfortable, rewarding world in order to be amply dumped on far away. Furthermore, animals tend to hate novelty. Put a rat in a new cage, give it a new feeding pattern, and it exhibits a stress response. Yet here young primates are risking life and limb for novelty. Old World monkeys have been known to transfer up to five times over their lifetime, or travel nearly 40 miles to a new troop. Why should any individual in its right mind want to do this?

I do not know why transfer occurs, but it is clearly very deeply rooted. Humans, in part because their diets are adaptable, are the most widely distributed mammal on Earth, inhabiting nearly every godforsaken corner of this planet. Among our primate relatives, those with the least finicky of diets, such as baboons, are also among the most widely distributed beasts on Earth (African baboons range from desert to rain forest, from mountain to savanna). Inevitably, someone had to be the first to set foot in each of those new worlds, an individual who transferred in a big way. And it is overwhelmingly likely a young individual who did that.

This love affair with risk and novelty seems to be why the young of all our primate species are the most likely to die of accidents, doing foolhardy things while their elders cluck over how they told them so. And it is also the reason that the young are most likely to discover something really new and extraordinary, whether in the physical or the intellectual realm. When the novel practice of washing food in seawater was discovered by snow monkeys in Japan, it was a youngster who did so, and it was her playmates who picked up the adaptation; hardly any of the older animals did. And when Darwin's ideas about evolution swept through academic primates in the midnineteenth century, it was the new, up-and-coming generation of scientists that embraced his ideas with the greatest enthusiasm.

You don't have to search far for other examples. Think of the tradition of near-adolescent mathematicians revolutionizing their fields, or of the young Picasso and Stravinsky galvanizing twentieth-century culture. Think about teenagers inevitably, irresistibly wanting to drive too fast, or trying out some new improvisatory sport guaranteed to break their necks, or marching off in an excited frenzy to whatever stupid war their elders have invented. Think of the endless young people leaving their homes, homes perhaps rife with poverty or oppression, but still their homes, to go off to find new worlds.

Part of the reason for the evolutionary success of primates, human or otherwise, is that we are a pretty smart collection of animals. What's more, our thumbs work in particularly fancy and advantageous ways, and we're more flexible about food than most. But our primate essence is more than just abstract reasoning, dexterous thumbs, and omnivorous diets. Another key to

our success must have something to do with this voluntary transfer process, this primate legacy of getting an itch around adolescence. How did voluntary dispersal evolve? What is going on with that individual's genes, hormones, and neurotransmitters to make it hit the road? We don't know, but we do know that following this urge is one of the most resonantly primate of acts. A young male baboon stands riveted at the river's edge; an adolescent female

chimp cranes to catch a glimpse of the chimps from the next valley. New animals, a whole bunch of 'em! To hell with logic and sensible behavior, to hell with tradition and respecting your elders, to hell with this drab little town, and to hell with that knot of fear in your stomach. Curiosity, excitement, adventure—the hunger for novelty is something fundamentally daft, rash, and enriching that we share with our whole taxonomic order.

The Mind of the Chimpanzee

Jane Goodall

Often I have gazed into a chimpanzee's eyes and wondered what was going on behind them. I used to look into Flo's, she so old, so wise. What did she remember of her young days? David Greybeard had the most beautiful eyes of them all, large and lustrous, set wide apart. They somehow expressed his whole personality, his serene self-assurance, his inherent dignity—and, from time to time, his utter determination to get his way. For a long time I never liked to look a chimpanzee straight in the eye—I assumed that, as is the case with most primates, this would be interpreted as a threat or at least as a breach of good manners. Not so. As long as one looks with gentleness, without arrogance, a chimpanzee will understand, and may even return the look. And then—or such is my fantasy—it is as though the eyes are windows into the mind. Only the glass is opaque so that the mystery can never be fully revealed.

I shall never forget my meeting with Lucy, an eight-year-old home-raised chimpanzee. She came and sat beside me on the sofa and, with her face very close to mine, searched in my eyes—for what? Perhaps she was looking for signs of mistrust, dislike, or fear, since many people must have been somewhat disconcerted when, for the first time, they came face to face with a grown chimpanzee. Whatever Lucy read in my eyes clearly satisfied her for she suddenly put one arm round my neck and gave me a generous and very chimp-like kiss, her mouth wide open and laid over mine. I was accepted.

For a long time after that encounter I was profoundly disturbed. I had been at Gombe for about fifteen years then and I was quite familiar with chimpanzees in the wild. But Lucy, having grown up as a human child, was like a changeling, her essential chimpanzee-ness overlaid by the various human behaviours she had acquired over the years. No longer purely chimp yet eons away from humanity, she was man-made, some other kind of being. I watched, amazed, as she opened the refrigerator and various cupboards, found bottles and a glass, then poured herself a gin and tonic. She took the drink to the TV, turned the set on, flipped from one channel to another then, as though in disgust, turned it off again. She selected a glossy magazine from the table and, still carrying her drink, settled in a comfortable chair. Occasionally, as she leafed through the magazine she identified something she saw, using the signs of ASL, the American Sign Language used by the deaf. I, of course, did not understand, but my hostess, Jane Temerlin (who was also Lucy's 'mother'), translated: 'That dog,' Lucy commented, pausing at a photo of a small white poodle. She turned the page. 'Blue,' she declared, pointing then signing as she gazed at a picture of a lady advertising some kind of soap powder and wearing a brilliant blue dress. And finally, after some vague hand movements—perhaps signed mutterings—'This Lucy's, this mine,' as she closed the magazine and laid it on her lap. She had just been taught, Jane told me, the use of the possessive pronouns during the thrice weekly ASL lessons she was receiving at the time.

The book written by Lucy's human 'father', Maury Temerlin, was entitled *Lucy, Growing Up Human*. And in fact, the chimpanzee is more like us than is any other living creature. There is close resemblance in the physiology of our two species and genetically, in the structure of the DNA, chimpanzees and humans differ by only just over one per cent. This is why medical research uses chimpanzees as experimental animals when they need substitutes for humans in the testing of some drug or vaccine. Chimpanzees can be infected with just about all known human infectious diseases including those, such as hepatitis B and AIDS, to which other non-human animals (except gorillas, orangutans and gibbons) are immune. There are equally striking similarities between humans and chimpanzees in the anatomy and wiring of the brain and nervous system, and—although many scientists have been reluctant to admit to this—in social behaviour, intellectual ability, and the emotions. The notion of an evolutionary continuity in physical structure from pre-human ape to modern man has long been morally acceptable to most scientists. That the same might hold good for mind was generally considered an absurd hypothesis—particularly by those who used, and often misused, animals in their laboratories. It is, after all, convenient to believe that the creature you are using, while it may react in disturbingly human-like ways, is, in fact, merely a mindless and, above all, unfeeling, 'dumb' animal.

When I began my study at Gombe in 1960 it was not permissible—at least not in ethological circles—to talk about an animal's mind. Only humans had minds. Nor was it quite proper to talk about animal personality. Of course everyone knew that they *did* have their own unique characters—everyone who had ever owned a dog or other pet was aware of that. But ethologists, striving to make theirs a 'hard' science, shied away from the task of trying to explain such things objectively. One respected ethologist, while acknowledging that there was 'variability between individual animals', wrote that it was best that this fact be 'swept under the carpet'. At that time ethological carpets fairly bulged with all that was hidden beneath them.

How naive I was. As I had not had an undergraduate science education I didn't realize that animals were not supposed to have personalities, or to think, or to feel emotions or pain. I had no idea that it would have been more appropriate to assign each of the chimpanzees a number rather than a name when I got to know him or her. I didn't realize that it was not scientific to discuss behaviour in terms of motivation or purpose. And no one had told me that terms such as *childhood* and *adolescence* were uniquely human phases of the life cycle, culturally determined, not to be used when referring to young chimpanzees. Not knowing, I freely made use of all those forbidden terms and concepts in my initial attempt to describe, to the best of my ability, the amazing things I had observed at Gombe.

I shall never forget the response of a group of ethologists to some remarks I made at an erudite seminar. I described how Figan, as an adolescent, had learned to stay behind in camp after senior males had left, so that we could give him a few bananas for himself. On the first occasion he had, upon seeing the fruits, uttered loud, delighted food calls: whereupon a couple of the older males had charged back, chased after Figan, and taken his bananas. And then, coming to the point of the story, I explained how, on the next occasion, Figan had actually suppressed his calls. We could hear little sounds, in his throat, but so quiet that none of the

others could have heard them. Other young chimps, to whom we tried to smuggle fruit without the knowledge of their elders, never learned such self-control. With shrieks of glee they would fall to, only to be robbed of their booty when the big males charged back. I had expected my audience to be as fascinated and impressed as I was. I had hoped for an exchange of views about the chimpanzee's undoubted intelligence. Instead there was a chill silence, after which the chairman hastily changed the subject. Needless to say, after being thus snubbed, I was very reluctant to contribute any comments, at any scientific gathering, for a very long time. Looking back, I suspect that everyone was interested, but it was, of course, not permissible to present a mere 'anecdote' as evidence for anything.

The editorial comments on the first paper I wrote for publication demanded that every *he* or *she* be replaced with *it,* and every *who* be replaced with *which*. Incensed, I, in my turn, crossed out the *its* and *whichs* and scrawled back the original pronouns. As I had no desire to carve a niche for myself in the world of science, but simply wanted to go on living among and learning about chimpanzees, the possible reaction of the editor of the learned journal did not trouble me. In fact I won that round: the paper when finally published did confer upon the chimpanzees the dignity of their appropriate genders and properly upgraded them from the status of mere 'things' to essential Beingness.

However, despite my somewhat truculent attitude, I did want to learn, and I was sensible of my incredible good fortune in being admitted to Cambridge. I wanted to get my PhD, if only for the sake of Louis Leakey and the other people who had written letters in support of my admission. And how lucky I was to have, as my supervisor, Robert Hinde. Not only because I thereby benefitted from his brilliant mind and clear thinking, but also because I doubt that I could have found a teacher more suited to my particular needs and personality. Gradually he was able to cloak me with at least some

of the trappings of a scientist. Thus although I continued to hold to most of my convictions—that animals had personalities; that they could feel happy or sad or fearful; that they could feel pain; that they could strive towards planned goals and achieve greater success if they were highly motivated—I soon realized that these personal convictions were, indeed, difficult to prove. It was best to be circumspect—at least until I had gained some credentials and credibility. And Robert gave me wonderful advice on how best to tie up some of my more rebellious ideas with scientific ribbon. 'You can't *know* that Fifi was jealous,' he admonished on one occasion. We argued a little. And then: 'Why don't you just say *If Fifi were a human child we would say she was jealous.*' I did.

It is not easy to study emotions even when the subjects are human. I know how I feel if I am sad or happy or angry, and if a friend tells me that he is feeling sad, happy or angry, I assume that his feelings are similar to mine. But of course I cannot know. As we try to come to grips with the emotions of beings progressively more different from ourselves the task, obviously, becomes increasingly difficult. If we ascribe human emotions to non-human animals we are accused of being anthropomorphic—a cardinal sin in ethology. But is it so terrible? If we test the effect of drugs on chimpanzees because they are biologically so similar to ourselves, if we accept that there are dramatic similarities in chimpanzee and human brain and nervous system, is it not logical to assume that there will be similarities also in at least the more basic feelings, emotions, moods of the two species?

In fact, all those who have worked long and closely with chimpanzees have no hesitation in asserting that chimps experience emotions similar to those which in ourselves we label pleasure, joy, sorrow, anger, boredom and so on. Some of the emotional states of the chimpanzee are so obviously similar to ours that even an inexperienced observer can understand what is going on. An infant who hurls himself screaming to the ground, face contorted, hitting out with his arms at any nearby object, banging his head, is clearly having a tantrum. Another youngster, who gambols around his mother, turning somersaults, pirouetting and, every so often, rushing up to her and tumbling into her lap, patting her or pulling her hand towards him in a request for tickling, is obviously filled with *joie de vivre*. There are few observers who would not unhesitatingly ascribe his behaviour to a happy, carefree state of well-being. And one cannot watch chimpanzee infants for long without realizing that they have the same emotional need for affection and reassurance as human children. An adult male, reclining in the shade after a good meal, reaching benignly to play with an infant or idly groom an adult female, is clearly in a good mood. When he sits with bristling hair, glaring at his subordinates and threatening them, with irritated gestures, if they come too close, he is clearly feeling cross and grumpy. We make these judgements because the similarity of so much of a chimpanzee's behaviour to our own permits us to empathize.

It is hard to empathize with emotions we have not experienced. I can imagine, to some extent, the pleasure of a female chimpanzee during the act of procreation. The feelings of her male partner are beyond my knowledge—as are those of the human male in the same context. I have spent countless hours watching mother chimpanzees interacting with their infants. But not until I had an infant of my own did I begin to understand the basic, powerful instinct of mother-love. If someone accidentally did something to frighten Grub, or threaten his well-being in any way, I felt a surge of quite irrational anger. How much more easily could I then understand the feelings of the chimpanzee mother who furiously waves her arm and barks in threat at an individual who approaches her infant too closely, or at a playmate who inadvertently hurts her child. And it was not until I knew the numbing grief that gripped me after the death of my second husband that I could even begin to appreciate the despair and sense of loss that can cause young chimps to pine

away and die when they lose their mothers.

Empathy and intuition can be of tremendous value as we attempt to understand certain complex behavioural interactions, provided that the behaviour, as it occurs, is recorded precisely and objectively. Fortunately I have seldom found it difficult to record facts in an orderly manner even during times of powerful emotional involvement. And 'knowing' intuitively how a chimpanzee is feeling—after an attack, for example—may help one to understand what happens next. We should not be afraid at least to try to make use of our close evolutionary relationship with the chimpanzees in our attempts to interpret complex behaviour.

Today, as in Darwin's time, it is once again fashionable to speak of and study the animal mind. This change came about gradually, and was, at least in part, due to the information collected during careful studies of animal societies in the field. As these observations became widely known, it was impossible to brush aside the complexities of social behaviour that were revealed in species after species. The untidy clutter under the ethological carpets was brought out and examined, piece by piece. Gradually it was realized that parsimonious explanations of apparently intelligent behaviours were often misleading. This led to a succession of experiments that, taken together, clearly prove that many intellectual abilities that had been thought unique to humans were actually present, though in a less highly developed form, in other, non-human beings. Particularly, of course, in the non-human primates and especially in chimpanzees.

When first I began to read about human evolution, I learned that one of the hallmarks of our own species was that we, and only we, were capable of making tools. *Man the Toolmaker* was an oft-cited definition—and this despite the careful and exhaustive research of Wolfgang Kohler and Robert Yerkes on the tool-using and tool-making abilities of chimpanzees. Those studies, carried out independently in the early twenties, were received with scepticism. Yet both Kohler and Yerkes were respected

scientists, and both had a profound understanding of chimpanzee behaviour. Indeed, Kohler's descriptions of the personalities and behaviour of the various individuals in his colony, published in his book *The Mentality of Apes,* remain some of the most vivid and colourful ever written. And his experiments, showing how chimpanzees could stack boxes, then climb the unstable constructions to reach fruit suspended from the ceiling, or join two short sticks to make a pole long enough to rake in fruit otherwise out of reach, have become classic, appearing in almost all textbooks dealing with intelligent behaviour in non-human animals.

By the time systematic observations of tool-using came from Gombe those pioneering studies had been largely forgotten. Moreover, it was one thing to know that humanized chimpanzees in the lab could use implements: it was quite another to find that this was a naturally occurring skill in the wild. I well remember writing to Louis about my first observations, describing how David Greybeard not only used bits of straw to fish for termites but actually stripped leaves from a stem and thus *made* a tool. And I remember too receiving the now oft-quoted telegram he sent in response to my letter: 'Now we must redefine *tool*, redefine *Man*, or accept chimpanzees as humans.'

There were, initially, a few scientists who attempted to write off the termiting observations, even suggesting that I had taught the chimps! By and large, though, people were fascinated by the information and by the subsequent observations of the other contexts in which the Gombe chimpanzees used objects as tools. And there were only a few anthropologists who objected when I suggested that the chimpanzees probably passed their tool-using traditions from one generation to the next, through observations, imitation and practice, so that each population might be expected to have its own unique tool-using culture. Which, incidentally, turns out to be quite true. And when I described how one chimpanzee, Mike, spontaneously solved a new problem by using a tool (he broke off a stick to knock a banana to the ground when he was too nervous to actually take it from my hand) I don't believe there were any raised eyebrows in the scientific community. Certainly I was not attacked viciously, as were Kohler and Yerkes, for suggesting that humans were not the only beings capable of reasoning and insight.

The mid-sixties saw the start of a project that, along with other similar research, was to teach us a great deal about the chimpanzee mind. This was Project Washoe, conceived by Trixie and Allen Gardner. They purchased an infant chimpanzee and began to teach her the signs of ASL, the American Sign Language used by the deaf. Twenty years earlier another husband and wife team, Richard and Cathy Hayes, had tried, with an almost total lack of success, to teach a young chimp, Vikki, to talk. The Hayes's undertaking taught us a lot about the chimpanzee mind, but Vikki, although she did well in IQ tests, and was clearly an intelligent youngster, could not learn human speech. The Gardners, however, achieved spectacular success with their pupil, Washoe. Not only did she learn signs easily, but she quickly began to string them together in meaningful ways. It was clear that each sign evoked, in her mind, a mental image of the object it represented. If, for example, she was asked, in sign language, to fetch an apple, she would go and locate an apple that was out of sight in another room.

Other chimps entered the project, some starting their lives in deaf signing families before joining Washoe. And finally Washoe adopted an infant, Loulis. He came from a lab where no thought of teaching signs had ever penetrated. When he was with Washoe he was given no lessons in language acquisition—not by humans, anyway. Yet by the time he was eight years old he had made fifty-eight signs in their correct contexts. How did he learn them? Mostly, it seems, by imitating the behaviour of Washoe and the other three signing chimps, Dar, Moja and Tatu. Sometimes, though, he received tuition from Washoe herself. One day, for example, she began to swagger about bipedally, hair bristling, signing *food!*

food! food! in great excitement. She had seen a human approaching with a bar of chocolate. Loulis, only eighteen months old, watched passively. Suddenly Washoe stopped her swaggering, went over to him, took his hand, and moulded the sign for *food* (fingers pointing towards mouth). Another time, in a similar context, she made the sign for *chewing gum*—but with *her* hand on *his* body. On a third occasion Washoe, apropos of nothing, picked up a small chair, took it over to Loulis, set it down in front of him, and very distinctly made the *chair* sign three times, watching him closely as she did so. The two food signs became incorporated into Loulis's vocabulary but the sign for chair did not. Obviously the priorities of a young chimp are similar to those of a human child!

When news of Washoe's accomplishments first hit the scientific community it immediately provoked a storm of bitter protest. It implied that chimpanzees were capable of mastering a human language, and this, in turn, indicated mental powers of generalization, abstraction and concept-formation as well as an ability to understand and use abstract symbols. And these intellectual skills were surely the prerogatives of *Homo sapiens*. Although there were many who were fascinated and excited by the Gardners' findings, there were many more who denounced the whole project, holding that the data was suspect, the methodology sloppy, and the conclusions not only misleading, but quite preposterous. The controversy inspired all sorts of other language projects. And, whether the investigators were sceptical to start with and hoped to disprove the Gardners' work, or whether they were attempting to demonstrate the same thing in a new way, their research provided additional information about the chimpanzee's mind.

And so, with new incentive, psychologists began to test the mental abilities of chimpanzees in a variety of different ways; again and again the results confirmed that their minds are uncannily like our own. It had long been held that only humans were capable of what is called 'cross-modal trans-

fer of information'—in other words, if you shut your eyes and someone allows you to feel a strangely shaped potato, you will subsequently be able to pick it out from other differently shaped potatoes simply by looking at them. And vice versa. It turned out that chimpanzees can 'know' with their eyes what they 'feel' with their fingers in just the same way. In fact, we now know that some other non-human primates can do the same thing. I expect all kinds of creatures have the same ability.

Then it was proved, experimentally and beyond doubt, that chimpanzees could recognize themselves in mirrors—that they had, therefore, some kind of self-concept. In fact, Washoe, some years previously, had already demonstrated the ability when she spontaneously identified herself in the mirror, staring at her image and making her name sign. But that observation was merely anecdotal. The proof came when chimpanzees who had been allowed to play with mirrors were, while anaesthetized, dabbed with spots of odourless paint in places, such as the ears or the top of the head, that they could see only in the mirror. When they woke they were not only fascinated by their spotted images, but immediately investigated, with their fingers, the dabs of paint.

The fact that chimpanzees have excellent memories surprised no one. Everyone, after all, has been brought up to believe that 'an elephant never forgets' so why should a chimpanzee be any different? The fact that Washoe spontaneously gave the name-sign of Beatrice Gardner, her surrogate mother, when she saw her after a separation of eleven years was no greater an accomplishment than the amazing memory shown by dogs who recognize their owners after separations of almost as long—and the chimpanzee has a much longer life span than a dog. Chimpanzees can plan ahead, too, at least as regards the immediate future. This, in fact, is well illustrated at Gombe, during the termiting season: often an individual prepares a tool for use on a termite mound that is several hundred yards away and absolutely out of sight.

2. PRIMATES

This is not the place to describe in detail the other cognitive abilities that have been studied in laboratory chimpanzees. Among other accomplishments chimpanzees possess pre-mathematical skills: they can, for example, readily differentiate between *more* and *less.* They can classify things into specific categories according to a given criterion—thus they have no difficulty in separating a pile of food into *fruits* and *vegetables* on one occasion, and, on another, dividing the same pile of food into *large* versus *small* items, even though this requires putting some vegetables with some fruits. Chimpanzees who have been taught a language can combine signs creatively in order to describe objects for which they have no symbol. Washoe, for example, puzzled her caretakers by asking, repeatedly, for a *rock berry.* Eventually it transpired that she was referring to Brazil nuts which she had encountered for the first time a while before. Another language-trained chimp described a cucumber as a *green banana,* and another referred to an Alka-Seltzer as a *listen drink.* They can even invent signs. Lucy, as she got older, had to be put on a leash for her outings. One day, eager to set off but having no sign for *leash,* she signalled her wishes by holding a crooked index finger to the ring on her collar. This sign became part of her vocabulary. Some chimpanzees love to draw, and especially to paint. Those who have learned sign language sometimes spontaneously label their works, 'This [is] apple'—or bird, or sweetcorn, or whatever. The fact that the paintings often look, to our eyes, remarkably unlike the objects depicted by the artists either means that the chimpanzees are poor draughtsmen or that we have much to learn regarding ape-style representational art!

People sometimes ask why chimpanzees have evolved such complex intellectual powers when their lives in the wild are so simple. The answer is, of course, that their lives in the wild are not so simple! They use—and need—all their mental skills during normal day-to-day life in their complex society. They are always having to make choices—where to go, or with whom to travel. They need highly developed social skills—particularly those males who are ambitious to attain high positions in the dominance hierarchy. Low-ranking chimpanzees must learn deception—to conceal their intentions or to do things in secret—if they are to get their way in the presence of their superiors. Indeed, the study of chimpanzees in the wild suggests that their intellectual abilities evolved, over the millennia, to help them cope with daily life. And now, the solid core of data concerning chimpanzee intellect collected so carefully in the lab setting provides a background against which to evaluate the many examples of intelligent, rational behaviour that we see in the wild.

It is easier to study intellectual prowess in the lab where, through carefully devised tests and judicious use of rewards, the chimpanzees can be encouraged to exert themselves, to stretch their minds to the limit. It is more meaningful to study the subject in the wild, but much harder. It is more meaningful because we can better understand the environmental pressures that led to the evolution of intellectual skills in chimpanzee societies. It is harder because, in the wild, almost all behaviours are confounded by countless variables; years of observing, recording and analysing take the place of contrived testing; sample size can often be counted on the fingers of one hand; the only experiments are nature's own, and only time—eventually—may replicate them.

In the wild a single observation may prove of utmost significance, providing a clue to some hitherto puzzling aspect of behaviour, a key to the understanding of, for example, a changed relationship. Obviously it is crucial to see as many incidents of this sort as possible. During the early years of my study at Gombe it became apparent that one person alone could never learn more than a fraction of what was going on in a chimpanzee community at any given time. And so, from 1964 onwards, I gradually built up a research team to help in the gathering of information about the behaviour of our closest living relatives.

Dian Fossey and Digit

Sy Montgomery

Every breath was a battle to draw the ghost of her life back into her body. At age forty-two it hurt her even to breathe.

Dian Fossey had been asthmatic as a child and a heavy smoker since her teens; X-rays of her lungs taken when she graduated from college, she remembered, looked like "a road map of Los Angeles superimposed over a road map of New York." And now, after eight years of living in the oxygen-poor heights of Central Africa's Virunga Volcanoes, breathing the cold, sodden night air, her lungs were crippled. The hike to her research camp, Karisoke, at 10,000 feet, took her graduate students less than an hour; for Dian it was a gasping two-and-a-half-hour climb. She had suffered several bouts of pneumonia. Now she thought she was coming down with it again.

Earlier in the week she had broken her ankle. She heard the bone snap when she fell into a drainage ditch near her corrugated tin cabin. She had been avoiding a charging buffalo. Two days later she was bitten by a venomous spider on the other leg. Her right knee was swollen huge and red; her left ankle was black. But she would not leave the mountain for medical treatment in the small hospital down in Ruhengeri. She had been in worse shape before. Once, broken ribs punctured a lung; another time she was bitten by a dog thought to be rabid. Only when her temperature reached 105 and her symptoms clearly matched those described in her medical book for rabies had she allowed her African staff to carry her down on a litter.

Dian was loath to leave the camp in charge of her graduate students, two of whom she had been fighting with bit-

terly. Kelly Steward and Sandy Harcourt, once her closest camp colleagues and confidantes, had committed the unforgivable error of falling in love with each other. Dian considered this a breach of loyalty. She yelled at them. Kelly cried and Sandy sulked.

But on this May day of 1974 Sandy felt sorry for Dian. As a gesture of conciliation, he offered to help her hobble out to visit Group 4. Splinted and steadied by a walking stick, she quickly accepted.

Group 4 was the first family of mountain gorillas Dian had contacted when she established her camp in Rwanda in September 1967. A political uprising had forced her to flee her earlier research station in Zaire. On the day she founded Karisoke—a name she coined by combining the names of the two volcanoes between which her camp nestled, Karisimbi and Visoke—poachers had led her to the group. The two Batwa tribesmen had been hunting antelope in the park—an illegal practice that had been tolerated for decades—and they offered to show her the gorillas they had encountered.

At that first contact, Dian watched the gorillas through binoculars for forty-five minutes. Across a ravine, ninety feet away, she could pick out three distinctive individuals in the fourteen-member group. There was a majestic old male, his black form silvered from shoulder to hip. This 350-pound silverback was obviously the sultan of the harem of females, the leader of the family. One old female stood out, a glare in her eyes, her lips compressed as if she had swallowed vinegar. And one youngster was "a playful little ball of disorganized black fluff . . . full of mischief and curiosity," as Dian would later describe

him in *Gorillas in the Mist.* She guessed then that he was about five years old. He tumbled about in the foliage like an animated black dustball. When the lead silverback spotted Dian behind a tree, the youngster obediently fled at his call, but Dian had the impression that the little male would rather have stayed for a longer look at the stranger. In a later contact she noticed the juvenile's swollen, extended middle finger. After many attempts at naming him, she finally called him Digit.

It was Digit, now twelve, who came over to Dian as she sat crumpled and coughing among the foliage with Sandy. Digit, a gaunt young silverback, served his family as sentry. He left the periphery of his group to knuckle over to her side. She inhaled his smell. A good smell, she noted with relief: for two years a draining wound in his neck had hunched his posture and sapped his spirit. Systemic infection had given his whole body a sour odor, not the normal, clean smell of fresh sweat. During that time Digit had become listless. Little would arouse his interest: not the sex play between the group's lead silverback and receptive females, not even visits from Dian. Digit would sit at the edge of the group for hours, probing the wound with his fingers, his eyes fixed on some distant spot as if dwelling on a sad memory.

But today Digit looked directly into Dian's eyes. He chose to remain beside her throughout the afternoon, like a quiet visitor to a shut-in, old friends with no need to talk. He turned his great domed head to her, looking at her solemnly with a brown, cognizant gaze. Normally a prolonged stare from a gorilla is a threat. But Digit's gaze bore no aggression. He seemed to say: I know. Dian would later write that she believed Digit understood she was sick. And she returned to camp that afternoon, still limping, still sick, still troubled, but whole.

"We all felt we shared something with the gorillas," one of her students would later recall of his months at Karisoke. And it is easy to feel that way after even a brief contact with these huge, solemn beings. "The face of a gorilla," wrote nature writer David Quammen after just looking at a picture of one, "offers a shock of what feels like total recognition." To be in the presence of a mountain gorilla for even one hour simply rips your soul open with awe. They are the largest of the great apes, the most hugely majestic and powerful; but it is the gaze of a gorilla that transfixes, when its eyes meet yours. The naturalist George Schaller, whose year-long study preceded Dian's, wrote that this is a look found in the eye of no other animal except, perhaps, a whale. It is not so much intelligence that strikes you, but understanding. You feel there has been an exchange.

The exchange between Digit and Dian that day was deep and long. By then Digit had known Dian for seven years. She had been a constant in his growing up from a juvenile to a young blackback and now to a silverback sentry. He had known her longer than he had known his own mother, who had died or left his group before he was five; he had known Dian longer than he had known his father, the old silverback who died of natural causes less than a year after she first observed him. When Digit was nine, his three age-mates in Group 4 departed: his half sisters were "kidnaped" by rival silverbacks, as often happens with young females. Digit then adopted Dian as his playmate, and he would often leave the rest of the group to amble to her side, eager to examine her gear, sniff her gloves and jeans, tug gently at her long brown braid.

As for Dian, her relationship with Digit was stronger than her bonds with her mother, father, or stepfather. Though she longed for a husband and babies, she never married or bore children. Her relationship with Digit endured

longer than that with any of her lovers and outlasted many of her human friendships.

In her slide lectures in the United States, Dian would refer to him as "my friend, Digit." "Friend," she admitted, was too weak a word, too casual; but she could find no other. Our words are something we share with other humans; but what Dian had with Digit was something she guarded as uniquely hers.

A mountain gorilla group is one of the most cohesive family units found among primates, a fact that impressed George Schaller. Adult orangutans live mostly alone, males and females meeting to mate. Chimpanzees' social groupings are so loosely organized, changing constantly in number and composition, that Jane Goodall couldn't make sense of them for nearly a decade. But gorillas live in tight-knit, clearly defined families. Typically a group contains a lead silverback, perhaps his adult brother, half brother, or nephew, and several adult females and their offspring.

A gorilla group travels, feeds, plays, and rests together. Seldom is an individual more than a hundred feet away from the others. The lead silverback slows his pace to that of the group's slowest, weakest member. All adults tolerate the babies and youngsters in the group, often with great tenderness. A wide-eyed baby, its fur still curly as black wool, may crawl over the great black bulk of any adult with impunity; a toddler may even step on the flat, leathery nose of a silverback. Usually the powerful male will gently set the baby aside or even dangle it playfully from one of his immense fingers.

When Dian first discovered Group 4, she would watch them through binoculars from a hidden position, for if they saw her they would flee. She loved to observe the group's three infants toddle and tumble together. If one baby found the play too rough, it would make a coughing sound, and its mother would lumber over and cradle it tenderly to her breast. Dian watched Digit and his juvenile sisters play:

wrestling, rolling, and chasing games often took them as far as fifty feet from the hulking adults. Sometimes a silverback led the youngsters in a sort of square dance. Loping from one palmlike *Senecio* tree to another, each gorilla would grab a trunk for a twirl, then spin off to embrace another trunk down the slope, until all the gorillas lay in a bouncing pileup of furry black bodies. And then the silverback would lead the youngsters up the slope again for another game.

Within a year, this cheerful silverback eventually took over leadership of the group, after the old leader died. Dian named him Uncle Bert, after her uncle Albert Chapin. With Dian's maternal aunt, Flossie (Dian named a Group 4 female after her as well), Uncle Bert had helped care for Dian after her father left the family when she was three. While Dian was in college Bert and Flossie gave her money to help with costs that her holiday, weekend, and summer jobs wouldn't cover. Naming the silverback after her uncle was the most tender tribute Dian could have offered Bert Chapin: his was the name given to the group's male magnet, its leader, protector—and the centerpiece of a family life whose tenderness and cohesion Dian, as a child, could not have imagined.

Dian was a lonely only child. Her father's drinking caused the divorce that took him out of her life; when her mother, Kitty, remarried when Dian was five, even the mention of George Fossey's name became taboo in the house. Richard Price never adopted Dian. Each night she ate supper in the kitchen with the housekeeper. Her stepfather did not allow her at the dinner table with him and her mother until she was ten. Though Dian's stepfather, a building contractor, seemed wealthy, she largely paid her own way through school. Once she worked as a machine operator in a factory.

Dian seldom spoke of her family to friends, and she carried a loathing for her childhood into her adult life. Long after Dian left the family home in California, she referred to her parents as "the Prices." She would spit on the ground whenever her stepfather's name was mentioned. When her Uncle Bert died, leaving Dian $50,000, Richard Price badgered her with cables to Rwanda, pressing her to contest the will for more money; after Dian's death he had her will overturned by a California court, claiming all her money for himself and his wife.

Her mother and stepfather tried desperately to thwart Dian's plans to go to Africa. They would not help her finance her lifelong dream to go on safari when she was twenty-eight. She borrowed against three years of her salary as an occupational therapist to go. And when she left the States three years later to begin her study of the mountain gorillas, her mother begged her not to go, and her stepfather threatened to stop her.

She chose to remain in the alpine rain forest, as alone as she had ever been. She chose to remain among the King Kong beasts whom the outside world still considered a symbol of savagery, watching their gentle, peaceful lives unfold.

Once Dian, watching Uncle Bert with his family, saw the gigantic male pluck a handful of white flowers with his huge black hands. As the young Digit ambled toward him, the silverback whisked the bouquet back and forth across the youngster's face. Digit chuckled and tumbled into Uncle Bert's lap, "much like a puppy wanting attention," Dian wrote. Digit rolled against the silverback, clutching himself in ecstasy as the big male tickled him with petals.

By the end of her first three months in Rwanda, Dian was following two gorilla groups regularly and observing another sporadically. She divided most of her time between Group 5's fifteen members, ranging on Visoke's southeastern slopes, and Group 4. Group 8, a family of nine, all adult, shared Visoke's western slopes with Group 4.

Dian still could not approach them. Gorilla families guard carefully against intrusion. Each family has at least one member who serves as sentry, typically posted at the periphery of the group to watch for danger—a rival silverback or

a human hunter. Gorilla groups seldom interact with other families, except when females transfer voluntarily out of their natal group to join the families of unrelated silverbacks or when rival silverbacks "raid" a neighboring family for females.

Adult gorillas will fight to the death defending their families. This is why poachers who may be seeking only one infant for the zoo trade must often kill all the adults in the family to capture the baby. Once Dian tracked one such poacher to his village; the man and his wives fled before her, leaving their small child behind.

At first Dian observed the animals from a distance, silently, hidden. Then slowly, over many months, she began to announce her presence. She imitated their contentment vocalizations, most often the *naoom, naoom, naoom,* a sound like belching or deeply clearing the throat. She crunched wild celery stalks. She crouched, eyes averted, scratching herself loud and long, as gorillas do. Eventually she could come close enough to them to smell the scent of their bodies and see the ridges inside the roofs of their mouths when they yawned; at times she came close enough to distinguish, without binoculars, the cuticles of their black, humanlike fingernails.

She visited them daily; she learned to tell by the contour pressed into the leaves which animal had slept in a particular night nest, made from leaves woven into a bathtub shape on the ground. She knew the sound of each individual voice belching contentment when they were feeding. But it was more than two years before she knew the touch of their skin.

Peanuts, a young adult male in Group 8, was the first mountain gorilla to touch his fingers to hers. Dian was lying on her back among the foliage, her right arm outstretched, palm up. Peanuts looked at her hand intently; then he stood, extended his hand, and touched her fingers for an instant. *National Geographic* photographer Bob Campbell snapped the shutter only a moment afterward: that the photo is blurry renders it dreamlike. The 250-pound gorilla's right hand still hangs in

midair. Dian's eyes are open but unseeing, her lips parted, her left hand brought to her mouth, as if feeling for the lingering warmth of a kiss.

Peanuts pounded his chest with excitement and ran off to rejoin his group. Dian lingered after he left; she named the spot where they touched Fasi Ya Mkoni, "the Place of the Hands." With his touch, Peanuts opened his family to her; she became a part of the families she had observed so intimately for the past two years. Soon the gorillas would come forward and welcome her into their midst.

Digit was almost always the first member of Group 4 to greet her. "I received the impression that Digit really looked forward to the daily contacts," she wrote in her book. "If I was alone, he often invited play by flopping over on his back, waving stumpy legs in the air, and looking at me smilingly as if to say, 'How can you resist me?' "

At times she would be literally blanketed with gorillas, when a family would pull close around her like a black furry quilt. In one wonderful photo, Puck, a young female of Group 5, is reclining in back of Dian and, with the back of her left hand, touching Dian's cheek—the gesture of a mother caressing the cheek of a child.

Mothers let Dian hold their infants; silverbacks would groom her, parting her long dark hair with fingers thick as bananas, yet deft as a seamstress's touch. "I can't tell you how rewarding it is to be with them," Dian told a New York crowd gathered for a slide lecture in 1982. "Their trust, the cohesiveness, the tranquility . . ." Words failed her, and her hoarse, breathy voice broke. "It is really something."

Other field workers who joined Dian at Karisoke remember similar moments. Photographer Bob Campbell recalls how Digit would try to groom his sleeves and pants and, finding nothing groomable, would pluck at the hairs of his wrist; most of the people who worked there have pictures of themselves with young gorillas on their heads or in their laps.

But with Dian it was different. Ian Redmond, who first came to Karisoke in 1976, remembers one of the first times he accompanied Dian to observe Group 4. It was a reunion: Dian hadn't been out to visit the group for a while. "The animals filed past us, and each one paused and briefly looked into my face, just briefly. And then each one looked into Dian's eyes, at very close quarters, for half a minute or so. It seemed like each one was queuing up to stare into her face and remind themselves of her place with them. It was obvious they had a much deeper and stronger relationship with Dian than with any of the other workers."

In the early days Dian had the gorillas mostly to herself. It was in 1972 that Bob Campbell filmed what is arguably one of the most moving contacts between two species on record: Digit, though still a youngster, is huge. His head is more than twice the size of Dian's, his hands big enough to cover a dinner plate. He comes to her and with those enormous black hands gently takes her notebook, then her pen, and brings them to his flat, leathery nose. He gently puts them aside in the foliage and rolls over to snooze at Dian's side.

Once Dian spotted Group 4 on the opposite side of a steep ravine but knew she was not strong enough to cross it. Uncle Bert, seeing her, led the entire group across the ravine to her. This time Digit was last in line. "Then," wrote Dian, "he finally came right to me and gently touched my hair. . . . I wish I could have given them all something in return."

At times like these, Dian wept with joy. Hers was the triumph of one who has been chosen: wild gorillas would come to her.

The great intimacy of love is onlyness, of being the loved One. It is the kind of love most valued in Western culture; people choose only one "best" friend, one husband, one wife, one God. Even our God is a jealous one, demanding "Thou shalt have no other gods before Me."

This was a love Dian sought over and over again—as the only child of parents who did not place her first, as the paramour of a succession of married lovers. The love she sought most

desperately was a jealous love, exclusive—not *agape,* the Godlike, spiritual love of all beings, not the uniform, brotherly love, *philia.* The love Dian sought was the love that singles out.

Digit singled Dian out. By the time he was nine he was more strongly attracted to her than were any of the other gorillas she knew. His only age-mates in his family, his half sisters, had left the group or been kidnaped. When Digit heard Dian belch-grunting a greeting, he would leave the company of his group to scamper to greet her. To Digit, Dian was the sibling playmate he lacked. And Dian recognized his longing as clearly as she knew her own image in a mirror.

Dian had had few playmates as a child. She had longed for a pet, but her stepfather wouldn't allow her to keep even a hamster a friend offered, because it was "dirty." He allowed her a single goldfish; she was devastated when it died and was never allowed another.

But Digit was no pet. "Dian's relationship with the gorillas is really the highest form of human-animal relationship," observed Ian Redmond. "With almost any other human-animal relationship, that involves feeding the animals or restraining the animals or putting them in an enclosure, or if you help an injured animal—you do something to the animal. Whereas Dian and the gorillas were on completely equal terms. It was nothing other than the desire to be together. And that's as pure as you can get."

When Digit was young, he and Dian played together like children. He would strut toward her, playfully whacking foliage; she would tickle him; he would chuckle and climb on her head. Digit was fascinated by any object Dian had with her: once she brought a chocolate bar to eat for lunch and accidentally dropped it into the hollow stump of a tree where she was sitting next to Digit. Half in jest, she asked him to get it back for her. "And according to script," she wrote her Louisville friend, Betty Schartzel, "Digit reached one long, hairy arm into the hole and retrieved the candy bar." But the chocolate didn't appeal to

him. "After one sniff he literally threw it back into the hole. The so-called 'wild gorillas' are really very discriminating in their tastes!"

Dian's thermoses, notebooks, gloves, and cameras were all worthy of investigation. Digit would handle these objects gently and with great concentration. Sometimes he handed them back to her. Once Dian brought Digit a hand mirror. He immediately approached it, propped up on his forearms, and sniffed the glass. Digit pursed his lips, cocked his head, and then uttered a long sigh. He reached behind the mirror in search of the body connected to the face. Finding nothing, he stared at his reflection for five minutes before moving away.

Dian took many photos of all the gorillas, but Digit was her favorite subject. When the Rwandan Office of Tourism asked Dian for a gorilla photo for a travel poster, the slide she selected was one of Digit. He is pictured holding a stick of wood he has been chewing, his shining eyes a mixture of innocence and inquiry. He looks directly into the camera, his lips parted and curved as if about to smile. "Come to meet him in Rwanda," exhorts the caption. When his poster began appearing in hotels, banks, and airports, "I could not help feeling that our privacy was on the verge of being invaded," Dian wrote.

Her relationship with Digit was one she did not intend to share. Hers was the loyalty and possessiveness of a silverback: what she felt for the gorillas, and especially Digit, was exclusive, passionate, and dangerous.

No animal, Dian believed, was truly safe in Africa. Africans see most animals as food, skins, money. "Dian had a compulsion to buy every animal she ever saw in Africa," remembers her friend Rosamond Carr, an American expatriate who lives in nearby Gisenyi, "to save it from torture." One day Dian, driving in her Combi van, saw some children on the roadside, swinging a rabbit by the ears. She took it from them, brought it back to camp, and built a spacious hutch for it. Another time it would be a chicken: visiting villagers sometimes brought one to camp, intending, of course, that it be eaten. Dian would keep it as a pet.

Dian felt compelled to protect the vulnerable, the innocent. Her first plan after high school had been to become a veterinarian; after failing chemistry and physics, she chose occupational therapy; with her degree, she worked for a decade with disabled children.

One day Dian came to the hotel in Gisenyi where Rosamond was working as a manager. Dian was holding a monkey. She had seen it at a market, packed in a carton. Rosamond remembers, "I look and see this rotten little face, this big ruff of hair, and I say, 'Dian. I'm sorry, you cannot have that monkey in this hotel!' But Dian spent the night with the animal in her room anyway.

"Luckily for me, she left the next day. I have never seen anything like the mess. There were banana peels on the ceiling, sweet potatoes on the floor; it had broken the water bottle, the glasses had been smashed and had gone down the drain of the washbasin. And with that adorable animal she starts up the mountain."

Kima, as Dian named the monkey, proved no less destructive in camp. Full grown when Dian brought her, Kima bit people, urinated on Dian's typewriter, bit the heads off all her matches, and terrorized students on their way to the latrine, leaping off the roof of Dian's cabin and biting them. Yet Dian loved her, built a hatchway allowing Kima free access to her cabin, bought her toys and dolls, and had her camp cook prepare special foods for her. Kima especially liked french fries, though she discarded the crunchy outsides and ate only the soft centers. "Everyone in camp absolutely hated that animal," Rosamond says. "But Dian loved her."

Another of Dian's rescue attempts occurred one day when she was driving down the main street of Gisenyi on a provisioning trip. Spotting a man walking a rack-ribbed dog on a leash, she slammed on the brakes. "I want to buy that dog," she announced. The Rwandan protested that it was not for

sale. She got out of her Combi, lifted up the sickly animal, and drove off with it.

Rosamond learned of the incident from a friend named Rita who worked at the American embassy. For it was to Rita's home that the Rwandan man returned that afternoon to explain why the dog, which he had been taking to the vet for worming, had never made it to its destination. "Madame, a crazy woman stopped and stole your dog, and she went off with it in a gray van."

"Rita got her dog back," Rosamond continues. Dian had taken it to the hotel where she was staying overnight; when Rita tracked her down, she was feeding the dog steak in her room. "And that was typical of Dian. She had to save every animal she saw. And they loved her—every animal I ever saw her with simply loved her."

When Dian first came to Karisoke, elephants frequently visited her camp. Rosamond used to camp with Dian in those early days before the cabin was built. The elephants came so close that she remembers hearing their stomachs rumble at night. Once she asked Dian if she undressed at night. "Of course not, are you crazy?" Dian replied. "I go to bed in my blue jeans. I have to get up six times at night to see what's happening outside."

One night an elephant selected Dian's tent pole as a scratching post. Another time a wild elephant accepted a banana from Dian's hand. The tiny antelopes called duiker often wandered through camp; one became so tame it would follow Dian's laying hens around. A family of seven bushbucks adopted Karisoke as home, as did an ancient bull buffalo she named Mzee.

Dian's camp provided refuge from the poacher-infested, cattle-filled forest. For centuries the pygmylike Batwa had used these volcanic slopes as a hunting ground. And as Rwanda's human population exploded, the Virungas were the only source of bush meat left, and poaching pressure increased. Today you will find no elephants in these forests; they have all been killed by poachers seeking ivory.

If you look at the Parc National des Volcans from the air, the five volca-

noes, their uppermost slopes puckered like the lips of an old woman, seem to be standing on tiptoe to withdraw from the flood of cultivation and people below. Rwanda is the most densely populated country in Africa, with more than 500 people per square mile. Almost every inch is cultivated, and more than 23,000 new families need new land each year. In rural Rwanda outside of the national parks, if you wander from a path you are more likely to step in human excrement than the scat of a wild animal. The Parc des Volcans is thoroughly ringed with *shambas,* little farm plots growing bananas, peanuts, beans, manioc, and with fields of pyrethrum, daisylike flowers cultivated as a natural insecticide for export. The red earth of the fields seems to bleed from all the human scraping.

The proud, tall Batutsi have few other areas to pasture their cattle, the pride of their existence; everywhere else are shambas. From the start Dian tried to evict the herders from the park, kidnaping their cows and sometimes even shooting them. On the Rwandan side of the mountain, cattle herds were so concentrated, she wrote, that "many areas were reduced to dustbowls." She felt guilty, but the cattle destroyed habitat for the gorillas and other wild animals the park was supposed to protect. Worse were the snares set by the Batwa. Many nights she stayed awake nursing a duiker or bushbuck whose leg had been mangled in a trap. Dian lived in fear that one of the gorillas would be next.

The Batwa do not eat gorillas; gorillas fall victim to their snares, set for antelope, by accident. But the Batwa have for centuries hunted gorillas, to use the fingers and genitals of silverbacks in magic rituals and potions. And now the hunters found a new reason to kill gorillas: they learned that Westerners would pay high prices for gorilla heads for trophies, gorilla hands for ashtrays, and gorilla youngsters for zoos.

In March 1969, only eighteen months into her study, a friend in Ruhengeri came to camp to tell Dian that a young gorilla had been captured from the southern slopes of Mount Karisimbi. All ten adults in the group had been killed so that the baby could be taken for display in the Cologne Zoo. The capture had been approved by the park conservator, who was paid handsomely for his cooperation. But something had gone wrong: the baby gorilla was dying.

Dian took the baby in, a three- to four-year-old female she named Coco. The gorilla's wrists and feet had been bound with wire to a pole when the hunters carried her away from the corpses of her family; she had spent two or three weeks in a coffinlike crate, fed only corn, bananas, and bread, before Dian came to her rescue. When Dian left the park conservator's office, she was sure the baby would die. She slept with Coco in her bed, awakening amid pools of the baby's watery feces.

A week later came another sick orphan, a four- to five-year-old female also intended for the zoo. Her family had shared Karisimbi's southern slope with Coco's; trying to defend the baby from capture, all eight members of her group had died. Dian named this baby Pucker for the huge sores that gave her face a puckered look.

It took Dian two months to nurse the babies back to health. She transformed half her cabin into a giant gorilla play-pen filled with fresh foliage. She began to take them into the forest with her, encouraging them to climb trees and vines. She was making plans to release them into a wild group when the park conservator made the climb to camp. He and his porters descended with both gorillas in a box and shipped them to the zoo in West Germany. Coco and Pucker died there nine years later, within a month of one another, at an age when, in the wild, they would have been mothering youngsters the same age they had been when they were captured.

Thereafter Dian's antipoaching tactics became more elaborate. She learned from a friend in Ruhengeri that the trade in gorilla trophies was flourishing; he had counted twenty-three gorilla heads for sale in that town in one year. As loyal as a silverback, as

wary as a sentry, Dian and her staff patrolled the forest for snares and destroyed the gear poachers left behind in their temporary shelters.

Yet each day dawned to the barking of poachers' dogs. A field report she submitted to the National Geographic Society in 1972 gave the results of the most recent gorilla census: though her study groups were still safe, the surrounding areas of the park's five volcanoes were literally under siege. On Mount Muhavura census workers saw convoys of smugglers leaving the park every forty-five minutes. Only thirteen gorillas were left on the slopes of Muhavura. On neighboring Mount Gahinga no gorillas were left. In the two previous years, census workers had found fresh remains of slain silverbacks. And even the slopes of Dian's beloved Karisimbi, she wrote, were covered with poachers' traps and scarred by heavily used cattle trails; "poachers and their dogs were heard throughout the region."

It was that same year, 1972, that a maturing Digit assumed the role of sentry of Group 4. In this role he usually stayed on the periphery of the group to watch for danger; he would be the first to defend his family if they were attacked. Once when Dian was walking behind her Rwandan tracker, the dark form of a gorilla burst from the bush. The male stood upright to his full height of five and a half feet; his jaw gaped open, exposing black gums and three-inch canines as he uttered two long, piercing screams at the terrified tracker. Dian stepped into view, shoving the tracker down behind her, and stared into the animal's face. They recognized each other immediately. Digit dropped to all fours and ran back to his group.

Dian wrote that Digit's new role made him more serious. No longer was he a youngster with the freedom to roll and wrestle with his playmate. But Dian was still special to him. Once when Dian went out to visit the group during a downpour, the young silverback emerged from the gloom and stood erect before his crouching human friend. He pulled up a stalk of wild celery—a favorite gorilla food

that Digit had seen Dian munch on many times—peeled it with his great hands, and dropped the stalk at her feet like an offering. Then he turned and left.

As sentry, Digit sustained the wound that sapped his strength for the next two years. Dian did not observe the fight, but she concluded from tracking clues that Digit had warded off a raid by the silverback leader of Group 8, who had previously kidnaped females from Group 4. Dian cringed each time she heard him coughing and retching. Digit sat alone, hunched and indifferent. Dian worried that his growth would be retarded. In her field notes she described his mood as one of deep dejection.

This was a time when Dian was nursing wounds of her own. She had hoped that Bob Campbell, the photographer, would marry her, as Hugo van Lawick had married Jane; but Bob left Karisoke for the last time at the end of May 1972, to return to his wife in Nairobi. Then she had a long affair with a Belgian doctor, who left her to marry the woman he had been living with. Dian's health worsened. Her trips overseas for primatology conferences and lecture tours were usually paired with hospital visits to repair broken bones and heal her fragile lungs. She feared she had tuberculosis. She noted her pain in her diary telegraphically: "Very lung-sick." "Coughing up blood." "Scum in urine."

When she was in her twenties, despite her asthma, Dian seemed as strong as an Amazon. Her large-boned but lanky six-foot frame had a coltish grace; one of her suitors, another man who nearly married her, described her as "one hell of an attractive woman," with masses of long dark hair and "eyes like a Spanish dancer." But now Dian felt old and ugly and weak. She used henna on her hair to try to cover the gray. (Dian told a friend that her mother's only comment about her first appearance on a National Geographic TV special was, "Why did you dye your hair that awful orange color?") In letters to friends Dian began to sign off as "The Fossil." She referred to her house as "the Mausoleum." In a cardboard album she made for friends from construction paper and magazine cut-outs, titled "The Saga of Karisoke," she pasted a picture of a mummified corpse sitting upright on a bed. She realized that many of her students disliked her. Under the picture Dian printed a caption: "Despite their protests, she stays on."

By 1976 Dian was spending less and less time in the field. Her lungs and legs had grown too weak for daily contacts; she had hairline fractures on her feet. And she was overwhelmed with paperwork. She became increasingly testy with her staff, and her students feared to knock on her door. Her students wouldn't even see her for weeks at a time, but they would hear her pounding on her battered Olivetti, a task from which she would pause only to take another drag on an Impala *filtrée* or to munch sunflower seeds. Her students were taking the field data on the gorillas by this time: when Dian went out to see the groups, she simply visited with them.

One day, she ventured out along a trail as slippery as fresh buffalo dung to find Group 4. By the time she found them, the rain was driving. They were huddled against the downpour. She saw Digit sitting about thirty feet apart from the group. She wanted to join him but resisted; she now feared that her early contact with him had made him too human-oriented, more vulnerable to poachers. So she settled among the soaking foliage several yards from the main group. She could barely make out the humped black forms in the heavy mist.

On sunny days there is no more beautiful place on earth than the Virungas; the sunlight makes the *Senecio* trees sparkle like fireworks in midexplosion; the gnarled old *Hagenias,* trailing lacy beards of gray-green lichen and epiphytic ferns, look like friendly wizards, and the leaves of palms seem like hands upraised in praise. But rain transforms the forest into a cold, gray hell. You stare out, tunnel-visioned, from the hood of a dripping raincape, at a wet landscape cloaked as if in evil enchantment. Each drop of rain sends a splintering chill into the flesh, and your muscles clench with cold; you can cut yourself badly on the razorlike cutty grass and not even feel it. Even the gorillas, with their thick black fur coats, look miserable and lonely in the rain.

Minutes after she arrived, Dian felt an arm around her shoulders. "I looked up into Digit's warm, gentle brown eyes," she wrote in *Gorillas in the Mist.* He gazed at her thoughtfully and patted her head, then sat by her side. As the rain faded to mist, she laid her head down in Digit's lap.

On January 1, 1978, Dian's head tracker returned to camp late in the day. He had not been able to find Group 4. But he had found blood along their trail.

Ian Redmond found Digit's body the next day. His head and hands had been hacked off. There were five spear wounds in his body.

Ian did not see Dian cry that day. She was almost supercontrolled, he remembers. No amount of keening, no incantation or prayer could release the pain of her loss. But years later she filled a page of her diary with a single word, written over and over: "Digit Digit Digit Digit . . ."

Sex and Society

Any account of hominid evolution would be remiss if it did not at least attempt to explain that most mystifying of all human experiences: our sexuality.

No other aspect of our humanity, whether it be upright posture, tool-making ability, or intelligence in general, seems to elude our intellectual grasp at least as much as it dominates our subjective consciousness. While we are a very long way from reaching a consensus as to why it arose and what it is all about, there is widespread agreement that our very preoccupation with sex is in itself one of the hallmarks of being human. Even as we experience it and analyze it, we exalt it and condemn it. Beyond seemingly irrational fixations, however, there is the further tendency to project our own values upon the observations we make and the data we collect.

There are many who argue quite reasonably that the human bias has been more male- than female-oriented and that the recent "feminization" of anthropology has resulted in new kinds of research and refreshingly new theoretical perspectives. (See "The Myth of the Coy Female" by Carol Tavris and "Sex and the Female Agenda" by Jared Diamond.) Not only should we consider the source when evaluating the old theories, so goes the reasoning, but we should also welcome the source when considering the new. To take one example, traditional theory would have predicted that the reproductive competitiveness of muriqui monkeys, as described in "These Are Real Swinging Primates" by Shannon Brownlee, would be associated with greater size and aggression among males. That this is not so, that making love can be more important than making war, and that females

do not necessarily have to live in fear of competitive males, just goes to show that, even among monkeys, nothing can be taken for granted. Just the very idea that females are helpless in the face of male aggression is called into question by Barbara Smuts in "Apes of Wrath."

Finally, there is the question of the social significance of sexuality in humans. Meredith Small shows in "What's Love Got to Do with It?" that the chimplike bonobos of Zaire use sex to reduce tensions and cement social relations and, in so doing, have achieved a high degree of equality between the sexes. Whether or not we see parallels in the human species, says Small, depends upon our willingness to interpret bonobo behavior as a "modern version of our own ancestors' sex play," and this, in turn, may revolve around our prior theoretical commitments.

Looking Ahead: Challenge Questions

How can muriqui monkeys be sexually competitive and yet gregarious and cooperative?

How does human sexuality differ from that of other creatures?

How has the increasing number of female scientists affected sociobiological assumptions?

What implications does bonobo sexual behavior have for understanding human evolution?

How and why do the reproductive strategies of male and female primates differ?

How do social bonds provide females with protection against abusive males?

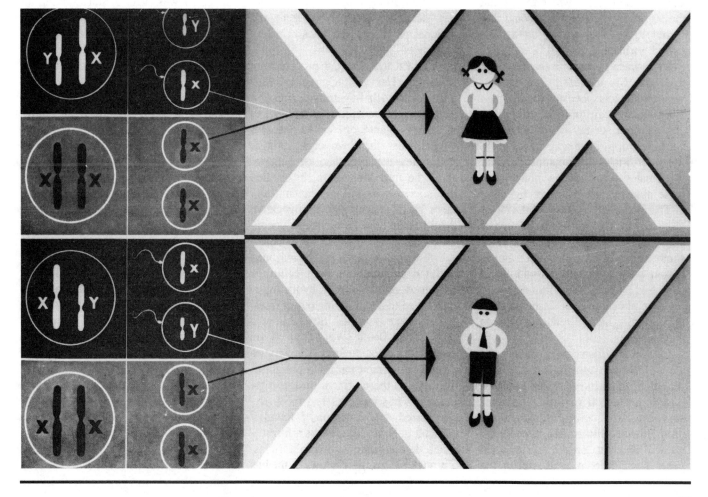

These Are Real Swinging Primates

There's a good evolutionary reason why the rare muriqui of Brazil should heed the dictum 'Make love, not war'

Shannon Brownlee

When I first heard of the muriqui four years ago, I knew right away that I had to see one. This is an unusual monkey, to say the least. To begin with, it's the largest primate in South America; beyond that, the males have very large testicles. We're talking gigantic, the size of billiard balls, which means that the 30-pound muriqui has *cojones* that would look more fitting on a 400-pound gorilla.

But it wasn't prurience that lured me to Brazil. My interest in the muriqui was intellectual, because more than this monkey's anatomy is extraordinary. Muriqui society is untroubled by conflict: troops have no obvious pecking order; males don't compete overtly for females; and, most un-monkeylike, these monkeys almost never fight.

The muriqui is also one of the rarest monkeys in the world. It lives in a single habitat, the Atlantic forest of southeastern Brazil. This mountainous region was once blanketed with forest from São Paulo to Salvador (*see map*), but several centuries of slash-and-burn agriculture have reduced it to fragments.

In 1969 Brazilian conservationist Alvaro Coutinho Aguirre surveyed the remaining pockets of forest and estimated that 2,000 to 3,000 muriquis survived. His data were all but ignored until Russell Mittermeier, a biologist, trained his sights on the muriquis ten years later. Known as Russel of the

Apes to his colleagues, Mittermeier, and American, directs the primate program for the World Wildlife Fund. He hopscotches from forest to forest around the world looking for monkeys in trouble and setting up conservation plans for them. In 1979 he and Brazilian zoologist Celio Valle retraced Aguirre's steps and found even fewer muriquis. Today only 350 to 500 are left, scattered among four state and national parks and six other privately held plots.

In 1981 Karen Strier, then a graduate student at Harvard, approached Mittermeier for help in getting permission to observe the muriqui. He took her to a coffee plantation called Montes Claros, near the town of Caratinga, 250 miles north of Rio de Janeiro. Over the next four years she studied the social behavior of the muriqui there—and came up with a provocative theory about how the monkey's unconventional behavior, as well as its colossal testicles, evolved. She reasoned that the evolution of both could be explained, at least in part, by the muriquis' need to avoid falling out of trees.

Last June I joined Strier, now a professor at Beloit (Wis.) College, on one of her periodic journeys to Montes Claros—clear mountains, in Portuguese. We arrived there after a disagreeable overnight bus trip over bad roads. As we neared the plantation, I found it difficult to believe there was a forest—much less a monkey—within miles. Through the grimy windows of the bus

I saw hillsides stripped down to russet dirt and dotted with spindly coffee plants and stucco farmhouses. There wasn't anything taller than a banana tree in sight. As the bus lurched around the last curve before our stop the forest finally appeared, an island of green amid thousands of acres of coffee trees and brown pastures.

Strier was eager to start looking for the muriquis—"There's a chance we won't see them the whole four days you're here," she said—so no sooner had we dropped our bags off at a cottage on the plantation than we set out along a dirt road into the forest. The trees closed around us—and above us, where they gracefully arched to form a vault of green filigree. Parrots screeched; leaves rustled; a large butterfly flew erratically by on transparent wings. By this time Strier had guided me onto a steep trail, along which she stopped from time to time to listen for the monkeys.

They appeared soon enough, but our first meeting was less than felicitous. After we had climbed half a mile, Strier motioned for me to stop. A muffled sound, like that of a small pig grunting contentedly, came from up ahead. We moved forward a hundred yards. Putting a finger to her lips, Strier sank to her haunches and looked up.

I did the same; twelve round black eyes stared back at me. A group of six muriquis squatted, silent, 15 feet above in the branches, watching us intently.

They began to grunt again. A sharp smell with undertones of cinnamon permeated the air. A light rain began to fall. I held out my palm to catch a drop. It was warm.

"Hey, this isn't rain!" I said.

Strier grinned and pointed to her head. "That's why I wear a hat," she said.

My enthusiasm for the muriquis waned slightly after that. We left them at dusk and retired to the cottage, where Strier described her arrival at Montes Claros four years earlier. Mittermeier acted as guide and interpreter during the first few days of her pilot study. He introduced her to the owner of the 5,000-acre plantation, Feliciano Miguel Abdala, then 73, who had preserved the 2,000-acre forest for more than 40 years. His is one of the only remaining tracts of Atlantic forest, and he agreed to let Strier use it as the site of her study. Then Mittermeier introduced her to the muriquis, assuring her they would be easy to see.

They weren't, and observing them closely is a little like stargazing on a rainy night: not only do you run the risk of getting wet, but you can also spend a lot of time looking up and never see a thing. Mittermeier was adept at spotting the monkeys in the forest, and helped Strier acquire this skill.

But brief glimpses of the monkeys weren't enough. "My strategy was to treat them like baboons, the only other species I'd ever studied," she says. "I thought I couldn't let them out of my sight." She tried to follow on the ground as they swung along in the trees. "They went berserk," she says. They threw branches, shrieked, urinated on her—or worse—and fled.

Even after the muriquis grew accustomed to her, keeping up with them wasn't easy. They travel as much as two miles a day, which is tough for someone picking her way through thick growth on the forest floor. As Strier and a Brazilian assistant learned the muriquis' habitual routes and daily patterns, they cleared trails. These helped, but the muriquis could still travel much faster than she could. "I've often thought the thing to have would be a jet pack," Strier says. "It would revolutionize primatology. Your National Science Foundation grant would include binoculars, pencils, and a jet pack."

Observing muriquis is like stargazing on a rainy night. You may get wet, and you can spend hours looking and seeing nothing.

The monkeys move by brachiating, swinging hand over hand from branch to branch, much like a child on a jungle gym. Only one other group of monkeys brachiates; the rest clamber along branches on all fours. The muriquis' closest relatives are two other Latin American genera, the woolly monkeys and the spider monkeys— hence woolly spider monkey, its English name. But the muriqui is so unlike them that it has its own genus, *Brachyteles,* which refers to its diminutive thumb, an adaptation for swinging through the trees. Its species name is *arachnoides,* from the Greek for spider, which the muriqui resembles when its long arms, legs, and tail are outstretched.

Brachiating is a specialization that's thought to have evolved because it enables primates to range widely to feed on fruit. Curiously, though, muriquis have a stomach designed for digesting leaves. Strier found that their diet consists of a combination of the two foods. They eat mostly foliage, low-quality food for a monkey, but prefer flowers and fruits, like figs and the *caja manga,* which is similar to the mango. Year after year they return to certain trees when they bloom and bear fruit. The rest of the time the muriquis survive on leaves by passing huge quantities of them through their elongated guts, which contain special bacteria to help them digest the foliage. By the end of the day their bellies are so distended with greenery that even the males look pregnant.

We returned to the trail the next morning just after dawn. Condensation trickled from leaves; howler monkeys roared and capuchins cooed and squeaked; a bird sang with the sweet, piercing voice of a piccolo. Then Strier had to mention snakes. "Watch out for snakes," she said blithely, scrambling on all fours up a steep bank. I followed her, treading cautiously.

The muriquis weren't where we had left them the day before. Strier led me along a ridge through a stand of bamboo, where a whisper of movement drifted up from the slope below. Maybe it was just the wind, but she thought it was the muriquis, so we sat down to wait. After a couple of hours, she confessed, "This part of research can get kind of boring."

By noon the faint noise became a distinct crashing. "That's definitely them," she said. "It's a good thing they're so noisy, or I'd never be able to find them." The monkeys, perhaps a dozen of them, swarmed uphill, breaking branches, chattering, uttering their porcine grunts as they swung along. At the crest of the ridge they paused, teetering in indecision while they peered back and forth before settling in some legume trees on the ridgetop. We crept down out of the bamboo to within a few feet of them, so close I noticed the cinnamon scent again—only this time I kept out of range.

Each monkey had its own feeding style. One hung upside down by its tail and drew the tip of a branch to its mouth; it delicately plucked the tenderest shoots with its rubbery lips. Another sat upright, grabbing leaves by the handful and stuffing its face. A female with twins—"Twins have never been seen in this species," Strier whispered as she excitedly scribbled notes—ate with one hand while hanging by the other and her tail. Her babies clung to the fur on her belly.

I had no trouble spotting the males. Their nether parts bulged unmistakably—blue-black or pink-freckled, absurd-looking monuments to monkey virility. I asked Strier what sort of obscene joke evolution was playing on the muriquis when it endowed them thus.

We were about to consider this question when a high-pitched whinnying began a few hundred yards away. Immediately a monkey just overhead pulled itself erect and let out an ear-splitting shriek, which set the entire troop to neighing like a herd of nervous horses. Then they took off down into the valley.

Strier and I had to plunge pell-mell into the underbrush or risk losing them for the rest of the day. "They're chasing the other troop," she said as we galloped downhill. A group of muriquis living on the opposite side of the forest had made a rare foray across the valley.

The monkeys we were observing swung effortlessly from tree to tree; we wrestled with thorny vines, and fell farther and farther behind. An impenetrable thicket forced us to backtrack in search of another route. By the time we caught up to the muriquis, they were lounging in a tree, chewing on unripe fruit and chuckling in a self-satisfied sort of way. The intruding troop was nowhere to be seen. "They must have scared the hell out of those other guys," said Strier, laughing.

Tolerance of another troop is odd behavior for monkeys, but not so odd as the fact that they never fight among themselves.

Such confrontations occur infrequently; muriquis ordinarily tolerate another troop's incursions. Strier thinks they challenge intruders only when there's a valuable resource to defend—like the fruit tree they were sitting in.

Tolerance of another troop is odd behavior for monkeys, but not as odd as the fact that members of a muriqui troop never fight among themselves. "They're remarkably placid," said Strier. "They wait in line to dip their hands into water collected in the bole of a tree. They have no apparent pecking order or dominance hierarchy. Males and females are equal in status, and males don't squabble over fe-

males." No other primate society is known to be so free of competition, not even that of gorillas, which have lately gained a reputation for being the gentle giants of the primate world.

Strier's portrayal of the muriqui brought to mind a bizarre episode that Katharine Milton, an anthropologist at the University of California at Berkeley, once described. While studying a troop of muriquis in another patch of the Atlantic forest, she observed a female mating with a half a dozen males in succession; that a female monkey would entertain so many suitors came as no surprise, but Milton was astonished at the sight of the males lining up behind the female "like a choo-choo train" and politely taking turns copulating. They continued in this manner for two days, stopping only to rest and eat, and never even so much as bared their teeth.

Primates aren't known for their graciousness in such matters, and I found Milton's report almost unbelievable. But Strier confirms it. She says that female muriquis come into heat about every two and a half years, after weaning their latest offspring, and repeatedly copulate during that five- to seven-day period with a number of males. Copulations, "cops" in animal-behavior lingo, last as long as 18 minutes, and average six, which for most primates (including the genus *Homo,* if Masters and Johnson are correct) would be a marathon. Yet no matter how long a male muriqui takes, he's never harassed by suitors-in-waiting.

Strier has a theory to explain the muriqui's benignity, based on a paper published in 1980 by Richard Wrangham, a primatologist at the University of Michigan. He proposed that the social behavior of primates could in large part be predicted by what the females eat.

This isn't a completely new idea. For years primatologists sought correlations between ecological conditions and social structure, but few patterns emerged—until Wrangham's ingenious insight that environment constrains the behavior of each sex differently. Specifically, food affects the sociability of females more than males.

Wrangham started with the generally accepted premise that both sexes in every species have a common aim: to leave as many offspring as possible. But each sex pursues this goal in its own way. The best strategy for a male primate is to impregnate as many females as he can. All he needs, as Wrangham points out, is plenty of sperm and plenty of females. As for the female, no matter how promiscuous she is, she can't match a male's fecundity. On average, she's able to give birth to only one offspring every two years, and her success in bearing and rearing it depends in part upon the quality of food she eats. Therefore, all other things being equal, male primates will spend their time cruising for babes, while females will look for something good to eat.

Wrangham's ingenious insight: the social behavior of primates can in large part be predicted by what the females eat.

Wrangham perceived that the distribution of food—that is, whether it's plentiful or scarce, clumped or evenly dispersed—will determine how gregarious the females of a particular species are. He looked at the behavior of 28 species and found that, in general, females forage together when food is plentiful and found in large clumps—conditions under which there's enough for all the members of the group and the clumps can be defended against outsiders. When clumps become temporarily depleted, the females supplement their diet with what Wrangham calls subsistence foods. He suggest that female savanna baboons, for example, live in groups because their favorite foods, fruits and flowers, grow in large clumps that are easy to defend. When these are exhausted they switch to seeds, insects, and grasses. The females form long-lasting relationships within their groups, and establish stable dominance hierarchies.

Chimpanzees provide an illustration of how females behave when their food isn't in clumps big enough to feed everybody. Female chimps eat flowers, shoots, leaves, and insects, but their diet is composed largely of fruits that are widely scattered and often not very plentiful. They may occasionally gather at a particularly abundant fruit tree, but when the fruit is gone they disperse to forage individually for other foods. Members of the troop are constantly meeting at fruit trees, splitting up, and gathering again.

These two types of female groups, the "bonded" savanna baboons and "fissioning" chimps, as Wrangham calls them, pose very different mating opportunities for the males of their species. As a consequence, the social behavior of the two species is different. For a male baboon, groups of females represent the perfect opportunity for him to get cops. All he has to do is exclude other males. A baboon troop includes a clan of females accompanied by a number of males, which compete fiercely for access to them. For baboons there are few advantages to fraternal cooperation, and many to competition.

Male chimpanzees fight far less over females than male baboons do, principally because there's little point—the females don't stick together. Instead,

the males form strong alliances with their fellows. They roam in gangs looking for females in heat, and patrol their troop's borders against male interlopers.

Wrangham's theory made so much sense, Strier says, that it inspired researchers to go back into the field with a new perspective. She saw the muriqui as an excellent species for evaluating the model, since Wrangham had constructed it before anyone knew the first thing about this monkey. His idea would seem all the more reasonable if it could predict the muriqui's behavior.

It couldn't, at least not entirely. Strier has found that the females fit Wrangham's predictions: they stick together and eat a combination of preferred and subsistence foods, defending the preferred from other troops. But the males don't conform to the theory. "Considering that the females are foraging together, there should be relatively low pressure on the males to cooperate," she says. "It's odd: the males should compete, but they don't."

She thinks that limitations on male competition may explain muriqui behavior. First, the muriquis are too big to fight in trees. "I think these monkeys are at about the limit of size for rapid brachiation," she says. "If they were bigger, they couldn't travel rapidly through the trees. They fall a lot as

it is, and it really shakes them up. I've seen an adult fall about sixty feet, nearly to the ground, before catching hold of a branch. That means that whatever they fight about has got to be worth the risk of falling out of a tree."

Moreover, fighting may require more energy than the muriquis can afford. Milton has estimated the caloric value of the food eaten by a muriqui each day and compared it to the amount of energy she would expect a monkey of that size to need. She concluded that the muriqui had little excess energy to burn on combat.

The restriction that rapid brachiation sets on the muriqui's size discourages competition in more subtle ways, as well. Given that muriquis are polygynous, the male should be bigger than the female, as is almost invariably the case among other polygynous species—but he's not. The link between larger males and polygyny is created by sexual selection, an evolutionary force that Darwin first recognized, and which he distinguished from natural selection by the fact that it acts exclusively on one sex. Sexual selection is responsible for the manes of male lions, for instance, and for the large canines of male baboons.

In a polygynous society, the advantages to being a large male are ob-

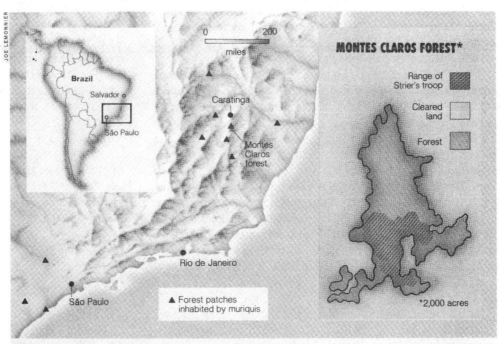

The 350 to 500 surviving muriquis live in ten patches of the Atlantic forest of southeastern Brazil.

vious: he who's biggest is most likely to win the battles over females—and pass on his genes for size. But sexual selection's push toward large males has been thwarted in the muriqui, says Strier. Any competitive benefits greater size might bring a male would be offset in part by the excessive demands on his energy and the costs of falling out of trees.

She believes that the constraints on the males' size have had a profound effect on the muriquis' social behavior. Most important, says Strier, with males and females being the same size, the females can't be dominated, which means they can pick their mates. Most female primates aren't so fortunate: if they copulate with subordinate males, they risk being attacked by dominant ones. But a female muriqui in heat can easily refuse a suitor, simply by sitting down or by moving away.

The size of the males has a profound effect on muriqui behavior. For one thing, they are simply too big to fight in trees.

Fighting not only doesn't help the male muriqui in his quest for cops; it may even harm his chances, since females can shun an aggressive male. Strier believes that females may also be responsible for the male muriquis' canine teeth not being oversized. As a rule, the male's canines are the same size as the female's only in monogamous primate species, but over the generations female muriquis may have mated more readily with males whose teeth were no bigger than their own. In sum, Strier thinks, for a male muriqui the costs of competing are far outweighted by the benefits of avoiding it.

But he has the means to vie for reproductive success and still come across as Mr. Nice Guy: his sperm. Sperm competition, as it's called, is a hot new idea in sociobiology, originally proposed to explain male bonding

in chimpanzees, and, as Milton was the first to suggest, it may explain why the muriqui has such enormous testicles.

The competition is something like a game of chance. Imagine a bucket with a hole in the bottom just big enough for a marble to pass through. People gather round, each with a handful of marbles. They drop their marbles in the bucket, mix them up, and one comes out the bottom. Whoever owns that marble is the winner.

In the sperm competition among male muriquis, the bucket is a female, the marbles are sperm, and winning means becoming a father. No male can be sure it will be his sperm that impregnates a female, since she mates with a number of his fellows. His chances are further complicated by the fact that the female muriqui, like all New World monkeys, gives no visible indication of ovulation; there may be nothing that signals the male (or the female) when during her heat that occurs. So it's to the male's advantage to continue mating as often as the female will have him.

This may sound like monkey heaven, but it puts the male on the horns of a dilemma. If he copulates as often as possible, he could run low on sperm just when the female is ovulating. On the other hand, if he refrains from copulating to save sperm, he may miss his chance at procreating altogether. Selection may have come to his aid, Strier reasons, by acting on his testicles.

Here's a plausible scenario. Suppose a male came along that could produce more sperm than the average muriqui because his testicles were bigger than average. That male would clean up in the reproductive arena. The ratio of testicle size to body weight has been correlated with high sperm count and repeated copulation over a short period in other mammals, and bigger testicles probably also increase the percentage of viable and motile sperm.

If the muriqui's testicles are anything like those of other species, then a male with extra big ones has a slight reproductive advantage. Like a player with more marbles to put in the bucket, a male that can produce more and

better sperm has a better than average chance of impregnating females and passing on this advantageous trait to his sons. Just as important, the outsized organs probably don't cost him much in metabolic energy. Thus, over generations, the muriqui's testicles have grown larger and larger.

Strier's theory has five years of data behind, it, and it's the kind of theory that will stimulate researchers to re-examine their ideas about other species. Yet it isn't her only concern; she concentrates equally on the muriqui's uncertain future. On our last day in the forest we watched the monkeys cross a six-foot gap in the canopy 60 feet above us. One by one they stood poised for a moment on the end of a branch before launching themselves. Strier counted them as they appeared in silhouette against a grey sky. The total was 33, including the twins. "They're up from twenty-two in 1982," she said. "That's a very fast increase."

The muriquis at Montes Claros make up almost one-tenth of the total population of the species, and they're critical to its survival—as are all the other isolated and widely separated troops. Each group's genetic pool is limited, and eventually the troops could suffer inbreeding depression, a decline in fecundity that often appears in populations with little genetic variability.

Strier and Mittermeier predict that one day muriquis will have to be managed, the way game species are in the U.S. They may be transported between patches of forest to provide some gene flow. But that's a dangerous proposition now. There are too few muriquis to risk it, and none has ever bred or survived for long in captivity. "Before my study, conservationists would probably have moved males between forests," Strier says. "That would've been a mistake. I have tentative evidence that in a natural situation the females may be the ones that do the transferring between groups."

For now, though, she thinks the biggest concern isn't managing the monkeys but preventing their habitat from disappearing. Preserving what remains of the Atlantic forest won't be easy, and no one knows this better than Feliciano Miguel Abdala, the man responsible for there being any forest at all at Montes Claros.

Abdala has little formal education, but he's rich; he owns nine plantations besides Montes Claros. His family lives in relative splendor in Caratinga, but he likes to spend the weekdays here. His house is just beyond the edge of the forest, and sunlight filters through the bougainvillea vine entwining the front porch. Chickens can be seen through the cracks in the floorboards, scratching in the dirt under the house. Electric cords are strung crazily from the rafters, and a bare bulb dangles in the center of his office. Abdala removes his straw hat decorously and places it on a chair before sitting at his desk.

Abdala bought the 5,000 acres of Montes Claros in 1944. The region was barely settled then, and smoke still rose from the great burning heaps of slash left from clearing the forest. Abdala's land included one of the last stands of trees. I ask him why he saved it. "I am a conservationist," he says. "For a long time the local people thought I was crazy because I wouldn't cut the forest. I told them not to shoot the monkeys, and they stopped. Now all my workers are crazy, too."

I ask Abdala about his plans for his forest. He rubs his head distractedly and says, vaguely. "I hope it will continue."

Abdala believes the government should buy Montes Claros—plantation and rain forest—to create a nature reserve. He'll probably maintain the forest as long as he lives, but the land is quite valuable, and his heirs might not share his lofty sentiments.

As important as the muriquis have become to understanding social systems, and as much as U.S. conservationists may wish to see these monkeys preserved, Strier thinks that in the end it's up to the Brazilians to save them. She's expecting a three-year grant from the National Science Foundation; part of the money will go toward allowing her to observe the monkeys in other forest patches, watching for variation in their behavior as a test of her ideas. Studies like hers will be critical not only for proving theories but also for ensuring that plans for managing the muriquis will work. The rest of the money will permit her to train seven Brazilian graduate students, because she says, "the future of the muriqui lies with the Brazilians."

The Myth of the Coy Female

Carol Tavris

[Thus] we arrived at the important conclusion that polygamy is the natural order among human beings, just as it is in most species of the animal kingdom. . . . monogamy is responsible for the high incidence of divorce and female grievances in modern society, as well as the genetic deevolution and behavioral degeneration of civilization as a whole. . . . Culture is to blame, and fortunately *culture can be changed.* Mating is the key. [Emphasis in original.]
—Sam Kash Kachigan, *The Sexual Matrix*

Sam Kash Kachigan is not a social scientist; he's just a regular fellow who thinks that the theories of sociobiology offer the best hope of improving relations between women and men. "Mating is the key," he argues. The mating he has in mind, it turns out, would (if we were truly to follow our evolutionary heritage) occur between rich old men and beautiful young girls. Among the annoying contemporary practices that Kachigan laments is the habit of beautiful young girls marrying boys their own age. To Kachigan, in any truly civilized society—that is, one in which our practices fit our sociobiological natures—girls would marry men who were old enough to demonstrate their "true potential":

In every respect, then, it makes much more sense for young women to mate with *older* men, who will have *proven* their genetic endowment as well as their financial and emotional capacity for raising children. [Emphasis in original.]

Why do I suspect that Kachigan is such a man?

The basic ideas behind sociobiology date back to Charles Darwin, who in 1871 described what he considered to be a basic dichotomy in the sexual natures of males and females of all species. Males actively pursue females; they are promiscuous; and those who are strongest, most fit in evolutionary terms, succeed in their sexual conquest. Females, said Darwin, are "comparatively passive"; they may choose their preferred suitor, but then remain monogamous and faithful. That this dichotomy conveniently fit Victorian dating and mating patterns was, naturally, pure coincidence.

For a century after Darwin, research on sexual selection and sexual behavior was based on the belief that males are passionate and undiscriminating (any female in a storm will do), whereas females are restrained, cautious, and highly discriminating in their choice of partner (only a male who meets her shopping list of qualifications will do). According to primatologist Sarah Blaffer Hrdy, this stereotype of "the coy female" has persisted in the public mind—and she adds a phrase that by now should be familiar to us—*"despite the accumulation of abundant openly available evidence contradicting it"* [my emphasis].

The stereotype of the coy female got a major boost in an important paper published in 1948 by Angus John Bateman. Bateman was a distinguished plant geneticist who did dozens of experiments with Drosophila, the tiny fruit fly that many people remember from science experiments in junior high school. Bateman found that successful male fruit flies could, with multiple matings, produce nearly three times as many offspring as the most reproductively successful female. As Hrdy explains, "whereas a male could always gain by mating just one more time, and hence benefit from a nature that made him undiscriminatingly eager to mate, a female, already breeding near capacity after just one copulation, could gain little from multiple mating and should be quite uninterested in mating more than once or twice."

What, you may ask, does a human man have in common with a fruit fly? When it comes to sexual strategies, said Bateman, the answer is everything. Generalizing from his sixty-four experiments with Drosophila to all species, Bateman concluded that there is a universally lopsided division in the sexual natures of all creatures, apart from "a few very primitive organisms." Quite simply, males profit, evolutionarily speaking, from frequent mating, and females do not. This is why, said Bateman, "there is nearly always a combination of an undiscriminating eagerness in the males and a discriminating passivity in the females."

The modern field of sociobiology took this idea still further, attempting to account for complex human social arrangements and customs—warfare and corporate raiding, feeding infants and giving children karate lessons—in terms of the individual's basic need to reproduce his or her genes. Women and men, sociobiologists believe, adopt highly different strategies in order to do this. Males compete with other males for access to desirable females, and their goal is to inseminate as many females as possible. Females, in contrast, are motivated to attach themselves to genetically "superior" males because of the female's greater "investment" in terms of time and energy in her offspring; this, according to sociobiologists, is why females are more faithful and nurturant than males. As biologist Ruth Hubbard observes, "Thus, from the seemingly innocent asymmetries between eggs and sperm [say the sociobiologists] flow such major social consequences as female fidelity, male promiscuity, women's disproportional contribution to the care of children, and the unequal distribution of labor by sex."

Sociobiological explanations of competitive, promiscuous men and choosy, inhibited but flirtatious women fit right in with many elements within the popular culture. "And so it was," Hrdy says, "that 'coyness' came to be the single most commonly mentioned attribute of females in the literature on sociobiology."

It all seems a cruel joke of nature. Certainly many people are convinced, as the King of Siam sings in *The King and I,* that the male is like the honeybee, flitting from flower to flower, "gathering all he can," whereas the female has "honey for just one man." But notice that it is the King who sings that song; until relatively recently, no one was asking Queens for their view of things. Nor were male observers asking why, if human females were so naturally chaste, coy, and monogamous, social taboos from ostracism to death had to be placed on females who indulged in forbidden sexual relationships. For that matter, why did nonmarital affairs need to be forbidden anyway, if females have "honey for just one man"?

Sociobiologists attempt to explain human social customs by drawing on research on nonhuman animals, from the fields of primatology, evolutionary biology, anthropology, and related disciplines. In the last two decades, however, there has been an explosion of new research that casts doubt on many sociobiological assumptions, a change that is largely a result of the growing numbers of women who have entered these fields. Most of the women saw

animal behavior in a different light from most of the male observers who had preceded them. Male primatologists, for example, had tended to observe and emphasize male-male competition and the number of times the male animals "got lucky"; the female animals, to the human men observing them, seemed mysterious and unpredictable. This is not unlike the ways in which human females have seemed mysterious and unpredictable to the human males who have observed *them.*

At first, women who went into these research fields saw the world as they had been taught to see it, through the academic perspective of their mentors. But after a while, they began to ask different questions and to bring different expectations to their observations. Hrdy recalls her own first glimpse of a female langur

> . . . moving away from her natal group to approach and solicit males in an all-male band. At the time, I had no context for interpreting behavior that merely seemed strange and incomprehensible to my Harvard-trained eyes. Only in time, did I come to realize that such wandering and such seemingly "wanton" behavior were recurring events in the lives of langurs.

Eventually, Hrdy learned that female langurs often leave their troops to join up with bands of males; and she also found that often a female, for reasons unknown, "simply takes a shine to the resident male of a neighboring troop." In fact, female langurs (and many other primate species) are able to shift from being in heat once a month to being continuously receptive for weeks at a time, a state not unlike the first phase of (human) love. In many primates, female receptivity is often *situation specific,* rather than being dependent exclusively on cyclical periods of being in heat.

As a result of the efforts of many pioneers like Hrdy, we now know that the females of many animal species do not behave like the patient, coy fruit fly. On the contrary, the females are sexually ardent and can even be called polyandrous (having many male partners). Further, their sexual behavior does not depend simply on the goal of

being fertilized by the male, because in many cases females actively solicit males when they are not ovulating, and even when they are already pregnant. Here are a few illustrations from hundreds of research studies:

- Many species of female birds are promiscuous. In one study, researchers vasectomized the "master" of a blackbird harem . . . but the females nevertheless conceived.
- Many species of female fish are promiscuous. A female shiner perch who is not ovulating will nevertheless mate with many males, collecting sperm and storing them internally until she is ready to ovulate.
- Many species of female cats, notably leopards, lions, and pumas, are promiscuous. A lioness may mate dozens of times with many different partners during the week she is in estrus.
- Many species of female primates are promiscuous. Among savanna baboons and Barbary macaques, females initiate many different brief sexual encounters. Among chimpanzees, Hrdy reports, some females form partnerships with one male, but others engage in communal mating with all males in the vicinity. And among wild tamarin monkeys, a species long thought to be monogamous (at least in captivity), supposedly faithful females will mate with several males. So do female Hanuman langurs, blue monkeys, and redtail monkeys, all primates that were formerly believed to be one-man women. The old notion that primate females typically form "one-male breeding units," as primatologists would say, is now seriously called into question.

In spite of rapidly accumulating evidence that females of many different and varied species do mate "promiscuously" (a word that itself has evaluative overtones), it was not until 1980 or so that researchers realized that this fact threw, well, a monkeywrench into traditional evolutionary theories. Why would females have more copulations than are necessary for conception? Why would they go off with some guy from a neighboring town, whom none of her friends approves of? Why risk losing the genetic father's support by joining the baboon equivalent of Hell's Angels? And the brooding question over all of them, why did female primates develop continuous sexual receptivity?

These questions stimulated a flurry of new theories to explain why female philandering would make as much survival sense as its male counterpart. Most of these new explanations directly resulted from considering the world from the female's point of view. Traditional theories of sexual selection, after all, were based exclusively on the perspective of the male: Males compete for *access* to the female, who apparently is just hanging around waiting to go out and party with the winner. And it's only from a male point of view that multiple female matings can be considered "excessive," or that female sexual interest is even described as her time of "receptivity." Is she passively "receptive" to the active intentions of the male? The word implies that she's just putting up with his annoying lustfulness yet again.

New hypotheses argue that there are genetic benefits for the offspring of sexually adventurous mothers. According to Hrdy's review of these explanations, the "fertility backup" hypothesis assumes that females need sperm from a number of males in order to assure conception by the healthiest sperm. The "inferior cuckold" hypothesis suggests that a female who has a genetically inferior mate will sneak off with a genetically superior male when she is likely to conceive. (I suppose she knows this by the size of his income.) And the "diverse paternity" hypothesis argues that when the environment is unpredictable, females diversify. Over a reproductive lifetime, females who have numerous partners, and thus different fathers for their offspring, improve their offspring's chances for survival.

Other theories look for the social and environmental benefits of female promiscuity to the mother and her infants. The "therapeutic hypothesis" suggests that having lots of partners and multiple orgasms (in some species) makes intercourse and conception more

pleasurable, and therefore more likely to occur. The "keep 'em around" hypothesis maintains that females actively solicit lower-status males (with the tacit approval of dominant males), a behavior that prevents weaker males from leaving the group. Hrdy's own favored theory is what she calls the "manipulation hypothesis," the idea that females mate with numerous males precisely because paternity becomes uncertain. The result is that male partners will be more invested in, and tolerant of, the female's infants. This idea, Hrdy explains,

grew out of a dawning awareness that, first of all, individual females could do a great deal that would affect the survival of their offspring, and second, that males, far from mere dispensers of sperm, were critical features on the landscape where infants died or survived. That is, females were more political, males more nurturing (or at least not neutral), than some earlier versions of sexual selection theory would lead us to suppose.

Both of these points are essential: Not only are females more than passive receptacles of sperm, but also males are more than "mere dispensers of sperm." They don't just mate and run. They have a key role in determining whether infants survive or die. Among primates, there is enormous variation in the extent to which males nurture and protect offspring:

- Among the ruffed lemur, the male tends the nest while the female forages for food.
- Among New World monkeys, males directly care for offspring in half of all species; often, the male is the primary caretaker, carrying the infant on his back, sharing food with it.
- In a rare study of a monogamous species of night monkey, an observer found that during one infant's first week of life, the mother carried it 33 percent of the time, the father 51 percent of the time, and a juvenile member of the troop the remaining time.
- Among baboons, males do not have much direct contact with infants, but they hover nearby protectively and offer what Hrdy calls "quality" time in a very real sense: They increase

the infant's chances of survival. They discourage attacks on the infant from males who are unknown, in both the literal and the Biblical sense, to the mother.

Hrdy's "manipulation hypothesis" assumes that primate males respond more benevolently to the offspring of females with whom they have mated, so the females derive obvious benefits from mating with more than one male. In numerous primate species, the mother's multiple sexual partners act like godfathers to the infant, as primatologist Jeanne Altmann calls them. Each of these males will help care for the female's offspring. Baboon males, many of whom could have served as the model for *Three Men and a Baby*, develop special relationships with the infant, carrying it on their backs in times of danger and protecting it from strangers and hazards. These affectionate bonds are possible because of the mother's closeness to the males, says Hrdy, and because the infant comes to trust these males and seek them out.

The manipulation hypothesis may or may not hold up with further research, as Hrdy acknowledges. It certainly does not apply to most human societies, where husbands do not look too kindly on their wives' "special relationships" with other men, let alone their previous lovers, husbands, and wooers. Hrdy's work, nonetheless, shows that theories depend, first and foremost, on what an observer *observes,* and then on how those observations can be blurred by unconscious expectations. Hrdy initially regarded those "wanton" female langurs as aberrations because their behavior did not fit the established theory. Not until researchers began to speculate on the potential benefits of female promiscuity did they come up with different questions and answers about female sexual behavior than had sociobiologists.

In evolutionary biology, if not in the popular press, the myth of the coy female (and, for that matter, the myth of the absent father) is dead. Hrdy is encouraged by the speed with which primatologists, once aware of the male bias that permeated their discipline, have produced "a small stampede by members of both sexes to study female reproductive strategies." This she takes to be a healthy sign, as do I. But Hrdy cautions against "substituting a new set of biases for the old ones":

That is, among feminist scholars it is now permissible to say that males and females are different, provided one also stipulates that females are more cooperative, more nurturing, more supportive—not to mention equipped with unique moral sensibilities. . . .

Perhaps it is impossible, as biologist Donna Haraway suggests, for any of us to observe the behavior of other species, let alone our own, in a way that does not mirror the assumptions of our own way of life. It is disconcerting, says Hrdy wryly, that primatologists were finding "politically motivated females and nurturing males at roughly

the same time that a woman runs for vice president of the United States and [Garry] Trudeau starts to poke fun at 'caring males' in his cartoons." Informally, scientists admit that their prejudices—such as the tendency to identify with the same sex of the species they are studying—affect their research. One woman primatologist told Hrdy, "I sometimes identify with female baboons more than I do with males of my own species."

The recognition of a male-centered bias in primatology and biology proved to be an enormous step forward, allowing scientists of both sexes to revise their theories of animal behavior. Sociobiologists (and their fans like Sam Kash Kachigan) can no longer justify traditional sex roles, particularly male dominance and female nurturance and

chastity, by appealing to the universality of such behavior in other species. Other species aren't cooperating.

But that is not the only moral of the Parable of the Primates. The female perspective is invaluable, but, as Hrdy warns, a female-centered bias will provide its own set of distortions. Cultural feminists who look to evolutionary biology to explain women's allegedly sweeter, more cooperative ways are on as shaky ground as the antifeminists they would replace.

If the sociobiological heroine is the coy female who is so different from males, the heroine of modern sexology is the lusty female who is just like them. I like her better, but I'm afraid that she, too, is (as a student of mine once inadvertently said) a fig leaf of the imagination. . . .

Sex and the Female Agenda

Most female mammals are anything but subtle when it comes to telling males it's time for sex. Not humans. For good evolutionary reasons, women have found it's much better to keep men in the dark.

Jared Diamond

SCENE ONE: A dimly lit bedroom; a handsome man lies in bed. A beautiful young woman, in nightgown, enters. A diamond wedding ring flashes virtuously on her left hand; her right clutches a small blue strip of paper. She bends, kissing the man's ear. She: "Darling! It's time!"

Scene Two: Same bedroom, same couple, making love; details obscured by dim lighting. Camera shifts to a calendar being flipped by a graceful hand wearing the same diamond wedding ring.

Scene Three: Same couple, blissfully holding smiling baby. He: "Darling! I'm so glad Ovustick told us when it was exactly the right time!"

Last Frame: Close-up of same graceful hand, clutching same small blue strip of paper. Caption reads: OVUSTICK. HOME URINE TEST TO DETECT OVULATION.

If baboons could understand our TV ads, they'd find that one especially hilarious. Neither a male nor a female baboon needs a hormonal test kit to detect the female's ovulation, the sole time when her ovary releases an egg and she can be fertilized. Instead, the skin around the female's vagina swells and turns bright pink. She gives off a distinctive smell. And in case a dumb male still misses the point, she also crouches in front of him and presents her hindquarters. Most other female animals are similar, advertising ovulation with equally bold visual signals, odors, or behaviors.

We consider female baboons with bright pink hindquarters an oddity. In fact, though, we humans are the odd ones—our scarcely detectable ovulations make us members of a small minority in the mammalian world. Granted, quite a few other primates—the group of mammals that includes monkeys, apes, and us—also conceal their ovulations. However, even among primates, baboon-style advertisement remains the majority practice. Human males, in contrast, have no means of detecting when their partners can be fertilized; nor did the women themselves until modern, scientific times.

We're also unusual in our continuous practice of sex, which is a direct consequence of our concealed ovulations. Most other animals confine sex to a brief period of estrus around the advertised time of ovulation. At estrus, a female baboon emerges from a month of sexual abstinence to copulate up to 100 times. A female Barbary macaque does it on an average of every 17 minutes, distributing her favors at least once to every adult male in her troop. Monogamous gibbon couples go several years without sex, until the female weans her most recent infant and comes into estrus again. The gibbons relapse into abstinence as soon as the female becomes pregnant.

We humans, though, practice sex on any day of the month. Hence most human copulations involve women who are unable to conceive at that moment. Not only do we have sex at the "wrong" time of the cycle, but we continue to have sex during pregnancy and after menopause, when we know for sure that fertilization is impossible.

Human sex does seem a monumental waste of effort from a "biological" point of view. After all, most other animals are sensibly stingy of copulatory effort, and for a simple reason—sex is expensive. Just count the ways: for males, sperm production is metabolically costly, so much so that mutant worms with few sperm live longer than normal sperm producing worms. Sex takes time that could otherwise be devoted to finding food. During the sex act itself, couples locked in embrace risk being surprised and killed by a predator or enemy. Finally, fights between males competing for a female often result in serious injury to the female as well as to the males.

So why don't human females behave the way most other animals do and give dear ovulatory signals that would let us restrict sex to moments when it could do us some good?

By now, you may have decided that I'm a prime example of an ivory-tower scientist searching unnecessarily for problems to explain. I can hear several million of you protesting, "There's no problem to explain, except why Jared Diamond is such an idiot. You don't understand why we have sex all the time? Because it's fun, of course!" Unfortunately, that answer isn't enough to satisfy scientists. Humans' concealed ovulations and unceasing receptivity must have evolved for good reasons, and ones that go beyond fun. While engaged in sex, animals, too, look as if they're having fun, to judge by their intense involvement. And with respect to *Homo sapiens,* the species unique in its self-consciousness, it's especially paradoxical that a female as smart and aware as a human should be unconscious of her own ovulation, when female animals as dumb as cows are aware of it.

In speculating about the reasons for our concealed ovulations, scientists tend to focus their attention on another of our unusual features: the helpless condition of our infants, which makes lots of parental care necessary for many years. The young of most mammals start to get their own food as soon as they're weaned and become fully independent soon afterward. Hence most female mammals can and do rear their young without any assistance from the father, whom the mother never sees again after copulation. For humans, though, most food is acquired by means of complex technologies far beyond the dexterity or mental ability of a toddler. As a result, our children have to have food brought to them for over a decade after weaning, and that job is much easier for two parents than for one. Even today, it's hard for a single human mother to rear kids unassisted. It was undoubtedly much harder for our prehistoric ancestors.

Just imagine what married life would be like if women did advertise their ovulations, like female baboons with bright pink derrieres.

Consider the dilemma facing an ovulating cavewoman who has just been fertilized. In many other mammal species, the male would promptly go off in search of another ovulating fe-

male. For the cave-woman, though, that would seriously jeopardize her child's survival. She's much better off if that man sticks around. But what can she do? Her brilliant solution: remain sexually receptive all the time! Keep him satisfied by copulating whenever he wants! In that way, he'll hang around, have no need to look for new sex partners, and will even share his daily hunting bag of meat.

That in essence is the theory that was formerly popular among anthropologists—among male anthropologists, anyway. Alas for that theory, there are numerous male animals that require no such sexual bribes to induce them to remain with their mate and offspring. I already mentioned that gibbons, seeming paragons of monogamous devotion, go years without sex. Male songbirds cooperate assiduously with their mates in feeding the nestlings, although sex ceases after fertilization. Even male gorillas with a harem of several females get only a few sexual opportunities each year because their mates are usually nursing or out of estrus. Clearly, these females don't have to offer the sop of constant sex.

But there's a crucial difference between our human couples and those abstinent couples of other animal species. Gibbons, most songbirds, and gorillas live dispersed over the landscape, with each couple or harem occupying its separate territory. That means few encounters with potential extramarital sex partners. Perhaps the most distinctive feature of traditional human society is that it consists of mated couples living within large groups of other couples, with whom we have to cooperate. A father and mother must work together for years to rear their helpless children, despite being frequently tempted by other fertile adults nearby. The specter of marital disruption by extramarital sex, with its potentially disastrous consequences for parental cooperation in child-rearing, is pervasive in human societies. Somehow we evolved concealed ovulation and constant receptivity to make possible our unique combination of marriage, coparenting, and adulterous temptation. How does that combination work?

More than a dozen new theories have emerged as possible explanations. From this plethora of possibilities, two—the father-at-home theory and the many fathers theory—have survived as most plausible. Yet they are virtually opposite.

The father-at-home theory was developed by University of Michigan biologist Richard Alexander and graduate student Katharine Noonan. To understand it, imagine what married life would be like if women did advertise their ovulations, like female baboons with bright pink derrieres. A husband would infallibly recognize the day on which his wife was ovulating. On that day he would stay home and assiduously make love, in order to fertilize her and pass on his genes. On all other days he would realize from his wife's pallid derriere that lovemaking with her was useless. He would instead wander off in search of other, unguarded pink-hued ladies so he could pass on even more of his genes. He'd feel secure in leaving his wife at home because he'd know she wasn't sexually receptive to men and couldn't be fertilized anyway.

The results of those advertised ovulations would be awful. Fathers wouldn't be at home to help rear the kids, mothers couldn't do the job unassisted, and babies would die in droves. That would be bad for both mothers and fathers because neither would succeed in propagating their genes.

Now let's picture the reverse scenario, in which a husband has no clue to his wife's fertile days. He then has to stay at home and make love with her on as many days of the month as possible if he wants to have much chance of fertilizing her. Another motive for him to stay around is to guard her against other men, since she might prove to be fertile on any day he's away. Besides, now he has less reason to wander, since he has no way of identifying when other women are fertile. The heartwarming outcome: fathers hang around and share baby care, and babies survive. That's good for both mothers and fathers, who have now succeeded in transmitting their genes. In effect, both gain: the woman, by recruiting an active co-parent; the man, because he acquires confidence that the kid he is helping to rear really carries his genes.

Naturally, infanticide horrifies us, but on reflection, one can see that the murderer gains a grisly genetic advantage.

Competing with the father-at-home theory is the many-fathers theory developed by anthropologist Sarah Hrdy of the University of California at Davis. Anthropologists have long recognized that infanticide used to be common in many human societies. Until field studies by Hrdy and others, though, zoologists had no appreciation for how often it occurs among other animals as well. Infanticide is especially likely to be committed by males against infants of females with whom they have never copulated—for example, by intruding males that have supplanted resident males and acquired their harem. The usurper "knows" that the infants killed are not his own. (Of course, animals don't carry out such subtle reasoning consciously; they evolved to behave that way instinctively.) The species in which infanticide has been documented now include our closest animal relatives, chimpanzees and gorillas, in addition to a wide range of other species from lions to African hunting dogs.

Naturally, infanticide horrifies us. But on reflection, one can see that the murderer gains a grisly genetic advantage. A female is unlikely to ovulate as long as she is nursing an infant. By killing the infant, the murderous intruder terminates the mother's lactation and stimulates her to resume estrous cycles. In most cases, the murderer proceeds to fertilize the bereaved mother, who then bears an infant carrying the murderer's own genes.

Infanticide is a serious evolutionary problem for these animal mothers, who lose their genetic investment in their murdered offspring. This problem would appear to be exacerbated if the female

has only a brief, conspicuously advertised estrus. A dominant male could easily monopolize her during that time. All other males would consequently know that the resulting infant was sired by their rival, and they'd have no compunctions about killing the infant.

Suppose, though, that the female has concealed ovulations and constant sexual receptivity. She can exploit these advantages to copulate with many males—even if she has to do it sneakily, when her consort isn't looking. (Hrdy, by the way, argues that the human female's capacity for repeated orgasms may have evolved to provide her with further motivation to do so.)

According to Hrdy's scenario, no male can be confident of his paternity, but many males recognize that they might have sired the mother's infant. If such a male later succeeds in driving out the mother's consort and taking her over, he avoids killing her infant because it could be his own. He might even help the infant with protection and other forms of paternal care. The mother's concealed ovulation will also serve to decrease fighting between males within her own troop, because any single copulation is unlikely to result in conception and hence is no longer worth fighting over.

In short where Alexander and Noonan view concealed ovulation as clarifying paternity and reinforcing monogamy, Hrdy sees it as confusing paternity and effectively undoing monogamy. Which theory is correct?

To find the answer, we turn to the comparative method, a technique often used by evolutionary biologists. By comparing primate species, we can learn which mating habits are shared by those species with concealed ovulation but absent from those with advertised ovulation. As we shall see, the reproductive biology of each species represents the outcome of an experiment, performed by nature, on the benefits and drawbacks of concealing ovulation.

This comparison was recently conducted by Swedish biologists Birgitta Sillén-Tullberg and Anders Møller. First

they tabulated the visible signs of ovulation for 68 species of higher primates (monkeys and apes). They found that some species, including baboons and our close relatives the chimpanzees, advertise ovulation conspicuously. Others, including our close relative the gorilla, exhibit slight signs. But nearly half resemble humans in lacking visible signs. Those species include vervets, marmosets, and spider monkeys, as well as one ape, the orangutan. Thus, while concealed ovulation is still exceptional among mammals in general, it nevertheless occurs in a significant minority of higher primates.

Next, the same 68 species were categorized according to their mating system. Some, including marmosets and gibbons, turn out to be monogamous. More, such as gorillas, have harems of females controlled by a single adult male. Humans are represented in both categories, with some societies being routinely monogamous and others having female harems. But most higher primate species, including chimpanzees, have a promiscuous system in which females routinely associate and copulate with multiple males.

Sillén-Tullberg and Møller then examined whether there was any tendency for more or less conspicuous ovulations to be associated with some particular mating system. Based on a naive reading of our two competing theories, concealed ovulation should be a feature of monogamous species if the father-at-home theory is correct, but of promiscuous species if the many-fathers theory holds. In fact, almost all monogamous primate species analyzed prove to have concealed ovulation. Not a single monogamous primate species has boldly advertised ovulations, which instead are mostly confined to promiscuous species. That seems to be strong support for the father-at-home theory. But the fit of predictions to theory is only a half-fit, because the reverse correlations don't hold up. Yes, most monogamous species have concealed ovulation, yet perpetually pallid derrieres are in turn no guarantee of monogamy. Out of 32 species that hide their ovulations, 22 aren't monogamous but promiscuous or live in harems.

So regardless of what caused concealed ovulation to evolve in the first place, it can evidently be maintained under varied mating systems.

Similarly, while most species with boldly advertised ovulations are promiscuous, promiscuity doesn't require flashing a bright pink behind once a month. In fact, most promiscuous primates either have concealed ovulation or only slight signs. Harem-holding species can have any type of ovulatory signal: invisible, slightly visible, or conspicuous.

These complexities warn us that concealed ovulation will prove to serve different functions according to the particular mating system with which it coexists. To identify these changes of function, Sillén-Tullberg and Møller got the bright idea of studying the family tree of living primate species. Their underlying rationale was that some modern species that are very closely related, and thus presumably derived from a recent common ancestor, differ in mating system or in strength of ovulatory signals. This implies recent evolutionary changes, and the two researchers hoped to identify the points where those changes had taken place.

Here's an example of how the reasoning works. Comparisons of DNA show that humans, chimps, and gorillas are still about 98 percent genetically identical. Measurements of how rapidly such gene changes accumulate, plus discoveries of dated ape and protohuman fossils, show that humans, chimps, and gorillas all stem from an ancestral "missing link" that lived around 9 million years ago. Yet those three modern descendants now exhibit all three types of ovulatory signal: concealed ovulation in humans, slight signals in gorillas, bold advertisement in chimps. This means that only one of those three descendants can be like the missing link, and the other two must have evolved different signals.

A strong hint of the problem's resolution is that many living species of primitive primates—creatures like tarsiers and lemurs—have slight signs of ovulation. The simplest interpretation, then, is that the missing link inherited slight signs from a primitive ancestor,

and that gorillas in turn inherited their slight signs unchanged from the missing link. Within the last 9 million years, though, humans must have lost even those slight signs to develop our present concealed ovulation, while chimps, in contrast, went on to evolve bolder signs.

Identical reasoning can be applied to other branches of the primate family tree, to infer the ovulatory signals of other now-vanished ancestors and the subsequent changes in their descendants. As it turns out, signal switching has been rampant in primate history. There have been several independent origins of bold advertisement (including the example in chimps); many independent origins of concealed ovulation (including humans and orangutans); and several reappearances of slight signs of ovulation, either from concealed ovulation (as in some howler monkeys) or from bold advertisement (as in many macaques).

All right, so that's how we can deduce past changes in ovulatory signals. When we now turn our attention to mating systems, we can use exactly the same procedure. Again, we discover that humans and chimps evolved in opposite directions, just as they did in their ovulatory signals. Studies of living primitive primate behavior suggest that ancestral primates of 60 million years ago mated promiscuously, and that our missing link of 9 million years ago had already switched to single-male harems. Yet if we look at humans, chimps, and gorillas as they are today, we find all three types of mating system represented. Thus, while gorillas may just have retained the harems of their missing link ancestor, chimps must have reinvented promiscuity and humans invented monogamy.

Overall, it appears that monogamy has evolved independently many times in higher primates: in us, in gibbons, and in numerous groups of monkeys. Harems also seem to have evolved many times, including in the missing link. Chimps and a few monkeys apparently reinvented promiscuity, after their recent ancestors had given up promiscuity for harems.

Thus Sillén-Tullberg and Møller have reconstructed both the type of mating system and the ovulatory signal that probably coexisted in numerous primates of the remote past. Now, finally, we can put all this information together to examine what the mating system was at each of the points in our family tree when concealed ovulation evolved.

What it boils down to is that concealed ovulation has repeatedly changed and reversed its function during primate evolutionary history.

Here's what one learns. In considering those ancestral species that did have ovulatory signals and that went on to lose those signals and evolve concealed ovulation, only one was monogamous. The rest of them were promiscuous or harem-holding—one species being the human ancestor that arose from the harem-holding missing link. We thus conclude that promiscuity or harems, not monogamy, are the mating systems associated with concealed ovulation. This conclusion is as predicted by Hrdy's many-fathers theory. It doesn't agree with the father-at-home theory.

But we can also ask the reverse question: What were the ovulatory signals prevailing at each point in our family tree when monogamy evolved? We find that monogamy never evolved in species with bold advertisement of ovulation. Instead, monogamy has usually arisen in species that already had concealed ovulation, and sometimes in species that had slight ovulatory signals. This conclusion agrees with predictions of Alexander and Noonan's father-at-home theory.

How can these two apparently opposite conclusions be reconciled? Recall that Sillén-Tullberg and Møller found that almost all monogamous primates today have concealed ovulation. That result must have arisen in two steps. First, concealed ovulation arose, in a promiscuous or harem-holding species. Then, with concealed ovulation already present, the species switched to monogamy.

Perhaps, by now, you're finding our sexual history confusing. We started out with an apparently simple question deserving a simple answer: Why do we hide our ovulations and have sex on any day of the month? Instead of a simple answer, you're being told that the answer is more complex and involves two steps.

What it boils down to is that concealed ovulation has repeatedly changed and actually reversed its function during primate evolutionary history. That is, both the father-at-home and the many-fathers explanations are valid, but they operated at different times in our evolutionary history. Concealed ovulation arose at a time when our ancestors were still promiscuous or living in harems. At such times, it let the ancestral woman distribute her sexual favors to many males, none of whom could swear that he was the father of her baby but each of whom knew that he might be. As a result, none of those potentially murderous males wanted to harm the baby, and some may actually have protected or helped feed it. Once the woman had

evolved concealed ovulation for that purpose, she then used it to pick a good man, to entice or force him to stay at home with her, and to get him to provide lots of help for her baby.

On reflection, we shouldn't be surprised at this shift of function. Such shifts are very common in evolutionary biology. Natural selection doesn't proceed in a straight line toward a distant perceived goal, in the way that an engineer consciously designs a new product. Instead, some feature that serves one function in an animal begins to serve some other function as well, gets modified as a result, and may even lose the original function. The consequence is frequent reinventions of similar adaptations, and frequent losses, shifts, or even reversals of function as living things evolve.

One of the most familiar examples involves vertebrate limbs. The fins of ancestral fishes, used for swimming, evolved into the legs of ancestral reptiles, birds, and mammals, used for running or hopping on land. The front legs of certain ancestral mammals and reptile-birds then evolved into the wings of bats and modern birds respectively, to be used for flying. Bird wings and

mammal legs then evolved independently into the flippers of penguins and whales respectively, thereby reverting to a swimming function and effectively reinventing the fins of fish. At least two groups of fish descendants independently lost their limbs, to become snakes and legless lizards. In essentially the same way, features of reproductive biology—such as concealed ovulation, boldly advertised ovulation, monogamy, harems, and promiscuity—have repeatedly changed function and been transmuted, reinvented, or lost.

Think of all this the next time you are having sex for fun. Chances are it will be at a nonfertile time of the ovulatory cycle and while you're enjoying the security of a lasting monogamous relationship. At such a time, reflect on how your bliss is made paradoxically possible by precisely those features of your physiology that distinguished your remote ancestors, condemned to harems or promiscuity. Ironically, those wretched ancestors had sex only on rare days of ovulation, when they discharged the biological imperative to fertilize, robbed of leisurely pleasure by their desperate need for swift results.

What's Love Got to Do With It?

Sex Among Our Closest Relatives Is a Rather Open Affair

Meredith F. Small

Maiko and Lana are having sex. Maiko is on top, and Lana's arms and legs are wrapped tightly around his waist. Lina, a friend of Lana's, approaches from the right and taps Maiko on the back, nudging him to finish. As he moves away, Lina enfolds Lana in her arms, and they roll over so that Lana is now on top. The two females rub their genitals together, grinning and screaming in pleasure.

This is no orgy staged for an X-rated movie. It doesn't even involve people—or rather, it involves them only as observers. Lana, Maiko, and Lina are bonobos, a rare species of chimplike ape in which frequent couplings and casual sex play characterize every social relationship—between males and females, members of the same sex, closely related animals, and total strangers. Primatologists are beginning to study the bonobos' unrestrained sexual behavior for tantalizing clues to the origins of our own sexuality.

In reconstructing how early man and woman behaved, researchers have generally looked not to bonobos but to common chimpanzees. Only about 5 million years ago human beings and chimps shared a common ancestor, and we still have much behavior in common: namely, a long period of infant dependency, a reliance on learning what to eat and how to obtain food, social bonds that persist over generations, and the need to deal as a group with many everyday conflicts. The assumption has been that chimp behavior

today may be similar to the behavior of human ancestors.

Bonobo behavior, however, offers another window on the past because they, too, shared our 5-million-year-old ancestor, diverging from chimps just 2 million years ago. Bonobos have been less studied than chimps for the simple reason that they are difficult to find. They live only on a small patch of land in Zaire, in central Africa. They were first identified, on the basis of skeletal material, in the 1920s, but it wasn't until the 1970s that their behavior in the wild was studied, and then only sporadically.

Bonobos, also known as pygmy chimpanzees, are not really pygmies but welterweights. The largest males are as big as chimps, and the females of the two species are the same size. But bonobos are more delicate in build, and their arms and legs are long and slender.

On the ground, moving from fruit tree to fruit tree, bonobos often stand and walk on two legs—behavior that makes them seem more like humans than chimps. In some ways their sexual behavior seems more human as well, suggesting that in the sexual arena, at least, bonobos are the more appropriate ancestral model. Males and females frequently copulate face-to-face, which is an uncommon position in animals other than humans. Males usually mount females from behind, but females seem to prefer sex face-to-face. "Sometimes the female will let a male start to mount from behind," says Amy Parish, a graduate student at the Uni-

versity of California at Davis who's been watching female bonobo sexual behavior in several zoo colonies around the world. "And then she'll stop, and of course he's really excited, and then she continues face-to-face." Primatologists assume the female preference is dictated by her anatomy: her enlarged clitoris and sexual swellings are oriented far forward. Females presumably prefer face-to-face contact because it feels better.

Like humans but unlike chimps and most other animals, bonobos separate sex from reproduction. They seem to treat sex as a pleasurable activity, and they rely on it as a sort of social glue,

---

"Sex is fun. Sex makes them feel good and keeps the group together."

---

to make or break all sorts of relationships. "Ancestral humans behaved like this," proposes Frans de Waal, an ethologist at the Yerkes Regional Primate Research Center at Emory University. "Later, when we developed the family system, the use of sex for this sort of purpose became more limited, mainly occurring within families. A lot of the things we see, like pedophilia and homosexuality, may be leftovers that some now consider unacceptable in our particular society."

Depending on your morals, watching bonobo sex play may be like watching humans at their most extreme and perverse. Bonobos seem to have sex more often and in more combinations than the average person in any culture, and most of the time bonobo sex has nothing to do with making babies. Males mount females and females sometimes mount them back; females rub against other females just for fun; males stand rump to rump and press their scrotal areas together. Even juveniles participate by rubbing their genital areas against adults, although ethologists don't think that males actually insert their penises into juvenile females. Very young animals also have sex with each other: little males suck on each other's penises or French-kiss. When two animals initiate sex, others freely join in by poking their fingers and toes into the moving parts.

One thing sex does for bonobos is decrease tensions caused by potential competition, often competition for food. Japanese primatologists observing bonobos in Zaire were the first to notice that when bonobos come across a large fruiting tree or encounter piles of provisioned sugarcane, the sight of food triggers a binge of sex. The atmosphere of this sexual free-for-all is decidedly friendly, and it eventually calms the group down. "What's striking is how rapidly the sex drops off," says Nancy Thompson-Handler of the State University of New York at Stony Brook, who has observed bonobos at a site in Zaire called Lomako. "After ten minutes, sexual behavior decreases by fifty percent." Soon the group turns from sex to feeding.

But it's tension rather than food that causes the sexual excitement. "I'm sure the more food you give them, the more sex you'll get," says De Waal. "But it's not really the food, it's competition that triggers this. You can throw in a cardboard box and you'll get sexual behavior." Sex is just the way bonobos deal with competition over limited resources and with the normal tensions caused by living in a group. Anthropologist Frances White of Duke University, a bonobo observer at Lomako since 1983, puts it simply: "Sex is fun. Sex makes them feel good and therefore keeps the group together."

Sexual behavior also occurs after aggressive encounters, especially among males. After two males fight, one may reconcile with his opponent by presenting his rump and backing up against the other's testicles. He might grab the penis of the other male and stroke it. It's the male bonobo's way of shaking hands and letting everyone know that the conflict has ended amicably.

Researchers also note that female bonobo sexuality, like the sexuality of female humans, isn't locked into a monthly cycle. In most other animals, including chimps, the female's interest in sex is tied to her ovulation cycle.

"Females rule the business. It's a good species for feminists, I think."

Chimp females sport pink swellings on their hind ends for about two weeks, signaling their fertility, and they're only approachable for sex during that time. That's not the case with humans, who show no outward signs that they are ovulating, and can mate at all phases of the cycle. Female bonobos take the reverse tack, but with similar results. Their large swellings are visible for weeks before and after their fertile periods, and there is never any discernibly wrong time to mate. Like humans, they have sex whether or not they are ovulating.

What's fascinating is that female bonobos use this boundless sexuality in all their relationships. "Females rule the business—sex and food," says De Waal. "It's a good species for feminists, I think." For instance, females regularly use sex to cement relationships with other females. A genital-genital rub, better known as GG-rubbing by observers, is the most frequent behavior used by bonobo females to reinforce social ties or relieve tension. GG-rubbing takes a variety of forms. Often one female rolls on her back and extends her arms and legs. The other female mounts her and they rub their swellings right and left for several seconds, massaging their clitorises against

each other. GG-rubbing occurs in the presence of food because food causes tension and excitement, but the intimate contact has the effect of making close friends.

Sometimes females would rather GG-rub with each other than copulate with a male. Parish filmed a 15-minute scene at a bonobo colony at the San Diego Wild Animal Park in which a male, Vernon, repeatedly solicited two females, Lisa and Loretta. Again and again he arched his back and displayed his erect penis—the bonobo request for sex. The females moved away from him, tactfully turning him down until they crept behind a tree and GG-rubbed with each other.

Unlike most primate species, in which males usually take on the dangerous task of leaving home, among bonobos females are the ones who leave the group when they reach sexual maturity, around the age of eight, and work their way into unfamiliar groups. To aid in their assimilation into a new community, the female bonobos make good use of their endless sexual favors. While watching a bonobo group at a feeding tree, White saw a young female systematically have sex with each member before feeding. "An adolescent female, presumably a recent transfer female, came up to the tree, mated with all five males, went into the tree, and solicited GG-rubbing from all the females present," says White.

Once inside the new group, a female bonobo must build a sisterhood from scratch. In groups of humans or chimps, unrelated females construct friendships through the rituals of shopping together or grooming. Bonobos do it sexually. Although pleasure may be the motivation behind a female-female assignation, the function is to form an alliance.

These alliances are serious business, because they determine the pecking order at food sites. Females with powerful friends eat first, and subordinate females may not get any food at all if the resource is small. When times are rough, then, it pays to have close female friends. White describes a scene at Lomako in which an adolescent female, Blanche, benefited from her established friendship with Freda. "I was following Freda and her boyfriend, and they found a tree that they didn't expect to be there. It was a small tree, heavily in fruit with one of their favorites. Freda went straight up the tree and made a food call to Blanche. Blanche came tearing over—she was quite far away—and went tearing up the tree to join Freda, and they GG-rubbed like crazy."

Alliances also give females leverage over larger, stronger males who otherwise would push them around. Females have discovered there is strength in numbers. Unlike other species of primates, such as chimpanzees or baboons (or, all too often, humans), where tensions run high between males and females, bonobo females are not afraid of males, and the sexes mingle peacefully. "What is consistently different from chimps," says Thompson-Handler, "is the composition of parties. The vast majority are mixed, so there are males and females of all different ages."

HIDDEN HEAT

Standing upright is not a position usually—or easily—associated with sex. Among people, at least, anatomy and gravity prove to be forbidding obstacles. Yet our two-legged stance may be the key to a distinctive aspect of human sexuality: the independence of women's sexual desires from a monthly calendar.

Males in the two species most closely related to us, chimpanzees and bonobos, don't spend a lot of time worrying, "Is she interested or not?" The answer is obvious. When ovulatory hormones reach a monthly peak in female chimps and bonobos, and their eggs are primed for fertilization, their genital area swells up, and both sexes appear to have just one thing on their mind. "These animals really turn on when this happens. Everything else is dropped," says primatologist Frederick Szalay of Hunter College in New York.

Women, however, don't go into heat. And this departure from our relatives' sexual behavior has long puzzled researchers. Clear signals of fertility and the willingness to do something about it bring major evolutionary advantages: ripe eggs lead to healthier pregnancies, which leads to more of your genes in succeeding generations, which is what evolution is all about. In addition, male chimps give females that are waving these red flags of fertility first chance at high-protein food such as meat.

So why would our ancestors give this up? Szalay and graduate student Robert Costello have a simple explanation. Women gave heat up, they say, because our ancestors stood up. Fossil footprints indicate that somewhere around 3.5 million years ago hominids—non-ape primates—began walking on two legs. "In hominids, something dictated getting up. We don't know what it was," Szalay says. "But once it did, there was a problem with the signaling system." The problem was that it didn't work. Swollen genital areas that were visible when their owners were down on all fours became hidden between the legs. The mating signal was lost.

"Uprightness meant very tough times for females working with the old ovarian cycle," Szalay says. Males wouldn't notice them, and the swellings themselves, which get quite large, must have made it hard for two-legged creatures to walk around.

Those who found a way out of this quandary, Szalay suggests, were females with small swellings but with a little less hair on their rears and a little extra fat. It would have looked a bit like the time-honored mating signal. They got more attention, and produced more offspring. "You don't start a completely new trend in signaling," Szalay says. "You have a little extra fat, a little nakedness to mimic the ancestors. If there was an ever-so-little advantage because, quite simply, you look good, it would be selected for."

And if a little nakedness and a little fat worked well, Szalay speculates, then a lot of both would work even better. "Once you start a trend in sexual signaling, crazy things happen," he notes. "It's almost like: let's escalate, let's add more. That's what happens in horns with sheep. It's a particular part of the body that brings an advantage." In a few million years human ancestors were more naked than ever, with fleshy rears not found in any other primate. Since these features were permanent, unlike the monthly ups and downs of swellings, sex was free to become a part of daily life.

It's a provocative notion, say Szalay's colleagues, but like any attempt to conjure up the past from the present, there's no real proof of cause and effect. Anthropologist Helen Fisher of the American Museum of Natural History notes that Szalay is merely assuming that fleshy buttocks evolved because they were sex signals. Yet their mass really comes from muscles, which chimps don't have, that are associated with walking. And anthropologist Sarah Blaffer Hrdy of the University of California at Davis points to a more fundamental problem: our ancestors may not have had chimplike swellings that they needed to dispense with. Chimps and bonobos are only two of about 200 primate species, and the vast majority of those species don't have big swellings. Though they are our closest relatives, chimps and bonobos have been evolving during the last 5 million years just as we have, and swollen genitals may be a recent development. The current unswollen human pattern may be the ancestral one.

"Nobody really knows what happened," says Fisher. "Everybody has an idea. You pays your money and you takes your choice."

—Joshua Fischman

Female bonobos cannot be coerced into anything, including sex. Parish recounts an interaction between Lana and a male called Akili at the San Diego Wild Animal Park. "Lana had just been introduced into the group. For a long time she lay on the grass with a huge swelling. Akili would approach her with a big erection and hover over her. It would have been easy for him to do a mount. But he wouldn't. He just kept trying to catch her eye, hovering around her, and she would scoot around the ground, avoiding him. And then he'd try again. She went around full circle." Akili was big enough to force himself on her. Yet he refrained.

In another encounter, a male bonobo was carrying a large clump of branches. He moved up to a female and presented his erect penis by spreading his legs and arching his back. She rolled onto her back and they copulated. In the midst of their joint ecstasy, she reached out and grabbed a branch from the male. When he pulled back, finished and satisfied, she moved away, clutching the branch to her chest. There was no tension between them, and she essentially traded copulation

for food. But the key here is that the male allowed her to move away with the branch—it didn't occur to him to threaten her, because their status was virtually equal.

Although the results of sexual liberation are clear among bonobos, no one is sure why sex has been elevated to such a high position in this species and why it is restricted merely to reproduction among chimpanzees. "The puzzle for me," says De Waal, "is that chimps do all this bonding with kissing and embracing, with body contact. Why do bonobos do it in a sexual manner?" He speculates that the use of sex as a standard way to underscore relationships began between adult males and adult females as an extension of the mating process and later spread to all members of the group. But no one is sure exactly how this happened.

It is also unclear whether bonobo sexuality became exaggerated only after their split from the human lineage or whether the behavior they exhibit today is the modern version of our common ancestor's sex play. Anthropologist Adrienne Zihlman of the University of California at Santa Cruz, who has used the evidence of fossil

bones to argue that our earliest known non-ape ancestors, the australopithecines, had body proportions similar to those of bonobos, says, "The path of human evolution is not a straight line from either species, but what I think is important is that the bonobo information gives us more possibilities for looking at human origins."

Some anthropologists, however, are reluctant to include the details of bonobo life, such as wide-ranging sexuality and a strong sisterhood, into scenarios of human evolution. "The researchers have all these commitments to male dominance [as in chimpanzees], and yet bonobos have egalitarian relationships," says De Waal. "They also want to see humans as unique, yet bonobos fit very nicely into many of the scenarios, making humans appear less unique."

Our divergent, non-ape path has led us away from sex and toward a culture that denies the connection between sex and social cohesion. But bonobos, with their versatile sexuality, are here to remind us that our heritage may very well include a primordial urge to make love, not war.

Apes of Wrath

Barbara Smuts

Barbara Smuts is a professor of psychology and anthropology at the University of Michigan. She has been doing fieldwork in animal behavior since the early 1970s, studying baboons, chimps, and dolphins. "In my work I combine research in animal behavior with an abiding interest in feminist perspectives on science," says Smuts. She is the author of Sex and Friendship in Baboons.

Nearly 20 years ago I spent a morning dashing up and down the hills of Gombe National Park in Tanzania, trying to keep up with an energetic young female chimpanzee, the focus of my observations for the day. On her rear end she sported the small, bright pink swelling characteristic of the early stages of estrus, the period when female mammals are fertile and sexually receptive. For some hours our run through the park was conducted in quiet, but then, suddenly, a chorus of male chimpanzee pant hoots shattered the tranquility of the forest. My female rushed forward to join the males. She greeted each of them, bowing and then turning to present her swelling for inspection. The males examined her perfunctorily and resumed grooming one another, showing no further interest.

At first I was surprised by their indifference to a potential mate. Then I realized that it would be many days before the female's swelling blossomed into the large, shiny sphere that signals ovulation. In a week or two, I thought, these same males will be vying intensely for a chance to mate with her.

The attack came without warning. One of the males charged toward us, hair on end, looking twice as large as my small female and enraged. As he rushed by he picked her up, hurled her to the ground, and pummeled her. She cringed and screamed. He ran off, rejoining the other males seconds later as if nothing had happened. It was not so easy for the female to return to normal. She whimpered and darted nervous glances at her attacker, as if worried that he might renew his assault

---

Some female primates use social bonds to escape male aggression. Can women?

In the years that followed I witnessed many similar attacks by males against females, among a variety of Old World primates, and eventually I found this sort of aggression against females so puzzling that I began to study it systematically—something that has rarely been done. My long-term research on olive baboons in Kenya showed that, on average, each pregnant or lactating female was attacked by an adult male about once a week and seriously injured about once a year. Estrous females were the target of even more aggression. The obvious question was, Why?

In the late 1970s, while I was in Africa among the baboons, feminists back in the United States were turning their attention to male violence against women. Their concern stimulated a wave of research documenting disturbingly high levels of battering, rape, sexual harassment, and murder. But although scientists investigated this kind of behavior from many perspectives, they mostly ignored the existence of similar behavior in other animals. My observations over the years have convinced me that a deeper understanding of male aggression against females in other species can help us understand its counterpart in our own.

Researchers have observed various male animals—including insects, birds, and mammals—chasing, threatening, and attacking females. Unfortunately, because scientists have rarely studied such aggression in detail, we do not know exactly how common it is. But the males of many of these species are most aggressive toward potential mates, which suggests that they sometimes use violence to gain sexual access.

Jane Goodall provides us with a compelling example of how males use violence to get sex. In her 1986 book, *The Chimpanzees of Gombe,* Goodall describes the chimpanzee dating game. In one of several scenarios, males gather around attractive estrous females and try to lure them away from other males for a one-on-one sexual expedition that may last for days or weeks. But females find some suitors more appealing than others and often resist the advances of less desirable males. Males often rely on aggression to counter female resistance. For example, Goodall describes how Evered, in "persuading" a reluctant Winkle to accompany him into the forest, attacked her six times over the course of five hours, twice severely.

Sometimes, as I saw in Gombe, a male chimpanzee even attacks an estrous female days before he tries to mate with her. Goodall thinks that a male uses such aggression to train a female to fear him so that she will be more likely to surrender to his subsequent sexual advances. Similarly, male hamadryas baboons, who form small harems by kidnapping child brides, maintain a tight rein over their females through threats and intimidation. If, when another male is nearby, a hamadryas female strays even a few feet from her mate, he shoots her a threatening stare and raises his brows. She usually responds by rushing to his side; if not, he bites the back of her neck. The neck bite is ritualized—the male does not actually sink his razor-sharp canines into her flesh—but the threat of injury is clear. By repeating this behavior hundreds of times, the male lays claim to particular females months or even years before mating with them. When a female comes into estrus, she solicits sex only from her harem master, and other males rarely challenge his sexual rights to her.

These chimpanzee and hamadryas males are practicing sexual coercion: male use of force to increase the chances that a female victim will mate with him, or to decrease the chances that she will mate with someone else. But sexual coercion is much more common in some primate species than in others. Orangutans and chimpanzees are the only nonhuman primates whose males in the wild force females to copulate, while males of several other species, such as vervet monkeys and bonobos (pygmy chimpanzees), rarely if ever try to coerce females sexually. Between the two extremes lie many species, like hamadryas baboons, in which males do not force copulation but nonetheless use threats and intimidation to get sex.

These dramatic differences between species provide an opportunity to investigate which factors promote or inhibit sexual coercion. For example, we might expect to find more of it in species in which males are much larger than females—and we do. However, size differences between the sexes are far from the whole story. Chimpanzee and bonobo males both have only a slight size advantage, yet while male chimps frequently resort to force, male bonobos treat the fair sex with more respect. Clearly, then, although size

matters, so do other factors. In particular, the social relationships females form with other females and with males appear to be as important.

In some species, females remain in their birth communities their whole lives, joining forces with related females to defend vital food resources against other females. In such "female bonded" species, females also form alliances against aggressive males. Vervet monkeys are one such species, and among these small and exceptionally feisty African monkeys, related females gang up against males. High-ranking females use their dense network of female alliances to rule the troop; although smaller than males, they slap persistent suitors away like annoying flies. Researchers have observed similar alliances in many other female-bonded species, including other Old World monkeys such as macaques, olive baboons, patas and rhesus monkeys, and gray langurs; New World monkeys such as the capuchin; and prosimians such as the ring-tailed lemur.

Females in other species leave their birth communities at adolescence and spend the rest of their lives cut off from their female kin. In most such species, females do not form strong bonds with other females and rarely support one another against males. Both chimpanzees and hamadryas baboons exhibit this pattern, and, as we saw earlier, in both species females submit to sexual control by males.

This contrast between female-bonded species, in which related females gang together to thwart males, and non-female-bonded species, in which they don't, breaks down when we come to the bonobo. Female bonobos, like their close relatives the chimpanzees, leave their kin and live as adults with unrelated females. Recent field studies show that these unrelated females hang out together and engage in frequent homoerotic behavior, in which they embrace face-to-face and rapidly rub their genitals together; sex seems to cement their bonds. Examining these studies in the context of my own research has convinced me that one way females use these bonds is to form alliances against males, and that, as a

consequence, male bonobos do not dominate females or attempt to coerce them sexually. How and why female bonobos, but not chimpanzees, came up with this solution to male violence remains a mystery.

Female primates also use relationships with males to help protect themselves against sexual coercion. Among olive baboons, each adult female typically forms long-lasting "friendships" with a few of the many males in her troop. When a male baboon assaults a female, another male often comes to her rescue; in my troop, nine times out of ten the protector was a friend of the female's. In return for his protection, the defender may enjoy her sexual favors the next time she comes into estrus. There is a dark side to this picture, however. Male baboons frequently threaten or attack their female friends—when, for example, one tries to form a friendship with a new male. Other males apparently recognize friendships and rarely intervene. The female, then, becomes less vulnerable to aggression from males in general, but more vulnerable to aggression from her male friends.

As a final example, consider orangutans. Because their food grows so sparsely adult females rarely travel with anyone but their dependent offspring. But orangutan females routinely fall victim to forced copulation. Female orangutans, it seems, pay a high price for their solitude.

Some of the factors that influence female vulnerability to male sexual coercion in different species may also help explain such variation among different groups in the same species. For example, in a group of chimpanzees in the Taï Forest in the Ivory Coast, females form closer bonds with one another than do females at Gombe. Taï females may consequently have more egalitarian relationships with males than their Gombe counterparts do.

Such differences between groups especially characterize humans. Among the South American Yanomamö, for instance, men frequently abduct and rape women from neighboring villages and severely beat their wives for suspected adultery. However, among the Aka people of the Central African Republic, male aggression against women has never been observed. Most human societies, of course, fall between these two extremes.

How are we to account for such variation? The same social factors that help explain how sexual coercion differs among nonhuman primates may deepen our understanding of how it varies across different groups of people. In most traditional human societies, a woman leaves her birth community when she marries and goes to live with her husband and his relatives. Without strong bonds to close female kin, she will probably be in danger of sexual coercion. The presence of close female kin, though, may protect her. For example, in a community in Belize, women live near their female relatives. A man will sometimes beat his wife if he becomes jealous or suspects her of infidelity, but when this happens, onlookers run to tell her female kin. Their arrival on the scene, combined with the presence of other glaring women, usually shames the man enough to stop his aggression.

Even in societies in which women live away from their families, kin may provide protection against abusive husbands.

Even in societies in which women live away from their families, kin may provide protection against abusive husbands, though how much protection varies dramatically from one society to the next. In some societies a woman's kin, including her father and brothers, consistently support her against an abusive husband, while in others they rarely help her. Why?

The key may lie in patterns of male-male relationships. Alliances between males are much more highly developed in humans than in other primates, and men frequently rely on such alliances to compete successfully against other men. They often gain more by supporting their male allies than they do by supporting female kin. In addition, men often use their alliances to defeat rivals and abduct or rape their women, as painfully illustrated by recent events in Bosnia. When women live far from close kin, among men who value their alliances with other men more than their bonds with women, they may be even more vulnerable to sexual coercion than many nonhuman primate females.

Like nonhuman primate females, many women form bonds with unrelated males who may protect them from other males. However, reliance on men exacts a cost—women and other primate females often must submit to control by their protectors. Such control is more elaborate in humans because allied men agree to honor one another's proprietary rights over women. In most of the world's cultures, marriage involves not only the exclusion of other men from sexual access to a man's wife—which protects the woman against rape by other men—but also entails the husband's right to complete control over his wife's sexual life, including the right to punish her for real or suspected adultery, to have sex with her whenever he wants, and even to restrict her contact with other people, especially men.

In modern industrial society, many men—perhaps most—maintain such traditional notions of marriage. At the same time, many of the traditional sources of support for women, including censure of abusive husbands by the woman's kinfolk or other community members, are eroding as more and more people end up without nearby kin

or long-term neighbors. The increased vulnerability of women isolated from their birth communities, however, is not just a by-product of modern living. Historically, in highly patriarchal societies like those found in China and northern India, married women lived in households ruled by their husband's mother and male kin, and their ties with their own kin were virtually severed. In these societies, today as in the past, the husband's female kin often view the wife as a competitor for resources. Not only do they fail to support her against male coercive control, but they sometimes actively encourage it. This scenario illustrates an important point: women do not invariably support other women against men, in part because women may perceive their interests as best served through alliances with men, not with other women. When men have most of the power and control most of the resources, this looks like a realistic assessment.

Decreasing women's vulnerability to sexual coercion, then, may require fundamental changes in social alliances. Women gave voice to this essential truth with the slogan SISTERHOOD IS POWERFUL—a reference to the importance of women's ability to cooperate with unrelated women as if they were indeed sisters. However, among humans, the male-dominant social system derives support from political, economic, legal, and ideological institutions that other primates can't even dream of. Freedom from male control—including male sexual coercion—therefore requires women to form alliances with one another (and with like-minded men) on a scale beyond that shown by nonhuman primates and humans in the past. Although knowledge of other primates can provide inspiration for this task, its achievement depends on the uniquely human ability to envision a future different from anything that has gone before.

The Hominid Transition

One of the most intriguing and perplexing gaps in the fossil record of human evolution lies in the transition from a common link between apes and humans to that which is clearly recognizable as a member of our own kind, the family *Hominidae*.

The issues regarding this "black hole" cannot be resolved by simply filling it in with fossil finds. Even if we had the physical remains of the earliest hominids in front of us, which we do not, there is no way such evidence could thoroughly answer the questions that physical anthropologists care most deeply about: How did these creatures move about and get their food? Did they cooperate and share? On what levels did they think and communicate? Did they have a sense of family, let alone a sense of self? In one way or another, all of the previous articles on primates relate to these issues, as do some of the subsequent ones on the fossil evidence. But what sets off this section from the others is that the various authors attempt to deal with these matters head on, even in the absence of direct fossil evidence. Christophe Boesch and Hedwige Boesch-Achermann (in "Dim Forest, Bright Chimps") indicate that some aspects of "hominization" (the acquisition of such humanlike qualities as cooperative hunting and food sharing) may have actually begun in the African rain forest rather than in the dry savanna, as has usually been proposed. They base their suggestions upon some remarkable first-hand observations of forest-dwelling chimpanzees.

As if to show that chimpanzee behavior may vary according to local circumstances, just as we know human behavior does, Craig Stanford (in "To Catch a Colobus") contrasts his observations of chimpanzee hunting in Gombe National Park with the findings of the Boeschs.

Recent research, discussed in "Ape Cultures and Missing Links" by Richard Wrangham, has shown some striking resemblances between apes and humans, hinting that such qualities might have been characteristic of our common ancestor. Following this line of reasoning, teaching a bonobo how to make and use stone tools (as revealed in "Ape at the Brink" by Sue Savage-Rumbaugh and Roger Lewin) allows us to make educated guesses as to the mental and physical processes of our hominid predecessors. There are, nevertheless, significant differences that need to be acknowledged as well. In this vein, Pete Wheeler, in "Human Ancestors Walked Tall, Stayed Cool," shows us how far we have come since our ancestors diverged from that of the apes.

Then there is the issue of the differing roles played by males and females in the transition to humanity and all that it implies with regard to bipedalism, toolmaking, and the origin of the family. As the article "Flesh and Bone," by Ellen Ruppel Shell, puts it, the question is

whether or not the primary theme of human evolution should be summed up as "man the hunter" or "woman the gatherer."

Taken collectively, the articles in this section show how far anthropologists are willing to go to construct theoretical formulations based upon limited data. Although making so much out of so little may be seen as a fault, and may generate irreconcilable differences among theorists, a readiness to entertain new ideas should be welcomed for what it is: a stimulus for more intensive and meticulous research.

Looking Ahead: Challenge Questions

What are the implications for human evolution of tool use, social hunting, and food sharing among Ivory Coast chimpanzees?

What kind of physical and mental skills are required in order to be a stone toolmaker?

How did the common ancestor of apes and humans probably get food?

What is the "man the hunter" theory? What is the "woman the gatherer" theory? What evidence is there for each?

What makes humans so different from the apes?

Why did our ancestors become bipedal?

Dim Forest, Bright Chimps

In the rain forest of Ivory Coast, chimpanzees meet the challenge of life by hunting cooperatively and using crude tools

Christophe Boesch and Hedwige Boesch-Achermann

Taï National Park, Ivory Coast, December 3, 1985. Drumming, barking, and screaming, chimps rush through the undergrowth, little more than black shadows. Their goal is to join a group of other chimps noisily clustering around Brutus, the dominant male of this seventy-member chimpanzee community. For a few moments, Brutus, proud and self-confident, stands fairly still, holding a shocked, barely moving red colobus monkey in his hand. Then he begins to move through the group, followed closely by his favorite females and most of the adult males. He seems to savor this moment of uncontested superiority, the culmination of a hunt high up in the canopy. But the victory is not his alone. Cooperation is essential to capturing one of these monkeys, and Brutus will break apart and share this highly prized delicacy with most of the main participants of the hunt and with the females. Recipients of large portions will, in turn, share more or less generously with their offspring, relatives, and friends.

In 1979, we began a long-term study of the previously unknown chimpanzees of Taï National Park, 1,600 square miles of tropical rain forest in the Republic of the Ivory Coast (Côte d'Ivoire). Early on, we were most interested in the chimps' use of natural hammers—branches and stones—to crack open the five species of hard-shelled nuts that are abundant here. A

sea otter lying on its back, cracking an abalone shell with a rock, is a familiar picture, but no primate had ever before been observed in the wild using stones as hammers. East Africa's savanna chimps, studied for decades by Jane Goodall in Gombe, Tanzania, use twigs to extract ants and termites from their nests or honey from a bees' nest, but they have never been seen using hammerstones.

As our work progressed, we were surprised by the many ways in which the life of the Taï forest chimpanzees differs from that of their savanna counterparts, and as evidence accumulated, differences in how the two populations hunt proved the most intriguing. Jane Goodall had found that chimpanzees hunt monkeys, antelope, and wild pigs, findings confirmed by Japanese biologist Toshida Nishida, who conducted a long-term study 120 miles south of Gombe, in the Mahale Mountains. So we were not surprised to discover that the Taï chimps eat meat. What intrigued us was the degree to which they hunt cooperatively. In 1953 Raymond Dart proposed that group hunting and cooperation were key ingredients in the evolution of *Homo sapiens*. The argument has been modified considerably since Dart first put it forward, and group hunting has also been observed in some social carnivores (lions and African wild dogs, for instance), and even some birds of prey. Nevertheless, many anthropologists still hold that hunting cooperatively and sharing food played a central role in the drama that enabled early hominids, some 1.8 mil-

lion years ago, to develop the social systems that are so typically human.

We hoped that what we learned about the behavior of forest chimpanzees would shed new light on prevailing theories of human evolution. Before we could even begin, however, we had to habituate a community of chimps to our presence. Five long years passed before we were able to move with them on their daily trips through the forest, of which "our" group appeared to claim some twelve square miles. Chimpanzees are alert and shy animals, and the limited field of view in the rain forest—about sixty-five feet at best—made finding them more difficult. We had to rely on sound, mostly their vocalizations and drumming on trees. Males often drum regularly while moving through the forest: pant-hooting, they draw near a big buttress tree; then, at full speed they fly over the buttress, hitting it repeatedly with their hands and feet. Such drumming may resound more than half a mile in the forest. In the beginning, our ignorance about how they moved and who was drumming led to failure more often than not, but eventually we learned that the dominant males drummed during the day to let other group members know the direction of travel. On some days, however, intermittent drumming about dawn was the only signal for the whole day. If we were out of earshot at the time, we were often reduced to guessing.

During these difficult early days, one feature of the chimps' routine proved to be our salvation: nut cracking is a noisy business. So noisy, in fact, that in the early days of French colonial rule, one officer apparently even proposed the theory that some unknown tribe was forging iron in the impenetrable and dangerous jungle.

Guided by the sounds made by the chimps as they cracked open nuts, which they often did for hours at a time, we were gradually able to get within sixty feet of the animals. We still seldom saw the chimps themselves (they fled if we came too close), but even so, the evidence left after a session of nut cracking taught us a great deal about what types of nuts they were eating, what sorts of hammer and anvil tools they were using, and—thanks to the very distinctive noise a nut makes when it finally splits open—how many hits were needed to crack a nut and how many nuts could be opened per minute.

After some months, we began catching glimpses of the chimpanzees before they fled, and after a little more time, we were able to draw close enough to watch them at work. The chimps gather nuts from the ground. Some nuts are tougher to crack than others. Nuts of the *Panda oleosa* tree are the most demanding, harder than any of the foods processed by present-day hunter-gatherers and breaking open only when a force of 3,500 pounds is applied. The stone hammers used by the Taï chimps range from stones of ten ounces to granite blocks of four to forty-five pounds. Stones of any size, however, are a rarity in the forest and are seldom conveniently placed near a nut-bearing tree. By observing closely, and in some cases imitating the way the chimps handle hammerstones, we learned that they have an impressive ability to find just the right tool for the job at hand. Taï chimps could remember the positions of many of the stones scattered, often out of sight, around a panda tree. Without having to run around rechecking the stones, they would select one of appropriate size that was closest to the tree. These mental abilities in spatial representation compare with some of those of nine-year-old humans.

To extract the four kernels from inside a panda nut, a chimp must use a hammer with extreme precision. Time and time again, we have been impressed to see a chimpanzee raise a twenty-pound stone above its head, strike a nut with ten or more powerful blows, and then, using the same hammer, switch to delicate little taps from a height of only four inches. To finish the job, the chimps often break off a small piece of twig and use it to extract the last tiny fragments of kernel from the shell. Intriguingly, females crack panda nuts more often than males, a gender difference in tool use that seems to be more pronounced in the forest chimps than in their savanna counterparts.

After five years of fieldwork, we were finally able to follow the chimpanzees at close range, and gradually, we gained insights into their way of hunting. One morning, for example, we followed a group of six male chimps on a three-hour patrol that had taken them into foreign territory to the north. (Our study group is one of five chimpanzee groups more or less evenly distributed in the Taï forest.) As always during these approximately monthly incursions, which seem to be for the purpose of territorial defense, the chimps were totally silent, clearly on edge and on the lookout for trouble. Once the patrol was over, however, and they were back within their own borders, the chimps shifted their attention to hunting. They were after monkeys, the most abundant mammals in the forest. Traveling in large, multi-species groups, some of the forest's ten species of monkeys are more apt than others to wind up as a meal for the chimps. The relatively sluggish and large (almost thirty pounds) red colobus monkeys are the chimps' usual fare. (Antelope also live in the forest, but in our ten years at Taï, we have never seen a chimp catch, or even pursue, one. In contrast, Gombe chimps at times do come across fawns, and when they do, they seize the opportunity—and the fawn.)

The six males moved on silently, peering up into the vegetation and stopping from time to time to listen for the sound of monkeys. None fed or groomed; all focused on the hunt. We followed one old male, Falstaff, closely,

for he tolerates us completely and is one of the keenest and most experienced hunters. Even from the rear, Falstaff set the pace; whenever he stopped, the others paused to wait for him. After thirty minutes, we heard the unmistakable noises of monkeys jumping from branch to branch. Silently, the chimps turned in the direction of the sounds, scanning the canopy. Just then, a diana monkey spotted them and gave an alarm call. Dianas are very alert and fast; they are also about half the weight of colobus monkeys. The chimps quickly gave up and continued their search for easier, meatier prey.

Shortly after, we heard the characteristic cough of a red colobus monkey. Suddenly Rousseau and Macho, two twenty-year-olds, burst into action, running toward the cough. Falstaff seemed surprised by their precipitousness, but after a moment's hesitation, he also ran. Now the hunting barks of the chimps mixed with the sharp alarm calls of the monkeys. Hurrying behind Falstaff, we saw him climb up a conveniently situated tree. His position, combined with those of Schubert and Ulysse, two mature chimps in their prime, effectively blocked off three of the monkeys' possible escape routes. But in another tree, nowhere near any escape route and thus useless, waited the last of the hunters, Kendo, eighteen years old and the least experienced of the group. The monkeys, taking advantage of Falstaff's delay and Kendo's error, escaped.

The six males moved on and within five minutes picked up the sounds of another group of red colobus. This time, the chimps approached cautiously, nobody hurrying. They screened the canopy intently to locate the monkeys, which were still unaware of the approaching danger. Macho and Schubert chose two adjacent trees, both full of monkeys, and started climbing very quietly, taking care not to move any branches. Meanwhile, the other four chimps blocked off anticipated escape routes. When Schubert was halfway up, the monkeys finally detected the two chimps. As we watched the colobus monkeys take off in literal panic, the appropriateness of the chimpanzees' scientific name—*Pan* came to mind: with a certain stretch of the imagination, the fleeing monkeys could be shepherds and shepherdesses frightened at the sudden appearance of Pan, the wild Greek god of the woods, shepherds, and their flocks.

Taking off in the expected direction, the monkeys were trailed by Macho and Schubert. The chimps let go with loud hunting barks. Trying to escape, two colobus monkeys jumped into smaller trees lower in the canopy. With this, Rousseau and Kendo, who had been watching from the ground, sped up into the trees and tried to grab them. Only a third of the weight of the chimps, however, the monkeys managed to make it to the next tree along branches too small for their pursuers. But Falstaff had anticipated this move and was waiting for them. In the following confusion, Falstaff seized a juvenile and killed it with a bite to the neck. As the chimps met in a rush on the ground, Falstaff began to eat, sharing with Schubert and Rousseau. A juvenile colobus does not provide much meat, however, and this time, not all the chimps got a share. Frustrated individuals soon started off on another hunt, and relative calm returned fairly quickly: this sort of hunt, by a small band of chimps acting on their own at the edge of their territory, does not generate the kind of high excitement that prevails when more members of the community are involved.

So far we have observed some 200 monkey hunts and have concluded that success requires a minimum of three motivated hunters acting cooperatively. Alone or in pairs, chimps succeed less than 15 percent of the time, but when three or four act as a group, more than half the hunts result in a kill. The chimps seem well aware of the odds; 92 percent of all the hunts we observed were group affairs.

Gombe chimps also hunt red colobus monkeys, but the percentage of group hunts is much lower: only 36 percent. In addition, we learned from Jane Goodall that even when Gombe chimps do hunt in groups, their strategies are different. When Taï chimps

arrive under a group of monkeys, the hunters scatter, often silently, usually out of sight of one another but each aware of the others' positions. As the hunt progresses, they gradually close in, encircling the quarry. Such movements require that each chimp coordinate his movements with those of the other hunters, as well as with those of the prey, at all times.

Coordinated hunts account for 63 percent of all those observed at Taï but only 7 percent of those at Gombe. Jane Goodall says that in a Gombe group hunt, the chimpanzees typically travel together until they arrive at a tree with monkeys. Then, as the chimps begin climbing nearby trees, they scatter as each pursues a different target. Goodall gained the impression that Gombe chimps boost their success by hunting independently but simultaneously, thereby disorganizing their prey; our impression is that the Taï chimps owe their success to being organized themselves.

Just why the Gombe and Taï chimps have developed such different hunting strategies is difficult to explain, and we plan to spend some time at Gombe in the hope of finding out. In the meantime, the mere existence of differences is interesting enough and may perhaps force changes in our understanding of human evolution. Most currently accepted theories propose that some three million years ago, a dramatic climate change in Africa east of the Rift Valley turned dense forest into open, drier habitat. Adapting to the difficulties of life under these new conditions, our ancestors supposedly evolved into cooperative hunters and began sharing food they caught. Supporters of this idea point out that plant and animal remains indicative of dry, open environments have been found at all early hominid excavation sites in Tanzania, Kenya, South Africa, and Ethiopia. That the large majority of apes in Africa today live west of the Rift Valley appears to many anthropologists to lend further support to the idea that a change in environment caused the common ancestor of apes and humans to evolve along a different line from those remaining in the forest.

Our observations, however, suggest quite another line of thought. Life in dense, dim forest may require more sophisticated behavior than is commonly assumed: compared with their savanna relatives, Taï chimps show greater complexity in both hunting and tool use. Taï chimps use tools in nineteen different ways and have six different ways of making them, compared with sixteen uses and three methods of manufacture at Gombe.

Anthropologist colleagues of mine have told me that the discovery that some chimpanzees are accomplished users of hammerstones forces them to look with a fresh eye at stone tools turned up at excavation sites. The important role played by female Taï chimps in tool use also raises the possibility that in the course of human evolution, women may have been decisive in the development of many of the sophisticated manipulative skills characteristic of our species. Taï mothers also appear to pass on their skills by actively teaching their offspring. We have observed mothers providing their young with hammers and then stepping in to help when the inexperienced youngsters encounter difficulty. This help may include carefully showing how to position the nut or hold the hammer properly. Such behavior has never been observed at Gombe.

Similarly, food sharing, for a long time said to be unique to humans, seems more general in forest than in savanna chimpanzees. Taï chimp mothers share with their young up to 60 percent of the nuts they open, at least until the latter become sufficiently adept, generally at about six years old. They also share other foods acquired with tools, including honey, ants, and bone marrow. Gombe mothers share such foods much less often, even with their infants. Taï chimps also share meat more frequently than do their Gombe relatives, sometimes dividing a chunk up and giving portions away, sometimes simply allowing beggars to grab pieces.

Any comparison between chimpanzees and our hominid ancestors can only be suggestive, not definitive. But our studies lead us to believe that the process of hominization may have begun independently of the drying of the environment. Savanna life could even have delayed the process; many anthropologists have been struck by how slowly hominid-associated remains, such as the hand ax, changed after their first appearance in the Olduvai age.

Will we have the time to discover more about the hunting strategies or other, perhaps as yet undiscovered abilities of these forest chimpanzees? Africa's tropical rain forests, and their inhabitants, are threatened with extinction by extensive logging, largely to provide the Western world with tropical timber and such products as coffee, cocoa, and rubber. Ivory Coast has lost 90 percent of its original forest, and less than 5 percent of the remainder can be considered pristine. The climate has changed dramatically. The harmattan, a cold, dry wind from the Sahara previously unknown in the forest, has now swept through the Taï forest every year since 1986. Rainfall has diminished; all the rivulets in our study region are now dry for several months of the year.

In addition, the chimpanzee, biologically very close to humans, is in demand for research on AIDS and hepatitis vaccines. Captive-bred chimps are available, but they cost about twenty times more than wild-caught animals. Chimps taken from the wild for these purposes are generally young, their mothers having been shot during capture. For every chimp arriving at its sad destination, nine others may well have died in the forest or on the way. Such priorities—cheap coffee and cocoa and chimpanzees—do not do the economies of Third World countries any good in the long run, and they bring suffering and death to innocent victims in the forest. Our hope is that Brutus, Falstaff, and their families will survive, and that we and others will have the opportunity to learn about them well into the future. But there is no denying that modern times work against them and us.

To Catch a Colobus

Chimpanzees in Gombe National Park band together to kill nearly a fifth of the red colobus monkeys in their range

Craig B. Stanford

Craig B. Stanford is an assistant professor of anthropology at the University of Southern California. His first fieldwork on primates was in Peru, where he studied tamarins. For his Ph.D. at the University of California, Berkeley, Stanford traveled to India and Bangladesh to investigate ecological influences on social behavior in capped langur monkeys. Stanford hopes to expand his research to the evolution of hunting behavior in primates, including humans.

On a sunny July morning, I am sitting on the bank of Kakombe Stream in Gombe National Park, Tanzania. Forty feet above my head, scattered through large fig trees, is a group of red colobus monkeys. This is J group, whose twenty-five members I have come to know as individuals during several seasons of fieldwork. Gombe red colobus are large, long-tailed monkeys, with males sometimes weighing more than twenty pounds. Both sexes have a crown of red hair, a gray back, and buff underparts. The highlight of this particular morning has been the sighting of a new infant, born sometime in the previous two days. As the group feeds noisily on fruit and leaves overhead, I mull over the options for possible names for the infant.

While I watch the colobus monkeys, my attention is caught by the loud and excited pant-hoots of a party of chimpanzees farther down the valley. I judge the group to be of considerable size and traveling in my direction. As the calls come closer, the colobus males begin to give high-pitched alarm calls, and mothers gather up their infants and climb higher into the tree crowns.

A moment later, a wild chorus of panthoots erupts just behind me, followed by a cacophony of colobus alarm calls, and it is obvious to both J group and to me that the chimps have arrived. The male chimps immediately climb up to the higher limbs of the tall albizia tree into which most of the colobus group have retreated. Colobus females and their offspring huddle high in the crown, while a phalanx of five adult males descends to meet the advancing ranks of four adult male chimpanzees, led by seventeen-year-old, 115-pound Frodo. Frodo is the most accomplished hunter of colobus monkeys at Gombe and the only one willing to take on several colobus males simultaneously in order to catch his prey. The other hunters keep their distance while Frodo first scans the group of monkeys, then advances upon the colobus defenders. Time and again he lunges at the colobus males, attempting to race past them and into the cluster of terrified females and infants. Each time he is driven back; at one point, the two largest males of J group leap onto Frodo's back until he retreats, screaming, a few yards away.

A brief lull in the hunt follows, during which the colobus males run to one another and embrace for reassurance, then part to renew their defense. Frodo soon charges again into the midst of the colobus males, and this time manages to scatter them long enough to pluck the newborn from its mother's abdomen. In spite of fierce opposition, Frodo has caught his quarry, and he now sits calmly and eats it while the other hunters and two female chimps—their swollen pink rumps a sign that they are in estrus, a period of sexual receptivity—sit nearby begging for meat. The surviving colobus monkeys watch nervously from a few feet away. Minutes later, the mother of the dead infant attempts to approach, perhaps to try to rescue her nearly consumed offspring. She is chased, falls from the tree to the forest floor, and is pounced upon and killed by juvenile chimpanzees that have been watching the hunt from below. Seconds later, before these would-be hunters have had a chance to begin their meal, Wilkie, the chimpanzee group's dominant male, races down the tree and steals the carcass from them. He shows off his prize by charging across the forest floor, dead colobus in hand, and then, amid a frenzy of chimps eager for a morsel, he sits down to share the meat with his ally Prof and two females from the hunting party.

Until Jane Goodall observed chimpanzees eating meat in the early 1960s, they were thought to be complete vegetarians. We now know that a small but regular portion of the diet of wild chimps consists of the meat of such mammals as bush pigs, small antelopes, and a variety of monkey species.

For example, chimpanzees in the Mahale Mountains of Tanzania, the Taï forest of Ivory Coast, and in Gombe all regularly hunt red colobus monkeys. Documenting the effect of such predation on wild primate populations, however, is extremely difficult because predators—whether chimps, leopards, or eagles—are generally too shy to hunt in the presence of people. The result is that even if predation is a regular occurrence, researchers are not likely to see it, let alone study it systematically.

Gombe is one of the few primate study sites where both predators and their prey have been habituated to human observers, making it possible to witness hunts. I have spent the past four field seasons at Gombe, studying the predator-prey relationship between the 45-member Kasakela chimpanzee community and the 500 red colobus monkeys that share the same twelve square miles of Gombe National Park. Gombe's rugged terrain is composed of steep slopes of open woodland, rising above stream valleys lush with riverine forest. The chimpanzees roam across these hills in territorial communities, which divide up each day into foraging parties of from one to forty animals. So far, I have clocked in more than a thousand hours with red colobus monkeys and have regularly followed the chimps on their daily rounds, observing some 150 encounters between the monkeys and chimps and more than 75 hunts. My records, together with those of my colleagues, show that the Gombe chimps may kill more than 100 red colobus each year, or nearly one-fifth of the colobus inhabiting their range. Most of the victims are immature monkeys under two years old. Also invaluable have been the data gathered daily on the chimps for the past two decades by a team of Tanzanian research assistants.

One odd outcome of my work has been that I am in the unique position of knowing both the hunters and their victims as individuals, which makes my research intriguing but a bit heart wrenching. In October 1992, for example, a party of thirty-three chimpanzees encountered my main study group, J, in upper Kakombe valley.

The result was devastating from the monkeys' viewpoint. During the hour-long hunt, seven were killed; three were caught and torn apart right in front of me. Nearly four hours later, the hunters were still sharing and eating the meat they had caught, while I sat staring in disbelief at the remains of many of my study subjects.

Determined to learn more about the chimp-colobus relationship, however, I continued watching, that day and many others like it. I will need several more field seasons before I can measure the full impact of chimpanzee hunting on the Gombe red colobus, but several facts about hunting and its effects on the monkeys have already emerged. One major factor that determines the outcome of a hunt in Gombe is the number of male chimps involved. (Although females also hunt, the males are responsible for more than 90 percent of all colobus kills.) Red colobus males launch a courageous counterattack in response to their chimpanzee predators, but their ability to defend their group is directly proportional to the number of attackers and does not seem to be related to the number of defenders. The outcome of a hunt is thus almost always in the hands of the chimps, and in most instances, the best the monkeys can hope to do is limit the damage to a single group member rather than several. Chimpanzees have a highly fluid social grouping pattern in which males tend to travel together while females travel alone with their infants. At times, however, twenty or more male and female chimpanzees forage together. When ten or more male chimps hunt together, they are successful nine times out of ten, and the colobus have little hope of escape.

Hunting success depends on other factors as well. Unlike the shy red-tailed and blue monkeys with which they share the forest (and which are rarely hunted by the chimps), red colobus do not flee the moment they hear or see chimps approaching. Instead, the red colobus give alarm calls and adopt a vigilant wait-and-see strategy, with males positioned nearest the potential attackers. The alarm calls increase in frequency and intensity as the

chimpanzees draw closer and cease only when the chimps are sighted beneath the tree. Then, the colobus sit quietly, watching intently, and only if the chimps decide to hunt do the colobus males launch a counterattack. The monkeys' decision to stand and fight rather than flee may seem maladaptive given their low rate of successful defense. I observed, however, that when the monkeys scatter or try to flee, the chimps nearly always pursue and catch one or more of them.

Fleeing red colobus monkeys are most likely to be caught when they have been feeding on the tasty new leaves of the tallest trees, the "emergents," which rise above the canopy. When these trees are surrounded by low plant growth, they frequently become death traps because the only way colobus can escape from attacking chimps is to leap out of the tree—often into the waiting arms of more chimpanzees on the ground below.

One of my primary goals has been to learn why a party of chimps will eagerly hunt a colobus group one day while ignoring the same group under seemingly identical circumstances on another. One determinant is the number of males in the chimp party: the more males, the more likely the group will hunt. Hunts are also undertaken mainly when a mother colobus carrying a small infant is visible, probably because of the Gombe chimps' preference for baby red colobus, which make up 75 percent of all kills. The situation is quite different in the Taï forest, where half of the chimp kills are adult colobus males (see "Dim Forest, Bright Chimps," Natural History, September 1991). Christophe and Hedwige Boesch have shown that the Taï chimps hunt cooperatively, perhaps because red colobus monkeys are harder to catch in the much taller canopy of the Taï rainforest. Successful Taï chimp hunters also regularly share the spoils. In contrast, each chimp in Gombe appears to have his own hunting strategy.

The single best predictor of when Gombe chimps will hunt is the presence of one or more estrous females in the party. This finding, together with the earlier observation by Geza Teleki (formerly of George Washington University) that male hunters tend to give meat preferentially to swollen females traveling with the group, indicates that Gombe chimps sometimes hunt in order to obtain meat to offer a sexually receptive female. Since hunts also occur when no estrous females are present, this trade of sex for meat cannot be the exclusive explanation, but the implications are nonetheless intriguing. Gombe chimps use meat not only for nutrition; they also share it with their allies and withhold it from their rivals. Meat is thus a social, political, and even reproductive tool. These "selfish" goals may help explain why the Gombe chimps do not cooperate during a hunt as often as do Taï chimps.

Whatever the chimps want the monkey meat for, their predation has a severe effect on the red colobus population. Part of my work involves taking repeated censuses of the red colobus groups living in the different valleys that form the hunting range of our chimpanzees. In the core area of the range, where hunting is most intense, predation by chimps is certainly the limiting factor on colobus population growth: red colobus group size in this area is half that at the periphery of the chimps' hunting range. The number of infant and juvenile red colobus monkeys is particularly low in the core area; most of the babies there are destined to become chimpanzee food.

The proportion of the red colobus population eaten by chimps appears to fluctuate greatly from year to year, and probably from decade to decade, as the number of male hunters in the chimpanzee community changes. In the early 1980s, for instance, there were five adult and adolescent males in the Kasakela chimp community, while today there are eleven; the number of colobus kills per year has risen as the number of hunters in the community has grown.

Furthermore, a single avid hunter may have a dramatic effect. I estimate that Frodo has single-handedly killed up to 10 percent of the entire red colobus population within his hunting range. I now want to learn if chimps living in forests elsewhere in Africa are also taking a heavy toll of red colobus monkeys. If they are, then they will add support to the theory that predation is an important limiting factor on wild primate populations and may also influence some aspects of behavior. Meanwhile, I will continue to watch in awe as Frodo and his fellow hunters attack my colobus monkeys and to marvel at the courageousness of the colobus males that risk their lives to protect the other members of their group.

Flesh & Bone

The story of human evolution has been largely written by male scientists, says Adrienne Zihlman. And they've left women out of the plot.

Ellen Ruppel Shell

Ellen Ruppel Shell is codirector of the program in science journalism at Boston University. This is her first article for DISCOVER.

A tour of Adrienne Zihlman's laboratories at the University of California at Santa Cruz is an exercise in the macabre. There's a hairy arm and ghostly white hand, the last vestiges of a chimp, poking over the rim of what looks like a stainless steel pasta pot. There's a pair of human cadavers laid out neatly under a sky-blue tarpaulin like slabs of bread dough beneath a towel. There's a sealed aquarium swarming with carnivorous beetles polishing off the last bits of flesh from a dog's skull. And then there are the bones.

"I collected most of these from road kills," Zihlman says, pulling drawer after drawer of animal skeletons, zipped neatly in thick plastic bags. "We've got skeletons of possum, lynx, fox, raccoon, and coyote."

The bones are here because Zihlman, a paleoanthropologist, contrives and tests ideas about the origins of humankind by studying the remains of living things. The dog skull, for instance, will be used to highlight differences between primates like us and other mammals for her anatomy students. And the human cadavers will become part of the university's burgeoning collection of primate skeletons.

Such remnants and fragments of life allow Zihlman to wrestle with some of the most thorny and fundamental issues in human evolution. Not content to tinker at the periphery of her field, she's challenged colleagues to rethink long-standing ideas about how people came to be. One of these cherished notions is that the initiation of hunting by males made us what we are today: it spurred us to stand on two feet and freed up our hands for toolmaking. Most important, it forged the first social contract between males and females.

"—the origin of the human line can be traced to a change in locomotion."

Zihlman has come up with evidence showing this is not necessarily the way things were. She has fashioned a convincing argument that activities pursued by females, such as food gathering and caring for infants, were just as likely as hunting to be behind two-legged walking and more stable social relationships. The major reason that male hunting has been portrayed as a seminal event in human development, she says, is that men—male anthropologists, in particular—were doing the portraying.

"Science has been characterized as a masculine activity," she says. "I think that is precisely the case."

Zihlman is firm in her belief that the evolutionary picture has been distorted by people who have yet to acknowledge their own biases. Much of this distortion occurs, she says, when researchers attempt to force the archeological and fossil record into the context of modern Western male-dominated culture.

For her views, Zihlman has endured more than a little criticism, ranging from thoughtless dismissals in academic journals to vilification at international meetings. Her ideas have caused her to clash with prominent researchers, such as Donald Johanson, famed as the discoverer of "Lucy," a 3-million-year-old ancestor and a cornerstone of the latest version of the male-hunting hypothesis. Although clearly shaken by these battles, Zihlman, at 50, shows no signs of retreat. "I don't have ulcers," she says, alternating dainty bites of avocado and yogurt in a lunch break wedged between meetings. "I give them to other people."

The daughter of working-class parents who felt that their children should be "exposed to everything," Zihlman has fond memories of trips to the Field Museum in Chicago, where she grew up, and to her grandmother's farm in Iowa. "My grandmother gave me my first lesson in neuroanatomy," she says. "I learned that a chicken really does run around after it gets its head cut off." Zihlman attended Miami University in Ohio, where, after reading Margaret Mead's *Coming of Age in Samoa* for a class, she decided to major in anthropology. When she found that Miami University had no such department, she transferred to the University of Colorado in Boulder, which did. She completed her degree and, in 1962, went on to do graduate work at Berkeley, where she set herself to the task of finding out how our ancestors began to walk.

"In monkeys," she explains, "seventy percent of bones, muscle, and skin are devoted to moving around. And almost everything about what humans are is about being bipeds. I was always interested in the anatomical basis of behavior, and locomotion is the key thing—the origin of the human line can be traced to a change in locomotion. It was the first feature to definitely indicate a hominid."

As part of her doctoral research, Zihlman traveled to the Transvaal Museum in Pretoria, South Africa, to measure, describe, and photograph the fossilized bones of our oldest preserved ancestors, the australopithecines. Her thesis compared chimpanzees with these hominids and detailed the changes in the angle of the hip sockets, the length and thickness of the thigh-bones, and other modifications that made bipedality possible for these creatures. And— ironically, in light of her current views—Zihlman included in her thesis a conjecture about the origins of the two-legged gait: it evolved, she wrote, to allow more efficient movement on long hunting trips through the African savanna. "Later I changed my mind

about the hunting part," she says, smiling.

That Zihlman included hunting at all is a measure of the pervasive influence of the idea at the time. Hunting, in the 1960s, had become the standard by which most prehistoric artifacts were judged, and upon which most theories of early humans were built. The objects that supported the "man the hunter" theory were pieces of sharpened bone found in close proximity to antelope skeletons in some South African caves—caves inhabited by australopithecines 2 million years ago. Zihlman saw these bones herself during her travels; she also met the man who found them, the late anthropologist Raymond Dart. "At the time I met Dart I received my own personal demonstration of how the bones were used to kill animals, a sort of reenactment of the film *2001*," she recalls.

And it was the males—assumed by Dart and most other anthropologists, including Zihlman's adviser, Sherwood Washburn, to be larger, more powerful, and unencumbered by the care of young children—who did the hunting. Anthropologists went on to reconstruct a strictly sex-specific picture of early human social life: males invented and built tools, hunted the food and dragged it home to hungry females, who were tied, helpless, to the hearth by demanding infants. Pair-bonds between males and females formed for the good of the species, monogamy giving a male more reason to defend his home and family.

But after completing her thesis in 1967, Zihlman got to thinking that there was something wrong with this picture of early human life. The reconstruction placed females at the mercy of the all-powerful male and gave them no purpose other than to reproduce and serve. In 1970 she heard a paper delivered by anthropologist Sally Linton entitled "Woman the Gatherer: Male Bias in Anthropology" that seemed to crystallize her thoughts. Linton argued that men's control and dominance of women should be seen as a modern institution, not a natural fact arising from our animal past.

That same year some holes in the man-the-hunter hypothesis started to appear when paleontologist C. K. Brain of the Transvaal Museum examined some bite and gnaw marks on animal bones in australopithecine caves near Dart's celebrated sites. Brain concluded that the bones had been dragged in by leopards, not hunted and killed by hominids. Similar marks on the hominid bones themselves led Brain to suggest that Dart had the food chain going in the wrong direction: australopithecines were more likely to be prey than predators.

"I was teaching a course in biology and the culture of sex roles at Santa Cruz at the time," Zihlman says, "and I had become alerted to the fact that women had essentially been invisible as far as evolutionary theory was concerned. The man-the-hunter theory has the male bringing home food to one female and to their offspring, and this pair-bond was key. But the data anthropologists were getting on the !Kung, a hunter-gatherer society in southern Africa, showed the women were pretty independent. They controlled the resources they collected."

"The whole idea of pair-bonding is completely overrated. It's a typical projection of the ideal American family life back in time."

!Kung women, according to studies by anthropologist Richard Lee, gathered the tubers, roots, and fruits that are the staples of the !Kung diet. No one was suggesting that the !Kung were living australopithecines, but they lived in a similar environment and had only rudimentary technology. So it was possible that early hominid female life resembled the life of !Kung women, who weren't tethered to a home base by child rearing. Instead they carried their young while walking miles across the savanna in search of food. And food gathering, Zihlman realized, was just as likely as hunting to have brought early hominids to their feet.

"A lot of the African vegetation went underground or grew thick coverings to protect itself through the dry season," she says. "Hominids needed tools to dig these fruits out or crack them open." Carrying these tools around, and using them to dig, required free hands. And that left only two feet for walking.

"Woman the gatherer," was not the absolute prehistoric truth, but it was a scenario at least as plausible as "man the hunter."

It also seemed less and less likely to Zihlman that the carnivorous, monogamous early hominids presumed by the hunting hypothesis would have evolved out of chimps or other apes who ate little meat and were rather fluid in their sexual relationships.

"I had done my dissertation on chimps," Zihlman says, "and I knew that chimps did not form stable pair-bonds and that the males came and went. Females and their offspring formed the core group within chimp societies. The whole idea of pair-bonding is completely overrated. It's a typical projection of the ideal American family life back in time. Gradually I was developing a view of human origins that took into consideration comparative anatomy, ape and human behavior, and the fossil record. And it firmly put women into the story of human evolution."

Zihlman began publishing a series of papers that drew these lines of evidence together to show gathering was an alternate route for human evolution

to travel. "Woman the gatherer," in Zihlman's view, was not the absolute prehistoric truth. But it was a scenario at least as plausible as "man the hunter."

Many of Zihlman's arguments rested on her contention that current primate behavior, particularly that of chimpanzees, provided a rough analogue to early hominid behavior. This reasoning was supported by studies done in the mid-1960s, comparing chimp and human blood proteins. Biochemists Vincent Sarich and the late Allan Wilson of Berkeley had used similarities in these proteins to show that chimps are our closest living primate relatives, probably diverging from a common ancestor 5 million years ago.

Zihlman became particularly intrigued by Sarich's speculation that the common ancestor must have looked something like a small chimpanzee (since animals tend to evolve into larger forms). To Zihlman, this called to mind the pygmy chimp, a species native to the Zaire River basin in equatorial Africa. The notion that pygmy chimps were "living links" to man's earliest ancestor was first put forward by Harvard zoologist Harold J. Coolidge in 1933. But it was never substantiated, partly because not enough was known of this rare and elusive animal to take the theory beyond the realm of speculation.

"There just weren't that many pygmy chimps around to study," Zihlman says. So in 1973, along with Douglas Cramer, a graduate student at the University of Chicago who was studying pygmy chimp cranial features, Zihlman visited the African Museum in Belgium (Zaire was a Belgian colony until 1960) to study the museum's relatively extensive collection of pygmy and common chimp skeletons. Zihlman and Cramer found that pygmy chimps differ from common chimps in a number of ways—their trunks are smaller, their arms are shorter, and their legs are a little longer.

Zihlman then observed pygmy chimps in action at the Yerkes Primate Center in Atlanta. She noticed that they often assumed a two-legged position when climbing, jumping, and standing. In essence, though arboreal

by nature, pygmy chimps seemed to her to be poised on the edge of bipedalism. At Yerkes, Zihlman also observed that pygmy chimps seemed more social and less aggressive—more "human"—than common chimps.

"All the differences were in the human direction," Zihlman says. "Here, it seemed to me, was an even better prototype for the ancestral human than the common chimpanzee. The pygmy chimp was a living ape that seemed to represent the 'transition' from quadrupedal to bipedal locomotion."

Zihlman went so far as to compare the pygmy chimpanzee with "Lucy," the hominid fossil skeleton found at Hadar in Ethiopia in 1974 by Donald Johanson, then at the Cleveland Museum of Natural History. The similarities between the two seemed striking. They were almost identical in brain and body size and stature, and the major differences, the hip and knee, could well be the outgrowth of Lucy's adaptation to bipedal walking. In an illustration Zihlman published in 1982 of Lucy's left side abutting the right side of a pygmy chimp, the two creatures looked almost like one image in a slightly cracked mirror.

One consequence of tying Lucy so tightly to pygmy chimp anatomy was that Zihlman theorized that males and females of Lucy's species were about the same size, as are male and female pygmy chimps. This innocuous-sounding conclusion unleashed a storm of controversy that's still raging today. For one of Johanson's cherished assertions about Lucy's kind is that males were much bigger than females.

Johanson and his colleague Tim White of Berkeley had taken Lucy's skeleton and similar bones from other hominids and put them into one species—the oldest one known, they claim, the ancestor to all other forms—called *Australopithecus afarensis*. Some of these individuals were much bigger than others, and Johanson and White accounted for this by saying that the big ones were males. "It was necessary for the females to be small," says Johanson, who is now president of the Institute of Human Origins in Berkeley. "If they were large, they wouldn't have been able to survive on the low quality food available to them and still nourish their fetus and their young. The males needed to be large in order to compete for the females and to protect the troop." Another of Johanson's colleagues, Owen Lovejoy of Kent State University, has proposed that these large males had begun to come down from the trees to hunt far and wide for food to bring up to their patiently waiting mates. So males invented walking, and man the hunter stalked again.

Zihlman, not surprisingly, doesn't buy this idea at all. No such extreme size difference between sexes has been noted before in other australopithecine species, she says, no such difference exists in chimps, and there is no con-

---

"Studies in anthropology, sociolinguistics, and psychology document that men and women communicate differently."

---

vincing evidence that it exists in Johanson's fossils. It's entirely possible, Zihlman argues, that Johanson has taken two or more different species, including a big one and a small one, and lumped them together.

"Johanson is asserting, not demonstrating, that there is this extreme size difference in *Australopithecus afarensis*," Zihlman says. "But he's never published a detailed argument with measurements to back this up. In modern humans, males and females can be distinguished most of the time by the pelvis, but in *Australopithecus afarensis,* with only one pelvis—Lucy's—there can be no comparisons. For all we know, Lucy might just as well have been a male as a female. As far as I'm concerned, it's a toss-up. All we know for sure is that Lucy was small."

Such statements infuriate Johanson and White, who have all but based their careers on the theory that *Australopithecus afarensis* is a single species. "What we are looking at in these samples is one geologic second in time," Johanson says. "And what we have

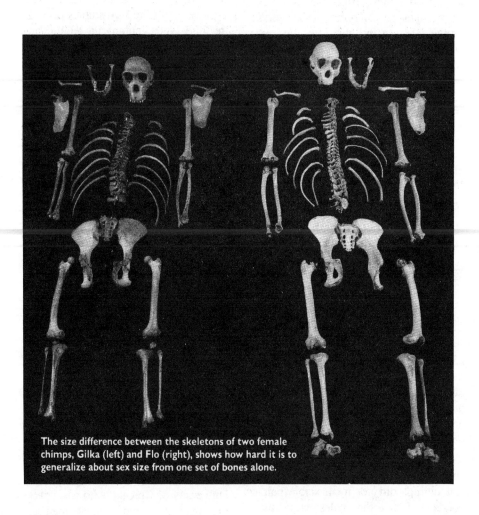

The size difference between the skeletons of two female chimps, **Gilka** (left) and **Flo** (right), shows how hard it is to generalize about sex size from one set of bones alone.

found in that slice are some rather large and some rather small specimens of the same species." In the first place, he says scornfully, anatomical comparisons show the pygmy chimp is no more closely related to Lucy than it is to modern humans. He argues that the teeth of pygmy chimps are much smaller than those of early hominids. Turning Zihlman's argument back on itself, he notes that while male and female pygmy chimps differ very little in anatomy, the fossil record shows dramatic differences between male and female hominids.

"I don't put a lot of emphasis on this

notion of a 'living link,' " Johanson scoffs. "But in any case, it is clear to me that the pygmy chimp does not appear to be it."

White goes even further, accusing Zihlman of distorting her science to fit her politics. "The bones that were found at Hadar don't have labels, so you can interpret them any way you want," White says. "You could also go to a cemetery, dig up the bones you find there, and say that each skeleton represents a different species. The question is whether the fossils show so much variation that we need to recognize them as two different species, and they don't. We've grounded our inference in the modern world. If Zihlman must accommodate the data of the real world to some politically correct manifesto, then she should write science fiction, not science."

Zihlman agrees that differences exist

between the early hominids and the pygmy chimp, especially when it comes to their teeth. But the chimp is only a model of the early ancestor, one that probably shared both common and pygmy chimp characteristics. "I never meant to suggest that pygmy chimps were exactly like the apes that gave rise to humans," she says. "But in terms of their body proportions, the early hominids are more like the pygmy chimp than any other ape."

As for the rest of the dispute, Zihlman contends that she is willing to defend her view in an open forum, but that so far she has not been asked to sit on the same podium with Johanson and White to argue her case. Zihlman says she tried to take measurements of the fossils herself, but when she asked Johanson for permission to see the collection when it was under his care at the Cleveland Museum, he said she could do so only if she gave him the right to review any paper she wrote on the fossils before she sent it to a journal. "The implication was that he had to approve it," Zihlman says. She felt that was a form of censorship and refused to work under those conditions. The collection has since been returned to Ethiopia.

Stalemates such as this, marked by displays of territoriality and possessiveness, have frustrated Zihlman to the point where this past year she decided to do something about it. With Mary Ellen Morbeck, an anthropologist at the University of Arizona, she organized a conference on female biology and evolution with the explicit purpose of encouraging free and open speech among the participants. To that end, the organizers invited only women researchers.

The move was immediately denounced as sexist by critics, both in her profession and in the press. However, Zihlman remains staunch in its defense, saying that what distinguished conference participants was not the possession of two X chromosomes but a supportive and cooperative attitude. "Studies in anthropology, sociolinguistics, and psychology document that men and women communicate differently," she says. "Men frequently use

language to dominate. My goal at the meeting was that language be used to communicate. And as it turned out, that is what happened. People didn't compete with one another, they didn't interrupt one another, they actually listened. We got down to the nitty-gritty very fast and could really discuss the issues."

" . . . fossils and bones are not enough—they just don't tell you all that much."

For Zihlman, one of the key issues was the effect females have on the evolution of their species. "Natural selection is operating at all stages of life, not just reproduction," she says. But most studies of the role of the individual in evolution focus on mating, she notes, on getting the genes into the next generation. "But mating is a male-dominated behavior," Zihlman says. "For females, that's just the beginning. They're involved with offspring for their whole lives."

This is particularly true for primates. "A primate lives a long life, with distinct stages of development," she says. "Chimps live twelve to thirteen years before they reproduce, and there are many things that happen during that time that can influence the health of their offspring. They can get sick or lose a parent or be injured. This is experiential, not genetic. To say genes are the be-all and end-all renders everything else—development, life experience, ecology—irrelevant. I don't think getting genes into the next generation is what it's all about. To reduce everything to genes is boring and simplistic, and I don't buy it for a minute. It might work for insects or birds—though I have my doubts—but it certainly does not work for primates." This is what Zihlman calls looking at the whole organism—and that, ulti-

mately, is what she is interested in.

"I knew early on that if I was going to survive in this business, I was going to have to diversify," Zihlman says. "If I had committed myself to studying fossils and only fossils, I would have failed, because when it comes to looking at fossils, access is everything and I knew I wouldn't get it. But fossils and bones are not enough—they just don't tell you all that much. For example, there's nothing in the bones of the goats in the Galápagos Islands that says they should be able to climb trees and eat vegetation. But they do. The whole point is trying to conceptualize what was on the bones and what it allowed individuals to do."

To illustrate the limitations of trying to reconstruct the life of an animal from its fossil remains, Zihlman walks back to one of the tall wooden bone chests in her laboratory and pulls out drawers filled with plastic bags that hold the remains of common chimps brought to her by Jane Goodall from her research center at Gombe National Park in Tanzania. Goodall has followed these chimps for 30 years, sometimes from birth to death, and has kept detailed records on the events that shaped their lives. Zihlman and Morbeck examined and measured the bones and skulls of the Gombe chimps to determine the extent to which these events also shaped their bodies.

For example, the bones of one chimp, "Gilka," are small and asymmetrical. If Gilka were the only female skeleton available, this might lead researchers to speculate that females of her species are much smaller than males. In fact, Gilka was stunted by a bout of polio suffered early in life. She bore four infants, all of whom died. By contrast "Flo," who lived to be 43, had a larger skeleton than many Gombe males and gave birth to five infants, three of whom survived to adulthood.

"The variation among individuals regardless of sex is enormous," Zihlman says. "What the Gombe studies show is the importance of the individual in evolution, that it's reductionist to focus on a few bones. Animals don't go from gene to protein to bone, there's a life that is lived in between. Bone is one of the most mobile of tissues, it is constantly being turned over and remodeled—the bone you have today is not the same bone you had six years ago."

Zihlman says she and Morbeck plan to use the data they glean from the Gombe bones in concert with Goodall's field notes to provide a basis for reevaluating what has been written about the early hominid fossil record. "Here we have information on the skeleton and information on the whole animal," she says. "From this we have a holistic view, we can learn what bones really tell us, and what they do not. There's a good chance we might overturn a lot of what's been accepted about the fossil record. Right now, it's only a work in progress, but of course, I hope it shakes things up."

It's likely to. Fossil hunters are often strongly wedded to their interpretations of their finds and are unlikely to accept criticism gracefully, particularly from an outsider who has not devoted her life to the dig. While not oblivious to the possibility of backlash, Zihlman is not overly concerned about it.

"In science, being outspoken and being a woman is an unforgivable combination," she says. "I've learned to live with the consequences. For me, there is no choice. I really don't know how to play the game, even if I wanted to."

Ape at the Brink

*Two and a half million years ago, an early human ancestor recognized
that in a stone lies the possibility of a tool. Four years ago a chimp
named Kanzi saw that, too.*

Sue Savage-Rumbaugh and Roger Lewin

*Sue Savage-Rumbaugh is a professor
of biology and psychology at Georgia
State University, at whose Language
Research Center she conducts her research with bonobos. She has written
over 100 scientific papers and two
books; her volume* Ape Language:
From Conditioned Response to Symbol *was published in 1986. Savage-
Rumbaugh's research is supported by
the National Institute of Child Health
and Human Development.*

*Roger Lewin is the author of numerous
books about human origins, including*
Origins, People of the Lake, *and* Origins Reconsidered, *all coauthored with
Richard Leakey. In 1989 he received
the inaugural Lewis Thomas Award for
excellence in the communication of the
life sciences, and in 1991 he was core-
cipient, with E. O. Wilson, of the Society for Conservation Biology's annual
award for services to conservation.*

Threading my way along the sandy
path toward the ocean shore, I sought
out the rhythmic sound of shifting surf.
The faint light of predawn arrived, and
I could see the rock coastline ahead,
then the silhouette of distant mountains. I was near the small coastal
village of Cascais, Portugal, attending
a meeting organized by the Wenner-
Gren Foundation, a group legendary in
anthropological circles. Scientists invited to these meetings are kept away
from the rest of the world and encouraged to examine each other's views in
small, intense discussions.

Walking along the beach, I mused
over the talk of the past few days. Bill
Calvin, a neurobiologist at the University of Washington, had been telling us
about the extraordinary accuracy and
power with which humans can throw.
We humans aren't the only primates
with the raw ability—chimpanzees and
gorillas can throw, too, as visitors to
zoos sometimes discover to their cha-
grin. Apes do not enjoy being stared at
and frequently throw things at visitors
in an attempt to make them leave. But
humans are far better at throwing than
apes are, and the development of this
skill, Bill had pointed out, was clearly
important during man's evolution from
an apelike ancestor. In particular, the
accurate hurling of stones became a
valuable means of hunting and self-
defense against predators.

Another scientist in our group, archeologist Nick Toth of Indiana University, was also interested in throwing,
but for a different reason. Nick, unlike
the rest of us, knew how to make the
stone tools that our prehuman ancestors had utilized.

Nick was not a typical scientist. I'd
recognized this right away when, in the
course of discussion, he began pulling
fist-size rocks out of his briefcase. He
riveted the group's attention with his
display and with his demonstrations of
how rocks can become tools. He explained the physics of conchoidal fracture by which rocks can be made to
yield good, sharp tools. Then he challenged us to accompany him to the
beach to try to make the "crude" stone
tools that our hominid ancestors made
2 million years ago. That afternoon I
gained a newfound respect for the feats
of my forebears.

It was my first attempt to emulate a
Paleolithic stone knapper, and I did not
find it an easy task. Neither I nor most
of the other "educated" scientists could
coax even a single flake from the
stones on the beach during our first
half hour of trying. We even resorted
to placing one stone on the ground and
slamming another against it, but to no
avail. Finally, instead of just watching
Nick, I began to look closely at what
he was doing. Why did the stones
break so easily when he struck them
together with such little force, while
they just made a loud thud when I
slammed them together as hard as I
could?

I gradually recognized that Nick was
not really hitting rocks together; instead
he was throwing the rock in his right
hand against the edge of the rock in his
left hand, letting the force of the controlled throw knock off the flake. The
"hammer rock" never really left his
right hand, but it was nonetheless thrown,
as a missile, against the "core," the rock
held in place in his left hand. What had I
been doing? Just slamming two rocks
together as though I were clapping my
hands with rocks in between.

Once I realized how Nick was actually flaking stone, I grasped the profound similarity between throwing and stone knapping. In each activity you must be able to snap the wrist rapidly forward at just the right moment during the downward motion of the forearm. This wrist-cocking action produces great force, either for achieving distance in throwing or for knocking a flake off a core. I also learned that it is important to deliver your blow to the core accurately. Several of us had bruised fingers after the afternoon's stone-knapping excursion, suggesting that, accurate though we might be as a species, as individuals we needed practice.

Bill Calvin was likely correct in his suggestion that throwing ability had been selected for in the course of human evolution. But now I saw that accurate throwers also had the potential skills for making stone tools. Could throwing as a defensive device have paved the way for the deliberate construction of stone tools?

Our conference was searching for evolutionary links between language, tools, and anatomy that could lead to the emergence of the bipedal, large-brained, technological creature that is *Homo sapiens*. The neurobiology of stone throwing and the skills of stone knapping were new to me, and as a psychobiologist, I was intrigued. Now as I walked on the beach, I attempted to integrate these ideas with my own knowledge of how apes understand language.

For the two decades I have known and studied chimpanzees, I have been attempting to discern the degree to which they can think and communicate as we do. The initial efforts of ape-language researchers, in the 1960s and early 1970s, were hurriedly greeted with acclaim. Newspapers and scientific journals declared the same message: apes can use symbols in a way that echoes the structure of human language, albeit in a modest manner. The symbols were not in the form of spoken words, of course, but were produced variously as hand gestures from American Sign Language, as col-

ored plastic shapes, and as arbitrary lexigrams on a computer keyboard.

But in the late 1970s and early 1980s this fascination turned to cynicism. Linguists asserted that apes were merely mimicking their caretakers and that they displayed no languagelike capacity at all. Most linguists and psychologists wanted to forget apes and move ahead with what they viewed as the "proper study of man"—generally typified by the analysis of the problem-solving strategies of freshman students.

From my earliest exposure to apes, I recognized that there would be considerable difficulty in determining whether or not they employed words with intent and meaning in the same way that we do. And so, in my research at the Language Research Center at Georgia State University, I searched for scientifically credible ways to approach the fundamental questions about apes and their intellectual and emotional capacities. By 1990, the year of the Wenner-Gren conference, I knew that at least some of this work was reaching an audience, or I would not have been invited to the conference. Perhaps there, I thought, I would have a chance to begin to tell my story—or, more accurately, Kanzi's story.

One ape out of the 11 that I have studied, a 150-pound bonobo (or pygmy chimpanzee) named Kanzi, began to learn language on his own, without drills or lessons. Kanzi, a male, was born on October 28, 1980, at the Yerkes Regional Primate Research Center's field station in Lawrenceville, Georgia. Before this time, no bonobo had been language trained. Matata, Kanzi's adoptive mother, was to be the first.

Matata proved to be a willing, though incompetent, study. She quickly understood that other chimpanzees used the keyboard to communicate and that pressing the lexigrams was what achieved this feat. However, after two years of training and 30,000 trials, she mastered only six symbols, in a limited way.

After Matata's departure, we set up the keyboard in the expectation that Kanzi would begin his language instruction—if he could learn to sit in

one place long enough. Kanzi, however, had his own opinion of the keyboard, and he began at once to make it evident. Not only was he using the keyboard as a means of communicating, but he also knew what the symbols meant. For example, one of the first things he did that morning was to activate the symbol for "apple," then "chase." He then picked up an apple, looked at me, and ran away with a grin on his face. I was hesitant to believe what I knew I was seeing. Kanzi appeared to know all the things we had attempted to teach Matata, yet we had not even been attending to him. Could he simply have picked up his understanding through social exposure, as children do?

For 17 months we kept a complete record of Kanzi's utterances, either directly on the computer when he was indoors, or manually while outdoors. By the end of the period, Kanzi had a vocabulary of about 50 symbols. He was already producing combinations of words—spontaneous utterances such as "Matata group-room tickle" to ask that his mother be permitted to join in a game of tickle in the group room.

We first detected what seemed like spoken word comprehension when Kanzi was one and a half years old. We began to notice that often, when we talked about lights, Kanzi would run to the switch on the wall and flip it on and off. Kanzi seemed to be "listening in" on conversations that had nothing to do with him, in a manner that I had not experienced in other apes—even in those who had been reared in human homes. As time passed, Kanzi appeared able to understand more and more spoken words. In response, we had to do what many parents do when they don't want their children to overhear: we began to spell out some words around Kanzi. We were able to determine that Kanzi understood 150 spoken words at the end of the 17-month period.

"If an ape can begin to comprehend spoken English without being so trained," I later wrote in a scientific paper, "it would appear that the ape possessed speech and language abilities similar to our own." The dual lesson we learned from the project was that chimpanzees can acquire language skills spontaneously, through social exposure to a language-rich environment, as human children do. And, again as for humans, early exposure is critical. As Elizabeth Bates comments, "The Berlin Wall is down, and so is the wall that separates man from chimpanzee."

It was the end of a long day at the Wenner-Gren conference, and we had all eaten dinner at a restaurant in the nearby town. On our return to the hotel, I was sitting near the rear of the bus, and Nick Toth was in the very back, legs stretched out, arms folded across his chest, eyes closed, apparently asleep. Suddenly he opened an eye and beckoned me to join him. "I have something I want to ask you," he said. "Do you think Kanzi could learn to make stone tools, like early humans did?"

His question seemed to come right out of the blue. It was something I had never thought of trying. From my long experience with chimpanzees, I had gained a great respect for their abilities. But making stone tools seemed light-years beyond them. Indeed, even I could not make a worthwhile stone tool, and I'd had Nick there to teach me.

Nevertheless, I was intrigued. "What do you have in mind?" I asked. Nick sat up and quickly explained.

In 1949 the British anthropologist Kenneth P. Oakley published a classic book, *Man the Tool-Maker.* This short volume encapsulated what was widely held to set humans apart as unique: "Possession of a great capacity for conceptual thought . . . is now generally regarded by comparative psychologists as distinctive of man," he wrote. "The systematic making of tools . . . required not only for immediate use but for future use, implies a marked capacity for conceptual thought." The notion of man the tool-maker struck a receptive chord: alone among the world's species, toolmaking *Homo sapiens* fashions an elaborate culture and manufactures a powerful technology,

through which the world is forever changed.

The shift to becoming a toolmaker has been seen as central to what differentiated humans from apes in an evolutionary sense. By definition, therefore, the very first members of the human family must have been toolmakers. This assumption has been challenged in the past several decades. The first members of the human family are now known to have evolved at least 5 millions years ago, perhaps as many as 8 million. And yet the first recognizable stone artifacts date only to around 2.5 million years ago. The appearance of these stone tools coincides with the first appearance of the genus *Homo,* which eventually gave rise to modern humans.

This raises an important question: Were the earliest toolmakers doing something that was beyond the cognitive ability of apes? Or were they merely bipedal apes who were applying their apelike cognitive skills to non-apelike activities?

Nick told me that he had been musing over this question for a long time, and that he had an idea in search of a collaborator. His proposal was to motivate Kanzi to make stone flakes, not to teach him with structured lessons. "We want to avoid the criticism of classical conditioning," he said. He suggested we would need a box with a transparent lid. Something enticing would be put in the box, and the lid would be secured with a length of string. Kanzi could be shown by example how to make flakes, by knocking two rocks together, but there would be no active teaching, no shaping of his hands, no breaking the task down into component parts.

I made some suggestions about how the design of the food box, or "tool site" as we came to call it, could be improved; Nick had underestimated Kanzi's ability to tear flimsy objects apart, especially if there is food inside. Nick promised to get in touch with me after we returned to the United States. This he did within a couple of weeks, and I told him that we had made a tool site to his specifications. A week later he arrived at the Language Research

Center in Atlanta with fellow archeologist Kathy Schick, their truck laden with a thousand pounds of rock.

At first we set up the tool site outside Kanzi's cage, so that Nick could show Kanzi how it was possible to gain access to the baited box. Nick struck a cobble with a hammerstone, selected a sharp flake, and then cut the string securing the lid to the box. Kanzi got the treat that was inside. Nick did this several times, after which we put the tool site inside Kanzi's enclosure. Nick knelt outside, making flakes. He handed sharp ones to me while I was inside with Kanzi, and I encouraged Kanzi to use them to cut the string. He very soon realized the utility of a sharp flake and eagerly took one from whoever was in with him. He then quickly went to the tool site to open the box. He even knocked two rocks together on several occasions, but in a rather desultory way, and without producing flakes. Nevertheless, he was clearly emulating Nick.

During that first afternoon, and throughout the project, Kanzi was never required to perform a task but was merely provided with the opportunity to participate if he wanted to. We wanted to motivate him to make and use flakes, and we hoped he would learn by example. As the days and weeks passed, he displayed a degree of persistence at the task that exceeded anything I'd seen him do.

Kanzi very quickly learned to discriminate between sharp flakes and dull ones, using visual inspection and his lips. On one occasion about three weeks into the project, one of our collaborators at Georgia State, psychologist Rose Sevcik, was striking a rock when—for the first time for her—it split, and several flakes flew off in different directions. Kanzi was watching closely and seemed to know which was the best of the flakes even before they had hit the ground. He let out a bonobo squeal of delight, rushed to pick up the sharpest flake, and was off to the tool site with it, all in one fluid motion.

Making flakes for himself, however, proved difficult. At first he was extremely tentative in the way he hit the rocks together. Almost always he used his right hand to deliver the hammer blow. He held the core in his left hand, often cradled against his chest, or sometimes braced against the floor, with his foot adding further support. Sometimes he put the core on the ground and simply struck it with the hammerstone. No one had demonstrated this "anvil" technique to him. But no matter how he held the core, he seemed unable or unwilling to deliver a powerful blow. Bonobos are three times stronger than a human of the same size, so there was no doubt that Kanzi had the muscle power to do the job. We wondered whether he was nervous about hitting his fingers; perhaps he lacked the correct wrist anatomy to produce a "snapping" action—the structure of a bonobo's arms, wrists, and hands is different from a human's (chimpanzees' wrists stiffened as they became adept knuckle walkers), and it constrains the animal's ability to deliver a sharp blow by snapping the wrist; or perhaps he was reluctant to deliver a hard blow because throughout his life we had discouraged him from slamming and breaking objects.

Then, one afternoon eight weeks into the project, I was sitting in my office when I was suddenly assailed with the sound of a BANG . . . BANG . . . BANG. I rushed to the tool-site room, and there was Kanzi, stone knapping with tremendous force. He had finally learned how to fracture rocks to make sharp flakes, albeit small ones.

One day Kanzi just sat there looking at me. Then at the rock. Then at me again, apparently reflecting. Suddenly he stood up and, with clear deliberation, threw the rock on the tile floor.

During the first three months of the project Kanzi became steadily more proficient at producing flakes, in part because he seemed to have learned to aim the hammer blows at the edge of the core. But despite his willingness to deliver harder blows than he had initially, he still wasn't hitting hard enough to produce flakes bigger than about an inch long. Nevertheless, he persisted with his newfound concentration, and we in turn made the string that secured the tool site thicker and thicker, so that small flakes would wear out before they cut the string.

One day during the fourth month, Kanzi was having only modest success at producing flakes. He turned to me and held out the rocks, as if to say, "Here, you do it for me." He did this from time to time, and mostly I would encourage him to try some more, which is what I did that day. He just sat there looking at me, then at the rock, then at me again, apparently reflecting. Suddenly he stood up and, with clear deliberation, threw the rock on the hard tile floor. The rock shattered, producing a whole shower of flakes. Kanzi vocalized ecstatically, grabbed one of the sharpest flakes, and headed for the tool site.

There was no question that Kanzi had reasoned through the problem and had found a better solution to making flakes. No one had demonstrated the efficacy of throwing. Kanzi had just worked it out for himself. I was delighted, because it demonstrated his ingenuity in the face of a difficult problem. I quickly telephoned Nick and told him what had happened. I was so excited that I didn't give a thought to the fact that Nick might not be delighted, too. He wasn't. He was disappointed. "The Oldowan toolmakers used hard-hammer percussion, not throwing," he said.

"Oldowan" is the name applied to the earliest known stone-tool assemblages, which were found in Africa and date to 2.5 million years ago. The artifacts that make up Oldowan assemblages were produced from small cobbles, and they include about half a dozen forms of so-called core tools—such as hammerstones, choppers, and scrapers—and small, sharp flakes. The toolmakers were assumed to have had

mental templates of these various tool types. The tools are often found in association with broken animal bones, which sometimes show signs of butchery. The clear inference is that, beginning about 2.5 million years ago, our human ancestors began exploiting their environment in a non-apelike way, by using stone tools as a means of including significant amounts of meat in their diet.

Until quite recently archeologists argued that the earliest toolmakers lived lives analogous to those of contemporary hunter-gatherers: they organized themselves into small, mobile bands, established temporary home bases, and divided the labor of hunting and gathering between male and female members of the band. This was a very humanlike way of life, albeit in primitive form, and most definitely unlike that of an ape.

In recent years, however, a reexamination of the archeological evidence has changed this picture dramatically, making it much less humanlike and more apelike. There is considerable debate over the extent to which these early members of the human family were active hunters as opposed to opportunistic scavengers. And the notion of home bases and a division of labor between the sexes has been abandoned as untenable. The earliest toolmakers are now viewed as bipedal apes who lived and foraged in social groups in a woodland-savanna environment, as baboons and chimpanzees do.

An equally important shift of perspective has taken place regarding the tool assemblages themselves. Nick Toth began a program of experimental archeology in the 1970s, in which he became a proficient maker of Oldowan artifacts himself. "My experimental findings suggest that far too much emphasis has been put on cores at the expense of flakes," he wrote. "It seems possible that the traditional relationship might be reversed: the flakes may have been the primary tools and the cores often (although not always) simply the by-product of manufacture. . . . Thus the shape of many early cores may have been incidental to the process of manufacture and therefore indicative of neither the maker's purpose nor the artifact's function."

Nick's reassessment of the Oldowan artifacts revolutionized African archeology and further changed the perception of the humanness of the earliest toolmakers. According to this new theory, the half-dozen different tool types in Oldowan assemblages were not the product of mental templates in the minds of sophisticated toolmakers. The only skill required, therefore, was that of striking flakes off a core using a hammerstone.

"If Kanzi throws the rocks, the percussion marks will be random, and we won't learn anything," Nick protested. Our different reactions reflected, I suppose, the different interests of the psychologist and the archeologist. Nick said I had to discourage Kanzi from throwing, and I pointed out that that would be difficult. "Try," said Nick. I agreed to try.

Rose Sevcik came up with the obvious suggestion, which was to cover the floor with soft carpeting. The first time Kanzi went into the carpeted room, he threw the rock a few times and looked puzzled when it didn't shatter as usual. He paused a few seconds, looked around until he found a place where two pieces of carpet met, pulled back a piece, and hurled the rock. We have assembled a videotape of the toolmaking project, which I show to scientific and more general audiences. Whenever the tape reaches this incident there is always a tremendous roar of approval as Kanzi—the hero—outwits the humans yet again.

By this time, spring was approaching, and we decided to take the tool site outdoors, where there was no hard floor to throw against. Forced to abandon his throwing technique, Kanzi steadily became more efficient at hard-hammer percussion, delivering more forceful and more precisely aimed blows. Very consistently now, Kanzi was hitting the edge of the core and was more successful at producing flakes. The resulting cores were sometimes very simple, with just a couple of flakes removed, or, if Kanzi had persistently hammered at them, they had many small flake scars and steep, bat-tered edges, some of which resembled eoliths, or "dawn stones," found in Europe in the decades around the turn of the century. There had been great controversy about these objects, with some arguing that they were true artifacts. They turned out to have been the product of natural forces, such as wave action or glaciation.

Just as Kanzi was becoming quite proficient at hard-hammer percussion, he foiled us yet again—which again delighted the psychologist and dismayed the archeologist. Kanzi discovered that even outside on soft ground he could exploit his throwing technique. This discovery seemed to be the result of a thoughtful analysis of the problem as well: he placed a rock carefully on the ground, stepped back, and took careful aim with the second rock, poised in his right hand. His aim was true, and the rock shattered. He continued to use this technique, and there was no way of stopping him. As far as I was concerned, we had presented Kanzi with a problem and he had figured out the best way to solve it—three times.

Kanzi had become a toolmaker. But how good a toolmaker? Could he have stood shoulder to shoulder with the makers of Oldowan tools, striking flakes off cores as effectively as they did?

Kanzi had become a toolmaker. But our question was, how good a toolmaker? Could he have stood shoulder to shoulder with the makers of Oldowan tools, striking flakes off cores as effectively as they did? Nick's experience as an Oldowan toolmaker offered us a way of addressing these questions. On that beach in Portugal, I had been impressed by how very difficult it is to produce flakes. The initial inclination of the naive stone knapper is to hit the core hard enough so that a flake will pop out of the core, as if it were being chiseled out. But as Nick demonstrated, the flakes come from the bottom of the core, not the top. The best everyday example of the principle of conchoidal fracture at work in stone toolmaking is the effect of a tiny pebble hitting a window: a cone of glass is punched out of the pane, and the exact shape of the cone is determined by the direction at which the stone hits the glass.

For effective flaking by hard-hammer percussion, three conditions have to be met. First, the core must have an acute edge (one with an angle of less than 90 degrees). Second, the core must be struck with a sharp, glancing blow, hitting about half an inch from the edge. And third, the blow must be directed through an area of high mass, such as a ridge or a bulge. With these conditions met, and starting with suitable raw material, you can form long, sharp flakes. Whatever forms are produced, they have the appearance of great simplicity. But as Nick correctly points out, "it is the process, not the product, that reveals the complexity of Oldowan toolmaking."

Nick and Kathy Schick recently drew up a list of criteria by which to assess the technological sophistication of simple tools. "It was necessary to get beyond relying on gut reaction for distinguishing between true artifacts and naturally fractured stone," explains Nick. The criteria include: flake angle, formed by its top and bottom surfaces; flake size, an indication of how efficiently flakes are being detached from the core; and the amount of step fractures and battering seen. Step fractures are unclean breaks. When a stone is hit at exactly the proper angle, a clean flake falls off, leaving the stone surface as smooth as if someone had run a knife through butter. If a stone is merely slammed into another hard surface, with little regard for the angle of the blow, it may break, but it will have a battered appearance. Well-flaked stone looks as though it has been sculpted or chiseled.

Measured against these criteria, the products of the earliest toolmakers score high. Their makers knew about angles required on the core, about sharp, glancing blows, and about seeking regions of high mass on the core. Therefore the Oldowan toolmakers displayed significant technological sophistication and perceptual skills.

What of Kanzi? His progress in hard-hammer percussion has been considerable, moving from the undirected, timid tapping together of rocks to forceful hammering. Nick describes the process of learning to make tools as being punctuational, with periods of slow change in between. "You suddenly get an insight into what is required and then slowly improve on that," he explains. Kanzi clearly had an insight into the importance of hitting the rock close to its edge; and he had important insights when he developed his throwing techniques. Despite this, however, he has not yet developed the stone-knapping skills of the Oldowan toolmakers.

Kanzi's relatively low degree of technological finesse seems to imply that these early humans had indeed ceased to be apes. It isn't yet certain, however, if Kanzi's poorer performance is the result of a cognitive or an anatomical limitation. I suspect that if Kanzi is limited in the quality of flaking through hard-hammer percussion, it is the result of biomechanical, not cognitive, constraints. Or simply lack of practice—certainly most of us working with Kanzi are unable to make stone tools ourselves. Without a good teacher and constant practice it is a very difficult skill to master. Making stone tools does not seem to be a skill that normal human beings acquire readily with little instruction, as we are asking Kanzi to do.

Nick hopes to learn whether or not Kanzi, with minimal demonstration, can acquire a skill that took, at best, many generations for our ancestors to perfect. If Kanzi does not succeed in matching the skills of the Oldowan toolmakers in the span of one research career, it would still be foolish to rule out the potential of the ape mind to do so, given a few generations of exposure to a need to use such tools.

The greatest surprise of the toolmaking project was Kanzi's development of throwing as a way of obtaining sharp edges. Not only did it reflect a problem-solving process in Kanzi's mind, but it also produced material that addresses an important archeological problem: What did early humans do *before* they made Oldowan tools? The criteria mentioned earlier to identify genuine artifacts as compared with naturally fractured stone would reject Kanzi's flakes and cores as tools. And yet they are artifacts, and they can be used as cutting tools.

Some of Kanzi's cores look rather similar to Oldowan core tools, acknowledges Nick, but most do not. "If I were surveying a Stone Age site and found some of these things, I'd definitely check them out, but I would almost certainly conclude they were naturally flaked," he says. "But after seeing these incipient flaking skills with Kanzi, we certainly have to consider it as a possible model for the earliest stone-tool making. He has taught us what we should be looking for."

Nick joked that Kanzi should be awarded an honorary doctorate, pointing out that he would need a small cap and a gown with long arms. He wasn't joking, though, when in the spring of 1991 he conferred on Kanzi the inaugural CRAFT annual award for outstanding research. Nick and Kathy are codirectors of CRAFT, the Center for Research into the Anthropological Foundations of Technology, at Indiana University. "The award is justified," says Nick, "because the work with Kanzi has given us one of our most important insights into Paleolithic technology. It has given us a view of what is possible with apes, and an insight into the cognitive background of what is necessary to go further."

FURTHER READING

Making Silent Stones Speak: Human Evolution and the Dawn of Technology. Kathy D. Schick and Nicholas Toth. Simon and Schuster, 1993. Two field researchers describe early tools and toolmakers and discuss how new technologies shape the course of human evolution.

Human Ancestors Walked Tall, Stayed Cool

Pete Wheeler

Hominids, or humanlike primates, first appeared in Africa five to seven million years ago, when that continent's climate was becoming increasingly arid and large tracts of woodland and savanna were replacing the unbroken canopy of the equatorial rain forest. While the ancestors of chimpanzees and gorillas remained in the moist forests, the hominids started to exploit the more open, drier habitats. The exact nature of the transition remains hidden, because the oldest-known hominid fossils (*Australopithecus afarensis*) are only four million years old. But the intense sunshine in the new environment, combined with a scarcity of drinking water, must have severely challenged the ability of early hominids to regulate their body temperature.

Many savanna mammals do not even attempt to dissipate all the additional heat they absorb during the day, allowing it instead to accumulate within their bodies until nightfall, when they can cool off without expending precious water. But this strategy works only if delicate tissues, such as the central nervous system, are protected from surges in body temperature. Most savanna mammals possess special physiological mechanisms to cool the brain—notably the carotid rete, a network of fine arteries near the base of the brain, coupled with venous circulation through the muzzle.

Humans, apes, and monkeys, however, lack these features. Although humans appear to have eventually evolved an alternative mechanism to help cool the surface of their enlarged brains, the first hominids could have prevented damaging elevations of brain temperature only by keeping their entire body cool. Any adaptations that either reduced the amount of heat absorbed from the environment or facilitated its rapid dissipation would have proved highly advantageous.

Walking on two feet—the unique mode of terrestrial locomotion that is widely recognized as the first key development in hominid evolution—conferred precisely these benefits. Bipedalism dramatically reduces exposure to direct solar radiation during the middle of the equatorial day. I have placed scale models of early australopithecines in quadrupedal and bipedal postures to measure how the sun would hit them. These experiments show that when the sun is high, bombarding the earth's surface with intense radiation (because the rays pass through less atmosphere), far less body surface is exposed on a biped than on a quadruped. When the sun is directly overhead, the heat load on an upright hominid is only about 40 percent of that received by a quadruped of similar size.

Bipedalism also raises most of the body well above the ground, so that the skin contacts cooler and faster-moving air currents. This favors heat dissipation through convection. Allowing for variation in environmental conditions and vegetation, I calculate that hominids would have lost about one-third more heat through convection by adopting a bipedal posture.

Finally, human bipedalism at low speeds uses less energy than does either true quadrupedalism or the knuckle walking used by African apes. This reduces both dietary requirements (and the time and effort spent foraging) and the rate at which heat is generated internally as a byproduct of muscular activity.

Taking these factors into account in calculating the overall energy and water budgets of the early hominids, I conclude that bipedalism significantly decreased early hominids' dependence on shade, allowing them to forage in the open for longer periods and at higher temperatures. Bipedalism also greatly reduced the amount of drinking water they needed for evaporative cooling through sweating. I estimate that a knuckle-walking ape, active throughout the day on the savanna, would typically need to drink about five pints of water. Just by assuming bipedal posture and locomotion, a hominid of similar size would get by with three pints daily.

Bipedalism appears to be an ideal mode of terrestrial locomotion for a mammal foraging in the equatorial savanna, where food and water resources are dispersed and far from abundant. But if so, why do we find bipedalism only in humans? Probably because all other mammals of the African savanna, including monkeys such as baboons, are descended from ancestors that were already true quadrupeds.

4. THE HOMINID TRANSITION

In contrast, humans, along with chimpanzees and gorillas, probably descended from tree-dwelling primates that brachiated, or swung from branches using their arms. These ancestors were not strongly committed to one particular mode of terrestrial locomotion and may have been predisposed to walking upright. As they moved into more open habitats, the overheating problems they encountered may have tipped the balance in favor of bipedalism. (An alternative possibility is that bipedalism was first perfected in the forest habitat for some entirely different reason, and that our ancestors just happened to be preadapted for the problems they would encounter on the expanding savanna.)

Following the acquisition of an upright posture, humans evolved in other ways that enabled them to keep cool. Average body weight rose, slowing dehydration under savanna conditions. Larger hominids would have been able to forage for longer periods, and across greater distances, before needing to drink.

Later hominids—members of our own genus, *Homo*—are also taller for their body weight than their stockier and rather more apelike ancestors, the australopithecines. By at least 1.6 million years ago, *H. erectus* had acquired the tall, linear physique, with relatively narrow shoulders and hips, characteristic of many human populations inhabiting hot, arid regions of the tropics today. A tall, thin body maximizes the skin area available for heat dissipation, while minimizing the exposure of these surfaces to the overhead sun. Longer legs help by raising the body still farther above the hot ground.

Scientists have long reasoned that one of the most obvious and unusual human features, the loss of insulating body hair, is an adaptation to the hot savanna. Although follicles are still densely distributed over most of the human body, the hairs they produce are so short and fine that the underlying skin is exposed directly to the flow of air, promoting the shedding of excess heat by convection and, when necessary, enhancing the effectiveness of sweating.

Angle of Sun above the Horizon

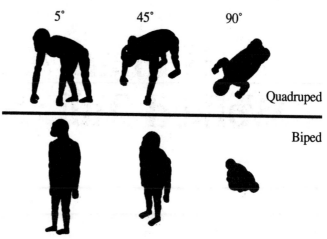

On all fours (top row), a hypothetical human progenitor exposes considerable body surface to direct solar radiation, whether the sun is low on the horizon, intermediate, or directly overhead. In contrast, the same creature in a bipedal posture is far less vulnerable to the intense rays of the midday sun (bottom row, right).
Pete Wheeler

The problem with this hypothesis has always been explaining why humans differ from other savanna mammals, which have retained dense coats of hair. In environments where mammals are exposed to strong solar radiation, the coat acts as a shield, reflecting and reradiating heat before it reaches the skin. For most mammals, the loss of this insulation would create more problems that it would solve: I calculate that on the savanna, naked quadrupeds would actually need to drink additional water to cope with the extra heat load. For a biped, in contrast, a naked skin saves water because so little skin surface is exposed to the sun. Mainly the head and upper shoulders are exposed, and these can be protected by the retention of a relatively small amount of hair cover. Bipedalism and the strategy of cooling the whole body (rather than just the brain) probably explain why humans evolved a naked skin, while other savanna mammals of comparable size did not.

The stability in body temperature provided by bipedalism and a naked skin may have been an essential step in allowing our large, heat-sensitive brains to evolve further. A parallel to this can

be seen in the development of modern computers. Information-processing systems—semiconductor as well as biological—generate substantial heat and are vulnerable to damage from overheating. This presents a major obstacle to electronics engineers attempting to build ever more capable machines. The circuits of the Cray 2 supercomputer, for example, are so densely packed that they must be immersed in a tank of fluorocarbon liquid maintained at about 65° F. As in the case of the evolution of the human brain, the development of such an elaborate cooling system does not inevitably lead to higher-performance machines, but it does make them possible.

As humans spread outward from Africa, they encountered different levels of heat, exposure, and moisture. Many studies suggest that these factors determined, at least in part, the variation we now observe in features as diverse as nose shape, limb proportions, hair structure, skin pigmentation, and eye color. Modern humans inhabiting savanna and desert environments near the equator, such as the Nilotic peoples of Africa and the Australian aborigines, commonly have tall, thin physiques resembling that of early

Homo erectus. Their skin, especially among groups that have traditionally worn little clothing, is generally very dark, owing to the high concentration of melanin pigment that protects underlying tissues from sunburn and the carcinogenic effects of ultraviolet radiation.

As humans migrated north into colder regions, where retaining heat became more vital, they evolved proportionately shorter limbs, a trend seen in many other groups of mammals. In these populations the skin has lost most of its pigmentation, apparently because of the milder impact of ultraviolet radiation at high latitudes. The reduction in pigment may simply reflect the relaxation of the need for it, or it may have been demanded to allow sufficient penetration of ultraviolet radiation (which humans need to synthesize essential vitamin D).

As they colonized—or recolonized—tropical rain forests, humans faced another obstacle. Although the canopy affords shade, the humidity inhibits the evaporation of sweat. The resultant dependence on convective heat loss favors a body form with a large surface area relative to volume. Unfortunately, the tall, linear physique that works so well in open equatorial habitats is not practical when negotiating dense vegetation. A better solution may be a small body, exemplified by the Mbuti Pygmies of the Congo Basin, who benefit from a high surface-to-volume ratio and can move with agility across the forest floor.

Ape Cultures and Missing Links

Richard W. Wrangham

Richard W. Wrangham, M. A. Oxford University (New College) 1970; Ph.D. Cambridge University (St. Johns College) 1975, is professor of Anthropology at Harvard University. He has held academic appointments at the University of Michigan, King's College (Cambridge, England), Stanford University, and Bristol University, and is on the Board of Trustees at the Center for Advanced Study of Behavioral Sciences, Stanford, the Dian Fossey Gorilla Foundation, and the Jane Goodall Institute. His current research interests are the nutritional ecology of chimpanzees compared to other primates, the role of chimpanzees in the frugivore community, and functional aspects of communication. Prof. Wrangham does two to seven months of fieldwork annually in western Uganda as Director of the Kibale Chimpanzee Project. In addition to numerous articles and chapters, his books include Current Problems in Sociobiology *(1982),* Ecology and Social Evolution: Birds and Mammals *(1986),* Primate Societies *(1987), and* Chimpanzee Cultures *(1994). He is a Fellow of the American Academy of Arts and Sciences, and received the Rivers Medal from the Royal Anthropological Institute in 1993.*

. . . In recognition of Gordon Getty's extraordinary reach, I'm going to address the three questions at the heart of

This paper was the first Getty Lecture of the Leakey Foundation, presented at the American Museum of Natural History on October 21, 1994.

the Leakey Foundation's mission. I'll frame those questions in a minute. But first, ladies and gentlemen, we've all had a long day, so please fill your glasses, sit back, and relax. And incidentally, as far as I'm concerned feel free to drink your wine with your fingers, or by dipping a napkin in it, or by sucking the tablecloth, or however you choose. I say this because I want to encourage you into the spirit of our ancestors . . . but, well, I'll come back to all that in a minute.

Last Saturday, six days ago, I was in Kibale Forest in western Uganda with a party of ten chimpanzees. About eight o'clock, we met a group of sixty red colobus monkeys. The high-ranking chimps stopped and stared. The younger adult males did the same. The colobus chirped in alarm. Some chimps started climbing. Others watched from the ground. Within minutes, chimps were hunting. Two drove a party of monkeys towards a third waiting in ambush fifty feet above the ground. The colobus did their best to file away through the tree-crowns, searching for an escape among the branches. But they found their path blocked. They turned, and tried another escape. The chimpanzees kept turning them back. The hunts went on for an hour and twenty minutes. At one point, thirty monkeys were trapped on a high branch, two chimps drove them higher, till one by one they jumped. There was a chimp waiting at the landing-point. The first three just escaped. The fourth was caught. The fracas went on. There were fourteen separate hunts in an hour and a half. By the end, three colobus were dead, three chimps had

killed, and five human observers were enthralled.

How things have changed. In 1959, 100 years after *The Origin of the Species* was published, humans were the only primate known to prey on mammals. Last week's observation would have been a paper in *Science*. Today, thanks to grantees of the Leakey Foundation, it's almost routine. We know now that chimpanzees everywhere kill and eat their own prey; that to do so, they often use elaborate cooperative strategies; that the meat is held by males, who share it with friends and lovers in exchange for favors; and that they can hunt so well and so often as to kill 15–30% of their prey population per year, a higher proportion than any carnivore does.

So what does this sort of observation mean for our history? Does it suggest a cooperatively hunting, killer-ape in our past? Some people think so. But why shouldn't we focus on other apes instead? For example, think about bonobos, the sister species to the chimpanzee. Bonobos live in similar forests with similar monkeys. They like to eat meat. But they don't cooperate in hunting monkeys. They don't even kill monkeys, even though they occasionally catch them and play with them like pets! And when they do eat meat, (meat of small antelopes), it's the females, not males that hold the carcass. Should we think, because of bonobos, that our male ancestors disdained the hunt, and ceded meat to females?

I'm not going to focus on hunting this evening. I use hunting just as an example. The same issues apply to any behaviors we're interested in. Whether

 From *Symbols*, Spring 1995, pp. 2-20. © 1995 by Richard W. Wrangham. Reprinted by permission.

Fig. 1. *Where Do We Come From? What Are We? Where Are We Going?*
Paul Gauguin (1848-1903) Museum of Fine Arts, Boston.

we're talking about hunting, or communicating, or tool-using, or anything else, we have to sort out what ape behavior today means for the human past.

In this lecture I'm going to argue that to be with chimpanzees in an African forest, is to climb into a time machine . . . that by stepping into the world of these extraordinary apes we move back six million years, to glimpse where we have come from. The glimpse isn't a perfect picture, but it's amazingly good. That's the argument.

Let's begin by looking back 25 years. In those first years of the Leakey Foundation, I couldn't have made *any* suggestion about apes as time machines without sounding very silly. At that time, with genetic and fossil data still poor, apes and humans were thought to be distantly related, not only to each other but also to their common ancestors.

Apes were certainly *fascinating* to visionaries like Louis Leakey, but then to that extraordinary man, everything was interesting. Happily, he supported Jane Goodall. And he was thrilled when she found chimpanzees modifying tools (and hunting prey), because this meant that chimps were a sort of bridge between humans and other primates. This gave flesh to the idea of evolution. But because at that time, 25 years ago, the kinship between humans and chimpanzees was thought to have ended in the distant past, maybe 15–20 million years ago, no-one was sure

what these observations meant for our history. And anyway, the idea of chimps as a bridge was undermined by an apparent gulf between apes and humans in certain critical aspects of behavior.

Certainly there were *some* similarities. Mothers were strongly attached to their infants. Many features were strikingly similar. But the parallels evaporated at a critical point: there was no evidence of serious aggression. Chimpanzees were seen to live wonderfully peaceful lives. So human society was something apart. Reviewing the chimpanzee studies of the 1960s, Robert Ardrey decisively affirmed the human-ape divide. The life of chimpanzees was an "arcadian existence of primal innocence."

This became the conventional wisdom for other apes. George Schaller and Dian Fossey found gorillas to be a gentle giant. Their new picture rightly challenged the view that gorillas were natural aggressors towards people. In so doing, it left them unconnected with modern human behavior. So the prevailing view was that "human forms of social life were largely unique to humans, created by us, subject to human manipulation according to our vision of human good."[1] Apes had nature; people had culture, and culture, it seemed, wasn't always so great.

In the first hundred years after Darwin, in every area of human thought, people were searching for new meanings

of human existence . . . and this was a common conclusion. Paul Gauguin was one of the first artists to do what the Leakey Foundation does, to search in the primitive. This painting (Figure 1) he considered his spiritual legacy. It looks to an imagined past, a primitive idyll where man and nature lived in harmony. It has on it, written in the top left-hand corner, the three questions of the Leakey Foundation, questions that go back to Thomas Carlyle's *Sartor Resartus*. On the right is a newborn child, representing "Where do we come from?" The figure plucking fruit in the centre shows our day to day existence: ("What are we?"). On the left, an old woman facing death symbolizes concern for the future: "Where are we going?"

You might think that, like ourselves today, Gauguin would have been inspired by his exploration of the human past, present and future. No; he was oppressed. Near the centre, you can see by the tree of knowledge two sinister figures. Their sombre colors show the suffering that comes from leaving nature, pain that Gauguin felt acutely. For Gauguin, human history was a story of acquired sin.

The challenge of completing the painting kept him alive during a period of depression over his daughter's death, but its conclusions left him empty. As soon as he'd finished his masterpiece, he walked out into the mountains, took a massive dose of arsenic, and lay down to wait for death. Should we feel the same depression from looking into the past? Was Gauguin right to see humans as figures of tragedy, doomed by the very abilities of brains and culture that represent the best of our achievements? No. We have new, more confident answers now, coming not from an imaginary vision of primitive Tahiti but from the real world of living primates. The story of human evolution that emerges is different from Gauguin's, still discomfiting, but much richer and more inspiring. It's a story of unfinished challenges. I'm going to address them by taking Gauguin's, and our Foundation's three questions in turn. Let's begin with the past. "Where do we come from?"

So what made a savannah-living, upright hominid out of a forest-living quadrupedal ape? And what was that ancestral species like, in how it looked and how it behaved? I claimed just now that our prehominid ancestor looked like a chimpanzee. Let me explain why I think so.

First, it's obvious that the three African apes, chimpanzees, gorillas, and bonobos, are all very similar, much more like each other than they are like any other species. The genetic evidence unambiguously supports our intuitions. Let's look at these three species.

Genetic evidence from Phil Morin, Maryellen Ruvolo and others show that West African chimps have been separate for about one-and-a-half million years from chimpanzees in East Africa. But morphologically, there's very little difference in chimpanzees across the continent. Like all the great apes, this a conservative species. Most gorillas are lowland gorillas. Recent Leakey Foundation studies are exciting because they are some of the first to watch lowland gorillas undisturbed. They are so similar to chimpanzees that people can find it hard to tell big chimpanzees and small gorillas apart.

Bonobos are the third African ape. They look so like chimpanzees that they weren't recognized to be different until 1933, when they were called "pygmy chimpanzees." But so-called pygmy chimpanzees are actually no

smaller than some chimpanzees. Most people prefer to call them bonobos. They live south of the Zaïre River, where there are no gorillas or chimpanzees. Chimpanzees live north of the Zaïre River, and share much of their range with gorillas.

The evolutionary relationship among these three apes is undisputed: chimpanzees and bonobos split most recently, around 2.5 m y ago, and their common ancestor split with gorillas much earlier, about 8–10 m y ago. So where do humans fit? Probably everyone here knows of the shocking genetic evidence now showing chimpanzees to be more closely related to humans than they are to gorillas. The last four years in particular give mounting confidence to this view, as every new nuclear or mitochondrial gene is looked at, currently more than 10 genes in detail as well as from DNA hybridisation looking at the genome as a whole. This means that human ancestors are no sister group to the apes, but instead arose within the African ape tree. Our hominid ancestors apparently split from the chimp-bonobo line *after* the split from gorillas. Louis Leakey, a great iconoclast, would have loved it. Now, this surprise gives us an unexpected bonus. It implies that our ancestral 6 m y species is likely to have been very like a modern-day chimpanzee. We can see why by reconstructing our various common ancestors.

First, what was the common ancestor of chimpanzees and bonobos like? The answer depends on comparisons with gorillas, the first ape to split off, Which is more similar to gorillas? Is it chimpanzees? or bonobos? The answer is clear: In characteristics that differ between chimpanzees and bonobos, chimpanzees are consistently more like gorillas. This is true for things we can see, such as the body build, the shape of the head, or the structure of the genitals, as well as those we can't, such as chromosomes and blood groups. Chimpanzees are like small gorillas, whereas bonobos are like changed chimpanzees. So the common ancestor of chimpanzees and bonobos should have looked like a chimpanzee.

What about the common ancestor of

chimpanzees and gorillas? Well, a gorilla is basically a big chimpanzee. The differences between chimpanzees and gorillas in morphology, as well as in feeding behavior, sexual anatomy, grouping patterns and social relationships, can [in large part] be explained simply by gorillas being larger. These two species are so similar that they should be in the same genus. So the common ancestor of chimpanzees and gorillas was surely an animal built on their body plan, more chimpanzee-like if it was smaller, more gorilla-like if it was larger.

Finally, the early, ape-like Australopithecine, *afarensis,* is sufficiently well-known for its body weight to be closely estimated. They were about the size of chimpanzees.

So our ape-like ancestor that gave rise to our hominid ancestors was presumably also the size of a chimpanzee, and built on the body plan of a chimpanzee. And with [*Ardipithecus*] *ramidus* suddenly presented to us, the earliest australopithecine is looking, as expected, more chimpanzee-like.

This is all very disturbing, and exciting. For years we were brought up to say that the living apes were interesting, but we mustn't think of them as our living ancestors. But now maybe one of them was!

So here's the scenario. At 8–10 m y a chimpanzee-like species gave rise to early gorillas; at 5–6 m y it calved off australopithecines; and at 2–3 m y it gave rise to bonobos; and it's still going. You *can* still argue, and some people do, that gorillas and chimpanzees are similar from parallel evolution rather than common phylogeny. If so, this argument fails. But the great thing is . . . that this question will eventually be settled when the astonishing fossil gap is filled. . . . The most reasonable view for the moment, however, is that chimpanzees are a conservative species and an amazingly good model for the ancestor of hominids. So . . . "What do we come from?" Our ancestor was likely a black-haired, knuckle-walking, large-brained, deep-voiced, heavily-built, big-mouthed, thin-enamelled fruit-eating, fission-fusion, male-bonded species living at low population density in the forests of equatorial Africa.

If we know what our ancestor looked like, naturally we get clues about how it behaved . . . that is, like modern-day chimpanzees. This helps in some ways of course. But . . . [we] can't just talk about The Chimpanzee: we have to talk about particular chimpanzee cultures, because chimps invent lots of different signals and different ways to live. For instance, look at the ways chimpanzees drink. They can put their lips to water. But they often make leaf-sponges, which they dip into water and suck. Sometimes they make drinking-brushes, dipped into narrow-holes. One population uses natural water-bottles. Another uses a pestle and mortar to smash up the juicy parts of a palm. And one, as Denise Wardill has seen this year in Burundi, uses whole leaves as bowls to scoop up water. These different drinking styles come from Guinea and Zaïre and Uganda and Tanzania and Burundi. So you make the call: what did an Ethiopian australopithecine do?

I love this list of drinking styles because it makes two other points. First, it shows how dynamic this field is. The stem-sponges were first seen less than 5 years ago, the pestle-and-mortar was reported this year, the moss-sponges and water-bowls haven't

Fig. 2. Adult female leaf-grooming. Photo: Richard Wrangham.

yet been published. People are moving into new chimpanzee populations and seeing new traditions all the time, not just in drinking but in eating, body care, signalling, play, everything! (Figure 2) Earlier this year, Rosalind Alp found chimpanzees in Sierra Leone using leafy branches like sandals: they do this when they climb along the thorn-studded branches of capok trees, holding their leafy sandals in their hands and feet to raise their soles and palms about the spines. So did Lucy sometimes wear shoes?

The inventiveness of chimpanzees is remarkable, and sometimes one can even see it directly. Last year, I watched a lonely boy chimpanzee, eight-year-old Kakama, playing for four hours with a log. He carried it on his back, on his belly, in his groin, on his shoulders. He took it with him every time he moved. He carried it up four trees, and down again. He lay in his nest and held it above him like a mother with her baby. And he made a special nest that he didn't use himself, except to put the log in. Three months later, he did it again, watched by two of my field assistants in Kibale Forest. They recovered the log, and pinned to it a description of the behavior. Their report was headed *'Kakama's toy baby.'* Imagination made wood.

As more chimpanzee populations are watched, each has its own culture. But the differences aren't understood. A tiny few can be attributed to simple ecological causes, but more appear arbitrary. The explanation of cultural differences is becoming an exciting challenge, and it involves explaining not only why traits are invented and passed on, but also why they go extinct. That's the first lesson of the drinking tools. And what it means for our big questions is both inspiring and annoying. It means that we can look to our past and see a cultural ape that could show a hundred or more inventions of tools and signs and ways to get food . . . but alas, an ape with so much invention that we can't easily predict where and what it did.

The second lesson is that some of the new observations are wonderfully suggestive about ape-hominid transi-

tions. People have argued that hominids were seed-eaters, making dramatic the hammer-tools used by chimps in West Africa. The fat-rich seeds made available by smashing nuts provide much of the calories for the Taï chimps, at some times of year. Did australopithecines harvest palm nuts along the fringes of a Pliocene swamp draining Lake Turkana? Here is an adaptation they could easily have brought with them from the forests.

Others think that hominids were root-eaters, using, like root-eating pigs, the seasonal stores of diverse savannah tubers. This is reasonable because roots could supply the fall-back food eaten when fruits were scarce. But could root-eating have started in the forest? Until the 1990s, there was no evidence of it, and it makes little sense . . . forests have few large storage organs, a tribute to their relatively even micro-climate. But now we have Annette Lanjouw's extraordinary observations of the root-eating chimpanzees of Tongo. The Tongo chimps, in eastern Zaïre, live on a lava flow. All water drains quickly: there are no streams or pools. [To get water] these chimps use their moss-sponges, up to 20 minutes a day, but it's laborious. So, when they're lucky, they have another trick. Sometimes they find a stem that excites them. Pulling the lava boulders away, they dig deep into the soil, maybe up to their shoulders, and extract a root. The prize is prized indeed. Like a prey monkey, the root is guarded by the possessor while around him his companions scream and hug and charge in joy. The root may be divided and shared. It can be carried for a kilometer or more, while it's slowly finished. What's in the root that excites them so? Its' saturated with water, according to Annette. She thinks it's a bottle.

So I like the idea of some strangely desiccated forest, on a lava flow, perhaps, or on an upland granite outcrop, leading an early Pliocene population of forest chimpanzees to become root-eaters—first for water, and only then for food . . . forest root-eating, precursor to savannah life.

And once on the savannah, can chimps help us imagine the past? In

Chambura Gorge in western Uganda, Cathy Poppenwimer's work in the last two years has uncovered a forest-based group of chimpanzees that come into the open savannahs for figs. They can nest in these isolated fig-trees. In the savannah grassland they chase the young antelope, the Uganda kob. Presumably they catch them sometimes. There are two lion dens in the gorge, but the chimps survive: leopards they chase in groups. And only two months ago, the first observations emerged of Ugandan chimpanzees using tools to fish for termites, out on the savannah rim of the gorge.

Nut-smashing, root-eating, savannah-using chimpanzees, resembling our ancestors, and capable by the way of extensive bipedalism. Using antwands, and sandals, and bowls, meat-sharing, hunting cooperatively. Strange paradox . . . a species trembling on the verge of hominization, but so conservative that it has stayed on that edge, little changed for 6 million years or more. It's hard to imagine what more one could ask for as pre-adaptations to a savannah life. But the history of chimpanzee studies shows that our imagination is limited only by what we know. We're still a long way from defining the limits of what chimpanzees do, and therefore from imagining the range of our ape ancestor's feats. We have a good answer, however, to "Where do we come from?" For one thing, we come from an ape with enough brains to invent novel cultural adaptations in every new environment.

The second of Gauguin's questions, "What are we?", goes to the heart of his anxieties. The big issue was the source of evil . . . human aggression and pain and misery. Gauguin, as we saw, thought it unnatural, the result of the loss of nature . . . a widespread romantic view, from Rousseau to Ardrey. But others saw deep roots. Dostoyevsky grappled with the question for a lifetime, and gave a stern answer in *The Brothers Karamazov:* "In every man, a demon lies hidden—the demon of rage, the demon of lustful heat at the screams of the tortured victim, the demon of lawlessness let off the chain . . ."[2] Who was right? Did humans get their

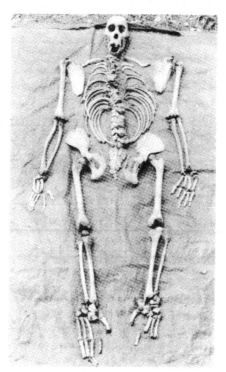

Fig. 3. Chimpanzee Ruwenzori's remains. Photo: Colin Chapman.

demons after leaving nature, or have we inherited them from our ancient forest lives?

The last two decades allow, at last, a reasonably confident comparison of human and chimpanzee behavior. The first similarities we find in the social behavior of chimpanzees and humans are those attractive ones from the era of Louis Leakey. Wherever chimpanzees are studied they form long-lasting individual social relationships, based on exchanges of gestures and favors in remarkably human-like patterns.

But the dramatic discoveries, of course, of the last two decades, have been of the violence that occasionally erupts to destroy Ardrey's "arcadian existence of primal innocence." I'm sure most people here know of the gut-wrenching episodes of male raiding that culminated in at least ten lethal attacks at Gombe and the mortal elimination of seven males that had recently set themselves up as their own independent group. Much was horrifying about that so-called warfare. It involved males that knew each other well. Associating as close companions before the split; victims were stalked and hunted like prey; the kills appeared the result of deliberate attempts to

maim often with extreme cruelty, such as the tearing of skin up an arm, or the twisting of a limb to break it.

Does this mean chimpanzees are naturally violent? Ten years ago it wasn't clear. The warfare was in Gombe, where chimpanzees were fed bananas. Maybe other populations, unaffected by human provisioning, would be found to have escaped the horror of cooperative male violence? Alas, the evidence is mounting, and it all points the same way. Here from my study site in Kibale (Figure 3), are the bones of the one of our chimpanzees killed by the neighbouring group during a period of feeding competition . . . the first [such] death known in an undisturbed population. In Mahale, border patrols, stalking, counter-chasing, and the extinction of the males of a community all suggest a comparable pattern of inter-group attacks. In Taï, reports of wounds from territorial encounters. In captivity, lethal gang attacks. In this cultural species, it may turn out that one of the least variable of all chimpanzee behaviors is the intense competition between males, the violent aggression they use against strangers, and their willingness to maim and kill those that frustrate their goals.

As the picture of chimpanzee society settles into focus, it now includes infanticide, rape, and regular battering of females by males. Some of these occur in other apes. If we leave Africa for a moment and go to Asia, we find that male orangutans rape regularly, so that perhaps half of their copulations involve force and patent resistance by the female. Orangutan rape has never been photographed in the wild, but something like it has been shown in captivity. And in the wild, adult male orangutans can't be together without violent aggression.

Back in Africa, the threat and practice of infanticide appears to lie at the heart of the mountain gorilla social system. Males fight violently for the control of groups, and can sometimes kill each other. The average female experiences infanticide at least once in her lifetime, and infanticide has been found responsible for 37% of infant deaths in these gentle giants. As in chimpanzees and orangutans, sexual coercion emerges readily in captivity. Males attack females, who copulate more willingly as a result.

There is a common theme to these relationships: male sexual aggression against females whose only defense is other males. The females of these species of ape live at risk of male brutality. The risk is not constant. For years on end a female gorilla may endure charmed days of relaxed relationships. But intermittent scenes of violence appear to pervade all their lives, so that all must be constantly on their guard.

What a change we see now from the 1968 view. Then, humans were an independent line, and the violence of our species represented novelty, perhaps arbitrary, perhaps random, perhaps a maladaptive trait, but at least without any evolutionary precedence.

Now, not merely do we see humans as descended from within the tightly related cluster of African apes, but the apes also show similar kinds of violence to ourselves. What makes this especially vivid is that these patterns of violence are generally uncommon in other primates and other animals. Deliberate raiding into neighbouring territories to ambush neighbours; sexual coercion, especially of females outside estrus . . . these are rare. The implication is that strong aspects of human violence have long evolutionary roots. "What are we?" In our aggressive urges we are not Gauguin's creatures of culture. We are apes of nature, cursed over six million years or more with a rare inheritance, a Dostoyevskyan demon.

It's a galling scenario. The implication is that for six million years or more, while we have been evolving from ape to australopithecine to human, through several foraging specialisations, while abandoning the trees and committing ourselves to earth, while brains expanded and faces shrunk and hair became short and fine, while sexuality shifted from promiscuity towards bonding, throughout all this we clung to a suite of characters so rare that it's not confirmed in any other species, and so dangerous that it threatens the survival of our species. Through all these

changes we retained intense rivalry between neighbouring groups of males, lethal coalitionary behavior, and a systematic use of violent sexual coercion. On another day, we could discuss the reasons, which look consistent and visceral: unbalanced power corrupts and pays. There's much still waiting to be explained about the conditions that lead to male-bonding. But one male-bonding is present, lethal aggression follows easily. The coincidence of demonic aggression in ourselves and our closest kin bespeaks its antiquity.

If that's what we are, "Where *are* we going?" The big issue, in taking up the third question, is whether we can go beyond our past. Gauguin eventually did. His suicide failed: (he threw up the arsenic). Eventually, he decided to send his picture to Paris, and it was his curiosity about the public response to it that dispelled his mood of morbid helplessness[3] and led to his painting a pastoral which was an optimistic counterpoint to the tragedy of his earlier fresco. The fourth ape gives us the equivalent to our Tahitian pastoral, our opportunity to be optimistic about controlling our natural demon.

Bonobos, as we saw, have apparently evolved from a chimpanzee ancestor. Yet, as we shall see, they have escaped the violence of chimpanzees. How has this happened?

Bonobos have been watched less than other apes, so generalizations are a little less secure. Still, from Kano's group in Wamba, the Stony Brook group in Lomako, and several studies in captivity, the overall pattern is clear. Bonobos have communities like chimpanzees, founded on a resident group of males and their sons. But the violence has died.

Male chimps commonly batter females. Male bonobos hardly ever attack females. And when they do, these occasional incidents suggest one main way that bonobos reduce male aggression. A female that is attacked screams, and what happens? Other females pour in on her side, and chase the offending male. Alliances among females keep males from getting out of hand. Kano saw them in Wamba. Amy Parish has been showing this very clearly in cap-

tivity, and just recently Barbara Fruth and Gottfried Hohmann have been seeing it in Lomako.

The extraordinary thing is that this doesn't happen in wild chimps. Why not? I mentioned that female chimps rarely travel together. So how can they help each other? But female bonobos are hardly ever apart: small parties are made up of *females* with the occasional male, whereas small parties of chimps are *males* with the occasional female. Do female bonobos support each other simply because they can spend time together? Yes—just like chimps in captivity. They also have to trust each other. Female bonobos invest a lot of time in developing friendly relationships with each other, using the most exotic means. If they're going to spend a lot of time together, supportive relationships are invaluable.

Bonobos have much else to recommend them, such as their famous sexual gymnastics, but I want to focus just on this use of alliances among females to deter male aggression. What does it do for the species? It means that sexual coercion doesn't pay. So males compete for mates not by being brutal, but by being socially attractive. This, I believe, lies at the heart of the bonobo changes from chimpanzees. Bonobos are neotenous, retaining a suite of juvenile characters into adulthood. They are slender, and their vocal repertoire is full of high-pitched, submissive-sounding calls. They have become sexy, friendly, mild. If only males assisted in parenting, they'd be a feminists's dream.

How did this change come about? The critical change, I believe, was the evolution of grouping patterns. Chimpanzee females travel together when fruits are abundant, but when fruits are scare they split up. That clearly suggests they travel alone to feed well. But bonobo females travel together all the time. Is there something different about the foods of bonobos?

Several years ago a number of us suggested that the key difference was that bonobos eat more piths from the forest floor. Pith-eating is a good thing if you can do it. The piths of forest herbs, like sugar-cane, provide good alternatives to fruits. And there's often a lot of it, so there's no need for foraging parties to break up if they can find a field of piths. Gorillas eat a lot of piths. It's the fields of pith that appear to allow the groups of lowland gorillas to forage together as a group.

But do bonobos eat more piths? Recently Richard Malenky and I compared pith densities and the amount of pith taken by bonobos and Lomako and chimpanzees in Zaïre. We found that bonobos passed much more pith than the chimps did over the year. They were consistently more focussed on the pith fields than chimps were. So they seem to have a good back-up food when fruits are few—and one that allows groups to stay together.

Let me, then, imagine one way that bonobos evolved from their chimp ancestors. Genetic evidence dates the split at 2–3 m y ago. We know from Liz Vrba and others that around 2.5 m y there was a major drying event. I suggest that south of the Zaïre River, gorillas and chimps, or ancestors very like them, lived together as they do now to the north of the river. Then the

drying event, and what happened? Only chimps survived. As we see today, in the more seasonal areas north of the Zaïre River, gorillas give out and only chimps remain.

Then the moistness returned, and with it, the piths that gorillas like to eat, as recent studies have been finding in Gabon. But there were no gorillas. So the chimps expanded to occupy the empty niche, including gorilla-foods—in other words, the piths—alongside their previous chimp-foods—that is, the tree-fruits. And as they adapted to the new combination of gorilla foods and chimp foods, they changed. They were rarely forced to travel alone. Females lived together. They developed supportive relationships. They attacked aggressive males. Aggressive males were failures as mates. Males were juvenilized.

The details of the process can barely be guessed at the moment. Certainly, a major role was played by the prolonged sexuality of bonobos, maybe involving concealed ovulation. But the principle will surely remain, that bonobos evolved from changed cir-

cumstance; and the way it happened was for a change in the environment to allow a political change. Bonobos weren't constrained by their chimpanzee past to keep their legacy of male violence. Social strategies have different pay-offs in different contexts. They can be easily changed when the contexts change. And a remarkable feature of the alliances among bonobo females is that they are developed among strangers. In other animals, alliances are linked to kinship. In bonobos, alliances are produced from recognition of common interest, a recognition that takes brains. The development of big brains and advanced cognition has brought with it the ability to escape from the constraints of biology, even in a species with little self-consciousness. Gauguin thought us tragic: the very skills that make us human, our intellect and emotions, also bring demons. But that romantic view is wrong, almost the reverse of history as we can see it now. Our demons come from our ape past, and we need our intellect and emotions to forge the alliances that can defeat the beast. It's common sense,

Fig. 4. Reassurance behavior between adult males. Photo: Richard Wrangham.

Fig. 5. Adult male inspecting tree for fruit. Photo: Richard Wrangham.

supported by the evidence.

What does it do for us, then, to know the behavior of our closest relatives? Chimpanzees and bonobos are an extraordinary pair. One, I suggest, shows us some of the worst aspects of our past and our present; the other shows an escape from it. In thinking creatively about our future, I hope we honor our sister species, who by being different from ourselves, emphasize the unity of our humanity.

Let me return to the extraordinary achievements of the Leakey Foundation. In this talk I've referred to perhaps twenty field studies. All have input from the Leakey Foundation. I should be referring to each by name, and honoring the individual scientists that make a broad review possible. But let me honor, instead, the trustees and supporters of the Leakey Foundation, who have put their time, their money, and their spirit into helping us all.

In a mere quarter-century, this imaginative group has presided over the golden age of biological anthropology, stimulated a range of exciting discoveries, brought academics face to face

with the public that supports them, and incidentally greatly benefited primate conservation efforts.

The knowledge so gained should help us, though some fear it. For Gauguin, "primitive" was good. Those who ate from the tree of knowledge suffered. For others today, "biology" (the primitive) is fearful. Many people reject the idea that we still follow rules that we can trace to the Pliocene. So we can pretend it's not true, but much good that may do us. Denial of our demons won't make them go away. But even if we're driven to accepting the evidence of a grisly past, we're not forced into thinking it condemns us to an unchanged future. There are many challenges.

For primatologists: to understand more precisely the conditions that favor male aggression, and the conditions that suppress it. Are there populations of chimpanzees that have evolved beyond violence? Are there bonobos that are violent like chimpanzees? We can expect some such local adaptations to special conditions—can we use them to explain the ill effects of testerone poisoning in our own ape lineage?

For psychologists: what has the long legacy of aggression done to our psyche? Has it made men specially vulnerable to deindividuation—that mindless loss of self, and acceptance of gang wisdom; . . . or to dehumanization—the cruel emotional deafness to the cries of outsiders? If it prepared us for a career of obedience to authority, of heroism and impulsivity, of quick acceptance of group norms, how can our understanding of history create an enlightened world? The human future may depend on taming the demonic male. It may involve the growing political power of women. But it will not happen in quite the bonobo way. We must look to nature not to copy but to learn.

It may be tempting to condemn the aggressive apes and overly praise the

bonobo. But of course apes are not humans, even though humans may be apes. Their failure to conform to a human morality is their problem, not ours, and they deserve sympathy, respect, and admiration, not disdain. Apes provide us both with a story of our ancestry and a glimpse of a better future. So let us celebrate their lives as instructive visions of other worlds. We still know little, but every population of apes teaches something new. Of course, those populations are disappearing fast. Even the vast forests of Zaïre, uncut though they may be, are being attacked: this year, when I was in Wamba, all mammals but the tabooed bonobo were gone; and the local population had already started killing and eating the bonobos. The same problems are everywhere. We have only a few decades to recover the extraordinary evidence waiting elusively in a hundred forests still unvisited by scientists. Future generations will think ill of us for letting them slide unknown into oblivion. But if we *can* get the observers into the field, and watch the apes in nature, we will surely continue to learn and to be inspired. In that way, the next version of this lecture (in 25 years' time) won't have to be retitled *'Ape Links . . . and Missing Cultures'*!

So ladies and gentlemen, for our sakes and theirs, the apes need all the support they can get. I ask you therefore to raise your glasses, or suck your table-cloths, in celebration of all that's been done, and will be done, by Gordon Getty and the Leakey Foundation!

NOTES

1. (adapted from R. Ardrey 1967, *'The Territorial Imperative'*, p. 232, Fontana).
2. Fyodor Dostoyevsky (1880) *The Brothers Karamazov*. Translated by Constance Garnett. Random House, New York (1950). Part I, Book V, Chapter IV: "Rebellion" (pp. 282–292). p. 287
3. Thomson B. 1987 *Gauguin*. London: Thames and Hudson.

The Fossil Evidence

One primary focal point of this book, as well as the whole of biological anthropology, is the search for, and interpretation of, the fossil evidence for hominid (meaning human or humanlike) evolution. Paleontologists are those who carry out this task by conducting the painstaking excavations and detailed analyses that serve as a basis for understanding our past. Every fragment found is cherished like a ray of light that may help to illuminate the path taken by our ancestors in the process of becoming "us." At least, this is what we would like to believe. In reality, each discovery leads to further mystery, and for every fossil-hunting paleoanthropologist who thinks his or her find supports a particular theory, there are many others anxious to express their disagreement.

How wonderful it would be, we sometimes think in moments of frustration with inconclusive data, if the fossils would just speak for themselves and every primordial piece of humanity were to carry with it a self-evident explanation for its place in the evolutionary story. Paleoanthropology would then be more a quantitative problem of amassing enough material to reconstruct our ancestral development than a qualitative problem of interpreting what it all means. It would certainly be a simpler process, but would it be as interesting? In "New Fossils Take Science Close to Dawn of Humans," for example, we are told of fossils that take us tantalizingly close to the common ancestor of both apes and hominids. But is it ape, hominid, or something else? Needless to say, it is too soon for consensus.

Most scientists tolerate, welcome, or even (dare it be said?) thrive on controversy, recognizing that diversity of opinion refreshes the mind, rouses students, and cap-

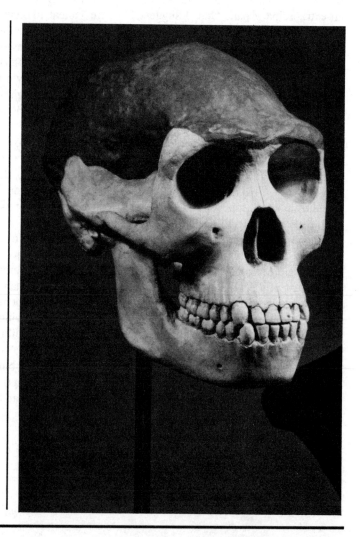

tures the imagination of the general public. After all, where would paleoanthropology be without the gadflies, the near-mythic heroes, and, lest we forget, the research funds they generate?

None of this is to say that all the research and theoretical speculation taking place in the field of paleoanthropology is so highly volatile. Most scientists, in fact, go about their work quietly and methodically, generating hypotheses that are much less explosive and yet have the cumulative effect of enriching our understanding of the details of human evolution. In the essay "Sizing Up Human Intelligence," Stephen Jay Gould shows that the significance of the human brain size is not truly revealed without a comparison with body size of a whole range of mammals, particularly primates. By studying the stratigraphic sequences of fossil remains of other species, Yves Coppens (in "East Side Story: The Origin of Humankind") is able to show how climatic change in East Africa had a significant impact on hominid evolutionary developments. In "Scavenger Hunt," Pat Shipman, furthermore, shows us how modern technology, in the form of the scanning electron microscope, combined with meticulous detailed analysis of cut marks on fossil animal bones, can help us better understand the locomotor and food-getting adaptations of our early hominid ancestors. In one stroke, she is able to challenge the traditional "man the hunter" theme that has pervaded most early hominid research and writing and simultaneously set forth an alternative hypothesis that will, in turn, inspire further research.

As we mull over the controversies outlined in this section, therefore, we should not take them to reflect upon an inherent weakness of the field of paleoanthropology,

but rather accept them as symbolic of its strength: the ability and willingness to scrutinize, question, and reflect on (seemingly endlessly) every bit of evidence. Even in the case of purposeful deception, as recounted in "Dawson's Dawn Man: The Hoax of Piltdown," by Kenneth Feder, it should be remembered that it was the skepticism of scientists themselves that finally led to the revelation of fraud.

Contrary to the way some would have it, the creationists coming to mind, an admission of doubt is not an expression of ignorance, but is simply a frank recognition of the imperfect state of our knowledge. If we are to improve our understanding of ourselves, we must maintain an atmosphere of free inquiry without preconceived notions and an unquestioning commitment to a particular point of view. To paraphrase Ashley Montagu, whereas creationism seeks certainty without proof, science seeks proof without certainty.

Looking Ahead: Challenge Questions

What effect did the Piltdown hoax have upon paleoanthropology?

What did the common ancestor of humans and apes probably look like?

What has climatic change in East Africa had to do with hominid evolution?

What evidence is there that human brain size is unprecedented in the natural world?

What is the "man the hunter" hypothesis and how might the "scavenging theory" better suit the early hominid data?

How would you draw the family tree?

Dawson's Dawn Man: The Hoax at Piltdown

Kenneth L. Feder

The Piltdown Man fossil is a literal skeleton in the closet of prehistoric archaeology and human paleontology. This single specimen seemed to turn our understanding of human evolution on its head and certainly did turn the heads of not just a few of the world's most talented scientists. The story of Piltdown has been presented in detail by Ronald Millar in his 1972 book *The Piltdown Men,* by J. S. Weiner in his 1955 work *The Piltdown Forgery,* and most recently in 1986 by Charles Blinderman in *The Piltdown Inquest.* The story is useful in its telling if only to show that even scientific observers can make mistakes. This is particularly the case when trained scientists are faced with that which they are not trained to detect—intellectual criminality. But let us begin before the beginning, before the discovery of the Piltdown fossil.

THE EVOLUTIONARY CONTEXT

We need to turn the clock back to Europe of the late nineteenth and early twentieth centuries. The concept of evolution—the notion that all animal and plant forms seen in the modern world had descended or evolved from earlier, ancestral forms—had been debated by scientists for quite some time (Greene 1959). It was not until Charles Darwin's *On the Origin of Species* was published in 1859, however, that a viable mechanism for evolution was proposed and supported with an enormous body of data. Darwin had meticulously studied his subject, collecting evidence from all over the world for more than thirty years in support of his evolutionary mechanism called *natural selection.* Darwin's arguments were so well reasoned that most scientists soon became convinced of the explanatory power of his theory. Darwin went on to apply his general theory to humanity in *The Descent of Man,* published in 1871. This book was also enormously successful, and more thinkers came to accept the notion of human evolution.

Around the same time that Darwin was theorizing about the biological origin of humanity, discoveries were being made in Europe and Asia that seemed to support the concept of human evolution from ancestral forms. In 1856, workmen building a roadway in the Neander Valley of Germany came across some remarkable bones. The head was large but oddly shaped (Figure 1). The cranium (the skull minus the mandible or jaw) was much flatter than a modern human's, the bones heavier. The face jutted out, the forehead sloped back, and massive bone ridges appeared just above the eye sockets. Around the same time, other skeletons were found in Belgium and Spain that looked very similar. The postcranial bones (all the bones below the skull) of these fossils were quite similar to those of modern humans.

There was some initial confusion about how to label these specimens. Some scientists concluded that they simply represented pathological freaks. Rudolf Virchow, the world's preeminent anatomist, explained the curious bony ridges above the eyes as the result of blows to the foreheads of the creatures (Kennedy 1975). Eventually, however, scientists realized that these creatures, then and now called *Neandertals* after their most famous find-spot, represented a primitive and ancient form of humanity.

The growing acceptance of Darwin's theory of evolution and the discovery of primitive-looking, though human-like, fossils combined to radically shift people's opinions about human origins. In fact, the initial abhorrence many felt concerning the entire notion of human evolution from lower, more primitive forms was remarkably changed in just a few decades (Greene 1959). By the turn of the twentieth century, not only were many people comfortable with the general concept of human evolution, but there actually was also a feeling of national pride concerning the discovery of a human ancestor within one's borders.

The Germans could point to their Neandertal skeletons and claim that the first primitive human being was a German. The French could counter that their own Cro-Magnon—ancient, though not as old as the German Neandertals—was a more humanlike and advanced ancestor; therefore, the first true human was a Frenchman. Fossils had also been found in Belgium and Spain, so Belgians and Spaniards could claim for themselves a place within the story of human origin and development. Even so small a nation as Holland could lay claim to a place in human evolutionary history since a Dutchman, Eugene Dubois, in 1891 had discovered the fossilized remains of a primitive human ancestor in Java, a Dutch-owned colony in the western Pacific.

However, one great European nation did not and could not participate fully in the debate over the ultimate origins of humanity. That nation was England. Very simply, by the beginning of the second decade of the twentieth century, no fossils of human evolutionary significance had been located in England. This lack of fossils led French scientists to label English human paleontology mere "pebble-collecting" (Blinderman 1986).

The English, justifiably proud of their cultural heritage and cultural evolution, simply could point to no evidence that humanity had initially developed within their borders. The conclusion reached by most was completely unpalatable to the proud English—no one had evolved in England. The English must have originally arrived from somewhere else.

At the same time that the English were feeling like a people with no evolutionary roots of their own, many other Europeans were still uncomfortable with the fossil record as it stood in the first decade of the twentieth century. While most were happy to have human fossils in their countries, they were generally not happy with what those fossils looked like and what their appearance implied about the course of human evolution.

Java Man (now placed in the category *Homo erectus* along with Peking Man), with its small cranium—its volume was about 900 cubic centimeters (cc), compared to a modern human average of about 1,450 cc—and large eyebrow ridges seemed quite apelike (see Figure 1). Neandertal Man, with his sloping forehead and thick, heavy brow ridges appeared to many to be

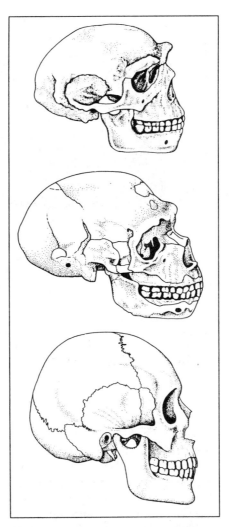

Figure 1 *Drawings showing the general differences in skull size and form between* Homo erectus *(Peking Man—500,000 years ago [top]), Neandertal Man (100,000 years ago [center]), and a modern human being [bottom]. Note the large brow ridges and forward-thrusting faces of* Homo erectus *and Neandertal, the rounded outline of the modern skull, and the absence of a chin in earlier forms. (Carolyn Whyte)*

quite ugly, stupid, and brutish. While the skulls of these fossil types were clearly not those of apes, they were equally clearly not fully human. On the other hand, the femur (thigh bone) of Java Man seemed identical to the modern form. While some emphasized what they perceived to be primitive characteristics of the postcranial skeleton of the Neandertals, this species clearly had walked on two feet; and apes do not.

All this evidence suggested that ancient human ancestors had primitive heads and, by implication, primitive

brains, seated atop rather modern-looking bodies. This further implied that it was the human body that evolved first, followed only later by the development of the brain and associated human intelligence.

Such a picture was precisely the opposite of what many people had expected and hoped for. After all, it was argued, it is intelligence that most clearly and absolutely differentiates humanity from the rest of the animal kingdom. It is in our ability to think, to communicate, and to invent that we are most distant from our animal cousins. This being the case, it was assumed that such abilities must have been evolving the longest; in other words, the human brain and the ability to think must have evolved first. Thus, the argument went, the fossil evidence for evolution should show that the brain had expanded first, followed by the modernization of the body.

Such a view is exemplified in the writings of anatomist Grafton Elliot Smith. Smith said that what most characterized human evolution must have been the "steady and uniform development of the brain along a well-defined course . . ." (as quoted in Blinderman 1986:36). Arthur Smith Woodward, ichthyologist and paleontologist at the British Museum of Natural History, later characterized the human brain as "the most complex mechanism in existence. The growth of the brain preceded the refinement of the features and of the somatic characters in general" (Dawson and Woodward 1913).

Put most simply, many researchers in evolution were looking for fossil evidence of a creature with the body of an ape and the brain of a human being. What was being discovered, however, was the reverse; both Java and Neandertal Man seemed more to represent creatures with apelike, or certainly not humanlike, brains but with humanlike bodies. Many were uncomfortable with such a picture.

A REMARKABLE DISCOVERY IN SUSSEX

Thus was the stage set for the initially rather innocuous announcement that appeared in the British science journal *Nature* on December 5, 1912, concerning a fossil find in the Piltdown section of Sussex in southern England. The notice read, in part:

> Remains of a human skull and mandible, considered to belong to the early Pleistocene period, have been discovered by Mr. Charles Dawson in a gravel-deposit in the basin of the River Ouse, north of Lewes, Sussex. Much interest has been aroused in the specimen owing to the exactitude with which its geological age is said to have been fixed. . . . (p. 390)

In the December 19 issue of *Nature,* further details were provided concerning the important find:

> The fossil human skull and mandible to be described by Mr. Charles Dawson and Dr. Arthur Smith Woodward at the Geological Society as we go to press is the most important discovery of its kind hitherto made in England. The specimen was found in circumstances which seem to leave no doubt of its geological age, and the characters it shows are themselves sufficient to denote its extreme antiquity. (p. 438)

According to the story later told by those principally involved, in February 1912 Arthur Smith Woodward at the British Museum received a letter from Charles Dawson—a Sussex lawyer and amateur scientist. Woodward had previously worked with Dawson and knew him to be an extremely intelligent man with a keen interest in natural history. Dawson informed Woodward in the letter that he had come upon several fragments of a fossil human skull. The first piece had been discovered in 1908 by workers near the Barcombe Mills manor in the Piltdown region of Sussex, England. In 1911, a number of other pieces of the skull came to light in the same pit, along with a fossil hippopotamus bone and tooth.

In the letter to Woodward, Dawson expressed some excitement over the discovery and claimed to Woodward that the find was quite important and might even surpass the significance of Heidelberg Man, an important specimen found in Germany just the previous year.

Due to bad weather, Woodward was not immediately able to visit Piltdown. Dawson, undaunted, continued to work

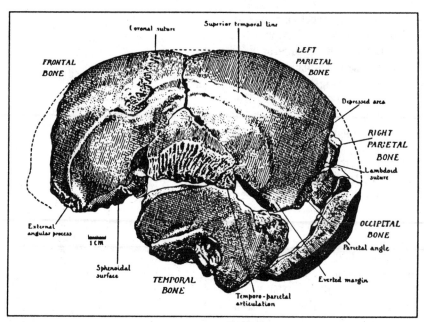

Figure 2 *This drawing with anatomical labels of the fragmentary remains of the Piltdown cranium appeared in a book written by one of the fossil's chief supporters. (From* The Evolution of Man, *by Grafton Elliot Smith, Oxford University Press)*

in the pit, finding fossil hippo and elephant teeth. Finally, in May 1912, he brought the fossil to Woodward at the museum. What Woodward saw was a skull that matched his own expectations and those of many others concerning what a human ancestor should look like. The skull, stained a dark brown from apparent age, seemed to be quite modern in many of its characteristics. The thickness of the bones of the skull, however, argued for a certain primitiveness. The association of the skull fragments with the bones of extinct animals implied that an ancient human ancestor indeed had inhabited England. By itself this was enormous news; at long last, England had a human fossil (Figure 2).

Things were to get even more exciting for English paleontologists. At the end of May 1912 Dawson, Woodward, and Pierre Teilhard de Chardin—a Jesuit priest with a great interest in geology, paleontology, and evolution whom Dawson had met in 1909—began a thorough archaeological excavation at the Piltdown site. . . . More extinct animal remains and flint tools were recovered. The apparent age of the fossils based upon comparisons to other sites indicated not only that Pilt-

down was the earliest human fossil in England, but also that, at an estimated age of 500,000 years, the Piltdown fossil represented potentially the oldest known human ancestor in the world.

Then, to add to the excitement, Dawson discovered one half of the mandible. Though two key areas—the chin, and the condyle where the jaw connects to the skull—were missing, the preserved part did not look anything like a human jaw. The upright portion or *ramus* was too wide, and the bone too thick. In fact, the jaw looked remarkably like that of an ape (Figure 3). Nonetheless, and quite significantly, the molar teeth exhibited humanlike wear. The human jaw, lacking the large canines of apes, is free to move from side to side while chewing. The molars can grind in a sideways motion in a manner impossible in monkeys or apes. The wear on human molars is, therefore, quite distinct from that of other primates. The Piltdown molars exhibited such humanlike wear in a jaw that was otherwise entirely apelike.

That the skull and the jaw had been found close together in the same geologically ancient deposit seemed to argue for the obvious conclusion that

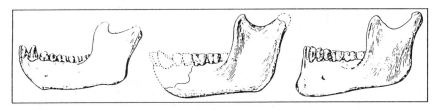

Figure 3 *Comparison of the mandibles (lower jaws) of a young chimpanzee [left], modern human [right], and Piltdown [center]. Note how much more similar the Piltdown mandible is to that of the chimp, particularly in the absence of a chin. The presence of a chin is a uniquely human trait. (From Dawson and Woodward, 1913, The Geological Society of London)*

they belonged to the same ancient creature. But what kind of creature could it have been? There were no large brow ridges like those of Java or Neandertal Man. The face was flat as in modern humans and not snoutlike as in the Neandertals. The profile of the cranium was round as it is in modern humans, not flattened as it appeared to be in the Java and Neandertal specimens (Figure 4). According to Woodward, the size of the skull indicated a cranial capacity or brain size of at least 1,100 cc (Dawson and Woodward 1913), much larger than Java and within the range of modern humanity. Anatomist Arthur Keith (1913) suggested that the capacity of the skull was actually much larger, as much as 1,500 cc, placing it close to the modern mean. But the jaw, as described above, was entirely apelike.

The conclusion drawn first by Dawson, the discoverer, and then by Woodward, the professional scientist, was that the Piltdown fossil—called *Eoanthropus dawsoni*, meaning Dawson's Dawn Man—was the single most important fossil find yet made anywhere in the world. Concerning the Piltdown discovery, the *New York Times* headline of December 19, 1912, proclaimed "Paleolithic Skull Is a Missing Link." Three days later the *Times* headline read "Darwin Theory Is Proved True."

The implications were clear. Piltdown Man, with its modern skull, primitive jaw, and great age, was the evidence many human paleontologists had been searching for: an ancient man with a large brain, a modern-looking head, and primitive characteristics below the important brain. As anatomist G. E. Smith summarized it:

The brain attained what may be termed the human rank when the jaws and face, and no doubt the body also, still retained much of the uncouthness of Man's simian ancestors. In other words, Man at first, so far as his general appearance and "build" are concerned, was merely an Ape with an overgrown brain. The importance of the Piltdown skull lies in the fact that it affords tangible confirmation of these inferences. (Smith 1927:105–6)

If Piltdown were the evolutionary "missing link" between apes and people, then neither Neandertal nor Java Man could be. Since Piltdown and Java Man lived at approximately the same time, Java might have been a more primitive offshoot of humanity that had

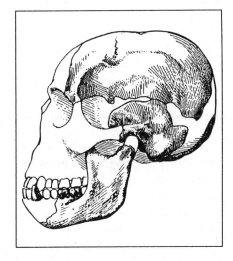

Figure 4 *Drawn reconstruction of the Piltdown skull. The portion of the skull actually recovered is shaded. As reconstructed, the cranium shows hominid (human) traits and the mandible shows pongid (ape) traits. Compare this drawing to those in Figure 1. With its humanlike head and apelike jaw, the overall appearance of the Piltdown fossil is far different from* Homo erectus, *Neandertal, or modern humans. (From* The Evolution of Man, *Grafton Elliot Smith, Oxford University Press)*

become extinct. Since Neandertal was much more recent than Piltdown, yet looked more primitive where it really counted (that is, the head), Neandertal must have represented some sort of primitive throwback, an evolutionary anachronism (Figure 5).

By paleontological standards the implications were breathtaking. In one sweeping blow Piltdown had presented England with its first ancestral human fossil, it had shown that human fossils found elsewhere in the world were either primitive evolutionary offshoots or later throwbacks to a more primitive type, and it had forced the rewriting of the entire story of human evolution. Needless to say, many paleontologists, especially those in England, were enthralled by the discovery in Sussex.

In March 1913, Dawson and Woodward published the first detailed account of the characteristics and evolutionary implications of the Piltdown fossil. Again and again in their discussion, they pointed out the modern characteristics of the skull and the simian appearance of the mandible. Their comments regarding the modernity of the skull and the apelike characteristics of the jaw, as you will see, turned out to be accurate in a way that few suspected at the time.

Additional discoveries were made at Piltdown. In 1913 a right canine tooth apparently belonging to the jaw was discovered by Teilhard de Chardin. It matched almost exactly the canine that had previously been proposed for the Piltdown skull in the reconstruction produced at the British Museum of Natural History. Its apelike form and wear were precisely what had been expected: "If a comparative anatomist were fitting out *Eoanthropus* with a set of canines, he could not ask for anything more suitable than the tooth in question," stated Yale University professor George Grant MacCurdy (1914: 159).

Additional artifacts, including a large bone implement, were found in 1914. Then, in 1915, Dawson wrote Woodward announcing spectacular evidence confirming the first discovery; fragments of another fossil human skull were found (possibly at a site just two miles from the first—Dawson never revealed the location). This skull, dubbed Piltdown II, looked just like the first with a rounded profile and thick cranial bones. Though no jaw was discovered, a molar recovered at the site bore the same pattern of wear as that seen in the first specimen.

Dawson died in 1916 and, for reasons not entirely clear, Woodward held back announcement of the second discovery until the following year. When the existence of a second specimen became known, many of those skeptical after the discovery of the first Piltdown fossil became supporters. One of those converted skeptics, Henry Fairfield Osborn, president of the American Museum of Natural History, suggested:

If there is a Providence hanging over the affairs of prehistoric man, it certainly manifested itself in this case, because the three minute fragments of this second Piltdown man found by Dawson are exactly those which we should have selected to confirm the comparison with the original type. (1921:581)

THE PILTDOWN ENIGMA

There certainly was no unanimity of opinion, however, concerning the significance of the Piltdown discoveries. The cranium was so humanlike and the jaw so apelike that some scientists maintained that they simply were the fossils of two different creatures; the skeptics suggested that the association of the human cranium and ape jaw was entirely coincidental. Gerrit S. Miller, Jr. (1915) of the Smithsonian Institution conducted a detailed analysis of casts of Piltdown I and concluded that the jaw was certainly that of an ape (See Figure 3). Many other scientists in the United States and Europe agreed. Anatomy professor David Waterson (1913) at the University of London, King's College, thought the mandible was that of a chimpanzee. The very well-known German scientist Franz Weidenreich concluded that Piltdown I was " . . . the artificial combination of fragments of a modern-human braincase with an orangutan-like mandible and teeth" (1943:273).

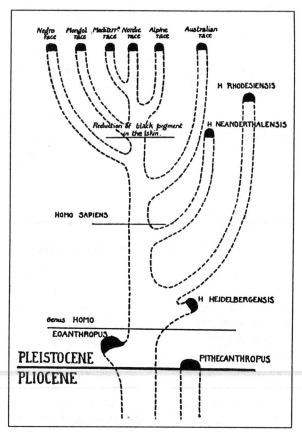

Figure 5 *Among its supporters,* Eoanthropus *(Piltdown Man) was seen as more directly ancestral to modern humanity than either* Homo erectus—*here labeled* Pithecanthropus *and depicted as an entirely separate evolutionary pathway—or Neandertal—shown here as a short-lived diversion off the main branch of human evolution. (From* The Evolution of Man, *Grafton Elliot Smith, Oxford University Press)*

Coincidentally or not, after Dawson's death no further discoveries were made in either the Piltdown I or II localities, though Woodward continued excavating at Piltdown through the 1920s. Elsewhere in the world, however, human paleontology became an increasingly exciting and fruitful endeavor. Beginning in the late 1920s as many as forty individuals of a species now called *Homo erectus* were unearthed at Zhoukoudian, a cave near Beijing in China (see Figure 1). Ironically, Davidson Black, anatomist at the Peking Union Medical College, who was instrumental in obtaining financial support for the excavation, had visited Grafton Elliot Smith's laboratory in 1914 and had become fascinated by the Piltdown find (Shapiro 1974). Further, Teilhard de Chardin participated in the excavation at the cave. The Zhoukoudian fossils were estimated to be one-half million years old. Also on Java,

another large group of fossils (close to twenty) were found at Sangiran; these were similar to those from Zhoukoudian.

Also in the 1920s, in Africa, the discovery was made of a fossil given the name *Australopithecus africanus.* It was initially estimated to be more than one million years old. In the 1930s and 1940s additional finds of this and other varieties of *Australopithecus* were made. In Europe the number of Neandertal specimens kept increasing; and even in England, in 1935, a fossil human ancestor was discovered at a place called Swanscombe.

Unfortunately for *Eoanthropus,* all of these discoveries seemed to contradict its validity. The Chinese and Sangiran *Homo erectus* evidence pointed to a fossil ancestor with a humanlike body and primitive head; these specimens were quite similar to Java Man in appearance (Java Man is also now considered to belong to the species *Homo erectus*), possessing large brow ridges, a flat skull, and a thrust-forward face while being quite modern from the neck down. Even the much older australopithecines showed clear evidence of walking on two feet; their skeletons were remarkably humanlike from the neck down, though their heads were quite apelike. Together, both of these species seemed to confirm the notion that human beings began their evolutionary history as upright apes, not as apelike people. *Eoanthropus* seemed more and more to be the evolutionary "odd man out."

How could Piltdown be explained in light of the new fossil evidence from China, Java, Europe, and Africa? Either Piltdown was a human ancestor, rendering all the manifold other discoveries members of extinct offshoots of the main line of human evolution, or else Piltdown was the remarkable coincidental find of the only known ape fossil in England within a few feet of a rather modern human skull that seemed to date back 500,000 years. Neither explanation sat well with many people.

UNMASKING THE HOAX

This sort of confusion characterized the status of Piltdown until 1949, when a new dating procedure was applied to the fossil. A measurement was made of the amount of the element fluorine in the bones. This was known to be a relative measure of the amount of time bone had been in the ground. Bones pick up fluorine in groundwater; the longer they have been buried, the more fluorine they have. Kenneth Oakley of the British Museum of Natural History conducted the test. While the fossil animal bones from the site showed varying amounts of fluorine, they exhibited as much as ten times more than did either the cranium or jaw of the fossil human. Piltdown Man, Oakley concluded, based on comparison to fluorine concentrations in bones at other sites in England, was no more than 50,000 years old (Oakley and Weiner 1955).

While this certainly cast Piltdown in

a new light, the implications were just as mysterious; what was a fossil human doing with an entirely apelike jaw at a date as recent as 50,000 years ago? Then, in 1953 a more precise test was applied to larger samples of the cranium and jaw. The results were quite conclusive; the skull and jaw were of entirely different ages. The cranium possessed .10 percent fluorine, the mandible less than .03 percent (Oakley 1976). The inevitable conclusion was reached that the skull and jaw must have belonged to two different creatures.

As a result of this determination, a detailed reexamination of the fossil was conducted and the sad truth was finally revealed. The entire thing had been a hoax. The skull was that of a modern human being. Its appearance of age was due, at least in part, to its having been artificially chemically stained. The thickness of the bone may have been due to a pathological condition (Spencer 1984) or the result of a chemical treatment that had been applied, perhaps to make it appear older than it was (Montague 1960).

Those scientific supporters of *Eoanthropus* who previously had pointed out the apelike character of the jaw were more right than they could have imagined; it was, indeed, a doctored ape jaw, probably that of an orangutan. When Gerrit Miller of the Smithsonian Institution had commented on the broken condyle of the mandible by saying, "Deliberate malice could hardly have been more successful than the hazards of deposition in so breaking the fossils as to give free scope to individual judgement in fitting the parts together" (1915:1), he was using a literary device and not suggesting that anyone had purposely broken the jaw. But that is likely precisely what happened. An ape's jaw could never articulate with the base of a human skull, and so the area of connection had to be removed to give "free scope" to researchers to hypothesize how the cranium and jaw went together. Otherwise the hoax would never have succeeded. Beyond this, the molars had been filed down to artificially create the humanlike wear pattern. The canine tooth had been

stained with an artist's pigment and filed down to simulate human wear; the pulp cavity had been filled with a substance not unlike chewing gum.

It was further determined that at least one of the fragments of the Piltdown II skull was simply another piece of the first one. Oakley further concluded that all the other paleontological specimens had been planted at the site; some were probably found in England, but others had likely originated as far away as Malta and Tunisia. Some of the ostensible bone artifacts had been carved with a metal knife.

The verdict was clear; as Franz Weidenreich (1943) put it, Piltdown was like the chimera of Greek mythology—a monstrous combination of different creatures. The question of Piltdown's place in human evolution had been answered: it had no place. That left still open two important questions: who did it and why?

WHODUNNIT?

The most succinct answer that can be provided for the question "Whodunnit?" is "No one knows." It seems, however, that every writer on the subject has had a different opinion.

Each of the men who excavated at Piltdown has been accused at one time or another. . . . Charles Dawson is an obvious suspect. He is the only person who was present at every discovery. He certainly gained notoriety; even the species name is *dawsoni*. Blinderman (1986) points out, however, that much of the evidence against Dawson is circumstantial and exaggerated. Dawson did indeed stain the fossil with potassium bichromate and iron ammonium sulfate. These gave the bones a more antique appearance, but such staining was fairly common. It was felt that these chemicals helped preserve fossil bone, and Dawson was quite open about having stained the Piltdown specimens. In an unrelated attack on his character, some have even accused Dawson of plagiarism in a book he wrote on Hastings Castle (Weiner 1955), but this seems to be unfair; as Blinderman points out, the book was explicitly a compilation of previous sources and Dawson did not attempt to take credit for the work of others.

Dawson's motive might have been the fame and notoriety that accrued to this amateur scientist who could command the attention of the world's most famous scholars. But there is no direct evidence concerning Dawson's guilt, and questions remain concerning his ability to fashion the fraud. And where would Dawson have obtained the orangutan jaw?

Arthur Smith Woodward certainly possessed the opportunity and expertise to pull off the fraud. His motive might have been to prove his particular view of human evolution. That makes little sense though, since he could not have expected the kind of confirming evidence he knew his colleagues would demand. Furthermore, his behavior after Dawson's death seems to rule out Woodward as the hoaxer. His fruitlessly working the original Piltdown pit in his retirement renders this scenario nonsensical.

Even the priest Teilhard de Chardin has been accused, most recently by Harvard paleontologist and chronicler of the history of science Stephen Jay Gould (1980). The evidence marshalled against the Jesuit is entirely circumstantial, the argument strained. The mere facts that Teilhard mentioned Piltdown but little in his later writings on evolution and was confused about the precise chronology of discoveries in the pit do not add up to a convincing case.

Others have had fingers pointed at them. W. J. Sollas, a geology professor at Oxford and a strong supporter of Piltdown, has been accused from beyond the grave. In 1978, a tape-recorded statement made before his death by J. A. Douglass, who had worked in Sollas's lab for some thirty years, was made public. The only evidence provided is Douglass's testimony that on one occasion he came across a package containing the fossil-staining agent potassium bichromate in the lab—certainly not the kind of stuff to convince a jury to convict.

Even Sir Arthur Conan Doyle has come under the scrutiny of would-be Piltdown detectives. Doyle lived near Piltdown and is known to have visited the site at least once. He may have held a grudge against professional scientists who belittled his interest in and credulity concerning the paranormal. Doyle, the creator of the most logical, rational mind in literature, Sherlock Holmes, found it quite reasonable that two young English girls could take photographs of real fairies in their garden. But why would Doyle strike out at paleontologists, who had nothing to do with criticizing his acceptance of the occult? Again, there is no direct evidence to implicate Doyle in the hoax.

The most recent name added to the roster of potential Piltdown hoaxers is that of Lewis Abbott, another amateur scientist and artifact collector. Blinderman (1986) argues that Abbott is the most likely perpetrator. He had an enormous ego and felt slighted by professional scientists. He claimed to have been the one who directed Dawson to the pit at Piltdown and may even have been with Dawson when Piltdown II was discovered (Dawson said only that he had been with a friend when the bones were found). Abbott knew how to make stone tools and so was capable of forging those found at Piltdown. Again, however, the evidence, though tantalizing, includes no smoking gun.

A definitive answer to the question "whodunnit" may never be forthcoming. The lesson in Piltdown, though, is clear. Unlike the case for the Cardiff Giant where scientists were not fooled, here many were convinced by what appears to be, in hindsight, an inelegant fake. It shows quite clearly that scientists, though striving to be objective observers and explainers of the world around them, are, in the end, human. Many accepted the Piltdown evidence because they wished to—it supported a more comfortable view of human evolution. Furthermore, perhaps out of naïveté, they could not even conceive that a fellow thinker about human origins would wish to trick them; the possibility that Piltdown was a fraud probably occurred to few, if any, of them.

Nevertheless, the Piltdown story, rather than being a black mark against science, instead shows how well it ultimately works. Even before its unmasking, Piltdown had been consigned by most to a netherworld of doubt. There was simply too much evidence supporting a different human pedigree than that implied by Piltdown. Proving it a hoax was just the final nail in the coffin lid for this fallacious fossil. As a result, though we may never know the hoaxer's name, at least we know this: if the goal was to forever confuse our understanding of the human evolutionary story, the hoax ultimately was a failure.

CURRENT PERSPECTIVES HUMAN EVOLUTION

With little more than a handful of cranial fragments, human paleontologists defined an entire species, *Eoanthropus,* and recast the story of human evolution. Later, in 1922, on the basis of a single fossil tooth found in Nebraska, an ancient species of man, *Hesperopithecus,* was defined. It was presumed to be as old as any hominid species found in the Old World and convinced some that thencurrent evolutionary models needed to be overhauled. The tooth turned out to belong to an ancient pig. Even in the case of Peking Man, the species was defined and initially named *Sinanthropus pekinensis* on the basis of only two teeth.

Today, the situation in human paleontology is quite different. The tapestry of our human evolutionary history is no longer woven with the filaments of a small handful of gauzy threads. We can now base our evolutionary scenarios (Figure 6) on enormous quantities of data supplied by several fields of science (see Feder and Park 1989 for a detailed summary of current thinking on human evolution).

Australopithecus afarensis, for example, the oldest known hominid, dating to more than 3.5 million years ago, is represented by more than a dozen fossil individuals. The most famous specimen, known as "Lucy," is more than 40 percent complete. Its pelvis is remarkably modern and provides clear evidence of its upright, and therefore

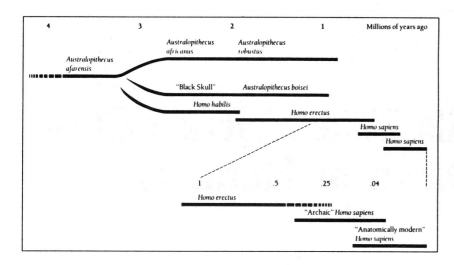

Figure 6 *Current human evolutionary chronologies are based on a large body of paleontological, archaeological, and genetic data. There is no room for—and no need for—a precociously large-brained human ancestor like* Eoanthropus *in the human pedigree. (From* Human Antiquity, *Feder and Park, Mayfield Publishing)*

humanlike, posture. Its skull, on the other hand, is quite apelike and contained a brain the size of a chimpanzee's. We even have a preserved pathway of footprints dating to the time when Lucy and her cohorts walked the earth, showing as dramatically as possible that they did so in a bipedal, humanlike fashion.

Homo erectus is known from dozens of individuals—forty from Zhoukoudian alone, nearly twenty from Java, and more than a dozen from Africa. In Kenya, the 80 percent complete skeleton of a twelve-year-old *Homo erectus* boy has been dated to more than 1.5 million years ago.

Archaic forms of *Homo sapiens,* especially the famous Neandertals, number in the hundreds. The fossil human record is rich and growing. Our evolu-

tionary scenarios are based, not on a handful of fragmentary bones, but on the remains of hundreds of individuals. Grafton Elliot Smith, Arthur Smith Woodward, and the others were quite wrong. The abundant evidence shows very clearly that human evolutionary history is characterized by the precedence of upright posture and the tardy development of the brain. It now appears that while our ancestors developed upright posture and humanlike bodies more than 3.5 million years ago, the modern human brain did not develop until as recently as 100,000 years ago.

Beyond this, human paleontologists are no longer restricted solely to the paleontological record. Exciting techniques of genetic analysis have allowed scientists to develop measures of dif-

ference between living species, including humans and our nearest extant relatives, the apes. Genetic "clocks" have been created from the results of such techniques.

For example, through DNA hybridization, scientists can quantify the difference between the genetic codes of people and chimpanzees. Here, an attempt is made to bond human and chimp DNA, much in the way the separate strands of the DNA double helix bond to produce the genetic code for a single organism. It turns out that the DNA of our two species is so similar that we can form a nearly complete bond. The opinion of most is that our two species could have split evolutionarily no more than five or six million years ago.

New dating techniques based on radioactive half-lives, biomechanical analysis of bones, scanning electron microscopy in bone and artifact examination, and many other new forms of analysis all make our evolutionary scenarios more concrete. It is to be expected that ideas will change as new data are collected and new analytical techniques are developed. Certainly our current views will be fine-tuned, and perhaps even drastic changes of opinion will take place. This is the nature of science. It is fair to suggest, however, that no longer could a handful of enigmatic bones that contradicted our mutually supportive paleontological, cultural, and genetic data bases cause us to unravel and reweave our evolutionary tapestry. Today, the discovery of a Piltdown Man likely would fool few.

New Fossils Take Science Close to Dawn of Humans

John Noble Wilford

Fossils of the oldest human ancestors have been discovered in Ethiopia, where these apelike creatures lived 4.4 million years ago on a forested flood plain. Not only do they represent an entirely new species, scientists said, but they also may well be the long-sought relatives who lived close to the fateful time when the lineages leading to modern apes and Homo sapiens went their separate ways.

"The discovery of these ancient fossils and their context signals a major step in our understanding of human origins," Dr. Tim D. White, a paleontologist at the University of California at Berkeley, said yesterday in an announcement of the findings.

Other scientists greeted the announcement with ringing endorsements. They said the evidence for identifying the new species was compelling. The species represented an enormous leap back of 800,000 years in reconstructing the prehuman fossil record. If genetic research by molecular biologists is correct, the find has taken scientists into that intriguing evolutionary time, estimated to be four million to six million years ago, when the apes and humans diverged.

The name assigned to the new species, Australopithecus ramidus, is a reflection of its presumed primal importance on the human family tree. In the Afar language of the region where the fossils were found, ramid is the word for root, and it applies to plants or people—thus humanity's root species.

Details about the fossils, excavated in the last two years at a site in the Ethiopian badlands called Aramis, are being reported in today's issue of the journal Nature in an article by Dr. White and his two principal colleagues, Dr. Gen Suwa, a paleontologist and expert in ancient teeth at the University of Tokyo, and Dr. Berhane Asfaw, an Ethiopian paleontologist. They described the fossils as "the most apelike hominid ancestor known," something scientists have been seeking for two decades, a closer "link in the evolutionary chain of species between humans and their African ape ancestors."

In a commentary accompanying the report, Dr. Bernard Wood, a paleontologist at the University of Liverpool in England, wrote, "The metaphor of a missing link has often been misused, but it is a suitable epithet for the hominid from Aramis."

The fact that the fossils were found in sediments of a previously wooded environment could also be of profound significance in reinterpreting the early stages of human evolution. It may even be the most important immediate consequence of the research.

"The most exciting thing about this discovery is the ecological context," Dr. Owen Lovejoy, a paleontologist at Kent State University in Ohio, said in an interview.

The assumption had been that when the climate changed and forests gave way to grasslands, the forces of natural selection favored those apes that could walk upright and adapt to the open country. These adaptations led to the first hominids. If the new species did indeed evolve in a forest, scientists will have to rethink these assumptions and, as Dr. White said, consider that it "was not the savannah that forced us along the evolutionary road."

As yet, there is only indirect evidence that these creatures, which were about the size of chimpanzees, were able to walk upright. Most of the fossils are of teeth, jaws, a cranial base and some arm bones. One of the objectives of the next excavations, to begin next month, is to search for pelvic, knee and foot bones that should be more revealing of the species' walking abilities.

The 4.4.-million-year-old bones have cast doubt on the path of evolution.

By shaking up conventional wisdom and extending the chronology of human ancestry, Dr. Lovejoy said, "This is the most exciting thing to happen since Lucy."

Until the new discoveries, the earliest known direct human ancestor was Australopithecus afarensis, the first and most famous specimen of which was found in 1974 and nicknamed Lucy. This partial skeleton was dated at 3.2 million years, and other finds showed that the same species lived between 3 and 3.6 million years ago, and perhaps even earlier, though the evidence is sparse and not well established. The fossil footprints that Mary Leakey, the noted Kenyan paleontologist, uncovered in Tanzania presumably were made by A. afarensis.

Although there are almost as many hypothesized human family trees as there are paleontologists, scholars generally agree that A. afarensis is the common ancestor to two subsequent lines of evolution. One is the heavy-jawed, small-brained australopithecines, which became extinct about one million years ago. The other line began with the emergence of the genus Homo about 2.5 million years ago, about the same time the first stone tools were made and used. The most immediate human ancestor was Homo erectus, from 1.8 million years to perhaps a few hundred thousand years ago.

After two decades of research, scientists recognized that the Lucy species still left them with a substantial gap in the initial evolution after the ape-hominid divergence. The search for a species ancestral to A. afarensis has been a central goal of fossil hunters.

Fossils of 17 individuals of the new species, A. ramidus, were excavated about 140 miles northeast of Addis Ababa and 45 miles south of Hadar, where the Lucy skeleton was found. Dr. Suwa made the initial discovery on Dec. 17, 1992. As he walked across the barren ground, his eye was caught by the glint of a molar tooth among the desert pebbles.

"I knew immediately that it was a hominid," Dr. Suwa said. "And because we had found other ancient animals that morning, I knew it was one of the oldest hominid teeth ever found."

Analyzing the fossils, the scientists realized that these individuals were more like chimpanzees, the apes that are the closest living relatives of humans, than were members of the afarensis species. But the reduced size and different shapes of certain teeth, particularly the canines and a lower first deciduous molar, one of the so-called milk teeth, showed that these creatures were more primitive than afarensis but had evolved from the same apes who had been their ancestors.

These were the remains of a species, Dr. Wood said, that "lies so close to the divergence between the lineages leading to the African apes and modern humans that its attribution to the human line is metaphorically, and literally, by the skin of its teeth."

Dr. Asfaw said: "The short cranial base and the hominid shapes of the canine and elbow show us that this species had already split from the apes. It had started to evolve towards human beings."

Since scientists had been expecting to find a species ancestral to afarensis, but much more primitive, said Dr. Donald C. Johanson, president of the Institute of Human Origins in Berkeley and, along with Dr. White, a discoverer of the Lucy skeleton, "There are no real surprises in the anatomy."

Dr. Johanson said the findings provided strong fossil support for the genetic studies suggesting that the split between apes and humans occurred relatively recently, perhaps no more than six million years ago. Many paleontologists had long held out for a much more ancient divergence, perhaps as much as 15 to 20 million years ago. Scientists said there could still be other transitional species closer to the common ancestor of apes and humans.

In another report in Nature, a team of geologists and anthropologists, led by Dr. Giday WoldeGabriel of the Los Alamos National Laboratory in New Mexico, described how the fossils lying under volcanic ash and glass were dated and noted that an abundance of fossil wood and arboreal seeds was identified. This and a substantial number of monkey fossils was offered as evidence that the new species had "lived and died in a woodland setting."

Like several scientists who have been challenging traditional thinking, Dr. Andrew Hill, a Yale University paleontologist, said: "This supports the hunches we have had that savannahs were not the major element in the origins of hominids. I would be happier if we knew it was a biped."

For other scientists to accept this revisionist view, the explorers at Aramis must come up with stronger evidence that A. ramidus could either walk upright or at least appears to have been evolving such a talent. Dr. White said the smaller canine teeth of the new species were consistent with characteristics of other hominids that had altered their social structure and were beginning to carry infants and food with their forearms, the first stage of upright walking. Other indirect evidence included characteristics of the cranial base that were different in some respects from apes, indicating that it had evolved in ways associated with upright walking.

Somewhat more direct evidence, Dr. White said, were the similarities in the arm bones of A. ramidus and the Lucy species. "This is not the arm of a knuckle-walker," he said, "but I want to hold the question of locomotion until more fossils are found."

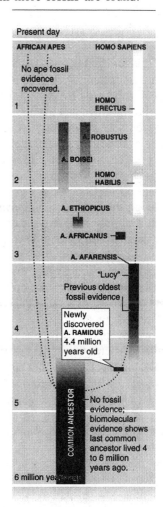

Fossils found in Aramis, Ethiopia, are believed to be from the oldest known hominid species. This is one theory of the approximate timetable.

Source: Dr. Tim D. White, University of California at Berkeley

Sizing Up Human Intelligence

Stephen Jay Gould

HUMAN BODIES

"Size," Julian Huxley once remarked, "has a fascination of its own." We stock our zoos with elephants, hippopotamuses, giraffes, and gorillas; who among you was not rooting for King Kong in his various battles atop tall buildings? This focus on the few creatures larger than ourselves has distorted our conception of our own size. Most people think that *Homo sapiens* is a creature of only modest dimensions. In fact, humans are among the largest animals on earth; more than 99 percent of animal species are smaller than we are. Of 190 species in our own order of primate mammals, only the gorilla regularly exceeds us in size.

In our self-appointed role as planetary ruler, we have taken great interest in cataloging the features that permitted us to attain this lofty estate. Our brain, upright posture, development of speech, and group hunting (to name just a few) are often cited, but I have been struck by how rarely our large size has been recognized as a controlling factor of our evolutionary progress.

Despite its low reputation in certain circles, self-conscious intelligence is surely the *sine qua non* of our current status. Could we have evolved it at much smaller body sizes? One day, at the New York World's Fair in 1964, I entered the hall of Free Enterprise to escape the rain. Inside, prominently displayed, was an ant colony bearing the sign: "Twenty million years of evolutionary stagnation. Why? Because the ant colony is a socialist, totalitarian system." The statement scarcely requires serious attention; nonetheless, I should point out that ants are doing very well for themselves, and that it is their size rather than their social structure that precludes high mental capacity.

In this age of the transistor, we can put radios in watchcases and bug telephones with minute electronic packages. Such miniaturization might lead us to the false belief that absolute size is irrelevant to the operation of complex machinery. But nature does not miniaturize neurons (or other cells for that matter). The range of cell size among organisms is incomparably smaller than the range in body size. Small animals simply have far fewer cells than large animals. The human brain contains several billion neurons; an ant is constrained by its small size to have many hundreds of times fewer neurons.

There is, to be sure, no established relationship between brain size and intelligence among humans (the tale of Anatole France with a brain of less than 1,000 cubic centimeters vs. Oliver Cromwell with well above 2,000 is often cited). But this observation cannot be extended to differences between species and certainly not to ranges of sizes separating ants and humans. An efficient computer needs billions of circuits and an ant simply cannot contain enough of them because the relative constancy of cell size requires that small brains contain few neurons. Thus, our large body size served as a prerequisite for self-conscious intelligence.

We can make a stronger argument and claim that humans have to be just about the size they are in order to function as they do. In an amusing and provocative article (*American Scientist,* 1968), F. W. Went explored the impossibility of human life, as we know it, at ant dimensions (assuming for the moment that we could circumvent—which we cannot—the problem of intelligence and small brain size). Since weight increases so much faster than surface area as an object gets larger, small animals have very high ratios of surface to volume: they live in a world dominated by surface forces that affect us scarcely at all. . . .

An ant-sized man might don some clothing, but forces of surface adhesion would preclude its removal. The lower limit of drop size would make showering impossible; each drop would hit with the force of a large boulder. If our homunculus managed to get wet and tried to dry off with a towel, he would be stuck to it for life. He could pour no liquid, light no fire (since a stable flame must be several millimeters in length). He might pound gold leaf thin enough to construct a book for his size, but surface adhesion would prevent the turning of pages.

Our skills and behavior are finely attuned to our size. We could not be twice as tall as we are, for the kinetic energy of a fall would then be 16 to 32 times as great, and our sheer weight (increased eightfold) would be more than our legs could support. Human giants of eight to nine feet have either died young or been crippled early by failure of joints and bones. At half our size, we could not wield a club with sufficient force to hunt large animals (for kinetic energy would decrease 16 to 32-fold); we could not impart sufficient momentum to spears and arrows; we could not cut or split wood with primitive tools or mine minerals with picks and chisels. Since these all were essential activities in our historical development, we must conclude that the path of our evolution could only have been followed by a creature very close to our size. I do not argue that we inhabit the best of all possible worlds, only that our size has limited our activities and, to a great extent, shaped our evolution.

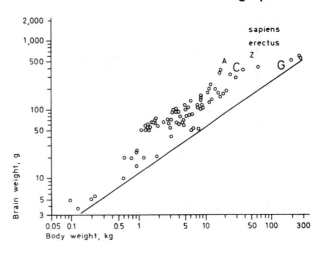

The correct criterion for assessing the superiority in size of our brains. The solid line represents the average relationship between brain weight and body weight for all body weights among mammals in general. Superiority in size is measured by upward deviation from this curve (i.e., "more" brain than an average mammal of the same body weight). Open circles represent primates (all have larger brains than average mammals). C is the chimpanzee, G the gorilla, and A the fossil hominid Australopithecus: erectus *covers the range of* Homo erectus *(Java and Peking Man);* sapiens *covers the field for modern humans. Our brains have the highest positive deviations of any mammal. (F. S. Szalay,* Approaches to Primate Paleobiology, *Contrib. Primat. Vol. 5, 1975, p. 267. Reproduced with the permission of S. Karger AG, Basel)*

HUMAN BRAINS

An average human brain weights about 1,300 grams (45.5 ounces); to accommodate such a large brain, we have bulbous, balloon-shaped heads unlike those of any other large mammal. Can we measure superiority by the size of our brains?

Elephants and whales have larger brains than ours. But this fact does not confer superior mental ability upon the largest mammals. Larger bodies need larger brains to coordinate their actions. We must find a way to remove the confusing influence of body size from our calculation. The computation of a simple ratio between brain weight and body weight will not work. Very small mammals generally have higher ratios than humans; that is, they have more brain per unit of body weight. Brain size does increase with body size, but it increases at a *much slower rate*.

If we plot brain weight against body weight for all species of adult mammals, we find that the brain increases at about two-thirds the rate of the body. Since surface areas also increase about two-thirds as fast as body weight, we

conjecture that brain weight is not regulated by body weight, but primarily by the body surfaces that serve as end points for so many innervations. This means that large animals may have absolutely larger brains than humans (because their bodies are bigger), and that small animals often have relatively larger brains than humans (because body size decreases more rapidly than brain size).

A plot of brain weight vs. body weight for adult mammals points the way out of our paradox. The correct criterion is neither absolute nor relative brain size—it is the difference between actual brain size and expected brain size at that body weight. To judge the size of our brain, we must compare it with the expected brain size for an average mammal of our body weight. On this criterion we are, as we had every right to expect, the brainiest mammal by far. No other species lies as far above the expected brain size for average mammals as we do.

This relationship between body weight and brain size provides important insights into the evolution of our brain. Our African ancestor (or at least close cousin), *Australopithecus afri-*

canus, had an average adult cranial capacity of only 450 cubic centimeters. Gorillas often have larger brains, and many authorities have used this fact to infer a distinctly prehuman mentality for *Australopithecus.* A recent textbook states: "The original bipedal apeman of South Africa had a brain scarcely larger than that of other apes and presumably possessed behavioral capacities to match." But *A. africanus* weighed only 50 to 90 pounds (female and male respectively—as estimated by Yale anthropologist David Pilbeam), while large male gorillas may weigh more than 600 pounds. We may safely state that *Australopithecus* had a much larger brain than other nonhuman primates, using the correct criterion of comparison with expected values for actual body weights.

The human brain is now about three times larger than that of *Australopithecus.* This increase has often been called the most rapid and most important event in the history of evolution. But our bodies have also increased greatly in size. Is this enlargement of the brain a simple consequence of bigger bodies or does it mark new levels of intelligence?

5. THE FOSSIL EVIDENCE

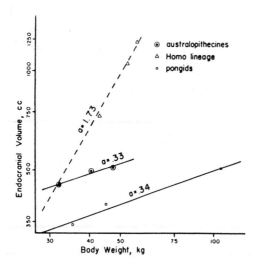

Evolutionary increase in human brain size (dotted line). The four triangles represent a rough evolutionary sequence: Australopithecus africanus, ER-1470 (Richard Leakey's new find with a cranial capacity just slightly less than 800 cc), Homo erectus (Peking Man), and Homo sapiens. The slope is the highest ever calculated for an evolutionary sequence. The two solid lines represent more conventional scaling of brain size in australopithecines (above) and great apes (below). ("Size and Scaling in Human Evolution," Pilbeam, David, and Gould, Stephen Jay, *Science* Vol. 186, pp. 892–901, Fig. 2, 6 December 1974. Copyright 1974 by the American Association for the Advancement of Science)

To answer this question, I have plotted cranial capacity against inferred body weight for the following fossil homids (representing, perhaps, our lineage): *Australopithecus africanus;* Richard Leakey's remarkable find with a cranial capacity of nearly 800 cubic centimeters and an antiquity of more than two million years (weight estimated by David Pillbeam from dimensions of the femur); *Homo erectus* from Choukoutien (Peking Man); and modern *Homo sapiens.* The graph indicates that our brain has increased much more rapidly than any prediction based on compensations for body size would allow.

My conclusion is not unconventional, and it does reinforce an ego that we would do well to deflate. Nonetheless, our brain has undergone a true increase in size not related to the demands of our larger body. We are, indeed, smarter than we were.

East Side Story: The Origin of Humankind

The Rift Valley in Africa holds the secret to the divergence of hominids from the great apes and to the emergence of human beings

Yves Coppens

Yves Coppens specializes in the study of human evolution and prehistory. He received his degrees from the Sorbonne, where he studied vertebrate and human paleontology. A member of many organizations, including the French Academy of Sciences and the National Academy of Medicine, Coppens is currently chair of paleoanthropology and prehistory at the College of France in Paris. He is also known for having done 20 years of extensive fieldwork in Africa, particularly in Chad and Ethiopia.

Humans are creatures whose roots lie in the animals. Accordingly, we find ourselves at the tip of one of the branches of an immense tree of life, a tree that has been developing and growing ever more diverse over a period of four billion years. From an evolutionary standpoint, it is important to locate the place and the time that our branch separated from the rest of the tree. It is these questions that the present article attempts to answer. When, where and why did the branch that led to us, the genus *Homo,* diverge from the branch that led to our closest cousin, the genus *Pan,* or the chimpanzee? Because this parting of the ways seems to unfold several million years before *Homo,* properly speaking, was born, the issue of our precise origin also needs to be

addressed. When, where and why did *Homo* appear in the bosom of a family, Hominidae, that was well planted in its ecosystem and well adapted to its environment?

I first realized in 1981 that it might be possible to find answers to these questions. The occasion was an international conference in Paris organized by UNESCO to celebrate the 100-year anniversary of the birth of Pierre Teilhard de Chardin. As an invited speaker, I gave a talk on the French paleontologist and philosopher's scientific work. Although this aspect of Teilhard's writing is often forgotten by biographers, who are essentially interested in his philosophical texts, he produced more than 250 scientific reports over the course of 40 years. His opus includes articles on the structural geology of Jersey, Somalia, Ethiopia and China; on the Paleocene and Eocene mammals of Europe; on the Tertiary and Quaternary mammals of the Far East; on the fossil men of China and Java; on the southern African australopithecines (a kind of prehuman, one that was already hominid, but not yet *Homo*); as well as on the Paleolithic and Neolithic tools of all those countries.

A member of the audience, whom I did not know at the time, came up to me after my talk and congratulated me very courteously, admitting that he had not known about this technical aspect of Father Teilhard's work. He asked me several questions about this science

of evolution that I practiced and about its state of development. My visitor ended this short interview with a precise question: Is there at present an important issue that is still being debated in your field?

Yes, I responded, there is a problem of chronology, as is often the case in historical sciences. Biochemists, struck by the great molecular proximity between humans and chimpanzees, place the beginning of the divergence of these two groups some three million years ago. This discipline also assigns a strictly African origin to humanity. In contrast, the field of paleontology describes a divergence that dates as far back as 15 million years ago. Paleontologists also postulate a broad origin, that is, one radiating from both the Asian and the African tropics.

The gentleman seemed interested, thanked me and left. Several months later I received a letter of invitation to a conference in Rome that he proposed to hold in May 1982. My questioner had been none other than Carlos Chagas, president of the Papal Academy of Sciences! In search of subjects that would have both current interest and important philosophical implications, he had considered what I had said and had organized, under the aegis of his institution, a confrontation between paleontologists and biochemists.

That meeting did take place and, although discreet, its influence on scientific thought was considerable. Two

	Hippopotamus	Struthionidae	Giraffidae		
Common ancestor of *Pan* and *Homo*	Deinotherium		Crocodilus	Gomphotherium	Hipparion

The Omo River Sequence

LATE MIOCENE	**AROUND EIGHT MILLION YEARS AGO**

significant facts, one paleontological and one biochemical, were presented to the participants. The first was the announcement by David Pilbeam, professor of paleontology at Harvard University, that his research group had discovered, in the Upper Miocene levels of the Potwar Plateau in Pakistan, the first known face of a ramapithecid. This face resembles an orangutan's much more closely than it does a chimpanzee's face. Pilbeam's data were particularly important because the ramapithecids had for many years been considered by some paleo-anthropologists to be the first members of the human family.

The second fact presented was a statement by Jerold M. Lowenstein of the University of California at San Francisco that active proteins had been discovered in the dental material of a ramapithecid. He had determined that activity by injecting extract from the ramapithecid teeth into a rabbit, where it brought on the formation of antibodies. Lowenstein then told us of the indisputable reaction of these antibodies to the antigens of orangutans. This strong reaction made it clear that some of the ramapithecid proteins were still preserved and that the creature seemed related to orangutans.

Before the discovery of the ramapithecid face, scientists had procured only some of this genus's teeth and jaw fragments. Although these features were certainly interesting, it is necessary to know that all the bones of a skeleton do not carry information of equal value. These pieces were less significant than the orbit area and the nose and upper jaw region found in the new Pakistani piece. Paleontologists use such facial fossils to draw anatomical comparisons with similar or contemporary fossils. A simple comparison of the face of this ramapithecid, an orangutan and a chimpanzee clearly revealed the similarities between the ramapithecid and the orangutan.

Rather than comparing anatomical attributes, biochemists examine molecular details. They look at DNA, at the proteins and chromosomal maps of current species—elements that are not usually conserved in fossils. Their work helps paleontologists, who can then arrange species in order of complexity and compare their protein maps. The progression from simple to complex and the sequence that emerges

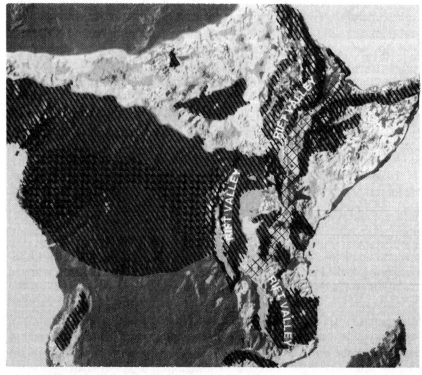

VEGETATION AND CLIMATE vary dramatically on either side of the Rift Valley: wet western woods (*striped areas*) give way to eastern grasslands (*light areas*). Reflecting these ecological differences, which arose millions of years ago, chimpanzees are distributed only to the west (*dotted area*), whereas hominid fossils are found only to the east (*cross-hatching*).

| | Gazella | | Giraffa | Hippopotamidae | | Australopithecus | |
| Deinotherium | | | Ceratotherium | Hyaenidae | Nyanzachoerus | Hipparion | Machairodontinae |

| AROUND SIX MILLION YEARS AGO | LOWER LOTHAGAMIAN (LOWER PLIOCENE) | FIVE MILLION YEARS AGO |

reproduces, in some fashion, the evolution of creatures in the fossil record. In the case of the ramapithecid, however, biochemistry had made, as never before, a foray back in time by examining fossil proteins.

Circumstances had come together in such a way that we could finally put the ramapithecid in his place. This hominoid had been known to be Eurasiatic, and he remained so. Now that his relationship to the great ape of Asia, the orangutan, had been brought to light, the geographic picture became clear. Indeed, it made complete sense, as so often happens when one has found the solution to a problem. The origin of humanity, as the molecular biologists had suspected, appeared to be Africa, and Africa alone. The question of our family's place of birth seemed settled.

But the question of the date of this birth remained to be addressed. Several paleontologists present at this congress continued to defend the great antiquity of the hominids, whereas the molecular biologists extolled the extraordinary brevity of the independent part of our branch. The most generous of the paleontologists had arrived in Rome convinced of the 15-million-year history of our family. The most extreme of the molecular biologists were sure that three million years, at most, would measure the length of existence of the human family. Both sides came to the conclusion—made, of course, with only the most serious considerations possible—that seven and a half million years was a good span. I dubbed this conclusion "the prehistoric compromise."

The two paleontological and biochemical announcements of the Rome meeting were not the only crucial items that came to light in the early 1980s. Another set of results further clarified our understanding of human origins. Twenty years of excavations in eastern Africa (between 1960 and 1980) had finally yielded a mass of information in which could be sought evolutionary sequences and patterns. This extensive material had not been looked at in such a way before because it takes time to study and identify fossils. Its

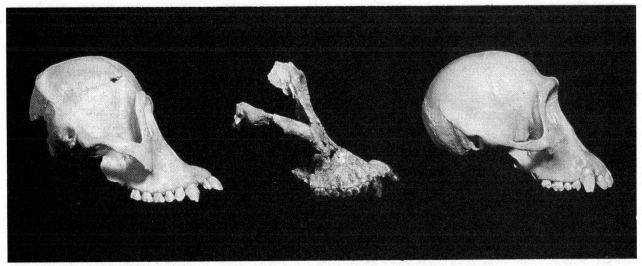

COMPARISON OF THREE HOMINOID SKULLS illustrates the proximity between two of the creatures. The ramapithecid (*center*) found in Pakistan resembles the great ape of Asia, the orangutan (*left*), much more closely than it does one of the African apes, the chimpanzee (*right*). Indeed, this very comparison led paleontologists to reject the Eurasiatic ramapithecids as close ancestors of humans and to focus on an African origin.

5. THE FOSSIL EVIDENCE

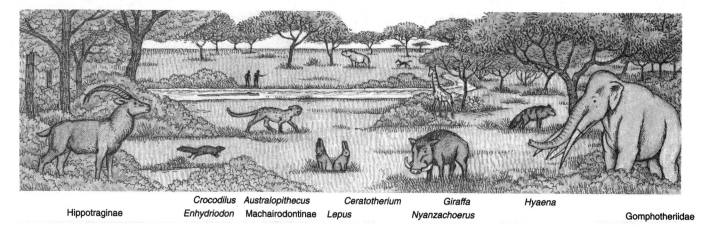

	Crocodilus	Australopithecus	Ceratotherium	Giraffa	Hyaena	
Hippotraginae	Enhydriodon	Machairodontinae	Lepus	Nyanzachoerus		Gomphotheriidae

FIVE MILLION YEARS AGO	**UPPER LOTHAGAMIAN (LOWER PLIOCENE)**	**3.5 MILLION YEARS AGO**

implications were vast, particularly when coupled with the information from the ramapithecid and the new-found consensus on dates.

The entry of paleoanthropologists into eastern Africa was actually an ancient affair. In 1935 Louis Leakey's expedition to Olduvai Gorge in Tanzania discovered remains attributed to *Homo erectus*. In 1939 the German team of Ludwig Kohl-Larsen found fossils that were named *Praeanthropus africanus*—later considered to be *Australopithecus*—near Lake Garusi, an area also called Laetoli, in Tanzania. In 1955 another Olduvai expedition led by Leakey revealed a single australopithecine tooth. These modest discoveries, however, did not command much interest.

It was not until the 1960s that the world eagerly turned its attention to eastern Africa. In 1959 Mary Leakey found at Olduvai an australopithecine skull equipped with all its upper teeth. This skull could be absolutely dated to about two million years ago by the volcanic tuff below which it had been enveloped. The new hominid was named *Zinjanthropus;* it was a small-brained bipedal hominid species that went extinct about one million years ago. After that significant finding, expeditions started to arrive in abundance: a new team came each year for the first 12 years, and each one excavated for 10 or 20 seasons. Never before had such an effort been de-ployed by paleontologists or paleo-anthropologists.

The results reflected the investment. Hundreds of thousands of fossils were discovered, of which about 2,000 were hominid remains. Yet, despite the constant work of preparation, analysis and identification of these fossils as they were unearthed, it is understandable that it was not until the 1980s that the first complete inventory of these thousands of finds was published. It is precisely this new information that, when added to the data received at the Rome conference, became essential to solving the mystery.

What emerged so clearly was that there was absolutely no sign of *Pan,* or one of its direct ancestors, in eastern Africa during the time of the australopithecines. Molecular biology, biochemistry and cytogenetics continued to demonstrate that humans and chimpanzees were molecularly extremely close, which meant, in evolutionary terms, that they had shared a common ancestor not very far back in time, geologically speaking. And fieldworkers had just revealed that Hominidae, as of seven or eight million years ago, were present in Ethiopia, Kenya and Tanzania. But during the same period, this region had not seen the least sign of the family Panidae, no precursor of the chimpanzee and no precursor of the gorilla. Even though one cannot base a hypothesis on a lack of evidence, the striking absence of these Panidae where Hominidae were abundant represented a sufficient contrast to cause concern—all the more so because the 200,000 to 250,000 vertebrate fossils that had been collected constituted a statistical base with a certain authority.

I had been thinking about this puzzle during the conference in Rome. A quite simple explanation came to mind when I opened an atlas marking the distribution of vertebrates. The map devoted to chimpanzees and gorillas showed a significant group of territories, including all the large forested regions of tropical Africa, but stopped, almost without overflow, at the great furrow that cuts perpendicularly across the equator from north to south: the Rift Valley. All the hominid sites that dated to more than three million years ago were found, without exception, on the eastern side of this furrow. Only one solution could explain how, at one and the same time, Hominidae and Panidae were close in molecular terms but never side by side in the fossil record. Hominidae and Panidae had never been together.

I therefore suggested the following model. Before Hominidae and Panidae had separated, the Rift Valley did not constitute an irregularity sufficient to divide equatorial Africa. From the Atlantic to the Indian Ocean, the African continent constituted one homogeneous biogeographical province in which the common ancestors of the future Hominidae and Panidae lived. Then, about eight million years ago, a tectonic

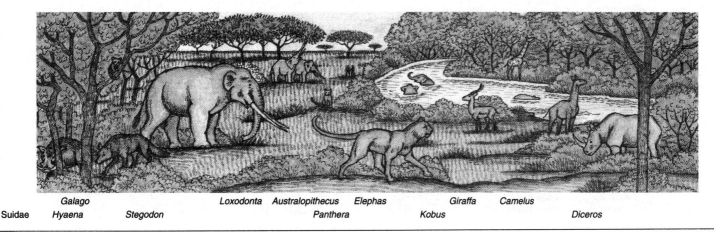

Suidae	Galago Hyaena	Stegodon	Loxodonta	Australopithecus Panthera	Elephas	Giraffa Kobus	Camelus	Diceros

3.5 MILLION YEARS AGO	LOWER SHUNGURIAN (UPPER PLIOCENE)	2.5 MILLION YEARS AGO

crisis arose that entailed two distinct movements: sinking produced the Rift Valley, and rising gave birth to the line of peaks forming the western rim of the valley.

The breach and the barrier obviously disturbed the circulation of air. The air masses of the west maintained, thanks to the Atlantic, a generous amount of precipitation. Those of the east, coming into collision with the barrier of the western rim of the Tibetan plateau, which also was rising, became organized into a seasonal system, today called the monsoon. Thus, the original extensive region was divided into two, each possessed of a different climate and vegetation. The west remained humid; the east became ever less so. The west kept its forests and its woodlands; the east evolved into open savanna.

By force of circumstance, the population of the common ancestor of the Hominidae and the Panidae families also found itself divided. A large western population existed, as did a smaller eastern one. It is extremely tempting to imagine that we have here, quite simply, the reason for the divergence. The western descendants of these common ancestors pursued their adaptation to life in a humid, arboreal milieu: these are the Panidae. The eastern descendants of these same common ancestors, in contrast, invented a completely new repertoire in order to adapt to their new life in an open environment: these are the Hominidae.

This uncomplicated model has the advantage of explaining why Hominidae and Panidae are so close in a genetic sense and yet never together geographically. It also has the advantage of offering, by means of a situation that is at first tectonic and then ecological, a variant of the situation found on islands. Compared to complex solutions about the movements of Hominidae from the forest to the savanna or about the movements of Pan-

idae from the savanna to the forest, the Rift Valley theory is quite straightforward.

It was only later, when I was reading the work of geophysicists, that I learned that the activity of the Rift Valley some eight million years ago was well known. Reading the studies of paleoclimatologists fortified me with the knowledge that the progressive desiccation of eastern Africa was also a well-known event, whose start-

MARY AND LOUIS LEAKEY examine the *Zinjanthropus* skull and upper jaw at Olduvai Gorge in Tanzania in 1959. Their discovery of a hominid fossil at this site led to a bone rush: paleontologists flooded in, and hundreds of thousands of fossils were excavated in subsequent decades.

5. THE FOSSIL EVIDENCE

Panthera	Deinotherium		Damaliscus	Diceros	Giraffa			Dinofelis	Australopithecus
Loxodonta	Homotherium		Lepus		Phacochoerus	Hipparion	Equus		Hyaena

2.5 MILLION YEARS AGO	UPPER SHUNGURIAN (UPPER PLIOCENE)	1.8 MILLION YEARS AGO

ing point had been placed at about eight million years ago. Finally, reading the declarations of paleontologists further reassured me, because they placed the emergence of eastern African animal life—a fauna labeled Ethiopian, to which the australopithecines belong—at about eight or 10 million years ago. Each discipline knew this date and in one way or another was familiar with the event or its consequences, but no interdisciplinary effort had brought them all into a synthesis. Adrian Kortlandt, a famous ethologist from the University of Amsterdam, had thought about such a possible scenario, but without any paleontological support, some years before.

The hypothesis lacked only a name. Three years later I was invited by the American Museum of Natural History

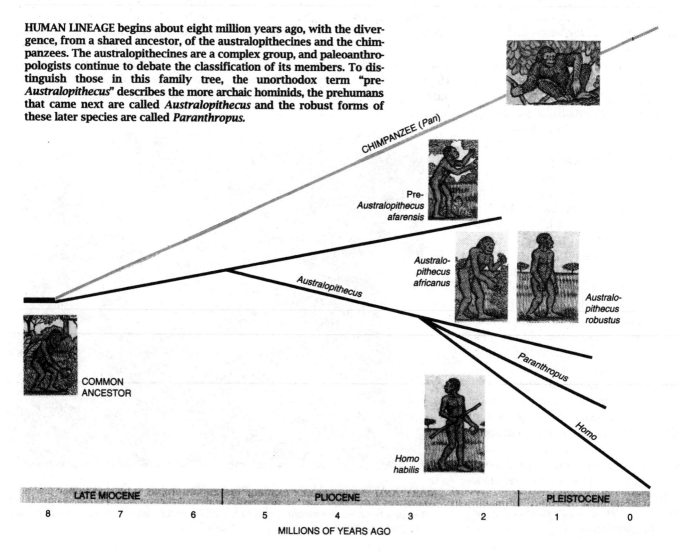

HUMAN LINEAGE begins about eight million years ago, with the divergence, from a shared ancestor, of the australopithecines and the chimpanzees. The australopithecines are a complex group, and paleoanthropologists continue to debate the classification of its members. To distinguish those in this family tree, the unorthodox term "pre-*Australopithecus*" describes the more archaic hominids, the prehumans that came next are called *Australopithecus* and the robust forms of these later species are called *Paranthropus*.

CHIMPANZEE (Pan)

Pre-*Australopithecus afarensis*

Australopithecus

Australopithecus africanus

Australopithecus robustus

Paranthropus

COMMON ANCESTOR

Homo

Homo habilis

LATE MIOCENE	PLIOCENE	PLEISTOCENE

| 8 | 7 | 6 | 5 | 4 | 3 | 2 | 1 | 0 |

MILLIONS OF YEARS AGO

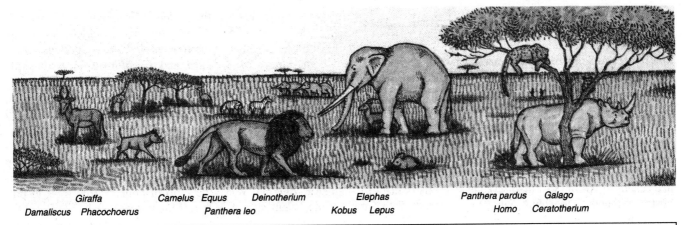

Giraffa   Camelus   Equus   Deinotherium   Elephas   Panthera pardus   Galago
Damaliscus Phacochoerus   Panthera leo   Kobus   Lepus   Homo   Ceratotherium

1.8 MILLION YEARS AGO   **PLEISTOCENE**   **ONE MILLION YEARS AGO**

in New York City to present the 55th James Arthur Lecture on the Evolution of the Human Brain. I also assumed a visiting professorship at the Mount Sinai School of Medicine of the City University of New York. The idea of giving this model a title that would be easy to remember and that would honor my hosts came to me then. I called it the East Side Story.

It is possible that the East Side Story has answered the first volley of questions: the when, where and why of our divergence from Panidae. Our phyletic branch, the one that now bears us, was marked off from the rest of the genealogical tree of living creatures eight million years ago in eastern Africa by reason of geographic isolation. The need for adaptation to the new habitat of the savanna, one that was drier and more bare than the preceding one, promoted further genetic divergence.

The second series of questions is more intricate: the when, where and why of the appearance of the genus *Homo* in the family Hominidae. The past eight million years during which our branch of the tree has grown have revealed themselves to be more complex than one might have imagined. The story begins with the diversification of a subfamily, the australopithecines. These creatures made very modest movements from eastern Africa to southern Africa. The story then continues from about three million years ago to today, with the emergence of another subfamily, the hominines. The hominines moved ex-

tensively, from eastern Africa across the entire planet. The last of the australopithecines coexisted for about two million years with the first of these hominines, which have only one genus, *Homo*.

The emergence of this hominine subfamily can be seen in a remarkable series of geologic beds and fossils found along the banks of the Omo River in Ethiopia. And, not surprisingly, because this is the second part of the East Side Story, the role of climate proves to be as powerful a force for change three million years ago as it did eight million years ago.

The Omo River tale began at the turn of this century, when a French geographic expedition proposed to cross Africa diagonally, from the Red Sea to the Atlantic. The Viscount du Bourg de Bozas directed the expedition. Having departed from Djibouti in 1901, the exploration was to end dramatically in the death of its leader from malaria on the banks of the Congo. The team nonetheless brought back from the journey, which followed the original itinerary, a fine harvest of fossils. Among the collection was a group of vertebrate remains gathered in what was then Abyssinia, on the eastern bank of the lower valley of the Omo River. The Omo lies on the eastern side of the Rift Valley.

Intrigued by this yield, which was described in two or three articles and in Émile Haug's geologic treatise in 1911, Camille Arambourg decided at the beginning of the 1930s to conduct a new expedition. Arambourg, future

professor of paleontology at the National Museum of Natural History in Paris, reached the Omo and stayed eight months in 1932. He returned to Paris with four tons of vertebrate fossils.

The next major operation—the Omo Research Expedition—was undertaken between 1967 and 1977. It was catalyzed, in part, by the bone rush of the 1960s and 1970s, described earlier, which had followed the 1959 find by Mary Leakey at Olduvai. A series of researchers conducted the 10-year Omo expedition in stages. In 1967 Arambourg and I worked on the site with Louis and Richard Leakey and Francis Clark Howell. Between 1968 and 1969 Richard Leakey left the expedition, and Arambourg, Howell and I continued the work. Finally, from 1970 until 1976, Howell and I dug there alone (Arambourg died in 1969).

From the very first expedition, the stratigraphy of this site was eminently visible, a superb column more than 1,000 meters deep. The fauna contained in these beds appeared to change so markedly as it progressed from base to summit that the site was obviously capable, even at mere glance, of telling a story. When dating by potassium-argon and by paleomagnetism finally became available, so that a chronological grid could be placed on this sequence, the history became clear.

Starting four million years ago (the age of the oldest Omo level, the Mursi formation) and ending one million years ago (the age of the most recent level, the top of the Shungura formation), the climate had clearly changed from humid to distinctly less humid. As a consequence, the vegetation had evolved from plants adapted to humidity to those capable of thriving in a drier climate. The fauna had also changed from one suited to a brushwood assemblage to one characteristic of a grassy savanna. And the Hominidae, subject like the other vertebrates to these climate fluctuations, had changed from so-called gracile australopithecines to robust australopithecines and, ultimately, to humans.

In 1975 I informed the international paleontological community of this clear correlation between the evolution of the climate and the evolution of the hominines. I did so in a note to the *Proceedings of the Academy of Sciences* in Paris and in a communication to a congress in London at the Royal Geological Society. The reaction was very skeptical.

Of all the great eastern African paleontological sites, the strata of Omo were the only ones that could have permitted such observations. This site alone offered a continuous sedimentary column that ran from four million years ago to one million years ago. It is precisely between three and two million years ago, or to be very exact between 3.3 to 2.4 million years ago, that the whole earth cooled and that eastern Africa became dry. (Laetoli and Hadar were too old, Olduvai was too young and East Turkana presented a stratigraphic gap at that point, so they could not offer the same demonstration.) We know this fact through several other tests conducted in various regions of the world.

This climatic crisis appears clearly in the fauna and flora records of the Omo sequence. By indexing, both qualitatively and quantitatively, the animals and plants gathered in the various levels, we can interpret the differences that emerge from these species, with regard to changes in the environment.

We know, for example, that the cheek teeth—that is, the premolars and molars—of herbivore vertebrates have a tendency to develop and become more complex when the diet becomes more grassy and less leafy. This change

takes place because grass wears down the teeth more than leaves do. We know also that the locomotion of these same herbivores becomes more digitigrade in open habitats in which they are more vulnerable: one runs better on tiptoe than in boots. A certain number of anatomical features corresponding to very precise functions can also be good indicators: the tree-dwelling feet of some rodents or the feet of others that are adapted to digging. We use, with appropriate caution, of course, a method called actualist; in other words, we believe that the varieties of animals or plants we are considering acted then as they act today.

Many examples demonstrate this transition to a drier environment, and they are extraordinary in their agreement. As one moves from the older strata on the bottom to the younger strata on the top, there is an increase in the hypsodonty—that is, in a tooth's height-to-width ratio—among Elephantidae (elephants close to the ones living in Asia today), Rhinocerotidae (specifically the white rhinoceros), *Hipparion* (ancestors of the horse), Hippopotamidae (precursors of the hippopotamus) and some pigs and antelopes. In other words, these groups exhibited the increasing complexity that we associate with a shift from a diet of leaves to a diet of grass. The Suidae, or precursors to swine, also show an increase in the number of cusps on their molars as they evolved.

On the lower strata are many antelopes—including Tragelaphinae and Reduncinae, which live among shrubs. All these creatures must have lived in an environment of wooded savanna close to water. On the top levels the true horse, *Equus*, appears, as do the high-toothed warthogs, *Phacochoerus* and *Stylochoeras*. We also see the development of the swift antelopes, *Megalotragus*, *Beatragus* and *Parmularius*, animals found on open grasslands.

On the bottom, three species of small *Galago*, or monkey, and the two Chiroptera, *Eidolon* and *Taphozous*, indicate a well-developed forest and a dense savanna. This conclusion is supported by the large number of Muridae rodents, such as *Mastomys*, as well as

the rodents *Grammomys*, *Paraxerus*, *Thryonomys* and *Golunda*. At the top, the rodents *Aethomys*, *Thallomys*, *Coleura* and *Gerbillurus* in conjunction with *Jaculus* and *Heterocephalus*, the Chiroptera, and the *Lepus*, or hare, replace the previous inhabitants. All the later rodents inhabit dry savanna.

Pollen specimens on the bottom indicate 24 taxa of trees, whereas the top is characterized by 11. At the bottom, the ratio of pollens from trees to pollens from grasses equals 0.4. But at the top, it is less than 0.01. At the bottom pollens from species that grow in humid conditions are abundant—they include *Celtis*, *Acalypha*, *Olea* and *Typha*. In the more recent strata, however, these pollens diminish considerably or even disappear from the record, whereas pollens from Myrica, a plant typical of dry climates, appear. The number of pollens transported by the wind, called allochtone pollens, dwindles from 21 percent at the bottom, where the forest edge is near the Omo River, to 2 percent at the top, where the Omo was low and the forest edge far away.

The story with the hominids is similar. They are clearly represented by *Australopithecus afarensis* on the lower strata. But the younger strata on the top reveal *A. aethiopicus*, *A. boisei* and *Homo habilis*. The oldest species of australopithecines, the graciles, are more ensconced in tree-filled habitats than are the more recent species, those called robust. As for humans, we are unquestionably a pure product of a certain aridity.

I called this climatic crisis "the (H)Omo event" using the simple play on words of Omo and *Homo*, because it permitted the emergence of humans—an event that affects us quite specifically—and because it was the Omo sequence that revealed it for the first time. Some years later the same data were reported from South Africa.

Thus, it appears strikingly clear that the history of the human family, like that of any other family of vertebrates, was born from one event, as it happens a tectonic one, and progressed under the pressure of another event, this one climatic.

These changes can be but quickly summarized here. Essentially, the first adaptation changed the structure of the brain but did not increase its volume, as suggested by the interpretation of endocasts, latex rubber casts of fossil skulls, done by Ralph L. Holloway of Columbia University. At the same time, the changes caused Hominidae to retain an upright stance as the most advantageous and to diversify the diet while keeping it essentially vegetarian. The second adaptation led in two directions: a strong physique and a narrow, specialized vegetarian diet for the large australopithecines and a large brain and a broad-ranging, opportunistic diet for humans.

Some hundreds of thousands of years later, it was the latter development that proved to be the more fruitful, and it is this one that prevailed. With a larger brain came a higher degree of reflection, a new curiosity. Accompanying the necessity of catching meat came greater mobility. For the first time in the history of the hominids, humanity spread out from its origin. And this mobility is the reason that in less than three million years, humanity has conquered this planet and begun the exploration of other worlds in the solar system.

FURTHER READING

EVOLUTION DES HOMINIDÉS ET DE LEUR ENVIRONNEMENT AU COURS DU PLIO-PLÉISTOCÈNE DANS LA BASSE VALLÉE DE L'OMO EN ETHIOPIE. Yves Coppens in *Comptes Rendus Hebdomadaires des Séances de l'Académie des Sciences,* Vol. 281, Series D, pages 1693–1696; December 3, 1975.

EARLIEST MAN AND ENVIRONMENTS IN THE LAKE RUDOLF BASIN: STRATIGRAPHY, PALEOECOLOGY AND EVOLUTION. Edited by Yves Coppens, F. Clark Howell, Glynn Ll. Isaac and Richard E. F. Leakey. University of Chicago Press, 1976.

RECENT ADVANCES IN THE EVOLUTION OF PRIMATES. Edited by Carlos Chagas. Pontificia Academia Scientiarum, 1983.

L'ENVIRONNEMENT DES HOMINIDÉS AU PLIO-PLÉISTOCÈNE. Edited by Fondation Singer-Polignac. Masson, Paris, 1985.

Scavenger Hunt

As paleoanthropologists close in on their quarry, it may turn out to be a different beast from what they imagined

Pat Shipman

Pat Shipman is an assistant professor in the Department of Cell Biology and Anatomy at The Johns Hopkins University School of Medicine.

In both textbooks and films, ancestral humans (hominids) have been portrayed as hunters. Small-brained, big-browed, upright, and usually mildly furry, early hominid males gaze with keen eyes across the gold savanna, searching for prey. Skillfully wielding a few crude stone tools, they kill and dismember everything from small gazelles to elephants, while females care for young and gather roots, tubers, and berries. The food is shared by group members at temporary camps. This familiar image of Man the Hunter has been bolstered by the finding of stone tools in association with fossil animal bones. But the role of hunting in early hominid life cannot be determined in the absence of more direct evidence.

I discovered one means of testing the hunting hypothesis almost by accident. In 1978, I began documenting the microscopic damage produced on bones by different events. I hoped to develop a diagnostic key for identifying the post-mortem history of specific fossil bones, useful for understanding how fossil assemblages were formed. Using a scanning electron microscope (SEM) because of its excellent resolution and superb depth of field, I inspected high-fidelity replicas of modern bones that

had been subjected to known events or conditions. (I had to use replicas, rather than real bones, because specimens must fit into the SEM's small vacuum chamber.) I soon established that such common events as weathering, root etching, sedimentary abrasion, and carnivore chewing produced microscopically distinctive features.

In 1980, my SEM study took an unexpected turn. Richard Potts (now of Yale University), Henry Bunn (now of the University of Wisconsin at Madison), and I almost simultaneously found what appeared to be stone-tool cut marks on fossils from Olduvai Gorge, Tanzania, and Koobi Fora, Kenya. We were working almost side by side at the National Museums of Kenya, in Nairobi, where the fossils are stored. The possibility of cut marks was exciting, since both sites preserve some of the oldest known archaeological materials. Potts and I returned to the United States, manufactured some stone tools, and started "butchering" bones and joints begged from our local butchers. Under the SEM, replicas of these cut marks looked very different from replicas of carnivore tooth scratches, regardless of the species of carnivore or the type of tool involved. By comparing the marks on the fossils with our hundreds of modern bones of known history, we were able to demonstrate convincingly that hominids using stone tools had processed carcasses of many different animals nearly two million years ago. For the first time, there was a firm link

between stone tools and at least some of the early fossil animal bones.

This initial discovery persuaded some paleoanthropologists that the hominid hunter scenario was correct. Potts and I were not so sure. Our study had shown that many of the cut-marked fossils also bore carnivore tooth marks and that some of the cut marks were in places we hadn't expected—on bones that bore little meat in life. More work was needed.

In addition to more data about the Olduvai cut marks and tooth marks, I needed specific information about the patterns of cut marks left by known hunters performing typical activities associated with hunting. If similar patterns occurred on the fossils, then the early hominids probably behaved similarly to more modern hunters; if the patterns were different, then the behavior was probably also different. Three activities related to hunting occur often enough in peoples around the world and leave consistent enough traces to be used for such a test.

First, human hunters systematically disarticulate their kills, unless the animals are small enough to be eaten on the spot. Disarticulation leaves cut marks in a predictable pattern on the skeleton. Such marks cluster near the major joints of the limbs: shoulder, elbow, carpal joint (wrist), hip, knee, and hock (ankle). Taking a carcass apart at the joints is much easier than breaking or cutting through bones. Disarticulation enables hunters to carry food back to a central place or camp, so that they can share it with others or cook it or even store it by placing portions in trees, away from the reach of carnivores. If early hominids were hunters who transported and shared their kills, disarticulation marks would occur near joints in frequencies comparable to those produced by modern human hunters.

Second, human hunters often butcher carcasses, in the sense of removing meat from the bones. Butchery marks are usually found on the shafts of bones from the upper part of the front or hind limb, since this is where the big muscle masses lie. Butchery may be carried out at the kill site—especially if the animal is very large and its bones very heavy—or it may take place at the base camp, during the process of sharing food with others. Compared with disarticulation, butchery leaves relatively few marks. It is hard for a hunter to locate an animal's joints without leaving cut marks on the bone. In contrast, it is easier to cut the meat away from the midshaft of the bone without making such marks. If early hominids shared their food, however, there ought to be a number of cut marks located on the midshaft of some fossil bones.

Finally, human hunters often remove skin or tendons from carcasses, to be used for clothing, bags, thongs, and so on. Hide or tendon must be separated from the bones in many areas where there is little flesh, such as the lower limb bones of pigs, giraffes, antelopes, and zebras. In such cases, it is difficult to cut the skin without leaving a cut mark on the bone. Therefore, one expects to find many more cut marks on such bones than on the flesh-covered bones of the upper part of the limbs.

Unfortunately, although accounts of butchery and disarticulation by modern human hunters are remarkably consistent, quantitative studies are rare. Further, virtually all modern hunter-gatherers use metal tools, which leave more cut marks than stone tools. For these reasons I hesitated to compare the fossil evidence with data on modern hunters. Fortunately, Diane Gifford of the University of California,

Santa Cruz, and her colleagues had recently completed a quantitative study of marks and damage on thousands of antelope bones processed by Neolithic (Stone Age) hunters in Kenya some 2,300 years ago. The data from Prolonged Drift, as the site is called, were perfect for comparison with the Olduvai material.

Assisted by my technician, Jennie Rose, I carefully inspected more than 2,500 antelope bones from Bed I at Olduvai Gorge, which is dated to between 1.9 and 1.7 million years ago. We made high-fidelity replicas of every mark that we thought might be either a cut mark or a carnivore tooth mark. Back in the United States, we used the SEM to make positive identifications of the marks. (The replication and SEM inspection was time consuming, but necessary: only about half of the marks were correctly identified by eye or by light microscope.) I then compared the patterns of cut mark and tooth mark distributions on Olduvai fossils with those made by Stone Age hunters at Prolonged Drift.

By their location, I identified marks caused either by disarticulation or meat removal and then compared their frequencies with those from Prolonged Drift. More than 90 percent of the Neolithic marks in these two categories were from disarticulation, but to my surprise, only about 45 percent of the corresponding Olduvai cut marks were from disarticulation. This difference is too great to have occurred by chance; the Olduvai bones did not show the predicted pattern. In fact, the Olduvai cut marks attributable to meat removal and disarticulation showed essentially the same pattern of distribution as the carnivore tooth marks. Apparently, the early hominids were not regularly disarticulating carcasses. This finding casts serious doubt on the idea that early hominids carried their kills back to camp to share with others, since both transport and sharing are difficult unless carcasses are cut up.

When I looked for cut marks attributable to skinning or tendon removal, a more modern pattern emerged. On both the Neolithic and Olduvai bones, nearly 75 percent of all cut marks

occurred on bones that bore little meat; these cut marks probably came from skinning. Carnivore tooth marks were much less common on such bones. Hominids were using carcasses as a source of skin and tendon. This made it seem more surprising that they disarticulated carcasses so rarely.

A third line of evidence provided the most tantalizing clue. Occasionally, sets of overlapping marks occur on the Olduvai fossils. Sometimes, these sets include both cut marks and carnivore tooth marks. Still more rarely, I could see under the SEM which mark had been made first, because its features were overlaid by those of the later mark, in much the same way as old tire tracks on a dirt road are obscured by fresh ones. Although only thirteen such sets of marks were found, in eight cases the hominids made the cut marks *after* the carnivores made their tooth marks. This finding suggested a new hypothesis. Instead of hunting for prey and leaving the remains behind for carnivores to scavenge, perhaps hominids were scavenging from the carnivores. This might explain the hominids' apparently unsystematic use of carcasses: they took what they could get, be it skin, tendon, or meat.

Man the Scavenger is not nearly as attractive an image as Man the Hunter, but it is worth examining. Actually, although hunting and scavenging are different ecological strategies, many mammals do both. The only pure scavengers alive in Africa today are vultures; not one of the modern African mammalian carnivores is a pure scavenger. Even spotted hyenas, which have massive, bone-crushing teeth well adapted for eating the bones left behind by others, only scavenge about 33 percent of their food. Other carnivores that scavenge when there are enough carcasses around include lions, leopards, striped hyenas, and jackals. Long-term behavioral studies suggest that these carnivores scavenge when they can and kill when they must. There are only two nearly pure predators, or hunters—the cheetah and the wild dog—that rarely, if ever, scavenge.

What are the costs and benefits of scavenging compared with those of predation? First of all, the scavenger avoids the task of making sure its meal is dead: a predator has already endured the energetically costly business of chasing or stalking animal after animal until one is killed. But while scavenging may be cheap, it's risky. Predators rarely give up their prey to scavengers without defending it. In such disputes, the larger animal, whether a scavenger or a predator, usually wins, although smaller animals in a pack may defeat a lone, larger animal. Both predators and scavengers suffer the dangers inherent in fighting for possession of a carcass. Smaller scavengers such as jackals or striped hyenas avoid disputes to some extent by specializing in darting in and removing a piece of a carcass without trying to take possession of the whole thing. These two strategies can be characterized as that of the bully or that of the sneak: bullies need to be large to be successful, sneaks need to be small and quick.

Because carcasses are almost always much rarer than live prey, the major cost peculiar to scavenging is that scavengers must survey much larger areas than predators to find food. They can travel slowly, since their "prey" is already dead, but endurance is important. Many predators specialize in speed at the expense of endurance, while scavengers do the opposite.

The more committed predators among the East African carnivores (wild dogs and cheetahs) can achieve great top speeds when running, although not for long. Perhaps as a consequence, these "pure" hunters enjoy a much higher success rate in hunting (about three-fourths of their chases end in kills) than any of the scavenger-hunters do (less than half of their chases are successful). Wild dogs and cheetahs are efficient hunters, but they are neither big enough nor efficient enough in their locomotion to make good scavengers. In fact, the cheetah's teeth are so specialized for meat slicing that they probably cannot withstand the stresses of bone crunching and carcass dismembering carried out by scavengers. Other carnivores are less successful at hunting, but have specializations of size, endurance, or

(in the case of the hyenas) dentition that make successful scavenging possible. The small carnivores seem to have a somewhat higher hunting success rate than the large ones, which balances out their difficulties in asserting possession of carcasses.

In addition to endurance, scavengers need an efficient means of locating carcasses, which, unlike live animals, don't move or make noises. Vultures, for example, solve both problems by flying. The soaring, gliding flight of vultures expends much less energy than walking or cantering as performed by the part-time mammalian scavengers. Flight enables vultures to maintain a foraging radius two to three times larger than that of spotted hyenas, while providing a better vantage point. This explains why vultures can scavenge all of their food in the same habitat in which it is impossible for any mammal to be a pure scavenger. (In fact, many mammals learn where carcasses are located from the presence of vultures.)

Since mammals can't succeed as fulltime scavengers, they must have another source of food to provide the bulk of their diet. The large carnivores rely on hunting large animals to obtain food when scavenging doesn't work. Their size enables them to defend a carcass against others. Since the small carnivores—jackals and striped hyenas—often can't defend carcasses successfully, most of their diet is composed of fruit and insects. When they do hunt, they usually prey on very small animals, such as rats or hares, that can be consumed in their entirety before the larger competitors arrive.

The ancient habitat associated with the fossils of Olduvai and Koobi Fora would have supported many herbivores and carnivores. Among the latter were two species of large saber-toothed cats, whose teeth show extreme adaptations for meat slicing. These were predators with primary access to carcasses. Since their teeth were unsuitable for bone crushing, the saber-toothed cats must have left behind many bones covered with scraps of meat, skin, and tendon. Were early hominids among the scavengers that exploited such carcasses?

All three hominid species that were present in Bed I times (*Homo habilis, Australopithecus africanus, A. robustus*) were adapted for habitual, upright bipedalism. Many anatomists see evidence that these hominids were agile tree climbers as well. Although upright bipedalism is a notoriously peculiar mode of locomotion, the adaptive value of which has been argued for years (see Matt Cartmill's article, "Four Legs Good, Two Legs Bad," *Natural History,* November 1983), there are three general points of agreement.

First, bipedal running is neither fast nor efficient compared to quadrupedal gaits. However, at moderate speeds of 2.5 to 3.5 miles per hour, bipedal *walking* is more energetically efficient than quadrupedal walking. Thus, bipedal walking is an excellent means of covering large areas slowly, making it an unlikely adaptation for a hunter but an appropriate and useful adaptation for a scavenger. Second, bipedalism elevates the head, thus improving the hominid's ability to spot items on the ground—an advantage both to scavengers and to those trying to avoid becoming a carcass. Combining bipedalism with agile tree climbing improves the vantage point still further. Third, bipedalism frees the hands from locomotive duties, making it possible to carry items. What would early hominids have carried? Meat makes a nutritious, easy-to-carry package; the problem is that carrying meat attracts scavengers. Richard Potts suggests that carrying stone tools or unworked stones for toolmaking to caches would be a more efficient and less dangerous activity under many circumstances.

In short, bipedalism is compatible with a scavenging strategy. I am tempted to argue that bipedalism evolved because it provided a substantial advantage to scavenging hominids. But I doubt hominids could scavenge effectively without tools, and bipedalism predates the oldest known stone tools by more than a million years.

Is there evidence that, like modern mammalian scavengers, early hominids had an alternative food source, such as either hunting or eating fruits and insects? My husband, Alan Walker, has shown that the microscopic wear on an animal's teeth reflects its diet. Early hominid teeth wear more like that of chimpanzees and other modern fruit eaters than that of carnivores. Apparently, early hominids ate mostly fruit, as the smaller, modern scavengers do. This accords with the estimated body weight of early hominids, which was only about forty to eighty pounds—less than that of any of the modern carnivores that combine scavenging and hunting but comparable to the striped hyena, which eats fruits and insects as well as meat.

Would early hominids have been able to compete for carcasses with other carnivores? They were too small to use a bully strategy, but if they scavenged in groups, a combined bully-sneak strategy might have been possible. Perhaps they were able to drive off a primary predator long enough to grab some meat, skin, or marrow-filled bone before relinquishing the carcass. The effectiveness of this strategy would have been vastly improved by using tools to remove meat or parts of limbs, a task at which hominid teeth are poor. As agile climbers, early hominids may have retreated into the trees to eat their scavenged trophies, thus avoiding competition from large terrestrial carnivores.

In sum, the evidence on cut marks, tooth wear, and bipedalism, together with our knowledge of scavenger adaptation in general, is consistent with the hypothesis that two million years ago hominids were scavengers rather than accomplished hunters. Animal carcasses, which contributed relatively little to the hominid diet, were not systematically cut up and transported for sharing at base camps. Man the Hunter may not have appeared until 1.5 to 0.7 million years ago, when we do see a shift toward omnivory, with a greater proportion of meat in the diet. This more heroic ancestor may have been *Homo erectus,* equipped with Acheulean-style stone tools and, increasingly, fire. If we wish to look further back, we may have to become accustomed to a less flattering image of our heritage.

Late Hominid Evolution

The most important aspect of human evolution is also the most difficult to decipher from the fossil evidence: our development as sentient, social beings capable of communicating by means of language. We detect hints of incipient humanity in the form of crudely chipped tools, the telltale signs of a home base, or the artistic achievements of ornaments and cave art, as in the reports "Ancient Odysseys" and "Rhinos and Lions and Bears (Oh, My!)." Yet, none of these indicators of a distinctly hominid way of life can provide us with the nuances of the everyday lives of these creatures, their social relations, or their supernatural beliefs, if any. Most of what remains is the rubble of bones and stones from which we interpret what we can of their lifestyle, thought processes, and communicating ability. Our ability to glean from the fossil record is not completely without hope, however. In fact, informed speculation is what makes possible such articles as "Hard Times among the Neanderthals" by Erik Trinkaus, and "Old Masters" by Pat Shipman. Each is a fine example of the kind of careful, systematic, and thought-provoking work that is based upon an increased understanding of hominid fossil sites as well as the more general environmental circumstances in which our predecessors lived.

Beyond the technological and anatomical adaptations, questions have arisen as to how our hominid forebears organized themselves socially and whether modern-day human behavior is inherited as a legacy of our evolutionary past or is a learned product of contemporary circumstances. Attempts to address these issues have given rise to the technique referred to as the "ethnographic analogy." This is a method whereby anthropologists use "ethnographies" or field studies of modern-day hunters and gatherers whose lives we take to be the best approximations we have to what life might have been like for our ancestors. While it is granted that these contemporary foragers have been living under conditions of environmental and social change just as industrial peoples have, it nevertheless seems that, at least in some aspects of their lives, they have not changed as much as we have, and that if we are to make any kind of enlightened assessments of prehistoric behavior patterns, we are better off looking at them than at ourselves.

As if to show that controversy over lineages is not limited to the earlier hominid period (see unit 5), in this unit we see how long-held beliefs about *Homo erectus* are being threatened by new fossil evidence (see "*Erectus* Arising" by James Shreeve), and we consider new evidence bearing upon the "Eve hypothesis," as addressed in "The Dating Game" and "The Neanderthal Peace," also by James Shreeve. In the case of the "Eve hypothesis," the issue of when and where the family tree of modern humans actually began has pitted the bone experts, on the one hand, against a new type of anthropologist specializing in molecular biology, on the other. Granted, for some scientists, the new evidence fits in quite comfortably with previously held positions; for others it seems that reputations, as well as theories, are at stake.

Looking Ahead: Challenge Questions

When, where, and why did *Homo erectus* evolve? Is it one species or two?

What evidence is there for hard times among the Neanderthals?

What were Cro-Magnons trying to say or do with their cave art?

Why is prehistoric art so specific as to time and place?

How do we measure evolutionary time?

Explain whether the Cro-Magnons were the first or the last modern sapiens to appear on Earth.

What are the strengths and weaknesses of the "Eve hypothesis"?

What do you think happened to the Neanderthals?

How would you draw the late hominid family tree?

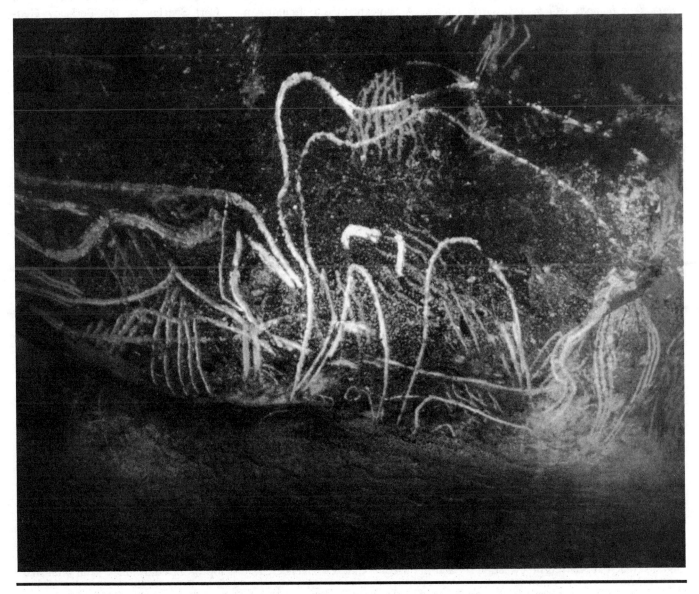

Erectus Rising

Oh No. Not This. The Hominids Are Acting Up Again . . .

James Shreeve

James Shreeve is the coauthor, with anthropologist Donald Johanson, of Lucy's Child: The Discovery of a Human Ancestor. *His book on the origins of modern humans will be published [in 1995], and he is at work on a novel that a reliable source calls "a murder thriller about the species question."*

Just when it seemed that the recent monumental fuss over the origins of modern human beings was beginning to quiet down, an ancient ancestor is once more running wild. Trampling on theories. Appearing in odd places, way ahead of schedule. Demanding new explanations. And shamelessly flaunting its contempt for conventional wisdom in the public press.

The uppity ancestor this time is *Homo erectus*—alias Java man, alias Peking man, alias a mouthful of formal names known only to the paleontological cognoscenti. Whatever you call it, *erectus* has traditionally been a quiet, average sort of hominid: low of brow, thick of bone, endowed with a brain larger than that of previous hominids but smaller than those that followed, a face less apelike and projecting than that of its ancestors but decidedly more simian than its descendants'. In most scenarios of human evolution, *erectus*'s role was essentially to mark time—a million and a half years of it—between its obscure, presumed origins in East Africa just under 2 million years ago and its much more recent evolution

into something deserving the name *sapiens*.

Erectus accomplished only two noteworthy deeds during its long tenure on Earth. First, some 1.5 million years ago, it developed what is known as the Acheulean stone tool culture, a technology exemplified by large, carefully crafted tear-shaped hand axes that were much more advanced than the bashed rocks that had passed for tools in the hands of earlier hominids. Then, half a million years later, and aided by those Acheulean tools, the species carved its way out of Africa and established a human presence in other parts of the Old World. But most of the time, *Homo erectus* merely existed, banging out the same stone tools millennium after millennium, over a time span that one archeologist has called "a period of unimaginable monotony."

Or so read the old script. These days, *erectus* has begun to ad-lib a more vigorous, controversial identity for itself. Research within the past year has revealed that rather than being 1 million years old, several *erectus* fossils from Southeast Asia are in fact almost 2 million years old. That is as old as the oldest African members of the species, and it would mean that *erectus* emerged from its home continent much earlier than has been thought—in fact, almost immediately after it first appeared. There's also a jawbone, found in 1991 near the Georgian city of Tbilisi, that resembles *erectus* fossils from Africa and may be as old as 1.8 million years, though that age is still in doubt. These new dates—and the debates they've engendered—

have shaken *Homo erectus* out of its interpretive stupor, bringing into sharp relief just how little agreement there is on the rise and demise of the last human species on Earth, save one.

"Everything now is in flux," says Carl Swisher of the Berkeley Geochronology Center, one of the prime movers behind the redating of *erectus* outside Africa. "It's all a mess."

Asian and African fossils were lumped into one far-flung taxon, a creature not quite like us but human enough to be welcomed into our genus: Homo erectus.

The focal point for the flux is the locale where the species was first found: Java. The rich but frustration-soaked history of paleoanthropology on that tropical island began just over 100 years ago, when a young Dutch anatomy professor named Eugène Dubois conceived the idée fixe that the "missing link" between ape and man was to be found in the jungled remoteness of the Dutch East Indies. Dubois had never left Holland, much less traveled to the Dutch East Indies, and his pick for the spot on Earth where humankind first arose owed as much to a large part of the Indonesian archipelago's being a Dutch colony as it did to any scientific evidence. He nevertheless found his missing link—the top of an oddly thick skull with massive browridges—in 1891 on the banks of the Solo River, near a community called Trinil in central Java. About a year later a thighbone that Dubois thought might belong to the same individual was found nearby; it looked so much like a modern human thighbone that Dubois assumed this ancient primate had walked upright. He christened the creature *Pithecanthropus erectus*—"erect ape-man"—and returned home in triumph.

Finding the fossil proved to be the easy part. Though Dubois won popular acclaim, neither he nor his "Java man" received the full approbation of the anatomists of the day, who considered his ape-man either merely an ape or merely a man. In an apparent pique, Dubois cloistered away the fossils for a quarter-century, refusing others the chance to view his prized possessions. Later, other similarly primitive human remains began to turn up in China and East Africa. All shared a collection of anatomical traits, including a long, low braincase with prominent browridges and a flattened forehead; a sharp angle to the back of the skull when viewed in profile; and a deep, robustly built jaw showing no hint of a chin. Though initially given separate regional names, the fossils were eventually lumped together into one far-flung taxon, a creature not quite like us but human enough to be welcomed into our genus: *Homo erectus*.

Over the decades the most generous source of new *erectus* fossils has been the sites on or near the Solo River in Java. The harvest continues: two more skulls, including one of the most complete *erectus* skulls yet known, were found at a famous fossil site called Sangiran just in the past year. Though the Javan yield of ancient humans has been rich, something has always been missing—the crucial element of time. Unless the age of a fossil can be determined, it hangs in limbo, its importance and place in the larger scheme of human evolution forever undercut with doubt. Until researchers can devise better methods for dating bone directly—right now there are no tech-

niques that can reliably date fossilized, calcified bone more than 50,000 years old—a specimen's age has to be inferred from the geology that surrounds it. Unfortunately, most of the discoveries made on the densely populated and cultivated island of Java have been made not by trained excavators but by sharp-eyed local farmers who spot the bones as they wash out with the annual rains and later sell them. As a result, the original location of many a prized specimen, and thus all hopes of knowing its age, are a matter of memory and word of mouth.

Despite the problems, scientists continue to try to pin down dates for Java's fossils. Most have come up with an upper limit of around 1 million years. Along with the dates for the Peking man skulls found in China and the Acheulean tools from Europe, the Javan evidence has come to be seen as confirmation that *erectus* first left Africa at about that time.

By the early 1970s most paleontologists were firmly wedded to the idea that Africa was the only human-inhabited part of the world until one million years ago.

There are those, however, who have wondered about these dates for quite some time. Chief among them is Garniss Curtis, the founder of the Berkeley Geochronology Center. In 1971 Curtis, who was then at the University of California at Berkeley, attempted to determine the age of a child's skull from a site called Mojokerto, in eastern Java, by using the potassium-argon method to date volcanic minerals in the sediments from which the skull was purportedly removed. Potassium-argon dating had been in use since the 1950s, and Curtis had been enormously successful with it in dating ancient African hominids—including Louis Leakey's famous hominid finds at Olduvai Gorge in Tanzania. The method takes advantage of the fact that a radioactive

isotope of potassium found in volcanic ash slowly and predictably decays over time into argon gas, which becomes trapped in the crystalline structure of the mineral. The amount of argon contained in a given sample, measured against the amount of the potassium isotope, serves as a kind of clock that tells how much time has passed since a volcano exploded and its ash fell to earth and buried the bone in question.

Applying the technique to the volcanic pumice associated with the skull from Mojokerto, Curtis got an extraordinary age of 1.9 million years. The wildly anomalous date was all too easy to dismiss, however. Unlike the ash deposits of East Africa, the volcanic pumices in Java are poor in potassium. Also, not unexpectedly, a heavy veil of uncertainty obscured the collector's memories of precisely where he had found the fossil some 35 years earlier. Besides, most paleontologists were by this time firmly wedded to the idea that Africa was the only human-inhabited part of the world until 1 million years ago. Curtis's date was thus deemed wrong for the most stubbornly cherished of reasons: because it couldn't possibly be right.

In 1992 Curtis—under the auspices of the Institute for Human Origins in Berkeley—returned to Java with his colleague Carl Swisher. This time he was backed up by far more sensitive equipment and a powerful refinement in the dating technique. In conventional potassium-argon dating, several grams' worth of volcanic crystals gleaned from a site are needed to run a single experiment. While the bulk of these crystals are probably from the eruption that covered the fossil, there's always the possibility that other materials, from volcanoes millions of years older, have gotten mixed in and will thus make the fossil appear to be much older than it actually is. The potassium-argon method also requires that the researcher divide the sample of crystals in two. One half is dissolved in acid and passed through a flame; the wavelengths of light emitted tell how much potassium is in the sample. The other half is used to measure the amount of argon gas that's released when the crystals are heated. This two-step process further increases the chance of error, simply by giving the experiment twice as much opportunity to go wrong.

The refined technique, called argon-argon dating, neatly sidesteps most of these difficulties. The volcanic crystals are first placed in a reactor and bombarded with neutrons; when one of these neutrons penetrates the potassium nucleus, it displaces a proton, converting the potassium into an isotope of argon that doesn't occur in nature. Then the artificially created argon and the naturally occurring argon are measured in a single experiment. Because the equipment used to measure the isotopes can look for both types of argon at the same time, there's no need to divide the sample, and so the argon-argon method can produce clear results from tiny amounts of material.

In some cases—when the volcanic material is fairly rich in potassium—all the atoms of argon from a single volcanic crystal can be quick-released by the heat from a laser beam and then counted. By doing a number of such single-crystal experiments, the researchers can easily pick out and discard any data from older, contaminant crystals. But even when the researchers are forced to sample more than one potassium-poor crystal to get any reading at all—as was the case at Mojokerto—the argon-argon method can still produce a highly reliable age. In this case, the researchers carefully heat a few crystals at a time to higher and higher temperatures, using a precisely controlled laser. If all the crystals in a sample are the same age, then the amount of argon released at each temperature will be the same. But if contaminants are mixed in, or if severe weathering has altered the crystal's chemical composition, the argon measurements will be erratic, and the researchers will know to throw out the results.

Curtis and Swisher knew that in the argon-argon step-heating method they had the technical means to date the potassium-poor deposits at Mojokerto

accurately. But they had no way to prove that those deposits were the ones in which the skull had been buried: all they had was the word of the local man who had found it. Then, during a visit to the museum in the regional capital, where the fossil was being housed, Swisher noticed something odd. The hardened sediments that filled the inside of the fossil's braincase looked black. But back at the site, the deposits of volcanic pumice that had supposedly sheltered the infant's skull were whitish in color. How could a skull come to be filled with black sediments if it had been buried in white ones? Was it possible that the site and the skull had nothing to do with each other after all? Swisher suspected something was wrong. He borrowed a penknife, picked up the precious skull, and nicked off a bit of the matrix inside.

"I almost got kicked out of the country at that point," he says. "These fossils in Java are like the crown jewels."

Luckily, his impulsiveness paid off. The knife's nick revealed white pumice under a thin skin of dark pigment: years earlier, someone had apparently painted the surface of the hardened sediments black. Since there were no other deposits within miles of the purported site that contained a white pumice visually or chemically resembling the matrix in the skull, its tie to the site was suddenly much stronger. Curtis and Swisher returned to Berkeley with pumice from that site and within a few weeks proclaimed the fossil to be 1.8 million years old, give or take some 40,000 years. At the same time, the geochronologists ran tests on pumice from the lower part of the Sangiran area, where erectus facial and cranial bone fragments had been found. The tests yielded an age of around 1.6 million years. Both numbers obviously shatter the 1-million-year barrier for erectus outside Africa, and they are a stunning vindication of Curtis's work at Mojokerto 20 years ago. "That was very rewarding," he says, "after having been told what a fool I was by my colleagues."

While no one takes Curtis or Swisher for a fool now, some of their colleagues won't be fully convinced by the new

dates until the matrix inside the Mojokerto skull itself can be tested. Even then, the possibility will remain that the skull may have drifted down over the years into deposits containing older volcanic crystals that have nothing to do with its original burial site, or that it was carried by a river to another, older site. But Swisher contends that the chance of such an occurrence is remote: it would have to have happened at both Mojokerto and Sangiran for the fossils' ages to be refuted. "I feel really good about the dates," he says. "But it has taken me a while to understand their implications."

The implications that can be spun out from the Javan dates depend on how one chooses to interpret the body of fossil evidence commonly embraced under the name Homo erectus. The earliest African fossils traditionally attributed to erectus are two nearly complete skulls from the site of Koobi Fora in Kenya, dated between 1.8 and 1.7 million years old. In the conventional view, these early specimens evolved from a more primitive, smaller-brained ancestor called Homo habilis, well represented by bones from Koobi Fora, Olduvai Gorge, and sites in South Africa.

If this conventional view is correct, then the new dates mean that erectus must have migrated out of Africa very soon after it evolved, quickly reaching deep into the farthest corner of Southeast Asia. This is certainly possible: at the time, Indonesia was connected to Asia by lower sea levels—thus providing an overland route from Africa—and Java is just 10,000 to 15,000 miles from Kenya, depending on the route. Even if erectus traveled just one mile a year, it would still take no more than 15,000 years to reach Java—a negligible amount of evolutionary time.

If erectus did indeed reach Asia almost a million years earlier than thought, then other, more controversial theories become much more plausible. Although many anthropologists believe that the African and Asian erectus fossils all represent a single species, other investigators have recently argued that

MEANWHILE, IN SIBERIA . . .

The presence of *Homo erectus* in Asia twice as long ago as previously thought has some people asking whether the human lineage might have originated in Asia instead of Africa. This long-dormant theory runs contrary to all current thinking about human evolution and lacks an important element: evidence. Although the new Javan dates do place the species in Asia at around the same time it evolved in Africa, all confirmed specimens of other, earlier hominids—the first members of the genus *Homo,* for instance, and the australopithecines, like Lucy—have been found exclusively in Africa. Given such an overwhelming argument, most investigators continue to believe that the hominid line began in Africa.

Most, but not all. Some have begun to cock an ear to the claims of Russian archeologist Yuri Mochanov. For over a decade Mochanov has been excavating a huge site on the Lena River in eastern Siberia—far from Africa, Java, or anywhere else on Earth an ancient hominid bone has ever turned up. Though he hasn't found any hominid fossils in Siberia, he stubbornly believes he's uncovered the next best thing: a trove of some 4,000 stone artifacts—crudely made flaked tools, but tools nonetheless—that he maintains are at least 2 million years old, and possibly 3 million. This, he says, would mean that the human lineage arose not in tropical Africa but in the cold northern latitudes of Asia.

"For evolutionary progress to occur, there had to be the appearance of new conditions: winter, snow, and, ac-companying them, hunger," writes Mochanov. "[The ancestral primates] had to learn to walk on the ground, to change their carriage, and to become accustomed to meat—that is, to become 'clever animals of prey.' " And to become clever animals of prey, they'd need tools.

Although he is a well-respected investigator, Mochanov has been unable to convince either Western anthropologists or his Russian colleagues of the age of his site. Until recently the chipped rocks he was holding up as human artifacts were simply dismissed as stones broken by natural processes, or else his estimate of the age of the site was thought to be wincingly wrong. After all, no other signs of human occupation of Siberia appear until some 35,000 years ago.

But after a lecture swing through the United States earlier this year—in which he brought more data and a few prime examples of the tools for people to examine and pass around—many archeologists concede that it is difficult to explain the particular pattern of breakage of the rocks by any known natural process. "Everything I have heard or seen about the context of these things suggests that they are most likely tools," says anthropologist Rick Potts of the Smithsonian Institution, which was host to Mochanov last January.

They're even willing to concede that the site might be considerably older than they'd thought, though not nearly as old as Mochanov estimates. (To date the site, Mochanov compared the tools with artifacts found early in Africa; he also employed an arcane dating technique little known outside Russia.) Preliminary results from an experimental dating technique performed on soil samples from the site by Michael Waters of Texas A&M and Steve Forman of Ohio State suggest that the layer of sediment bearing the artifacts is some 400,000 years old. That's a long way from 2 million, certainly, but it's still vastly older than anything else found in Siberia—and the site is 1,500 miles farther north than the famous Peking man site in China, previously considered the most northerly home of *erectus.*

"If this does turn out to be 400,000 years old, it's very exciting," says Waters. "If people were able to cope and survive in such a rigorous Arctic environment at such an early time, we would have to completely change our perception of the evolution of human adaptation."

"I have no problem with hominids being almost anywhere at that age—they were certainly traveling around," says Potts. "But the environment is the critical thing. If it was really cold up there"—temperatures in the region now often reach −50 degrees in deep winter—"we'd all have to scratch our heads over how these early hominids were making it in Siberia. There is no evidence that Neanderthals, who were better equipped for cold than anyone, were living in such climates. But who knows? Maybe a population got trapped up there, went extinct, and Mochanov managed to find it." He shrugs. "But that's just arm waving."

—*J. S.*

the two groups are too different to be so casually lumped together. According to paleoanthropologist Ian Tattersall of the American Museum of Natural History in New York, the African skulls traditionally assigned to *erectus* often lack many of the specialized traits that were originally used to define the species in Asia, including the long, low cranial structure, thick skull bones, and robustly built faces. In his view, the African group deserves to be placed in a separate species, which he calls *Homo ergaster.*

Most anthropologists believe that the only way to distinguish between species in the fossil record is to look at the similarities and differences between bones; the age of the fossil should not play a part. But age is often hard to ignore, and Tattersall believes that the new evidence for what he sees as two distinct populations living at the same time in widely separate parts of the Old World is highly suggestive. "The new dates help confirm that these were indeed two different species," he says.

"In my view, *erectus* is a separate variant that evolved only in Asia."

Other investigators still contend that the differences between the African and Asian forms of *erectus* are too minimal to merit placing them in separate species. But if Tattersall is right, his theory raises the question of who the original emigrant out of Africa really was. *Homo ergaster* may have been the one to make the trek, evolving into *erectus* once it was established in Asia. Or perhaps a population of some even more primitive, as-yet-unidentified common ancestor ventured forth, giving rise to *erectus* in Asia while a sister population evolved into *ergaster* on the home continent.

Furthermore, no matter who left Africa first, there's the question of what precipitated the migration, a question made even more confounding by the new dates. The old explanation, that the primal human expansion across the hem of the Old World was triggered by the sophisticated Acheulean tools, is no longer tenable with these dates, simply because the tools had not yet been invented when the earliest populations would have moved out. In hindsight, that notion seems a bit shopworn anyway. Acheulean tools first appear in Africa around 1.5 million years ago, and soon after at a site in the nearby Middle East. But they've never been found in the Far East, in spite of the abundant fossil evidence for *Homo erectus* in the region.

Until now, that absence has best been explained by the "bamboo line." According to paleoanthropologist Geoffrey Pope of William Paterson College in New Jersey, *erectus* populations venturing from Africa into the Far East found the land rich in bamboo, a raw material more easily worked into cutting and butchering tools than recalcitrant stone. Sensibly, they abandoned their less efficient stone industry for one based on the pliable plant, which leaves no trace of itself in the archeological record. This is still a viable theory, but the new dates from Java add an even simpler dimension to it: there are no Acheulean tools in the Far East because the first wave of *erectus*

to leave Africa didn't have any to bring with them.

So what *did* fuel the quick-step migration out of Africa? Some researchers say the crucial development was not cultural but physical. Earlier hominids like *Homo habilis* were small-bodied creatures with more apelike limb proportions, notes paleoanthropologist Bernard Wood of the University of Liverpool, while African *erectus* was built along more modern lines. Tall, relatively slender, with long legs better able to range over distance and a body better able to dissipate heat, the species was endowed with the physiology needed to free it from the tropical shaded woodlands of Africa that sheltered earlier hominids. In fact, the larger-bodied *erectus* would have required a bigger feeding range to sustain itself, so it makes perfect sense that the expansion out of Africa should begin soon after the species appeared. "Until now, one was always having to account for what kept *erectus* in Africa so long after it evolved," says Wood. "So rather than raising a problem, in some ways the new dates in Java solve one."

Of course, if those dates are right, the accepted time frame for human evolution outside the home continent is nearly doubled, and that has implications for the ongoing debate over the origins of modern human beings. There are two opposing theories. The "out of Africa" hypothesis says that *Homo sapiens* evolved from *erectus* in Africa, and then—sometime in the last 100,000 years—spread out and replaced the more archaic residents of Eurasia. The "multiregional continuity" hypothesis says that modern humans evolved from *erectus* stock in various parts of the Old World, more or less simultaneously and independently. According to this scenario, living peoples outside Africa should look for their most recent ancestors not in African fossils but in the anatomy of ancient fossils within their own region of origin.

As it happens, the multiregionalists have long claimed that the best evidence for their theory lies in Australia,

which is generally thought to have become inhabited around 50,000 years ago, by humans crossing over from Indonesia. There are certain facial and cranial characteristics in modern Australian aborigines, the multiregionalists say, that can be traced all the way back to the earliest specimens of *erectus* at Sangiran—characteristics that differ from and precede those of any more recent, *Homo sapiens* arrival from Africa. But if the new Javan dates are right, then these unique characteristics, and thus the aborigines' Asian *erectus* ancestors, must have been evolving separately from the rest of humankind for almost 2 million years. Many anthropologists, already skeptical of the multiregionalists' potential 1-million-year-long isolation for Asian *erectus*, find a 2-million-year-long isolation exceedingly difficult to swallow. "Can anyone seriously propose that the lineage of Australian aborigines could go back that far?" wonders paleoanthropologist Chris Stringer of the Natural History Museum in London, a leading advocate of the out-of-Africa theory.

The multiregionalists counter that they've never argued for *complete* isolation—that there's always been some flow of genes between populations, enough interbreeding to ensure that clearly beneficial *sapiens* characteristics would quickly be conferred on peoples throughout the Old World. "Just as genes flow now from Johannesburg to Beijing and from Melbourne to Paris, they have been flowing that way ever since humanity evolved," says Alan Thorne of the Australian National University in Canberra, an outspoken multiregionalist.

Stanford archeologist Richard Klein, another out-of-Africa supporter, believes the evidence actually *does* point to just such a long, deep isolation of Asian populations from African ones. The fossil record, he says, shows that while archaic forms of *Homo sapiens* were developing in Africa, *erectus* was remaining much the same in Asia. In fact, if some *erectus* fossils from a site called Ngandong in Java turn out to be as young as 100,000 years, as some researchers believe, then *erectus* was still alive on Java at the same time that fully modern human beings were living in Africa and the Middle East. Even more important, Klein says, is the cultural evidence. That Acheulean tools never reached East Asia, even after their invention in Africa, could mean the inventors never reached East Asia either. "You could argue that the new dates show that until very recently there was a long biological and cultural division between Asia on one hand, and Africa and Europe on the other," says Klein. In other words, there must have been two separate lineages of *erectus,* and since there aren't two separate lineages of modern humans, one

of those must have gone extinct: presumably the Asian lineage, hastened into oblivion by the arrival of the more culturally adept, tool-laden *Homo sapiens.*

Naturally this argument is anathema to the multiregionalists. But this tenacious debate is unlikely to be resolved without basketfuls of new fossils, new ways of interpreting old ones—and new dates. In Berkeley, Curtis and Swisher are already busy applying the argon-argon method to the Ngandong fossils, which could represent some of the last surviving *Homo erectus* populations on Earth. They also hope to work their radiometric magic on a key

erectus skull from Olduvai Gorge. In the meantime, at least one thing has become clear: *Homo erectus,* for so long the humdrum hominid, is just as fascinating, contentious, and elusive a character as any other in the human evolutionary story.

FURTHER READING

Eugène Dubois & the Ape-Man from Java. Bert Theunissen. Kluwer Academic, 1989. When a Dutch army surgeon, determined to prove Darwin right, traveled to Java in search of the missing link between apes and humans, he inadvertently opened a paleontological Pandora's box. This is Dubois's story, the story of the discovery of *Homo erectus.*

Hard Times Among the Neanderthals

Although life was difficult, these prehistoric people may not have been as exclusively brutish as usually supposed

Erik Trinkaus

Throughout the century that followed the discovery in 1856 of the first recognized human fossil remains in the Neander Valley (*Neanderthal* in German) near Düsseldorf, Germany, the field of human paleontology has been beset with controversies. This has been especially true of interpretations of the Neanderthals, those frequently maligned people who occupied Europe and the Near East from about 100,000 years ago until the appearance of anatomically modern humans about 35,000 years ago.

During the last two decades, however, a number of fossil discoveries, new analyses of previously known remains, and more sophisticated models for interpreting subtle anatomical differences have led to a reevaluation of the Neanderthals and their place in human evolution.

This recent work has shown that the often quoted reconstruction of the Neanderthals as semierect, lumbering caricatures of humanity is inaccurate. It was based on faulty anatomical interpretations that were reinforced by the intellectual biases of the turn of the century. Detailed comparisons of Neanderthal skeletal remains with those of modern humans have shown that there is nothing in Neanderthal anatomy that conclusively indicates locomotor, manipulative, intellectual, or linguistic abilities inferior to those of modern humans. Neanderthals have therefore been added to the same spe-

cies as ourselves—*Homo sapiens*—although they are usually placed in their own subspecies, *Homo sapiens neanderthalensis.*

Despite these revisions, it is apparent that there are significant anatomical differences between the Neanderthals and present-day humans. If we are to understand the Neanderthals, we must formulate hypotheses as to why they evolved from earlier humans about 100,000 years ago in Europe and the Near East, and why they were suddenly replaced about 35,000 years ago by peoples largely indistinguishable from ourselves. We must determine, therefore, the behavioral significance of the anatomical differences between the Neanderthals and other human groups, since it is patterns of successful behavior that dictate the direction of natural selection for a species.

In the past, behavioral reconstructions of the Neanderthals and other prehistoric humans have been based largely on archeological data. Research has now reached the stage at which behavioral interpretations from the archeological record can be significantly supplemented by analyses of the fossils themselves. These analyses promise to tell us a considerable amount about the ways of the Neanderthals and may eventually help us to determine their evolutionary fate.

One of the most characteristic features of the Neanderthals is the exaggerated massiveness of their trunk and limb bones. All of the preserved bones

suggest a strength seldom attained by modern humans. Furthermore, not only is this robustness present among the adult males, as one might expect, but it is also evident in the adult females, adolescents, and even children. The bones themselves reflect this hardiness in several ways.

First, the muscle and ligament attachment areas are consistently enlarged and strongly marked. This implies large, highly developed muscles and ligaments capable of generating and sustaining great mechanical stress. Secondly, since the skeleton must be capable of supporting these levels of stress, which are frequently several times as great as body weight, the enlarged attachments for muscles and ligaments are associated with arm and leg bone shafts that have been reinforced. The shafts of all of the arm and leg bones are modified tubular structures that have to absorb stress from bending and twisting without fracturing. When the habitual load on a bone increases, the bone responds by laying down more bone in those areas under the greatest stress.

In addition, musculature and body momentum generate large forces across the joints. The cartilage, which covers joint surfaces, can be relatively easily overworked to the point where it degenerates, as is indicated by the prevalence of arthritis in joints subjected to significant wear and tear over the years. When the surface area of a joint is increased, the force per unit area or a crest, especially the muscles used in grasping objects. In fact, Neanderthal hand bones frequently have clear bony crests, where on modern human ones it is barely possible to discern the attachment of the muscle on the dried bone.

In addition, the flattened areas on the ends of the fingers, which provide support for the nail and the pulp of the finger tip, are enormous among the Neanderthals. These areas on the thumb and the index and middle fingers are usually two to three times as large as those of similarly sized modern human hands. The overall impression is one of arms to rival those of the mightiest blacksmith.

Neanderthal legs are equally massive; their strength is best illustrated in the development of the shafts of the leg bones. Modern human thigh and shin bones possess characteristic shaft shapes adapted to the habitual levels and directions of the stresses acting upon them. The shaft shapes of the Neanderthals are similar to those in modern humans, but the cross-sectional areas of the shafts are much greater. This implies significantly higher levels of stress.

Further evidence of the massiveness of Neanderthal lower limbs is provided by the dimensions of their knee and ankle joints. All of these are larger than in modern humans, especially with respect to the overall lengths of the bones.

The development of their limb bones suggests that the Neanderthals frequently generated high levels of mechanical stress in their limbs. Since most mechanical stress in the body is produced by body momentum and muscular contraction, it appears that the Neanderthals led extremely active lives. It is hard to conceive of what could have required such exertion, especially since the maintenance of vigorous muscular activity would have required considerable expenditure of energy. That level of energy expenditure would undoubtedly have been maladaptive had it not been necessary for survival.

The available evidence from the archeological material associated with

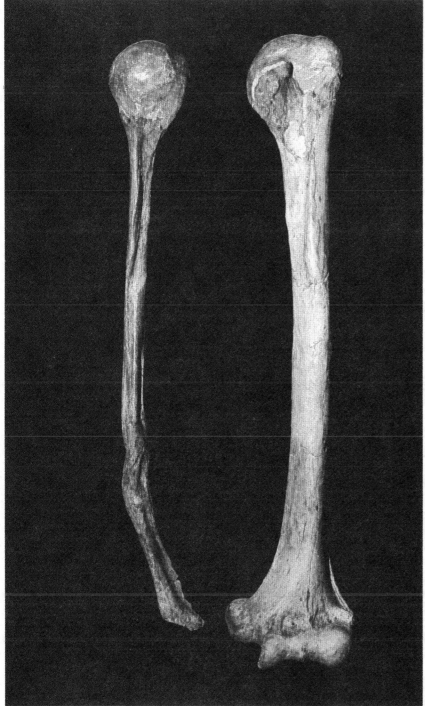

Diagonal lines on these two arm bones from Shanidar 1 are healed fractures. The bone on the right is normal. That on the left is atrophied and has a pathological tip, caused by either amputation or an improperly healed elbow fracture.

area of cartilage is reduced, decreasing the pressure on the cartilage.

Most of the robustness of Neanderthal arm bones is seen in muscle and ligament attachments. All of the muscles that go from the trunk or the shoulder blade to the upper end of the arm show massive development. This applies in particular to the muscles responsible for powerful downward movements of the arm and, to a lesser extent, to muscles that stabilize the shoulder during vigorous movements.

Virtually every major muscle or ligament attachment on the hand bones is clearly marked by a large roughened the Neanderthals is equivocal on this matter. Most of the archeological evidence at Middle Paleolithic sites concerns stone tool technology and hunting activities. After relatively little change in technology during the Middle Paleolithic (from about 100,000 years to 35,000 years before the present), the advent of the Upper Paleolithic appears to have brought significant technological advances. This transition about 35,000 years ago is approximately coincident with the replacement of the Neanderthals by the earliest anatomically modern humans. However, the evidence for a significant

change in hunting patterns is not evident in the animal remains left behind. Yet even if a correlation between the robustness of body build and the level of hunting efficiency could be demonstrated, it would only explain the ruggedness of the Neanderthal males. Since hunting is exclusively or at least predominantly a male activity among humans, and since Neanderthal females were in all respects as strongly built as the males, an alternative explanation is required for the females.

Some insight into why the Neanderthals consistently possessed such massiveness is provided by a series of

partial skeletons of Neanderthals from the Shanidar Cave in northern Iraq. These fossils were excavated between 1953 and 1960 by anthropologist Ralph Solecki of Columbia University and have been studied principally by T. Dale Stewart, an anthropologist at the Smithsonian Institution, and myself. The most remarkable aspect of these skeletons is the number of healed injuries they contain. Four of the six reasonably complete adult skeletons show evidence of trauma during life.

The identification of traumatic injury in human fossil remains has plagued paleontologists for years. There has been a tendency to consider any form of damage to a fossil as conclusive evidence of prehistoric violence between humans if it resembles the breakage patterns caused by a direct blow with a heavy object. Hence a jaw with the teeth pushed in or a skull with a depressed fracture of the vault would be construed to indicate blows to the head.

The central problem with these interpretations is that they ignore the possibility of damage after death. Bone is relatively fragile, especially as compared with the rock and other sediment in which it is buried during fossilization. Therefore when several feet of sediment caused compression around fossil remains, the fossils will almost always break. In fact, among the innumerable cases of suggested violence between humans cited over the years, there are only a few exceptional examples that cannot be readily explained as the result of natural geologic forces acting after the death and burial of the individual.

One of these examples is the trauma of the left ninth rib of the skeleton of Shanidar 3, a partially healed wound inflicted by a sharp object. The implement cut obliquely across the top of the ninth rib and probably pierced the underlying lung. Shanidar 3 almost certainly suffered a collapsed left lung and died several days or weeks later, probably as a result of secondary complications. This is deduced from the presence of bony spurs and increased density of the bone around the cut.

The position of the wound on the

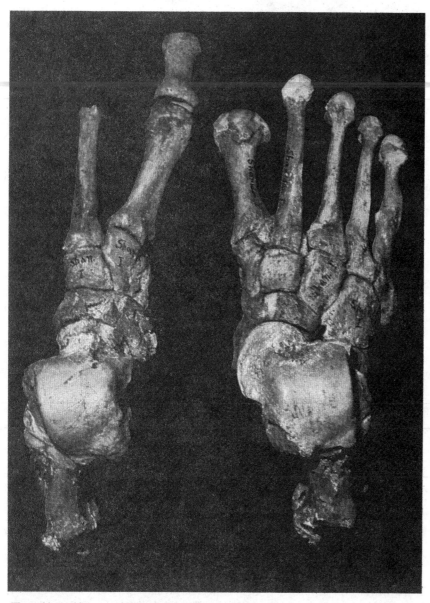

The ankle and big toe of Shanidar 1's right foot show evidence of arthritis, which suggests an injury to those parts. The left foot is normal although incomplete.

The scar on the left ninth rib of Shanidar 3 is a partially healed wound inflicted by a sharp object. This wound is one of the few examples of trauma caused by violence.

rib, the angle of the incision, and the cleanness of the cut make it highly unlikely that the injury was accidentally inflicted. In fact, the incision is almost exactly what would have resulted if Shanidar 3 had been stabbed in the side by a right-handed adversary in face-to-face conflict. This would therefore provide conclusive evidence of violence between humans, the *only* evidence so far found of such violence among the Neanderthals.

In most cases, however, it is impossible to determine from fossilized remains the cause of an individual's death. The instances that can be positively identified as prehistoric traumatic injury are those in which the injury was inflicted prior to death and some healing took place. Shortly after an injury to bone, whether a cut or a fracture, the damaged bone tissue is resorbed by the body and new bone

tissue is laid down around the injured area. As long as irritation persists, new bone is deposited, creating a bulge or spurs of irregular bone extending into the soft tissue. If the irritation ceases, the bone will slowly re-form so as to approximate its previous, normal condition. However, except for superficial injuries or those sustained during early childhood, some trace of damage persists for the life of the individual.

In terms of trauma, the most impressive of the Shanidar Neanderthals is the first adult discovered, known as Shanidar 1. This individual suffered a number of injuries, some of which may be related. On the right forehead there are scars from minor surface injuries, probably superficial scalp cuts. The outside of the left eye socket sustained a major blow that partially collapsed that part of the bony cavity, giving it a flat rather than a rounded contour. This injury possibly caused loss of sight in the left eye and pathological alterations of the right side of the body.

Shanidar 1's left arm is largely preserved and fully normal. The right arm, however, consists of a highly atrophied but otherwise normal collarbone and shoulder blade and a highly abnormal upper arm bone shaft. That shaft is atrophied to a fraction of the diameter of the left one but retains most of its original length. Furthermore, the lower end of the right arm bone has a healed fracture of the atrophied shaft and an irregular, pathological tip. The arm was apparently either intentionally amputated just above the elbow or fractured at the elbow and never healed.

This abnormal condition of the right arm does not appear to be a congenital malformation, since the length of the bone is close to the estimated length of the normal left upper arm bone. If, however, the injury to the left eye socket also affected the left side of the brain, directly or indirectly, by disrupting the blood supply to part of the brain, the result could have been partial paralysis of the right side. Motor and sensory control areas for the right side are located on the left side of the brain, slightly behind the left eye socket. This would explain the atrophy

of the whole right arm since loss of nervous stimulation will rapidly lead to atrophy of the affected muscles and bone.

The abnormality of the right arm of Shanidar 1 is paralleled to a lesser extent in the right foot. The right ankle joint shows extensive arthritic degeneration, and one of the major joints of the inner arch of the right foot has been completely reworked by arthritis. The left foot, however, is totally free of pathology. Arthritis from normal stress usually affects both lower limbs equally; this degeneration therefore suggests that the arthritis in the right foot is a secondary result of an injury, perhaps a sprain, that would not otherwise be evident on skeletal remains. This conclusion is supported by a healed fracture of the right fifth instep bone, which makes up a major portion of the outer arch of the foot. These foot pathologies may be tied into the damage to the left side of the skull; partial paralysis of the right side would certainly weaken the leg and make it more susceptible to injury.

The trauma evident on the other Shanidar Neanderthals is relatively minor by comparison. Shanidar 3, the individual who died of the rib wound, suffered debilitating arthritis of the right ankle and neighboring foot joints, but lacks any evidence of pathology on the left foot; this suggests a superficial injury similar to the one sustained by Shanidar 1. Shanidar 4 had a healed broken rib. Shanidar 5 received a transverse blow across the left forehead that left a large scar on the bone but does not appear to have affected the brain.

None of these injuries necessarily provides evidence of deliberate violence among the Neanderthals; all of them could have been accidentally self-inflicted or accidentally caused by another individual. In either case, the impression gained of the Shanidar Neanderthals is of a group of invalids. The crucial variable, however, appears to be age. All four of these individuals died at relatively advanced ages, probably between 40 and 60 years (estimating the age at death for Neanderthals beyond the age of 25 is extremely difficult); they therefore had considerable time to accumulate the scars of past injuries. Shanidar 2 and 6, the other reasonably complete Shanidar adults, lack evidence of trauma, but they both died young, probably before reaching 30.

Other Neanderthal remains, all from Europe, exhibit the same pattern. Every fairly complete skeleton of an elderly adult shows evidence of traumatic injuries. The original male skeleton from the Neander Valley had a fracture just below the elbow of the left arm, which probably limited movement of that arm for life. The "old man" from La Chapelle-aux-Saints, France, on whom most traditional reconstructions of the Neanderthals have been based, suffered a broken rib. La Ferrassi 1, the old adult male from La Ferrassie, France, sustained a severe injury to the right hip, which may have impaired his mobility.

In addition, several younger specimens and ones of uncertain age show traces of trauma. La Quina 5, the young adult female from La Quina, France, was wounded on her right upper arm. A young adult from Sala, Czechoslovakia, was superficially wounded on the right forehead just above the brow. And an individual of unknown age and sex from the site of Krapina, Yugoslavia, suffered a broken forearm, in which the bones never reunited after the fracture.

This evidence suggests several things. First, life for the Neanderthals was rigorous. If they lived through childhood and early adulthood, they did so bearing the scars of a harsh and dangerous life. Furthermore, this incidence of trauma correlates with the massiveness of the Neanderthals; a life style that so consistently involved injury would have required considerable strength and fortitude for survival.

There is, however, another, more optimistic side to this. The presence of so many injuries in a prehistoric human group, many of which were debilitating and sustained years before death, shows that individuals were

taken care of long after their economic usefulness to the social group had ceased. It is perhaps no accident that among the Neanderthals, for the first time in human history, people lived to a comparatively old age. We also find among the Neanderthals the first intentional burials of the dead, some of which involved offerings. Despite the hardships of their life style, the Neanderthals apparently had a deep-seated respect and concern for each other.

Taken together, these different pieces of information paint a picture of life among the Neanderthals that, while harsh and dangerous, was not without personal security. Certainly the hardships the Neanderthals endured were beyond those commonly experienced in the prehistoric record of human caring and respect as well as of violence between individuals. Perhaps for these reasons, despite their physical appearance, the Neanderthals should be considered the first modern humans.

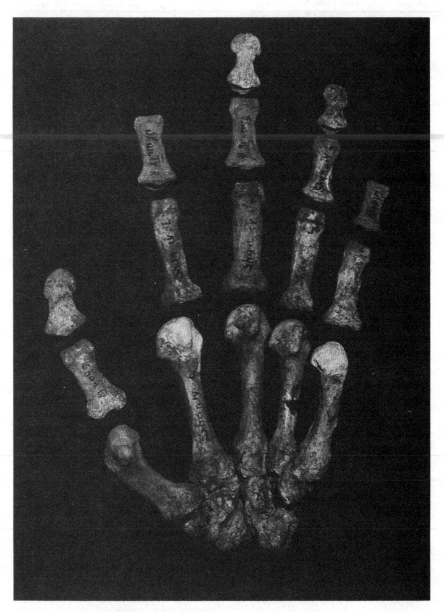

The right hand of Shanidar 4 demonstrates the enlarged finger tips and strong muscle markings characteristic of Neanderthal hands.

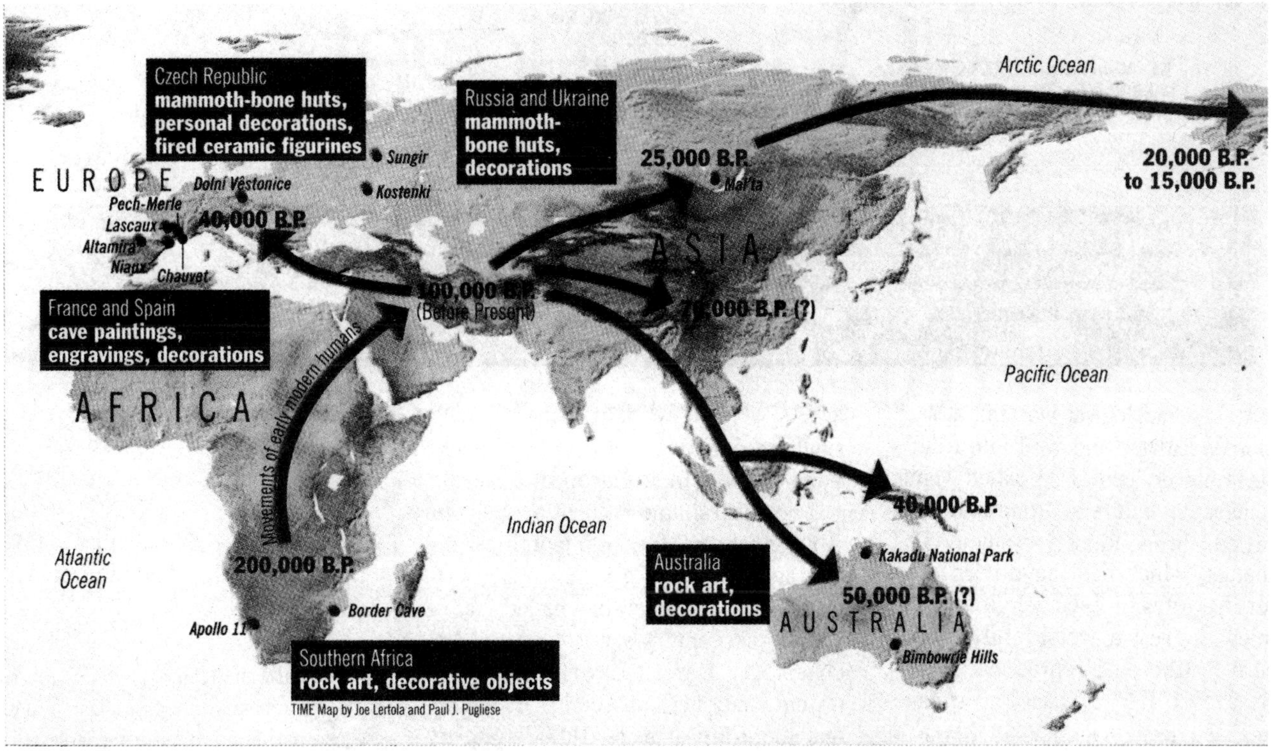
Czech Republic
mammoth-bone huts, personal decorations, fired ceramic figurines
Russia and Ukraine
mammoth-bone huts, decorations
Arctic Ocean
Sungir
Kostenki
EUROPE
Dolní Věstonice
Pech-Merle
Lascaux
Altamira
Chauvet
25,000 B.P.
20,000 B.P. to 15,000 B.P.
ASIA
France and Spain
cave paintings, engravings, decorations
(Before Present)
Pacific Ocean
AFRICA
Movements of early modern humans
Indian Ocean
40,000 B.P.
Atlantic Ocean
200,000 B.P.
Australia
rock art, decorations
Kakadu National Park
50,000 B.P. (?)
Border Cave
Apollo 11
AUSTRALIA
Southern Africa
rock art, decorative objects
TIME Map by Joe Lertola and Paul J. Pugliese

Ancient Odysseys

As early humans migrated around the globe, image making spread rapidly

Michael D. Lemonick

The human mind can't easily comprehend huge expanses of time. Once the years run into the tens of thousands, our brain lumps them together into an undifferentiated mass. The catchall term prehistoric art works perfectly with this sort of thinking. It sounds like just another episode in art history—modern art, Renaissance art, Byzantine art, prehistoric art.

In reality, the artworks created before history began—prior, say, to about 10,000 B.P. (before the present)—cover a much longer time span than what has come afterward. Southwestern European cave painting, only the most familiar expression of ancient creativity, was done over a period of at least 10,000 years. And when Paleolithic people first crawled into the Chauvet cave to daub the walls with images of rhinos and bears, nearly half of all art history was already over with.

When art first appeared, presumably around 40,000 B.P., it spread quickly. Within a mere 5,000 years—barely the blink of an eye on paleontological time scales—the work of early artists popped up in several corners of the globe. Archaeologists have found more than 10,000 sculpted and engraved objects in hundreds of locations across Europe, southern Africa, northern Asia and Australia. The styles range from realistic to abstract, and the materials include stone, bone, antler, ivory, wood, paint, teeth, claws, shells and clay that have been carved, sculpted and painted to represent animals, plants, geometric forms, landscape features and human beings—virtually every medium and every kind of subject that artists would return to thousands of years later.

This creative explosion is best documented in Europe, largely because that is where most of the excavations have taken place. Early body decoration, for example, was found in the 1950s by Soviet archaeologists at Sungir, near the Russian city of Vladimir. From graves dating back to 28,000 B.P., they unearthed the remains of a 10-year-old girl, a 12-year-old boy and a 60-year-old man. The three are festooned with beads, more than 14,000 all told. But each is adorned in a different way, evidence that body decoration was used to emphasize gender and age distinctions in social groups. In addition to the beads, the girl has delicate snowflake-like carvings around her head and torso. The boy has no snowflakes but wears a belt made from 240 fox canine teeth. And the man is wearing a single pendant made of stone in the middle of his chest. Another distinction: the beads on the children's bodies are approximately two thirds the size of those the man is wearing.

At about the same time that the three were being buried—give or take a few millenniums—a new sort of artifact begins to appear in the prehistorical

From *Time*, February 13, 1995, pp. 64, 66-67. © 1995 by Time Inc. Magazine Company. Reprinted by permission.

Art through the Prehistoric Ages

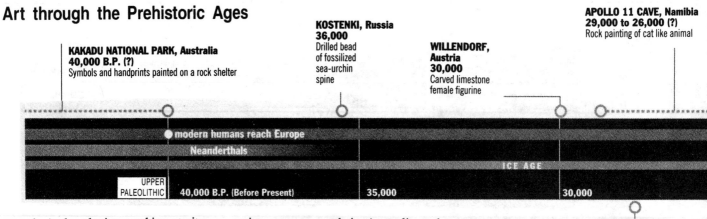

**KAKADU NATIONAL PARK, Australia
40,000 B.P. (?)**
Symbols and handprints painted on a rock shelter

**KOSTENKI, Russia
36,000**
Drilled bead
of fossilized
sea-urchin
spine

**WILLENDORF,
Austria
30,000**
Carved limestone
female figurine

**APOLLO 11 CAVE, Namibia
29,000 to 26,000 (?)**
Rock painting of cat like animal

modern humans reach Europe

Neanderthals

ICE AGE

UPPER PALEOLITHIC

40,000 B.P. (Before Present)

35,000

30,000

**SUNGIR, Russia
28,000**
Ivory animal pendant
with traces of paint

record. Archaeologists working at sites all across Europe and well into Russia have found dozens of so-called Venus figurines: miniature sculptures of big-breasted, broad-hipped women. The statuettes, which may have been used in fertility rites or even religious ceremonies, suggest a worshipful attitude toward fertility and reproduction.

By 22,000 B.P., archaeologists have found, the first evidence of the cave paintings that appeal so strongly to modern eyes begins to appear. The paintings, some of them realistic portraits of animals, others depicting half-human, half-animal figures or abstract symbols, soon became the dominant form of prehistoric European art. They remained important until 10,000 B.P., when, along with the glaciers of the last Ice Age, they seem to have melted away from human consciousness.

Those are the broad outlines, at least, of early art history. The details are much messier: it's not as though one phase gave way smoothly to another. Beadwork and statuette carving didn't stop just because cave painting began—and the presence of caves didn't automatically inspire people to cover them with images. Says Jean Clottes, one of France's pre-eminent authorities on prehistoric art: "There are a lot of caves in Yugoslavia, for example, but no paintings in them." Moreover, there is enormous regional variation in what sorts of art were produced at what times.

The story is even less straightforward in other parts of the world. Not only have extensive explorations been less common outside Europe, but also what's been found has proved difficult to date. Nonetheless, it is clear that

artists were at work in Australia and southern Africa, at least, at roughly the same time as their European cousins.

The Australian continent abounds in Aboriginal rock art, both paintings and engravings. Much of it lies in a 1,500-mile-long, boomerang-shaped area across the country's north coast. Archaeologist Darrell Lewis of the Australian National University estimates that there are at least 10,000 rock-art sites on the Arnhem Land plateau alone, in the Northern Territory. "Each of these sites," he says, "can have several hundred paintings." But unlike early inhabitants of Europe, who frequently decorated caves over a short period and then abandoned them, the Australian Aborigines would return over and over to the same sites—a practice that still goes on today. Unraveling the history of a single site can thus be extremely complicated.

How old is Australia's art? Some archaeologists insist that certain paintings of human hands and life-size crocodiles and kangaroos were done 50,000 years ago, but these experts may be overconfident of their dating techniques. Another controversial assertion is the claim by anthropologist Alan Thorne of the Australian National University that a small piece of red ochre (a kind of clay), dated to 50,000 B.P., was worn down on one side like a piece of chalk by humans. "Whether it was ground to paint a shelter or a person or part of a wall, I don't think anyone would disagree that it is evidence of art," says Thorne. Even if Australia's art is not as ancient as Thorne thinks, there is strong evidence that at least two rock carvings found in the Bimbowrie Hills are more than

40,000 years old, and that scores of others in the area fall between 30,000 and 20,000 B.P.

Southern Africa's artistic record is much sparser. Scientists have unearthed a pendant made from a seashell that may be more than 40,000 years old, carved bones and beads made from ostrich eggshells that probably date from around 27,000 B.P., and paintings on slabs of rock in a Namibian cave that may be nearly as old. But like Australia's Aborigines, southern Africa's indigenous people carried on their rock-art tradition into modern times, confusing anthropologists' tasks considerably.

And in the rest of the world . . . nothing. Not in the Middle East, not in Southeast Asia, not in China or Japan or Korea, and not in North Africa before 15,000 B.P. at the very earliest—although there is ample evidence of an ancient human presence in all these areas. This may mean the people there weren't interested in art, or it may simply be that they painted or carved on wood or animal skins, which have long since rotted away.

Nobody can do more than speculate about the answer. That uncertainty, along with the spottiness of the archaeological record—even in an intensively studied area like southern France—makes it hard to know whether art, once invented, was a universal practice. Probably not, argues archaeologist Olga Soffer, of the University of Illinois at Urbana-Champaign: "Art is

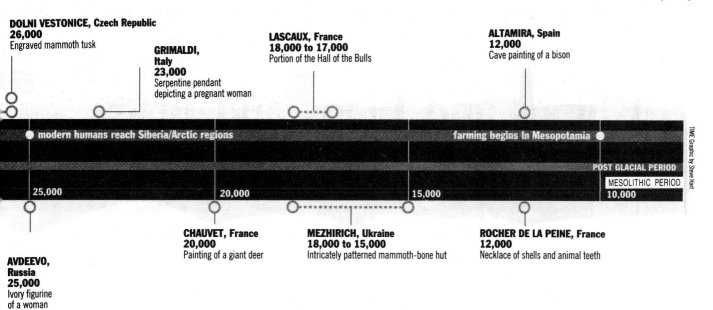

DOLNI VESTONICE, Czech Republic
26,000
Engraved mammoth tusk

GRIMALDI,
Italy
23,000
Serpentine pendant
depicting a pregnant woman

LASCAUX, France
18,000 to 17,000
Portion of the Hall of the Bulls

ALTAMIRA, Spain
12,000
Cave painting of a bison

modern humans reach Siberia/Arctic regions   farming begins In Mesopotamia

POST GLACIAL PERIOD

MESOLITHIC PERIOD

25,000   20,000   15,000   10,000

TIME Graphic by Steve Hart

AVDEEVO,
Russia
25,000
Ivory figurine
of a woman

CHAUVET, France
20,000
Painting of a giant deer

MEZHIRICH, Ukraine
18,000 to 15,000
Intricately patterned mammoth-bone hut

ROCHER DE LA PEINE, France
12,000
Necklace of shells and animal teeth

a social phenomenon that appears and disappears and, in some places, may not arise at all." But many anthropologists counter that the term art is usually defined too narrowly. What paleolithic humans really invented, they say, is symbolic representation, and by that definition art may well appear in every culture—though it might not be easy for us to recognize.

It's also difficult to say whether art originated in a specific part of the world. By the time of humanity's great artistic awakening, Homo sapiens had probably already traveled from its African homeland through most of Europe and Asia. The urge to make art could have arisen in any of these places and spread throughout the world, or it could have happened in many areas independently.

There are problems with either scenario, however. "The pattern is puzzling," observes anthropologist Randall White. "One of the most common forms of body adornment in Western Europe during this early period is canine teeth from carnivores, drilled with holes and worn as dangling ornamentation. And damned if in Australia, some 35,000 to 40,000 years ago this isn't exactly what they're doing too." It might seem like an unremarkable coincidence—after all, carnivores must have loomed large in every culture. But an-

thropologists have learned that such coincidences are actually quite rare. If art did spread around the world, it moved with astonishing speed (on a paleontological time scale, that is), and, says White, "it's a long way from southern France to Australia."

One possible explanation: art was percolating along for tens of thousands of years before most of the known examples show up. Perhaps the original Homo sapiens populations in Africa invented art and carried it to other regions. The reasons nothing much has been found dating before 40,000 B.P., goes the argument, are that scientists haven't looked hard enough and most of the evidence has perished. As appealing as it may seem though, this art-is-older-than-we-think theory has attracted little support; the demarcation line at 40,000 B.P. is just too sharp.

New discoveries like the one at the Chauvet cave, and more intensive study of existing sites, are constantly giving archaeologists more information to work with. Also, dating techniques are becoming more refined. It used to be that scientists needed to test a large sample of paint to pinpoint its age. And, says anthropologist Margaret Conkey, "no one was willing to scrape a bison's rump off the wall." Now it takes only a tiny sample. French prehistory expert Arlette Leroi-Gourhan

estimates dates by using pollen particles preserved on cave floors.

The results of all these studies, while always enlightening, don't necessarily simplify things for scientists. A new analysis of the Cosquer cave on the French Riviera, for example, has shown that painted handprints on the walls date to 27,000 B.P., while images of horses and other animals came some 9,000 years later. Rather than being decorated in a single, prolonged burst of creativity, the cavern was painted over scores of centuries, quite possibly by artists who had no connection of any kind with one another, unlike Aborigines, whose culture has direct links to the distant past.

Prehistoric art was created over so long a period by so many different humans in so many parts of the world, and presumably for so many different reasons, that it may never fit into a tidy catalog. These ancient masterpieces are telling us that our prehistoric forebears had modes of expression more varied than we once imagined—and also that we'll never truly understand just how rich their lives must have been.

—Reported by David Bjerklie and Andrea Dorfman/New York, Tim Blair/Melbourne, Peter Hawthorne/ Cape Town and Thomas Sancton/ Paris

Rhinos and Lions and Bears (Oh, My!)

An archeologist explores the newly discovered Chauvet Cave

Jean Clottes

Jean Clottes is scientific adviser for prehistoric rock art studies at the French Ministry of Culture and chairman of the International Committee for Rock Art. An archeologist by training, Clottes served for twenty-one years as director of prehistoric antiquities for the Midi-Pyrénées region, where he studied and helped to conserve the painted caves. His current research involves the application of new laboratory techniques for analyzing ancient art: he is also interested in other archeological evidence that may throw light on the artists' motivations, technology, and culture.

On Thursday, December 29, 1994, I was at my home in Foix, France, preparing for a New Year's celebration. My three children, their spouses, and my seven grandchildren (ranging in age from six months to ten years) were arriving that day and the next for a crowded family week-end. At noon the phone rang. Jean-Pierre Daugas, the regional conservator in charge of archeology for the Rhône-Alpes region, was calling to tell me that there had been a major discovery in the Ardèche Valley in southeast France. A few days before, on Christmas, three men had discovered a big cave with hundreds of paintings and engravings representing lions, rhinos, bears, horses, bison, and even a leopard and a hyena. By chance, they had felt a draft through stone rubble that blocked a small hole at the foot of a cliff in the valley. After moving the stones, they managed to wriggle through a narrow passage into a hitherto unknown painted cave and believed they were the first humans to enter it in 20,000 years.

Leopards and hyenas were unknown in Paleolithic cave art, and lions, rhinos, and bears were rare. Situated near the town of Vallon-Pont d'Arc, the cave is in a very touristy area where more than a million visitors, including many cave explorers, roam every summer. Could this be a hoax? Daugas insisted it was not. One of the discoverers, Jean-Marie Chauvet, was well known to him, as he was employed by the Ministry of Culture as a guard at the painted caves in the Ardèche region. He was trustworthy and so were his two companions, Eliette Deschamps and Christian Hillaire, who had discovered several minor painted or engraved caves in the Ardèche and Gard areas during the past ten years. I said I would go the following week. But Daugas pressed me, saying, "This looks extremely important and I really wish you could come right away." Reluctantly, I decided to disappoint my family and go check out the cave. The same afternoon I packed my cave overalls, miner's lamp, helmet, camera, and flashlight and drove to Vallon-Pont d'Arc, about 250 miles away.

The next morning, Daugas, along with one of his colleagues and the three cave explorers, met me at the hotel and we set off for the cave. I felt duty bound to tell them that I would have to question everything because my first concern was to ascertain whether such a spectacular discovery could be a fake. They just laughed and said they were not worried.

It was a bleak winter day, and heavy fog shrouded the normally beautiful countryside. We climbed briskly through thick woods to the foot of a cliff. After following along its base for a while and passing several small caves, we reached an unpromising cavity, several feet wide, which my guides said was our entry point. We scrambled down the sloping hole for about thirty feet to a heap of loose rocks that covered a much narrower opening. It was here that the discoverers had first noticed the air current rising. When they first came upon this much deeper hole, they had to spend an entire day removing rocks that had been blocking it. Before leaving the site, however, they had stacked enough rocks over the entrance to hide it again. Now they removed this small pile and crawled into the cave. Then it was my turn. The seven-foot passage was so narrow that I had to strip down to my overalls before attempting to go through. After a difficult ten minutes, gelling stuck repeatedly and creeping forward only while exhaling, I emerged on the other side, where

I descended a thirty-foot hanging ladder they had left there. At the bottom I found myself inside a vast chamber.

Obviously, the Paleolithic artists had not used the access we had been through, which opened into the ceiling of the cave. Hours later, we found the cave's original entrance some hundreds of feet on the other side of the chamber. It had long been blocked by a huge pile of rocky debris, perhaps soon after the cave had been visited by humans. This blocked entrance will remain as it is, so as not to change the climatic conditions inside the cavern.

My first impression of the cave was that it was vast, pristine, and beautiful. Stalactites and stalagmites sparkled everywhere under our lights. The ground seemed untrodden, and on the other side of the chamber I could distinguish a first panel of red dots. We went over to it, and I examined it closely. The dots were large (two and a half to three inches in diameter) and numerous, resembling those in the cave of Pech-Merle in Quercy. The ancient paint had long ago penetrated into the wall, and a thin veil of calcite covered a few dots. They were undoubtedly authentic. We followed Jean-Marie Chauvet closely, stepping where he told us in order not to destroy any traces or even dirty the ground. He carefully unrolled long slips of black plastic in front of us, choosing a path where the ground was solid rock or covered with thick calcite, and skirting the soft places where prints might be preserved.

In the first chambers, most of the art consisted of red figures. Next to a few hand stencils and red dots, we saw only one black horse, half-hidden under an old layer of calcite. In a smaller gallery, the outlined head of a red deer was followed by three cave bear images and one of a horse. In creating one of the bears, the prehistoric artist had utilized the natural relief of the wall as a three-dimensional shoulder for the animal. Elsewhere, three rhinos followed one another in a long frieze. As is always the case in Paleolithic painted caves, there were many geometric signs: several panels of dots, similar to the one we had first seen; a semicircle of much smaller dots; and a few cryptic drawings. Two of these strange geometrics resembled birds or bats, while others were reminiscent of insects with multiple legs.

The recognizable creatures painted in red included several rhinos, bears, and lions, at least one ibex, four mammoths, one bovid, and two other animals close to each other. One was indisputably a leopard, recognizable by its spots and its tail, which was devoid of the tuft all lions possess. The other one was bigger. At first, I identified it as a bear, but I was bothered by its spindly legs, its shortened hindquarters, and the spots on the front part of the body. I then let myself be persuaded that it might indeed be a hyena, as Chauvet had said in the first place. If it really was a hyena, it would be the first depiction of that animal in Paleolithic art, just as the leopard is the first known example of its kind. However, I am far from certain what it is; it still could be a bear.

After a low passage full of stalactites, we reached other chambers. In one of them, the ground had collapsed, and a deep crater about thirty feet wide had opened up. Above it, an owl, two mammoths, and a horse had been engraved on an overhang at a time when it was easy to reach. Now the engravings stood about fifteen feet above the bottom of the crater. This was further evidence that no forger could have been at work on the walls.

Farther on, we came to several extensive panels crowded with numerous black figures. These paintings were truly astonishing: on the whole they were well preserved and distinct. Most of the animals were recognizable as to species and sometimes even as to sex or behavior. Contrary to what can be seen in most painted caves, these animal depictions seem to be grouped into compositions. For example, one of the main panels appears to be organized on both sides of a small recess, inside of which a horse, a mammoth, and a rhino have been painted. On the right, there is another, young-looking mammoth, several rhinos, and some bison followed by a group of fourteen lions with their heads stretching in the direction of other animals. Behind the lions is a solitary rhino. On the other side of the recess is a spectacular series of at least thirteen or fourteen rhinos, some superimposed on the others; most are facing left while two face right. Then there are four big lions all on the alert and looking to the right. In the middle of the group, one sees a reindeer and at least two series of red spots of various sizes—the smaller ones in a line; the bigger ones in a sort of semicircle.

Could this really be a composition rather than the placing of unrelated animals on the same walls? Already I thought of what would have to be done to try and find an answer to this question. Analyses of paint constituents might reveal whether all the animals had been done at the same time, with the same paint. All the images would have to be traced carefully and the techniques used by the artists investigated. We could not go up to that panel because the ground in front of it was untrodden and fragile, so we stayed about thirty feet back and examined it from a distance.

We could, however, get close to another one, equally complex and beautiful. There, on one wall, animals of different species had also been represented in black, and some of the images had been superimposed on others. Detailed chemical analysis would in time tell us which animals had been done first or last and enable us to establish the different phases in the composition. A first examination showed, for instance, that some small rhinos had been partly covered by four big aurochs, while another rhino was on top of one of the aurochs and four horses' heads were on top of this rhino. Two other male rhinos seemed to be fighting; such a scene is unique in Paleolithic rock art.

While I was gazing at the panel, trying to distinguish the succession of the images and, in particular, looking closely at the splendid heads of the four horses, I was suddenly overcome with emotion. I felt a deep and clear certainty that here was the work of one of the great masters, a Leonardo da Vinci of the Solutrean revealed to us for the first time. It was both humbling and exhilarating. Humbling because of the admiration one could not help but feel for the artist, forever unknown, whose works had spanned the millennia, and because the discovery underlined the immensity of our ignorance. If after more than a century of research such original and important paintings could still come to light, how many had been destroyed or were still unknown in the depths of concealed caves? On the other hand, I was thoroughly exhilarated to be there, one of the fortunate few to first behold such a masterpiece.

After a whole day spent in the cave it was possible to make a preliminary assessment. The authenticity of the paintings and engravings is beyond question. The cave is a major discovery because of the number of animals represented on its walls, their esthetic quality, and their originality. Of course, years of study lie ahead. For now, nothing can be said as to the precise dates for the works of art, the activities of prehistoric people in the cave, the meaning of the paintings, or the choice of panels. That will come later. But the indisputable authenticity makes the Chauvet Cave, as the discoverers want to call it, one of the great archeological finds of the century.

I saw more than 150 animal images that day, and I probably missed many more, as it was impossible to walk to the other side of some chambers in which the ground was littered with cave bear bones and where undisturbed prints could be seen on the surface. Across one of those chambers, we could just make out the outlines of more images, unrecognizable from a distance. Most probably, when the cave is explored in detail, there will be 200 to 300 animal figures and possibly even more. In comparison, among French caves considered among the most important in Paleolithic cave art, 145 animal paintings or engravings have been found in the Cosquer Cave near Marseille (*see* "Neptune's Ice Age Gallery," *Natural History,* April 1993) and 110 in Niaux, in the Ariège.

Most of the animals in the Chauvet Cave are rhinos, lions, and bears, which is very surprising. Generally, those most often represented at the time were horses, bison, aurochs, mammoths, deer, and ibexes. Images of these animals are also present in the cave, but the emphasis on predatory animals that were probably not hunted testifies to a regional difference in the Ardèche culture during that time.

Exact dates for the paintings are still a matter of conjecture. However, some details point to a pre-Magdalenian period—the Solutrean, about 18,000 to 21,000 years ago, which is already represented in the Ardèche caves but is rare elsewhere. The panels of big dots and at least one deer are similar to the ones in Pech-Merle, a cave where stenciled red hands have also been painted and which is generally attributed to the Solutrean. Several bison are pictured with their horns facing front, while their bodies are shown in profile and their heads in three-quarters view. The style reminded me of a similar bison in the recently discovered Cosquer Cave, which is half-submerged in a seacliff on the Mediterranean and has been radiocarbondated to about 18,500 years ago. Three animals that appear to be Irish elk—an extinct deer with giant antlers—have been painted in the Chauvet Cave. Those animals appear very rarely in Paleolithic art but happen to be present in several caves dated to the Solutrean or even earlier times, such as Cougnac and Pech-Merle in the Lot region, just south of the Massif Central, and again in the Cosquer Cave. If the Chauvet Cave is indeed Solutrean, which we shall know after radiocarbon analyses and archeological studies have been done, it will be the most important sanctuary ever discovered for that culture. In any case, the Ardèche, and more generally the southeast of France, is no longer a minor area for rock art. It now ranks among the best, along with the Pèrigord, the Pyrenees, and Cantabria.

Finally, the Chauvet Cave stands out because it has been so well preserved. The discoverers were extremely careful to walk where they would cause no damage. In places, the remains of fires can still be seen. Elsewhere, the ancient soil is covered with bear and human prints. Cave bear bones litter the whole cave. It will be necessary to determine whether the bears hibernated in the cave thousands of years before humans came or were present at the same time. An in-depth study of all traces should also tell us whether children went there with the adults and possibly what sorts of activities went on. In one chamber, for example, a cave bear skull has been placed on top of a big block of stone in a very dramatic way. What could this mean? Have any other bear bones been moved? And why? Did the bears go back into the cave after humans had decorated the walls? Many such questions are unanswered for the time being.

In the months and years to come, much research will be carried out in the cave. However, our first priority will have to be its preservation. A discovery such as this is exceptional from many points of view, and exceptional care is therefore in order. We have often regretted that the excavation of such caves as Lascaux and Altamira destroyed their archeological context, either through carelessness or to answer some questions of the time. In future years, our successors will have different theories and models, and they will use different techniques. Nothing should be done to destroy the primary evidence. Strict precautions must be taken against vandalism, and some restrictions placed on research. After preservation, scientific study will be our second priority. Research will take years to complete and must be nondestructive. Our third priority is to respond to the enormous public demand for films, CD-ROMs, and replicas of the images. These will become possible in time, but there is no hurry. After all, what are a few years to wait for a cave that has waited for us for fifteen or twenty millennia!

OLD MASTERS

Brilliant paintings brightened the caves of our early ancestors. But were the artists picturing their mythic beliefs or simply showing what they ate for dinner?

Pat Shipman

Pat Shipman wrote about killer bamboo in [Discover,] February [1990].

Fifty years ago, in a green valley of the Dordogne region of southwest France, a group of teenage boys made the first claustrophobic descent into the labyrinthine caverns of Lascaux. When they reached the main chamber and held their lamps aloft, the sight that flickered into view astonished them. There were animals everywhere. A frieze of wild horses, with chunky bodies and fuzzy, crew-cut manes, galloped across the domed walls and ceiling past the massive figure of a white bull-like creature (the extinct aurochs). Running helter-skelter in the opposing direction were three little stags with delicately drawn antlers. They were followed by more bulls, cows, and calves rounding the corner of the chamber.

Thousands have since admired these paintings in Lascaux's Hall of the Bulls, probably the most magnificent example of Ice Age art known to us today. In fact, by 1963 so many tourists wanted to view the cave that officials were forced to close Lascaux to the general public; the paintings were being threatened as the huge influx of visitors warmed the air in the cave and brought in corrosive algae and pollen. (Fortunately, a nearby exhibit called Lascaux II faithfully reproduces the

The image of Paleolithic humans moving by flickering lamps, singing, chanting, and drawing their knowledge of their world is hard to resist.

paintings.) After I first saw these powerful images, they haunted me for several months. I had looked at photographs of Lascaux in books, of course, so I knew that the paintings were beautiful; but what I didn't know was that they would reach across 17,000 years to grab my soul.

Lascaux is not an Ice Age anomaly. Other animal paintings, many exquisitely crafted, adorn hundreds of caves throughout the Dordogne and the French Pyrenees and the region known as Cantabria on the northern coast of Spain. All these images were created by the people we commonly call Cro-Magnons, who lived during the Upper Paleolithic Period, between 10,000 and 30,000 years ago, when Europe lay in the harsh grip of the Ice Age.

What did this wonderful art mean, and what does it tell us about the prehistoric humans who created it? These questions have been asked since the turn of the century, when cave paintings in Spain were first definitively attributed to Paleolithic humans. Until recently the dominant answers were based on rather sweeping symbolic interpretations—attempts, as it were, to read the Paleolithic psyche.

These days some anthropologists are adopting a more literal-minded approach. They are not trying to empathize with the artists' collective soul—a perilous exercise in imagination, considering how remote Cro-Magnon life must have been from ours. Rather, armed with the tools of the late twentieth century—statistics, maps, computer analyses of the art's distribution patterns—the researchers are trying to make sense of the paintings by piecing together their cultural context.

This is a far cry from earlier attempts at interpretation. At the beginning of the century, with little more to go on than his intuition, the French amateur archeologist Abbé Henri Breuil suggested that the pictures were a form of hunting magic. Painting animals, in other words, was a magical way of capturing them, in the hope that it would make the beasts vulnerable to hunters. Abstract symbols painted on the walls were interpreted as hunting paraphernalia. Straight lines drawn to the animals' sides represented spears, and V and O shapes on their hides were seen as wounds. Rectangular grids, some observers thought, might have been fences or animal traps.

In the 1960s this view was brushed aside for a much more complex, somewhat Freudian approach that was brought into fashion by anthropologist André Leroi-Gourhan. He saw the cave paintings as a series of mythograms, or symbolic depictions, of how Paleolithic people viewed their world—a world split between things male and female. Femaleness was represented by animals such as the bison and aurochs (which were sometimes juxtaposed with human female figures in the paintings), and maleness was embodied by such animals as the horse and ibex (which, when accompanied by human figures, were shown only with males). Female images, Leroi-Gourhan suggested, were clustered in the central parts of the dark, womblike caves, while male images either consorted with the female ones or encircled them in the more peripheral areas.

Leroi-Gourhan also ascribed sex to the geometric designs on the cave walls. Thin shapes such as straight lines, which often make up barbed, arrowlike structures, were seen as male (phallic) signs. Full shapes such as ovals, V shapes, triangles, and rectangles were female (vulval) symbols. Thus, an arrow stuck into a V-shaped wound on an animal's hide was a male symbol entering a complementary female one.

Leroi-Gourhan was the first to look for structure in the paintings system-

atically, and his work reinforced the notion that these cave paintings had underlying designs and were not simply idle graffiti or random doodles. Still, some scholars considered his *"perspective sexomaniaque"* rather farfetched; eventually even he played down some of the sexual interpretations. However, a far bigger problem with both his theory and Breuil's was their sheer monolithic scope: a single explanation was assumed to account for 20,000 years of paintings produced by quite widely scattered groups of people.

Yet it is at least as likely that the paintings carried a number of different messages. The images' meaning may have varied depending on who painted them and where. Increasingly, therefore, researchers have tried to relate the content of the paintings to their context—their distribution within a particular cave, the cave's location within a particular region, and the presence of other nearby dwelling sites, tools, and animal bones in the area.

Anthropologist Patricia Rice and sociologist Ann Paterson, both from West Virginia University, made good use of this principle in their study of a single river valley in the Dordogne

> *. . . animals may have been depicted more or less frequently depending on how aggressive they were to humans.*

region, an area that yielded 90 different caves containing 1,955 animal portrayals and 151 dwelling sites with animal bone deposits. They wanted to find out whether the number of times an animal was painted simply reflected how common it was or whether it revealed further information about the animals or the human artists.

By comparing the bone counts of the various animals—horses, reindeer, red deer, ibex, mammoths, bison, and au-

rochs—Rice and Paterson were able to score the animals according to their abundance. When they related this number to the number of times a species turned up in the art, they found an interesting relationship: Pictures of the smaller animals, such as deer, were proportionate to their bone counts. But the bigger species, such as horses and bison, were portrayed more often than you'd expect from the faunal remains. In fact, it turned out that to predict how often an animal would appear, you had to factor in not just its relative abundance but its weight as well.

A commonsense explanation of this finding was that an animal was depicted according to its usefulness as food, with the larger, meatier animals shown more often. This "grocery store" explanation of the art worked well, except for the ibex, which was portrayed as often as the red deer yet was only half its size and, according to the bone counts, not as numerous. The discrepancy led Rice and Paterson to explore the hypothesis that animals may have also been depicted more or less frequently depending on how aggressive they were to humans.

To test this idea, the researchers asked wildlife-management specialists to score the animals according to a "danger index." The feisty ibex, like the big animals, was rated as highly aggressive; and like these other dangerous animals, it was painted more often than just the numbers of its remains would suggest. Milder-tempered red deer and reindeer, on the other hand, were painted only about as often as you'd expect from their bones. Rice and Paterson concluded that the local artists may have portrayed the animals for both "grocery store" and "danger index" reasons. Maybe such art was used to impress important information on the minds of young hunters—drawing attention to the animals that were the most worthwhile to kill, yet balancing the rewards of dinner with the risks of attacking a fearsome animal.

One thing is certain: Paleolithic artists knew their animals well. Subtle physical details, characteristic poses, even seasonal changes in coat color or texture, were deftly observed. At Lascaux bison are pictured shedding their dark winter pelts. Five stags are shown swimming across a river, heads held high above the swirling tide. A stallion is depicted with its lip curled back, responding to a mare in heat. The reddish coats, stiff black manes, short legs, and potbellies of the Lascaux horses are so well recorded that they look unmistakably like the modern Przhevalsky's horses from Mongolia.

New findings at Solutré, in east-central France, the most famous horse-hunting site from the Upper Paleolithic, show how intimate knowledge of the animal's habits was used to the early hunter's advantage. The study, by archeologist Sandra Olsen of the Virginia Museum of Natural History, set out to reexamine how vast numbers of horses—from tens to hundreds of thousands, according to fossil records—came to be killed in the same, isolated spot. The archeological deposits at Solutré are 27 feet thick, span 20,000 years, and provide a record of stone tools and artifacts as well as faunal remains.

The traditional interpretation of this site was lots of fun but unlikely. The Roche de Solutré is one of several high limestone ridges running east-west from the Saône River to the Massif Central plateau; narrow valleys run between the ridges. When the piles of bones were discovered, in 1866, it was proposed that the site was a "horse jump" similar to the buffalo jumps in the American West, where whole herds of bison were driven off cliffs to their death. Several nineteenth-century paintings depict Cro-Magnon hunters driving a massive herd of wild horses up and off the steep rock of Solutré. But Olsen's bone analysis has shown that the horse jump scenario is almost certainly wrong.

For one thing, the horse bones are not at the foot of the steep western end of Solutré, but in a natural cul-de-sac along the southern face of the ridge. For the horse jump hypothesis to work, one of two fairly incredible events had to occur. Either the hunters drove the horses off the western end and then dragged all the carcasses around to the southern face to butcher

them or the hunters herded the animals up the steep slope and then forced them to veer off the southern side of the ridge. But behavioral studies show that, unlike bison, wild horses travel not in herds but in small, independent bands. So it would have been extremely difficult for our Cro-Magnons on foot to force lots of horses together and persuade them to jump en masse.

Instead the horse behavior studies suggested to Olsen a new hypothesis. Wild horses commonly winter in the lowlands and summer in the highlands. This migration pattern preserves their forage and lets them avoid the lowland's biting flies and heat in summer and the highland's cold and snow in winter. The Solutré horses, then, would likely have wintered in the Saône's floodplain to the east and summered in the mountains to the west, migrating through the valleys between the ridges. The kill site at Solutré, Olsen notes, lies in the widest of these valleys, the one offering the easiest passage to the horses. What's more, from the hunters' point of view, the valley has a convenient cul-de-sac running off to one side. The hunters, she proposes, used a drive lane of brush, twigs, and rocks to divert the horses from their migratory path into the cul-de-sac and then speared the animals to death. In deed, spear points found at the site support this scenario.

The bottom line in all this is that Olsen's detailed studies of this prehistoric hunting site confirm what the cave art implies: these early humans used their understanding of animals' habits, mating, and migration patterns to come up with extremely successful hunting strategies. Obviously this knowledge must have been vital to the survival of the group and essential to hand down to successive generations. Perhaps the animal friezes in the cave were used as a mnemonic device or as a visual teaching aid in rites of initiation—a means for people to recall or rehearse epic hunts, preserve information, and school their young. The emotional power of the art certainly suggests that this information was cru-

cial to their lives and could not be forgotten.

The transmission of this knowledge may well have been assisted by more than illustration. French researchers Iégor Reznikoff and Michel Dauvois have recently shown that cave art may well have been used in rituals accompanied by songs or chants. The two studied the acoustic resonances of three caves in the French Pyrenees by singing and whistling through almost five octaves as they walked slowly through each cave. At certain points the caves resonated in response to a particular note, and these points were carefully mapped.

For all the finely observed animal pictures, we catch only the sketchiest glimpses of humans, in the form of stick figures or stylized line drawings.

When Reznikoff and Dauvois compared their acoustic map with a map of the cave paintings, they found an astonishing relationship. The best resonance points were all well marked with images, while those with poor acoustics had very few pictures. Even if a resonance point offered little room for a full painting, it was marked in some way—by a set of red dots, for example. It remains to be seen if this intriguing correlation holds true for other caves. In the meantime, the image of Paleolithic humans moving by flickering lamps, singing, chanting, and drawing their knowledge of their world indelibly into their memories is so appealing that I find it hard to resist.

Yet the humans in this mental image of mine are shadowy, strangely elusive people. For all the finely observed animal pictures, we catch only the sketchiest glimpses of humans, in the form of stick figures or stylized line drawings. Still, when Rice and Paterson turned to study these human images in French and Spanish caves, a few striking patterns did emerge. Of the 67 images studied, 52 were male and a mere 15 were female. Only men were depicted as engaged in active behavior, a category that included walking, running, carrying spears, being speared, or falling. Females were a picture of passivity; they stood, sat, or lay prone. Most women were shown in close proximity to another human figure or group of figures, which were always other women. Seldom were men featured in social groups; they were much more likely to be shown facing off with an animal.

These images offer tantalizing clues to Paleolithic life. They suggest a society where males and females led very separate lives. (Male-female couples do not figure at all in Paleolithic art, for all the sexual obsessions of earlier researchers.) Males carried out the only physical activities—or at least the only ones deemed worthy of recording. Their chief preoccupation was hunting, and from all appearances, what counted most was the moment of truth between man and his prey. What women did in Paleolithic society (other than bear children and gather food) remains more obscure. But whatever they did, they mostly did it in the company of other women, which would seem to imply that social interaction, cooperation, and oral communication played an important role in female lives.

If we could learn the sex of the artists, perhaps interpreting the social significance of the art would be easier. Were women's lives so mysterious because the artists were male and chauvinistically showed only men's activities in their paintings? Or perhaps the artists were all female. Is their passive group activity the recording and encoding of the information vital to the group's survival in paintings and carvings? Did they spend their time with other women, learning the songs and chants and the artistic techniques that transmitted and preserved their knowledge? The art that brightened the caves of the Ice Age endures. But the artists who might shed light on its meaning remain as enigmatic as ever.

The Dating Game

**By tracking changes in ancient atoms, archeologists are establishing
the astonishing antiquity of modern humanity.**

James Shreeve

James Shreeve wrote fiction before turning to science writing. He is the coauthor (with anthropologist Donald Johanson) of Lucy's Child: The Discovery of a Human Ancestor *and the author of* Nature: The Other Earthlings.

Four years ago archeologists Alison Brooks and John Yellen discovered what might be the earliest traces of modern human culture in the world. The only trouble is, nobody believes them. Sometimes they can't quite believe it themselves.

Their discovery came on a sun-soaked hillside called Katanda, in a remote corner of Zaire near the Ugandan border. Thirty yards below, the Semliki River runs so clear and cool the submerged hippos look like giant lumps of jade. But in the excavation itself, the heat is enough to make anyone doubt his eyes.

Katanda is a long way from the plains of Ice Age Europe, which archeologists have long believed to be the setting for the first appearance of truly modern culture: the flourish of new tool technologies, art, and body ornamentation known as the Upper Paleolithic, which began about 40,000 years ago. For several years Brooks, an archeologist at George Washington University, had been pursuing the heretical hypothesis that humans in Africa had invented sophisticated technologies even earlier, while their European counterparts were still getting by with

the same sorts of tools they'd been using for hundreds of thousands of years. If conclusive evidence hadn't turned up, it was only because nobody had really bothered to look for it.

"In France alone there must be three hundred well-excavated sites dating from the period we call the Middle Paleolithic," Brooks says. "In Africa there are barely two dozen on the whole continent."

One of those two dozen is Katanda. On an afternoon in 1988 John Yellen—archeology program director at the National Science Foundation and Brooks's husband—was digging in a densely packed litter of giant catfish bones, river stones, and Middle Paleolithic stone tools. From the rubble he extricated a beautifully crafted, fossilized bone harpoon point. Eventually two more whole points and fragments of five others turned up, all of them elaborately barbed and polished. A few feet away, the scientists uncovered pieces of an equally well crafted daggerlike tool. In design and workmanship the harpoons were not unlike those at the very end of the Upper Paleolithic, some 14,000 years ago. But there was one important difference. Brooks and Yellen believe the deposits John was standing in were at least five times that old. To put this in perspective, imagine discovering a prototypical Pontiac in Leonardo da Vinci's attic.

"If the site is as old as we think it is," says Brooks, "it could clinch the

argument that modern humans evolved in Africa."

Ever since the discovery the couple have devoted themselves to chopping away at that stubborn little word *if*. In the face of the entrenched skepticism of their colleagues, it is an uphill task. But they do have some leverage. In those same four years since the first harpoon was found at Katanda, a breakthrough has revived the question of modern human origins. The breakthrough is not some new skeleton pulled out of the ground. Nor is it the highly publicized Eve hypothesis, put forth by geneticists, suggesting that all humans on Earth today share a common female ancestor who lived in Africa 200,000 years ago. The real advance, abiding quietly in the shadows while Eve draws the limelight, is simply a new way of telling time.

To be precise, it is a whole smorgasbord of new ways of telling time. Lately they have all converged on the same exhilarating, mortifying revelation: what little we thought we knew about the origins of our own species was hopelessly wrong. From Africa to the Middle East to Australia, the new dating methods are overturning conventional wisdom with insolent abandon, leaving the anthropological community dazed amid a rubble of collapsed certitudes. It is in this shell-shocked climate that Alison Brooks's Pontiac in Leonardo's attic might actually find a hearing.

"Ten years ago I would have said it was impossible for harpoons like these to be so old," says archeologist Michael Mehlman of the Smithsonian's National Museum of Natural History. "Now I'm reserving judgment. Anything can happen."

An archeologist with a freshly uncovered skull, stone tool, or bone Pontiac in hand can take two general approaches to determine its age. The first is called relative dating. Essentially the archeologist places the find in the context of the surrounding geological deposits. If the new discovery is found in a brown sediment lying beneath a yellowish layer of sand, then, all things being equal, it is older than the yellow sand layer or any other deposit higher up. The fossilized remains of extinct animals found near the object also provide a "biostratigraphic" record that can offer clues to a new find's relative age. (If a stone tool is found alongside an extinct species of horse, then it's a fair bet the tool was made while that kind of horse was still running around.) Sometimes the tools themselves can be used as a guide, if they match up in character and style with tools from other, better-known sites. Relative dating methods like these can tell you whether a find is older or younger than something else, but they cannot pin an age on the object in calendar years.

The most celebrated *absolute* method of telling archeological time, radiocarbon dating, came along in the 1940s. Plants take in carbon from the atmosphere to build tissues, and other organisms take in plants, so carbon ends up in everything from wood to woodchucks. Most carbon exists in the stable form of carbon 12. But some is made up of the unstable, radioactive form carbon 14. When an organism dies, it contains about the same ratio of carbon 12 to carbon 14 that exists in the atmosphere. After death the radioactive carbon 14 atoms begin to decay, changing into stable atoms of nitrogen. The amount of carbon 12, however, stays the same. Scientists can look at the amount of carbon 12 and—based on the ratio—deduce how much carbon 14 was originally present. Since the decay rate of carbon 14 is constant and steady (half of it disappears every 5,730 years), the difference between the

amount of carbon 14 originally in a charred bit of wood or bone and the amount present now can be used as a clock to determine the age of the object.

Conventional radiocarbon dates are extremely accurate up to about 40,000 years. This is far and away the best method to date a find—as long as it is younger than this cutoff point. (In older materials, the amount of carbon 14 still left undecayed is so small that even the slightest amount of contamination in the experimental process leads to highly inaccurate results.) Another dating technique, relying on the decay of radioactive potassium rather than carbon, is available to date volcanic deposits *older* than half a million years. When it was discovered in the late 1950s, radiopotassium dating threw open a window on the emergence of the first members of the human family—the australopithecines, like the famous Lucy, and her more advanced descendants, *Homo habilis* and *Homo erectus*. Until now, however, the period between half a million and 40,000 years—a stretch of time that just happens to embrace the origin of *Homo sapiens*—was practically unknowable by absolute dating techniques. It was as if a geochronological curtain were drawn across the mystery of our species' birth. Behind that curtain the hominid lineage underwent an astonishing metamorphosis, entering the dateless, dark centuries a somewhat precocious bipedal ape and emerging into the range of radiocarbon dating as the culturally resplendent, silver-tongued piece of work we call a modern human being.

Fifteen years ago there was some general agreement about how this change took place. First, what is thought of as an *anatomically* modern human being—with the rounded cranium, vertical forehead, and lightly built skeleton of people today—made its presence known in Europe about 35,000 years ago. Second, along with those first modern-looking people, popularly known as the Cro-Magnons, came the first signs of complex human

behavior, including tools made of bone and antler as well as of stone, and art, symbolism, social status, ethnic identity, and probably true human language too. Finally, in any one region there was no overlap in time between the appearance of modern humans and the disappearance of "archaic" humans such as the classic Neanderthals, supporting the idea that one group had evolved from the other.

"Thanks to the efforts of the new dating methods," says Fred Smith, an anthropologist at Northern Illinois University, "we now know that each of these ideas was wrong."

The technique doing the most damage to conventional wisdom is called thermoluminescence, TL for short. (Reader take heed: the terrain of geochronology is full of terms long enough to tie between two trees and trip over, so acronyms are a must.) Unlike radiocarbon dating, which works on organic matter, TL pulls time out of stone.

If you were to pick an ordinary rock up off the ground and try to describe its essential rockness, phrases like "frenetically animated" would probably not leap to mind. But in fact minerals are in a state of constant inner turmoil. Minute amounts of radioactive elements, both within the rock itself and in the surrounding soil and atmosphere, are constantly bombarding its atoms, knocking electrons out of their normal orbits. All this is perfectly normal rock behavior, and after gallivanting around for a hundredth of a second or two, most electrons dutifully return to their normal positions. A few, however, become trapped en route— physically captured within crystal impurities or electronic aberrations in the mineral structure itself. These tiny prisons hold on to their electrons until the mineral is heated, whereupon the traps spring open and the electrons return to their more stable position. As they escape, they release energy in the form of light—a photon for every homeward-bound electron.

Thermoluminescence was observed way back in 1663 by the great English physicist Robert Boyle. One night Boyle took a borrowed diamond to bed with him, for reasons that remain obscure. Resting the diamond "upon a warm part of my Naked Body," Boyle noticed that it soon emitted a warm glow. So taken was he with the responsive gem that the next day he delivered a paper on the subject at the Royal Society, noting his surprise at the glow since his "constitution," he felt, was "not of the hottest."

Three hundred years later another Englishman, Martin Aitken of Oxford University, developed the methods to turn thermoluminescence into a geophysical timepiece. The clock works because the radioactivity bombarding a mineral is fairly constant, so electrons become trapped in those crystalline prisons at a steady rate through time. If you crush the mineral you want to date and heat a few grains to a high enough temperature—about 900 degrees, which is more body heat than Robert Boyle's constitution could ever have produced—all the electron traps will release their captive electrons at once, creating a brilliant puff of light. In a laboratory the intensity of that burst of luminescence can easily be measured with a device called a photomultiplier. The higher the spike of light, the more trapped electrons have accumulated in the sample, and thus the more time has elapsed since it was last exposed to heat. Once a mineral is heated and all the electrons have returned "home," the clock is set back to zero.

Now, our lineage has been making flint tools for hundreds of thousands of years, and somewhere in that long stretch of prehistory we began to use fire as well. Inevitably, some of our less careful ancestors kicked discarded tools into burning hearths, setting their electron clocks back to zero and opening up a ripe opportunity for TL timekeepers in the present. After the fire went out, those flints lay in the ground, pummeled by radioactivity, and each trapped electron was another tick of the clock. Released by laboratory heat, the electrons flash out photons that reveal time gone by.

In the late 1980s Hélène Valladas, an archeologist at the Center for Low-Level Radioactivity of the French Atomic Energy Commission near Paris, along with her father, physicist Georges Valladas, stunned the anthropological community with some TL dates on burned flints taken from two archeological sites in Israel. The first was a cave called Kebara, which had already yielded an astonishingly complete Neanderthal skeleton. Valladas dated flints from the Neanderthal's level at 60,000 years before the present.

In itself this was no surprise, since the date falls well within the known range of the Neanderthals' time on Earth. The shock came a year later, when she used the same technique to pin a date on flints from a nearby cave called Qafzeh, which contained the buried remains of early modern human beings. This time, the spikes of luminescence translated into an age of around 92,000 years. In other words, the more "advanced" human types were a full 30,000 years older than the Neanderthals they were supposed to have descended from.

If Valladas's TL dates are accurate, they completely confound the notion that modern humans evolved from Neanderthals in any neat and tidy way. Instead, these two kinds of human, equally endowed culturally but distinctly different in appearance, might have shared the same little nook of the Middle East for tens of thousands of years. To some, this simply does not make sense.

"If these dates are correct, what does this do to what else we know, to the stratigraphy, to fossil man, to the archeology?" worries Anthony Marks, an archeologist at Southern Methodist University. "It's all a mess. Not that the dates are necessarily wrong. But you want to know more about them."

Marks's skepticism is not entirely unfounded. While simple in theory, in practice TL has to overcome some devilish complications. ("If these new techniques were easy, we would have thought of them a long time ago," says geochronologist Gifford Miller of the University of Colorado.) To convert into calendar years the burst of luminescence when a flint is heated, one has to know both the sensitivity of that particular flint to radiation and the dose of radioactive rays it has received each year since it was "zeroed" by fire. The sensitivity of the sample can be determined by assaulting it with artificial radiation in the lab. And the annual dose of radiation received from *within* the sample itself can be calculated fairly easily by measuring how much uranium or other radioactive elements the sample contains. But determining the annual dose from the environment *around* the sample—the radioactivity in the surrounding soil, and cosmic rays from the atmosphere itself—is an iffier proposition. At some sites fluctuations in this environmental dose through the millennia can turn the "absolute" date derived from TL into an absolute nightmare.

Fortunately for Valladas and her colleagues, most of the radiation dose for the Qafzeh flints came from within the flints themselves. The date there of 92,000 years for the modern human skeletons is thus not only the most sensational number so far produced by TL, it is also one of the surest.

"The strong date at Qafzeh was just good luck," says Valladas. "It was just by chance that the internal dose was high and the environmental dose was low."

More recently Valladas and her colleague Norbert Mercier turned their TL techniques to the French site of Saint-Césaire. Last summer they confirmed that a Neanderthal found at Saint-Césaire was only 36,000 years old. This new date, combined with a fresh radiocarbon date of about 40,000 years tagged on some Cro-Magnon sites in northern Spain, strongly suggests that the two types of humans shared the same corner of Europe for several thousand years as the glaciers advanced from the north.

While Valladas has been busy in Europe and the Middle East, other TL timekeepers have produced some astonishing new dates for the first human occupation of Australia. As recently as the 1950s, it was widely believed that Australia had been colonized only some five thousand years ago. The reasoning was typically Eurocentric:

since the Australian aborigines were still using stone tools when the first white settlers arrived, they must have just recently developed the capacity to make the difficult sea crossing from Indonesia in the first place. A decade later archeologists grudgingly conceded that the date of first entry might have been closer to the beginning of the Holocene period, 10,000 years ago. In the 1970s radiocarbon dates on human occupation sites pushed the date back again, as far as 32,000 years ago. And now TL studies at two sites in northern Australia drop that first human footstep on the continent—and the sea voyage that preceded it—all the way back to 60,000 years before the present. If these dates stand up, then the once-maligned ancestors of modern aborigines were building ocean-worthy craft some 20,000 years *before* the first signs of sophisticated culture appeared in Europe.

"Luminescence has revolutionized the whole period I work in," says Australian National University archeologist Rhys Jones, a member of the team responsible for the new TL dates. "In effect, we have at our disposal a new machine—a new time machine."

With so much at stake, however, nobody looks to TL—or to any of the other new "time machines"—as a geochronological panacea. Reputations have been too badly singed in the past by dating methods that claimed more than they could deliver. In the 1970s a flush of excitement over a technique called amino acid racemization led many workers to believe that another continent—North America—had been occupied by humans fully 70,000 years ago. Further testing at the same American sites proved that the magical new method was off by one complete goose egg. The real age of the sites was closer to 7,000 years.

"To work with wrong dates is a luxury we cannot afford," British archeologist Paul Mellars intoned ominously earlier this year, at the beginning of a London meeting of the Royal Society to showcase the new dating technologies. "A wrong date does not simply inhibit research. It could conceivably throw it into reverse."

Fear of just such a catastrophe—not to mention the risk that her own reputation could go up in a puff of light—is what keeps Alison Brooks from declaring outright that she has found exquisitely crafted bone harpoons in Zaire that are more than 40,000 years older than such creations are supposed to be. So far the main support for her argument has been her redating of another site, called Ishango, four miles down the Semliki River from the Katanda site. In the 1950s the Belgian geologist Jean de Heinzelin excavated a harpoon-rich "aquatic civilization" at Ishango that he thought was 8,000 years old. Brooks's radiocarbon dating of the site in the mid-1980s pushed the age back to 25,000. By tracing the layers of sediment shared between Ishango and Katanda, Brooks and her colleagues are convinced that Katanda is much farther down the stratigraphy—twice as old as Ishango, or perhaps even more. But even though Brooks and Yellen talk freely about their harpoons at meetings, they have yet to utter such unbelievable numbers in the unforgiving forum of an academic journal.

"It is precisely because no one believes us that we want to make our case airtight before we publish," says Brooks. "We want dates confirming dates confirming dates."

Soon after the harpoons were discovered, the team went to work with thermoluminescence. Unfortunately, no burned flints have been found at the site. Nevertheless, while TL works best on materials that have been completely zeroed by such extreme heat as a campfire, even a strong dose of sunlight can spring some of the electron traps. Thus even ordinary sediments surrounding an archeological find might harbor a readable clock: bleached out by sunlight when they were on the surface, their TL timers started ticking as soon as they were buried by natural processes. Brooks and Yellen have taken soil samples from Katanda for TL, and so far the results are tantalizing—but that's all.

"At this point we think the site is quite old," says geophysicist Allen Franklin of the University of Mary-

land, who with his Maryland colleague Bill Hornyak is conducting the work. "But we don't want to put a number on it."

As Franklin explains, the problem with dating sediments with TL is that while some of the electron traps might be quickly bleached out by sunlight, others hold on to their electrons more stubbornly. When the sample is then heated in a conventional TL apparatus, these stubborn traps release electrons that were captured perhaps millions of years before the sediments were last exposed to sunlight-teasing date-hungry archeologists with a deceptively old age for the sample.

Brooks does have other irons in the dating fire. The most promising is called electron spin resonance—or ESR, among friends. Like TL, electron spin resonance fashions a clock out of the steadily accumulating electrons caught in traps. But whereas TL measures that accumulation by the strength of the light given off when the traps open, ESR literally counts the captive electrons themselves while they still rest undisturbed in their prisons.

All electrons "spin" in one of two opposite directions—physicists call them up and down. (Metaphors are a must here because the nature of this "spinning" is quantum mechanical and can be accurately described only in huge mathematical equations.) The spin of each electron creates a tiny magnetic force pointing in one direction, something like a compass needle. Under normal circumstances, the electrons are paired so that their opposing spins and magnetic forces cancel each other out. But trapped electrons are unpaired. By manipulating an external magnetic field placed around the sample to be dated, the captive electrons can be induced to "resonate"—that is, to flip around and spin the other way. When they flip, each electron absorbs a finite amount of energy from a microwave field that is also applied to the sample. This loss of microwave energy can be measured with a detector, and it is a direct count of the number of electrons caught in the traps.

ESR works particularly well on tooth

enamel, with an effective range from a thousand to 2 million years. Luckily for Brooks and Yellen, some nice fat hippo teeth have been recovered from Katanda in the layer that also held the harpoons. To date the teeth, they have called in Henry Schwarcz of McMaster University in Ontario, a ubiquitous, veteran geochronologist. In the last ten years Schwarcz has journeyed to some 50 sites throughout Europe, Africa, and western Asia, wherever his precious and arcane services are demanded.

Schwarcz also turned up at the Royal Society meeting, where he explained both the power and the problems of the ESR method. On the plus side is that teeth are hardy remains, found at nearly every archeological site in the world, and that ESR can test a tiny sample again and again—with the luminescence techniques, it's a one-shot deal. ESR can also home in on certain kinds of electron traps, offering some refinement over TL, which lumps them all together.

On the minus side, ESR is subject to the same uncertainties as TL concerning the annual soaking of radiation a sample has received from the environment. What's more, even the radiation from *within* a tooth cannot be relied on to be constant through time. Tooth enamel has the annoying habit of sucking up uranium from its surroundings while it sits in the ground. The more uranium the tooth contains, the more electrons are being bombarded out of their normal positions, and the faster the electron traps will fill up. Remember: you cannot know how old something is by counting filled traps unless you know the rate at which the traps were filled, year by year. If the tooth had a small amount of internal uranium for 50,000 years but took in a big gulp of the hot stuff 10,000 years ago, calculations based on the tooth's current high uranium level would indicate the electron traps were filled at a much faster rate than they really were. "The big question is, When did the uranium get there?" Schwarcz says. "Did the tooth slurp it all up in three days, or did the uranium accumulate gradually through time?"

One factor muddying the "big question" is the amount of moisture present around the sample during its centuries of burial: a wetter tooth will absorb uranium faster. For this reason, the best ESR sites are those where conditions are driest. Middle Eastern and African deserts are good bets. As far as modern human origins go, the technique has already tagged a date of about 100,000 years on some human fossils from an Israeli cave called Skhul, neatly supporting the TL date of 92,000 from Qafzeh, a few miles away. If a new ESR date from a Neanderthal cave just around the corner from Skhul is right, then Neanderthals were also in the Middle East at about the same time. Meanwhile, in South Africa, a human jawbone from the site of Border Cave—"so modern it boggles the mind," as one researcher puts it—has now been dated with ESR at 60,000 years, nearly twice as old as any fossil like it in Europe.

But what of the cultural change to modern human behavior—such as the sophisticated technological development expressed by the Katanda harpoons? Schwarcz's dating job at Katanda is not yet finished, and given how much is at stake, he too is understandably reluctant to discuss it. "The site has good potential for ESR," he says guardedly. "Let's put it this way: if the initial results had indicated that the harpoons were not very old after all, we would have said 'So what?' to them and backed off. Well, we haven't backed off."

There are other dating techniques being developed that may, in the future, add more certainty to claims of African modernity. One of them, called uranium-series dating, measures the steady decay of uranium into various daughter elements inside anything formed from carbonates (limestone and cave stalactites, for instance). The principle is very similar to radiocarbon dating—the amount of daughter elements in a stalactite, for example, indicates how long that stalactite has been around—with the advantage that uranium-series dates can stretch back half a million years. Even amino acid racemization, scorned for the last 15 years, is making a comeback, thanks to the

discovery that the technique, unreliable when applied to porous bone, is quite accurate when used on hard ostrich eggshells.

In the best of all possible worlds, an archeological site will offer an opportunity for two or more of these dating techniques to be called in so they can be tested against each other. When asked to describe the ideal site, Schwarcz gets a dreamy look on his face. "I see a beautiful human skull sandwiched between two layers of very pure flowstone," he says, imagining uranium-series dating turning those cave limestones into time brackets. "A couple of big, chunky hippo teeth are lying next to it, and a little ways off, a bunch of burned flints."

Even without Schwarcz's dream site, the dating methods used separately are pointing to a common theme: the alarming antiquity of modern human events where they are not supposed to be happening in the first place. Brooks sees suggestive traces of complexity not just at Katanda but scattered all over the African continent, as early as 100,000 years before the present. A classic stone tool type called the blade, long considered a trademark of the European Upper Paleolithic, appears in abundance in some South African sites 40,000 to 50,000 years before the Upper Paleolithic begins. The continent may even harbor the earliest hints of art and a symbolic side to human society: tools designed with stylistic meaning; colorful, incandescent minerals, valueless but for their beauty, found hundreds of miles away from their source. More and more, the Cro-Magnons of Europe are beginning to look like the last modern humans to show themselves and start acting "human" rather than the first.

That's not an easy notion for anthropologists and archeologists to swallow. "It just doesn't fit the pattern that those harpoons of Alison's should be so old," says Richard Klein, a paleoanthropologist at the University of Chicago. Then he shrugs. "Of course, if she's right, she has made a remarkable discovery indeed."

Only time will tell.

The Neanderthal Peace

For perhaps 50,000 years, two radically different types of human lived side by side in the same small land. And for all those millennia, the two apparently had nothing whatsoever to do with each other. Why in the world not?

James Shreeve

James Shreeve is a contributing editor of Discover. *His previous book,* Lucy's Child: The Discovery of a Human Ancestor, *was coauthored with anthropologist Donald Johansen.*

I met my first Neanderthal in a café in Paris, just across the street from the Jussieu metro stop. It was a wet afternoon in May, and I was sitting on a banquette with my back to the window. The cafe was smoky and charmless. Near the entrance a couple of students were thumping on a pinball machine called Genesis, which beeped approval every time they scored. The place was packed with people—foreign students, professors, young professionals, French workers, Arabs, Africans, and even a couple of Japanese tourists, all thrown together by the rain. Our coffee had just arrived, and I found that if I tucked my elbow down when raising my cup, I could drink it without poking the ribs of a bearded man sitting at the table next to me, who was deep into an argument.

Above the noise of the pinball game and the din of private conversations, a French anthropologist named Jean-Jacques Hublin was telling me about the anatomical unity of man. It was he who had brought along the Neanderthal. When we had come into the cafe, he had placed an object wrapped in a soft rag on the table and had ignored it ever since. Like anything so carefully neglected, it was beginning to monopolize my attention.

"Perhaps you would be interested in this," he said at last, whisking away the rag. There, amid the clutter of demi-

tasses and empty sugar wrappers, was a large human lower jawbone. The teeth, worn and yellowed by time, were all in place. Around us, I felt the café raise a collective eyebrow. The hubbub of talk sank audibly. The bearded man next to me stopped in midsentence, looked at the jaw, looked at Hublin, and resumed his argument. Hublin gently nudged the fossil to the center of the table and leaned back.

"What is it? " I asked.

"It is a Neanderthal from a site called Zafarraya, in the south of Spain," he said. "We have only this mandible and an isolated femur. But as you can see, the jaw is almost complete. We are not sure yet, but it may be that this fossil is only 30,000 years old."

"Only" 30,000 years may seem an odd way of expressing time, but coming from a paleoanthropologist, it is like saying that a professional basketball player is *only* 6 foot 4. Hominids—members of the exclusively human family tree—have been on Earth for at least 4 million years. Measured against the earliest members of our lineage, the mineralized piece of bone on the table was a mewling newborn. Even compared with others of its kind, the jaw was astonishingly young. Neanderthals were supposed to have disappeared fully 5,000 years before this one was born, and I had come to France to find out what might have happened to them.

The Neanderthals are the best known and least understood of all human ancestors. To most people, the name instantly brings to mind the image of a hulking brute, dragging his mate around by her coif. This stereotype, born al-

most as soon as the first skeleton was found in a German cave in the middle of the last century, has been refluffed in comic books, novels, and movies so often that it has successfully passed from cliché to common parlance. But what actually makes a Neanderthal a Neanderthal is not its size or its strength or any measure of its native intelligence but a suite of exquisitely distinct physical traits, most of them in the face and cranium.

Like all Neanderthal mandibles, for example, the one on the table lacked the bony protrusion on the rim of the jaw called a mental eminence—better known as a chin. The places on the outside of the jaw where chewing muscles had once been attached were grossly enlarged, indicating tremendous torque in the bite. Between the last two molars and the upward thrust of the rear of the jaw, Hublin pointed to gaps of almost a quarter inch, an architectural nicety shifting the business of chewing farther toward the front.

In these and in several other features the jaw was uniquely, quintessentially Neanderthal; no other member of the human family before or since shows the same pattern. With a little instruction the Neanderthal pattern is recognizable even to a layman like me. But unlike Hublin, whose expertise allowed him to sit there calmly sipping coffee while the jaw of a 30,000-year-old man rested within biting distance of his free hand, I felt like stooping down and paying homage.

Several years before, based on a comparison of DNA found in the mitochondria of modern human cells, a team of biochemists in Berkeley, California, had concluded that all humans on Earth could trace their ancestry back to a woman who had lived in Africa only 200,000 years earlier. Every living branch and twig of the human family tree had shot up from this "mitochondrial Eve" and spread like kudzu over the face of the globe, binding all humans in an intimate web of relatedness.

To me the Eve hypothesis sounded almost too good to be true. If all living people can be traced back to a common ancestor just 200,000 years ago, then the entire human population of the globe is really just one grand brother-and-sisterhood, despite the confounding embellishments of culture and race. Thus on a May afternoon, a cafe in Paris could play host to clientele from three or four continents, but the scene still amounted to a sort of ad hoc family reunion.

But Eve bore a darker message too. The Berkeley study suggested that at some point between 100,000 and 50,000 years ago, people from Africa began to disperse across Europe and Asia, eventually populating the Americas as well. These people, and these alone, became the ancestors of all future human generations. When they arrived in Eurasia, however, there were thousands, perhaps millions, of other human beings already living there—including the Neanderthals. What happened to them all? Eve's answer was cruelly unequivocal: the Neanderthals—including the Zafarraya population represented by the jaw on the table—were pushed aside, outcompeted, or otherwise driven extinct by the new arrivals from the south.

What fascinates me about the fate of the Neanderthals is the paradox of their promise. Appearing first in Europe about 150,000 years ago, the Neanderthals flourished throughout the increasing cold of an approaching ice age; by 70,000 years ago they had spread throughout Europe and western Asia. As for Neanderthal appearance, the stereotype of a muscled thug is not completely off the mark. Thick-boned, barrel-chested, a healthy Neanderthal male could lift an average NFL linebacker over his head and throw him through the goalposts. But despite the

Neanderthal's reputation for dim-wittedness, there is nothing that clearly distinguishes its brain from that of a modern human except that, on average, the Neanderthal version was slightly *larger*. There is no trace of the thoughts that animated those brains, so we do not know how much they resembled our own. But a big brain is an expensive piece of adaptive equipment. You don't evolve one if you don't use it. Combining enormous physical strength with manifest intelligence, the Neanderthals appear to have been outfitted to face any obstacle the environment could put in their path. They could not lose.

And then, somehow, they lost. Just when the Neanderthals reached their most advanced expression, they suddenly vanished. Their demise coincides suspiciously with the arrival in western Europe of a new kind of human: taller, thinner, more modern-looking. The collision of these two human populations—us and the other, the destined parvenu and the doomed caretaker of a continent—is as potent and marvelous a part of the human story as anything that has happened since.

By itself, the half-jaw on the table in front of me had its own tale to tell. Hublin had said that it was perhaps as young as 30,000 years old. A few months before, an American archeologist named James Bischoff and his colleagues had also announced astonishing ages for some objects from Spanish caves. After applying a new technique to date some modern human-style artifacts, they declared them to be 40,000 years old. This was 6,000 years *before* there were supposed to have been modern humans in Europe. If both Bischoff's and Hublin's dates were right, it meant that Neanderthals and modern humans had been sharing Spanish soil for 10,000 years. That didn't make sense to me.

"At 30,000 years," I asked Hublin, "wouldn't this jaw be the last Neanderthal known?"

"If we are right about the date, yes," he said. "But there is still much work to be done before we can say how old the jaw is for certain."

"But Bischoff says modern humans were in Spain 10,000 years before then," I persisted. "I can understand how a population with a superior technology might come into an area and quickly dominate a less sophisticated people already there. But 10,000 years doesn't sound very quick even in evolutionary terms. How can two kinds of human being exist side by side for that long without sharing their cultures? Without sharing their genes?"

Hublin shrugged in the classically cryptic French manner that means either "The answer is obvious" or "How should I know?"

Among all the events and transformations in human evolution, the origins of modern humans were, until recently, the easiest to account for. Around 35,000 years ago, signs of a new, explosively energetic culture in Europe marked the beginning of the period known as the Upper Paleolithic. They included a highly sophisticated variety of tools, made out of bone and antler as well as stone. Even more important, the people making these tools—usually known as Cro-Magnons, a name borrowed from a tiny rock shelter in southern France where their skeletons were first found, in 1868—had discovered a symbolic plane of existence, evident in their gorgeously painted caves, carved animal figurines, and the beads and pendants adorning their bodies. The Neanderthals who had inhabited Europe for tens of thousands of years had never produced anything remotely as elaborate. Coinciding with this cultural explosion were the first signs of the kind of anatomy that distinguishes modern human beings: a well-defined chin; a vertical forehead lacking pronounced brow-ridges; a domed braincase; and a slender, lightly built frame, among other, more esoteric features.

The skeletons in the Cro-Magnon cave, believed to be between 32,000 and 30,000 years old, provided an exquisite microcosm of the joined emergence of culture and anatomy. Five skeletons, including one of an infant, were found buried in a communal grave, and all exhibited the anatomical characteristics of modern human beings. Scattered in the grave with them were hundreds of artificially pierced seashells and animal teeth, clearly the vestiges of necklaces, bracelets, and other body ornaments. The nearly simultaneous appearance of modern culture and modern anatomy provided a readymade explanation for the final step in the human journey. Since they happened at the same time, the reasoning went, obviously one had caused the other. It all made good Darwinian sense. A more efficient technology emerged to take over the survival role previously provided by brute strength, relaxing the need for the robust physiques and powerful chewing apparatus of the Neanderthals. Voilà. Suddenly there was clever, slender Cro-Magnon man. That this first truly modern human should be indigenous to Europe tightened the evolutionary narrative: modern man appeared in precisely the region of the world where culture—according to Europeans—later reached its zenith. Prehistory foreshadowed history. The only issue to sort out was whether the Cro-Magnons had come from somewhere else or whether the Neanderthals had evolved into them.

The latter scenario, of course, assumes that modern humans and Neanderthals didn't coexist, at least not for any appreciable amount of time. But the jawbone from Zafarraya challenged that neat supposition. Even more damaging were some strange findings in the Mideast. Recent discoveries there too suggest that Neanderthals and modern humans may have inhabited the same land at the same time, and for far, far longer than in Spain.

In Israel, on the southern edge of the Neanderthal range, a wooded rise of limestone issues abruptly out of the Mediterranean below Haifa, ascending in an undulation of hills. This is the Mount Carmel of the Song of Solomon, where Elijah brought down the false priests of Baal, and Deborah laid rout to the Canaanites. In subsequent centuries, armies, tribes, and whole cultures tramped through its rocky passes and over its fertile flanks, bringing Hittites, Persians, Jews, Romans, Mon-

gols, Muslims, Crusaders, Turks, the modern meddling of Europeans—one people slaughtered or swallowed by the next but somehow springing up again and gaining strength enough to slaughter or swallow in its turn.

The story in the Levant never made sense. Here, how modern a hominid looked said nothing about how modernly it behaved.

My interest here is in more ancient confrontations. Mount Carmel lies in the Levant, a tiny hinge of habitability between the sea and the desert, linking the two great landmasses of Africa and Eurasia. A million years ago a massive radiation of large mammals moved through the Levant from Africa toward the temperate latitudes to the north. Among these mammals were some ancestral humans. Time passed. The humans evolved, diversified. The ones in Europe came to look very different from their now-distant relatives who had remained in Africa. The Europeans became the Neanderthals. Then, still long before history began to scar the Levant with its sieges and slaughters, some Neanderthals from Europe and other humans from Africa wandered into this link between their homelands, leaving their bones on Mount Carmel. What happened when they met? How did two kinds of human respond to each other?

Reaching the Stone Age in Israel is easy; I simply rented a car in Tel Aviv and drove a couple of hours up the coastal road. My destination was the cave of Kebara, an excavation hunched above a banana plantation on the sea-weathered western slope of the mountain.

Inside the cave the present Mideast, with all its political complexities, disappeared—here there was only a cool, sheltered emptiness, greatly enlarged by decades of archeological probing. Scattered through the excavation were a dozen or so scientists and students;

an equal number were working at tables along the rim. The atmosphere was one of hushed, almost monkish concentration, like that of a reading room in a great library.

The Kebara excavation began ten years ago, picking up on the previous work of Moshe Stekelis of Hebrew University in the 1950s and early 1960s. Stekelis exposed a sequence of Paleolithic deposits and, before his sudden death, discovered the skeleton of an infant Neanderthal. A greater treasure emerged in 1983. After Stekelis's time, the sharp vertical profiles of the excavation crumbled under the feet of a generation of kibbutz children and assorted other slow ravages. A graduate student named Lynne Schepartz was assigned the mundane task of cleaning up the deteriorated exposures by cutting them a little deeper. One afternoon she noticed what appeared to be a human toe bone peeking out of a fused clod of sediments. The next morning her whisk broom exposed a pearly array of human teeth: the lower jaw of an adult Neanderthal skeleton. Stekelis's team had missed it by two inches.

Lynne Schepartz was no longer a graduate student, but she was still spending her summers at Kebara. I found her and asked her how it felt to uncover the fossil. "Unprintable," she said. "I was jumping up and down and screaming."

She had reason to react unprintably. Her discovery turned out to be not just any Neanderthal but the most complete skeleton ever found: the first complete Neanderthal spinal column, the first complete Neanderthal rib cage, the first complete pelvis of any early hominid known. She showed me a plaster cast of the fossil—affectionately known as Moshe—lying on an adjacent table. The bones were arranged exactly as they had been found. Moshe was resting on his back, his right arm folded over his chest, his left hand on his stomach, in a classic attitude of burial. The only missing parts were the right leg, the extremity of the left, and except for the lower jaw, the skull.

Schepartz led me down ladders to Moshe's burial site, a deep rectangular pit near the center of the excavation. On this July morning, the Neanderthal's grave was occupied by a modern human named Ofer Bar-Yosef, who peered back up at me from behind thick glasses, magnifying my sense that I had disturbed the happy toil of a cavernicolous hobbit. He seemed evolved to the task, nimble and gnomishly compact, the better to fit into cramped quarters.

Bar-Yosef told me that he had directed his first archeological excavation at the age of 11, rounding up a crew of his friends in his Jerusalem neighborhood to help him unearth a Byzantine water system. He had not stopped digging since. Kebara was the latest of three major excavations under his direction. "My daughter has been coming to this site since she was a fetus," he told me. "She used to have a playpen set up right over there."

Throughout his career, Bar-Yosef has dug for answers to two personal obsessions: the origins of Neolithic agricultural societies and—the point where our obsessions converge—the twisting conundrum of modern human origins.

The story in the Levant never really made much sense. In the old days, back when everybody "knew" that modern humans first appeared in western Europe, where the really modern folks still live, you could identify a hominid by the kind of tools he left behind. Bulky Neanderthals made bulky flakes, while svelte Cro-Magnons made slim "blades." Narrowness is, in fact, the very definition of a blade, which in paleoarcheology means nothing more than a stone tool twice as long as it is wide. In Europe a new, efficient way of producing blades from a flint core appeared as part of the "cultural explosion" that coincided with the appearance of the Cro-Magnon people. Here in the Levant, however, the arrival of anatomically modern humans was marked by no fancy new tools not to mention no painted caves, beaded necklaces, or other evidence of exploding Cro-Magnon couture. In this part of the world, how modern a hominid looked in its body said nothing about how modernly it behaved.

Just a couple of bus stops up the coastal road from Kebara is the cave of Tabun, with over 80 vertical feet of deposits spanning more than 100,000

years of human occupation. The treasures of Tabun, like those of Kebara, are Neanderthals. Literally around the corner from Tabun is another cave, called Skhul, where some fairly modern-looking humans were found in the 1930s. And a few miles inland from Kebara on a hill in lower Galilee is Qafzeh, where in 1965 a young French anthropologist named Bernard Vandermeersch found a veritable Middle Paleolithic cemetery of distinctly modern humans. But though the bones in these caves include both Neanderthals and modern humans, the tools found with the bones are all pretty much the same.

In 1982, Arthur Jelinek of the University of Arizona made an inspired attempt to massage some sense into the nagging paradox of Mount Carmel. As in Europe later on, he argued, tools get thinner along with the bodies of the people who make them. Only in this case, the reduction is front to back rather than side to side.

The fattest flakes, he showed, came from a layer near the bottom of Tabun cave, where a partial skeleton of a Neanderthal woman had turned up; if flake thickness was indeed a true measure of time, then she was the oldest in the group. The next oldest would be the Neanderthal infant that Stekelis had found at Kebara. The modern humans of Skhul yielded flake tools that were flatter. And the flattest of all belonged to the moderns of Qafzeh cave. Although the physically modern Skhul-Qafzeh people might not have crossed the line into full-fledged, blade-based humanness, they appeared, as Jelinek wrote, "on the threshold of breaking away.

"Our current evidence from Tabun suggests an orderly and continuous progress of industries in the southern Levant," he went on, "paralleled by a morphological progression from Neanderthal to modern man." According to this scenario, the Neanderthals simply evolved into modern humans. There was no collision of peoples or cultures; two kinds of human never met, because there was really only one kind, changing through time.

If Jelinek's conventional chronology based on slimming tool forms was right, the fossils found in Qafzeh could

be "proto-Cro-Magnons," the evolutionary link between a Neanderthal past and a Cro-Magnon future—and thence to the present moment. But the dating methods he used were *relative,* merely inferring an age for the skeletons by where they fell in an overall chronological scheme. What was needed was a new way of measuring time, preferably an *absolute* dating technique that could label the Mount Carmel hominids with an age in actual calendar years.

The most celebrated absolute dating method is radiocarbon dating, which measures time by the constant, steady decay of radioactive carbon atoms. Developed in the 1940s, radiocarbon dating is still one of the most accurate ways to pin an age on a site, so long as it is younger than around 40,000 years. In older materials the amount of radioactive carbon still left undecayed is so small that even the slightest amount of contamination leads to highly inaccurate results. Another technique, relying on the decay of radioactive potassium instead of carbon, has been used since the late 1950s to date volcanic deposits older than half a million years. Radiopotassium was the method of choice for dating the famous East African early hominids like Lucy, as well as the new "root hominid," *Australopithecus ramidus,* announced in 1994. Until recently, though, everything that lived between the ranges of these two techniques—including the moderns at Qafzeh and the Neanderthals at Kebara—fell into a chronological black hole.

In the early 1980s, however, Hélène Valladas, a French archeologist, used a new technique called thermoluminescence, or TL, to date flints from the Kebara and Qafzeh caves. As applied to these flints, the technique is based on the fact that minerals give off a burst of light when heated to about 900 degrees. It is also based on the certainty that past humans, like present ones, were sometimes careless. In the Middle Paleolithic, some flint tools happened to lie around in the path of careless feet, and some tools got kicked into fires, opening up an exquisite opportunity for absolute dating. When a flint tool was heated sufficiently by the fire, it gave up its thermoluminescent energy. Over thousands of years, that energy slowly built up again. The dating of fire-charred tools is thus, in principle, straightforward: the brighter a bit of flint glows when heated today, the longer since the time it was last used.

By 1987, Valladas and her physicist father, Georges, had squeezed an age of 60,000 years out of the burnt tools found beside Moshe at Kebara. That number pleased everybody, since it agreed with time schemes arrived at through relative dating methods. The shocker came the following year, when Valladas and her colleagues announced the results of their work at Qafzeh: the "modern" skeletons were 92,000 years old, give or take a few thousand.

Several other Neanderthal and modern human sites have since been dated with TL, and the one at Qafzeh remains not only the most sensational but the surest. Key sites in the Levant have also been dated by a "sister" technique called electron-spin resonance (ESR). Large mammal teeth found near the Qafzeh skeletons came back with an ESR date even older than Valladas's thermoluninescent surprise. The skeletons were at least 100,000 and perhaps 115,000 years old. "People said that TL had too many uncertainties," Bernard Vandermeersch told me. "So we gave them ESR. By now it is very difficult to dispute that the first modern humans in the Levant were here by 100,000 years ago."

Clearly, if modern humans were inhabiting the Levant 40,000 years before the Neanderthals, they could hardly have evolved from them. If the dates are indeed correct, it is hard to see what else one can do with the venerated belief in our Neanderthal ancestry but chuck it, once and for all.

Case closed? On the contrary, the dates only twist the mystery on Mount Carmel even tighter. Presuming that the moderns did not just come for a visit 100,000 years ago and then politely withdraw, they must have been around when the Neanderthals arrived 40,000 years later—if the Neanderthals as well weren't there to begin with: the latest ESR dates for the Tabun Neanderthal woman place her there 110,000 years ago. Either way, two distinct

kinds of human were apparently squeezed together in an area not much larger than the state of New Jersey, and for a long time—at least 25,000 years and perhaps 50,000 or more.

Rather than resolving the paradox, the new dating techniques only teased out its riddles. If two kinds of human were behaving the same way in the same place at the same time, how can we call them different? If modern humans did not descend from the Neanderthals but replaced them instead, why did it take them so long to get the job done?

At Kebara, I took the paradox with me to mull over outside, on a still summer afternoon, where the horizon manifested the present moment in the silhouette of an oil tanker, far out at sea. If the names "Neanderthal" and "modern human" are meaningful distinctions, if they have as much reality, say, as the oil tanker pasted onto the horizon, then they cannot be blended, any more than one can blend the sea and the sky. But what if they are mere edges after all, edges that might have had firm content in France and Spain but not here, not in *this* past; edges whose contents spilled over and leaked into each other so profusely that no true edges can be said to exist at all?

In that case, there would be no more mystery. The Levantine paradox would be a trick knot; pull gently from both ends and it unravels on its own. Think of one end of the rope as cultural. Every species has its own ecological niche, its unique set of adaptations to local habitats. The "principle of competitive exclusion" states that two species cannot squeeze into the same niche: the slightly better adapted one will eventually drive the other one out. Traditionally, the human niche has been defined by culture, so it would be impossible for two kinds of human to coexist using the same stone tools to compete for the same plant and animal resources. One would drive the other into extinction, or never allow it to gain a foothold.

"Competitive exclusion would preclude the coexistence of two different kinds of hominid in a small area over a

40,000- or 50,000-year period unless they had different adaptations," says Geoffrey Clark of Arizona State University. "But as far as we can tell, the adaptations were identical at Kebara and Qafzeh." Clark adds to the list of common adaptations the use of symbols—or lack of it. Perhaps Neanderthals lacked complex social symbols like beads, artwork, and elaborate burial. But so, he believes, did their skinny contemporaries down the road at Qafzeh. If *neither* was littering the landscape with signs of some new mental capacity, by what right do we favor the skinny one with a brilliant future and doom the other to dull extinction?

This leads to the morphological end of the rope. If the two human types cannot be distinguished on the basis of their tools, then the only valid way of telling a Neanderthal from a modern human is to declare that one looks "Neanderthalish" and the other doesn't. If you were to take all the relevant fossils and line them up, could you really separate them into two mutually exclusive groups, with no overlap? A replacement advocate might think so, but a believer in continuity like Geoffrey Clark insists that you could not. He thinks the lineup might better be characterized as one widely variable population, running the gamut from the most Neanderthal to the most modern. The early excavators at Tabun and Skhul saw the fossils there as an intermediate grade between archaic and modern *Homo sapiens*. Perhaps they were right. "The skeletal material is anything but clearly 'Neanderthal' and clearly 'modern,' " Clark maintains, "whatever those terms mean in the first place, which I don't think is much."

This view preserves the traditional idea of continuity but abandons the *process:* there was no evolution from one kind of human to another—from Neanderthal to modern—because there was, in fact, no "other." But for all its appeal, the "oneness" solution to the Levantine paradox is fundamentally flawed. Nobody disputes that the tool kits of the two human types are virtually identical. But it does not logically follow that the toolmakers must be identical as well. Middle Paleolithic tool kits are associated in our minds with Neanderthals because they are the best known human occupants of the Middle Paleolithic. But if people with modern anatomy turn out to have been living back then, too, why *wouldn't* they be using the same culture as the Neanderthals?

"If you ask me, forget about the stone tools," Ofer Bar-Yosef told me. "They can tell you nothing, zero. At most they say something about how they were preparing food. But is what you do in the kitchen all of your life? Of course not. Being positive people, we are not willing to admit that some of the missing evidence might be the crucial evidence we need to solve this problem."

Whatever the tools suggest, the skeletons of moderns and Neanderthals look different, and the pattern of their differences is too consistent to dismiss. As anthropologist Erik Trinkaus of the University of New Mexico has shown, those skeletal differences clearly reflect two distinct patterns of behavior, however alike the archeological leavings may be. Furthermore, the two physical types do not follow one from the other, nor do they meet in a fleeting moment before one triumphs and the other fades. They just keep on going, side by side but never mingling. In his behavioral approach to bones, Trinkaus purposely disregards the features that might best discriminate Neanderthals and moderns from each other genetically. By definition, these traits are poor indicators of the effects of lifestyle on bone, since their shape and size are decided by heredity, not by use. But there is one profoundly important aspect of human life where behavior and heredity converge: the act that allows human lineages to continue in the first place.

Humans love to mate. They mate all the time, by night and by day, through all the phases of the female's reproductive cycle. Given the opportunity, humans throughout the world will mate with any other human. The barriers between races and cultures, so cruelly evident in other respects, melt away when sex is at stake. Cortés began the systematic annihilation of the Aztec

people—but that did not stop him from taking an Aztec princess for his wife. Blacks have been treated with contempt by whites in America since they were first forced into slavery, but some 20 percent of the genes in a typical African American are "white." Consider James Cook's voyages in the Pacific in the eighteenth century. "Cook's men would come to some distant land, and lining the shore were all these very bizarre-looking human beings with spears, long jaws, browridges," archeologist Clive Gamble of Southampton University in England told me. "God, how odd it must have seemed to them. But that didn't stop the Cook crew from making a lot of little Cooklets."

Project this universal human behavior back into the Middle Paleolithic. When Neanderthals and modern humans came into contact in the Levant, they would have interbred, no matter how "strange" they might initially have seemed to each other. If their cohabitation stretched over tens of thousands of years, the fossils should show a convergence through time toward a single morphological pattern, or at least some swapping of traits back and forth.

But the evidence just isn't there, not if the TL and ESR dates are correct. Instead the Neanderthals stay staunchly themselves. In fact, according to some recent ESR dates, the least "Neanderthalish" among them is also the oldest. The full Neanderthal pattern is carved deep at the Kebara cave, around 60,000 years ago. The moderns, meanwhile, arrive very early at Qafzeh and Skhul and never lose their modern aspect. Certainly, it is possible that at any moment new fossils will be revealed that conclusively demonstrate the emergence of a "Neandermod" lineage. From the evidence in hand, however, the most likely conclusion is that Neanderthals and modern humans were not interbreeding in the Levant.

Of course, to interbreed, you first have to meet. Some researchers have contended that the coexistence on the slopes of Mount Carmel for tens of thousands of years is merely an illusion created by the poor archeological record. If moderns and Neanderthals were physically isolated from each

other, then there is nothing mysterious about their failure to interbreed. The most obvious form of isolation is geographic. But imagine an isolation in time as well. The climate of the Levant fluctuated throughout the Middle Paleolithic—now warm and dry, now cold and wet. Perhaps modern humans migrated up into the region from Africa during the warm periods, when the climate was better suited to their lighter, taller, warm-adapted physiques. Neanderthals, on the other hand, might have arrived in the Levant only when advancing glaciers cooled their European range more than even their cold-adapted physiques could stand. Then the two did not so much cohabit as "time-share" the same pocket of landscape between their separate continental ranges.

Humans love to mate. The barriers between races, so cruelly evident in other respects, melt away when sex is at stake.

While the solution is intriguing, there are problems with it. Hominids are remarkably adaptable creatures. Even the ancient *Homo erectus*—who lacked the large brain, hafted spear points, and other cultural accoutrements of its descendants—managed to thrive in a range of regions and under diverse climatic conditions. And while hominids adapt quickly, glaciers move very, very slowly, coming and going. Even if one or the other kind of human gained sole possession of the Levant during climatic extremes, what about all those millennia that were neither the hottest nor the coldest? There must have been long stretches of time—perhaps enduring as long as the whole of recorded human history—when the Levant climate was perfectly suited to both Neanderthals and modern humans. What part do these in-between periods play in the time-sharing scenario? It doesn't make sense that one human population should politely vacate Mount Carmel just before the other moved in.

If these humans were isolated in neither space nor time but were truly contemporaneous, then how on earth did they fail to mate? Only one solution to the mystery is left. Neanderthals and moderns did not interbreed in the Levant because they *could* not. They were reproductively incompatible, separate species—equally human, perhaps, but biologically distinct. Two separate species, who both just happened to be human at the same time, in the same place.

Cohabitation in the Levant in the last ice age conjures up a chilling possibility. It forces you to imagine two equally gifted, resourceful, emotionally rich human entities weaving through one tapestry of landscape—yet so different from each other as to make the racial diversity of present-day humans seem like nothing. Take away the sexual bridge and you end up with two fully sentient human species pressed into one place, as mindless of each other as two kinds of bird sharing the same feeder in your backyard.

When paleoanthropologists bicker over whether Neanderthal anatomy is divergent enough to justify calling Neanderthals a separate species from us, they are using a *morphological* definition of a species. This is a useful pretense for the paleoanthropologists, who have nothing but the shapes of bone to work with in the first place. But they admit that in the real, vibrantly unruly natural world, bone morphology is a pitifully poor indication of where one species leaves off and another begins. Ian Tattersall, an evolutionary biologist at the American Museum of Natural History, points out that if you stripped the skin and muscle off 20 New World monkey species, their skeletons would be virtually indistinguishable. Many other species look the same even with their skins still on.

The most common definition of *biological* species, as opposed to the morphological make-believes paleontologists have to work with, is a succinct utterance of the esteemed evolutionary biologist Ernst Mayr: "Species are groups of actually or potentially interbreeding natural populations that are reproductively isolated from other such groups." The key phrase is *reproductively isolated:* a species is something that doesn't mate with anything but itself. The evolutionary barriers that prevent species from wantonly interbreeding and producing a sort of organismic soup on the landscape are called isolating mechanisms. These can be any obstructions that prevent otherwise closely related species from mating to produce fertile off-spring. The obstructions may be anatomical. Two species of hyrax in East Africa share the same sleeping holes, make use of common latrines, and raise their young in communal "play groups." But they cannot interbreed, at least in part because of the radically different shapes of the males' penises. Isolating mechanisms need not be so conspicuous. Two closely related species might have different estrous cycles. Or the barrier might come into play after mating: the chromosomes are incompatible or perhaps recombine into an offspring that is incapable of breeding, an infertile hybrid like a mule.

It is easy to see why paleoanthropologists despair over trying to apply Mayr's biological concept of species to ancient hominids. The characteristics needed to recognize a biological species—the isolating mechanism—are not the kind that usually turn up as fossils. How can an estrous cycle be preserved? What does an infertile hybrid, reduced to a few fragments of its skeleton, look like? How does a chromosomal difference turn into stone?

But there is another way of looking at species that might offer hope. The biological-species concept is a curiously negative one: what makes a species itself is that it doesn't mate with anything else. A few years ago a South African biologist named Hugh Patterson turned the biological-species concept inside out, proposing a view of a species based on not with whom it *doesn't* mate but with whom it *does.* Species, according to Patterson, are groups of individuals in nature that share "a common system of fertilization mechanisms."

With reproduction at its core, Patterson's concept is just as "biological" as Mayr's. But he turns the focus away from barriers preventing interbreeding and throws into relief the adaptations that together ensure the successful meeting of a sperm and an egg. Obviously, sex and conception are fertilization mechanisms, as is the genetic compatibility of the two parents' chromosomes. But long before a sperm cell gets near a receptive egg, the two sexes must have ways of recognizing each other as potential mates. And therein, perhaps, lies a solution to the mystery of Mount Carmel.

Every mating in nature begins with a message. It may be chemically couched: eggs of the brown alga *Ascophyllum nodosum,* for example, send out a chemical that attracts the sperm of *A. nodosum* and no other. It may be a smell. As any dog owner knows, a bitch in heat lures males from all over the neighborhood. Note that the scent does not draw squirrels, tomcats, or teenage boys. Many birds use vocal signals to attract and recognize the opposite sex, but only of their own species. "A female of one species might *hear* the song of the male of another," explains Judith Masters, a colleague of Patterson's at the University of Witwatersrand, "but she won't make any response. There's no need to talk about what *prevents* her from mating with that male. She just doesn't see what all the fuss is about."

A species' mate-recognition system is extremely stable compared with adaptations to the local habitat. A sparrow born with a slightly too short beak may or may not be able to feed its young as well as another with an average-size beak. But a sparrow who sings an unfamiliar song will not attract a mate and is not going to have any young at all. He will be plucked from the gene pool of the next generation, leaving no evolutionary trace of his idiosyncratic serenade. The same goes, of course, for any sparrow hen who fails to respond to potential mates singing the "correct" tune. With this kind of price for deviance, everybody is a conservative. "The only time a species' mate-recognition system will change is when something really dramatic happens," Masters says.

For the drama to unfold, a population must be geographically isolated from its parent species. If the population is small enough and the habitat radically different from what it was previously, even the powerful evolutionary inertia of the mate-recognition system may be overcome. This change in reproduction may be accompanied by new adaptations to the environment. Or it may not. Either way, the only shift that marks the birth of a new species is the one affecting the recognition of mates. Once the recognition threshold is crossed, there is no going back. Even if individuals from the new population and the old come to live in the same region again—let's say in a well-trafficked corridor of fertile land linking their two continental ranges— they will no longer view each other as potential mates.

The human mate-recognition system is overwhelmingly visual. "Love comes in at the eye," wrote Yeats, and the locus of the human body that lures the eye most of all is the face—a trait our species shares with many other primates. "It is a common Old World anthropoid ploy," says Masters. "Cercopithecoid monkeys have a whole repertoire of eyelid flashes. Forest guenons have brightly painted faces with species-specific patterns, which they wave like flags in the forest gloom. Good old evolution tinkering away, providing new variations on a theme."

Faces are exquisitely expressive instruments. Behind our facial skin lies an intricate web of musculature, concentrated especially around the eyes and mouth, evolved purely for social communication—expressing interest, fear, suspicion, joy, contentment, doubt, surprise, and countless other emotions. Each emotion can be further modified by the raise of an eyebrow or the slight flick of a cheek muscle to express, say, measured surprise, wild surprise, disappointed surprise, feigned surprise, and so on. By one estimate, the 22

expressive muscles on each side of the face can be called on to produce 10,000 different facial actions or expressions.

Among this armory of social signals are stereotyped, formal invitations to potential mates. The mating display we call flirtation plays the same on the face of a New Guinean tribeswoman and a *lycéenne* in a Parisian cafe: a bashful lowering of the gaze to one side and down, followed by a furtive look at the other's face and a coy retreat of the eyes. A host of other sexual signals are communicated facially—the downward tilt of the chin, the glance over the shoulder, the slight parting of the mouth. The importance of the face as an attractant is underscored by the lengths to which humans in various cultures go to embellish what is already there. But the underlying message is communicated by the anatomy of the face itself. "'Tis not a lip, or eye, we beauty call, / but the joint force and full result of all," wrote Alexander Pope. And it is that "joint force"—over generations—that keeps our species so forcefully joined.

This brings us back to the Levant: two human species in a tight space for a long time. The vortex of anatomy where Neanderthals and early moderns differ most emphatically, where a clear line can be drawn between *them* and *us* by even the most rabid advocate of continuity is, of course, the face. The Neanderthal's "classic" facial pattern—the midfacial thrust picked up and amplified by the great projecting nose, the puffed-up cheekbones, the long jaw with its chinless finish, the large, rounded eye sockets, the extra-thick browridges shading it like twin awnings—is usually explained as a complex of modifications relating to a cold climate, or as a support to heavy chewing forces delivered to the front teeth. Either way it is assumed to be an environmental adaptation. But what if these adaptive functions of the face were not the reason they evolved in the first place? What if the peculiarities evolved instead as the underpinnings of a totally separate, thoroughly Neanderthal mate-recognition system?

Although it is merely a speculation, the idea fits some of the facts and

solves some of the problems. Certainly the Neanderthals' ancestors were geographically cut off from other populations enough to allow some new mate-recognition system to emerge. During glacial periods, contact through Asia was blocked by the polar glaciers and vast uninhabitable tundra. Mountain glaciers between the Black and Caspian Seas all but completed a barrier to the south. "The Neanderthals are a textbook case for how to get a separate species," archeologist John Shea told me. "Isolate them for 100,000 years, then melt the glaciers and let 'em loose."

If mate recognition lay behind a species-level difference between Neanderthals and moderns, the Levantine paradox can finally be put to rest. Their cohabitation with moderns no longer needs explanation. Neanderthals and moderns managed to coexist through long millennia, doing the same human-like things but without interbreeding, simply because the issue never really came up.

The idea seems scarcely imaginable. Continuity believers cannot credit the idea of two human types coexisting in sexual isolation. Replacement advocates cannot conceive of such a long period of coexistence without competition, if not outright violent confrontation. They would rather see Neanderthals and moderns pushing each other in and out of the Levant, in an extended struggle finally won by our own ancestors. Of course, if the Neanderthals were a biologically separate species, something must have happened to cause their extinction. After all, we are still here, and they are not.

Why they faded and we managed to survive is a separate story with its own shocks and surprises. But what happened on Mount Carmel might be more remarkable still. It is something that people today are not prepared to comprehend, especially in places like the Levant. Two human species, with far less in common than any two races or ethnic groups now on the planet, may have shared a small, fertile piece of land for 50,000 years, regarding each other the whole time with steady, untroubled, peaceful indifference.

Living with the Past

Anthroplogy continues to evolve as a discipline, in terms of the tools and techniques of the trade as well as in terms of the application of whatever knowledge we stand to gain about our selves. It is in this context that Patrick Huyghe, in "Profile of an Anthropologist: No Bone Unturned," describes "forensic anthropology," a whole new field involving the use of physical similarities and differences between people in order to identify human remains. In the same practical vein, John Horgan discusses the validity of, and the methods behind, a new field called "behavioral genetics" (in "Eugenics Revisited"), and, finally, Edward Humes, in "The DNA Wars,"

discusses the legal ramifications of the use of DNA in criminal law. If there is one theme that ties the articles of this section together, then, it is that they have as much to do with the present as with the past.

An axiom in evolutionary theory called the "law of irrevocability" holds that no species completely revokes or sheds the vestiges of even its distant ancestors. Given the fact that each of us is a product of that which went before, we carry with us a certain amount of "evolutionary baggage." Some of this "baggage" may present problems that will not go away—any more than the baboons described by Jim Bell (in "Farmers and Baboons in the Taita Hills: Inter-Species Warfare in Southeastern Kenya") or the macaques described by Meredith Small (in "Macaque See, Macaque Do"). Our primate relatives have been a part of the human evolutionary scene since time immemorial. We can make adjustments, however, if for no other reason than for the sake of human safety and efficiency.

Sometimes an awareness of our biological and behavioral past may even make the difference between life and death, as Meredith Small writes in "A Reasonable Sleep." Recent research indicates that the sleeping arrangement of mothers and their young, that is, whether or not they conform to the traditional pattern of bedding down together, has a contributing effect on the incidence of Sudden Infant Death Syndrome. Meanwhile, at the other end of the human life cycle, Jared Diamond argues in "The Saltshaker's Curse" that a physiological adaptation that once helped American blacks survive slavery may now be predisposing their descendants to an early death from hypertension.

As we reflect upon where we have been and how we came to be as we are in the evolutionary sense, the inevitable question arises as to what will happen next. This is the most difficult issue of all, since our biological future depends so much upon long-range ecological trends that no one seems to be able to predict. Some will wonder if we will even survive long enough as a species to experience any significant biological changes. Perhaps our capacity for knowledge is outstripping the wisdom to use it wisely, and the consequent destruction of our earthly environments and wildlife is placing us in ever greater danger of creating the circumstances of our own extinction.

Counterbalancing this pessimism is the view that, since it has been our conscious decision making (and not the genetically predetermined behavior that characterizes some species) that has gotten us into this mess, then it will be the conscious will of our generation and future generations that will get us out. But, can we wait much longer for humanity to collectively come to its senses? Or is it already too late?

Looking Ahead: Challenge Questions

What is "forensic anthropology"?

What social policy issues are involved in the nature vs. nurture debate?

How reliable is DNA matching in criminal cases?

Why has the conflict between humans and baboons intensified over time?

How can the demands of tourism and the needs of primates be reconciled for mutual benefit?

How might sleeping patterns in the United States be contributing to the incidence of Sudden Infant Death Syndrome?

What is the "saltshaker's curse," and why are some people more affected by it than others?

Profile of an Anthropologist
No Bone Unturned

Patrick Huyghe

The research of some physical anthropologists and archaeologists involves the discovery and analysis of old bones (as well as artifacts and other remains). Most often these bones represent only part of a skeleton or maybe the mixture of parts of several skeletons. Often these remains are smashed, burned, or partially destroyed. Over the years, physical anthropologists have developed a remarkable repertoire of skills and techniques for teasing the greatest possible amount of information out of sparse material remains.

Although originally developed for basic research, the methods of physical anthropology can be directly applied to contemporary human problems. . . . In this profile, we look briefly at the career of Clyde C. Snow, a physical anthropologist who has put these skills to work in a number of different settings. . . .

As you read this selection, ask yourself the following questions:
- *Given what you know of physical anthropology, what sort of work would a physical anthropologist do for the Federal Aviation Administration?*
- *What is anthropometry? How might anthropometric surveys of pilots and passengers help in the design of aircraft equipment?*
- *What is forensic anthropology? How can a biological anthropologist be an expert witness in legal proceedings?*

Clyde Snow is never in a hurry. He knows he's late. He's always late. For Snow, being late is part of the job. In fact, he doesn't usually begin to work until death has stripped some poor individual to the bone, and no one—neither the local homicide detectives nor the pathologists—can figure out who once gave identity to the skeletonized remains. No one, that is, except a shrewd, laconic, 60-year-old forensic anthropologist.

Snow strolls into the Cook County Medical Examiner's Office in Chicago on this brisk October morning wearing a pair of Lucchese cowboy boots and a three-piece pin-striped suit. Waiting for him in autopsy room 160 are a bunch of naked skeletons found in Illinois, Wisconsin, and Minnesota since his last visit. Snow, a native Texan who now lives in rural Oklahoma, makes the trip up to Chicago some six times a year. The first case on his agenda is a pale brown skull found in the garbage of an abandoned building once occupied by a Chicago cosmetics company.

Snow turns the skull over slowly in his hands, a cigarette dangling from his fingers. One often does. Snow does not seem overly concerned about mortality, though its tragedy surrounds him daily.

"There's some trauma here," he says, examining a rough edge at the lower back of the skull. He points out the area to Jim Elliott, a homicide detective with the Chicago police. "This looks like a chopping blow by a heavy bladed instrument. Almost like a decapitation." In a place where the whining of bone saws drifts through hallways and the sweet-sour smell of death hangs in the air, the word surprises no one.

Snow begins thinking aloud. "I think what we're looking at here is a female, or maybe a small male, about thirty to forty years old. Probably Asian." He turns the skull upside down, pointing out the degree of wear on the teeth. "This was somebody who lived on a really rough diet. We don't normally find this kind of dental wear in a modern Western population."

"How long has it been around?" Elliott asks.

Snow raises the skull up to his nose. "It doesn't have any decompositional odors," he says. He pokes a finger in the skull's nooks and crannies. "There's no soft tissue left. It's good and dry. And it doesn't show signs of having been buried. I would say that this has been lying around in an attic or a box for years. It feels like a souvenir skull," says Snow.

Souvenir skulls, usually those of Japanese soldiers, were popular with U.S. troops serving in the Pacific during World War II; there was also a trade in skulls during the Vietnam War years. On closer inspection, though, Snow begins to wonder about the skull's Asian origins—the broad nasal aperture and the jutting forth of the upper-tooth-bearing part of the face suggest Melanesian features. Sifting through the objects found in the abandoned building with the skull, he finds several loose-leaf albums of 35-millimeter transparencies documenting life among the highland tribes of New Guinea. The slides, shot by an anthropologist, include graphic scenes of ritual warfare. The skull, Snow concludes, is more likely to be a trophy from one of these tribal battles than the result of a local Chicago homicide.

"So you'd treat it like found property?" Elliott asks finally. "Like somebody's garage-sale property?"

"Exactly," says Snow.

Clyde Snow is perhaps the world's most sought-after forensic anthropologist. People have been calling upon him to identify skeletons for more than a quarter of a century. Every year he's involved in some 75 cases of identification, most of them without fanfare. "He's an old scudder who doesn't have to blow his own whistle," says Walter Birkby, a forensic anthropologist at the University of Arizona. "He know's he's good."

Yet over the years Snow's work has turned him into something of an unlikely celebrity. He has been called upon to identify the remains of the Nazi war criminal Josef Mengele, reconstruct the face of the Egyptian boy-king Tutankhamen, confirm the authenticity of the body autopsied as that of President John F. Kennedy, and examine the skeletal remains of General Custer's men at the battlefield of the Little Bighorn. He has also been involved in the grim task of identifying the bodies in some of the United States' worst airline accidents.

Such is his legend that cases are sometimes attributed to him in which he played no part. He did not, as the *New York Times* reported, identify the remains of the crew of the *Challenger* disaster. But the man is often the equal of his myth. For the past four years, setting his personal safety aside, Snow has spent much of his time in Argentina, searching for the graves and identities of some of the thousands who "disappeared" between 1976 and 1983, during Argentina's military regime.

Snow did not set out to rescue the dead from oblivion. For almost two decades, until 1979, he was a physical anthropologist at the Civil Aeromedical Institute, part of the Federal Aviation Administration in Oklahoma City. Snow's job was to help engineers improve aircraft design and safety features by providing them with data on the human frame.

One study, he recalls, was initiated in response to complaints from a flight attendants' organization. An analysis of accident patterns had revealed that inadequate restraints on flight attendants' jump seats were leading to deaths and injuries and that aircraft doors weighing several hundred pounds were impeding evacuation efforts. Snow points out that ensuring the survival of passengers in emergencies is largely the flight attendants' responsibility. "If they are injured or killed in a crash, you're going to find a lot of dead passengers."

Reasoning that equipment might be improved if engineers had more data on the size and strength of those who use it, Snow undertook a study that required meticulous measurement. When his report was issued in 1975, Senator William Proxmire was outraged that $57,800 of the taxpayers' money had been spent to caliper 423 airline stewardesses from head to toe. Yet the study, which received one of the senator's dubious Golden Fleece Awards, was firmly supported by both the FAA and the Association of Flight Attendants. "I can't imagine," says Snow with obvious delight, "how much coffee Proxmire got spilled on him in the next few months."

It was during his tenure at the FAA that he developed an interest in forensic work. Over the years the Oklahoma police frequently consulted the physical anthropologist for help in identifying crime victims. "The FAA figured it was a kind of community service to let me work on these cases," he says.

The experience also helped to prepare him for the grim task of identifying the victims of air disasters. In December 1972, when a United Airlines plane crashed outside Chicago, killing 43 of the 61 people aboard (including the wife of Watergate conspirator Howard Hunt, who was found with $10,000 in her purse), Snow was brought in to help examine the bodies. That same year, with Snow's help, forensic anthropology was recognized as a specialty by the American Academy of Forensic Sciences. "It got a lot of anthropologists interested in forensics," he says, "and it made a lot of

pathologists out there aware that there were anthropologists who could help them."

Each nameless skeleton poses a unique mystery for Snow. But some, like the second case awaiting him back in the autopsy room at the Cook County morgue, are more challenging than others. This one is a real chiller. In a large cardboard box lies a jumble of bones along with a tattered leg from a pair of blue jeans, a sock shrunk tightly around the bones of a foot, a pair of Nike running shoes without shoelaces, and, inside the hood of a blue windbreaker, a mass of stringy, blood-caked hair. The remains were discovered frozen in ice about 20 miles outside Milwaukee. A rusted bicycle was found lying close by. Paul Hibbard, chief deputy medical examiner for Waukesha County, who brought the skeleton to Chicago, says no one has been reported missing.

Snow lifts the bones out of the box and begins reconstructing the skeleton on an autopsy table. "There are two hundred six bones and thirty-two teeth in the human body," he says, "and each has a story to tell." Because bone is dynamic, living tissue, many of life's significant events—injuries, illness, childbearing—leave their mark on the body's internal framework. Put together the stories told by these bones, he says, and what you have is a person's "osteobiography."

Snow begins by determining the sex of the skeleton, which is not always obvious. He tells the story of a skeleton that was brought to his FAA office in the late 1970s. It had been found along with some women's clothes and a purse in a local back lot, and the police had assumed that it was female. But when Snow examined the bones, he realized that "at six foot three, she would have probably have been the tallest female in Oklahoma."

Then Snow recalled that six months earlier the custodian in his building had suddenly not shown up for work. The man's supervisor later mentioned to Snow, "You know, one of these days when they find Ronnie, he's going to be dressed as a woman." Ronnie, it turned out, was a weekend transvestite. A copy of his dental records later confirmed that the skeleton in women's clothing was indeed Snow's janitor.

The Wisconsin bike rider is also male. Snow picks out two large bones that look something like twisted oysters—the innominates, or hipbones, which along with the sacrum, or lower backbone, form the pelvis. This pelvis is narrow and steep-walled like a male's, not broad and shallow like a female's. And the sciatic notch (the V-shaped space where the sciatic nerve passes through the hipbone) is narrow, as is normal in a male. Snow can also determine a skeleton's sex by checking the size of the mastoid processes (the bony knobs at the base of the skull) and the prominence of the brow ridge, or by measuring the head of an available limb bone, which is typically broader in males.

From an examination of the skull he concludes that the bike rider is "predominantly Caucasoid." A score of bony traits help the forensic anthropologist assign a skeleton to one of the three major racial groups: Negroid, Caucasoid, or Mongoloid. Snow notes that the ridge of the boy's nose is high and salient, as it is in whites. In Negroids and Mongoloids (which include American Indians as well as most Asians) the nose tends to be broad in relation to its height. However, the boy's nasal margins are somewhat smoothed down, usually a Mongoloid feature. "Possibly a bit of American Indian admixture," says Snow. "Do you have Indians in your area?" Hibbard nods.

Age is next. Snow takes the skull and turns it upside down, pointing out the basilar joint, the junction between the two major bones that form the underside of the skull. In a child the joint would still be open to allow room for growth, but here the joint has fused—something that usually happens in the late teen years. On the other hand, he says, pointing to the zigzagging lines on the dome of the skull, the cranial sutures are open. The cranial sutures, which join the bones of the braincase, begin to fuse and disappear in the mid-twenties.

Next Snow picks up a femur and looks for signs of growth at the point where the shaft meets the knobbed end. The thin plates of cartilage—areas of incomplete calcification—that are visible at this point suggest that the boy hadn't yet attained his full height. Snow double-checks with an examination of the pubic symphysis, the joint where the two hipbones meet. The ridges in this area, which fill in and smooth over in adulthood, are still clearly marked. He concludes that the skeleton is that of a boy between 15 and 20 years old.

"One of the things you learn is to be pretty conservative," says Snow. "It's very impressive when you tell the police, 'This person is eighteen years old,' and he turns out to be eighteen. The problem is, if the person is fifteen you've blown it—you probably won't find him. Looking for a missing person is like trying to catch fish. Better get a big net and do your own sorting."

Snow then picks up a leg bone, measures it with a set of calipers, and enters the data into a portable computer. Using the known correlation between the height and length of the long limb bones, he quickly estimates the boy's height. "He's five foot six and a half to five foot eleven," says Snow. "Medium build, not excessively muscular, judging from the muscle attachments that we see." He points to the grainy ridges that appear where muscle attaches itself to the bone. The most prominent attachments show up on the teenager's right arm bone, indicating right-handedness.

Then Snow examines the ribs one by one for signs of injury. He finds no stab wounds, cuts, or bullet holes, here or elsewhere on the skeleton. He picks up the hyoid bone from the boy's throat and looks for the tell-tale fracture signs that would suggest the boy was strangled. But, to Snow's frustration, he can find no obvious cause of death. In hopes of identifying the missing teenager, he suggests sending the skull, hair, and boy's description to Betty Pat Gatliff, a medical illustrator and sculptor in Oklahoma who does facial reconstructions.

Six weeks later photographs of the boy's likeness appear in the *Milwaukee Sentinel*. "If you persist long enough," says Snow, "eighty-five to ninety percent of the cases eventually get positively identified, but it can take anywhere from a few weeks to a few years."

Snow and Gatliff have collaborated many times, but never with more glitz than in 1983, when Snow was commissioned by Patrick Barry, a Miami orthopedic surgeon and amateur Egyptologist, to reconstruct the face of the Egyptian boy-king Tutankhamen. Normally a facial reconstruction begins with a skull, but since Tutankhamen's 3,000-year-old remains were in Egypt, Snow had to make do with the skull measurements from a 1925 postmortem and X-rays taken in 1975. A plaster model of the skull was made, and on the basis of Snow's report—"his skull is Caucasoid with some Negroid admixtures"—Gatliff put a face on it. What did Tutankhamen look like? Very much like the gold mask on his sarcophagus, says Snow, confirming that it was, indeed, his portrait.

Many cite Snow's use of facial reconstructions as one of his most important contributions to the field. Snow, typically self-effacing, says that Gatliff "does all the work." The identification of skeletal remains, he stresses, is often a collaboration between pathologists, odontologists, radiologists, and medical artists using a variety of forensic techniques.

One of Snow's last tasks at the FAA was to help identify the dead from the worst airline accident in U.S. history. On May 25, 1979, a DC-10 crashed shortly after takeoff from Chicago's O'Hare Airport, killing 273 people. The task facing Snow and more than a dozen forensic specialists was horrific. "No one ever sat down and counted," says Snow, "but we estimated ten thousand to twelve thousand pieces or parts of bodies." Nearly 80 percent of the victims were identified on the basis of dental evidence and fingerprints. Snow and forensic radiologist John Fitzpatrick later managed to identify two dozen others by comparing postmortem X-rays with X-rays taken during the victim's lifetime.

Next to dental records, such X-ray comparisons are the most common way of obtaining positive identifications. In 1978, when a congressional committee reviewed the evidence on John F. Kennedy's assassination, Snow used X-rays to show that the body autopsied at Bethesda Naval Hospital was indeed that of the late president and had not—as some conspiracy theorists believed—been switched.

The issue was resolved on the evidence of Kennedy's "sinus print," the scalloplike pattern on the upper margins of the sinuses that is visible in X-rays of the forehead. So characteristic is a person's sinus print that courts throughout the world accept the matching of antemortem and postmortem X-rays of the sinuses as positive identification.

Yet another technique in the forensic specialist's repertoire is photo superposition. Snow used it in 1977 to help identify the mummy of a famous Oklahoma outlaw named Elmer J. McCurdy, who was killed by a posse after holding up a train in 1911. For years the mummy had been exhibited as a "dummy" in a California funhouse—until it was found to have a real human skeleton inside it. Ownership of the mummy was eventually traced back to a funeral parlor in Oklahoma, where McCurdy had been embalmed and exhibited as "the bandit who wouldn't give up."

Using two video cameras and an image processor, Snow superposed the mummy's profile on a photograph of McCurdy that was taken shortly after his death. When displayed on a single monitor, the two coincided to a remarkable degree. Convinced by the evidence, Thomas Noguchi, then Los Angeles County coroner, signed McCurdy's death certificate ("Last known occupation: Train robber") and allowed the outlaw's bones to be returned to Oklahoma for a decent burial.

It was this technique that also allowed forensic scientists to identify the remains of the Nazi "Angel of Death," Josef Mengele, in the summer of 1985. A team of investigators, including Snow and West German forensic anthropologist Richard Helmer, flew to Brazil after an Austrian couple claimed that Mengele lay buried in a grave on a São Paulo hillside. Tests revealed that the stature, age, and hair color of the unearthed skeleton were consistent with information in Mengele's SS files; yet without X-rays or dental records, the scientists still lacked conclusive evidence. When an image of the reconstructed skull was superposed on 1930s photographs of Mengele, however, the match was eerily compelling. All doubts were removed a few months later when Mengele's dental X-rays were tracked down.

In 1979 Snow retired from the FAA to the rolling hills of Norman, Oklahoma, where he and his wife, Jerry, live in a sprawling, early-1960s ranch house. Unlike his 50 or so fellow forensic anthropologists, most of whom are tied to academic positions, Snow is free to pursue his consultancy work full-time. Judging from the number of miles that he logs in the average month, Snow is clearly not ready to retire for good.

His recent projects include a reexamination of the skeletal remains found at the site of the Battle of the Little Bighorn, where more than a century ago Custer and his 210 men were killed by Sioux and Cheyenne warriors. Although most of the enlisted men's remains were moved to a mass grave in 1881, an excavation of the battlefield in the past few years uncovered an additional 375 bones and 36 teeth. Snow, teaming up again with Fitzpatrick, determined that these remains belonged to 34 individuals.

The historical accounts of Custer's desperate last stand are vividly confirmed by their findings. Snow identified one skeleton as that of a soldier between the ages of 19 and 23 who weighed around 150 pounds and stood about five foot eight. He'd sustained gunshot wounds to his chest and left forearm. Heavy blows to his head had fractured his skull and sheared off his teeth. Gashed thigh bones indicated that his body was later dismembered with an ax or hatchet.

Given the condition and number of the bodies, Snow seriously questions the accuracy of the identifications made by the original nineteenth-century burial crews. He doubts, for example, that the skeleton buried at West Point is General Custer's.

For the last four years Snow has devoted much of his time to helping two countries come to terms with the horrors of a much more recent past. As part of a group sponsored by the American Association for the Advancement of Science, he has been helping the Argentinian National Commission on Disappeared Persons to determine the fate of some of those who vanished during their country's harsh military rule: between 1976 and 1983 at least 10,000 people were systematically swept off the streets by roving death squads to be tortured, killed, and buried in unmarked graves. In December 1986, at the invitation of the Aquino government's Human Rights Commission, Snow also spent several weeks training Philippine scientists to investigate the disappearances that occurred under the Marcos regime.

But it is in Argentina where Snow has done the bulk of his human-rights work. He has spent more than 27 months in and around Buenos Aires, first training a small group of local medical and anthropology students in the techniques of forensic investigation, and later helping them carefully exhume and examine scores of the *desaparecidos,* or disappeared ones.

Only 25 victims have so far been positively identified. But the evidence has helped convict seven junta members and other high-ranking military and police officers. The idea is not necessarily to identify all 10,000 of the missing, says Snow. "If you have a colonel who ran a detention center where maybe five hundred people were killed, you don't have to nail him with five hundred deaths. Just one or two should be sufficient to get him convicted." Forensic evidence from Snow's team may be used to prosecute several other military officers, including General Suarez Mason. Mason is the former commander of the I Army Corps in Buenos Aires and is believed to be responsible for thousands of disappearances. He was recently extradited from San Francisco back to Argentina, where he is expected to stand trial this winter [1988].

The investigations have been hampered by a frustrating lack of antemortem information. In 1984, when commission lawyers took depositions from relatives and friends of the disappeared, they often failed to obtain such basic information as the victim's height, weight, or hair color. Nor did they ask for the missing person's X-rays (which in Argentina are given to the patient) or the address of the victim's dentist. The problem was compounded by the inexperience of those who carried out the first mass exhumations prior to Snow's arrival. Many of the skeletons were inadvertently destroyed by bulldozers as they were brought up.

Every unearthed skeleton that shows signs of gunfire, however, helps to erode the claim once made by many in the Argentinian military that most of the *desaparecidos* are alive and well and living in Mexico City, Madrid, or Paris. Snow recalls the case of a 17-year-old boy named Gabriel Dunayavich, who disappeared in the summer of 1976. He was walking home from a movie with his girlfriend when a Ford Falcon with no license plates snatched him off the street. The police later found his body and that of another boy and girl dumped by the roadside on the outskirts of Buenos Aires. The police went through the motions of an investigation, taking photographs and doing an autopsy, then buried the three teenagers in an unmarked grave.

A decade later Snow, with the help of the boy's family, traced the autopsy reports, the police photographs, and the grave of the three youngsters. Each of them had four or five closely spaced bullet wounds in the upper chest—the signature, says Snow, of an automatic weapon. Two also had wounds on their arms from bullets that had entered behind the elbow and exited from the forearm.

"That means they were conscious when they were shot," says Snow. "When a gun was pointed at them, they naturally raised their arm." It's details like these that help to authenticate the last moments of the victims and bring a dimension of reality to the judges and jury.

Each time Snow returns from Argentina he says that this will be the last time. A few months later he is back in Buenos Aires. "There's always more work to do," he says. It is, he admits quietly, "terrible work."

"These were such brutal, cold-blooded crimes," he says. "The people who committed them not only murdered; they had a system to eliminate all trace that their victims even existed."

Snow will not let them obliterate their crimes so conveniently. "There are human-rights violations going on all around the world," he says. "But to me murder is murder, regardless of the motive. I hope that we are sending a message to governments who murder in the name of politics that they can be held to account."

TRENDS IN BEHAVIORAL GENETICS

EUGENICS REVISITED

Scientists are linking genes to a host of complex human disorders and traits, but just how valid—and useful—are these findings?

John Horgan, *senior writer*

"How to Tell If Your Child's a Serial Killer!" That was the sound bite with which the television show *Donahue* sought to entice listeners February 25. On the program, a psychiatrist from the Rochester, N.Y., area noted that some men are born with not one Y chromosome but two. Double-Y men, the psychiatrist said, are "at special risk for antisocial, violent behavior." In fact, the psychiatrist had recently studied such a man. Although he had grown up in a "Norman Rockwell" setting, as an adult he had strangled at least 11 women and two children.

"It is not hysterical or overstating it," Phil Donahue told his horrified audience, "to say that we are moving toward the time when, quite literally, just as we can anticipate . . . genetic predispositions toward various physical diseases, we will also be able to pinpoint mental disorders which include aggression, antisocial behavior and the possibility of very serious criminal activity later on."

Eugenics is back in fashion. The message that genetics can explain, predict and even modify human behavior for the betterment of society is promulgated not just on sensationalistic talk shows but by our most prominent scientists. James D. Watson, co-discoverer of the double-helix structure of DNA and former head of the Human Genome Project, the massive effort to map our entire genetic endowment, said recently, "We used to think that our fate was in our stars. Now we know, in large part, that our fate is in our genes."

Daniel E. Koshland, Jr., a biologist at the University of California at Berkeley and editor of *Science*, the most influential peer-reviewed journal in the U.S., has declared in an editorial that the nature/nurture debate is "basically over," since scientists have shown that genes influence many aspects of human behavior. He has also contended that genetic research may help eliminate society's most intractable problems, including drug abuse, homelessness and, yes, violent crime.

Some studies cited to back this claim are remarkably similar to those conducted over a century ago by scientists such as Francis Galton, known as the father of eugenics. Just as the British polymath studied identical twins in order to show that "nature prevails enormously over nurture," so do modern researchers. But the primary reason behind the revival of eugenics is the astonishing successes of biologists in mapping and manipulating the human genome. Over the past decade, investigators have identified genes underlying such crippling diseases as cystic fibrosis, muscular dystrophy and, this past spring, Huntington's disease. Given these advances, researchers say, it is only a matter of time before they can lay bare the genetic foundation of much more complex traits and disorders.

The political base for eugenics has also become considerably broader in recent years. Spokespersons for the mentally ill believe demonstrating the genetic basis of disorders such as schizophrenia and manic depression—and even alcoholism and drug addiction—will lead not only to better diagnoses and

treatments but also to more compassion toward sufferers and their families. Some homosexuals believe society will become more tolerant toward them if it can be shown that sexual orientation is an innate, biological condition and not a matter of choice.

But critics contend that no good can come of bad science. Far from moving inexorably closer to its goals, they point out, the field of behavioral genetics is mired in the same problems that have always plagued it. Behavioral traits are extraordinarily difficult to define, and practically every claim of a genetic basis can also be explained as an environmental effect. "This has been a huge enterprise, and for the most part the work has been done shoddily. Even careful people get sucked into misinterpreting data," says Jonathan Beckwith, a geneticist at Harvard University. He adds, "There are social consequences to this."

The skeptics also accuse the media of having created an unrealistically optimistic view of the field. Richard C. Lewontin, a biologist at Harvard and a prominent critic of behavioral genetics, contends that the media generally give much more prominent coverage to dramatic reports—such as the discovery of an "alcoholism gene"—than to contradictory results or retractions. "Skepticism doesn't make the news," Lewontin says. "It only makes the news when you find a gene." The result is that spurious findings often become accepted by the public and even by so-called experts.

The claim that men with an extra Y chromosome are predisposed toward violence is a case in point. It stems from a survey in the 1960s that found more extra-Y men in prison than in the general population. Some researchers hypothesized that since the Y chromo-

"EERIE" PARALLELS between identical twins raised apart—such as Jerry Levey (*left*) and Mark Newman, who both became firefighters—are said to support genetic models of human behavior. Yet skeptics say the significance of such coincidences has been exaggerated.

some confers male attributes, men with an extra Y become hyperaggressive "supermales." Follow-up studies indicated that while extra-Y men tend to be taller than other men and score slightly lower on intelligence tests, they are otherwise normal. The National Academy of Sciences concluded in a report published this year that there is no evidence to support the link between the extra Y chromosome and violent behavior.

Minnesota Twins

No research in behavioral genetics has been more eagerly embraced by the press than the identical-twin studies done at the University of Minnesota. Thomas J. Bouchard, Jr., a psychologist, initiated them in the late 1970s, and since then they have been featured in the *Washington Post, Newsweek,* the *New York Times* and other publications worldwide as well as on television. *Science* has favorably described the Minnesota team's work in several news stories and in 1990 published a major article by the group.

The workers have studied more than 50 pairs of identical twins who were separated shortly after birth and raised in different households. The assumption is that any differences between identical twins, who share all each other's genes, are caused by the environment; similarities are attributed to their shared genes. The group estimates the relative contribution of genes to a given trait in a term called "heritability." A trait that stems entirely from genes, such as eye color, is defined as 100 percent heritable. Height is 90 percent heritable; that is, 90 percent of the variation in height is accounted for by genetic variation, and the other 10 percent is accounted for by diet and other environmental factors.

The Minnesota group has reported finding a strong genetic contribution to practically all the traits it has examined. Whereas most previous studies have estimated the heritability of intelligence (as defined by performance on intelligence tests) as roughly 50 percent, Bouchard and his colleagues arrived at a figure of 70 percent. They have also found a genetic component underlying such culturally defined traits as religiosity, political orientation (conservative versus liberal), job satisfaction, leisure-time interests and proneness to divorce. In fact, the group concluded in *Science,* "On multiple measures of personality and temperament...monozygotic twins reared apart are about as similar as are monozygotic twins reared together." (Identical twins are called monozygotic because they stem from a single fertilized egg, or zygote.)

The researchers have buttressed their statistical findings with anecdotes about "eerie," "bewitching" and "remarkable" parallels between reunited twins. One case involved Oskar, who was raised as a Nazi in Czechoslovakia, and Jack, who was raised as a Jew in Trinidad. Both were reportedly wearing shirts with epaulets when they were reunited by the Minnesota group in 1979. They also both flushed the toilet before as well as after using it and enjoyed deliberately sneezing to startle people in elevators.

Some other celebrated cases involved two British women who wore seven rings and named their firstborn sons Richard Andrew and Andrew Richard; two men who both had been named Jim, named their pet dogs Toy, married women named Linda, divorced them and remarried women named Betty; and two men who had become firefighters and drank Budweiser beer.

Other twin researchers say the significance of these coincidences has been greatly exaggerated. Richard J. Rose of Indiana University, who is collaborating on a study of 16,000 pairs of twins in Finland, points out that "if you bring together strangers who were born on the same day in the same country and ask them to find similarities between them, you may find a lot of seemingly astounding coincidences."

Rose's collaborator, Jaakko Kaprio of the University of Helsinki, notes that the Minnesota twin studies may also be biased by their selection method. Whereas he and Rose gather data by combing birth registries and sending questionnaires to those identified as twins, the Minnesota group relies heavily on media coverage to recruit new twins. The twins then come to Minnesota for a week of study—and, often, further publicity. Twins who are "interested in publicity and willing to support it," Kaprio says, may be atypical. This self-selection effect, he adds, may explain why the Bouchard group's estimates of heritability tend to be higher than those of other studies.

One of the most outspoken critics of

the Minnesota twin studies—and indeed all twin studies indicating high heritability of behavioral traits—is Leon J. Kamin, a psychologist at Northeastern University. In the 1970s Kamin helped to expose inconsistencies and possible fraud in studies of separated identical twins conducted by the British psychologist Cyril Burt during the previous two decades. Burt's conclusion that intelligence was mostly inherited had inspired various observers, notably Arthur R. Jensen, a psychologist at the University of California at Berkeley, to argue that socioeconomic stratification in the U.S. is largely a genetic phenomenon.

In his investigations of other twin studies, Kamin has shown that identical twins supposedly raised apart are often raised by members of their family or by unrelated families in the same neighborhood; some twins had extensive contact with each other while growing up. Kamin suspects the same may be true of some Minnesota twins. He notes, for example, that some news accounts suggested Oskar and Jack (the Nazi and the Jew) and the two British women wearing seven rings were reunited for the first time when they arrived in Minnesota to be studied by Bouchard. Actually, both pairs of twins had met previously. Kamin has repeatedly asked the Minnesota group for detailed case histories of its twins to determine whether it has underestimated contact and similarities in upbringing. "They've never responded," he says.

Kamin proposes that the Minnesota twins have particularly strong motives to downplay previous contacts and to exaggerate their similarities. They might want to please researchers, to attract more attention from the media or even to make money. In fact, some twins acquired agents and were paid for appearances on television. Jack and Oskar recently sold their life story to a film producer in Los Angeles (who says Robert Duvall is interested in the roles).

Even the Minnesota researchers caution against overinterpretation of their work. They agree with their critics that high heritability should not be equated with inevitability, since the environment can still drastically affect the expression of a gene. For example, the genetic disease phenylketonuria, which causes profound retardation, has a heritability of 100 percent. Yet eliminating the amino acid phenylalanine from the diet of affected persons prevents retardation from occurring.

Such warnings tend to be minimized in media coverage, however. Writers often make the same inference that Koshland did in an editorial in *Science:* "Bet-

ter schools, a better environment, better counseling and better rehabilitation will help some individuals but not all." The prime minister of Singapore apparently reached the same conclusion. A decade ago he cited popular accounts of the Minnesota research in defending policies that encouraged middle-class Singaporeans to bear children and discouraged childbearing by the poor.

Smart Genes

Twin studies, of course, do not indicate which specific genes contribute to a trait. Early in the 1980s scientists began developing powerful ways to unearth that information. The techniques stem from the fact that certain stretches of human DNA, called polymorphisms, vary in a predictable way. If a polymorphism is consistently inherited together with a given trait—blue eyes, for example—then geneticists assume it either lies near a gene for that trait or actually is the gene. A polymorphism that merely lies near a gene is known as a marker.

In so-called linkage studies, investigators search for polymorphisms co-inherited with a trait in families unusually prone to the trait. In 1983 researchers used this method to find a marker linked to Huntington's disease, a crippling neurological disorder that usually strikes carriers in middle age and kills them within 10 years. Since then, the same technique has pinpointed genes for cystic fibrosis, muscular dystrophy and other diseases. In association studies, researchers compare the relative frequency of polymorphisms in two unrelated populations, one with the trait and one lacking it.

Workers are already using both methods to search for polymorphisms associated with intelligence, defined as the ability to score well on standardized intelligence tests. In 1991 Shelley D. Smith of the Boys Town National Institute for Communication Disorders in Children, in Omaha, and David W. Fulker of the University of Colorado identified polymorphisms associated with dyslexia in a linkage study of 19 families exhibiting high incidence of the reading disorder.

Behavioral Genetics: A Lack-of-Progress Report

CRIME: Family, twin and adoption studies have suggested a heritability of 0 to more than 50 percent for predisposition to crime. (Heritability represents the degree to which a trait stems from genetic factors.) In the 1960s researchers reported an association between an extra Y chromosome and violent crime in males. Follow-up studies found that association to be spurious.

MANIC DEPRESSION: Twin and family studies indicate heritability of 60 to 80 percent for susceptibility to manic depression. In 1987 two groups reported locating different genes linked to manic depression, one in Amish families and the other in Israeli families. Both reports have been retracted.

SCHIZOPHRENIA: Twin studies show heritability of 40 to 90 percent. In 1988 a group reported finding a gene linked to schizophrenia in British and Icelandic families. Other studies documented no linkage, and the initial claim has now been retracted.

ALCOHOLISM: Twin and adoption studies suggest heritability ranging from 0 to 60 percent. In 1990 a group claimed to link a gene—one that produces a receptor for the neurotransmitter dopamine—with alcoholism. A recent review of the evidence concluded it does not support a link.

INTELLIGENCE: Twin and adoption studies show a heritability of performance on intelligence tests of 20 to 80 percent. One group recently unveiled preliminary evidence for genetic markers for high intelligence (an IQ of 130 or higher). The study is unpublished.

HOMOSEXUALITY: In 1991 a researcher cited anatomic differences between the brains of heterosexual and homosexual males. Two recent twin studies have found a heritability of roughly 50 percent for predisposition to male or female homosexuality. These reports have been disputed. Another group claims to have preliminary evidence of genes linked to male homosexuality. The data have not been published.

Two years ago Robert Plomin, a psychologist at Pennsylvania State University who has long been active in behavioral genetics, received a $600,000 grant from the National Institute of Child Health and Human Development to search for genes linked to high intelligence. Plomin is using the association method, which he says is more suited than the linkage technique to identifying genes whose contribution to a trait is relatively small. Plomin is studying a group of 64 schoolchildren 12 to 13 years old who fall into three groups: those who score approximately 130, 100 and 80 on intelligence tests.

Plomin has examined some 25 polymorphisms in each of these three groups, trying to determine whether any occur with greater frequency in the "bright" children. The polymorphisms have been linked to genes thought to have neurological effects. He has uncovered several markers that seem to occur more often in the highest-scoring children. He is now seeking to replicate his results in another group of 60 children; half score above 142 on intelligence tests, and half score less than 74 (yet have no obvious organic deficiencies). Plomin presented his preliminary findings at a meeting, titled "Origins and Development of High Ability," held in London in January.

At the same meeting, however, other workers offered evidence that intelligence tests are actually poor predictors of success in business, the arts or even advanced academic programs. Indeed, even Plomin seems ambivalent about the value of his research. He suggests that someday genetic information on the cognitive abilities of children might help teachers design lessons that are more suited to students' innate strengths and weaknesses.

But he also calls his approach "a fishing expedition," given that a large number of genes may contribute to intelligence. He thinks the heritability of intelligence is not 70 percent, as the Minnesota twin researchers have claimed, but 50 percent, which is the average finding of other studies, and at best he can only find a gene that accounts for a tiny part of variance in intelligence. "If you wanted to select on the basis of this, it would be of no use whatsoever," he remarks. These cautions did not prevent the *Sunday Telegraph*, a London newspaper, from announcing that Plomin had found "evidence that geniuses are born not made."

Evan S. Balaban, a biologist at Harvard, thinks Plomin's fishing expedition is doomed to fail. He grants that there may well be a significant genetic compo-

nent to intelligence (while insisting that studies by Bouchard and others have not demonstrated one). But he doubts whether investigators will ever uncover any specific genes related to high intelligence or "genius." "It is very rare to find genes that have a specific effect," he says. "For evolutionary reasons, this just doesn't happen very often."

The history of the search for markers associated with mental illness supports Balaban's view. Over the past few decades, studies of twins, families and adoptees have convinced most investigators that schizophrenia and manic depression are not caused by psychosocial factors—such as the notorious "schizophrenogenic mother" postulated by some Freudian psychiatrists—but by biological and genetic factors. After observing the dramatic success of linkage studies in the early 1980s, researchers immediately began using the technique to isolate polymorphic markers for mental illness. The potential value of such research was enormous, given that schizophrenia and manic depression each affect roughly one percent of the global population.

They seemed to have achieved their first great success in 1987. A group led by Janice A. Egeland of the University of Miami School of Medicine claimed it had linked a genetic marker on chromosome 11 to manic depression in an Amish population. That same year another team, led by Miron Baron of Columbia University, linked a marker on the X chromosome to manic depression in three Israeli families.

The media hailed these announcements as major breakthroughs. Far less attention was paid to the retractions that followed. A more extensive analysis of the Amish in 1989 by a group from the National Institute of Mental Health turned up no link between chromosome 11 and manic depression. This year Baron's team retracted its claim of linkage with the X chromosome after doing a new study of its Israeli families with more sophisticated markers and more extensive diagnoses.

Schizophrenic Results

Studies of schizophrenia have followed a remarkably similar course. In 1988 a group headed by Hugh M. D. Gurling of the University College, London, Medical School announced in *Nature* that it had found linkage in Icelandic and British families between genetic markers on chromosome 5 and schizophrenia. In the same issue, however, researchers led by Kenneth K. Kidd of Yale University reported seeing no such

linkage in a Swedish family. Although Gurling defended his result as legitimate for several years, additional research has convinced him that it was probably a false positive. "The new families showed no linkage at all," he says.

These disappointments have highlighted the problems involved in using linkage to study mental illness. Neil Risch, a geneticist at Yale, points out that linkage analysis is ideal for studying diseases, such as Huntington's, that have distinct symptoms and are caused by a single dominant gene. Some researchers had hoped that at least certain subtypes of schizophrenia or manic depression might be single-gene disorders. Single-gene mutations are thought to cause variants of breast cancer and of Alzheimer's disease that run in families and are manifested much earlier than usual. But such diseases are rare, Risch says, because natural selection quickly winnows them out of the population, and no evidence exists for distinct subtypes of manic depression or schizophrenia.

Indeed, all the available evidence suggests that schizophrenia and manic depression are caused by at least several genes—each of which may exert only a tiny influence—acting in concert with environmental influences. Finding such genes with linkage analysis may not be impossible, Risch says, but it will be considerably more difficult than identifying genes that have a one-to-one correspondence to a trait. The difficulty is compounded by the fact that the diagnosis of mental illness is often subjective—all the more so when researchers are relying on family records or recollections.

Some experts now question whether genes play a significant role in mental illness. "Personally, I think we have overestimated the genetic component of schizophrenia," says E. Fuller Torrey, a psychiatrist at St. Elizabeth's Hospital in Washington, D.C. He argues that the evidence supporting genetic models can be explained by other biological factors, such as a virus that strikes in utero. The pattern of incidence of schizophrenia in families often resembles that of other viral diseases, such as polio. "Genes may just create a susceptibility to the virus," Torrey explains.

The Drink Link

Even Kidd, the Yale geneticist who has devoted his career to searching for genes linked to mental illness, acknowledges that "in a rigorous, technical, scientific sense, there is very little proof that schizophrenia, manic depression" and other psychiatric disorders have a genetic origin. "Virtually all the evidence supports a genetic explanation, but there are always other explanations, even if they are convoluted."

The evidence for a genetic basis for alcoholism is even more tentative than that for manic depression and schizophrenia. Although some studies discern a genetic component, especially in males, others have reached the opposite conclusion. Gurling, the University College investigator, found a decade ago that identical twins were slightly *more* likely to be discordant for alcoholism than fraternal twins. The drinking habits of some identical twins were strikingly different. "In some cases, one drank a few bottles a day, and the other didn't drink at all," Gurling says.

Nevertheless, in 1990 a group led by Kenneth Blum of the University of Texas Health Science Center at San Antonio announced it had discovered a genetic marker for alcoholism in an association study comparing 35 alcoholics with a control group of 35 nonalcoholics. A page-one story in the *New York Times* portrayed the research as a potential watershed in the diagnosis and treatment of alcoholism without mentioning the considerable skepticism aroused among other researchers.

The Blum group claimed that its marker, called the A1 allele, was associated with a gene, called the D2 gene, that codes for a receptor for the neurotransmitter dopamine. Skeptics noted that the A1 allele was actually some 10,000 base pairs from the dopamine-receptor gene and was not linked to any detectable variation in its expression.

Since the initial announcement by Blum, three papers, including an additional one by Blum's group, have presented more evidence of an association between the A1 allele and alcoholism. Six groups have found no such evidence (and received virtually no mention in the popular media).

In April, Risch and Joel Gelernter of Yale and David Goldman of the National Institute on Alcohol Abuse and Alcoholism analyzed all these studies on the A1 allele in a paper in the *Journal of the American Medical Association.* They noted that if Blum's two studies are cast aside, the balance of the results shows no association between the D2 receptor and alcoholism, either in the disor-

BRAIN OF SCHIZOPHRENIC (*right*) appears different from the brain of his identical twin in these magnetic resonance images. Such findings suggest that factors that are biological but not genetic—such as viruses—may play a significant role in mental illness.

der's milder or most severe forms. "We therefore conclude that no physiologically significant association" between the A1 allele and alcoholism has been proved, the group stated. "It's a dead issue," Risch says.

Gelernter and his colleagues point out that association studies are prone to spurious results if not properly controlled. They suggest that the positive findings of Blum and his colleagues may have derived from a failure to control for ethnic variation. The limited surveys done so far have shown that the incidence of the A1 allele varies wildly in different ethnic groups, ranging from 10 percent in certain Jewish groups to about 50 percent in Japanese.

Blum insists that the ethnic data, far from undermining his case, support it, since those groups with the highest prevalence of the A1 allele also exhibit the highest rates of "addictive behavior." He contends that the only reason the Japanese do not display higher rates of alcoholism is that many also carry a gene that prevents them from metabolizing alcohol. "They're pretty compulsive," explains Blum, who recently obtained a patent for a genetic test for alcoholism.

These arguments have been rejected even by Irving I. Gottesman of the University of Virginia, who is a strong defender of genetic models of human behavior. He considers the papers cited by Blum to support his case to be ambiguous and even contradictory. Some see an association only with alcoholism that leads to medical complications or even death; others discern no association with alcoholism but only with "polysubstance abuse," including cigarette smoking. "I think it is by and large

garbage," Gottesman says of the alleged A1-alcoholism link.

By far the most controversial area of behavioral genetics is research on crime. Last fall complaints by civil-rights leaders and others led the National Institutes of Health to withdraw its funding from a meeting entitled "Genetic Factors in Crime: Findings, Uses and Implications." The conference brochure had noted the "apparent failure of environmental approaches to crime" and suggested that genetic research might yield methods for identifying and treating potential criminals—and particularly those prone to violence—at an early age.

Critics contend that such investigations inevitably suggest that blacks are predisposed to crime, given that blacks in the U.S. are six times more likely than whites to be arrested for a violent crime. In fact, some prominent scientists, notably Richard J. Herrnstein, a psychologist at Harvard, have made this assertion. Others reject this view but insist biological research on attributes linked to violent crime, such as aggression, may still have some value. "People who are unwilling to address genetic and biochemical factors are just putting their heads in the sand," says Goldman, the alcoholism expert. "It is not fair to say that just because there have been geneticists who have had a very narrow view of this in the past, we shouldn't explore this now."

In fact, investigations of the biology of violent crime continue, albeit quietly. Workers at City of Hope Hospital in Duarte, Calif., claim to have found an association between the A1 allele—the alleged alcoholism marker—and "criminal aggression." Last year a group led

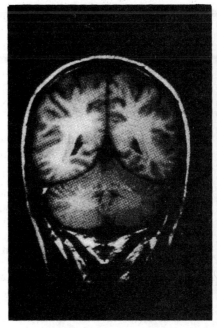
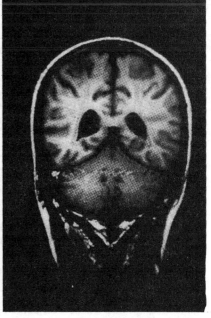

by Markus J. P. Kruesi of the University of Illinois at Chicago presented evidence of an association between low levels of the neurotransmitter serotonin and disruptive-behavior disorders in children. Kruesi concedes there is no way to determine whether the serotonin levels are genetically influenced. In fact, the serotonin levels might be an effect—a reaction to an environmental trauma—rather than a cause. "This might be a scar marker," he says.

One reason such research persists is that studies of families, twins and adoptees have suggested a genetic component to crime. Glenn D. Walters, a psychologist at the Federal Correctional Institution in Schuylkill, Pa., recently reviewed 38 of these studies, conducted from the 1930s to the present, in the journal *Criminology*. His meta-analysis turned up a small genetic effect, "but nothing to get excited about." He observes that "a lot of the research has not been very good" and that the more recent, better-designed studies tended to turn up less evidence. "I don't think we will find any biological markers for crime," he says. "We should put our resources elsewhere."

Gay Genes

The ostensible purpose of investigations of mental illness, alcoholism and even crime is to reduce their incidence. Scientists studying homosexuality have a different goal: simply to test whether homosexuality is innate, as many homosexuals have long professed. That claim was advanced by a report in *Science* in 1991 by Simon LeVay of the Salk Institute for Biological Studies in San Diego. LeVay has acknowledged both that he is gay and that he believes evidence of biological differences between homosexuals and heterosexuals will encourage tolerance toward gays.

LeVay, who recently left the Salk Institute to found the Institute of Gay and Lesbian Education, focused on a tiny neural structure in the hypothalamus, a region of the brain known to control sexual response. He measured this structure, called the interstitial nucleus, in autopsies of the brains of 19 homosexual males, 16 heterosexual males and six heterosexual women. LeVay found that the interstitial nucleus was almost twice as large in the heterosexual males as in the homosexual males or in the women. He postulated that the interstitial nucleus "is large in individuals oriented toward women"—whether male or female.

Of course, LeVay's finding only addresses anatomic differences, not nec-

The Huntington's Disease Saga: A Cautionary Tale

The identification of the gene for Huntington's disease, which was announced in March, was hailed as one of the great success stories of modern genetics. Yet it provides some rather sobering lessons for researchers seeking genes linked to more complex human disorders and traits.

The story begins in the late 1970s, when workers developed novel techniques for identifying polymorphisms, sections of the human genome that come in two or more forms. Investigators realized that by finding polymorphisms linked—always and exclusively—to diseases, they could determine which chromosome the gene resides in. Researchers decided to test the polymorphism technique on Huntington's disease, a devastating neurological disorder that affects roughly one in 10,000 people. Scientists had known for more than a century that Huntington's was caused by a mutant, dominant gene. If one parent has the disease, his or her offspring have a 50 percent chance of inheriting it.

One of the leaders of the Huntington's effort was Nancy Wexler, a neuropsychologist at Columbia University whose mother had died of the disease and who therefore has a 50 percent chance of developing it herself. She and other researchers focused on a poor Venezuelan village whose inhabitants had an unusually high incidence of the disease. In 1983, through what has now become a legendary stroke of good fortune, they found a linkage with one of the first polymorphisms they tested. The linkage indicated that the gene for Huntington's disease was somewhere on chromosome 4.

The finding led quickly to a test for determining whether offspring of carriers—either in utero or already born—have inherited the gene itself. The test requires an analysis of blood samples from several members of a family known to carry the disease. Wexler herself has declined to say whether she has taken the test.

Researchers assumed that they would quickly identify the actual gene in chromosome 4 that causes Huntington's disease. Yet it took 10 years for six teams of workers from 10 institutions to find the gene. It is a so-called expanding gene, which for unknown reasons gains base pairs (the chemical "rungs" binding two strands of DNA) every time it is transmitted. The greater the expansion of the gene, researchers say, the earlier the onset of the disease. The search was complicated by the fact that workers had no physical clues about the course of the disease to guide them. Indeed, Wexler and others emphasize that they still have no idea how the gene actually causes the disease; treatments or cures may be years or decades away.

The most immediate impact of the new discovery will be the development of a better test for Huntington's, one that requires blood only from the person at risk

essarily genetic ones. Various other researchers have tried to establish that homosexuality is not just biological in its origin—caused, perhaps, by hormonal influences in utero—but also genetic. Some have sought evidence in experiments with rats and other animals. A group headed by Angela Pattatucci of the National Cancer Institute is studying a strain of male fruit flies—which wags have dubbed either "fruity" or "fruitless"—that court other males.

In December 1991 J. Michael Bailey of Northwestern University and Richard C. Pillard of Boston University announced they had uncovered evidence of a genetic basis for male homosexuality in humans. They studied 161 gay men, each of whom had at least one identical or fraternal twin or adopted brother. The researchers determined that 52 percent of the identical twins were both

homosexual, as compared with 22 percent of the fraternal twins and 11 percent of the adopted brothers.

Bailey and Pillard derived similar results in a study of lesbians published this year in the *Archives of General Psychiatry*. They compared 147 gay women with identical or fraternal twins or adopted sisters: 48 percent of the identical twins were both gay, versus 16 percent of the fraternal twins (who share only half each other's genes) and 6 percent of the adopted sisters. "Both male and female sexual orientation appeared to be influenced by genetic factors," Bailey and Pillard concluded.

This conclusion has disturbed some of Bailey and Pillard's own subjects. "I have major questions about the validity of some of the assumptions they are making," says Nina Sossen, a gay woman living in Madison, Wis., whose identical twin is heterosexual. Her doubts

"Hierarchy of Worthlessness"

NANCY WEXLER helped to find the gene responsible for Huntington's disease by studying a population in Venezuela that has been ravaged by the disorder.

and not other family members. By measuring the length of the mutant gene, the test might also predict more accurately when carriers will show symptoms.

As difficult as it was to pinpoint the gene for Huntington's, it will be almost infinitely harder to discover genes for behavioral disorders, says Evan S. Balaban, a biologist at Harvard University. Unlike Huntington's disease, he notes, disorders such as schizophrenia and alcoholism cannot be unambiguously diagnosed. Furthermore, they stem not from a single dominant gene but from many genes acting in concert with environmental effects. If researchers do find a statistical association between certain genes and a trait, Balaban says, that knowledge may never be translated into useful therapies or tests. "What does it mean to have a 10 percent increased risk of alcoholism?" he asks.

are shared by William Byne, a psychiatrist at Columbia University. He notes that in their study of male homosexuality Bailey and Pillard found more concordance between unrelated, adopted brothers than related (but non-twin) brothers. The high concordance of the male and female identical twins, moreover, may stem from the fact that such twins are often dressed alike and treated alike—indeed, they are often mistaken for each other—by family members as well as by others.

"The increased concordance for homosexuality among the identical twins could be entirely accounted for by the increased similarity of their developmental experiences," Byne says. "In my opinion, the major finding of that study is that 48 percent of identical twins who were reared together were discordant for sexual orientation."

Byne also criticizes LeVay's conclusion that homosexuality must be biological—although not necessarily genetic—because the brains of male homosexuals resemble the brains of women. That assumption, Byne points out, rests on still another assumption, that there are significant anatomic differences between heterosexual male and female brains. But to date, there have been no replicable studies showing such sexual dimorphism.

Byne notes that he has been suspected of having an antigay motive. Two reviewers of an article he recently wrote criticizing homosexuality research accused him of having a "right-wing agenda," he says. He has also been contacted by conservative groups hoping he will speak out against the admittance of homosexuals to the military. He emphasizes that he supports gay rights and thinks homosexuality, whatever its cause, is not a "choice." He adds that genetic models of behavior are just as likely to foment bigotry as to quell it.

Despite the skepticism of Byne and others, at least one group, led by Dean Hamer of the National Cancer Institute, is searching not merely for anatomic or biochemical differences in homosexuals but for genetic markers. Hamer has done a linkage study of numerous small families, each of which has at least two gay brothers. He says his study has turned up some tentative findings, and he plans to submit his results soon. Hamer's colleague Pattatucci is planning a similar study of lesbians.

What purpose will be served by pinpointing genes linked to homosexuality? In an information sheet for prospective participants in his study, Hamer expresses the hope that his research may "improve understanding between people with different sexual orientations." He adds, "This study is not aimed at developing methods to alter either heterosexual or homosexual orientation, and the results of the study will not allow sexual orientation to be determined by a blood test or amniocentesis."

Yet even Pillard, who is gay and applauds Hamer's work, admits to some concern over the potential uses of a genetic marker for homosexuality. He notes that some parents might choose to abort embryos carrying such a marker. Male and female homosexuals might then retaliate, he says, by conceiving children and aborting fetuses that lacked such a gene.

Balaban, the Harvard biologist, thinks the possible dangers of such research—assuming it is successful—outweigh any benefits. Indeed, he sees behavioral genetics as a "hierarchy of worthlessness," with twin studies at the bottom and linkage studies of mental illness at the top. The best researchers can hope for is to find, say, a gene associated with a slightly elevated risk of schizophrenia. Such information is more likely to lead to discrimination by insurance companies and employers than to therapeutic benefits, Balaban warns.

His colleague Lewontin agrees. In the 1970s, he recalls, insurance companies began requiring black customers to take tests for sickle cell anemia, a genetic disease that primarily affects blacks. Those who refused to take the test or who tested positive were denied coverage. "I feel that this research is a substitute for what is really hard—finding out how to change social conditions," Lewontin remarks. "I think it's the wrong direction for research, given that we have a finite amount of resources."

Paul R. Billings, a geneticist at the California Pacific Medical Center, shares some of these concerns. He agrees that twin studies seem to be inherently ambiguous, and he urges researchers seeking markers for homosexuality to consider what a conservative government—led by Patrick Buchanan, for example—might allow to be done with such information. But he believes some aspects of behavioral genetics, particularly searches for genes underlying mental illness, are worth pursuing.

In an article published in the British journal *Social Science and Medicine* last year, Billings and two other scientists offered some constructive criticism for the field. Researchers engaged in association and linkage studies should establish "strict criteria as to what would constitute meaningful data." Both scientists and the press should emphasize the limitations of such studies, "especially when the mechanism of how a gene acts on a behavior is not known." Billings and his colleagues strive to end their article on a positive note. "Despite the shortcomings of other studies," they say, "there is relatively good evidence for a site on the X chromosome which is associated with [manic depression] in some families." This finding was retracted earlier this year.

"Better Breeding"

Fairly or not, modern genetics research is still haunted by the history of eugenics. "It offers a lot of cautionary lessons," says Daniel J. Kevles, a historian at the California Institute of Technology, who wrote the 1985 book *In the Name of Eugenics*. The British scientist Francis Galton, cousin to Charles Darwin, first proposed that human society could be improved "through better breeding" in 1865 in an article entitled "Hereditary Talent and Character." He coined the term "eugenics," from the Greek for "good birth," in 1883.

Galton's proposal had broad appeal. The American sexual libertarian John Humphrey Noyes bent eugenics into an ingenious argument for polygamy. "While the good man will be limited by his conscience to what the law allows," Noyes said, "the bad man, free from moral check, will distribute his seed beyond the legal limit."

A more serious advocate was the biologist Charles B. Davenport, founder of Cold Spring Harbor Laboratory and of the Eugenics Record Office, which gathered information on thousands of American families for genetic research. After demonstrating the heritability of eye, skin and hair color, Davenport went on to "prove" the heritability of traits such as "pauperism," criminality and "feeble-mindedness." In one monograph, published in 1919, he asserted that the ability to be a naval officer is an inherited trait, composed of subtraits for thalassophilia, or love of the sea, and hyperkineticism, or wanderlust. Noting the paucity of female naval officers, Davenport concluded that the trait is unique to males.

Beginning in the 1920s the American Eugenics Society, founded by Davenport and others, sponsored "Fitter Families Contests" at state fairs around the U.S. Just as cows and sheep were appraised by judges at the fairs, so were human entrants (such as the family shown above at the 1925 Texas State Fair). Less amusingly, eugenicists helped to persuade more than 20 U.S. states to authorize sterilization of men and women in prisons and mental hospitals, and they urged the federal government to restrict the immigration of "undesirable" races.

No nation, of course, practiced eugenics as enthusiastically as Nazi Germany, whose program culminated in "euthanasia" ("good death") of the mentally and physically disabled as well as Jews, Gypsies, Catholics and others. As revelations of these atrocities spread after World War II, popular support for eugenics programs waned in the U.S. and elsewhere.

The DNA Wars

Touted as an infallible method of identifying criminals, DNA matching has mired courts in a vicious battle of expert witnesses.

Edward Humes

Edward Humes is the author of "Murderer With a Badge," published by Dutton. He won a 1989 Pulitzer Prize for specialized reporting while at the Orange County Register.

The ambush was waiting for Prof. Laurence Mueller long before he arrived at the courthouse with his bar charts and slides and other hieroglyphs of science. You could see it in the deputy D.A.'s bear-trap smile, in the pile of dog-eared files he had amassed on Mueller's past courtroom performances, in the patiently highlighted inconsistencies ferreted out of those transcripts. The prosecutor and his experts were even making book—inaccurately, it turned out—that the good professor would wear his trademark tweed blazer, a coat that announces academe faster than any resume.

Mueller, a professor of evolutionary biology at UC Irvine, had been hired on behalf of an accused rapist to testify on the potentially eye-glazing subject of population genetics as it applies to that *Wunderkind* police technology, DNA "fingerprinting." With such a topic, his main concern should have been keeping the jury awake.

He needn't have worried. By the time Mueller left that courtroom in Santa Ana last spring, science, the presumptive subject of the day, had taken a back seat to more personal, and far more heated, topics. In short order, Mueller was branded a hired gun devoid of principles because he has earned more as an expert witness in DNA cases than as a university professor. As for his opinions, Mueller wasn't just proclaimed mistaken, he was accused of attempting to "lie with statistics" and of making deliberately erroneous conclusions with false data, a cardinal sin in the scientific world. (Mueller and his colleagues say his only sin was disagreeing with the government's experts.) Finally, Mueller was mocked for daring to apply lessons from his experiments with fruit flies to human genetics, even though the lowly fruit fly, with its prodigious birth rate, has been a staple of genetic science for most of this century.

LAURENCE MUELLER: The professor's opposition to DNA evidence has prompted vitriolic personal attacks.

The two-fisted, in-your-face cross-examination had jurors on the edges of their chairs and the defense lawyer itching to fling a similar attack at the prosecution's three experts. Which he did, with the same sort of biting accusations Mueller had withstood, charging the experts with ignoring data to reach false conclusions.

Funny thing was, Mueller declared the experience one of his milder courtroom bouts to date. More often than not, the verbal body blows get a lot nastier. "It was heated, yes, but not as bad as some," Mueller said. Later he added, "And I've taken a few other jackets out of mothballs."

Genetic printing, a once seemingly unassailable technology for identifying criminals through their DNA, has been stripped of its luster by a series of furious academic debates, vicious legal battles and highly personal attacks on scientists nationwide. Mueller's experience has become the rule, not the exception, and people on either side of the equation say that both justice and science are the ultimate casualties of this war.

DNA printing, it turns out, though an undeniably powerful tool for the police, is not the nearly infallible magic bullet for solving crimes its proponents once claimed. Bottom line: Much of the time this method of comparing a suspect's DNA to blood, semen or hair found at crime scenes works, sometimes it doesn't. And the close calls—when the spotty, ink-blot-like patterns of deoxyribonucleaic acid are blurred or faint—become so subjective that their utility is questionable. Matching a suspect's DNA to evidence from a crime scene becomes an art, not a science, with lives and liberty hanging in the balance.

This simple realization has created chaos in the courts. Judges and juries with no scientific training are being asked to decide which scientists are right: those who believe DNA printing works well, or those who believe it is fatally flawed. Each side is sincere. Each cites reams of data. Each boasts

From *Los Angeles Times Magazine*, November 29, 1992, pp. 20-22, 24, 26, 54-57. © 1992 by Edward Humes. Reprinted by permission.

impeccable resumes, and equally impeccable reasons for slamming those who disagree. So how do jurors know whether a complex technology is being used to convict the guilty, or to railroad the innocent? They can listen to hours of testimony and still not know. Innocents might be sent to Death Row, while killers are set free. It all depends on which side has the cleverest lawyers and the most persuasive scientists. Across the country, the confusion is so great that one judge can allow DNA printing as evidence while another, in the same state or even the same courthouse, could rule that the technology is still too unreliable.

And so, perhaps inevitably, a strange thing has happened as lawyers jockey for the sympathies of juries and jurists. Instead of the science, the scientists themselves are being challenged with unprecedented venom. Reputations have been tarnished, accusations of government conspiracies and defense lawyers' cabals have been thrown onto the fire and bitter rifts among researchers have arisen, making it increasingly difficult for them to work together to resolve the very debate causing the courtroom combat.

The reason for this lies in a long-standing legal principle that judges may admit new scientific evidence in the courtroom only when there is no significant debate within the scientific community over its validity. That means government prosecutors and experts who want to use DNA to convict people cannot simply disagree with scientists who question the reliability of genetic printing. They must discredit and denounce the critics, questioning their motives, ethics and abilities to show that there really is no legitimate debate. Defense lawyers have responded in kind, attacking with equal zest.

Scientists accustomed to the sterility of the laboratory and the decorum of university conferences have been left blinking in anger, and sometimes fear, at the withering attacks. Allegations of perjury and hidden conflicts of interest, smirking remarks about sexual orientation, insinuations about tax audits and immigration status—nothing is off-limits. Many researchers now simply

refuse to testify rather than face being shredded on the stand.

"It's not about science," says a rueful Mueller. "They are interested in dirty laundry."

ROCKNE HARMON: The deputy D.A. is noted for his use of DNA matching—and for discrediting its opponents.

"I'm not ashamed," counters Alameda County Deputy Dist. Atty. Rockne Harmon, a nationally prominent expert at using DNA evidence in court who has been equally prominent in efforts to discredit Mueller and other scientists critical of the technology. During charitable moments, he calls Mueller a "knucklehead." "A dangerous criminal," he says, "could be set free to rape, rob or kill people."

In short, the battle over DNA fingerprinting has become the most entertaining and bewildering legal spectacle around. With jurors and judges unsure just whom to believe, resolution is nowhere in sight.

By the end of last year, the FBI had performed 4,000 DNA comparisons in criminal cases, with private, state and county labs adding thousands more. In about a third of those cases, the tests cleared the suspect. But hundreds of people were prosecuted using DNA evidence in more than 40 states.

Most of these defendants were convicted, a testament to the power of this new scientific evidence. But even when DNA tests were ruled inadmissible, the suspects usually were still found guilty. In part, that is because prosecutors chose slam-dunk cases for their first DNA trials, under the theory that obviously guilty individuals were less likely to pursue appeals of the DNA portion of their cases. Only now are numbers of cases beginning to appear in which DNA is the key piece of evidence, the only link between a suspect and a crime.

In the earlier mold, one case stands out. In New York, a handyman by the name of Joseph Castro was accused of fatally stabbing a pregnant South Bronx woman and her 2-year-old daughter in February, 1987. Lifecodes Corp. of Valhalla, N.Y., one of three private labs in the United States that does forensic genetics testing, was hired by prosecutors to do a DNA analysis. Lifecodes' tests said the DNA from a tiny bloodstain on Castro's wristwatch matched the woman's genes, and that the odds against the blood belonging to someone else were 1 in 100 million.

But the Castro case represented the first full-blown challenge to DNA evidence. Castro's lawyers amassed a team of prestigious scientists, who examined Lifecodes' test results and found numerous errors. Even one of the prosecution experts, after conferring with the defense scientists, reversed himself and said that the vaunted 1 in 100 million match was wrong. The judge hearing Castro's case kicked the DNA evidence out.

Yet prosecutors also proclaimed a victory: Castro later pleaded guilty, admitting that the blood on his watch really had come from the victim. Prosecutors say the Castro case, in which the tests were accurate but ruled inadmissible, raises the specter of criminals' going free. Had there not been other, damning evidence in the case, they say, a double murderer would have walked. (In fact, although no national statistics are kept, experts on both sides of the DNA issue could recall only three or four defendants who won acquittals after DNA evidence was excluded.) Defense attorneys counter that bogus DNA evidence could just as easily convict an innocent person.

The prosecution of David Hicks, meanwhile, demonstrates another extreme—a case where DNA was the pivotal evidence despite problems with the test results. A young, unskilled laborer now on Death Row for the murder-rape of his grandmother in rural Freestone County, Tex., Hicks lacked the expert witnesses and skilled attorneys Castro had. The blurry DNA prints obtained in his case, and the 96 million to 1 probability of guilt announced by prosecution experts, again from Lifecodes, were barely challenged. The one expert hired for Hicks' defense, former UC Irvine geneticist Simon Ford, said he got such limited and late access to lab data that he was unprepared when he testified. Yet the defense attorney appointed to represent Hicks declined to ask for more time.

After Hicks was convicted in early 1989 and sentenced to death, Ford and other scientists, Laurence Mueller among them, reviewed the Lifecodes lab work and concluded that the DNA match was improperly done and vastly overstated. An accurate analysis, Ford estimates, would show not a 96 million to 1 probability that Hicks was the killer, but something on the order of hundreds to 1. Furthermore, in Furney-Richardson, Tex., population 300, where Hicks was born and lived, many residents are genetically related. Families have lived there, married their neighbors and passed around the same genetic patterns, the same DNA, for generations. Therefore, people in the community are far more likely to share DNA prints with Hicks—and the killer. Indeed, relatives of Hicks were suspects early in the case, raising an even greater possibility that the killer's DNA pattern could appear to match Hicks', yet not be his.

Hicks' jury never heard any of this because Ford never had a chance to do his analysis before the trial. Had they known, Hicks might easily have been acquitted, since there was little more than circumstantial evidence against him and no eyewitnesses, says William C. Thompson, the attorney and UC Irvine professor now helping Hicks to find legal representation for his appeal. Because of the certainty the 96 million to 1 finding implied, "the jurors were told that there was no way anyone other than Hicks could have been the killer," Thompson says. "That simply is not true."

Hicks' prosecutor, Robert W. Gage, said in a letter to The Sciences magazine that he was convinced Hicks received a fair trial. Gage also asserted that Ford and Thompson, who together have written articles on DNA printing,

have less than altruistic motives behind their criticism. They "profit by traveling around the country and testifying for desperate defendants about the pitfalls of DNA identification," Gage claimed, noting that Ford and Thompson, thanks to their DNA work for defendants, are known to prosecutors nationwide as the "Combine from Irvine."

Both Ford and Thompson say such remarks are examples of widespread harassment against DNA critics. Thompson, who is married and lives with his wife and children near the UC Irvine campus, says opponents are spreading false rumors among the DNA litigation set that he and Ford are lovers using their DNA legal fees to build a home in Laguna Beach. He has also endured bar complaints filed by prosecutors in New Mexico and California, accusing him of conflict of interest for publishing academic articles on cases in which he had been a lawyer. The complaints were ruled groundless, he says.

Ford also complains of prosecutorial harassment and, though still active as a consultant in DNA cases, now avoids testifying in court. A British national, Ford was on the witness stand in an Arizona murder case two years ago when an FBI lawyer abruptly asked about his visa status. Ford was then trying to obtain a permanent resident "green card." Though the judge quickly silenced the attorney for straying into irrelevant areas, Ford saw it as a veiled threat from a federal official.

"It definitely was chilling," Ford recalls. The judge in the Arizona case eventually dealt a stinging blow to the FBI, by finding that its DNA methods were not generally accepted by the scientific community and so could not be used in court. A state appeals court is currently considering whether to ban DNA evidence throughout Arizona.

In Texas, however, David Hicks remains on Death Row, convicted on similar evidence, insisting he is innocent, but garnering few sympathetic ears. Thompson believes Hicks might well be an innocent man convicted wrongly by his own DNA. But given the current conservative climate in ap-

pellate courts, Thompson concedes, stopping Hicks' date with lethal injection will be an uphill battle. Yet the question his case poses is a haunting one: How can evidence be too unreliable in Arizona, yet be used to put a man to death in Texas?

To keep defense experts at bay, an informal network of prosecutors and scientists who wholeheartedly support DNA printing has sprung up across the country. Rockne Harmon, the Alameda County deputy district attorney, is its unofficial clearinghouse. To help discredit defense experts, network members regularly fax articles, transcripts and other tidbits to one another, including, at times, unpublished papers that DNA experts have tried to keep confidential.

Researchers critical of the technology say they have been pressured to alter or withdraw scientific papers from publication. When pressure on individual scientists has failed, government officials and the experts they employ have lobbied publications, including the prestigious journal Science, to reject articles that challenge DNA fingerprinting. In one highly publicized case last December, Science—after pressure from DNA proponents—published an unprecedented, simultaneous rebuttal to an article criticizing the government's theories on DNA printing.

"I never expected that the government would attempt to interfere in my scholarly activities or publications," wrote Daniel L. Hartl, a co-author of the Science article and a professor of genetics at Washington University School of Medicine in St. Louis, in a sworn affidavit. James Wooley, a federal prosecutor from an organized crime strike force in Ohio, obtained the article before it was published, then telephoned Hartl, who had been a defense witness in a case Wooley prosecuted. According to the professor, Wooley "proceeded to badger me for almost an hour asserting that the article would do incalculable harm to government prosecutions and the criminal justice system. . . . I was particularly disturbed when Mr. Wooley . . . asked me whether I was afraid of having my taxes audited."

Wooley denies any attempt to stifle Hartl's, or anyone else's, academic freedom, saying he may have made some sarcastic remarks toward the end of his telephone conversation with Hartl, but that the scientist was being paranoid.

Perhaps more than anyone, Laurence Mueller has been a favorite whipping boy in the DNA debate. Deputy Dist. Atty. Harmon has written harsh letters questioning the quality and accuracy of his testimony, not only to various scientific journals to which Mueller has submitted articles, but to his department chairman and the UC Irvine chancellor. Editors at Science even informed Harmon by mail that they had rejected an article by Mueller before they told the scientist of their decision. "It sounds like they respect me more than they do him," Harmon says.

The government is not the only side getting down and dirty: Defense lawyers active in DNA cases also have their own network of litigators and scientists, and the government's "pro-DNA" experts have begun to complain that they, too, are being harassed by harsh attacks on their integrity.

In U.S. vs. Yee, an Ohio murder case, both sides of the DNA war pulled out all stops. Last spring, New York defense lawyers Barry Scheck and Peter Neufeld filed a motion for a new trial, charging the government with conducting a national campaign to harass and stifle DNA critics. At the same time, the two attorneys launched an attack of their own: The motion accuses two prominent Texas genetics researchers of warping their scientific opinions in favor of DNA printing in order to garner $500,000 in Justice Department grants.

Scheck and Neufeld's broadside also accuses the FBI's chief expert in DNA printing, Bruce Budowle, of citing a nonexistent study to support convictions in the Yee case. The lawyers have demanded an investigation of this alleged perjury by the FBI, the nation's preeminent purveyor of DNA printing. Budowle did not return repeated phone messages, but his boss, FBI Assistant

Director John W. Hicks, defended the DNA expert, saying that Budowle knows that teams of defense lawyers and experts will scrutinize every word he says on the witness stand. "He knows not to say something dumb."

Not even Hicks is immune from attack: Yee lawyers say he tried to destroy evidence that could aid defendants in DNA cases—allegations that Hicks hotly denies, although government memos do show that he wanted to destroy certain files that might have contained information on FBI lab errors. They also criticized Hicks for attempting to influence a recent report by a committee of the prestigious National Academy of Sciences, which in April issued a qualified endorsement of the use of DNA fingerprinting in court, but rejected certain crucial techniques used by the FBI. Hicks calls the allegations raised in the Yee case "a witch hunt."

Finding common ground between the opposing sides has been nearly impossible, in part because of the way DNA evidence was first presented to the courts and the public: as a magic bullet.

The technique first was used in 1985 in Great Britain, when blood was taken from more than 4,000 men to identify a rapist-murderer who had killed two 15-year-old girls in two neighboring villages. The DNA fragments extracted from these blood samples were then compared to DNA from semen found in the victims; police found their man when he tried to get someone else to contribute a blood sample for him.

Proponents of the technique claimed that the genetic comparison was so exact that the odds of a false match were 1 in hundreds of millions. In other words, they said, the odds of a mistake were so minuscule that DNA was as good as a fingerprint.

By 1987, the technology had crossed the Atlantic, with three private laboratories offering DNA analyses in criminal cases. The FBI soon followed with labs in Washington and Quantico, Va., and various state and local government

DNA laboratories came on line in the next two years. DNA printing became a growth industry.

Its appeal was enormous, especially in rape and murder cases. Previously, forensic scientists charged with finding evidence at crime scenes could only compare blood types, or a somewhat more refined analysis of blood enzymes. Semen or blood found in the victims or at the crime scenes was collected and compared to blood from suspects. If there was a different blood type, a suspect was exonerated. If there was a match, however, it often proved little; millions of people share the same blood type or enzyme.

"Before DNA, if we got a figure of 1 in 4, maybe 1 in 10, we were lucky. One in 100, we were ecstatic," says John Hartmann of the Orange County sheriff-coroner's DNA lab, one of the most respected in the nation. "It was not very discriminating."

Then, suddenly, a quantum advance occurred. Compare DNA, proponents of the new technology announced, and you could be sure you had the right culprit. To men like Hartmann, who genuinely agonized at the thought of criminals' going free because their lab work was too inexact, DNA printing represented a law-enforcement "home run." Now rapists who might have gone free because of the vagaries of eyewitness testimony or the lack of hard proof could be prosecuted. Serial murderers who left no living witnesses would no longer prey on society with impunity. Their DNA, with the help of the knowing, dispassionate men in white lab coats who analyzed it, would answer the questions of guilt and innocence. And the odds that they might be wrong would be 1 in millions, maybe billions. It almost seemed too good to be true.

It was.

Even the term genetic "fingerprint" turned out to be a misnomer, granting an unwarranted aura of infallibility to the technique. Now many jurisdictions prohibit the term's use in court out of concern that it misleads juries, using instead DNA "profiling" or "typing."

Jurors can look at a projection of conventional fingerprint comparisons and say, yeah, they really do look alike. Furthermore, it is uncontrovertible that no two people possess the same fingerprints, not even twins.

Neither is true with DNA prints.

Unlike fingerprints, a person's entire DNA is not examined in the technique—current technology is too primitive. Instead, scientists analyze only a few areas of the long, complex chains of deoxyribonucleic acid that contain the genetic blueprint for all organisms, bacteria to Homo sapiens. The regions of the DNA molecule that are studied, fragments called VNTRs, serve no known purpose other than linking other portions of DNA, like empty boxcars in the middle of a freight train.

When semen, blood or hair is left by a rapist or killer at a crime scene, the DNA can be chemically removed and broken up into fragments in a solution of organic solvents and enzymes. The purified DNA that results is poured into an electrified gel, which spreads out the fragments according to their length. After several more steps, another chemical solution called a "probe" is added, which mates with a specific group of VNTRs, highlighting it with a radioactive tag. The final step uses radiation-sensitive film to record the VNTR pattern. The resulting "autoradiograph" bears a passing resemblance to a very sloppy bar code like that on most grocery labels. The crime-scene autorad can then be compared to a suspect's autorad. Theoretically, different patterns mean innocence; a match means guilt.

Sounds a lot like fingerprinting. And proponents and critics agree that the technique is theoretically sound. But in practice, the autorads are occasionally hazy and incomplete, due in part to the decomposition that typically occurs before forensic evidence is gathered. The blurry images that can result may lead one expert to see a match where another sees none. Many matches are clear-cut; others are so subjective that the certainty DNA printing is supposed to convey simply vanishes. Worse, jurors and judges at times don't know what they're really looking at when the scientists start passing out the auto-

rads. So one focus of the debate is whether a match can be declared reliably in each and every case.

The hottest battle, though, revolves around what it means when DNA prints do clearly match. Does a match really mean that only one person matches the criminal's DNA print, or are there other people walking around with the same patterns? Proponents of the technology say the odds of more than one person bearing the same VNTR patterns are extremely small. Critics say prosecutors and their witnesses are vastly overstating this certainty level.

To understand this aspect of the debate, you have to understand how the chemical "probes" work. There are several kinds, and each probe examines a different grouping of genetic "boxcars"—the VNTRs. According to FBI population studies of several thousand people who gave blood samples, one VNTR grouping may occur in 1 out of 100 people. Another grouping may occur in 1 out of 17 individuals, another, 1 in 2,000. By using three, four or more such probes, then multiplying the odds together, incredibly small probabilities are generated, anywhere from 1 in 100,000 to 1 in billions. Thus, the image of DNA printing as magic bullet was born.

In the Hicks case in Texas, for example, Lifecodes declared a six-probe match in calculating the 96 million to 1 probability that he raped and murdered his grandmother. In theory, this should be irrefutable evidence. But defense witness Ford's analysis showed that four of the six VNTR patterns contained in a vaginal swab of the victim could have come from the grandmother's cells, not the killer's—there was no way of telling them apart in this case. As relatives, Hicks and his grandmother had identical VNTR groupings in four places. Using only the two VNTR groupings that must have come from the killer and that do match Hicks, the odds of Hicks' being the guilty party, Ford says, are a few hundred to 1, nothing close to the level of certainty represented to the jury that convicted Hicks. By Ford's estimate, millions of others could have commit-

ted the crime, including many people in Hicks' insular hometown.

The possibility that such communities might contain people with common VNTR patterns is another hot point of contention in the DNA wars. Defense attorneys recently sought to embarrass one of the government's most prominent DNA experts, Kenneth Kidd, a professor of genetics, psychiatry and biology at Yale University for claiming that a four-probe match between two different people was virtually impossible. This claim was refuted—with Kidd's own research on an isolated Amazonian Indian tribe called the Karitiana, in which about a third of the 54 people tested had identical DNA patterns for four different probes. (Hicks was sent to Death Row on the basis of two distinct probes.) Once confronted with his own data, Kidd and prosecutors dismissed the inbred Karitiana community as an aberration that does not apply to the much larger gene pool of U.S. populations.

"That's what they say now," Thompson argues. "But before, they said it couldn't happen at all, anywhere."

The DNA critics say such findings dictate that more conservative probabilities should be used to explain to juries what a DNA match means. Prosecutors resist this, saying the FBI and other labs already build in error factors that give defendants the benefit of the doubt. Obviously, they also oppose change because less dramatic odds leave too much room for doubt about a suspect's guilt. The magic bullet turns into a blank.

The recent National Academy of Sciences report, however, urges somewhat more conservative numbers than the FBI and other labs generate—striking a rare compromise between the two DNA factions. It remains to be seen if either side adopts the report's recommendations. So far, the FBI is resisting change, while defense lawyers lobby for probabilities more in their favor. A series of recent appellate court decisions against DNA evidence, including one in Massachusetts and two in California, cite the academy report and side with the critics.

"Really, when you get down to it, there's not much difference between a million to 1 and 100 million to 1, or a million to 1 and a 100,000 to 1, which is really what they're arguing about," Orange County's John Hartmann says. "Either way, we've hit a home run."

If such arguments were all there was to it, the viciousness that marks DNA court battles probably wouldn't have erupted. Each side merely would amass its experts, let them testify, and the judge and jury would decide. But the battle also revolves around a legal precedent set by a federal appeals court in 1923, the Frye Rule, which governs the admissibility of new scientific evidence in many, though not all, jurisdictions. The legal rule was first established to examine (and ultimately bar from court) lie-detector tests, but 70 years later, it provides an uneasy fit with the state-of-the-art technology of DNA printing. In DNA cases, Frye's peculiarities make the intense attacks on scientists' integrity all but inevitable.

According to the Frye decision, scientific discoveries should be admitted only when there is no substantial debate about them within the relevant scientific communities—in this case, geneticists, molecular biologists and statisticians. Under Frye, judges aren't supposed to decide who is right in a scientific debate—they aren't qualified—but merely whether a legitimate debate exists.

That explains the vicious attacks on the scientists, and why so many complaints of harassment have been generated. If government officials can halt articles and paint DNA critics as unethical charlatans, judges may decide there is no legitimate debate.

Naturally, defense lawyers respond in kind, attempting to prove the government experts are the real charlatans whenever they testify that there is no debate about DNA printing. "It's trench warfare, no doubt about that," Hartmann says.

Until recently, prosecutors have won most of the skirmishes: DNA evidence has been admitted in most cases, with decisive results. Only one state's Supreme Court has ruled DNA inadmissible—Massachusetts—while one other, Minnesota, severely limits the way it can be used. Numerous other states, including California, are reconsidering its admissibility. The U.S. Supreme Court has yet to specifically rule on the issue.

At the trial court level, the results are more contradictory. In the same courthouse, one judge may admit a DNA test while another finds a legitimate scientific dispute exists, rendering the DNA evidence inadmissible. Justice, when it comes to DNA evidence, is unequal, varying from state to state and judge to judge. The U.S. 2nd Circuit Court of Appeals (with jurisdiction over New York, Vermont and Connecticut), for instance, recently approved the use of DNA evidence without lengthy admissibility hearings; at the same time, a District of Columbia judge barred prosecutors from using DNA printing in court.

Another example: last year, one division of the California Court of Appeal upheld DNA evidence in a Ventura murder case, which could have set a precedent for all of California. But a month before that ruling, Los Angeles County Superior Court Judge C. Robert Simpson Jr. ruled in a different murder case that DNA evidence was too questionable to be admitted. "There is a profound, significant and honestly held disagreement among these men of science," Simpson wrote. Because that case developed after the Ventura prosecution, Simpson's decision was not undone by the appellate court's embrace of DNA evidence. The two at-odds rulings stand, their illogic intact.

In August, a different division of the state Court of Appeal, citing the national academy report, ruled that DNA evidence was not admissible. Now the state Supreme Court has been asked to rule definitively.

An Orange County rape trial earlier this year, in which Mueller and Kidd were lambasted, shows the kind of balancing act juries must perform to deal with the attacks, disputes and contradictions. Frank Lee Soto was charged with raping his neighbor, an elderly woman in Westminster. The only hard evidence against him was a DNA test of his blood—he provided it voluntarily—that showed a clear match with the rapist's semen. (The victim, too ill to testify, told police Soto didn't do it.)

Soto's attorney, Paul Stark, fought bitterly with Deputy Dist. Atty. Dennis Bauer over what the DNA match meant. Bauer, with Yale's Kidd and several other of the most prominent pro-DNA printing experts in the country, said the odds were 189 million to 1 that Soto was the right man. Equally prominent experts suggested the numbers should be more favorable to Soto; in particular, biology professor William Shields of the State University of New York at Syracuse said the correct number was between 65,000 to 1 and 23,000 to 1. Given Orange County's population, that meant 17 other potential suspects were running around, five times that in all of Southern California.

Both sides sounded certain and sincere. Both had the charts and the numbers and other paraphernalia to support their positions. Both sides impugned the abilities and motives of the opposing experts in typical vitriolic fashion. There was literally no way for the jurors (or the judge, for that matter) to know whom to believe.

Doing what the scientists refused to do, the jurors sought compromises. Their statements after the trial showed that they accepted the smaller defense numbers put forward by Shields, and so convicted Soto of the lesser charge of attempted rape. Had Soto not been a neighbor, they said, they would have acquitted him. But 65,000 to 1, coupled with the fact that he lived next door, was enough to cinch the case. Soto received a three-year prison sentence, but, because of the uncertainties revolving around the DNA issue, he is free on bail while he appeals.

Hartmann, whose Orange County lab performed the tests on Soto's blood, applauded the jury's decision that DNA evidence alone is insufficient to convict. His attitude is among the most reasonable of any expert in the field and though he is ardent in his support for DNA printing, he does not believe that it should on its own determine anyone's fate: "If I was on that jury, I would have had a real problem with it, too. . . . No one should be convicted solely on the basis of DNA evidence, not even a billion to 1. If there was no other evidence, I would vote not guilty, too."

But for most of the combatants, the DNA debate has assumed the aspect of a religious argument, each side certain it is right, each incapable of seeing the other's point of view. Voices of compromise are drowned out.

There is one unique case in Virginia that calls into question the sincerity of these head-butting positions. Joseph R. O'Dell III was convicted of a vicious and sensational murder in Virginia Beach in 1985. O'Dell was seen at the bar where the murder victim had been on the night of her death, though no one saw them arrive or leave together. Later, police seized bloody men's clothes in O'Dell's garage after they received an angry call from his girlfriend. O'Dell, who had a robbery conviction and other legal run-ins behind him, told police his shirt and jacket got bloody from a bar fight that night, but detectives figured they had

found their man. Lab results seemed to confirm their opinion. The case predates DNA printing, but less sophisticated blood enzyme tests showed that the blood on O'Dell's clothes was consistent with the victim's blood. O'Dell was convicted and sentenced to death.

Since then, with the advent of DNA testing, his appellate lawyers petitioned the court for new tests. The result: the more refined DNA technology shows the blood on O'Dell's clothing cannot be matched to the victim's, according to briefs filed in his appeal. Key evidence against O'Dell apparently has been invalidated, a case where DNA printing seemingly exonerates rather than convicts.

But O'Dell remains on Death Row. He has been unable to win a new trial. Prosecutors, who in other courtrooms have championed the use of DNA evidence against defendants, are so convinced of O'Dell's guilt that they have opposed its use in his case, even as defense attorneys want the test results admitted.

The prosecution is winning so far, keeping the Virginia appellate courts from considering the DNA evidence in O'Dell's case by focusing on a technicality. O'Dell's out-of-state lawyers filed an appeal petition that lacked a

table of contents and a memorandum of facts summarizing the case (a formulaic introduction to the appeal). The prosecution seized on this procedural gaffe as a means of throwing out the entire appeal. By the time the defense lawyers noticed the oversight, a filing deadline had passed by three days, and the Virginia Supreme Court refused to consider the case.

Recently, three justices of the U.S. Supreme Court suggested that the Virginia courts ought to think again. Although the full court declined to hear O'Dell's direct appeal, Harry A. Blackmun, John Paul Stevens and Sandra Day O'Connor decided that putting a man to death because his lawyers forgot a table of contents was going too far, especially if he might be innocent. In an unusual letter handed down in the case, they instructed lower federal courts in Virginia to give careful consideration to O'Dell's next appeal, a habeas corpus petition to be filed this year, "because of the gross injustice that would result if an innocent man were sentenced to death." And there it stands.

O'Dell remains on Death Row, waiting for his case to be heard, even as prosecutors across the country continue to use DNA evidence to send him companions.

Farmers and Baboons in the Taita Hills: Inter-Species Warfare in Southeastern Kenya

Jim Bell

ABSTRACT: *In a mountainous region of southeastern Kenya, horticulturists and troops of wandering baboons have engaged in inter-species warfare for countless generations. Such warfare has been over food and territory. Often, the battles are not just confined to elements of protecting, or stealing food from garden plots, or capturing territories, but they are psychological contests involving a show of will and "clever" strategies in which mankind does not necessarily prevail. This paper is a humorous view of a confrontation between one set of men and a single baboon troop in the East African bush, an insight into conflict resolution between man and monkey in modern times.*

INTRODUCTION

East Africa, ancestral origin of humankind, has long served as a battleground between animal species in their quest for survival. This region's river valleys, plateau plains, rift valley, seemingly endless savannahs, and deep upland forests have all witnessed the daily aggression and mortal combat between those animals that are hunted and those that hunt. Among the most successful animal populations to survive such aggression through the millennia in East Africa have been various primate species.

Paleontologists suggest that primate species may have a long history of violent competition between one another for the nutritional resources of a local area. And, as their territories become smaller in contemporary times, zoologists and primatologists discuss food competition between modern primate species. Of course, topping the list of successful primate competitors at the moment is *Homo sapiens*.

One can easily observe that human beings have overwhelming control of the earth's food resources, especially those resources in East Africa, where other primate species live. There is, however, at least one of these other species who seems not in total agreement with this observation: the common, or savannah, baboon. Baboons usually view all food stuffs within the troop's range as theirs. This simple, yet irritating, fact was made clear to me while investigating the affects of local socialization practices on the academic performance of primary school children in southeastern Kenya.

On several occasions during my research, I had an opportunity to observe first-hand the foraging methods of baboons as they went into local garden plots and stole crops intended for humans. On one such occasion, I had the misfortune of being part of this inter-species warfare; a confrontation as old as the domestication of plants in the region and, perhaps, as old as the two species themselves.

The following is offered as a sometimes humorous view of a rather serious aspect of life in the bush-lands of East Africa. Such conflict between these particular anthropoids does provide some indication as to mankind's rise above the lower primates and, at the same time, serves to illustrate how the alleged domination of our species over these other animals may owe more to dumb luck than to brain size or superior intellect and fighting skills.

THE SETTING

The Taita Hills are a cluster of mountain groups located in the southern portion of Kenya, slightly less than 192 miles (309 kilometers) southeast of the nation's capital of Nairobi and

From *California Anthropologist*, Vol. 19, No. 1, 1992, pp. 1-6. Reprinted by permission of *California Anthropologist*, Department of Anthropology, California State University, Los Angeles, CA.

where the eastern-most fingers of the Serengeti extend into the western edge of the coastal plateau. Here, too, lies Kenya's famous Tsavo National Game Park. Free-roaming baboon troops constantly wander away from the game park and raid *shambas* (garden plots) of the people living in, and around, the Taita Hills. The residents of these isolated inselbergs in the midst of the plateau plains refer to themselves as *Wataita, Taita,* or "The People." Their native language, Kitaita, is one of several Bantu tongues common to this part of East Africa. Owing to their colonial past, many Wataita are proficient in English, and all are fluent in Kiswahili as well.

Cultivation of cash crops, such as vegetables and coffee, and wage labor, both in their homeland and in far off urban centers like Mombasa and Nairobi, are the major sources of income for the Wataita. Small herds of cattle, goats, and sheep serve as a source of income, but cash crops and wage labor are the primary means of acquiring wealth.

Taita men are the principle landowners, and they are most often in control of those agricultural duties connected with the production of cash crops. One of these duties includes protecting the *shambas* from raids by others. Women usually concentrate on cultivating the grains, varieties of peas and beans, and the root crops used in the local diet. In general, the Wataita live in scattered nuclear and/or extended family units which are located within easy access to one or two of the many compact village communities found throughout the Taita Hills.

Descent among the Wataita is patrilineal, with many living in extended family groups consisting of brothers and their wives and children. At a higher level of social organization, the Wataita also possess a fictive kin-group they refer to as *Kichuku*. Many Wataita also use the English term "clan" when referring to *Kichuku*. Members of a *Kichuku* usually live in close proximity to each other so that they can assist one another in times of trouble.

It is in this setting, and among these people, that I experienced one of this century's most hard-fought, yet fruit-less, battles. A *shamba* belonging to my friend and key informant became the ground for hostilities between man and monkey.

THE RAID ON SIKUKU'S *SHAMBA*

I had been living in the Taita Hills slightly over a month when I was initiated *(blooded)* into one of the most sacred male rituals associated with farming in this part of the world. I and a young Wataita, Sikuku, who was my key informant and friend, sat just inside of the open door of his small two-room home. We were planning our next day's research problem, drinking beer, and watching the sun accentuate the various hues of green in the valley below. His younger female cousin, Mwakio, ran past the door delivering a panicky message in a high-pitched Kitaita no one could initially understand. She was told to calm down and repeat herself. The girl managed, in a squealing voice, to relay her bulletin. I did not understand the meaning; the presentation was much too fast for my limited Kitaita at the time, but the tone indicated serious trouble.

"Quickly!," Sikuku snapped. So away we went, bolting through the door and down a narrow path toward the valley. "We must remove those ones from the *shamba!,"* he shouted to me. I ran head-long down the path, trying to keep up with this younger man who had travelled this trail a thousand times in a single year. He knew it well. I, on the other hand, was moving on unfamiliar terrain.

"Remove who? What? How?," I yelled while traversing the steep path.

Sikuku said nothing. He just seemed to increase his speed as I tried to coordinate the rate of my descent with the movement of my feet. I had to keep my feet under my body, or I would fall on my face. Whatever we had to remove from the *shamba,* I wanted to arrive in one piece.

Mwakio was far above us squealing out more alarms, calling on members of Sikuku's *Kichuku* to assist at the *shamba*. A man from a nearby household joined us. He too was moving with great speed and he, like Sikuku, made it look easy. My feet, the path, and my body were still at odds with one another. We continued down and down, turning and twisting, jumping over felled trees, trying to avoid toppling head-over-heels toward God-only-knew what. I tried to maintain some dignity in my demeanor. I did not want anyone to say I did not have a "handle" on the situation.

"How many of these notorious creatures are there?," a calm voice behind me asked.

"I do not know," I replied, huffing and puffing like an old steam engine. Three of Sikuku's male cousins passed me on the right and another two men shot by on my left. "Whose *shamba* is it?," I questioned, but no one answered. Everyone was busy trying to maintain his balance as the incline steepened.

"My *shamba* is under attack," Sikuku finally answered.

Immediately I began to gear down, trying to slow my descent, but to no avail. "Under attack?" Noticing that none of the men carried weapons of any kind, no bows and arrows, not even the all-purpose *ponga* (machete), I simply asked, "By what?"

"By nasty baboons," one of the men explained.

After descending approximately three-quarters of a mile, we reached a small hillock overlooking Sikuku's larger *shamba*. He was growing maize and beans on a little less than half an acre of prime bottom land. Scattered throughout the *shamba* was a troop of baboons. There were seven of us on the hillock. We picked up rocks, sticks, bits and pieces of decaying palm-leaves, or anything we thought suitable as a weapon. I still wondered why the men did not bring *pongas* or bows and arrows, but I thought it best not to ask. I had already made a fool of myself coming down the path. This was war time. Quickly devised estimates of the enemy's number came forth. Some of the men calculated perhaps 25 to 30 baboons in the *shamba,* with 6 or 7 on the outskirts of the plot. Others guessed the creatures were at least 30 to 40 strong, including some 20 adult males, because they believed this troop had raided the *shamba* in the past. I figured there were in the neighborhood of several hundred, probably because I had never been so close to baboons before, and they were larger than I had thought they would be.

Of course, as with most military campaigns, no one was really sure of the enemy's numbers. The confusion, coupled with fear and panic, caused an inflation in the estimates of enemy strength. If we had taken the time to count their correct numbers, we would have found only 19 of the "nasty creatures," as my Taita mates called them. Most of the enemy, it later turned out, were females and their offspring. There were four alpha males and five or six adolescent beta-sized males trying to stay out of everyone else's way. These little details were not available to us until after the battle. But, knowing how war-stories have a tendency to grow with the passage of time, my original guess of several hundred baboons on the field of honor that bygone day seems nearer the correct number as the years pass. Their strengths increase at each retelling of the event.

Sikuku's older cousin and a man from his *Kichuku* came up behind us. "What do we do?.," I wished to know. I was hoping for some definite answer steeped in the wisdom of traditionally proven strategies, an answer that came from Wataita ancestors, an answer that was handed down from the ancient gods of the Old Ones. I wanted something that would allow us to best these animals and evict them from the *shamba*. My knees were hurting from the rapid descent, and I missed the comfort of Sikuku's house. I was not ready for any major exertion.

Instead, I got puzzled looks and the most wonderful of East African rationales for an answer: "Of course, we must remove these rascals from the *shamba*." I was now sure this man, Sikuku's cousin, thought me a fool. The logic was masterful. If only I could say as much for the question.

The nine of us were simply going to attack. We moved toward the *shamba* secure in the knowledge of our ten thousand years or so of experience

expelling unwanted pests from cultivated lands and millions of years of evolution. We advanced with determination and a sense of quick victory.

"Charge them, but do not go directly at them or chase one for any long time," Sikuku advised me over the shouts and yells of the other men.

As we stormed the *shamba*, I shouted back to him, "Why not?"

"They will bite you," Sikuku warned just before disappearing into a row of maize plants.

My pace immediately slowed to a cautious walk. I suddenly realized that the baboons had also been evolving for millions of years, and they also had thousands of years of experience to count upon. I crept slowly into the maize row. An adolescent male faked an attack; I yelled. There we were, two horrified combatants trying to decide what came next. I continued yelling, threw one of the small rocks I had brought from the hillock, and he retreated out of sight. Round one was mine, and my confidence was building. Deeper in the maize field, I encountered two small females and another adolescent male. They retreated without any challenge from me. As I continued to the next row, a large alpha male shot past me like a bullet.

"Baboons," I thought aloud, "are not suppose to move that fast." I froze in fear, unable to retreat or go forward. Fortunately, one of the fellows came up behind me and, with a proper shove, got me moving again.

We were nine representatives of the earth's most dominant primate species, running back and forth, in and out of maize rows, chasing baboons that barked, displayed their canines, flashed their eye-lids, engaged in mock attacks, or simply sat on their haunches yawning. In short, they were handling us better than we were controlling them. Some of the braver animals actually retrieved the smaller stones thrown at them to see if they were edible.

We had been stumbling around for five or ten minutes, a lifetime it seemed, in an effort to wrest Sikuku's fields and crops from these primates, who should have, in my estimation,

run at our first appearance. Since they did not, we continued to score direct hits, only on each other, with our rocks and sticks. One of our party had been beaten over the head by another member with a dead palm-branch by mistake. The victim refused to speak to his attacker for several days. After being struck twice with missiles myself, I developed a quick appreciation for the absence of bows and arrows, *pongas*, and spears in this endeavor.

We pulled back to the hillock for a bit of rest and regrouping. It was, "Really not a retreat," I was informed by one of the men. I suppose one could say it was a strategic withdrawal to assess the damage and to reevaluate the course of action. At the time, I believed it to be a retreat not fully completed. I felt that we should have returned to the village, and not stopped at the hillock. I knew that safety and rest were further up the mountain-side.

Most of the baboons collected in the open area of the *shamba*, where the beans grew, and where they could see us more clearly. Still, many of them continued to eat some of the crops. They were, however, very agitated and began snapping at one another as they watched us. The largest of the alpha males, and the one who was clearly the leader, was exerting his dominance over the others within a five yard radius. We humans seemed as agitated as the baboons. Two of the men, exhibiting a paroxysmal fear, blamed the rest of us for not adhering to their verbal commands during the first phase of the battle. It became our collective fault that the baboons remained in the *shamba*. We, like the enemy, were short tempered and confused about the next tactic to be employed. Each time failures were cited, my name was mentioned and my maneuvers were metaphorically likened to cow dung.

Sikuku and his cousin, Mwandawa, devised a plan whereby we would form a semi-circle of sorts and progress into the *shamba* in three teams of three men each. This plan called for three men to flank the baboons on the right, three men on the left, and three men to come at them straight-on. This would force the animals out of the *shamba* and push them further down into the valley. Loading up with more ammunition, we set out to drive the enemy from "our" land.

The baboons became more agitated as we drew near their position in the *shamba.* We divided ourselves into our three-man teams and proceeded with our flanking movement. As we came closer, the females with infants clustered around the leader. Three alpha males spread out so that one was confronting each of our teams. They could keep our separate units under intense scrutiny. As we approached, adolescent males moved toward us in mock attacks. Then, the second phase of the campaign was underway. Again, two primate species were in full combat.

The men, yelling and screaming, inched forward. Rocks and sticks were thrown in every direction. The baboons barked, bared their teeth, and bounced on all fours with furor. Both sides meant serious business. I sensed that saving the crops was no longer the point of our spirited charge. Demonstrating our dominance over the arrogant little "beasties" was the rationale of the contest. How dare they refuse to run before their superiors!

Within a matter of minutes, our superior strategy and tactics gave way to confusion and panic. Baboons, except for three females and their infants, bolted in alarm and scattered throughout the *shamba.* This sudden movement was so unexpected that we too scattered in fright. Again, we humans pelted one another with stones. All five of the adolescent males had broken through our lines and threatened our retreat to the hillock. We were out-maneuvered and, seemingly, out-smarted. The more the enemy scampered about, criss-crossing in front and behind us, the less able we were to secure clear targets. Fortunately, the adolescent males at our rear were not confident enough, or large and mature enough, to charge us. The alpha males in front of us, however, were getting closer with each of their mock attacks. It was time for another strategic withdrawal. We had to fight our way past the adolescent males, while holding the three alpha males at a safe distance, and keeping an eye on the few females who

had tried to join the engagement. At a time like this, one's senses increase ten-fold. Colors became more vivid, sounds increased in clarity, and the air seemed alive with differing odors that were concentrated just in the *shamba.* It was one of those moments when time is motionless, when one is at once part of, and apart from, the action that is taking place. One is a participant and, yet, one can view one's performance from a distance at the same time.

On Sikuku's cousin's command, we ran for home base (the hillock). My heart was pumping, my mouth was dry, and my legs worked only half as well as they should have. But, I managed to reach the hillock and collapse with the other men. My wind was lost somewhere back in the *shamba.* My head throbbed, my throat was raw, and my body felt like it had been crushed by an eighteen-wheeler. We lay on the hillock for what seemed forever.

Finally, after about 15 or 20 minutes, an additional four men from Sikuku's *Kichuku* arrived to help. We prepared for another attack. One of the new arrivals noticed the baboons departing down the slope toward the deeper reaches of the valley floor. "Let us give chase!," exclaimed another of the new men.

"No brother," Sikuku replied, "let them go."

Another of the newly arrived warriors looked us over carefully, saw our dusty appearance, noticed our fatigue, lack of fighting spirit, and said, "Ahy! You have let those ones defeat you!" Not one of us contradicted him.

Almost one-third of Sikuku's crops were eaten or destroyed. Nine of us had formed an alliance, a partnership with each other, and a covenant with the ancestors to battle another species to save our food resources. We had pledged to defend "our" land from the enemy, and to maintain dominance over so-called "lesser creatures." All had not gone quite the way we had envisioned. We had not really wrested the *shamba* from the baboons. They left in their own good time. However, two-thirds of Sikuku's crops were saved from destruction and damage, which counted for something. That

alone keeps us humans ahead on overall points, and maybe that is how it has been for millennia in this region.

CONCLUSION

The events in Sikuku's *shamba* are a continuation of a centuries-old struggle in this part of the world between those that have and those that have not. Man and beast alike are the offended and offender in this ritual of life and survival. The very nature of farming in East Africa, during the past ten thousand years or so, would have been marked by such encounters. Human primates toil in the sun, turn the land, plant and weed the fields, and wait for the earth to bring forth food. These crops are a means of securing the survival of the species *Homo sapiens* and, in some instances, the excess food produced is employed to maintain economic and political ties to other human populations. Once in a while mankind's more distant relatives claim some of the fruits of this difficult labor.

In the past, the farmers of the Taita Hills lost portions of their production efforts to nomadic herders like the Maasai and some Galla groups. The baboon, perhaps the most persistent of the local animal population to raid their *shambas,* added to these losses as well. Today, an occasional human family may steal from a lowland garden, or one midway up into the foothills, but the baboon continues to pillage *shambas* throughout large areas of the Taita Hills. Baboons, like their human counterparts, have the right to exploit the environment. After all, each species views the world as theirs to control. Conflict mounts when the one cannot maintain control over the other. Humans have infringed on baboon territory in the Taita region for ten or more millennia, and it only seems fair that baboons exploit the labors of their human invaders in return.

Macaque See, Macaque Do

*At tourist sites in Bali, humans are teaching their fellow
primates some bad habits*

Meredith F. Small

*Meredith F. Small is an associate pro-
fessor of anthropology at Cornell. Her
book* Female Choices: Sexual Behavior of Female Primates *was published
by Cornell University Press.*

Early last July, I boarded a plane for a
thirty-six-hour journey to Bali, the
tropical island vacation spot. Contrary
to what most of my friends thought,
this eight-week trip to Indonesia was
not really intended as a holiday of sun,
surf, and shopping—my assignment
was to evaluate the effect of tourism on
the native Balinese monkey, the long-
tailed macaque.

My last research project on monkey
behavior had taken place five years
earlier, and I felt a surge of excitement
when I reached my primary research
site, the Sangeh Monkey Forest in the
center of Bali. As I walked down a
winding cement path through a lovely
patch of nutmeg forest to Sangeh's
central temple, Pura Bukit Sari, I suddenly saw them, scampering among
the tourists, leaping over temple walls,
and generally acting like monkeys—
curious, social, and full of energy.

Watching them, I felt the old observation skills click back into gear: That
one with a bent tail will be easy to
identify again. The female over there is
in heat. Two babies are less than three
months old. I see at least four young
infants. This group has few subadult
males.

Lost in this primatological reverie, I
failed to see an adult female approach-

ing to my left. Suddenly she streaked
past me, a blur of green-gray fur so
close I could smell the familiar monkey
odor. In mid-leap, her tiny fingers
gripped the earpiece of my brand-new
sunglasses. She unceremoniously yanked them off my face and sped into the
forest.

I was stunned. The swiftness of her
calculated thievery was breathtaking.
(More important, how could I spend
day after day recording the minute
details of monkey behavior without a
decent pair of shades?) Accompanied
by a temple guard, I tracked my as-
sailant deep into the woods. She finally
stopped running, only to sit and chew
contemplatively on my glasses, her
brown eyes shifting back and forth
between her pursuers. The guard tossed
her a few bags of peanuts. Needing
both hands to collect this booty, she
dropped the glasses in favor of something more digestible and sped away.

"You must not wear glasses near the
monkeys," instructed the guard. "They
also steal wallets, money, hair ribbons,
and handkerchiefs. And don't try to
hide anything in your pockets, because
they will find it." His description
sounded more applicable to big-city
pickpockets than to monkeys on their
home turf. As I returned to the main
area, I noticed tourists holding on to
their possessions for dear life, and
monkeys clearly poised for thievery.
Animals stood up on two legs and
yanked on clothes. They jumped on
people, pulled hair, and rifled pockets.
These normally gentle and friendly animals had turned into beggars and

thieves. Something had gone terribly
wrong at Sangeh.

As my study progressed, I realized
that I had been a victim of a monkey
mugging only because the monkeys
were victims themselves. Bad management of a tourist site, coupled with
uneducated visitors with no appreciation of macaques as fellow primates,
had resulted in a twisted relationship
between the visitors and the very animals they had come to see.

All monkeys have a special place in
Hindu religion. This reverence stems
partly from the role of the monkey
god, Hanuman, in the classic Hindu
epic *Ramayana*. According to the story,
Prince Rama's beloved wife, Sita, was
kidnapped by the evil giant King
Rawana. The monkey king, Sugriva,
had once aided Prince Rama, so Sugriva's general, Hanuman, was enlisted
to gather an army, wreak havoc, and
rescue the princess.

Sangeh itself also features impor-
tantly in the Balinese version of the
Ramayana story. Clever Hanuman and
his monkey battalions capture Mount
Mahameru and use the two halves of
the holy mountain to crush the giant.
Part of the mountain falls to earth and
lands at Sangeh with a troop of monkeys hanging tight.

Monkeys thus retain the status of
privileged visitors, especially on temple grounds, where they are treated
with great tolerance. Like all living
objects, monkeys also embody the
spirits of Hindu gods, both good and
evil. When a monkey leaps onto a
temple altar, destroying carefully placed

palm baskets of sacred offerings and gorging on the fruit and rice intended for higher powers, the Balinese ignore the vandalism—after all, a spirit might now reside in that monkey and might need the food.

Macaques are highly adaptable monkeys that live in deep forests, on high mountains, or along the seaside. About five million years ago, the genus *Macaca,* of which longtails are one of nineteen species, radiated out of North Africa into Europe and east into Asia. Macaques now inhabit Morocco and Algeria, India, Pakistan, China, most of Southeast Asia, and Japan; and long-tailed macaques (*Macaca fascicularis*) have lived on Bali longer than humans. Although they eat just about anything, they prefer fruits and vegetables. In a sense, they are the cockroaches of the primate world, able to adapt well to changes, move into new environments, and scrounge when food gets scarce.

Their humanlike sociality makes these monkeys tourist attractions. We aren't as genetically related to macaques as we are to the apes, such as chimpanzees, but we see ourselves in their behavior—the constant social interactions, the jostling for hierarchical position, the bickering and making up are all similar to the daily machinations of human society. This connection between humans and the macaques either fascinates or repels tourists, and I saw both types of visitors in Bali.

During my weeks at Sangeh, I watched monkeys eat 409 peanuts, 67 bits of bread, 49 chunks of fruit, and endless quantities of crackers, cookies, and candy. I saw them chew on cigarettes, suck on matchsticks, rip apart film boxes, and play with discarded plastic bags. Feeding the animals was encouraged by locals outside the forest; at dozens of stalls, men and women relentlessly hawked both monkey food and souvenirs. Huge buses and smaller minivans disgorged more than a thousand people a day to view the monkeys. Although many of the tourists were Asian, Australian, or European, by far the greatest number of visitors were from other Indonesian islands, such as Java.

After a few days of observation, I understood why the monkeys were so badly behaved—they have been taught to be obnoxious. At the entrance to the temple at the Sangeh Monkey Forest, about thirty men who call themselves "guides" sit and wait for the tourists. Although dressed in appropriate temple garb—a sarong and scarf wound at the waist—they are not officials of the temple; this is a business. Each man owns a Polaroid camera, and his job is to manipulate the tourist into buying a photograph. The method is simple: As a tourist enters, a guide tags along offering tidbits of information (mostly incorrect) about monkey behavior. At the first sight of a monkey, the guide pulls bits of food out of his pack and puts it on the tourist's shoulder. The monkey, of course, leaps up. The animal quietly munches away, and the Polaroid camera flashes. The monkey is then shooed off, often hit, and the guide demands 6,000 rupia (about $4).

In most cases, people are amused and give the money. But sometimes the clammy toes of a monkey on an unsuspecting neck cause real terror. The tourist will twist and turn, while the monkey, tossed about and confused, becomes agitated and bites. These protest bites never break the skin, but they do hurt and bruise—I know from personal experience (about thirty bites).

The guides—I called them the Polaroid gang—also foster mass thievery among the monkeys. When a monkey steals a nonfood item, such as a pair of glasses, it gets rewarded with a bunch of bananas or a bag of peanuts from the guide. The purpose is to distract the thief and grab the goods back. From the monkey's point of view, stealing translates into an edible reward. This destructive cycle instigated by the Polaroid gang guides, who are just trying to make a living in a poor country, has been going on for over a decade.

The scene at Sangeh brings out the worst in both human and monkey behavior—stealing, screaming, injury, and intimidation. The day I was attacked by a large subadult male who gnawed on my neck to get my glasses, I decided it was time to leave. I was

beginning to hate my subjects—the tourists *and* the monkeys.

I expected the situation at Sangeh to be repeated all across Bali because of the pressure of tourism. The island is the starting point for most tours of Indonesia. It is easily accessible from Asia and Australia and has been known for decades to European tourists as the land of perfect beaches. Bali also has cultural allure, revolving around its own brand of Hinduism. To visit Bali is to see a delicate ballet accompanied by a mystical gamelan orchestra, watch women with huge loads of fruit balanced on their heads move in an undulating line toward a temple, or bargain with fine craftsmen for carved wooden masks or intricately cut shadow puppets. Until now, the Balinese have been able to retain their culture, despite the onslaught of two million tourists annually. But as the monkeys of Sangeh demonstrate, the relationship between Bali and its tourists is wearing thin.

I left Sangeh and headed south to one of the more remote temples, Pura Uluwatu. Perched on the southwestern tip of the island, the temple looks like the prow of a ship thrust into the sea. A troop of about fifty longtails come and go here, wandering through the low scrub and out on the cliffs. "I feed them whenever I see them," the guard told me, "but that isn't every day." He pointed out that there are monkeys living along the edge of the sea on the cliffs, undisturbed by the surfers who come from all corners of the world to work the waves of Uluwatu Beach.

My time at Uluwatu was spent in peaceful reflection. The monkeys came around, checked me out, took a few peanuts from the hundred or so tourists that passed by daily, and left. They only became aggressive when they spied a plastic water bottle. To these inhabitants of the dry Bukit Peninsula, water—not food—was the limiting resource. Monkeys would sneak up to tourists, grab bottles right from their hands, and empty them. Monkeys only sat on people—myself included—to get a good view of other group members or maybe to groom their hosts, systematically flicking through hair in search of dry flakes of skin.

Uluwatu is the opposite of Sangeh. The wheels of tourism have not yet been set into motion at Uluwatu. Consequently, fewer tourists are around to lure the monkeys with food, and there are fewer hawkers and no Polaroid camera guides.

Evidence of a peaceful monkey–human interaction made me wonder how an area could develop from the low-key situation at Uluwatu to the intense arena at Sangeh. I began hearing about another temple, Alas Kedaton where, according to many travelers, "the monkeys are nice." This I had to see—a highly visible tourist site with "nice" monkeys?

Alas Kedaton is a tiny scrap of forest near the city of Tabanan, west of Sangeh. In addition to two troops of monkeys, several hundred flying foxes, or fruit bats, inhabit the trees. The site doesn't yet have the constant influx of tourists that Sangeh has, but a visit to Alas Kedaton now appears on many day-tour packages. The major difference between Sangeh and Alas Kedaton, however, is the attitude of the people in charge. The nearby village of Kukuh has taken an active interest in the welfare of both the tourists and the monkeys. As a result, this site offers the most pleasant interaction between humans and their primate cousins.

Like Sangeh, the approach to Alas Kedaton is flanked by rows of souvenir shops. But no one harasses the traveler into buying food for monkeys, a cold drink, or yet another sarong. Instead, the community has installed a system to tone down the pressure on tourists. A designated guide, usually a woman, accompanies each group of tourists into the forest. She encourages the tourists to buy only potatoes for the monkeys from one vendor. ("It's better for the monkeys," she will say, and this is true.) The guide then puts tourists through explicit monkey-feeding paces. "Bend down, open your hand, give only one piece at a time."

Although no tourist could possibly imitate the graceful genuflection of a Balinese woman, the action does put the giver on the same level as the monkey. As a result, monkeys never jump on anyone. In addition, the guides are constantly on the alert for actions that might harm the animals. They seem to know how to say "Don't touch the monkeys" in about five languages. When the guide has taken the visitors on a short stroll to see the flying foxes, and once around its small temple, she requests a visit to her shop. If the tourists say no, they are free to head for the parking lot.

Nyoman Oka, nicknamed Juli, is the principal monkey-food seller. Her husband is responsible for the organization and growth of Alas Kedaton as a tourist attraction. She explained to me, over a lunch of hot Balinese chicken and rice: "If any shop owner bothers a tourist, they are fined 25,000 rupia [about $12]. It isn't nice for tourists to always have someone asking them to buy things." When I inquired about the rows and rows of new shops appearing near the gate, thinking only of the pressure of more human traffic on the monkeys, she laughed. "Those aren't new shops. We are moving the ones here out there, and we will build more forest or perhaps a garden here." In their ambition to increase the flow of tourists through the area, the people of Kukuh have taken into consideration not only what the visit will be like for tourists, but also what will be best for the monkeys. With the appropriate controls, monkeys and tourists can have a reasonable experience.

A comparison of the three temples gave me the data I needed as an academic, but my memories of the summer were of more than maps of forests and counts of peanuts snatched from pockets. Most of all, I remember time spent with the animals, deep in the forest away from the intrusive gaze of tourists. I often sat quietly with a group of females as they groomed one another, and smiled as babies made their first wobbly steps away from mom. Sometimes I ran after screaming males as they fought out a hierarchical disagreement.

I also remember moments with my other subjects, the tourists. At all three sites, I was repeatedly asked about my research. I always responded with my most used Indonesian sentence, "Saya menyedlidiki monyet" (I study monkeys), followed by a quick natural history of macaques. I emphasized the macaque's attachment to family and friends and explained specific behaviors as they unfolded right in front of us. Balinese tour guides often sat with me and watched me watch monkeys while their human charges wandered through the temple grounds. We talked together about the long history of macaques on Bali and compared notes on the different sites around the island. I soon realized that educating an eager public was as much my job as collecting data for analysis. Obviously, the best way to save the monkeys from exploitation and extinction is to create a mutually respectful alliance between the tourists and the animals.

Back home, a carving of the monkey god Hanuman, hangs over my desk and watches as I enter endless columns of numbers into my computer. Hanuman laughs because he knows that these data mean little in the real world of his monkey armies. Once more, he is needed to battle an evil foe, but this time, the monkeys themselves need Hanuman's protection.

A Reasonable Sleep

Meredith F. Small

Three-month-old Jenny lies in the crook of her mother's arm. As the infant twitches in her sleep, ten thin wires taped to her face and bald head wiggle in all directions, giving her a baby Medusa look. Jenny's mother opens her sleepy eyes in the dimly lit room and stares blankly into the tiny face only inches away. The matching wires on the mother's head nod toward her baby as she unconsciously reaches out and pats Jenny reassuringly a few times. She adjusts the baby's blanket, and they both drift back into a deeper level of sleep.

One room away James McKenna watches the needles on a 12-channel polygraph jump in tandem as Jenny and her mother experience this mutual arousal. An elfin grin spreads across his face. He's recorded so many of these unconscious stirrings that they seem to him to map out a nightlong dance.

McKenna, an anthropologist at Pomona College, has come to the nearby Sleep Disorders Laboratory at the University of California at Irvine to test a hypothesis: he believes that the Western practice of placing babies in their own beds at night is at odds with human nature—so odd that sudden infant death syndrome (SIDS), the mysterious killer of babies, can more easily come stalking. But he is just as interested in the vast majority of babies who don't succumb to SIDS. Sleeping in isolation affects them too, he suspects, though more subtly than in the rare cases of SIDS. Jenny and her mother are providing the numbers to support what McKenna has been advocating for the past eight years: "If you have a baby, sleep with it."

His idea developed from years of watching infant monkeys cling to their mothers day and night. He also knew that babies sleep with their parents in the vast majority of human cultures. Both facts suggested to McKenna that it's inconsistent with our evolutionary roots to put babies in their own beds at

---

Evolution suggests that if we sleep with our babies, we might help some of them escape sudden infant death syndrome.

---

night. What's more, he points out, the current Western practice is only a century or two old, "just a wink" in human history. As an anthropologist with no formal medical training, however, McKenna hesitated to push for co-sleeping. Most pediatricians, after all, thought babies should sleep alone. Yet as he began to talk about his ideas, he found a receptive audience. His words, some parents told him, finally gave them "permission" to do what seemed to come naturally—sleep with their babies.

Many parents have fears about the safety of co-sleeping. They've been told that bed-sharing puts a squirming baby at risk of being suffocated by well-meaning but exhausted parents. This is probably no more than an old wives' tale. As McKenna points out, most babies worldwide sleep with an adult without ill effects. Other parents feel that they need a break from the baby's constant demands, or they crave time for intimacy. And current advice books uniformly reinforce the idea that sleep practices should accommodate parents, not babies.

Parenting advice in the 1990s, post–Dr. Spock, tends to be permissive. But in one area discipline survives: when, where, and how much babies should sleep. In *The Well Baby Book,* a popular guide, Mike and Nancy Samuels give parents hints to aid their quest to get tiny infants to sleep through the night. "Don't bring the baby into the parents' bed and let it sleep there till morning," they say. "It is more likely to be disturbed." Penelope Leach, in *Babyhood,* admits that babies sleep better when snuggled between adults. But Leach also writes that parents are often disturbed by the baby's fidgeting, and many are uncomfortable with an infant in the "marital bed." What's worse, she and other authorities claim, co-sleeping establishes a dependency that will be difficult to break, making it hard for the older child to fall asleep when alone, although there is no evidence to support this.

McKenna believes the notion that solitary sleep is healthier for babies in the long run is based not on biology but on a recent adoption of urban-industrial values. Modern society requires "good" citizens—independent people not making too many demands on others. In this scenario, autonomy must be fostered as soon as possible. We begin early, McKenna claims, by placing babies alone at night so that busy parents can get on with their lives. "In our modern day," he says, "the biological interests of the infants might not coincide with the best interests of the parents. But evolution never promised us a rose garden."

McKenna's observation of mothers and infants began decades ago, with his training in primate behavior. "As a junior at U.C. Berkeley in 1969, I took

In the natural state, monkey and ape babies always sleep with their mother, clinging to her belly until the infant *initiates independence.*

a course in primatology," he says. "I learned that monkeys and apes need so much physical attention and contact. I remember thinking, when I have a baby, I'm going to give it as much affection as it can take. You cannot understand primates without coming to appreciate that very early physical contact is everything. It's what we're all about."

Now, at 43, he realizes that his later diversion to sleep research has even earlier origins. "I grew up in a large family of six children. There weren't enough beds in my house and we all shared beds. I slept at my brother Tommy's feet for over a year!" But it wasn't until the birth of his son Jeffrey, in 1978, that McKenna put those research interests together.

"I noticed that one way to get Jeff to sleep was to nap with him. I'd lie down with him and breathe as if I was asleep." He breathes in and out, in and out, pumping his chest up and down as if baby Jeff were still bundled on top of him. "I became really skilled at getting him to sleep. I also found it totally amusing." But the scholar in McKenna was intrigued. "I noticed he was so responsive to these breathing cues. And then I wondered why I was surprised. Here was a primate baby, undeveloped at birth, selected to be responsive to parental contact and care. The fact that he *was* responsive to my sounds and breathing patterns was

everything the last ten years of anthropological research had told me he would be."

McKenna soon realized the implications of what he'd observed. In the United States one in every 500 babies is found dead during the first year of life, most often between two and four months of age. These babies usually show no previous signs of illness, and no known cause of death can be determined at autopsy—although recent research suggests that abnormalities in fetal development may predispose some infants to an early death. But it now occurred to McKenna that the absence of cues from co-sleeping parents might also play a role.

Since the medical community concentrates on physiological causes for SIDS, McKenna knew that any suggestion of a cultural influence would be considered radical. He knew he would need to explain how co-sleeping had evolved—how it contributed to a baby's physical well-being. "The difficulty is explaining to medically trained specialists what it means to apply evolutionary theory in the context of infancy and parenthood. That's where I thought I could fill a role—making evolution alive and meaningful in the context of clinical research."

There were experiments McKenna could cite. As several psychologists showed in the 1960s, the infant's physical dependence on its mother is a primate universal, and it involves more than simple providing. When infant macaque monkeys were separated from their mothers, even for a few hours, they experienced physiological effects such as changes in heart rate and body temperature, sleep disturbances, increases in cardiac arrhythmias, and signs of clinical depression. In short the animals' immature nervous systems just didn't function as well. In the natural state, McKenna adds, monkey and ape babies always sleep with their mother, clinging to her belly until the *infant* initiates independence.

Human babies are even more dependent on adults. No other animal needs

so much nurturing and takes so long to mature. The advantage to being so unformed at birth is the great capacity for learning and social interaction.

As with other primates, McKenna speculates, in humans the strong mother-infant bond was selected for because it helped babies get through their long formative period. But human babies are so helpless they can't even cling to their mothers like monkeys. Instead, they are carried. In humans, McKenna says, "infant sleep evolved against a background of being jerked up and down in the back of a sling." Even today you can see babies carried this way throughout Africa and Asia: mothers out hoeing in the garden, baby sleeping on their back. "There is a physicality in the relationship," he says. "We can't go on assuming that there are no physiological consequences to sleeping alone."

McKenna suggests that all human babies benefit from hearing their parents breathe, feeling their parents' touches, and just being close to adults. Although the long-term effects of solitary versus co-sleeping are unknown, McKenna suspects there's a connection between nocturnal closeness and mental health later on, even into adulthood. "A feeling of social-psychological connectedness allows infants to later become more independent from parents. It may also result in higher self-esteem

"Mothers usually say the time in the lab is the first reasonable night's sleep they've had since the baby was born."

and a good sense of empathy for others. These infants might also be able to better monitor nonverbal cues given by others."

More dramatically, McKenna believes, co-sleeping may be important in avoiding the particularly human problem of SIDS. Humans, he notes, are different from other primates in a way that makes us vulnerable: we rely so heavily on speech that we use "voluntary," or controlled, breathing far more than any other mammal. We have to learn how to modulate our breathing to talk, though we never lose the ability to return to automatic pilot—the involuntary, reflexive breathing we use during sleep or reading.

Human babies begin switching back and forth from automatic to controlled breathing between two and four months of age. At this developmental stage, the infant neocortex, the higher brain, becomes functionally connected to the primitive brain stem. Behavior becomes less a series of reflex actions and more voluntary. Babies start to smile because they want to, and their vocalizations are no longer mere reactions to hunger or wet diapers. They begin to manipulate their breathing by changing airflow rates, air pressure, and lung volume. A cry will suddenly carry specific information to a carefully listening parent; it's a form of speech-breathing that will later become talking. This is also a susceptible time for infants. Most do fine, but McKenna thinks some can't manage the flip-flop between the two types of breathing. They stop, and succumb to SIDS.

To support his claims about the importance of co-sleeping, McKenna knew he would first need to show that babies are physically affected when they spend the night in contact with an adult. His co-sleeping hypothesis works only if infants sleep differently—presumably better—when tucked in with Mom.

One day in 1984 McKenna walked into the first open door in the pediatrics department at the University of California at Irvine and bent the ear of pediatrician Claibourne Dungy. Dungy quickly assembled what McKenna recalls as "four people in white lab coats staring at me skeptically." One of them was Sarah Mosko, a clinical psychologist, a sleep expert, and most important for McKenna, a trained polysomnographer—a person who knows how to wire sleepers and interpret the squiggles on the polygraph. McKenna asked if she'd like to collaborate with him on his research. "It didn't take much for

me to say yes," recalls Mosko, who now works as a sleep-disorders consultant in addition to her research with McKenna.

Together McKenna and Mosko have collected sleep data on eight mother and infant pairs at the Sleep Disorders Lab. In the first study, conducted from 1986 to 1987, five mother-infant pairs were tracked for one night. In the second study, finished last year, three mothers and infants spent the first two nights sleeping alone but in adjacent rooms, so that the mothers could get up and feed the babies. The third night each mother and baby slept in the same bed—an unusual event for two of the pairs.

Mothers and their infants report to the lab at 8:00 p.m. The sleep room, with a hospital bed and blackout curtains, seems to them an inviting haven. "These are sleep-deprived new mothers," says Mosko. "They usually say the time in the lab is the first reasonable night's sleep they've had since the baby was born."

Before mother and baby settle down for the night, each has four wires taped to the head to record electroencephalographic, or brain wave, signals. Another two wires, placed close to each eye orbit, monitor eye movements, and three more wires on the chin measure muscle relaxation. Heartbeats are picked up by two wires on the chest. A thin wire placed beneath the nose monitors breathing by sensing the temperature of the passing air; exhaled air is warmer than inhaled air. (Breathing is also recorded as chest-wall movement.)

The data from all these sources help differentiate the five levels of sleep a person traverses during the night. Rapid eye movement, or REM, sleep is the most active—the eyes flicker, the face and limbs twitch as muscles tense and relax, brain waves come faster but with lower voltage, and breathing and heart rate become less regular. This is a dreaming state, although dreams sometimes occur in other stages. There are four non-REM levels; deep sleep occurs in levels three and four. Individuals vary in the amount of time they spend at each stage, and infants have

fewer distinct levels—at three months they typically have three. In any case, several cycles through the various levels seem to be important for a satisfying snooze.

As McKenna and Mosko's subjects sleep, impulses from the wires travel to the recording room, where inked needles leave tracks on long sheets of paper. Later Mosko gathers the pages and marks out sleep levels in 30-second intervals. She determines if each subject is sleeping at a certain level, awake, or experiencing transient arousal—moving into lighter levels of sleep but not to full wakefulness. McKenna, with his animal-behavior background, scores the videotape—baby lifts head, mother opens eyes, and so on. The two researchers eventually compare mothers and babies sleeping alone and together, interval by interval.

These data choreograph the nocturnal dance of mothers and babies—the dance McKenna had predicted—but with mutual promptings and responses. It's not that mothers regulate their babies' breathing. The sleepers are, instead, physiologically entwined; the movements and breathing of each partner affect the other. When one arouses, the other often wakes up a bit, too.

McKenna proposes that transient arousals are especially important because they give babies practice in waking up. All babies experience apneas, or pauses in breathing, several times a night. If a pause becomes prolonged, a healthy baby will wake up to breathe. Many researchers believe that SIDS babies have some deficiency that inhibits their arousal. When they stop breathing, they're less apt to wake up—and thus more likely to die. But if aroused more often by a parent, McKenna reasons, they may learn better how to do it on their own, and wake up one night when it really matters.

McKenna also suggests that co-sleeping helps a baby master breathing techniques. During sleep, just as during wakefulness, adults shift through periods of controlled or automatic breathing, switching between neocorti-

Medical Research on SIDS

Each year hundreds of papers are published on SIDS, pointing the finger at a host of possible culprits. Mothers who smoke during pregnancy, for example, have been told they're upping their baby's risk of SIDS about threefold. Babies may also be at higher risk if they are born prematurely or of low birth weight, as a sibling rather than a first born, or to a young mother. Babies who lie on their stomach have a higher risk; more babies die of SIDS in winter; elevated body temperature from a stuffy room or overdressing may be a factor.

Still, none of this explains the actual cause of sudden death. "Risk factors are simply things that may make a baby more vulnerable," explains Marian Willinger, who directs SIDS research for the National Institute of Child Health and Human Development. "Just because cigarette smoking is linked with an increased risk doesn't mean that cigarette smoking causes SIDS. A lot of SIDS babies' mothers don't smoke. There's something about the baby itself that predisposes it to SIDS."

Pinning down that something, however, has so far proved impossible. "At this point," explains Willinger, "SIDS is a diagnosis of exclusion. If you can't find any other cause of death after a full postmortem, then it's called SIDS—so by definition we're starting without much to help us."

Nevertheless, some strides have been made. The most popular theory is that something is wrong with the way vulnerable babies arouse themselves from sleep—they're supposed to wake up when they stop breathing for an unusual length of time, but they don't. To investigate this idea, neurophysiologist Ron Harper and his colleagues at UCLA checked the records of nearly 7,000 babies whose heartbeats and breathing were recorded in a British study. Sixteen of those babies later died of SIDS; Harper found that they had gone through far fewer short respiratory pauses while sleeping than the ones who were still alive. Although the reason for this difference is not yet known, it is a true disparity.

Other researchers are looking at where respiration is controlled—in the brain. The brains of all newborns are still developing; for instance, the neurons are not all covered by their protective sheaths of myelin. Early last year Hannah Kinney of Children's Hospital in Boston and her colleagues showed that myelination in the brains of 61 infants who died of SIDS lagged significantly behind myelination in 89 children who died of other causes—though again this is so far just a clue.

Of course, a disease with such a nebulous definition can easily fool you. Researchers are fairly certain that 3 to 10 percent of SIDS cases are actually the result of inborn metabolic defects. And a study published last summer showed that a few babies diagnosed as succumbing to SIDS —fewer than 1 percent—might have suffocated on soft bedding such as beanbag cushions.

Yet researchers do feel that SIDS is a discrete entity with its own physiological mechanism, not just a conglomeration of other syndromes that simply need to be teased apart. "The scientists really believe that after all is said and done there will be a core of babies with a certain characteristic abnormality that makes them vulnerable to sudden death," says Willinger. "We won't keep peeling away layers of onion until there is nothing left."

—*Lori Oliwenstein*

cal-driven breaths and brain stem-operated breaths. Babies undergo that flip-flop each time they wake up. When sleeping with Mom, a baby reacts to her movements and wakes up more times during the night—an average of 24 percent more, McKenna finds, than when sleeping alone—thus getting more practice in the repeated hop from one kind of breathing to the other. "Sleep has evolved against these interruptions," says McKenna, "and they may serve as practice for the baby when it has more serious, internally based interruptions in breathing."

Such fitful sleep may, in fact, be the norm for adults as well. The mothers in McKenna's experiments passed through transient arousals 60 percent more frequently when sleeping with their babies then when sleeping alone.

"We Westerners have the 'die' theory of sleep," McKenna says, laughing. "You close your eyes, fall asleep, and basically die—you become totally unconscious until you wake up in the morning—and you hope for the best. If there's anything in between, there's something wrong with you. Other people in the world don't sleep like that. The !Kung bushmen, for example, get up, tend the fire, talk, then go back to sleep. Western culture has streamlined what we think is normal. And if people can't conform, there's disease out there for them—it's called insomnia. A small group of sleep researchers have also admitted that humans are not monophasic sleepers—they are biphasic. The afternoon nap is biologically based."

His point is that cultures dictate norms unrelated to what might or might not be evolutionarily natural— that is, bred into human physiology. He feels that the extreme American emphasis on individualism, and the view that husband and wife have a relationship apart from the children, have reinforced notions that infants are born too dependent and should sleep by themselves as soon as possible. In contrast, Japanese infants normally sleep with their parents. This, too, is a culturally bound notion, but instead of opting for independence, the Japanese foster interdependence. Interestingly enough, the rate of SIDS is significantly lower in Japan than in the United States: less than one per 1,000 births.

Data for immigrant populations in the United States suggest that such cultural differences may indeed play a role. For example, Chinese immigrants in California have an incidence of SIDS 38 times higher than nonimmigrant Chinese in Hong Kong. Among other Asian-American populations the SIDS rates vary, but the rate increases the longer a group has lived in the United States. The Vietnamese, for example, arrived later than the Japanese, and their SIDS rate is lower. McKenna feels that the pattern may be explained by immigrants' adopting the American style of placing babies in their own beds. His speculation cannot be confirmed, of course, until other possible influences—such as changes in feeding practices—are ruled out.

McKenna began giving talks about his ideas in the early eighties. Then, in 1986, he published a massive paper on his work, which attracted a lot of attention. So far the response from the medical community has not been as critical as McKenna first feared. Marian Willinger, who directs SIDS research at the National Institute of Child Health and Human Development, says, "In general this is a new area for infant and child health—tying parenting styles with physiology—and therefore McKenna and Mosko's basic research is important for *all* babies."

One medical researcher was deeply impressed. "I think their work is terrific," says Jeffrey Laitman, an anatomist at New York's Mount Sinai School of Medicine. His own research on the development of the throat and voice box in infants supports McKenna's hunch that SIDS is linked to the evolution of speech making. "In newborns, as in many animals, the larynx locks into the back of the nasal cavity," Laitman explains. "This enables them to breathe and swallow at roughly the

---

"We Westerners have the 'die' theory of sleep. You close your eyes, fall asleep, and basically die—you become unconscious and hope for the best."

---

same time. But in humans the larynx begins to drop down into the throat in the first few months of life. No other mammal goes through such a tremendous metamorphosis, and there's a great possibility of miscues"—as well as a far greater ability to make the wide range of sounds used in talking.

But McKenna's not just out to prevent SIDS; his approach has always been more anthropological than medical. His larger goal is to show that early sleeping practices are important to everyone's health. This past January he and Mosko brought the first of 30 mother-baby pairs, including 15 co-sleepers, into the lab to investigate whether the sleep and breathing patterns of the co-sleeping babies are dif-

ferent from those of the babies who habitually sleep alone. McKenna expects to finish this study by the end of the year, but even then he'll be a long way from proving that co-sleeping is best for everyone in the long run. His argument that it seems to work well in traditional cultures cuts two ways. After all, most American babies, with their background of solitary sleeping, also grow up apparently healthy.

For now, McKenna aims to prove that co-sleeping is natural and normal for the average baby, a reasonable option rather than a dangerous, misguided practice that should be discouraged, as stated in current advice books. "Should a parent or parents feel good about co-sleeping, elect it as a favored strategy, and it is done responsibly," he writes, "nothing could be better for their infant or child."

He is also philosophical about his potential role as a revolutionary in American parenting styles. "There is nothing profound about what I am trying to document or argue for—it's based on evolutionary history. It doesn't take any genius to know there may be some naturalistic interactions between co-sleeping babies and mothers, or babies and caretakers. Like those who have discovered in the twentieth century that breast-feeding is good for babies, I spend all my time documenting the obvious."

The Saltshaker's Curse

Physiological adaptations that helped American blacks survive slavery may now be predisposing their descendants to hypertension

Jared Diamond

Jared Diamond is a professor of physiology at UCLA Medical School.

On the walls of the main corridor at UCLA Medical School hang thirty-seven photographs that tell a moving story. They are the portraits of each graduating class, from the year that the school opened (Class of 1955) to the latest crop (Class of 1991). Throughout the 1950s and early 1960s the portraits are overwhelmingly of young white men, diluted by only a few white women and Asian men. The first black student graduated in 1961, an event not repeated for several more years. When I came to UCLA in 1966, I found myself lecturing to seventy-six students, of whom seventy-four were white. Thereafter the numbers of blacks, Hispanics, and Asians exploded, until the most recent photos show the number of white medical students declining toward a minority.

In these changes of racial composition, there is of course nothing unique about UCLA Medical School. While the shifts in its student body mirror those taking place, at varying rates, in other professional groups throughout American society, we still have a long way to go before professional groups truly mirror society itself. But ethnic diversity among physicians is especially important because of the dangers inherent in a profession composed of white practitioners for whom white biology is the norm.

Different ethnic groups face different health problems, for reasons of genes as well as of life style. Familiar examples include the prevalence of skin cancer and cystic fibrosis in whites, stomach cancer and stroke in Japanese, and diabetes in Hispanics and Pacific islanders. Each year, when I teach a seminar course in ethnically varying disease patterns, these by-now-familiar textbook facts assume a gripping reality, as my various students choose to discuss some disease that affects themselves or their relatives. To read about the molecular biology of sickle-cell anemia is one thing. It's quite another thing when one of my students, a black man homozygous for the sickle-cell gene, describes the pain of his own sickling attacks and how they have affected his life.

Sickle-cell anemia is a case in which the evolutionary origins of medically important genetic differences among peoples are well understood. (It evolved only in malarial regions because it confers resistance against malaria.) But in many other cases the evolutionary origins are not nearly so transparent. Why is it, for example, that only some human populations have a high frequency of the Tay-Sachs gene or of diabetes? . . .

Compared with American whites of the same age and sex, American blacks have, on the average, higher blood pressure, double the risk of developing hypertension, and nearly ten times the risk of dying of it. By age fifty, nearly half of U.S. black men are hypertensive. For a given age and blood pressure, hypertension more often causes heart disease and especially kidney failure and strokes in U.S. blacks than whites. Because the frequency of kidney disease in U.S. blacks is eighteen times that in whites, blacks account for about two-thirds of U.S. patients with hypertensive kidney failure, even though they make up only about one-tenth of the population. Around the world, only Japanese exceed U.S. blacks in their risk of dying from stroke. Yet it was not until 1932 that the average difference in blood pressure between U.S. blacks and whites was clearly demonstrated, thereby exposing a major health problem outside the norms of white medicine.

What is it about American blacks that makes them disproportionately likely to develop hypertension and then to die of its consequences? While this question is of course especially "interesting" to black readers, it also concerns all Americans, because other ethnic groups in the United States are not so far behind blacks in their risk of hypertension. If *Natural History* readers are a cross section of the United States, then about one-quarter of you now have high blood pressure, and more than half of you will die of a heart attack or stroke to which high blood pressure predisposes. Thus, we all have valid reasons for being interested in hypertension.

First, some background on what those numbers mean when your doctor inflates a rubber cuff about your arm, listens, deflates the cuff, and finally pronounces, "Your blood pressure is 120 over 80." The cuff device is called a sphygmomanometer, and it measures the pressure in your artery in units of millimeters of mercury (that's the height to which your blood pressure would force up a column of mercury in case, God forbid, your artery were suddenly connected to a vertical mercury column). Naturally, your blood pressure varies with each stroke of your heart, so the first and second numbers refer, respectively, to the peak pressure at each heartbeat (systolic pressure) and to the minimum pressure between beats (diastolic pressure). Blood pressure varies somewhat with position, activity, and anxiety level, so the measurement is usually made while you are resting flat on your back. Under those conditions, 120 over 80 is an average reading for Americans.

There is no magic cutoff between normal blood pressure and high blood pressure. Instead, the higher your blood pressure, the more likely you are to die of a heart attack, stroke, kidney failure, or ruptured aorta. Usually, a pressure reading higher than 140 over 90 is arbitrarily defined as constituting hypertension, but some people with lower readings will die of a stroke at age fifty, while others with higher readings will die in a car accident in good health at age ninety.

Why do some of us have much higher blood pressure than others? In about 5 percent of hypertensive patients there is an identifiable single cause, such as hormonal imbalance or use of oral contraceptives. In 95 percent of such cases, though, there is no such obvious cause. The clinical euphemism for our ignorance in such cases is "essential hypertension."

Nowadays, we know that there is a big genetic component in essential hypertension, although the particular genes involved have not yet been identified. Among people living in the same household, the correlation coefficient for blood pressure is 0.63 between identical twins, who share all of their genes. (A correlation coefficient of 1.00 would mean that the twins share identical blood pressures as well and would suggest that pressure is determined entirely by genes and not at all by environment.) Fraternal twins or ordinary siblings or a parent and child,

who share half their genes and whose blood pressure would therefore show a correlation coefficient of 0.5 if purely determined genetically, actually have a coefficient of about 0.25. Finally, adopted siblings or a parent and adopted child, who have no direct genetic connection, have a correlation coefficient of only 0.05. Despite the shared household environment, their blood pressures are barely more similar than those of two people pulled randomly off the street. In agreement with this evidence for genetic factors underlying blood pressure itself, your risk of actually developing hypertensive disease increases from 4 percent to 20 percent to 35 percent if, respectively, none or one or both of your parents were hypertensive.

But these same facts suggest that environmental factors also contribute to high blood pressure, since identical twins have similar but not identical blood pressures. Many environmental or life style factors contributing to the risk of hypertension have been identified by epidemiological studies that compare hypertension's frequency in groups of people living under different conditions. Such contributing factors include obesity, high intake of salt or alcohol or saturated fats, and low calcium intake. The proof of this approach is that hypertensive patients who modify their life styles so as to minimize these putative factors often succeed in reducing their blood pressure. Patients are especially advised to reduce salt intake and stress, reduce intake of cholesterol and saturated fats and alcohol, lose weight, cut out smoking, and exercise regularly.

Here are some examples of the epidemiological studies pointing to these risk factors. Around the world, comparisons within and between populations show that both blood pressure and the frequency of hypertension increase hand in hand with salt intake. At the one extreme, Brazil's Yanomamö Indians have the world's lowest-known salt consumption (somewhat above 10 milligrams per day!), lowest average blood pressure (95 over 61!), and lowest incidence of hypertension (no cases!). At the opposite extreme, doc-

tors regard Japan as the "land of apoplexy" because of the high frequency of fatal strokes (Japan's leading cause of death, five times more frequent than in the United States), linked with high blood pressure and notoriously salty food. Within Japan itself these factors reach their extremes in Akita Prefecture, famous for its tasty rice, which Akita farmers flavor with salt, wash down with salty miso soup, and alternate with salt pickles between meals. Of 300 Akita adults studied, not one consumed less than five grams of salt daily, the average consumption was twenty-seven grams, and the most salt-loving individual consumed an incredible sixty-one grams—enough to devour the contents of the usual twenty-six-ounce supermarket salt container in a mere twelve days. The *average* blood pressure in Akita by age fifty is 151 over 93, making hypertension (pressure higher than 140 over 90) the norm. Not surprisingly, Akita's frequency of death by stroke is more than double even the Japanese average, and in some Akita villages 99 percent of the population dies before age seventy.

Why salt intake often (in about 60 percent of hypertensive patients) leads to high blood pressure is not fully understood. One possible interpretation is that salt intake triggers thirst, leading to an increase in blood volume. In response, the heart increases its output and blood pressure rises, causing the kidneys to filter more salt and water under that increased pressure. The result is a new steady state, in which salt and water excretion again equals intake, but more salt and water are stored in the body and blood pressure is raised.

At this point, let's contrast hypertension with a simple genetic disease like Tay-Sachs disease. Tay-Sachs is due to a defect in a single gene; every Tay-Sachs patient has a defect in that same gene. Everybody in whom that gene is defective is certain to die of Tay-Sachs, regardless of their life style or environment. In contrast, hypertension involves several different genes whose molecular products remain to be identified. Because there are many causes of raised blood pressure, different hypertensive patients may owe their condition to different gene combinations. Furthermore, whether someone genetically predisposed to hypertension actually develops symptoms depends a lot on life style. Thus, hypertension is not one of those uncommon, homogeneous, and intellectually elegant diseases that geneticists prefer to study. Instead, like diabetes and ulcers, hypertension is a shared set of symptoms produced by heterogeneous causes, all involving an interaction between environmental agents and a susceptible genetic background.

Since U.S. blacks and whites differ on the average in the conditions under which they live, could those differences account for excess hypertension in U.S. blacks? Salt intake, the dietary factor that one thinks of first, turns out on the average not to differ between U.S. blacks and whites. Blacks do consume less potassium and calcium, do experience more stress associated with more difficult socioeconomic conditions, have much less access to medical care, and are therefore much less likely to be diagnosed or treated until it is too late. Those factors surely contribute to the frequency and severity of hypertension in blacks.

However, those factors don't seem to be the whole explanation: hypertensive blacks aren't merely like severely hypertensive whites. Instead, physiological differences seem to contribute as well. On consuming salt, blacks retain it on average far longer before excreting it into the urine, and they experience a greater rise in blood pressure on a high-salt diet. Hypertension is more likely to be "salt-sensitive" in blacks than in whites, meaning that blood pressure is more likely to rise and fall with rises and falls in dietary salt intake. By the same token, black hypertension is more likely to be treated successfully by drugs that cause the kidneys to excrete salt (the so-called thiazide diuretics) and less likely to respond to those drugs that reduce heart rate and cardiac output (so-called beta blockers, such as propanolol). These facts suggest that there are some qualitative differences between the causes of black and white hypertension, with black hypertension more likely to involve how the kidneys handle salt.

Physicians often refer to this postulated feature as a "defect": for example, "kidneys of blacks have a genetic defect in excreting sodium." As an evolutionary biologist, though, I hear warning bells going off inside me whenever a seemingly harmful trait that occurs frequently in an old and large human population is dismissed as a "defect." Given enough generations, genes that greatly impede survival are extremely unlikely to spread, unless their net effect is to increase survival and reproductive success. Human medicine has furnished the best examples of seemingly defective genes being propelled to high frequency by counterbalancing benefits. For example, sickle-cell hemoglobin protects far more people against malaria than it kills of anemia, while the Tay-Sachs gene may have protected far more Jews against tuberculosis than it killed of neurological disease. Thus, to understand why U.S. blacks now are prone to die as a result of their kidneys' retaining salt, we need to ask under what conditions people might have benefited from kidneys good at retaining salt.

That question is hard to understand from the perspective of modern Western society, where saltshakers are on every dining table, salt (sodium chloride) is cheap, and our bodies' main problem is getting rid of it. But imagine what the world used to be like before saltshakers became ubiquitous. Most plants contain very little sodium, yet animals require sodium at high concentrations in all their extracellular fluids. As a result, carnivores readily obtain their needed sodium by eating herbivores, but herbivores themselves face big problems in acquiring that sodium. That's why the animals that one sees coming to salt licks are deer and antelope, not lions and tigers. Similarly, some human hunter-gatherers obtained enough salt from the meat that they ate. But when we began to take up farming ten thousand years ago, we either had to evolve kidneys superefficient at conserving salt or learn to extract salt at great effort or trade for it at great expense.

Examples of these various solutions abound. I already mentioned Brazil's Yanomamö Indians, whose staple food is low-sodium bananas and who excrete on the average only 10 milligrams of salt daily—barely one-thousandth the salt excretion of the typical American. A single Big Mac hamburger analyzed by Consumer Reports contained 1.5 grams (1,500 milligrams) of salt, representing many weeks of intake for a Yanomamö. The New Guinea highlanders with whom I work, and whose diet consists up to 90 percent of low-sodium sweet potatoes, told me of the efforts to which they went to make salt a few decades ago, before Europeans brought it as trade goods. They gathered leaves of certain plant species, burned them, scraped up the ash, percolated water through it to dissolve the solids, and finally evaporated the water to obtain small amounts of bitter salt.

Thus, salt has been in very short supply for much of recent human evolutionary history. Those of us with efficient kidneys able to retain salt even on a low-sodium diet were better able to survive our inevitable episodes of sodium loss (of which more in a moment). Those kidneys proved to be a detriment only when salt became routinely available, leading to excessive salt retention and hypertension with its fatal consequences. That's why blood pressure and the frequency of hypertension have shot up recently in so many populations around the world as they have made the transition from being self-sufficient subsistence farmers to members of the cash economy and patrons of supermarkets.

This evolutionary argument has been advanced by historian-epidemiologist Thomas Wilson and others to explain the current prevalence of hypertension in American blacks in particular. Many West African blacks, from whom most American blacks originated via the slave trade, must have faced the chronic problem of losing salt through sweating in their hot environment. Yet in West Africa, except on the coast and certain inland areas, salt was traditionally as scarce for African farmers as it has been for Yanomamö and New Guinea farmers. (Ironically, those Africans who sold other Africans as slaves often took payment in salt traded from the Sahara.) By this argument, the genetic basis for hypertension in U.S. blacks was already widespread in many of their West African ancestors. It required only the ubiquity of salt-shakers in twentieth-century America for that genetic basis to express itself as hypertension. This argument also predicts that as Africa's life style becomes increasingly Westernized, hypertension could become as prevalent in West Africa as it now is among U.S. blacks. In this view, American blacks would be no different from the many Polynesian, Melanesian, Kenyan, Zulu, and other populations that have recently developed high blood pressure under a Westernized life style.

But there's an intriguing extension to this hypothesis, proposed by Wilson and physician Clarence Grim, collaborators at the Hypertension Research Center of Drew University in Los Angeles. They suggest a scenario in which New World blacks may now be at more risk for hypertension than their African ancestors. That scenario involves very recent selection for super-efficient kidneys, driven by massive mortality of black slaves from salt loss.

Grim and Wilson's argument goes as follows. Black slavery in the Americas began about 1517, with the first imports of slaves from West Africa, and did not end until Brazil freed its slaves barely a century ago in 1888. In the course of the slave trade an estimated 12 million Africans were brought to the Americas. But those imports were winnowed by deaths at many stages, from an even larger number of captives and exports.

First, slaves captured by raids in the interior of West Africa were chained together, loaded with heavy burdens, and marched for one or two months, with little food and water, to the coast. About 25 percent of the captives died en route. While awaiting purchase by slave traders, the survivors were held on the coast in hot, crowded buildings called barracoons, where about 12 percent of them died. The traders went up and down the coast buying and loading slaves for a few weeks or months until a ship's cargo was full (5 percent more died). The dreaded Middle Passage across the Atlantic killed 10 percent of the slaves, chained together in a hot, crowded, unventilated hold without sanitation. (Picture to yourself the result of those toilet "arrangements.") Of those who lived to land in the New World, 5 percent died while awaiting sale, and 12 percent died while being marched or shipped from the sale yard to the plantation. Finally, of those who survived, between 10 and 40 percent died during the first three years of plantation life, in a process euphemistically called seasoning. At that stage, about 70 percent of the slaves initially captured were dead, leaving 30 percent as seasoned survivors.

Even the end of seasoning, however, was not the end of excessive mortality. About half of slave infants died within a year of birth because of the poor nutrition and heavy workload of their mothers. In plantation terminology, slave women were viewed as either "breeding units" or "work units," with a built-in conflict between those uses: "These Negroes breed the best, whose labour is least," as an eighteenth-century observer put it. As a result, many New World slave populations depended on continuing slave imports and couldn't maintain their own numbers because death rates exceeded birth rates. Since buying new slaves cost less than rearing slave children for twenty years until they were adults, slave owners lacked economic incentive to change this state of affairs.

Recall that Darwin discussed natural selection and survival of the fittest with respect to animals. Since many more animals die than survive to produce offspring, each generation becomes enriched in the genes of those of the preceding generation that were among the survivors. It should now be clear that slavery represented a tragedy of unnatural selection in humans on a gigantic scale. From examining accounts of slave mortality, Grim and Wilson argue that death was indeed selective: much of it was related to unbalanced salt loss, which quickly brings on collapse. We think immediately of salt loss by sweating under hot conditions: while slaves were working, marching, or confined in unventilated barracoons or ships' holds. More body salt may have been spilled with vomiting from seasickness. But the biggest salt loss at every stage was from diarrhea due to crowding and lack of sanitation—ideal conditions for the spread of gastrointestinal infections. Cholera and other bacterial diarrheas kill us by causing sudden massive loss of salt and water. (Picture your most recent bout of *turista,* multiplied to a diarrheal fluid output of twenty quarts in one day, and you'll understand why.) All contemporary accounts of slave ships and plantation life emphasized diarrhea, or "fluxes" in eighteenth-century terminology, as one of the leading killers of slaves.

Grim and Wilson reason, then, that slavery suddenly selected for super-efficient kidneys surpassing the efficient kidneys already selected by thousands of years of West African history. Only those slaves who were best able to retain salt could survive the periodic risk of high salt loss to which they were exposed. Salt supersavers would have had the further advantage of building up, under normal conditions, more of a salt reserve in their body fluids and bones, thereby enabling them to survive longer or more frequent bouts of diarrhea. Those superkidneys became a disadvantage only when modern medicine began to reduce diarrhea's lethal impact, thereby transforming a blessing into a curse.

Thus, we have two possible evolutionary explanations for salt retention by New World blacks. One involves slow selection by conditions operating in Africa for millennia; the other, rapid recent selection by slave conditions within the past few centuries. The result in either case would make New World blacks more susceptible than whites to hypertension, but the second explanation would, in addition, make them more susceptible than African blacks. At present, we don't know the relative importance of these two explanations. Grim and Wilson's provocative hypothesis is likely to stimulate medical and physiological comparisons of American blacks with African blacks and thereby to help resolve the question.

While this piece has focused on one medical problem in one human population, it has several larger morals. One, of course, is that our differing genetic heritages predispose us to different diseases, depending on the part of the world where our ancestors lived. Another is that our genetic differences reflect not only ancient conditions in different parts of the world but also recent episodes of migration and mortality. A well-established example is the decrease in the frequency of the sickle-cell hemoglobin gene in U.S. blacks compared with African blacks,

because selection for resistance to malaria is now unimportant in the United States. The example of black hypertension that Grim and Wilson discuss opens the door to considering other possible selective effects of the slave experience. They note that occasional periods of starvation might have selected slaves for superefficient sugar metabolism, leading under modern conditions to a propensity for diabetes.

Finally, consider a still more universal moral. Almost all people alive today exist under very different conditions from those under which every human lived 10,000 years ago. It's remarkable that our old genetic heritage now permits us to survive at all under such different circumstances.

But our heritage still catches up with most of us, who will die of life style related diseases such as cancer, heart attack, stroke, and diabetes. The risk factors for these diseases are the strange new conditions prevailing in modern Western society. One of the hardest challenges for modern medicine will be to identify for us which among all those strange new features of diet, life style, and environment are the ones getting us into trouble. For each of us, the answers will depend on our particular genes, hence on our ancestry. Only with such individually tailored advice can we hope to reap the benefits of modern living while still housed in bodies designed for life before saltshakers.

Index

Credits/ Acknowledgments

Cover design by Charles Vitelli

1. Natural Selection
Facing overview—New York Public Library illustration.

2. Primates
Facing overview—United Nations photo by George Love.

3. Sex and Society
Facing overview—WHO photo.

4. The Hominid Transition
Facing overview—The American Museum of Natural History photo. 118—*Discover* photo by Andy Freeberg. © 1991 by The Walt Disney Company.

5. The Fossil Evidence
Facing overview—The American Museum of Natural History photo. 154—*Scientific American* map by Johnny Johnson. 154-159—*Scientific American* illustrations by Patricia J. Wynne. 155—Photo by Yves Coppens. 157—Photo by Des Bartlett/Photo Researchers.

6. Late Hominid Evolution
Facing overview—AP/Wide World photo by Jean Clottes. 175-178—*Natural History* photos by Erik Trinkaus.

7. Living with the Past
Facing overview—Photo by Napoleon Chagnon/Anthro Photo. 210—© 1995 by Bob Sacha. 213—Photo courtesy of Drs. E. Fuller Torrey and Daniel R. Weinberger, NIMH Neuroscience Center, Washington, DC. 215—Photo courtesy of Nick Kelsh. 216—Photo courtesy of the American Philosophical Society.

ANNUAL EDITIONS ARTICLE REVIEW FORM

■ NAME: _____ DATE: _____

■ TITLE AND NUMBER OF ARTICLE: _____

■ BRIEFLY STATE THE MAIN IDEA OF THIS ARTICLE: _____

_____

■ LIST THREE IMPORTANT FACTS THAT THE AUTHOR USES TO SUPPORT THE MAIN IDEA:

_____

_____

_____

_____

_____

_____

■ WHAT INFORMATION OR IDEAS DISCUSSED IN THIS ARTICLE ARE ALSO DISCUSSED IN YOUR TEXTBOOK OR OTHER READING YOU HAVE DONE? LIST THE TEXTBOOK CHAPTERS AND PAGE NUMBERS:

_____

_____

_____

_____

_____

_____

■ LIST ANY EXAMPLES OF BIAS OR FAULTY REASONING THAT YOU FOUND IN THE ARTICLE:

_____

_____

_____

_____

■ LIST ANY NEW TERMS/CONCEPTS THAT WERE DISCUSSED IN THE ARTICLE AND WRITE A SHORT DEFINITION:

_____

_____

_____

_____

_____

ANNUAL EDITIONS: PHYSICAL ANTHROPOLOGY 96/97
Article Rating Form

Here is an opportunity for you to have direct input into the next revision of this volume. We would like you to rate each of the 43 articles listed below, using the following scale:

1. **Excellent: should definitely be retained**
2. **Above average: should probably be retained**
3. **Below average: should probably be deleted**
4. **Poor: should definitely be deleted**

Your ratings will play a vital part in the next revision. So please mail this prepaid form to us just as soon as you complete it.
Thanks for your help!

Annual Editions revisions depend on two major opinion sources: one is our Advisory Board, listed in the front of this volume, which works with us in scanning the thousands of articles published in the public press each year; the other is you—the person actually using the book. Please help us and the users of the next edition by completing the prepaid article rating form on this page and returning it to us. Thank you.

Rating	Article	Rating	Article
	1. The Growth of Evolutionary Science		25. Dawson's Dawn Man: The Hoax at Piltdown
	2. The Struggle for the Schools		26. New Fossils Take Science Close to Dawn of Humans
	3. Curse and Blessing of the Ghetto		27. Sizing Up Human Intelligence
	4. The Arrow of Disease		28. East Side Story: The Origin of Humankind
	5. The Future of AIDS		29. Scavenger Hunt
	6. Black, White, Other		30. *Erectus* Rising
	7. Racial Odyssey		31. Hard Times among the Neanderthals
	8. Machiavellian Monkeys		32. Ancient Odysseys
	9. What Are Friends For?		33. Rhinos and Lions and Bears (Oh, My!)
	10. Gut Thinking		34. Old Masters
	11. The Young and the Reckless		35. The Dating Game
	12. The Mind of the Chimpanzee		36. The Neanderthal Peace
	13. Dian Fossey and Digit		37. Profile of an Anthropologist: No Bone Unturned
	14. These Are Real Swinging Primates		38. Eugenics Revisited
	15. The Myth of the Coy Female		39. The DNA Wars
	16. Sex and the Female Agenda		40. Farmers and Baboons in the Taita Hills: Inter-Species Warfare in Southeastern Kenya
	17. What's Love Got to Do with It?		41. Macaque See, Macaque Do
	18. Apes of Wrath		42. A Reasonable Sleep
	19. Dim Forest, Bright Chimps		43. The Saltshaker's Curse
	20. To Catch a Colobus		
	21. Flesh and Bone		
	22. Ape at the Brink		
	23. Human Ancestors Walked Tall, Stayed Cool		
	24. Ape Cultures and Missing Links		

(Continued on next page)

ABOUT YOU

Name _____ Date _____

Are you a teacher? ❑   Or student? ❑

Your School Name _____

Department _____

Address _____

City _____ State _____ Zip _____

School Telephone # _____

YOUR COMMENTS ARE IMPORTANT TO US!

Please fill in the following information:

For which course did you use this book? _____

Did you use a text with this Annual Edition? ❑ yes ❑ no

The title of the text? _____

What are your general reactions to the Annual Editions concept?

Have you read any particular articles recently that you think should be included in the next edition?

Are there any articles you feel should be replaced in the next edition? Why?

Are there other areas that you feel would utilize an Annual Edition?

May we contact you for editorial input?

May we quote you from above?

ANNUAL EDITIONS: PHYSICAL ANTHROPOLOGY 96/97

No Postage
Necessary
if Mailed
in the
United States

BUSINESS REPLY MAIL

First Class   Permit No. 84   Guilford, CT

Postage will be paid by addressee

**Dushkin Publishing Group/
Brown & Benchmark Publishers**
Sluice Dock
Guilford, Connecticut 06437